D0982543

DATE DUE

MAY 1 3 2018	

BRODART, CO.　　　　　　　Cat. No. 23-221

IN SEARCH OF THE BLACK FANTASTIC

TRANSGRESSING BOUNDARIES

Studies in Black Politics and Black Communities
Cathy Cohen and Fredrick Harris, Series Editors

In Search of the
Black Fantastic

POLITICS AND POPULAR CULTURE
IN THE POST–CIVIL RIGHTS ERA

RICHARD ITON

OXFORD
UNIVERSITY PRESS
2008

OXFORD
UNIVERSITY PRESS

Oxford University Press, Inc., publishes works that further
Oxford University's objective of excellence
in research, scholarship, and education.

Oxford   New York
Auckland   Cape Town   Dar es Salaam   Hong Kong   Karachi
Kuala Lumpur   Madrid   Melbourne   Mexico City   Nairobi
New Delhi   Shanghai   Taipei   Toronto

With offices in
Argentina   Austria   Brazil   Chile   Czech Republic   France   Greece
Guatemala   Hungary   Italy   Japan   Poland   Portugal   Singapore
South Korea   Switzerland   Thailand   Turkey   Ukraine   Vietnam

Copyright © 2008 by Oxford University Press, Inc.

Published by Oxford University Press, Inc.
198 Madison Avenue, New York, NY 10016

www.oup.com

Oxford is a registered trademark of Oxford University Press

Library of Congress Cataloging-in-Publication Data
Iton, Richard.
In search of the Black fantastic :
politics and popular culture in the post–Civil Rights era
/ Richard Iton.
p. cm. — (Transgressing boundaries)
Includes bibliographical references and index.
ISBN 978-0-19-517846-3
1. African Americans—Politics and government—20th century.
2. African Americans—Politics and government—21st century.
3. African Americans in popular culture.
4. Popular culture—Political aspects—United States.
5. African Americans—Race identity—Political aspects.
6. African Americans—Intellectual life.
7. United States—Race relations—Political aspects.
8. Political culture—United States. I. Title.
E185.625.I76 2008
323.1196'0730904—dc22
2007041197

9   8   7   6   5   4   3   2   1

Printed in the United States of America
on acid-free paper

For Ms. Laura Buscoigne
October 24, 1902–February 15, 2005
still/always

CONTENTS

IN SEARCH OF THE BLACK FANTASTIC

Most certainly the black element is indispensable in developing a race's artistic genius. This is my point of departure. —Count Joseph-Arthur de Gobineau (1855)

The Negro is primarily an artist, loving life for its own sake. His *metier* is expression rather than action. He is, so to speak, the lady among the races. —Robert E. Park (1924)

I as a black writer, must in some way represent you. Now, you didn't elect me, and I didn't ask for it, but here we are. —James Baldwin (1963)

[M]y Negro friends recognize a certain division of labor among the members of the tribe. Their demands are that I publish more novels. —Ralph Ellison (1964)

1

KNOWN RIVERS/NEW FORMS

It is a familiar dilemma. How do the excluded engage the apparently dominant order? Does progress entail that the marginalized accept mainstream norms and abandon transformative possibilities? These questions, of course, become more complicated once we recognize that the excluded are never simply excluded and that their marginalization reflects and determines the shape, texture, and boundaries of the dominant order and its associated privileged communities. The identities of the latter are inevitably defined in opposition to, and as a negation of, the representations of the marginalized, and in certain respects, the outside is always inside: invisible perhaps, implicated and disempowered, unrecognized but omnipresent. In this context, how do the outcast imagine and calibrate progress, and assess options?

For blacks in the United States and elsewhere, this outside/inside dynamic has often been experienced asymmetrically: as political disfranchisement on the one hand and overemployment in the arenas of popular culture on the other.[1] Accordingly, in trying to map out the most effective strategies for emancipation, African Americans have had to try to understand the precise nature of the linkage between popular culture and this thing we call politics. What kinds of politics can cultural actors make if blacks, as it is commonly asserted, have a unique relationship with the cultural realm, a positioning that has been celebrated by some, and cursed and refused by others? My aim here is to identify exactly how we might situate popular culture in general, and black popular culture in particular, in relation to both the formally and informally political. Second, I want to consider the implications of reading culture as politics in the context of the post–civil rights era.[2]

One of the most intriguing aspects of contemporary black politics is the relationship among the realms of formal political activity involving black elected officials and organized interest groups; state-focused "protest" organizations such as the National Urban League, the National Association for the Advancement of Colored People (NAACP), the Rainbow Coalition, and the National Action Network; extrastate mobilization characterized by the programs of the Black Panther Party and the Nation of Islam; and the media of religiosity and popular culture. With the significant increase in organic and sympathetic elected representation following the end of Jim Crow, one might expect that the means by which African American interests are conceived and articulated (and the urgency with which they are expressed) would change. It is interesting that—despite the 1964 Civil Rights Act, which suggested a commitment to policies of anti-discrimination, and the 1965 Voting Rights Act, legislation that significantly enhanced black voting power—the realms of protest activity, extrastate and often nationalist engagement, and African American religiosity and popular culture have continued to be politically relevant. In other words, at the same time that blacks markedly increased their access to the arenas of formal political decision-making, and despite expectations that legalistic triumphs would orient most political energies toward these arenas, informal politics has continued to play a major role in mobilizing and shaping (and containing and circumscribing) black politics.[3] In particular, the negotiation, representation, and reimagination of black interests through cultural symbols has continued to be a major component in the making of black politics.

The expectation that progress on the legal front would and should bring about the routinization of black politics partly rested on the implicit assumptions that integration was the logical path to follow, that all African Americans would benefit from the opportunities made available in the new era, and that mainstreaming the means by which blacks made their politics would increase their ability to transform the public agenda. "[T]he civil rights movement will be advanced only to the degree that social and economic welfare gets to be inextricably linked with civil rights," wrote Bayard Rustin, the key strategist of the later phases of the civil rights campaign, in *Commentary* in 1965. He was making this observation at a time when a certain degree of optimism was justified. The major foundations of the Jim Crow order had been toppled, and for the first time since Reconstruction it seemed possible that a progressive and racially inclusive coalition might prevail in American politics. Rustin also predicted that a civil rights/labor/liberal coalition would be able to bring about "revolutionary" and "radical change," given that adequate "forms of political democracy [now] exist[ed]" in the United States. Beyond the "peripheral" gains of the civil rights movement, Rustin suggested that a deliberate move to exploit these opportunities would result in the full "package deal": "employment, housing, school integration, police protection, and so forth." In order to realize these possibilities, Rustin urged that the movement cease "confus[ing] political institutions with lunch counters," downplay protest, recognize compromise as inevitable, and embrace political action within the Democratic Party.[4]

Rustin's formulation hardly represented an "adjust[ment] to the status quo" and indeed offered what could only be seen as a comprehensive proposal for remaking the American republic.[5] His argument, though, was predicated on a model of the routine that clearly overlooked—and, given his own strategic commitments at the time, deliberately chose to minimize—the limits of legal discourse, the racialized foundation and irrational character of American politics, and the extent to which protest politics, and informal politics in general, were hardly unique to black communities. Not surprisingly, the civil rights/labor/liberal coalition collapsed by the end of the decade, and Rustin's confidence regarding the progressive capacity of American democracy proved to be largely misplaced.

Among blacks, even before this point, there was some uncertainty about the wisdom of placing so much faith in the institutions of the state and the formal political realm. Underlying this doubt was the perception that the transition to "politics" might not work equally well for all. Although class issues would prove to be the first visible axis of conflict—as indicated by the debate regarding the importance of launching a poor people's movement—other fronts would soon open up as well. For those not granted access and whose circumstances were not materially improved by the developments of the era—and, of course, those who were never persuaded by the integrationist argument in the first place—informal politics, other-directed politics, and protest politics would be important strategic options. Cultural politics, albeit in a modified form, would also continue to represent a significant aspect of black expression, despite optimism regarding the progressive possibilities of working within the "rules of the game." Indeed, one can read what some might cast as a continued overinvestment in cultural politics (and the various forms of informal and protest politics) as a response to the perceived inadequacies of the American state (and the nation-state as a general concept); the shortcomings of the civil rights movement on a variety of fronts, including most prominently class, gender, and sexuality; and the restructuring of the sentimental economy that had previously sustained solidaristic attachments among different black subconstituencies.

For African Americans, partly because of their marginal status and often violent exclusion from the realms of formal politics, popular culture was an integral and important aspect of the making of politics throughout the pre–civil rights era and the civil rights era itself—"a time when it was almost impossible," film historian Donald Bogle contends, "to keep politics and aesthetics apart."[6] Indeed, in the absence of any significant space for black participation in the institutionalized realm (outside of, perhaps, the machine politics associated with the city of Chicago), the notion that politics and art might not be intimately connected was rarely suggested. In this context, the cultural products that mainstream outlets created and propagated—such as the minstrel shows of the nineteenth century, films including *The Birth of a Nation*, Al Jolson's *Jazz Singer*, and *Gone with the Wind*, and the radio version of *Amos 'n' Andy*—often provoked criticism and outrage on the part of blacks who interpreted the promotion of images they saw as unfavorable, as a roadblock to their struggle for equal citizenship.

"Art was at one time the only voice we had to declare our humanity," the actor, playwright, and director Ossie Davis suggested in the late 1990s. Furthermore, he asserted, "Art among us blacks has always been a statement about our condition, and therefore it has always been political." Making specific reference to Marian Anderson's concert at the Lincoln Memorial on April 16, 1939 (after she was prevented from playing Constitution Hall by the Daughters of the American Revolution), Davis wrote: "It was for me an act of definition as well as defiance, with its own salute to the black Struggle. It married in my mind forever the performing arts as a weapon in the struggle for freedom. It made a connection that, for me and thousands of other artists, has never been severed. It was a proclamation and a commitment. . . . That voice focused me and gave me my marching orders. It reminded me that whatever I said and whatever I did as an artist was an integral part of my people's struggle to be free."[7]

Given the recognized connection between the cultural and political realms, it is not surprising that both W. E. B. Du Bois and Walter White of the NAACP wrote novels; that labor leader A. Philip Randolph initially came to New York City inspired by Du Bois's pioneering fusion of culture and politics, *The Souls of Black Folk*, to become engaged in radical politics and to become a stage actor; or that political leaders of the pre–civil rights era felt comfortable and indeed obligated to comment on African American cultural efforts.[8] As a consequence, actors involved in protest and electoral activity made frequent efforts to shape the contributions (or, if necessary, silence the voices) of individuals working in the various cultural arenas. In a 1928 *Negro World* editorial, Marcus Garvey stated, "Our race, within recent years, has developed a new group of writers who have been prostituting their intelligence, under the direction of the white man, to bring out and show up the worst traits of our people." Specifically, Garvey castigated Paul Robeson for his participation in the film version of *Show Boat* and for allowing "his genius to appear in pictures and plays that tend to dishonor, mimic, discredit and abuse the cultural attainments of the Black Race," and characterized Claude McKay's vernacular-based and sexually explicit *Home to Harlem* as "a damnable libel against the Negro."[9] Du Bois, cofounder of the NAACP, was also among the most vociferous critics of McKay's novel, and his review in the NAACP's *Crisis*—wherein he reported that the book "nauseates me, and after the dirtier parts of its filth I felt distinctly like taking a bath"—prompted McKay to reply that Du Bois was too removed "from contact with real life" to make such judgments and to contend that Du Bois had mistaken "the art of life for nonsense and [was trying] to pass off propaganda as life in art!"[10] Indeed, by that point Du Bois had developed his own clear views about the proper relationship between art and politics. In a piece published in 1926, entitled "Criteria of Negro Art," he argued: "[A]ll art is propaganda and ever must be, despite the wailing of the purists. I stand in utter shamelessness and say that whatever art I have for writing has been used always for propaganda for gaining the right of black folk to love and enjoy. I do not care a damn for any art that is not used for propaganda."[11]

THE AGONY AND THE ECSTASY: POPULAR CULTURE AND AFRICAN AMERICAN EXCEPTIONALISM

Although many artists might claim that their work is not "political"—"Nothing about politics," asserted Luther Vandross, arguably the most gifted male vocalist of his generation, "I don't write about politics"—that they are driven purely by aesthetic considerations, or that they seek to entertain and provide escape from "reality" for their audiences, political intention adheres to every cultural production.[12] Sometimes such stances are a response to the perception that "politics" narrowly understood—that is, formal politics and the individuals who operate in that domain—is inherently corrupt and corrupting, and devoid of real substance. In this spirit, South African vocalist Miriam Makeba states, "I've always said, 'I don't sing politics; I sing the truth.' I sang about the suffering we endured. It was not political, it was *honest*."[13] Artists might also claim not to be "political" to avoid the unwanted scrutiny of the state and other associated authorities in the realm of formal politics. As often, these kinds of assertions are meant to refer to the artist's disengagement from the issues driving formal political activity, although songs about romance and novels about family life, for example, certainly are political in the broadest sense. Love itself, the subversive gift, is an important public good, and loving is a significant political act, particularly among those stigmatized and marked as unworthy of love and incapable of deep commitment.

The suggestions that art and politics should be divorced also depend on a notion of the aesthetic as a realm that by definition should not be implicated with the political. Accordingly, in 1994, critic Arlene Croce disparaged the work of dancer-choreographer Bill T. Jones, and specifically his piece "Still/Here" focusing on the devastation wrought by the AIDS crisis, as "utilitarian art" inspired by "sixties permissiveness . . . [the] campaigns of the multicultural-ists, the moral guardians, and the minority groups." Throughout her review, Croce implied that art should be separated from "community outreach," and that there is something improper about infusing art with political intention.[14] In contrast, it can be argued that the "art for art's sake" position depends on an arguably false and impossible dichotomy. Political communication is not divorced from the same kinds of considerations that determine our responses to artistic work: imagine Malcolm X, for instance, without his comic timing and his sense of humor. There are aesthetic grammars that determine the relative success of political interactions and the impact of political communication in the cultural realm: signs, styles, and performances whose qualities transcend the political and artistic realms. In other words, the suggestion that aesthetics cannot be divorced from politics does not imply that we cannot make aesthetic judgments regarding creative and political work; the point is that aesthetic judgments should not be confined to the artistic realm and cannot be detached from political considerations. Accordingly, we should not resist the erasure of the lines distinguishing the politics of poetry and the poetics of the political.[15] Intentional silences also have significance: to *say nothing* suggests acceptance of, or satisfaction with, existing arrangements, and implicitly represents the expression of a political preference. If we agree that politics is, among other things, a contest about what matters and ought to be subject to consideration and debate, we will recognize both the assertion of the aesthetic and the suggestion that art is a self-contained realm "above" politics as political arguments of a particular normative type (similar to the corresponding claims that are made with regard to science).[16]

The specific relationship between popular culture and black politics also has to be understood in the broader context of the uncertainty about the status of black citizenship and specifically the question of whether African Americans are permanent outsiders, the penultimate American other.[17] Among the allegedly queer characteristics of black political behavior that provoke this type of reaction are the supposed overdependence of blacks on (male) charismatic leadership (e.g., Marcus Garvey, Adam Clayton Powell Jr., Malcolm X, Martin Luther King Jr., Jesse Jackson); the implication that blacks, unlike other groups, vote as a bloc (for the Democratic Party) and that this is somehow irrational and evidence of a lack of sophistication; the ritualistic engagement in demonstrations, protest marches, and, perhaps, riots; and the ongoing significance of the black churches in the making of black politics.[18]

Regarding this last aspect, there has been a long-running debate concerning the merits of African American religiosity and the predominant role of "the black church." This discourse can be traced back to the Marxist supposition that religion merely assisted in the obfuscation of class realities and prevented the working classes from understanding the true nature of their situation. This *opiate theory*, as Fredrick C. Harris writes, "insists that Afro-Christianity promotes otherworldliness functioning as an instrument of political pacification," and rejects the assumptions of the *inspiration theory,* which would include the civil rights movement among the political accomplishments of the black church (the frequency with which churches were targeted and destroyed by opponents of the civil rights movement obviously supports this interpretation).[19] It is not surprising, then, that Du Bois would claim "Our religion holds us in superstition" or that black ministers would be depicted as hustlers and sellouts in the films of Oscar Micheaux (e.g., *Within Our Gates* [1919], and *Body and Soul* [1924] starring Paul Robeson, a minister's son) and the comedy of Pigmeat Markham (e.g., *The Crap Shootin' Rev*).[20] "The majority black church did not support [Martin Luther] King's leadership," adds Houston Baker, in reference to the situation after World War II. "[I]ndeed, the multi-million-member National Baptist Convention relentlessly *opposed* a civil rights agenda."[21] There is also, of course, Adolph Reed Jr.'s depiction of the implications of a black politics driven by black religiosity and a dependence on faith-based institutions, in his discussion of Jesse Jackson's 1984 campaign for the presidency: "This model of [clerical] authority is fundamentally antiparticipatory and antidemocratic; in fact it is grounded on a denial of the rationality that democratic participation requires." At another point he observes, "Exceptionalist approaches to black politics typically are fed by the mystique of black churchliness and religiosity, which postulates a peculiarly racial basis of participation and representation."[22]

The suggestion that popular culture, and the various manifestations of "Saturday night's" activities, should be seen as relevant to black politics provokes many of the same reactions and potentially legitimate concerns as have assertions regarding the political significance of the black churches, black church life, and Sunday morning's rituals. At the most basic level, there is the contention that an emphasis on black popular culture as a political medium encourages exceptionalist understandings of African American political behavior. In this normative matrix, investigations and certainly celebrations of any linkages between the two realms might reinforce the notion that blacks lie outside of the (standard, masculinist) American mainstream. "[T]he ideology of race," as Hortense Spillers notes, "is founded upon the fundamental assumption that one is not a 'man'" (or, more broadly, as Valentin Mudimbe has observed, "the colonial library disseminates the concept of deviation as the best symbol of the idea of Africa").[23] "Normal" Americans, then, make their politics by collecting information through rational and regularized processes. Blacks, in contrast, pursue means that are irregular, inappropriate, probably

ineffective, and possibly in the eyes of some (e.g., the always anxious comprador class) improper, embarrassing, and shameful. On this point, Reed contends that a focus on popular culture

> boils down to nothing more than an insistence that authentic,
> meaningful political engagement for black Americans is expressed
> not in relation to the institutions of public authority—the state—or
> the workplace—but in the clandestine significance assigned
> to apparently apolitical rituals. Black people, according to this
> logic, don't mobilize through overt collective action. They do it
> surreptitiously when they look like they're just dancing. . . . This is
> don't-worry, be-happy politics.[24]

Certainly, to the extent that an emphasis on the cultural realm can encourage
facile commodification, accommodation, and incorporation into status quo
arrangements as the intriguingly expressive, the exotic, or the interesting and
entertaining other, such a strategy can produce conservative outcomes.

Claims about the political salience of black popular culture also raise concerns about the degree to which these practices can be routinized. Although
performances need not be insincere or merely calculating, and are sometimes
simply a matter of amplification (making one's intentions and message as
clear as possible), popular culture thrives on, and indeed demands, nuance,
dadaesque ambiguity, and contrapuntality as it resists fixedness in its moves
between the grounded and the fantastic. "The work that I do frequently falls,
in the minds of most people, into that realm of fiction called fantastic, or
mythic, or magical, or unbelievable," the novelist Toni Morrison suggests. "I'm
not uncomfortable with these labels."[25] Going further, Ralph Ellison contends:
"The novel at its best demands a sort of complexity of vision which politics
doesn't like."[26] While intentions are not always easily known, the effects of a
vote or a decision can be more clearly ascertained. The inclination in formal
politics toward the quantifiable and the bordered, the structured, ordered,
policeable, and disciplined is in fundamental tension with popular culture's
willingness to embrace disturbance, to engage the apparently mad and mad-
dening, to sustain often slippery frameworks of intention that act sublimi-
nally, if not explicitly, on distinct and overlapping cognitive registers, and to
acknowledge meaning in those spaces where speechlessness is the common
currency.[27] Moreover, popular culture's willingness not to know, its frequent
preference for experience over explanation, and its deployment of omission as
method and silence as meaning, as in the work of Ahmad Jamal, Miles Davis,

and Shirley Horn, mark its expressions and manifestations as distinct from the ambitions of the formally political. Finally, the ways the performative challenges the truth claims of the formally political and casts it as itself just another mode of performance explain many of the disjunctions between the two realms, and the characteristic disavowal of any intimate connection with the cultural on the part of the political narrowly understood.

It is specifically because of this disjunction between the political and cultural realms that one of the arguments Ellison and his intellectual progeny raise is so unconvincing: the obvious influence of African Americans on mainstream American culture (i.e., the blues and jazz) and the possibility that all Americans are cultural mulattoes do not translate into acceptance of blacks in the formal political structures of the (white) republic. Evidence of the implausibility of this position would include the dissonant cultural and political traditions that have developed in Memphis, the blues affectations of the late race-baiting Lee Atwater, and the code-switching abilities of former president Bill Clinton (indeed, *Juneteenth*, Ellison's posthumous novel, speaks to this kind of possibility). "We do have institutions," Ellison asserted in the early 1970s, "We have the Constitution and the Bill of Rights. *And we have jazz*."[28] While all three might share a certain bluesaic quality, the operations of the Constitution and the Bill of Rights have rarely been as amenable to the interests of African Americans, nor as reflective of their aspirations in practice, as the thing Ellison calls jazz. Furthermore, given the Ellisonian preference for jazz in its pre-bebop forms, this version of the blues aesthetic has had trouble recognizing the work of John Coltrane (post–*A Love Supreme*), Albert Ayler, Jimi Hendrix, Funkadelic, Rudy Ray Moore, Gayl Jones, and Toni Morrison as falling squarely "within the tradition."[29] The engagement with and interpellation via cultural representations of black life by (white) American citizens historically has been quite compatible with the marginalization and disfranchisement of African Americans as political subjects and potential members of the republican community. Just as the mythology of racial democracy in the Brazilian instance obscures as much as it reveals, the simple equation of the racial and ideological dynamics of the blues perspective and the jazz world with the operations of American democracy—a rhetorical stance frequently endorsed by Albert Murray, Stanley Crouch, and Wynton Marsalis—cannot be supported empirically. Rather, the Ellisonian paradigm, especially in its later iterations, is seemingly energized by an urge to curtail the political, to push it out of the frame of the artistic and the creative, a move that itself necessitates a restriction of the imaginative and a denial of the full range of the possible, intentional, and significant.[30] Ellison's rhetorical half-stepping, and his resistance to the aesthetic bleeding into the political, and vice versa, suggest, ironically, a fear of engaging the real complexities and fluidities he reserves as the domain of the creative, and a reluctance to acknowledge and struggle with the rigidities of the formally political world.

Let me now take up the broader underlying question of the anxiety about African American exceptionalism. At the most superficial level, this concern overlooks the reality that the realms of formal political activity and cultural expression are joined in a number of complicated and mundane ways, not just in the making of black politics but in the making of politics in general. That being the case, nervousness with regard to the possibility of black difference and the related desires to maintain respectability need, then, to be contextualized, and their roots and implications understood.[31]

These desires not to be excluded from the community of the "normal," often underwritten by a particular form of vindicationist spirit, can translate into an avoidance of struggle and the abandonment of transformative possibilities. The ambition to be included in mainstream spaces can necessitate accepting alienation and subordination as the price of the ticket (to use James Baldwin's term).[32] If modernity, that bundle of cultural, political, philosophical, and technological iterations and reiterations of the Renaissance, the Enlightenment, and the Industrial Revolution, "requires an alterity," as Michel-Rolph Trouillot suggests, if it implies and requires antonymic and problematic others—if it, to put it bluntly, needs "the nigger"—can those others constituted and marginalized in this manner viably challenge their circumstances without questioning the logic and language of their exclusion?[33] The apparent absence of a thickly transformative dialectic within modernity's matrix (e.g., the Hegelian blueprint); its seeming inability to shake itself free of its embedded sexism and racism; its primal tendency to read issues that make race salient as pointing toward either the premodern or antimodern; and the ways it makes, excludes, and yet exploits and contains black bodies, raise doubts about the feasibility of any simplistic reconciliation of the modern and the black (however constructed), and the more superficial depictions of the Afro-modernity and Afro-modernism projects.[34]

Given these constraints, the labor that has been devoted to making the texts of modernity self-evident and operational and the "commonsensical" exclusions and misrepresentations that render "civilization" feasible need to be exposed and acknowledged. Accordingly, those actors who are committed to changing substantively the situation of blacks are required to make plain, to borrow from Achille Mbembe, modernity's capacity to "legitimize the violence of its irrationality in the very name of reason," to contemplate abandoning any attachment to the "rules of the game," and to seek strategies, and employ whatever means available, that might destabilize and transcend the norms and assumptions underpinning the projects of modernity, despite their attractiveness, ubiquity, and apparent inescapability.[35] Among these understandings would be the privileging of the national that renders "the modern nation-state"—the "paramount structural effect of the modern social world," as Timothy Mitchell observes—natural, convenient, coherent, and appealing; and the fencing off of the aesthetic from the political.[36] The complex of imperatives imposed on nonwhites regarding economic function, cultural identity, sexuality, and civil status are constructions that those engaged by the discursive traditions and agenda that define black communities must recognize; resist through the circulation of competing narratives; and, beyond that, hopefully transcend.[37]

At one level, what I am making is a simple language claim. If modernity is more than just a flat trope representing the "new" (in other words, a benign temporal marker), if it is in fact "premised," as Wendy Brown contends, "on the notion of emergence *from* darker times and places," and accordingly continues to reconstitute peoples of African descent as subaltern others—even demanding such an arrangement—then endorsing the term would not seem to allow much room for blacks to imagine a significant improvement in their circumstances.[38] I am working here with the assumptions that underpin Toni Morrison's suggestion that "[M]odern life begins with slavery," and Paul Gilroy's conceptualization of the black Atlantic as being necessarily a counterculture of modernity.[39] In other words, in the language game staked out by the modern, blacks are uniquely locked into a relationship that allows few possibilities for agency, autonomy, or substantive negotiation. One could argue that no word in and of itself has a fixed connotation and that the meanings attached to particular terms can be challenged and revised—witness Savion Glover's efforts to redefine the art of tap dancing and free it from any embedded minstrel subtexts. While there is some validity to this point—the suggestion that the meaning of terms can float—one has to question the probability that the term "modernity" can be divested of its progressive assumptions and hierarchical designs. "Concepts have a way of carrying their etymologies with them forever," submits Walter Ong.[40] Furthermore, whether investing energy in these kinds of rehabilitative endeavors is sensible, given the range of other work that needs to be done, is open to debate, as is the wisdom of seeking emancipation through reaction.

At another level, I am obviously talking about more than just a simple language claim. There is a corresponding set of material institutions and practices that reflect the ambitions and horizons that the language envisions and demands: processes, mechanisms, and arenas that are viscerally addicted to ascriptive rankings, unavoidably colonial in their appetites, and immune to deep egalitarian reimagining and restructuring. It is these dynamics that have trifurcated black sensibilities—among various invented, static and stigmatized pasts; unevenly across the centers and margins of contemporary life; and, in response to the multiple crises that mark the modernity/slavery nexus, into the unscripted but attractive-by-default postmodern and beyond.[41] Given these dislocating logics, whether blacks are capable of functioning as modern subjects is, again, a question whose assumptions need to be interrogated, especially given the ways blackness is a constitutively modern albeit unstable formation (i.e., its commitments to possibilities in excess of and beyond modernity).

By raising the possibility that the norms, assumptions, and constructions of the modern need to be superseded, I am not overlooking the fact that blacks can rightly claim co-ownership as stockholders in the projects of modernity (and copyright holders with regard to the definition of many of these endeavors) or contending that modern developments are uniformly problematic and that there is some easy alternative. The pursuit of genuine emancipatory schemes is not a simple matter of escaping or even resisting existing arrangements (in the manner, perhaps, that new world blacks could conceivably in some past time establish maroon communities). The processes of exclusion that have defined the black experience of modernity have not allowed those of African descent to avoid the transfiguring and scarring aspects of the extended moment or complicity in its present conditions. These dynamics have also demanded sensibilities that recognize that solidarities are always contingent and essentialisms at best pragmatic, positional, and strategic.[42] Opting out, then, is not a viable—or available—response.

The logic of this argument makes the possible challenge offered by the articulation of a black aesthetic, or an explicitly ethnicized aesthetic, a less attractive course of action. The aesthetic in blackface, otherwise unreconfigured, would still leave in place the sanctity of the aesthetic and the aesthetic/political boundary. The objective, in the spirit of the arguments raised by artist-theorist Sylvia Wynter, cultural historian Clyde Taylor, and filmmaker Julio García Espinosa, is not to pluralize the aesthetic but rather to supplant it, while still leaving room for the possibility of more broadly embedded aesthetic registers.[43] For my purposes here, this stance would correspond with the reluctance to engage in the shadow discourses of Afro- or alternative modernities (indeed, the two positions are intimately linked).[44] If the aesthetic is understood as a science of beauty that forecloses substantive political engagement or challenge, it must be recognized as a key brick in the wall of modernity and one of the cornerstones of the racialized edifice that has so effectively contained and restricted black life chances. Given the synchronic political marginalization of black peoples and cultural hyperdeployment of representations of blackness, a transformative approach would have to move far beyond the conjoined and overlapping imperatives of the aesthetic and the modern.

My suggestive reference to a black fantastic, then, is meant to refer to the minor-key sensibilities generated from the experiences of the underground, the vagabond, and those constituencies marked as deviant—notions of being that are inevitably aligned within, in conversation with, against, and articulated beyond the boundaries of the modern.[45] The surrealist movements of the early and mid-twentieth century and the broader neosurrealist tradition, in their attempts to fuse dream worlds and everyday practices and bridge the politics/culture divide, are obvious reference points and sources of sustenance. (Indeed, one might suggest that representations of blackness are always surreal, given the inevitably irregular and provocative qualities of these efforts and the "source material" itself in a broader context in which the nonblack is thoroughly normalized.) We might also think here of the struggles to establish and maintain space for substantive, open-ended deliberative activity and the related commitment to the nurturing of potentially subversive forms of interiority through and by which private geographies are made available to the public. The *black* in black fantastic, in this context, signifies both a generic category of underdeveloped possibilities and the particular "always there" interpretations of these agonistic, postracial, and post-colonial visions and practices generated by subaltern populations.[46]

The effort here is to identify meaningful and social as well as consciously imperfect and in-process notions of autonomy and emancipation that can survive the challenge of those who legitimately critique the hidden imperialisms that underwrite too many of our notions of progress, cosmopolitanism, the human and the universal.[47] The hope is that these contingent, evolving, and uncommon thick particularisms in the aggregate represent an appealing and viable alternative to the inevitable frustrations and racially bound, unproductive labor associated with the efforts to work within the standard narratives of modernity. By bringing into view and into the field of play practices and ritual spaces that are often cast as beyond the reasonable and relevant—to the point, indeed, of being unrecognizable as politics—these visions might help us gain normative traction in an era characterized by the dismissal of any possibilities beyond the already existing.

My concern is to identify the ways these sensibilities and activities in and around the joints of the politics/popular culture matrix, derived from a particular understanding of the relationship between blackness and modernity, might transcend the prevailing notions of the aesthetic and the predominance of the state as the sole frame for subject formation and progressive and transformative discourse and mobilization. The fantastic in this context would entail unsettling these governmentalities and the conventional notions of the political, the public sphere, and civil society that depend on the exclusion of blacks and other nonwhites from meaningful participation and their ongoing reconstitution as raw material for the naturalization of modern arrangements. These perspectives and practices would require, then, both decentering the state and overriding the aesthetic and, in the process, pushing to the surface exactly those tensions and possibilities that are necessarily suppressed and denied in the standard respectability discourses associated with the preservation of the modern.

Returning to the anxieties regarding black difference, then, the fusion of the realms of politics and popular culture in mainstream American life *does* at one level present a unique array of dilemmas, problems, and opportunities for blacks. Nevertheless, the claim that the integration of cultural actors into the framework of black politics legitimizes exceptionalist understandings of African American inclinations overlooks the possibility that being exceptional in relation to the standard practices and norms prevailing in American life need not necessarily be a bad thing; naturalizes a national frame that deserves troubling; and arguably misses the point. Hyperactivity on the cultural front usually occurs as a response to some sort of marginalization from the processes of decision-making or exercising control over one's own circumstances; what might appear to be an overinvestment in the cultural realm is rarely a freely chosen strategy. American blacks are not "different" in this respect because they have chosen to be but because of the exclusionary and often violent practices that have historically defined black citizenship and public sphere participation as problematic and because of the recognition that the cultural realm is always in play and already politically significant terrain. In other words, not engaging the cultural realm, whether defensively or assertively, would be, to some degree, to concede defeat in an important—and relatively accessible—arena. "Precisely because African Americans historically have had more control over their own culture than many other aspects of their world," historian Waldo

Martin Jr. adds, "culture has always been a critical battleground in their freedom struggle."[48] The factors, then, that might provoke such (perceived) overinvestments and the implications of such developments need to be acknowledged and investigated, as the logical error of reading these choices outside of their causal fields must be avoided.

Anxieties about institutionalizing and celebrating difference aside, another significant concern that underlies many of the objections to the reading of popular culture as a form of politics is normative. On one level, the desirability of incorporating specifically *popular* culture into formal politics is complicated by the extent to which the images of black life that have had an impact in mainstream circles have tended often to promote distorted notions of black humanity (e.g., minstrelsy, *The Adventures of Huckleberry Finn*, the signifying black smile, *The Birth of a Nation*, Elvis, Madonna, and the work of Quentin Tarantino), despite their occasionally transgressive qualities. Given the constant containment aspect that has been historically characteristic of these forms of entertainment, and their frequent deployment of black bodies as punctuation, it would not appear sensible to encourage the further merging of the realms of formal politics and popular culture. Indeed, one could instead urge their further disentanglement; for what kinds of politics are likely to be encouraged by processes in which cultural actors play a significant role, especially given the often dialectic tension between the qualifier "black" and the term "popular culture" and the symbolically (and problematically) loaded nature of what are perceived to be black performances, in the broadest sense, for nonblack audiences?[49]

Clearly, the messages emanating from the arenas of popular culture can generate action and inaction, and encourage reactionary as well as progressive mindsets. Reed writes that popular culture does not qualify as politics, that "the beauty of cultural politics . . . [is that] it can coexist comfortably with any kind of policy orientation," but he does not grapple with the reality that there is a need to at least acknowledge the status quo–oriented and reactionary perspectives that can gain sustenance within the realms of popular culture.[50] The ways popular culture can mobilize or demobilize—for instance, the way much of turn-of-the-century black pop (ranging from rapper Jay-Z's "Hard Knock Life [Ghetto Anthem]" to gospel vocalist Donnie McClurkin's "We Fall Down") naturalized economic hardship and specifically black poverty—need to be integrated into any effective framework for understanding the development of black politics. If we are to understand black politics fully, from an empirical or academic perspective, we cannot overlook those spaces that generate difficult data. Similarly, those committed to progressive change must also engage with those arenas and voices that promote regressive and discomforting narratives.

Regardless of the content and impact of these communications, their significance, and the pattern of their effects, if any, need to be considered. To the extent that simple recognition is an important political goal for political actors, the different media of popular culture provide a means by which this need can be satisfied. While simply *being seen*, in and of itself, is rarely translated into an acknowledgment of the legitimacy of one's interests or action on behalf of those concerns, pop culture's ability to render the invisible visible (in an Ellisonian sense perhaps) or the unheard audible—and possibly, to borrow from Ellison and Fred Moten, the invisible audible and the unheard visible—gives it a certain political legitimacy.[51] In those instances where recognition itself is the intended end point of political activity, cultural politics often might suffice.[52] Finally, popular culture's ability—and tendency—to redefine the political, and cross the gendered and racialized borders distinguishing the public and private realms, should not be overlooked, nor should its status with regard to questions of political economy.

It is extremely rare—though not impossible—for actions undertaken by creative artists alone to bring about specific substantive public policy reorientations on the part of state authorities. Rather, the discursive disruptions artists instigate and the meanings read into their actions and creations are most likely to have a more diffuse, symbolic impact, at least in the external domain. Although music, films, and books are capable to some degree of generating attention around a specific issue, generally popular culture is about the mobilization of broader and less coherent sentiments.[53] At the same time, political movements' and campaigns' effectiveness in achieving particular policy objectives is affected by the broader atmospheric and symbolic discourses taking place. Indeed, it could be argued that the development of broader solidaristic sensibilities, which are crucial to sustaining a progressive politics in an era of neoliberal individuation, is *best* accomplished by means of the actions of creative artists.

SOME SING, SOME DANCE: FUNCTION, FORM, AND DOMAIN

One of the important functions popular culture has played has involved providing a location for the discussion of issues of concern and the making of black politics.[54] This role became even more significant over the course of the decades following the civil rights era because of the marked transformation of the accessible, structured spaces for intramural black discourse. Indeed, some analysts have suggested that a viable black counterpublic has not existed for the last three decades. "[S]uch a public sphere did exist within the Black community as recently as the early 1970s," observed Michael Dawson in the mid-1990s, "if by that we mean a set of institutions, communication networks and practices which facilitate debate of causes and remedies to the current combination of political setbacks and economic devastation facing major segments of the Black community, and which facilitate the creation of oppositional formations and sites." As a result of the processes unleashed by the civil rights movement, though, he asserted, "A Black public sphere does not exist in contemporary America," although he would later modify this claim somewhat and refer to the black counterpublic as "severely undermined" and being in a state of "disintegration."[55]

Although black dialogical spaces and media were significantly reordered over the course of the 1970s, it was only toward the end of this period that previously marginalized constituencies within the black community were able to mobilize and develop their own communicative networks (e.g., the formation of the National Black Feminist Organization and the Combahee River Collective, in 1973 and 1975, respectively, and later the National Coalition of Black Lesbians and Gays in 1978). The concerns of African American women, gays and lesbians, and lower-income cohorts rose to the surface—if only briefly in some instances—in a way that was largely impossible during the supposed glory days of the black public sphere that Dawson and others have highlighted.[56] A more accurate account might suggest that the conventional wisdom equates the viability and efficacy of black deliberative autonomy with the promotion of the interests of primarily straight, middle-class (or aspiring to be middle-class) men and overlooks other constituencies (as well as more local processes and micropublics that, in contrast to national arenas, are more likely to feature women in decision-making roles). This revised narrative is also suggestive in the same way that the coincidence of the implosion of the Left in the United States and the peak of the civil rights movement provokes questions about American progressives: what does it mean that the black public sphere—to use Dawson's terminology—is seen as collapsing at the same time that lower-income constituencies, women, lesbians, and gays start to mobilize?[57] That said, one might argue that black spaces continue to operate under constant pressure of erasure while resisting the assertion that an across-the-board collapse of some sort occurred at some point in the 1970s.

With regard to the activities taking place in these reconfigured public spaces, it is important not to exaggerate the distinction between the external and internal dimensions of the politics/popular culture nexus in the shaping and expression of African American politics. The blurring of the clear lines that demarcated black spaces is one of the legacies of the civil rights movement. There is currently a limited ability for blacks to discuss issues in arenas not accessible to others. Black life has, in many respects, become intensely public, partly as a result of the dramas that unfolded in the early 1990s, featuring in quick and painful succession Clarence Thomas, Anita Hill, Rodney King, and O. J. Simpson, among others. Accordingly, the actor-director Charles Dutton recalls that the singer Dionne Warwick told him she left before the completion of a performance of August Wilson's play *The Piano Lesson* in which he was appearing because "[S]he couldn't take it anymore.... [W]e were letting white folks in on all of our sacred little things."[58] To some extent, similar concerns underpinned the controversies surrounding the popular 2002 film *Barbershop* and the mocking references made by one of its lead characters to Rosa Parks, Martin Luther King Jr., and Jesse Jackson. "I was surprised it [i.e., the debate about the film] went straight to the media," noted O'Shea "Ice Cube" Jackson, one of the film's stars.[59]

This translucence is, of course, not entirely new: consider Booker T. Washington's double performance in Atlanta in 1895. Washington's simultaneous engagement of southern black and white audiences (and, to some extent, northern whites as well) with his famous Exposition speech downplaying the importance of civil rights while in a lower register encouraging black economic autonomy exemplifies a problematic Clyde Taylor has identified: "The speaker in this position attempts to master a language and thematic understandable by the majority while also speaking to affirm the values and interests of the in-house group." Continuing, Taylor asks the question that underpins most of the anxieties regarding black life and discourse played out in public and that animated most of the analyses of Washington's speech: "[W]hich of two masters does the text most effectively serve?"[60] In this respect, the Atlanta address and the responses it generated, and Washington's subsequent intentionally public role through the Tuskegee Machine in promoting a script that sought to restrict the substantive contours of black discourse foreshadowed later developments in the post–civil rights era. While Washington operated in a period in which black politics and popular culture remained largely behind the veil, to use Du Bois's terminology, developments in the last two decades of the twentieth century fundamentally challenged any assumptions about the sanctity of the black counterpublic/white public sphere divide and provoked even deeper concerns with respect to the implications of black deliberative engagements and performances being accessible to nonblack audiences.

The remaking of the racial architecture that occurred post-1965 also suggests that the traditional frameworks for discussing and distinguishing black politics and discourses might need to be abandoned or, at the very least, troubled. On a superficial level, it has long been a common practice for black actors and movements to draw in varying degrees from both the integrationist and nationalist traditions, depending on the audience in question and the prevailing circumstances. While this is not a new phenomenon, it becomes much less remarkable and awkward after the civil rights movement. This is particularly true following the gradual domestication of the nationalist agenda, as evidenced in the transition in emphasis from emigration in the nineteenth century to the support of segregated development within the United States, and to the community control projects that emerged in the post–civil rights era. The diminished coherence of the integrationist stance in the face of successive white backlashes and withdrawals should also be considered a contributing factor to the decreased resonance of the integrationist/nationalist divide. It is useful to recall that integrationism itself only becomes an explicit goal of organizations such as the NAACP in the 1940s in the context of the struggle to desegregate the military—previously the goal had been identified as a matter of achieving civil rights.

It is perhaps in the contemporary production and consumption of black cultural politics that the displacement of relatively procedural questions of location and orientation becomes most obvious. Operating in deterritorialized arenas—for example, radio, television, and the internet—that confound the older understandings of the distinction between integrated and segregated spaces, artists in the post–civil rights era have been major contributors to the recalibration of the black discursive agenda. In their choices regarding whether to conform or transform, resist or embrace, confront or disengage, the distinct substantive dimensions of political and cultural existence become more salient and germane. Questions of geography and genealogy have less purchase on black thought as the inside and outside; the local, transnational, and global; and the past, present and future become conjoined and in some respects conflated. Moreover, beyond the cataloguing of geographical presences and genealogical connections, there is the possibility of approaching black identifications conceptually: as a matter of indexing a related set of sensibilities that resist quantification, physical or temporal classifications, and corporeal boundaries.

As a result of this paradigm shift, and the related reordering of the black counterpublic, the primacy and stridency of the integrationist/nationalist debate subsides, as other concerns related to class, gender, sexuality, generation, and blackness in the aggregate emerge and become predominant. Clearly, the absorption with questions of segregation and assimilation has not dissipated completely; it lies just below the surface of almost every issue that attracts the interest of colored America (and the rest of the country as well). Furthermore, these questions are driven by very real substantive concerns: who are we if we make our politics and our selves over there as opposed to right here? It is hardly inconceivable that the integrationist/nationalist cleavage might reemerge as the most salient axis of African American discourse. That said, it is still remarkable how rarely contemporary black concerns are articulated in the terms of the earlier categorical language and how antiquated in some respects the inside/outside framework appears in the current moment, particularly if we consider the issue from the vantage point of the popular culture/politics nexus.[61]

Following this realignment, in choosing to *say something,* black artists can seek both to influence outcomes and to redefine the terms of debate, within and outside their immediate communities, and to bring attention to—and perhaps confer legitimacy on—the spaces in which they operate (whether these are black-community-specific or not). This merging of the substantive and the procedural—the support of certain agendas and the maintenance of viable dialogical spheres—can occur simultaneously inside and outside black spaces (to the extent, again, that such spaces can be identified). Alternately, these efforts can be strategically ordered, for example, by focusing first on intracommunity campaigns before deciding to intervene in broader discursive processes. Regardless of strategic preferences, cultural media and the actors involved in these arenas have played an increasingly crucial role in defining the aggregate black agenda and determining which issues will move from the internal arenas to the broader national stage (and possibly the international stage) with the perceived support of most African Americans.[62]

Regarding the issue of intentionality, cultural productions, moments, and gestures can have political and social meanings attributed to them regardless of their creators' objectives—for example, the "Burn, Baby! Burn!" exclamation identified with radio deejay the Magnificent Montague, and Aretha Franklin's "Respect." "I'm not a politician or political theorist," contends Franklin. "I don't make it a practice to put my politics into my music or social commentary. But the fact that 'Respect' naturally became a battle cry and an anthem for a nation shows me something."[63] In this context, consider the interpretations of Martha and the Vandellas' 1964 recording "Dancing in the Street." "Few blacks," suggests Gerald Early, "accepted the song on its face, insisting that it was a metaphorical theme song for black unity and . . . revolution."[64] In 1965, Rolland Snellings, at the time a member of the Revolutionary Action Movement and subsequently (as Askia Muhammad Touré) one of the more prominent poets associated with the Black Arts movement, invoked the recording as a "Riot-song": "We sing in our young hearts, we sing in our angry Black Souls: WE ARE COMING UP! WE ARE COMING UP! And it's reflected in the Riot-song that symbolized Harlem, Philly, Brooklyn, Rochester, Patterson, Elizabeth; this song of course, 'Dancing in the Streets'—making Martha and the Vandellas legendary. . . . OUR songs are turning from 'love,' turning from being 'songs,' turning into WAYS, into WAYS, into 'THINGS.'"[65]

In contrast, Martha Reeves, the group's lead singer, contends that the song, released on July 31, 1964, "actually came out just after the riots occurred but, even so, the rumor got stirred up. It offended me because I would never be a part of anything like that. I've always promoted love, my songs are about heartbreak not [the] beating up of heads or breaking down of buildings and destroying anyone's property." Reeves, who would subsequently be elected to Detroit's city council, is correct to note that the riots that took place in Harlem and Rochester that summer happened before the release of the single (although other conflicts, including those in Jersey City, Elizabeth, and Paterson, New Jersey, and Philadelphia—one of the cities mentioned in the lyrics—occurred the same summer, after the song's release).[66] Despite her understanding of the recording and the group's intentions, though, it is not surprising that others uncovered different possibilities: distinct readings she would have to consider in her subsequent performances of the composition (at least in the mid- and late 1960s). The song does feature a certain post-King sensibility, and in its reclaiming of the streets, its references to (mostly) northern cities, and its propulsive, assertive rhythm, one can detect some sense of the changes that were taking place at the time (e.g., the campaign to open up the Democratic Party at its convention in Atlantic City the same summer). Marvin Gaye, one of the song's coauthors, offers that "of all the acts back then, I thought Martha and the Vandellas came closest to really saying something. It wasn't a conscious thing, but when they sang numbers like 'Quicksand' or 'Wild One' or 'Nowhere to Run' or 'Dancing in the Street,' they captured a spirit that felt political to me."[67] Indeed, a unique pent-up energy radiates throughout many of the group's classic singles that could be easily translated and adapted to the broader circumstances pertaining in that particular era. Cultural work, then, must be understood as a result of the interactions of the creative process and its embedded intentions; the potentially quite distinct and even contrasting—but equally creative—use made of them by others; and the feedback mechanisms and interpolative possibilities linking these various stages (in both senses of the word).[68]

If, as political theorists often insist, the opportunity to debate and the quality of deliberation are important, the arenas of popular culture offer more accessible spaces for engagement than the officially recognized mechanisms of decision-making.[69] This is especially true in light of the developments during the 2000 and 2004 national elections (i.e., the fact that there is no guarantee that one's vote will even be counted), and given the limited number of other effective means for substantive political debate among African Americans in the electoral realm. The concerns of certain black constituencies have not been responded to, and indeed been avoided, by black elected officials. The silences and evasions, which have been at times encouraged by other blacks, have not been as audible or apparent in the formal political realms—nor for that matter in the original added content provided by what remains of the black press, black-oriented radio, or the newer black media—as they have been in the aggregated arenas of popular culture.[70] In other words, the agenda-setters controlling these black-oriented media outlets have been on the whole reluctant to reproduce unfiltered the intracommunity negotiations and conflicts taking place within African American popular culture.

A number of factors can explain these circumstances: the absence of structured and recognized mechanisms within black communities for expression of internal disagreements, local political structures sufficiently sensitive to intracommunity conflicts, and a significant political movement to the left of the Democratic Party; disenfranchisement and continued black mis- and underrepresentation; and the ways the workings of race in American life have discouraged the slightest manifestations of "black disunity."[71] With regard to the logic underlying this last point, Charles Hamilton argued in 1970:

> If we would understand the nature of The Modern Political Struggle,
> we would understand that its essence lies not in traditional debates
> among ourselves that our very gallant forefathers of necessity had to
> engage in. We would quickly resolve those differences and move to a
> new level—a level occasioned by new times and new needs and new
> possibilities. For example: The mass media is a new variable. How
> are we going to organize to use it? To continue to debate and blast
> each other—to the entertainment of white people? Or to carefully
> politicize masses of Black people?[72]

Hamilton's analysis speaks to a sensibility that assumes that public discourse among blacks is problematic and, with its confident deployment of collective pronouns, assumes that race itself is a legitimate marker of community lines. For black public officials persuaded, understandably, by these sorts of sentiments, there is little inclination to engage in open debate with regard to the options available to African Americans. Actors in the cultural arenas, then, like early twentieth-century soapbox orators, have often been the primary public generators of black conventional wisdoms, and the main protagonists in the evolving battles concerning the negotiation of the boundaries of black community, and the definition of the aggregate black agenda. African American elected officials have been less often called on to play these roles; unwilling to get involved beyond engaging in the overlapping theatrics associated with performing blackness and performing accountability; discouraged, overcommitted, or powerless; or simply unable to respond in any useful manner or contemplate possibilities beyond the already existing.

This characterization of the limitations of contemporary black electoral politics needs to be further contextualized. Black elected officials are not deficient or retrograde in comparison to their colleagues in the legislative branch. Indeed, they—especially the members of the Congressional Black Caucus (CBC)—have consistently been the most likely to promote liberal and democratic alternatives, and the most reliable defenders of black interests in congressional debates. Although some subconstituencies are neglected and underserved, black elected officials are also, in the aggregate, more economically and socially liberal and progressive than the communities they represent. At the same time, the ability and capacity of black representatives to risk public deliberations among themselves is restricted by the relative size of the black contingent in the formal realm, strategic considerations, and the racially polarized foundation on which American politics rests. This last point is important. Because race is still a major, arguably *the* major, structuring contributor to the shape and substance of American politics, black politics still operate under some serious constraints, and crossracial coalitions are still extremely difficult to sustain.[73]

The choices made by black elected officials have also illustrated the salience of the processes of linked fate and secondary marginalization, developed by political scientists Michael Dawson and Cathy Cohen, respectively.[74] Although belatedly in some instances, inclusive movements of the sort Dawson describes have developed in response to cases of police brutality, reparations, racial profiling, voting rights infractions, and other race-related civil rights violations, and been accompanied by movements within black popular culture (e g., the numerous recordings generated by the murder of Amadou Diallo).[75] Despite the fault lines that have become magnified within black communities since the end of the civil rights era (including class, which is the focus of most of Dawson's attention), issues perceived to be linked directly to race have continued to mobilize significant support among African Americans and black elected officials.[76]

In contrast, issues regarding class, gender, sexuality, and the "boundaries" of American blackness, to use Cohen's term, have not, for the most part, generated the same level of interest from, or cohesion among, black elected officials or black publics. On those occasions when these actors have been engaged by these issues, the responses have lacked intensity and enthusiasm (as evidenced in the debates about welfare reform and AIDS policy). Indeed, as Cohen notes, these concerns and their advocates have often been (actively) marginalized within black communities. The literal and emotional redistricting that has taken place in the post–civil rights era has not been nearly as apparent in the realms of formal political activity—nor, for that matter, the realms of protest and extrastate activity—as it has been in black music, film, comedy and comic strips (i.e., *The Boondocks*), literature, video, athletics, and to a lesser degree, television (particularly Black Entertainment Television [BET]), theatre, and the fine arts. Indeed, beyond deliberation, I will argue that official politics have been pulled into vernacular spaces and that de facto decisions have been made in the cultural realm regarding issues of clear political significance.

TELLING STORIES

The broad question with which I started, of how the marginalized should respond to the shifting terms of their exclusion, is closely related to the narrower concern underlying this book. What happens to the assumption that popular culture and politics are intimately and optimally linked after the paradigm shift that marks the end of the civil rights era with its post-nationalist, post-soul, post-black, and anti-nigger echoes? Both questions speak not only to the dilemmas facing black communities and their representatives throughout the diaspora but to the character, salience and viability of diasporic identifications themselves. African Americans, defined broadly, European blacks, and continental Africans are all currently grappling with distinct but overlapping forms of demoralization, Afro-pessimism, and postcolonial melancholia, to borrow—out of context—a phrasing from Paul Gilroy, and with a hegemonic incentive structure that posits that black imaginations should neither trouble the aesthetic/politics boundary nor exceed nation-state borders. The current moment is characterized much more by its acceptance of these dominant scripts of modernity than by a willingness to challenge the slippery and changing bases on which blacks have been excommunicated by the reification and deification of the modern. At the beginning of the twenty-first century, we seem to have agreed that there is no escaping this modernity—so wide we can't get around it—and, accordingly, its problematics and implicit margins. Even our references to alternative modernities suggest a primary template that might at best allow certain variations on a relatively fixed score. My goal here is to understand what role popular culture has played in getting us to this point, and perhaps pushing against the grain, the potentially transformative, thickly emancipatory and substantively post-colonial visions these black performances might offer in their lower registers: their capacity to displace modernity as a master signifier within black and global discourse, along with its norms and modal infrastructures.

Throughout the book, I aim to bring together a number of distinct disciplines and fields of study—political science and cultural studies, African American studies and diaspora studies, American studies and postcolonial studies, among others—in order to insert the African American and American examples more explicitly into discourses that tend to overlook the particular significance of American data for our understanding of our modern circumstances. And vice versa: I am interested in placing the study of the United States in a comparative framework as well as one that attends to the artificiality of national boundaries. Toward these ends, Chapter 2 examines the political developments within black popular culture in the period after the Red Scare and the efforts to create forms of blackness from outside and from within that might align more easily with the borders and ambitions of the modern American project. In particular, I argue that the Cold War marks an important turn with regard to the pressures to separate the roles of creative artist and political activist by focusing on the experiences of, among others, Paul Robeson, Lorraine Hansberry, and Harry Belafonte and the related changes that took place in the relationship between black politics and popular culture between 1945 and 1965. Chapter 3 considers the emergence of the Black Arts Movement and its impact on African American politics leading up to the 1972 National Black Political Assembly. The focus is on the various attempts to renegotiate the relationship between actors in the cultural arena and those in the realm of formal politics and the resulting contest over the location and substance of politics. Despite efforts to restrict black political energies within the boundaries of formal politics, I argue that actors in the cultural realm continue to resist arrangements that confine black deliberative activity spatially and temporally to the places and rhythms preferred by the increasing ranks of black elected officials. In Chapter 4, I suggest that the technological changes occurring in the 1980s—especially with regard to the visual arts—challenge intracommunity assumptions about the inheritability of black political traditions and indeed the sustainability of a coherent black politics. Chapter 5 follows chronologically and thematically from the previous chapter and examines the ways shifts in black discourse, situated in popular culture, might have affected, and not just reflected, the way blacks responded to the welfare reform debates of the mid-1990s (i.e., regarding the reform/abolition of Aid to Families with Dependent Children [AFDC]). I seek to establish in this section that black deliberative activity cannot be captured or understood by focusing only on that which happens in the arenas of formal politics and policy making. In this chapter, and the next, I also contend that the standard discourses of citizenship might be questioned in light of their dependence on the trope of the nigger. Chapter 6 examines the intersection of the two primary concerns of this book: the relationship between the aesthetic and the political and that between the national and the diasporic. In a discussion that considers the boundary work and play that link Garveyism, modernism, reggae, and the emergence of hip-hop, I also consider the question of the relationship between deliberative space and black politics from a perspective that does not posit the nation-state as the only or final frontier. Where the previous chapter hints at the instability of modern infrastructures, in this chapter I discuss more explicitly the transgressibility of the modernity/coloniality matrix and, specifically, diaspora's capacity through cultural exchange to challenge modern narratives that obscure their colonial underpinnings. Chapter 7 is presented as a sort of remix of the previous chapter in its examination of the gendered dynamics and colonial narratives that have underpinned diasporic relations and attempts to map and temporalize the ways African American (cultural) politics have been energized and limited by certain identifications in the realms of gender and sexuality. Here, I propose that exchange in the cultural arena has the potential not only to upset the nation—in at least two senses—but also to counter the masculinist norms that often structure both state-centered and diasporic politics. The last chapter is a brief overview of the book's central claims. Here, as in the rest of the book, my intention is to be suggestive rather than comprehensive, given the range of topics and artistic media under consideration. The goal is to highlight the possible ways a deep engagement with popular culture might enhance our understanding of developments in the formal political arena and to suggest that greater attention to a fuller range of deliberative practices and spaces might compel a revision of our notions of the political.

Whereof we cannot speak thereof we must be silent.

—Ludwig Wittgenstein, *Tractatus Logico-Philosophicus*

What now emerges into prominence is the family

considered as an element internal to population, and as a

fundamental instrument in its government.

—Michel Foucault, "Governmentality"

2

REMEMBERING THE FAMILY

If modern sensibilities suggest that those of African descent are outliers, it is not surprising that some of those so designated would seek to establish their credentials as able citizens deserving of equal treatment without challenging the terms on which their marginalization occurred. In the context of the struggle over the proper definition of black politics, the black agenda, and blackness itself that has occurred since World War II, this reluctance manifested itself as a hegemonic bundle of inclinations and efforts to render the already said unsaid and unimaginable. This dominant set of impulses informed the steady rhetorical retreat that has characterized black politics since the Cold War: the splitting of the civil rights movement from the Left that occurred in the 1940s and 1950s; the associated disconnection of the domestic civil rights campaign from other international and diasporic anticolonial movements; the resistance to second wave feminism as it was enunciated by women of color in the 1960s, 1970s, and 1980s; the related increasingly ambivalent response to the call for progressive policy reform within the framework of the liberal welfare state; and recently, to a significantly lesser extent, the questioning of the value and appropriateness of antiracist mobilization. Consistent with these campaigns were the celebration of pragmatism, instrumentalism, and compromise; the abandonment of the convention movement, black counterpublics, and shared spaces, once they are used to broaden rather than constrict black possibilities; and the rhetorical shunning and shaming of protest activities, political engagement on the part of the black churches, and the efforts to imagine and seek change via the cultural realm.[1]

These investments can be linked in some respects to the shared sentiments that informed Ralph Ellison's pre–civil rights era American Negroism; the former Popular Front singer Bayard Rustin's arguments and increasingly Habermasian commitments regarding the irrationality of protest strategies in the mid-1960s; and Adolph Reed's post–civil rights concerns about what he has cast as problematic evidence of African American exceptionalism. Common to these perspectives is also a certain liminal pessimism with regard to the implications of the (black) popular. Like the anxious and cross-pressured finance ministers of indebted states that have been ordered to undergo structural readjustment by the International Monetary Fund, these actors are for the most part committed to integrating black communities into the American body politic and the modern order, on the terms they imagine—or feel compelled to suggest—that these entities and constructions operate. Working in a broader rhetorical context in which alternatives to American liberalism and modernity increasingly seem to be lacking and fantastical, this valorization of black realpolitik, even by progressives, appears "rational" and justified.

By suggesting that Rustin's calls for downplaying protest are part of a broader cycle, I do not mean to imply that he was opposed to black internationalism or a welfare state oriented toward institutionalizing comprehensive and redistributive public goods or that he supported the maintenance of the prevailing status quos with regard to questions of gender and sexuality. In all of these instances, Rustin's commitments were generally progressive and, on occasion, transformative. Similarly, Ellison's and Reed's politics in the aggregate are hardly conservative. While their prescriptions were not nearly as effectively conservative as those proposed publicly by Booker T. Washington as part of a similar earlier campaign, what does resonate in the arguments these strategists have made is a certain emerging caution with regard to the trajectory of black politics and the scope of black claims, ambitions, and practices. Given their suggestion that mainstream practices should be the yardstick against which the wisdom of black strategies should be assessed, the emphasis on "normalizing" black politics and practices corresponded, and possibly contributed implicitly, to a rhetorical reticence and inevitable substantive retreat on the part of black publics. To the extent that the approximation of mainstream American norms becomes a priority—and at points *the* priority—such commitments imply a logic that can have logarithmic effects and implications (and is, at the very least, in tension with some of their other positions). Progressive and transformative proposals, in this logical matrix, only become acceptable if they correspond to the patterns and practices prevalent in the American national context. Blacks, accordingly, should never unilaterally dissent or "act out."

In this context, it might be useful to think of the anxiety regarding the blurring of the lines that distinguish politics and popular culture as not just exemplary of the modern/black dilemma but crucial and perhaps central to an understanding and investigation of that broader problematic. Figures engaged in both popular culture and politics put into question the frames that have been constituted and reified to keep these realms alienated and apart. Also disrupted is the enforcement of other norms that have been rendered as conventional wisdoms with regard to appropriate performances of class status, gender, and sexuality, as the boundary transgressor or space traitor takes things to places they do not belong, carrying materials and sentiments that are quotidian in one arena into contexts where they become unavoidably surplus and intrinsically provocative. Such displays would mitigate, for example, against the nation-state's attempts to naturalize the splitting of the self into that which is—always incompletely—integrated into the state as citizen and that which haunts that project by imagining ways of being and communal identifications that transcend, ignore, displace, upend, or undermine the singular predominance of these administrative investments and arrangements. This double consciousness, to invoke a familiar reference, is especially evident in the interpellation of nonwhite subjects. To understand, then, the unstable text that is the black/modern and the nature of the shifting connections between politics and popular culture, a good starting point is the status of the artist-activist, that presence that must be read as an implicit rejection of these compelled and internalized binary estrangements and, in general, as a challenge to the promotion of both the aesthetic and the national as signifiers of respectability.

My aim in this chapter is to trace the developments in the Cold War, civil rights, and immediate post–civil rights eras regarding the viability of the artist-activist as other civil rights leaders rooted in the protest tradition—narrowly defined—and elected officials sought to establish their legitimacy as the most appropriate representatives of black interests. Black political leadership in this period largely lay outside the halls of Congress and, for that matter, the state legislatures and municipal administrations that determined the policies that affected black communities. During this time, there were only four black members of Congress (all Democrats): William L. Dawson, from Chicago, who was first elected in 1943 and served until 1970; Adam Clayton Powell Jr., who represented Harlem from 1945 until 1967 (and then again from 1969 to 1971); and later Detroit's Charles C. Diggs Jr. (1955–80) and Philadelphia's Robert N. C. Nix (1958–79).[2] In the absence of significant representation within electoral politics, civil rights leaders and cultural actors provided much of the public leadership of black communities.

Much of this leadership came from the left side of the political spectrum. In the 1930s and 1940s, the Communist Party had established closer links with the civil rights movement than any other progressive movement in American history. As a result of the connections among the Congress of Industrial Unions, the major civil rights groups, and the left wing of the Democratic Party, the Left was at its peak in terms of its influence on American politics, especially if we include left-of-center movements operating outside of the Communist Party of the United States (CPUSA), for instance, the anti-Communist, originally socialist-oriented work of A. Philip Randolph within the Brotherhood of Sleeping Car Porters, the mainstream labor movement, disaffected but still left-leaning former communists, Marxists, Trotskyists, and socialists, of various hues.

The CPUSA was hardly the ideal partner in the civil rights venture, given its ties to the foreign policy concerns of the Soviet Union, and subsequently Joseph Stalin's pogroms, through the Comintern; its chronic inability to reckon with black autonomy (whether expressed institutionally as nationalism or in artistic, cultural, and religious forms); and its willingness at a moment's notice to "go slow" with regard to, or abandon, the civil rights cause.[3] The Party did provide, though, a space for the development of alternatives to the American status quo on both the class and race fronts. "The reality of the day was that anyone who took an active interest in the plight of black people was naturally drawn toward the Communist Party—not as a member, necessarily, but at least as a friend and ally, owing to the fact that the Communists historically had been out front in the struggle for civil rights," recollects Coleman Young, an activist in the labor movement:

> The prevailing paranoia about communism was consequently
> translated into a paranoia about civil rights—although in retrospect,
> it is difficult to say which was the predominant phobia. It seemed
> that the government was unable to make any distinction between
> civil rights and communism, and by extension, between civil rights

and subversion. . . . It was all but impossible for a black person to avoid the Communist label as long as he or she advocated civil rights with any degree of vigor.[4]

By explicitly challenging American mores and espousing an internationalist rhetoric, the communist Left opened up American domestic arrangements and foreign policies—and the connections between the two—for scrutiny in a way that no purely domestic movement could have managed. In this way, by destabilizing the mechanisms that constrained American political practice and the thinking about the nation's various colonial investments, the Left represented a natural ally for civil rights activists, especially as both movements were stigmatized and attacked by the same forces. This cooperation was further enabled by the fact that economic marginalization and skepticism about the natural and exclusive sovereignty claims of the state had always been embedded subtexts in the civil rights movement defined broadly—that is, including the abolitionist and emigration movements and the Reconstruction effort of the nineteenth century—throughout its history. Moreover, it is important to recognize that anticommunism was never just about the Soviet Union or the CPUSA; it also operated as a metaphor and proxy for the demonization of any forms of dissent or deviance.

Operating, then, in a moment in which civil rights and communism were conflated in the American mind, it was predictable that the actor Canada Lee's efforts to distinguish himself from the Left while maintaining and indeed publicly deepening his commitment to the civil rights cause in the United States and South Africa (where he had filmed *Cry, the Beloved Country* with Sidney Poitier) would fail to save him from being effectively blacklisted.[5] Although elements in the broader civil rights movement made attempts to challenge only the racial status quo, the degree to which such projects were logically— and, by others, deliberately—connected to questions of class and economic status made such efforts rather difficult to sustain. The hardly coincidental linkage of these two forms of "un-American" activity—dissent on the economic and racial fronts—was hardly new in the broader sweep of the history of the United States and created a polarized environment that allowed for little middle-ground or moderate maneuvering.[6]

Perhaps the most significant personality in this period was the actor, singer, and activist Paul Robeson. Along with W. E. B. Du Bois, and Canada Lee, Robeson was one of the major targets of the Red Scare investigations that would develop after World War II and the emergence of antagonisms between the two former allies, the United States and the Soviet Union. Although he was never actually a member, Robeson was strongly identified with the CPUSA, the Soviet Union, and the Left in general and embodied the fusion of the civil rights movement, the anticolonial effort (through his work with Du Bois and others on the Council on African Affairs), the Left and the union movement, and in particular the left-leaning and—in this period—actively antiracist Congress of Industrial Organizations (CIO). Moreover, the combination of his artistic accomplishments and his political engagements made him exactly the kind of transgressive figure that would trouble, at some fundamental level, the arrangements on which the American modern depended. It was precisely this admixture that marked him as not only an enemy of the Right but a major symbol and hero of many progressives as well.

Accordingly, it is not surprising that Robeson emerged as a focal point in the Cold War drama and that so many African Americans saw him as one of their most cherished leaders. "I was in awe of him," offers West Coast jazz artist Buddy Colette:

> He was one of the first to speak out in that way, and that really did
> a lot for me to see that. And he wasn't afraid. Being around him, it
> was a turning point for me. I loved it, I really did. . . . A lot of people
> don't realize the inspiration he was for a lot of the black people who
> were leaders, who were able to stand up. Because it can be costly if
> you stand up and say, "I believe in this."[7]

Trinidadian expatriate C. L. R. James would argue in retrospect that Robeson possessed the unique ability to attract and mobilize black support:

> [I]f Paul had wanted to he would have built a movement in the
> United States that would have been the natural successor to the
> Garvey movement. . . . [T]he movement would have been of a far
> higher intellectual quality than was the Garvey movement. . . . There
> were numbers of people, dozens and scores of people, who would
> have been ready to work with him if he had begun, and the mass of
> the black population would have followed him as they were ready to
> follow him everywhere he went.[8]

Reflecting his own brand of anti-Soviet Marxism, James would lament, though, Robeson's steadfast attachment to the Soviet Union, observing that Robeson "felt himself committed to the doctrines and the policies of the Communist Party. The Black movement which could have burst and swept the United States around Paul Robeson did not come because Paul did not see it that way."[9] Great man theories of history aside, James's characterization of Robeson's potential speaks to the standing he had within black communities in this period.

Robeson had reached the apex of his popularity with American audiences in 1939 with his radio performance of Earl Robinson's "Ballad for Americans," a song that attempted to construct a linear progressive narrative out of the materials of American history. Ten years later, though, a speech he gave in April 1949 at the Congress of the World Partisans of Peace in Paris was widely interpreted as a suggestion that African Americans would not support the United States in a war with the Soviet Union.[10] "We colonial peoples have contributed to the building of the United States and are determined to share in its wealth," Robeson stated, according to the Associated Press.

> We denounce the policy of the United States government, which
> is similar to that of Hitler and Goebbels. . . . It is unthinkable that
> American Negroes would go to war on behalf of those who have
> oppressed us for generations against a country [the Soviet Union]
> which in one generation has raised our people to the full dignity of
> mankind.[11]

Robeson and those in attendance would recall his speech slightly differently. Suggesting that the wealth of the United States had been built "on the backs of the white workers from Europe . . . and on the backs of millions of blacks," he is reported to have warned,

> We are resolved to share it equally among our children. And we shall
> not put up with any hysterical raving that urges us to make war on
> anyone. Our will to fight for peace is strong. We shall not make war
> on anyone. We shall not make war on the Soviet Union.[12]

While the references to Nazi Germany—and perhaps the implicit suggestion that American blacks were "colonial peoples"—contained in the Associated Press dispatch undoubtedly accounted for some of the subsequent uproar, the main focus was on Robeson's assertion, common to both versions of his speech, that American blacks would not take up arms against the Soviet Union.

In a process that has since become quite familiar, prominent blacks were called on to perform patriotic fidelity and denounce Robeson and his supposedly seditious utterances. At the State Department's request, the NAACP's Walter White wrote an article in *Ebony* ("The Strange Case of Paul Robeson") characterizing the singer/activist as "a bewildered man who is more to be pitied than damned" with "innumerable contradictions . . . which are only understandable to himself and possibly a psychologist." White also challenged Robeson's commitment to African Americans and suggested that he was more preoccupied with his own personal circumstances.[13] In quick succession, Robeson was also criticized by Roy Wilkins, also of the NAACP, A. Philip Randolph, the civil rights attorney Charles H. Houston, Adam Clayton Powell Jr., Sugar Ray Robinson, and educator Mary McLeod Bethune, who had founded the National Council of Negro Women and served in the Roosevelt administration.[14]

As the decision was made in the civil rights leadership that it was necessary that Robeson be thoroughly repudiated, most of these declarations were coordinated, after a call from Wilkins, by Randolph and his top aide, Bayard Rustin. In a later interview, Rustin would invoke an intriguing and expanded version of the dirty laundry principle and contend, "There's a sort of unwritten law that if you want to criticize the United States you do it at home; it's a corollary of the business where you're just a nigger if you stand up and criticize colored folks in front of white folks—it's not done. . . . We have to prove we're patriotic."[15] Walter White would make a similar suggestion with regard to the Paris speech, contending that Robeson had implicitly broken faith with his blood kin: "A member of the family is obligated to correct the faults of his family *within the family* before he calls in the neighbors or the police."[16]

Rustin also questioned, as did others, Robeson's legitimacy as a representative of African American opinion. In his view, Robeson

> did not ever take any organizational responsibility for what was happening in the black community. . . . Here is a man who is making some other country better than ours, and we've got to sit here and take the gaff, while he is important enough to traipse all over the country, to be lionized by all these white people, saying things for which he will not take any responsibility.[17]

In this last comment, one can detect early traces of an argument Rustin would make more explicitly fifteen years after the Paris speech controversy: the notion that artist-activists—and, indeed, all activists not tethered to recognized institutions—lacked mandates and functional legitimacy.[18]

The most public and significant rebuttal to Robeson came from Jackie Robinson, who had been accepted as the first black baseball player in the major leagues in 1947 (partly because of the interventions of Robeson and others), who testified before the House Un-American Activities Committee (HUAC).

That Robinson's critique is remembered as central to the black anti-Robeson campaign underscores his own highly symbolic status and more generally the extent to which figures outside of formal politics were seen as appropriate representatives of the black general will. The Brooklyn Dodgers' second baseman suggested that Robeson's comments did not reflect the views of American blacks:

> I've been asked to express my views on Paul Robeson's statement in
> Paris to the effect that American Negroes would refuse to fight in
> any war against Russia because we love Russia so much. I haven't
> any comment to make on that statement except that if Mr. Robeson
> actually made it, it sounds very silly to me.[19]

The points Robinson, and others, made regarding the need for more effort on the civil rights front were, of course, overlooked in the subsequent media reports as the headlines focused on the issue of Robeson's comments.

As a result of the campaign to identify and isolate suspected communists, the labor movement, under the influence of Walter Reuther, sought to purge itself of suspected communists, a process that led to the expulsion of prominent Detroit activists Coleman Young and George Crockett from the CIO and United Auto Workers (UAW), respectively, among others. The mainstream civil rights organizations undertook a housecleaning of their own, a process that exacerbated the tensions between the NAACP's director, Walter White, and its cofounder, W. E. B. Du Bois (and led to the suspension of the charter of the association's San Francisco branch).[20] In the entertainment industry, a number of black artists were blacklisted, including Lena Horne, Hazel Scott, and the actors Frederick O'Neal, William Marshall, and Dick Campbell. Others had their passport privileges rescinded. The latter process spoke to the recognition on the part of state authorities in the United States and elsewhere of the need to domesticate blackness and prevent racialized subjects from interacting across national borders as much as it reflected an effort to disable leftist internationalism.

In order to save their careers, some of these individuals chose to cooperate with HUAC and testify, make announcements to the press declaring their "innocence," leave the country—for example, Hazel Scott—or stay abroad (for example, the artist Elizabeth Catlett). Josh White, whose vocal group featured Bayard Rustin for a period, appeared before Congress—after telling Robeson, in tears, that he felt he had no choice but to try and clear his name—and asserted that he had been fooled into appearing in leftist-affiliated programs and shows.

He elaborated on this claim in an article for *Negro Digest* entitled "I Was a Sucker for the Communists" in which he wrote "Artists are not often smart about politics." With regard to Robeson's alleged statements, White offered:

> I have a great admiration for Mr. Robeson as an actor and great
> singer, but if what I read in the papers is true, I feel sad over the help
> he's been giving to people who despise America. . . . I stand ready to
> fight Russia or any enemy of America.

Finally, he invoked the same principle that Rustin and Walter White cited with regard to the propriety of American blacks criticizing the United States from outside of the country. In reference to his refusal to acknowledge foreign audiences' requests by for him to play his version of Billie Holiday's "Strange Fruit," White notes:

> I tried to make them understand that America is the best and freest
> country in the world. . . . It's one thing to complain of lynching
> in America, where your listeners know that it does not detract
> from your loyalty and love for your country. It seemed to me quite
> another thing to complain of it abroad, where the listeners might
> think it's the whole story. . . . [I]t's our family affair, to be solved by
> Americans in the peaceful, democratic American way.[21]

The reliance on the same awkward metaphors indeed suggests that Robeson's critics were working from a common script. The poet and playwright Langston Hughes, who had written a piece called "Good Morning Revolution" and *Scottsboro Limited* (a play about the case of the Scottsboro Boys), deleted W. E. B. Du Bois's entry from his *Famous American Negroes* and Robeson's biography from his *Famous Negro Music Makers*.[22] Referring to Hughes's revisions and the dilemmas White and Canada Lee faced, the actor Ossie Davis lamented: "Some of these black heroes had to publicly attack Paul Robeson, or at least swear that Paul had duped them."[23]

The NAACP, and the civil rights movement as a whole, seeking to avoid being cast as anti-American and unpatriotic precisely because of the attention they brought to the issues of race, would find themselves in a paradoxical situation partly of their own choosing, trying awkwardly to make progress on the Jim Crow front while defending the country against charges from abroad that it had a "race problem." The latter effort obviously blunted their effectiveness on the domestic front, as significant energy was consumed responding to the various allegations made by the Soviet Union in the context of its propaganda battle with the United States for favor among the world's nonwhite peoples. As a result of these kinds of commitments, Walter White had managed to prevent the critical report Du Bois had assembled in 1947 regarding the situation of blacks in the United States—*An Appeal to the World*—from being discussed at the United Nations. Similar forces contributed to the nonresponse to *We Charge Genocide,* a document edited by William Patterson, largely based on research done by the NAACP, and issued as part of the CPUSA's effort to reestablish its credentials with African Americans after the Party's abandonment of civil rights causes.

At the same time, American blacks were discouraged from linking their situation with the anticolonial struggles taking place elsewhere, and given the prevailing incentive structures, many engaged in speech acts that must be read in the context of the times as closer to compelled rather than frank expression. Accordingly, while Walter White, Josh White, and Rustin, in invoking the family metaphor, do not name the "father," it is implied that there is some power that has encouraged them to express their loyalties and frame their identities in one way rather than another. Similar effects can be detected in the work of Roi Ottley, who was forced to leave the Federal Writers' Project because of the antired tide. Writing in 1951, he argued in *No Green Pastures*, his travel journal exploring the racial situation outside the United States,

> If Negroes were a primitive people, living beyond the borders of
> the country, and the color question had a colonial-imperialist basis,
> perhaps the equation would make sense to Europeans. But since
> the Negro is a full-fledged citizen, his separation from the white
> community bewilders the average person abroad, astonishes the
> sophisticated and delights the anti-American elements.

Despite the prevalence of Jim Crow, which in the same period provided a model for the shaping of South Africa's apartheid system, Ottley's assertion that American citizenship categorically distinguished U.S. blacks from those elsewhere would become a common assumption in public discourse in the early Cold War years, as would the contention that colonialism had no relevance to American domestic arrangements. He would also invoke the (national) family to explain the pleasurable experience of being overseas:

> I felt the lift and magnitude of being an American abroad—Negro
> though I am. I shared abundantly the esteem, admiration and
> affection often lavished upon white men in America. . . . I realized

that to be born an American citizen today is to be part of a real good thing—like being born into a rich and powerful family. America is the greatest success story in human history.... [M]y colored countrymen and I enjoy a share of material things which most white people do not enjoy elsewhere in the world today.[24]

SEPIA AMBASSADORS

In the decade following the Manchester Pan-African Congress of 1945, probably the high point in terms of the political mobilization of a black, consciously internationalist, counterpublic, and against the backdrop of the Red Scare, which impacted not only the Left and the civil rights movement, conventionally defined, but the anticolonial campaign as well, pressures were placed on African Americans to endorse and reproduce the norms associated with the promotion of American interests. Accordingly, while the American government was imprisoning noncitizen Caribbean immigrants, including CPUSA member and pioneering feminist Claudia Jones, labor leader Ferdinand Smith, and C. L. R. James, at Ellis Island, under the Immigration and Nationality Act of 1952 (otherwise known as the McCarran-Walter Act) on the basis of their leftist affiliations, and subsequently deporting them, and the State Department was restricting Robeson and Du Bois from traveling abroad, efforts were made to replace and displace the Robesonian example and present an impression to the world that blacks were fully and happily incorporated into the American polity. In *The Pleasures of Exile*, the Barbadian poet and novelist George Lamming remarked on the effect of these efforts on his own travels and comportment in the United States in the early 1950s, remembering his own guarantee to American customs officials that he would "not and would never ... overthrow the Government of the United States," and his decision to avoid conversations about McCarthy during his stay. Mobility and personal conduct became circumscribed in ways in this period that encouraged blacks—natives and nonnatives throughout the anglophone Americas—to work with, rather than against, the dominant authorities.[25]

Responding to these cues, Adam Clayton Powell suggested to the Eisenhower administration that it send a delegation of observers to the upcoming Asian-African Conference of Nonaligned Nations to be held in Bandung, Indonesia, in the spring of 1955.[26] Furthermore, he advised that it would be a good idea to send a diverse group that optimally would include some representation from the black members of Congress—of which there were three at the time—including himself, given his acumen and training in the area of foreign affairs. In a letter to White House aide Maxwell Rabb, seeking the sponsorship of the State Department, he asserted, "I know personally many of the Chiefs of State and members of the foreign offices of these countries, both in Africa and in Asia, and I can assure you that the appearance in Indonesia at that time of American officials, both Negro and white, will be of tremendous value."[27] The conference, which was to bring together those countries not aligned with either the Soviet Union or the United States, Powell argued, would be a setting conducive to the Americans, indicating, through their attendance, their support for these newly independent nations and potential allies. The Eisenhower administration decided against sending any such delegation; Powell announced that he would go at his own expense. (He also received press credentials and reported for the *New York Age* and the *Pittsburgh Courier*, although he did indeed cover his own costs.)

In Bandung, in response to a question from a Ceylonese correspondent— "How can the U.S. be expected to take a firm stand against South African racial policies when it practices racism at home?"—Powell represented the United States as moving toward full and equal citizenship for all, regardless of race, and dismissed suggestions that the Soviet bloc offered a more progressive approach to questions of ethnic and racial difference.[28] In the *New York Herald Tribune*, he was quoted as saying,

> Second class citizenship is on the way out. . . . It is a mark of
> distinction in the United States to be a Negro. To be a Negro is no
> longer a stigma. A Negro has been elected to a city-wide office in
> Atlanta. Negroes are in office in Richmond and Norfolk.[29]

Powell also strongly urged the United States that it was in its interests to support the anticolonial cause if it was sincerely seeking to improve its standing in the nonaligned world.

Given Powell's participation in the anti-Robeson effort six years earlier, it is not surprising that he characterized American race relations in such a strikingly rosy fashion. His actions also undoubtedly reflected a desire to separate himself as much as possible from any red taint remaining from his wife Hazel Scott being blacklisted; and his own associations with communists such as Benjamin Davis (who replaced Powell on the New York City council when Powell was elected to Congress), and William Patterson. Furthermore, beyond rehabilitation, he likely calculated, quite accurately as it turned out, that his performance would make him a hero in certain circles back home. Toward this end, he was quoted in the *New York Times* highlighting the role he had played in Indonesia in protecting the United States from charges of racial discrimination:

> I was able to stand up in front of them as an American Negro and
> tell them in a straightforward and factual way that racial problems
> had been great in the United States, but that they were now on the
> mend. I plainly knew more on the subject than they did, and since
> the first day no one at a press conference has mentioned the problem
> of racial discrimination in the United States.

Upon returning to Congress, he was welcomed with applause and warm praise from his colleagues in the House of Representatives.[30]

"The Congressman gave us Americans a cleaner bill of health than we deserve," suggested Richard Wright, who was also present at Bandung.[31] Excited, though, by the experience of witnessing a heterogeneous congregation affiliated with neither the Left nor the Right, the author of *Native Son* also commented on what he saw as the broader significance of Powell's actions:

> The astounding aspect of Congressman Powell's appearance at
> Bandung was that he *felt the call, felt its meaning.* . . . At the very
> moment when the United States was trying to iron out the brutal
> kinks of its race problem, there came along a world event which
> reawakened in the hearts of its "23,000,000 colored citizens" [the
> figure Powell cited with regard to all American nonwhites] the
> feeling of *race*, a feeling which the racial mores of American whites
> had induced deep in their hearts. If a man as sophisticated as
> Congressman Powell felt this, then one can safely assume that in less
> schooled and more naïve hearts it went profoundly deep.[32]

The other "call" Powell felt—the urge to defend the United States against charges of racism—is arguably more remarkable, especially given that his own government had not asked him to attend the conference. Indeed, there was an over-the-top quality to Powell's statements, even if one factors in the afterglow that prevailed in the period between the initial *Brown* Supreme Court decision in May 1954 and the *Brown* II "all deliberate speed" formulation that was announced at the end of May 1955. As Percival "P. L." Prattis wrote in the *Pittsburgh Courier*, addressing Powell,

[T]he colored writers aren't ... certain you have meant all you said. ...
I can't see where I'm distinguished today. If you visit any American
city, you find me living in the slums. If you visit most mills and
factories, and find me at all, I'm doing the dirtiest and heaviest work
for the lowest pay.[33]

On the paper's editorial page, it was suggested that Powell had turned his back
on Left causes in order to court the favor of Southern legislators.[34] Horace
Cayton, also writing in the *Courier*, avoided the issue of the Powell's motives
and simply identified his trip as evidence of the need for "the State Department
to take a more realistic look at the possible use of more and more Negroes in
our foreign service."[35]

In response to such pleas, plans were also laid to support the travel of jazz
musicians abroad to assist the country in its efforts to woo the citizenries of
the nonaligned countries who might be swayed by the appeals and propaganda
of the Soviet Union. At a point when Jim Crow was still in effect—indeed, was
being reinforced, in reaction to the *Brown* decision—it was perceived that the
American government needed to actively challenge the image of the country
as racist. An influential front-page story in the *New York Times* on November 6,
1955, included the comment "America's secret weapon is a blue note in a minor
key. Right now its most effective ambassador is Louis (Satchmo) Armstrong."
The story, written by Felix Belair, the paper's Stockholm correspondent,
extolled the power of American jazz over European listeners and suggested that
the music's "individuality of expression" accounted for its popularity. Given its
appeal, he observed, "What many thoughtful Europeans cannot understand is
why the United States Government, with all the money it spends for so-called
propaganda to promote democracy, does not use more of it to subsidize the
continental travels of jazz bands and the best exponents of the music."[36]

The State Department–sponsored tours by jazz musicians were also partly
the result of Powell's lobbying efforts, enhanced undoubtedly by the credibility he had earned at Bandung as a seemingly reliable defender of American
national interests. Familiar with the jazz world, and married to a jazz musician, Powell was concerned that the acts being chosen to represent the United
States abroad did not reflect the full range of the country's talents. "The State
Department has allotted $5,000,000 for an international cultural exchange,"
Powell announced in December 1955. "I have convinced them that instead of
emphasizing ballet dancers and classical music, they can get real value out
of spending the vast majority of the money on jazz and other Americana such

as folk music, mambos, spirituals, American Indian dancers, Hawaiian music, and so forth." Accordingly, the *New York Times* noted, "Before long, jazz will become an arm of this country's foreign policy in such places as the Far East, Middle East, and Africa. . . . Bands will go into countries where communism has a foothold."[37]

The first "goodwill ambassador" from the jazz realm chosen by the State Department to tour was John Birks "Dizzy" Gillespie. As trumpet player Quincy Jones reports, Powell told Gillespie, "Birks, if you put together a big band, I'll have the State Department sponsor it and send it abroad. It'll be a first."[38] Committed to another tour and therefore unable to assemble a big band on short notice, Gillespie asked Jones, as a young but increasingly respected arranger, to do it for him. The ensemble Jones created was both racially integrated—as it included altoist Phil Woods and trombonist Rod Levitt—and gender inclusive, as it featured Melba Liston, a trombonist and accomplished arranger in her own right, and vocalist Dottie Saulter.

The twenty-two-member band's first stop was originally scheduled to be in India. That changed after Jawaharlal Nehru, the country's prime minister, announced that India would align itself with neither the Soviets nor the Americans. A new itinerary called for the tour to begin in Iran. As historian Penny Von Eschen notes,

> It was no accident that the first State Department jazz performance
> of the hundreds that would occur over the next two decades took
> place at the heart of the former British Empire, in a country rich
> in that coveted Cold War commodity, oil. Three years earlier, Iran
> had been the site of the first CIA-backed coup of that decade—a
> coup that ousted the nationalist government of Prime Minister
> Muhammad Musaddiq and installed the shah. As a result, American
> firms gained entry into the Iranian oil industry and acquired a share
> of profits from selling Iranian crude and refined products on the
> world market.[39]

The tour dates in 1956 were set with the objective of presenting the United States as a benign benefactor distinct from, and not responsible for, the imperial excesses of the European powers and a more attractive partner—partly on account of its natural and peaceful heterogeneity—than the Soviet Union. As the United States sought to manage the increasingly dispersed territorial possessions it had accumulated (peopled largely by nonwhites), it needed the assistance of American blacks, especially given the increasingly public demonstrations of southern etiquette—for example, the newspaper accounts of the Emmett Till lynching in the fall of 1955—that were being transmitted across the globe. There was, accordingly, an unstated recognition that blacks had to be conscripted as part of the effort to maintain the desired image of the peaceful diversity and inclusiveness—and the might—of the United States in the global arena.

Gillespie, for his part, was hardly a dyed-in-the-wool supporter of American foreign policy objectives. He was one of the musicians whose creativity converted Paul Robeson into a fan of jazz—at least as it was reconfigured during the bebop revolution—and was a relatively close friend and deep admirer of Robeson. Robeson was indeed, and would remain, his hero.[40] Gillespie had also been a member of the Communist Party, although he would later explain that affiliation as a matter of pragmatism, stating, "I was a card-carrying communist because it was directly associated with my work."[41] Despite his former leftist affiliations and associations with elements of the Popular Front, Gillespie claimed to be on board with the general goal of the tours, although it is important his statements be read against the broader punitive context in which he was operating. As he observed in a telegram to President Eisenhower, reprinted in the *Pittsburgh Courier*, "Our trip through the Middle East proved conclusively that our interracial group was powerfully effective against Red propaganda. Jazz is our own American folk music that communicates with all peoples regardless of language or social barriers."[42] While he appeared committed to the superficial goals of the State Department, Gillespie was also quite aware of the reason jazz musicians were being deployed in this manner and uninterested in downplaying the realities of the American racial state. As he writes in his autobiography, "I sort of liked the idea of representing America, but I wasn't going to apologize for the racist policies of America. . . . I know what they've done to us and I'm not going to make any excuses."[43] It is also important to acknowledge that, in the same manner that affiliating with communists might have been a practical move at one point on Gillespie's part, the State Department support gave Gillespie not only employment but an opportunity to tour with a big band again, an experience he had not had, on account of the changes in the economics of the jazz industry, since 1950.[44]

Adam Clayton Powell had also suggested to the officials at the State Department that they consider Louis Armstrong as a jazz ambassador, an idea they were keen to put into action. Initial plans for a tour by Armstrong were abandoned, though, after the trumpet player spoke out against the administration's failure to challenge Orval Faubus's resistance to school integration in Arkansas in 1957. As reported in the *New York Times*, Armstrong, who had just returned from a trip to Ghana, rejected the planned tours to the Soviet Union and South America because "the way they are treating my people in the South, the Government can go to hell." Eisenhower, in Armstrong's view, was "two-faced" and had "no guts," while Faubus was an "uneducated plow boy." At the end of the item, it was recognized: "Mr. Armstrong was regarded by the State Department as perhaps the most effective unofficial goodwill ambassador this country had. They said Soviet propagandists undoubtedly would seize on Mr. Armstrong's words." The next day, September 20, 1957, the *Times* ran a small piece entitled "Armstrong May Tour," based solely on the statements of his manager, Pierre Tallerie, who reassured the concerned parties, "Louie isn't mad at anybody. He couldn't stay mad for more than a few seconds, anyway." Despite his manager's proclamation, Armstrong held out until Eisenhower did commit to intervening in the Little Rock crisis, after which he sent a note to the president stating that the United States was "the greatest country," adding, "If you decide to walk into the schools with the colored kids, take me along, daddy. God bless you."[45]

Armstrong eventually performed as an official goodwill ambassador. In 1960 and 1961, under the auspices of the State Department, he returned to Ghana and appeared at shows in Nyasaland, Rhodesia, Tanganyika, Kenya, Uganda, Cameroon, Nigeria, and the Republic of the Congo. During the tour he avoided making statements that might explicitly embarrass American authorities or, as the *Times* put it, he "showed his diplomacy when he ruled out political questions from newsmen." "I don't know anything about it [politics]," he replied to a Kenyan reporter, "I'm just a trumpet player. The reason I don't bother with politics is the words is so big by the time they break them down to my size the joke is over." In response to another question—"Do you feel like an American in Africa or an African in America?"—he offered, "I just feel in place, man."[46] While his answers were designed to superficially avoid disturbing American propaganda efforts, there was an obvious excessive quality to his rejoinders that allowed those who were so inclined and capable of doing so to read between the lines. "Beneath that gravel voice and that shuffle, under all that mouth, wide as a satchel with more grinning teeth than a piano got keys," as Ossie Davis would later suggest regarding Armstrong, "was a horn that could kill a man."[47]

Given the possibility of this sort of play, it is also important to consider the illogics of empire, the impossibility of achieving the specific outcomes anticipated by the Eisenhower administration. For instance, the State Department's efforts were complicated by the conflicting concerns of the varied audiences they were attempting to satisfy. Significant constituencies within the United States, and particularly Congress, were opposed to government funds being used to sponsor the travels of American blacks and the mere suggestion that somehow these jazz and bebop musicians might actually represent some aspect of the cultural essence of the United States. As Allen J. Ellender, a prosegregationist senator from Louisiana, argued in Congress, "I never heard so much noise in all my life. . . . I can assure you that instead of doing good [these tours] will do harm and the people will really believe we are barbarians."[48] In the face of such concerns, as with the gradual introduction of blacks into the military and the propaganda efforts of the Office of War Information during World War II, efforts were made to prevent southern whites and their sympathizers from being exposed to exactly those things the State Department wanted blacks in the United States and foreign audiences to see: evidence of interracial intimacy, harmony, and cooperation, among Americans.

The jazz ambassadorial projects also depended on the negotiation of a form of blackness that would serve the conflicting needs of the American state: a blackness that was in some sense credible and appealing to foreign audiences but at the same time would not disable the precise calibrations of the broader national mission. In other words, a blackness that traveled well but avoided the internationalist and diasporic paths laid out by Marcus Garvey, Du Bois, Robeson, James, and Jones, among others. In that context, Louis Armstrong's reaction to Eisenhower's initial refusal to intervene in Arkansas—"It's getting almost so bad, a colored man hasn't got any country"—especially coming from Armstrong, who had a significant audience both inside the United States and abroad, and was seen as one of the more genial and pliable African American artists of his generation, likely engendered real anxiety among Eisenhower administration officers, given their eagerness to avoid exactly the kinds of nascent diasporic consciousness underlying Armstrong's frustration.[49]

Frantz Fanon, who was based in Accra, Ghana, at the time of Armstrong's tour, as the permanent representative of the Provisional Government of the Republic of Algeria, read these jazz tours as precisely the workings of the American imperial machine.[50] He wrote:

The specter of the West, the European tinges, was everywhere present
and active. The French, English, Spanish, Portuguese areas remained
living. Oxford as opposed to the Sorbonne, Lisbon to Brussels, the
English bosses to the Portuguese bosses, the pound to the franc,
the Catholic Church to Protestantism or to Islam. *And above all*

this, the United States has plunged in everywhere, dollars in the
vanguard, with Armstrong as herald and American Negro diplomats,
scholarships, the emissaries of the Voice of America.[51]

Armstrong, for his part, recalls that "they stopped fighting to hear me play."
However, when one contemplates the reality that his appearance in Katanga
Province in the Congo coincided with the imprisonment and torture of Patrice
Lumumba, and that Lumumba was killed while Armstrong was still engaged
elsewhere on the continent—a series of acts carried out with the cooperation of American authorities—Fanon's interpretation of the role of the Negro
ambassadors rings even more true.[52]

Nonetheless, the effort to identify and market a safe and reliable sepia pro-
totype was bound to fail in some respects. The tours by Gillespie, Armstrong,
and subsequently Duke Ellington exposed audiences outside the United States
to colored formations that could only have troubled, in some respects, the
attempts by American authorities to avoid the kinds of interactions Robeson's
work typically engendered. Gillespie, on a later tour to South America, would
make connections in Brazil that would, as with his Afro-Cuban engagements
of the 1940s, have profound cultural effects both in the United States and in
the Latin American republic. The pianist Randy Weston, who was involved in
later tours, established strong linkages with West and North African musicians
that would inform all his subsequent work. The musicians, vocalists, and dancers featured in these concerts contributed to a heightened, more developed
sense of diasporic consciousness than would have otherwise been the case.
Moreover, it must be recognized that communication does not solely depend
on physical encounter. The State Department's attempts to limit the mobility
of certain black bodies hardly addressed the many other forms of exchange on
which communities and diasporas rely. That said, it is clear that even at their
most effective and connective, the explicit political content—and, in particular, the leftist and anticolonial substance—of the exchanges initiated and models proposed by Du Bois, Jones, James, and Robeson were not easily replicated
in the post–Cold War era.

The developments at the Congress of Black Artists and Writers must be placed
alongside Bandung—to which a number of those in attendance referred—and
the jazz ambassadors program. Convened in Paris at the Sorbonne in September
1956 under the umbrella of the journal *Présence Africaine*, the meeting provided
yet another space for the performance of this new Cold War blackness. Aimé
Césaire would provoke some of the attendees by arguing, "Even our American

brothers, as a result of racial discrimination, find themselves within a great modern nation in an artificial situation that can only be understood in reference to colonialism."[53] John A. Davis, an American delegate, responded:

> I would like to say that it is undoubtedly true that American Negroes have a tremendous sympathy for and a working interest in the freeing of Negroes everywhere in the world from various states. It is inevitable, both as Americans *and* as Negroes. America has always taken an anti-colonial position; from George Washington down to Dwight Eisenhower, every president has taken this position. I don't have to tell you how difficult our relationships have been with our allies because of this, and one reads the papers: one hears how the British and the French talk about us. . . . [W]e are accused of all sorts of "back-door" pressure in this regard.

James Ivy, representing the NAACP, asserted,

> The basic problem of the 15 million American Negroes is one of integration. It is not a colonial problem. The Negroes of the United States are the most quintessential of Americans. They are biologically as much European as African and culturally more Europe-American [*sic*] than Afro-American.

Together, Davis's intriguing celebration of the anticolonial credentials of American presidents throughout history and Ivy's wholesale investment in a "strictly American heritage" speak to the anxieties American blacks faced abroad; their unwillingness to be caught—especially in the shadows of the Robeson debacle—speaking ill of the United States and its policies; and the ways colonial values can be internalized and reproduced.[54] These pronouncements are even more impressive if we remember that the Eisenhower administration would have resisted being classified as "anticolonial" and consider how few Americans would have willingly recognized Davis and Ivy as fellow citizens.

Du Bois, unable to attend the conference because of the State Department restrictions, sent a message to the convention:

> I am not present at your meeting because the United States Government will not give me a passport for travel abroad. Any Negro-American who travels abroad today must either not discuss race conditions in the United States or say the sort of thing which our State Department wishes the world to believe. The government

especially objects to me because I am a socialist and because I believe in peace with Communist States like the Soviet Union.[55]

"We had a message today that hurt me," Richard Wright, who had helped organize the conference and the launching of *Présence Africaine*, and invited some members of the American delegation, offered in response to Du Bois's comment. At another point, he muttered, "When my role [is] finished in this conference, I would appreciate it if you would tell me what governments paid me," a comment not only on the congress itself but the rumors circulating that because he still had an American passport, he was working for the Central Intelligence Agency (CIA). Wright would find himself depressed and generally dispirited after the meetings.[56]

James Baldwin, for his part, characterized Du Bois's comments as "extremely ill-considered" and wrote afterward of the ways the conference deepened his sense of being an American. As he recorded in *Nobody Knows My Name*,

> [W]hat, at bottom, distinguished the Americans from the Negroes
> who surrounded us, men from Nigeria, Senegal, Barbados,
> Martinique—so many names for so many disciplines—was the
> banal and abruptly quite overwhelming fact that we had been born
> in a society, which, in a way quite inconceivable for Africans, and no
> longer real for Europeans, was open, and, in a sense which has nothing
> to do with justice or injustice, was free. It was a society, in short, in
> which nothing was fixed and we had therefore been born to a greater
> number of possibilities, wretched as those possibilities seemed at the
> instant of our birth.

Regarding Césaire's speech, Baldwin found himself "stirred in a very strange and disagreeable way." His further suggestion that "Césaire's case against Europe . . . was watertight [and] a very easy case to make" can be interpreted as an implicit argument for the exceptionality of the United States and the incomparability of the situation of African Americans and blacks elsewhere.[57] While one might read these notes of a self-identified native son against the grain in search of some liminal traces of doubt about the relative value and character of American freedom, the visceral and oddly parochial quality of Baldwin's responses is, in the end, all the more remarkable given his frequent suggestions that it was only in exile in Paris that he came into his own as a writer.

These disavowals of possible colonial linkages between the situations of American blacks and blacks outside of the United States in Cold War–era literary circles would reach their apogee in the work of Ralph Ellison, who turned down an invitation to attend the conference (despite being based at the time in Rome). Although Ellison's scholarship troubled domestic understandings with his assertions that blacks might be read as lawgivers in the American context, he combined this provocation with a disinclination to challenge the nationalist assumptions underlying U.S. discourse. Accordingly, as Danielle Allen has noted, he offered a largely effective rebuttal to Hannah Arendt's contention vis-à-vis the Little Rock crisis of 1957 that black parents and the NAACP had failed to act heroically by allowing children to be exposed to such potential violence and her further suggestion that school integration should not be such a priority and that intermarriage laws represented a more suitable target.[58] In response, invoking one of his favorite tropes, Ellison would highlight the discipline required of all blacks during Jim Crow, regardless of age, and the necessity for blacks to introduce their children to this reality at a young age.[59] While Ellison was successful in exposing the absurdity of Arendt's central claims, he let pass—not surprisingly—a remarkable assertion she makes at the beginning of her piece. "The color question," she wrote,

> was created by the one great crime in America's history and is soluble only within the political and historical framework of the Republic. The fact that this question has also become a major issue in world affairs is sheer coincidence as far as American history and politics are concerned; for the color problem in world politics grew out of the colonialism and imperialism of European nations—that is, the one great crime in which America was never involved.

Going further, and noting the Cold War backdrop, she added, "The tragedy is that the unsolved color problem within the United States may cost her the advantages she otherwise would rightly enjoy as a world power."[60]

Ellison's resistance to imagining Negro life beyond the formal borders of the United States prevented him from finding fault with Arendt's placement of the United States outside of the colonial (and, apparently, outside history). Indeed, in his work, taken as a whole, there was a constant resistance to any attempts to position American blackness in relation to anything other the West and more specifically American articulations of Western possibilities. In *Shadow and Act* Ellison would write,

> [T]he American Negro people is North American in origin and has evolved under specifically American conditions. . . . [T]here is no

other "Negro" culture. . . . It is not culture which binds the peoples who are of partially African origin now scattered throughout the world, but an identity of passions. . . . But even this identification is shared by most non-white peoples, and while it has political value of great potency, its cultural value is almost nil.[61]

As Jerry Gafio Watts notes,

Ellison was at the forefront of emphatically denying any significant Afro-American cultural connection with Africa. . . . and almost fanatical in proclaiming a lack of personal interest in Africa and Africans. . . . Equally conspicuous is Ellison's omission of the cultural connection between West Indians and indigenous black Americans.

Continuing, Watts proposes: "Perhaps Ellison thought that an identification with Africa would be self-stigmatizing. Such internalized racist thoughts concerning Africa were frequently held by black intellectuals of his generation."[62]

"The world's getting bluesier all the time, as Joe Williams and Count [Basie] well know," Ellison observed in a 1957 letter to his friend and colleague Albert Murray, "and even though those Africans have Ghana they still haven't developed to the point where the blues start." At another point in the same exchange, he asks, "Who the hell dreamed up Louie [Armstrong]?" Reflecting his commitment to the view that American Negroes should not identify with the diaspora and his condescension toward blacks elsewhere, he replied, "[H]e's a mask for a lyric poet who is much greater than most now writing. That's a mask . . . to study . . .; only I know enough not to miss my train by messing around . . . looking over in Africa or even down in the West Indies [for an explanation]." Almost two decades later, he would state with emphasis, "I've *never* identified with Africa."[63]

FELLOWS TRAVELING

"I got a telephone call from the late Era Bell Thompson, a managing editor of *Ebony*," journalist Carl Rowan recalls.

"Mr. Johnson [publisher John H.] says Paul Robeson is getting a raw deal in the media and everyplace else. Nobody will tell his side of the story. He says you're the only journalist in America who can write the truth and not get destroyed by the McCarthyites. Will you consider it?"[64]

Rowan agreed, and the article did indeed feature a rather extensive and, given the existing broader climate, balanced assessment of Robeson's claims against the federal government regarding the withholding of his passport and his complaints regarding the actions of black leadership.[65]

In the feature, published in October 1957, seven months after Ghana's independence, Robeson situated the African American struggle in an international and diasporic context. In response to a question from Rowan about the possibility of working within the boundaries of the United States, he stated, "I think the Negro should solve his problems within the American framework, and he is definitely on the way to dignity and equality. But he never will achieve integration until the time comes when all Negroes show complete solidarity, backed by all the colored people of the world."[66]

With regard to the civil rights leadership's role in his marginalization, Robeson argued, "The State Department could not have done this had Negro leaders spoken out. Instead, Walter White, Jackie Robinson and other Negroes blasted me without even talking to me to find out what I had really said and why I had said it."[67] Robeson also contended that the responses generated within the African American community reflected a class divide and that his affiliation had long been with the working classes. "I came to my present viewpoint between 1928 and 1940, and not in Russia but in London," he told Rowan. "I first went to Russia in 1934, not as a politician but as an artist. It was the British labor struggle that shaped my political philosophy. That is why in this country my identification is with the Negro working class, not with the black bourgeoisie."[68]

On this same point, W. E. B. Du Bois suggested that, somewhat to his surprise, very little support was forthcoming for Robeson, himself, and the other targets of the McCarthy era from the black middle classes, and specifically the "Talented Tenth" that he had previously identified as the "future of the race." He did concede that a "dichotomy in the Negro group, [the] development of class structure, was to be expected" and that the size of these gaps would increase "as discrimination against Negroes as such decreases." Nevertheless, he was still struck by the unwillingness of middle-class blacks to resist the government's efforts at censorship. "The reaction of Negroes," he wrote, "revealed a distinct cleavage not hitherto clear in American Negro opinion." Somewhat in the spirit of comments E. Franklin Frazier would later make in *Black Bourgeoisie*, Du Bois added,

> Negroes of intelligence and prosperity had become American in
> their acceptance of exploitation as defensible, and in their imitation

of American "conspicuous expenditure." They proposed to make money and spend it as pleased them.... They hated "Communism" and "Socialism" as much as any white American. Their reaction toward Paul Robeson was typical: they simply could not understand his surrendering a thousand dollars a night for a moral conviction.[69]

Within African American communities, Robeson clearly drew more support from working-class blacks, and particularly union members, than from the colored middle classes. The former phenomenon can be partly explained by Robeson's contributions to the National Negro Labor Council (NNLC), which was established in 1951 and affiliated with the UAW and the CIO, and his strong identification with the labor movement as a whole.[70] The class skew with regard to support for Robeson also reflected the different political orientations of the black working classes and the black middle classes. In many respects, the pro-Robeson/anticommunist debate was a proxy for a more explicit and direct class debate among blacks as to the proper salience of issues related to economic justice and the direction the civil rights movement should take. The NAACP's reluctance to get involved in the Scottsboro Boys case in 1931—because of the accusations of rape and interracial sex associated with the arrests—in contrast with the CPUSA's involvement symbolized this class divide and the ways diverging notions of respectability bifurcated the black polity.[71]

The year after the *Ebony* interview saw the publication of Robeson's *Here I Stand*, which suggested a certain deemphasis on his part of his Soviet affiliations. This turn might be read largely as a response to Khrushchev's revelations regarding Stalin's regime at the twentieth congress of the Communist Party of the Soviet Union in February 1956, and one can imagine that by this point Robeson had become frustrated with some aspects of Comintern policy, even if he was unwilling to express these reservations publicly. This shift, though, was likely just as connected to Robeson's desire to reestablish his authenticity and credentials with African American audiences.[72] His effort to geographically locate himself within the larger black community is evident in the first paragraph of the book's foreword: "I am a Negro. The house I live in is in Harlem—this city within a city, Negro metropolis of America. And now as I write of things that are urgent in my mind and heart, I feel the press of all that is around me here where I live, at home among my people."[73] With his references to his brother and father as ministers, and the repeated refrain "I've got a home in that rock," he also identified himself with the black church and the religious foundations of black social and political life.

Although he did not shy away from his commitment to "scientific socialism" and the significance of the Soviet model, the dominant theme was his devotion to, and involvement in, the black liberation struggle, albeit defined more broadly than most civil rights leaders suggested in this period. Accordingly, he cited the relevance of the anticolonial movement; his encounters with Kwame Nkrumah, Jomo Kenyatta, and Nnamdi Azikiwe in London; the Bandung conference; and the importance of African Americans' right and willingness to travel so that they might generate broader coalitions for the improvement of the circumstances of blacks throughout the diaspora. To sustain this last claim and his implicit rejection of the particular version of the family metaphor Walter White and others endorsed, Robeson situated his efforts in a tradition extending back to Frederick Douglass's trans-Atlantic abolitionist work. "To the Negro artist, as well as to the Negro spokesman," he wrote, "the 'moral support of England and Europe' has been of great importance and, indeed, the right to travel has been a virtual necessity for the Negro artist." Robeson, in many respects quite rightly, also emphasized the racial character of his predicament, observing: "[T]he controversy concerning my views and actions had its origin not among the Negro people but among the white folks on top who have directed at me the thunderbolts of their displeasure and rage." Against this backdrop, he highlighted the role race played with regard to the deprivation of his passport privileges and cited a State Department brief asserting that if the

> passport was cancelled solely because of the applicant's recognized status as spokesman for large sections of Negro Americans, we submit that this would not amount to an abuse of discretion in view of appellant's frank admission that he has been for years extremely active politically in behalf of independence of the colonial people of Africa.[74]

The passport restrictions and domestic sanctions by this point had made it nearly impossible for Robeson's career to proceed (his income dropped from over $100,000 in 1947 to less than 2 percent of that figure in 1950), and his marginalization within black leadership circles was virtually complete by the time the book was published.[75] Later that year, however, after the *Kent et al. v. Dulles* decision in 1958, which made the deprivation of passport privileges of suspected communists unconstitutional on First Amendment grounds, Robeson and Du Bois, among others, had their passports restored.[76] Both immediately left the country. Du Bois, at age ninety, departed in August to Eastern Europe, the Soviet Union, China, the United Kingdom, the Netherlands, the Virgin Islands, and Nigeria. Three years later, on October 1, 1961, he would apply to join the CPUSA and embark for Ghana, where he would die two years later at age ninety-five on August 27, 1963, the eve of the March on Washington. Robeson headed to England, where he was greeted on landing by Claudia Jones and the Guyanese anticolonialist Cheddi Jagan, among others. Although his right to travel was restored, the civil rights movement had shifted firmly southward under the leadership of the Southern Christian Leadership Conference and Martin Luther King Jr. (a development Du Bois celebrated at first but came to lament, on account of what he felt was insufficient attention to economic issues). Outside of a few appearances, and suffering from a protracted illness, Robeson would effectively retire from public life by the early 1960s.

It is interesting to trace Robeson's legacy as an artist-activist in the work of his admirers and the substantive complexion of the kinds of issues raised in the cultural arena after his silencing. Although a number of the younger artists were quite devoted to Robeson, he made an effort to discourage them from publicly associating with him, given the attempts by the government to identify and excommunicate those perceived to be "fellow travelers" of the Left. As Dizzy Gillespie remembers, "One time I was playing at the Apollo Theatre at the height of the McCarthy era and I received a telegram from him saying that he had come by to see me but that he didn't come backstage because he didn't want to put pressure on me."[77] In reference to a Robeson show during this period, Coleman Young recalls,

W]hen we staged a rally across the river from Harlem . . . Harry Belafonte showed up. . . . [and] told Paul that he was going out on the stage to sing. . . . Robeson . . . kindly advised Belafonte not to go out there, knowing that such an appearance could abort a young singer's career before it really started. "You don't need to do that to prove your support of me," Paul said. . . . Harry cried, but he took Robeson's advice.[78]

Poitier, who writes in his own biography that in this period he was "inclined toward the left of center," notes, "I remember times when [Harry] and I would meet Robeson in a bar on Fifth Avenue just off a Hundred and Twenty-fifth Street, and sit there and talk. He was very fond of Harry. And Harry loved him." At another point, he adds, "I got to know him well enough that he became concerned about me, urging me to be careful in my association with him."[79]

For the young artists among Robeson's supporters, the attempts to isolate Robeson created a serious dilemma. As Ossie Davis observes, "We young ones in the theater, trying to fathom even as we followed, were pulled this way and that, by the swirling currents of these new dimensions of the Struggle, which split us down the middle." Davis also recalls that these divisions had a class dimension to them: "Black revolutionaries fighting, just like the Russians, to liberate the workers and save the world, against the black bourgeoisie fighting, at the behest of rich white folks, to defeat the Communist menace and save the world." In this context, for Davis, the proper course of action was clear. "I, for one, had no trouble identifying which side I was on. I was on the side with Paul Robeson and W. E. B. Du Bois."[80]

Despite Robeson's efforts to protect his friends and supporters from investigation and harassment, many of the younger artists became targets of the broader Red Scare. Actor Ruby Dee, Davis's wife, was included among leftists suspected by Ed Sullivan, and Davis himself attracted attention from New York state authorities. Poitier, who had been involved in the theatre group associated with the left-affiliated Committee for the Negro in the Arts, was asked to sign a loyalty statement disavowing Robeson and Canada Lee before he was allowed to appear in *Blackboard Jungle* in 1953. Although he was told that his name was "on a list of people whose loyalty is questionable," he declined to sign the statement and was not challenged when he showed up for work on the film set. A similar request was made of him before he could appear in the NBC broadcast *A Man Is Ten Feet Tall*. "I was torn inside," he states.

> How could I not be proud of Paul Robeson? How could I repudiate
> a relationship with Canada Lee, from whom I had learned so much
> about life? Torn between my desire to get on with my career and my
> revulsion at what they were asking me to do, I broke down and cried.
> When I cry—I get angry. . . . [I said] what I felt couldn't remain
> unsaid: "I have nothing but respect for Paul Robeson—and that's the
> truth. And if you see my respect for him as un-American, then I am
> fucking un-American."[81]

Again, Poitier was allowed to appear in the movie, although he had not signed the loyalty oath.

Belafonte, also an affiliate of the Committee for the Negro in the Arts, experienced problems on this front as well. In order to get a lead role in *Carmen Jones* (1954) alongside Dorothy Dandridge, he told the antileft publication *Counterattack* that he "hated" communism and that he was not aware that the Committee for the Negro in the Arts was one of the Party's organizations.[82] When he was invited to appear on *The Ed Sullivan Show*, whose host was known as one of the more prominent enforcers of the blacklist, it was assumed in some quarters that he must have "named names." "A lot of people on the left turned against me, because they thought there was no way I could get on the Sullivan show if I hadn't talked to the Committee [HUAC]," Belafonte remembers. "Sidney Poitier saved me one night at a bar in Harlem from a man with a knife who came at me—he was part of the left—because he thought, how could I have possibly gotten on the Ed Sullivan show unless I finked?"[83]

In their subsequent work, Belafonte and Poitier would, in a sense, carry on the twin legacies Robeson had established: the search for dignified roles for black actors, as embodied in Poitier's work throughout the late 1950s and 1960s, and the activism—arguably energized by a desire for redemption—characteristic of Belafonte's efforts, particularly during the civil rights movement. Absent, though, would be the explicit leftist/Popular Front political aesthetic and the diasporic consciousness that had defined the older activist's work, and one has to imagine that, like a number of individuals who sought to establish and maintain careers in the McCarthy era and afterward, Belafonte and Poitier made conscious efforts to distance themselves from any possible red taint or radical association.

Belafonte's activism did not prevent him from pursuing a successful career as a singer and actor, and Poitier was certainly involved in the civil rights movement (though never as deeply and publicly immersed as Belafonte). Nevertheless, their paths do suggest the difficulty of pursuing both goals. Indeed, Belafonte, implicitly identifying his own situation with Robeson's, would criticize Poitier for failing to make more political use of his social capital:

> In the early days, Sidney participated in left affairs, but once he
> became anointed he gave it up. Sidney was always more pliable,
> more accommodating. He handpicked each one of those pictures to
> continue to exercise that beauty and make sure that he never, never,
> ever disturbed the white psyche in anything he did. Not once. Not
> in public utterance or in private utterance. I put script after script
> before people who just rejected them out of hand, and I just said
> there's no point in trying to change this monster. They would not
> listen to my gods.[84]

Despite his frustrations on the cultural front, Belafonte emerged as a major figure in the shaping of black political aspirations during the southern phase of the civil rights movement. Perceptions that he might still be committed to the Left, though, troubled his relationship with some elements in this period, including particularly the NAACP. As Ella Baker, who would be indispensable with regard to the conception and formation of the Student Nonviolent Co-ordinating Committee (SNCC)—as well as the organization of the Southern Christian Leadership Conference (SCLC)—and a former leftist herself, recalls, "I was told that they had banned [Belafonte]. . . . They may have thought of him as 'Red.' I think it was an anti-communist reaction on the part of the NAACP."[85]

On the question of Poitier's political commitments, and indeed the issue of how the creative artists of his generation, including Belafonte, made the transition from being identified with the Left and Robeson to become significant players in the mainstream, post–Popular Front arts world, it is important to consider the dramatic changes that took place in the period between the early 1950s and the early 1960s. The rhetorical terrain changed substantially in this period, as the Left disappeared as a significant force in American life and the civil rights movement shifted southward under the leadership of the church, the one institution with which the Communist Party had the least patience. Recognizing that the game had changed for a number of this cohort, Martin Luther King Jr., despite his early tendency to use the specter of communism to encourage American authorities to respond to the civil rights agenda, represented in many respects a continuation of the work done and example set by Robeson. "Paul Robeson was the 'gate' to Martin Luther King," contends Gillespie.[86] Those young actors who were closest to Robeson—such as Belafonte, Poitier, Dee, and Davis—would also become relatively close to King.

In this light, it is worth remembering that there were also instrumental, pragmatic reasons for African Americans to associate with the communist cause: the Left was attractive because it challenged for a period the racial status quo. As Ossie Davis writes, "I never was a Communist, but I was a fellow traveler. Though layered, my loyalty was never split; always at the bottom, even if I did have to constantly shuffle my tactics, was black itself. I was 'red' only when I thought it was a better way of being 'black.'"[87] While a number of individuals were certainly committed to both leftism and the civil rights cause, others were quite willing to leave the broader ideological questions behind, especially given the incentive structure put in place by the combination of the Red Scare and the slight openings created by the success of the largely southern integrationist movement. It should also be noted that many of the people who invested in the civil rights movement were hardly regular churchgoing

Christians either, despite the prominence of the church in the movement itself (or, for that matter, committed to nonviolence). In other words, involvement with the CPUSA and its affiliated causes and support for the southern church-based civil rights movement both represented instrumental means by which black civil rights could be achieved. In this light, we can understand Robeson's references to the church in *Here I Stand* (while noting that he was hardly an atheist), and A. Philip Randolph's earlier decision to use religious language and engage the black churches in the launching of the Brotherhood of Sleeping Car Porters (even though he was not a believer).[88]

Finally, pragmatic considerations aside, although it is impossible to determine the significance of an absence, in the biographies of this generation, it is noticeable that there is little mention of how the transition was made from the Robeson era to the later civil rights era.[89] The rearrangement, then, of the visceral scaffolding of black progressive politics is generally cloaked in silence, with the effect of marginalizing the intensity and significance of the earlier commitments to such an extent that, in many instances, they have simply been forgotten and rendered unremarkable and for all intents and purposes irretrievable. The maps that might help us trace the connections between the pre- and post-Robeson moments do not exist, leaving the rather overpowering silence—the unpublished retraction—that has marked the borders and boundaries of the Popular Front era and classic, southern-based civil rights era politics.

A FAMILY AFFAIR

One of the key subtexts of this paradigmatic reorientation was gender. The Popular Front was, in general, rather inattentive to issues of gender, reflecting in many respects the backlash against first wave feminism that characterized the decades after World War I on both sides of the Atlantic; the belief that gender discrimination and the "woman question" were basically manifestations of a more significant class oppression; and the go-slow policies of the CPUSA as it pursued a more reformist path in the immediate prewar years. While issues related to gender and race and—largely through the efforts of Claudia Jones—the intersection of the two were given a higher profile in the late 1940s and the 1950s, the common problematic linkages drawn between issues of gender and race mitigated against the explicit consideration of sexuality in Popular Front representations.[90] The mainstream civil rights movement, at this point anchored in the North and led by the NAACP and Urban League, was equally disinclined to engage issues related to gender dynamics and sexuality within black communities, especially given the longstanding narratives that cast blacks as licentious, undisciplined, and lacking in sexual restraint.

As a result, it is difficult to distinguish the artistic products of the era, and particularly those generated by individuals associated with the Popular Front, from those that followed in the decades afterward, in terms of their treatment and depictions of African Americans and certainly black sexuality. Hollywood's cultural left tended to either pursue a relatively benign integrationist approach to racial issues or, as was more often the case, avoid race completely (hence the black invisibility characteristic of American film until the early 1970s). At the same time, in his artistic and political work, it is apparent that apart from his mastery of what was perceived to be the black folk voice, a large part of Robeson's power lay in his signifying masculinity, whether it was used as a trope for the shaping of American modernism in the photographs of Nickolas Muray, the sculptures of Antonio Salemme, and the films *The Emperor Jones* (1933) and *Showboat* (1936); to justify and naturalize British imperialism, as in *Sanders of the River* (1935) and *Song of Freedom* (1936); to energize the attacks on him during the Red Scare; or functioned as a mobilizing factor in the making of red and black politics in the 1940s and 1950s.[91]

Some sense of the role Robeson's physical appeal and his embodiment of manhood played in this era is reflected in the following statement from Ossie Davis:

> My experience with Paul Robeson was on more levels than one. On a personal level, he was an immediate mentor and hero for those of us in the theatre who wanted to be actors. We wanted to be some degree like he was. He was huge, he was beautiful, he could sing and he was an athlete and he was sexy. He had all of the positive things a young man and a young woman could be inspired by. Paul represented to us that top moment, that top possibility.[92]

While he virtually disappeared from the stages of American and, to a lesser degree, African American life, as a consequence of the Red Scare, battles would emerge over his legacy that revealed not only class divisions but differences regarding the role of gender—and gender parity—in the making of a transformative black politics.

Indeed, among Robeson's protégés, a certain hypermasculinist turn is observable in the period immediately following the McCarthy era—undoubtedly informed by the developments in American society at the time, as evidenced in the work of Norman Mailer and others in American letters in the 1950s. In the course of this paradigm shift, subtext would become overtext and the implicit would be denaturalized, transfigured, and renaturalized as first fact. This reconfiguration linked the Robesonian era to both the southern civil rights movement and the nationalism of the black arts and Black Power movements. In an article Davis published in *Freedomways* in 1962 regarding his play *Purlie Victorious*, he would make explicit reference to the significance of the feature as a means of enabling masculinity: "[I]t is not enough to be only a Negro in this world . . . one must, and more importantly, also be, a man," he added. "Purlie showed me that, whatever I was, I was not a man . . . not yet! . . . Purlie told me my *manhood* was hidden within my Negroness, and that I could never find the one without fully, and passionately, embracing the other."[93] He would famously express similar sentiments with regard to Malcolm X after his murder, making reference to the slain activist as "our manhood, our living black manhood" in his eulogy, and again in *The Autobiography of Malcolm X*:

> Malcolm was a man! . . . He also knew that every Negro who did
> not challenge on the spot every instance of racism, overt or covert,
> committed against him and his people, who chose instead to
> swallow his spit and go on smiling, was an Uncle Tom and a traitor,
> without balls or guts, or any other commonly accepted aspects of
> manhood.[94]

It is in this matrix that Sidney Poitier's work—on stage and behind the scenes—in the first black-authored Broadway production, *A Raisin in the Sun*, is intriguing. For Poitier, his political work was his acting: his conscious investment in representing "positive" images of black masculinity. It is his—and Hollywood's—investment in a cool, dignified, clearly restrained, and at most suggestive masculinism that represents Poitier's most significant and well-known contribution to representations of black life in the post–Red Scare era. His embodiment of a certain understated black manhood also stood in contrast with the more sensuous, explicit, albeit exoticized possibilities Belafonte would engage in his film work and music. That said, Poitier's performance in *Raisin* is not consistent with the persona he established in the 1960s with *Pressure Point, Lilies of the Field, A Patch of Blue, To Sir With Love*, and *Guess Who's Coming to Dinner?* and first introduced in *No Way Out* in 1950.[95] *Raisin* features a more naked, earnest and less calculated take on black male possibilities, the id to the iconic and extratextual Sidney's almost Robesonesque superego; and a less ambitious exposition of denaturalized masculinity that is asked to do a kind of work one would not immediately associate with the artist-activist who was by that point retired. The rawer Poitier would emerge in films that featured all-black or nearly all-black settings; the more saintly persona, not surprisingly, was likely to appear in integrated spaces.

A Raisin in the Sun, which drew its title from a line in Langston Hughes's poem "Harlem," was about a family awaiting an insurance settlement of $10,000 and its struggles over how the money should be spent: the son played by Poitier wants to buy a liquor store, and the mother, played by Claudia McNeil, is interested in providing support for her daughter, Beneatha (Diana Sands), to go to medical school and in buying a house for the extended family in an otherwise all-white neighborhood in Chicago. Although the successful Broadway production, which debuted on March 11, 1959, was technically a product of the civil rights era, one can see elements of the Old Left, an awareness of diaspora and the civil rights/anticolonial nexus (in the relationship between Beneatha and her suitor, the Nigerian Joseph Asagai, played by Ivan Dixon), and the issues that would come to dominate post–civil rights black public discourse, including class and gender: the second wave feminist sensibility that informs Ruth Younger's deliberations about whether or not she should have an abortion, Beneatha's professional aspirations, and Poitier's enactment of an anomic masculinism.

The play's creator, Lorraine Hansberry, was raised in an upper-middle-class Chicago family. As she writes, "I recall being the only child in my class who did not come from the Rooseveltian atmosphere of the homes of the Thirties. Father ran for Congress as a Republican. He believed in private enterprise."[96] Hansberry would rebel against her upbringing and her alienation from the majority of blacks:

> I have remained throughout the balance of my life a creature formed
> in a community atmosphere where I was known as—a "rich" girl. . . .
> [M]y mother sent me to kindergarten in white fur in the middle of the
> depression; the kids beat me up; and I think it was from that moment
> I became—a rebel.[97]

Influenced by her uncle William Leo Hansberry, professor of African history at Howard University and mentor to Nigerian anticolonialist Nnamdi Azikiwe, Hansberry became a contributor to both Robeson's newspaper *Freedom* during its run in the early 1950s and the left-leaning journal *Freedomways*, launched in 1961, and was thoroughly acquainted with the issues that defined the black corridors of the Popular Front. An early issue of *Freedom* recognized her service as "subscription clerk, receptionist, typist, and editorial assistant," and during the newspaper's existence she wrote articles on the anti-colonial effort, the Red Scare, and the mobilization of black women against racism, among other topics.[98] She also had her passport privileges rescinded during the Cold War. "I knew her only as a politically aware, contemporary black American who was fairly close to Paul Robeson," recalls Poitier.[99] In other words, like Poitier, she could lay claim to a part of Robeson's legacy. Given the changing currents, though, it was predictable that gender as well as class would distinguish Hansberry's and Poitier's understandings of black possibilities in the post–Cold War era and that they would struggle over the proper interpretation of the script.

For Poitier, the play as originally drafted did not portray black men in a sufficiently positive light: "The playwright's [Hansberry's] sympathies were completely against me," the actor suggests.

> She saw the play as weighted toward the mother; that's how she'd
> *written* it. She was a very intelligent young black woman, and she
> came from a family of achievers. Her whole family were achievers,
> especially the women, and she had a certain mindset about women
> and their potential, especially black women in America. So she
> wrote a play about a matriarch faced with this dilemma. But in that
> formulation the son is just a ne'er-do-well.

For Poitier, the product of an economically humble background, the stakes were personal: "My father was with me every moment as I performed in *A Raisin in the Sun*. The themes, too, seemed like so many threads from my own life. . . . My work is *me*." At another point, almost in anticipation of the Moynihan report, Poitier adds,

> The simple truth of the matter was that if the play is told from the
> point of view of the mother, and you don't have an actor playing the
> part of Walter Lee [Poitier's role] strongly, then the end result may
> very well be a negative comment on the black male.

Not interested in following that script, Poitier recalls that he formed an alliance with another actor, Ruby Dee, who played Ruth, Walter Lee's wife, to reorient the production:

> I had an ally—the talented, highly intelligent Ruby Dee. We
> decided on an approach, and conspired to keep the strength in the

character of Walter Lee Younger, which meant my playing *against* Claudia McNeil [the mother], who is a tower of strength as a stage personality. I had to change my whole performance to prevent the mother character from so dominating the stage that it would cast a negative focus on the black male.[100]

Ruby Dee, for her part, seems to have been intimidated by Hansberry and speaks of feeling "uncomfortable [and] patronized." She adds, "I felt like I was in the presence of a superior intellect."[101] Ossie Davis, who was Poitier's understudy, suggests that he and Dee both shared Poitier's concerns and zero-sum calculations:

> *A Raisin in the Sun* was a hit. . . . I liked it, too, but Ruby and I had a basic bone to pick. In our opinion, this play was meant to be a warning, as Langston's poem ["Harlem"] suggested. . . . [S]omehow, in the production, that clear intent became subverted. Sure, Walter, goaded by dreams of what he could not have in America because of racism, was about to explode; but not to worry. Lena, his mother, the strong and domineering head of the household, was totally in charge. America could depend on her to keep Walter under control, no matter what.[102]

Dee also found herself in direct conflict with Claudia McNeil. There is a scene in the play in which the mother slaps the daughter, Beneatha, played by Diana Sands, for questioning the existence of the Christian God. Sands had mastered the art of dodging the full impact of McNeil's blow—a necessary skill, given that McNeil had no apparent interest in pulling her punches on stage—but her understudy, Billie Allen, had not. When Sands left the play, McNeil's slaps landed without restriction, prompting Dee to mutter to McNeil on stage, "You hit that girl one more time like that and I'll knock you on your ass!"[103] The deliberations with regard to gender, then, cut across the cast and production crew in a manner that did not simply pit the women against the men.

Ironically, although Poitier believed that his concerns regarding the script were being ignored, Hansberry was frustrated by what she saw as Poitier's inability to bring the Walter Lee character to life as the main protagonist of the play. Though she would subsequently regret that the play was not effectively structured in terms of identifying a clear protagonist—"A central character as such is certainly lacking from *Raisin*. . . . I consider it an enormous dramatic fault if no one else does"—she resisted changing the script and hoped the director Lloyd Richards would be able to coax Poitier into making the play his own.[104]

Beyond the explicit gender and generational tensions, the play and movie were also significant because they were interpreted as pointing to and endorsing integrationism as the primary objective of the black community. Although the play suggests some anxieties about the implications of integration, the received thrust of both iterations of Hansberry's script was to normalize, in many respects, black families within the American social context.[105] Hansberry's work, taken in the aggregate, does not support such a reading. In *Les Blancs*, which she began writing in the early 1960s as a response in part to Jean Genet's play *The Blacks* and the dilemmas brought to the surface by Lumumba's assassination, and possibly the meanings ascribed to *Raisin in the Sun*, her commitment to a black transnational politics that exceeded integrationist principles is clear. Indeed, Hansberry has the lead character in that play, Tshembe Matoseh, distinguishing himself from "simpering American Negroes sitting around and discussing admission to country clubs!"[106] Nina Simone, who attributed the major part of her politicization to her friend Hansberry— "[W]hen we got together, it was always Marx, Lenin and revolution . . . real girls' talk"—suggests that the playwright "saw civil rights as only a part of the wider racial and class struggle."[107]

In this light, it is worth noting that some scenes were cut from the script for *Raisin in the Sun* as it was reworked in rehearsal before it reached Broadway, including the discussion of a black family's house being bombed in an all-white part of the city; a scene in which the son, Travis, who was portrayed by a young Glynn Turman, is playing with a rat; and the reactions to Beneatha's getting a "natural." Hansberry's attempts to further complicate the narrative when she was writing the movie script—adding a scene with the mother interacting with her employer as a maid, and a soapbox orator making connections between conditions in Africa, the American South, and Chicago—were deleted by the executives at Columbia, the studio that was making the film. Although some of these cuts were justified as attempts to maintain narrative clarity, they also reinforced a certain notion of what the appropriate narrative should be. Accordingly, the studio executives argued that "the addition of race issue material . . . should be avoided [as it might] lessen the sympathy of the audience, give the effect of propagandistic writing, and so weaken the story, not only as dramatic entertainment, but as propaganda too" and that the references to colonialism were "surplus . . . and potentially troublesome to no purpose."[108]

The resulting product established a blueprint, a particular sentimental economy, with regard to prevailing understandings of black class relations.

In the story of the Younger family, one saw the fusion of black working-class realities with African American middle-class aspirations and expectations—an implied solidaristic relationship that rendered different black economic sub-constituencies indistinguishable. On the economic front, the Youngers contained all and represented all in a context in which one might safely assume every black fate was linked. *A Raisin in the Sun* and the diverging interpretations of its proper meanings also represent the temporal and paradigmatic shifts distinguishing the black Popular Front and much of the northern civil rights movement from the politics, aesthetics, and geographies of the movement activism that followed.[109] The downplaying, and in some instances suppression, of themes related to anticolonialism, diasporic consciousness, and intraracial class distinctions, along with the implicit engagement of gender relations, mark her creation as a significant turning point in both black politics and popular culture, as do the broader pressures to decouple race and the questions of coloniality, as if such an operation were logically possible. Especially given the Popular Front backgrounds of Hansberry, Poitier, and Dee, the borderline intratextual dissonance lying just below the play's surface, and the symbolic importance attributed to the success of the play and the subsequent movie, *Raisin* has to be seen as a crucial moment in terms of the negotiation of the transition from the Robesonian era to the final phases of the southern-inflected and integration-oriented civil rights movement.

BIRMINGHAM

"If I thought it would do some good, I'd leave some of the shows I have to do, lose thousands of dollars, and join Dr. Martin Luther King and other integration leaders in my native state of Alabama," Nat King Cole asserted in the spring of 1963. Speaking in response to an idea floated by Edwin Berry of the Chicago branch of the National Urban League that black artists should actively join the civil rights effort, and the widely publicized involvement of comedian Dick Gregory and former Ellington vocalist Al Hibbler in the broader campaign, Cole asked, "What good, except for his own publicity, has it done for Dick Gregory to go down there? Gregory's act is based upon racial satire. Hibbler needed the publicity. Harry Belafonte, who has not gone down there yet, is a professional integrationist. We don't see eye-to-eye."[110] In an interview published in the *Chicago Defender*, Cole argued for a clear separation of the roles of entertainer and political activist:

I do not see why or how some of our professional civil rights fighters come up every so often with the idiotic idea that Negro entertainers should lead the way. . . . [E]ntertainers, for the most part, are not trained in such fighting. They spend their lives weaving dreams. In my audiences I might have a Nazi, a Communist, a Bilbo [i.e., Mississippi governor, U.S. senator, and segregationist Theodore G. Bilbo] and people of many colors and faiths. I try to build for them an entertaining illusion, taking them away from the cares of the day.[111]

Cole observed that Thurgood Marshall had called him an "Uncle Tom," despite his having taken the "first integrated unit . . . into the South," and lamented, again, the suggestion that artists should lead political movements: "I am a singer of songs. I am not a public speaker. Our ministers, lawyers, and other *vocally trained* professional civil rights fighters are the ones for the job. With money I earn from my songs, I do and will continue to help their fight, which is also my fight."[112]

The same concerns Cole raised about functional miscegenation and the desire to separate the roles of artist and politician arguably inform—albeit in a lighthearted manner—the following item published in the *Afro-American*'s "Grapevine News" during the same period with regard to Dick Gregory: "Dick Gregory's a Number One guy for many reasons, but we can't believe that he's seriously thinking of running for Congress in his Chicago district next year."[113] At this time there were still very few black representatives in Congress—five at this point—and of that small number, California's Augustus Hawkins had only just been elected, while two others were effectively missing in action: Philadelphia's Robert Nix and Chicago's William Dawson. Dawson, closely tied to the patronage network that controlled the second city's politics, "used his . . . personal power to enhance his political position and influence in Congress and did not serve blacks in general," suggests political scientist Hanes Walton.[114] After the Chicago branch of the NAACP criticized him for his silence regarding the lynching of Emmett Till and his failure to support Adam Clayton Powell's effort to prohibit federal support for segregated schools (in the wake of the *Brown* decision), Dawson exercised his influence to remove the NAACP's leadership in the city and marginalize it within local politics.[115] He would later oppose King's efforts to establish the SCLC in Chicago, stating, "What does he [King] mean coming in here trying to tell our citizens that we are segregated? Chicagoans know what's best for Chicagoans."[116] Powell, Harlem's representative and the black elected official most committed to the arts of explicit performance, was certainly engaged on the civil rights front, construed broadly, but he was consumed at this point with his own battle with the NAACP—he had criticized the organization for being, in his view, controlled by whites—and was moving toward a "black power" position. There was also tension between Powell and the South-oriented SCLC. For Powell, his ability as chair of the House Committee on Education and Labor to raise the minimum wage was more important than any gains southern protesters might make.[117] In general, Powell seemed as committed to protecting his turf as black America's preeminent representative as to cooperating with the effort to change the conditions under which many of his constituents, in the broadest sense, lived. Detroit's Charles Diggs was involved with the struggle on the ground and was actually in the South during the 1963 campaign on a "fact-finding tour." While staying at the home of Aaron Henry, the president of the Mississippi branch of the NAACP, Diggs assisted in putting out a fire that was ignited by two bombs thrown at the house. Telling reporters that he intended to ask the House Judiciary Committee to conduct an investigation of conditions in the region, he added that he planned to testify himself and that the "hearings would have great psychological impact which would be of great benefit to both sides."[118] In other words, while some of the black members of Congress were willing to represent the concerns of the civil rights community within the arenas of formal politics, there was a shortage in terms of human capital. Moreover, as often as these elected officials were working toward the same goals as the movement, they were at odds with those engaged in explicit protest activity. In this light, serious or not, a campaign for Congress by Gregory in his home district in Chicago was hardly far-fetched, especially given the inactivity of some of these elected officials (especially Dawson) and their marginal status with regard to the making of black politics in this period.[119]

Underlying Nat King Cole's statements was some concern about the impact of civil rights activism on his career, especially given the punishment Robeson received on the financial front. This real and understandable fear, which Lorraine Hansberry had identified in a speech the previous fall, explains Cole's references to "los[ing] thousands of dollars" and being "finish[ed] in the only life [he] knew."[120] Five months earlier, New Orleans native and pianist Antoine "Fats Domino" Dominique had expressed similar reservations about the financial and professional implications of public civil rights activism, stating that he would begin playing segregated venues again. "I've lost thousands and thousands of dollars in the past because I've gone along with the NAACP, and it has hurt my reputation as a performer," he told the press. "I won't do it anymore." After being roundly criticized by blacks, Domino backpedaled a little bit and a week later asserted, "I know from my heart that the NAACP is the greatest friend of the minorities."[121]

Beyond financial concerns, Cole and others also had serious doubts about the ability of the SCLC and other civil rights groups to bring about real change and the effectiveness of the nonviolent approach. "If, now," he calculated, "the non-violence approach used by the NAACP and Dr. King, despite the current success, would break down and we as Negroes had to defend ourselves, I'd be right on the firing line."[122] This particular worry was based on real-life experience. In April 1956, in the middle of a show in Birmingham, Alabama, for an all-white audience—a show later that evening would be for blacks only—Cole was physically assaulted by five men. "Man, I love show business, but I don't want to die for it," he would comment afterward, while stating that he would continue to play venues that barred blacks and leave politics "to the other guys." This pronouncement led to plans by black audiences to boycott Cole's shows and recordings—in response to which he purchased a $500 lifetime membership with the NAACP.[123]

In the same issue of the *Defender* that carried Cole's interview, there was a short piece entitled "Gregory Tells [of] Beating in Birmingham Jail," detailing the comedian's treatment at the hands of the city's police. "You leave the world when you go into the Birmingham jail," he wrote with regard to the extralegal character of southern jails. "It was the most miserable experience of my entire life." Showing reporters the "six to eight-inch welt on his left forearm," the St. Louis native stated that he and "an estimated 500 prisoners" had been assaulted by officers "using billy clubs, hammers and sawed-off pool sticks." Gregory, who had been initially invited to get involved in the southern campaign by Medgar Evers, was arrested while leading a group of teenagers who were protesting segregation. And his contract was terminated at the Galaxy night club in St. Albans, New York, because, in his view, he had committed publicly to devote his "entire weekly salary, $5,500 . . . to help voter registration efforts in Greenwood." Gregory, in an effort to use the Cold War propaganda contest in support of the relatively narrow ambitions of this phase of the civil rights movement, said, "This is the only way to get freedom. They call us Communists. Well, I say the Negro in the South is treated like the East Germans who want the freedom of West Berlin." Of course, while elements of the American press were indirectly red-baiting civil rights activists and encouraging them to reject the internationalist commitments of Robeson's cohort, "[t]he Communist press throughout Europe," the *Defender* observed, "[was] bitterly attack[ing] the United States for its racial troubles in Birmingham, Ala."[124]

Other artists were more reluctant to participate on the front lines of the movement. Against the backdrop of the Birmingham campaign, popular balladeer and South Carolina native Brook Benton, expressed reservations about the philosophy of nonviolence. Accordingly, he suggested that he might not be the best candidate to participate on the front lines of the movement as he was "not a non-violent Negro."[125] Performers such as Josh White and Ray Charles expressed similar reservations, while Mahalia Jackson, the Staple Singers, former Drifter Clyde McPhatter, and Sam Cooke raised funds and awareness by other means.[126]

Along with the Impressions and their lead singer and songwriter, Curtis Mayfield, perhaps the artist whose recordings were most likely to be found on movement turntables was Nina Simone. Emerging in the late 1950s within the rhythm and blues field, albeit classically trained and quite singular in the context of the genre, Simone found herself resisting the restrictions characteristic of the music industry and inspired by her interactions with individuals such as Lorraine Hansberry, James Baldwin, and Langston Hughes. As a result of these interactions, Simone wrote "To Be Young, Gifted and Black," with Weldon Irvine, referencing the title of the play Hansberry was working on before her death from cancer in 1965 at age thirty-four.[127] By this point, Simone had also added to the public record the most explicit civil rights–oriented composition of the period, the self-explanatory "Mississippi Goddamn." In her autobiography, she recalls that after the murder of Medgar Evers and the infamous church bombing in Birmingham in September 1963 that killed four young girls, "I had it in my mind to go out and kill someone, I didn't know who, but someone I could identify as being in the way of my people getting some justice for the first time in three hundred years." Persuaded by her husband that she "knew nothing about killing," she writes, "I did know about music. I sat down at my piano. An hour later I came out of my apartment with the sheet music for 'Mississippi Goddamn' in my hand. It was my first civil rights song, and it erupted out of me quicker than I could write it down." Indeed the recording sounds as if it was written in a rage, with its staccato rhythm and take-no-prisoners lyrical thrust. Simone subsequently became a regular featured performer at civil rights benefits in support of SNCC, including, at some risk to her personal safety, at venues on the front lines of the South. She was, though, concerned about the possibility of harm and was quite resistant to not being compensated for her efforts: "It's all well and good, but I'm not gonna get myself killed and I'm not gonna give up my life to please this group or that group. I'm doing what I'm doing; I want to make some money."[128]

The artist most closely identified with the civil rights cause in this period was Harry Belafonte, who met King in 1956. Their close friendship was reflected in Belafonte's participation in the Committee to Defend Martin Luther King, formed when Alabama sought to prosecute King for tax evasion. Belafonte also supported the King family by paying the premiums for a life insurance policy for King (at a time when few companies were willing to provide affordable coverage for him). Having formed a relationship with and endorsed John F. Kennedy in 1960, he also provided a link between the SCLC and the White House. Moreover, Belafonte played a crucial role, along with Sammy Davis Jr., in getting members of the liberal Hollywood community to appear at civil rights benefits (which might help explain, given the social distance between the black music industry and the filmmaking business in this period, the underrepresentation of the gospel and rhythm and blues communities in movement activities).

Belafonte was also present in the South and active in ways that made a favorable impression on those engaged in the trenches. Arguing with his long-time friend Sidney Poitier about the wisdom of making a trip to Mississippi to deliver money to SNCC members, Belafonte said, "Our presence there will be a very forceful morale booster for a lot of kids who have been in that area all summer. . . . It would be good for them to see us." Indeed, it is estimated that Belafonte devoted roughly one-fifth of his income to funding a range of activities, including SNCC. Within the broader civil rights movement itself, as a member of the Council of Advisors of the SCLC, and an important contact person for SNCC (an organization toward which he contributed start-up funds) and the southern campaign as a whole, Belafonte's connections also allowed him to function as a costrategist at points and an effective arbitrator when disputes arose between the SCLC and SNCC and indeed most of the other civil rights groups (with the previously noted exception of the NAACP).[129]

In contrast to Belafonte's example, Ralph Ellison continued to posit that the roles of artist and politician should remain separate, and—consistent with his reading of the blues as political theory—that American blacks ultimately did not have the means to determine or change their circumstances. "[T]he outcome of the struggle in the South," he suggested with regard to the Birmingham campaign, "rests in the hands of those who have the power of violence in their hands. And that is not the Negroes." While he offered verbal support for King, and hoped that the marches would be "carried on into the North," he noted that his appointment at Rutgers University would prevent him from actually marching. Responding to the poet Robert Lowell's decision not to attend a 1965 event sponsored by the Johnson administration for fear that it might look like an endorsement of the country's increasing military commitments in Vietnam, Ellison contended, "I think this was unfortunate. The President wasn't telling

Lowell how to write his poetry and I don't think he's in any position to tell the President how to run the government." His claims to the contrary, though, it should be noted that Ellison's support for the war was partly tied to his conviction that any other stance would weaken an administration that seemed committed to desegregation. In other words, Ellison's position, at root, was not an argument against artists taking political positions but rather a rejection of those who supported policies with which he was not comfortable.[130]

Ellison would also function as the presence against which many in the emerging Black Arts movement would define their identities and objectives. To the extent that he rejected any ties to African sources—however constituted and defined—and argued often in a tortured manner for the disentanglement of the creative arts and politics, he provided an easy target for a movement that saw art as a political weapon and a generation that was committed to reimagining the place of Africa and Africanisms in the making of black culture in the United States. Signaling the tension that would characterize the relationship between Ellison and the subsequent generation of black writers was his review of LeRoi Jones's 1963 dissertation on the evolution of African American music. "*Blues People*," he wrote,

> like much that is written by Negro Americans at the present
> moment, takes on an inevitable resonance from the Freedom
> Movement, but is in itself characterized by a straining for a note
> of militancy which is, to say the least, distracting. Its introductory
> mood of scholarly analysis frequently shatters into a dissonance of
> accusation, and one gets the impression that while Jones wants to
> perform a crucial task which he feels *someone* should take on—as
> indeed someone should—he is frustrated by the restraint demanded
> of the critical pen and would like to pick up a club.[131]

In his implicitly disdainful reference to artistic work influenced by the civil rights campaign and the more pointed suggestion that Jones might be more drawn to the club than the pen, one can detect Ellison's characteristic resistance to the idea of the fusion of the creative and political arts. Indeed, with regard to Birmingham, Jones expressed doubt that the SCLC's policy of nonviolence would work and whether he himself would be able to "control [him]self and bow down when ordered to pray and remain submissive when attacked."[132]

Ellison also chided Jones for neglecting the familial linkages, to use Walter White's preferred construction, that bound all Americans:

Jones has stumbled over that ironic obstacle which lies in the path of any who would fashion a theory of American Negro culture while ignoring the intricate network of connections which binds Negroes to the larger society. To do so is to attempt a delicate brain surgery with a switch-blade. And it is possible that any viable theory of Negro American culture obligates us to fashion a more adequate theory of American culture as a whole. The heel bone is, after all, connected, through its various linkages, to the head bone.[133]

Bodily metaphors aside, as I will discuss in the next chapter, the generation Jones and his colleagues represented would reject both Ellison's almost primal attachment to the American project and his resistance to the joining of the creative arts and politics.

CODA: PRODIGAL SONS

Paul Robeson died on January 23, 1976, at seventy-seven. The following year, the actor James Earl Jones, who had appeared in both Jean Genet's *The Blacks* and Lorraine Hansberry's *Les Blancs*, was asked to appear in a play based on Robeson's life, and accepted. *Paul Robeson*, in its final incarnation, turned out to be a two-act play written by Phillip Hayes Dean and directed by Lloyd Richards. It described Robeson's development from childhood through his singing and stage successes, his activism, and his persecution. The play toured the country to mixed reviews.[134]

Robeson's son opposed the production. As Jones recalls, at virtually every performance of the play in every part of the country, he would encounter Paul Jr. outside the theatre. As a result of his disapproval, the production was unable to use recordings of Robeson's voice or any of the materials controlled by the Robeson estate. This resistance reached its peak in January 1978 with the publication of a two-page advertisement in *Variety* just before the play's scheduled opening on Broadway. Titled "A Statement of Conscience," this "open letter to the entertainment industry" stated:

> Shortly, the play "Paul Robeson" will open on Broadway. We the undersigned members of the Black community, having seen the production or read versions in progress, regretfully feel compelled to take the extraordinary step of alerting all concerned citizens to what we believe to be, however unintended, a pernicious perversion of the essence of Paul Robeson.

In the body of the text, Robeson's achievements were noted as well as his commitments: "Robeson . . . believed that his art and his being were inseparable from his race and his politics, and he adamantly insisted on using his great gifts as a revolutionary instrument in the case of the liberation of the Blacks of America and of Africa, and the oppressed of all nations." Acknowledging that "[w]e cannot in this brief statement begin to establish the total dimensions—physical, intellectual, artistic and spiritual—of the man," the statement discussed the outlines of the American government's persecution of Robeson: the economic deprivation, the denial of passport privileges, the efforts to expunge him from the historical record to create a "non-person."[135]

The play itself was characterized as

a rewriting of history as perverse in its way as the original attempt to erase history: a tissue of invention and distortions ranging from the most elementary facts of the man's youth, aspirations and development; of the role of his father, his brothers, his wife; to the simplest chronological events of his life and career—all presumably in the effort to create "acceptable" motivation to soften the genuine ones.

Although the play itself was seen as problematic, Jones's acting was praised:

We make this statement *despite the fact that the magnificent acting of James Earl Jones* elevates the portrait to sympathetic and commanding levels. There will be many persons, unknowing of the true dimensions of Robeson or the full extent of what was done to him, who may be grateful for what is given. But it is precisely here that the greatest danger lies. For we in the Black community have repeatedly seen the giants among us reduced from REVOLUTIONARY heroic dimensions to manageable, sentimentalized size. If they cannot be co-opted in life, it is simple enough to tailor their images in death.[136]

The ad was sponsored by the National Ad Hoc Committee (in formation) to End the Crimes against Paul Robeson.[137] Among the signatories were Alvin Ailey, Maya Angelou, James Baldwin, then city councilman Marion Barry, law professor Derrick Bell, *Ebony*'s Lerone Bennett Jr., then Georgia state senator Julian Bond, historian John Bracey, activist Elombe Brath, Gwendolyn Brooks, playwright Alice Childress, John Henrik Clarke, playwright Lonnie Elder III, Nikki Giovanni, Ewart Guinier, novelist Rosa Guy, political scientists Charles

Hamilton, Mack Jones, and Ronald Walters, John O. Killens, Coretta Scott King, Paule Marshall, Alvin Poussaint, members of Congress John Conyers and Charles Rangel, poet Quincy Troupe, Coleman Young—by this point mayor of Detroit—and Paul Robeson Jr.[138]

Baldwin, who had struggled to get support for his movie script detailing the life and times of Malcolm X, wrote a separate piece in the *Village Voice* explaining his displeasure with the Robeson production.[139] He acknowledged that he had not yet witnessed a performance of the play but contended that he could still judge the production as "Plays are read and judged—*seen*, in the mind's eye— long before they are produced: indeed, this is *how* they are produced." Noting the ironic dimensions of the campaign, given the concerted effort to silence Robeson the activist despite the First Amendment, Baldwin argued,

> It is tempting to dismiss the Robeson Ad Hoc Committee as an
> "un-black activities committee," but this is inaccurate and unfair.
> The accusation is not supported either by the tone, or the language,
> of the committee's statement. This statement was, after all, drawn
> up by writers, and every writer loathes and distrusts this sort of
> controversy. . . . I hope I do not have to say that no one wishes to burn
> the script and no one is willing to stone the writer: we have all been
> stoned too often.

In common with many of the play's critics, he praised Jones's acting abilities, recognizing that "if one reads the play knowing that James Earl Jones is going to play Paul Robeson, one can almost feel the electricity with which Jones will fill the theatre. The Jones incandescence would beautifully transform the script." Finally, he highlighted what he felt was the inaccurate and inappropriate rendering of Robeson's career and significance and lamented "the trivialization of Robeson" and "the debasement of his legacy." At the end of the statement, he asserted,

> The man the play presents is not Paul Robeson. That is all that
> we are saying. There is much, much more than this to say, for this
> controversy raises enormous questions, questions within questions:
> of life versus entertainment, life versus art, of awaking or sleeping, of
> warring responsibilities with which we will be struggling until we die.
> Yet, at the moment, it must be said: this man is not Paul Robeson. We
> *must* say this, since we are here, we are living, and we knew him.[140]

James Earl Jones himself had been frustrated with aspects of the play's second act, particularly what he sensed was a lack of coherence in the material.

Nevertheless, he was generally satisfied that the production did a good job of representing Robeson, a man he admired. Indeed, he had longstanding personal reasons to be committed to portraying Robeson accurately. His father, Robert Earl Jones, an acquaintance of Robeson and a stage actor, had been called to testify before HUAC and subsequently blacklisted. As the son would recall in his autobiography, "He had been called up because of his involvement with the leftist movement in the late 1930s." At the same time, his father's experience made the younger Jones wary of political activism:

> I was aware that when the Army was doing my security clearance [in 1953], I had not been declared guilty by association because Robert Earl had not raised me. . . . From that time on, I did not want to be political. When I met Robert Earl in New York, we talked only briefly about his politics. We agreed that the less I knew about his past activities, the better. I did not know whether he was a Communist or not. He denied that in public. I didn't want to know anything that would require me to compromise myself.[141]

Jones also argued that the work of an actor should be distinguished from political concerns. "I believe the profession of being an actor should transcend the politics and the social order of the times," he wrote, adding later, "I have never been an activist."[142] He also cited Robeson's own words in defense of the play. In an essay Robeson wrote for the National Urban League's journal *Opportunity* in 1924, in response to critics of his appearance in Eugene O'Neill's *All God's Chillun,* he asserted that blacks were "too self-conscious, too afraid of showing all phases of our life—especially those phases which are of greatest dramatic value."[143] Moreover, proposed Jones, some of the individuals who lent their names to the protest against the play did so because they were seeking to "make amends" for having insufficiently supported Robeson during his lifetime and the "play became the vehicle for their expiation."[144] Finally, Jones questioned the legitimacy and character of some of the protesters. In reference to a public forum that was held to discuss the play at Hunter College in New York (in March 1978), which he attended with his father, Jones chided Baldwin for being an absentee race man—"Baldwin flew in from . . . somewhere . . . as was his habit in crucial moments when he decided there was a need for a spokesman"—and Ossie Davis, another participant, whom he suspected was one of the ringleaders of the protest.[145]

The debate regarding *Paul Robeson* also raised the question of the relationship between form and political content. While Jones, Richards, Dean, and undoubtedly others were seeking to create a moving drama about one particular and obviously quite remarkable individual, there was also the issue of whether the theatre and drama constituted the most appropriate way to engage Robeson's legacy, especially so soon after his death. As with issues such as slavery, and personalities such as Malcolm X and Martin Luther King Jr., the dramatic urge arguably works against the political (narrowly understood), given its focus on the individual and the sentimental in ways—or, more accurately, to a degree—that, for example, the documentary form does not. As Paul Robeson Jr. and the other supporters of the protest contended, Jones's skill as an actor could be seen as increasing the possibility that audiences would engage the character of Paul Robeson minus the deeper political significance of his times. Robeson himself was reported to have preferred to have his story conveyed in the form of "a documentary with authentic footage."[146]

The most interesting aspect of the protest and the advertisement campaign against the play is the characterization of Robeson's significance. The "open letter to the entertainment industry" characterizes Robeson almost solely in racial terms, as a race man, to use the canonical term. Besides one brief reference to "the oppressed and exploited of all nations," there is no hint in the text that Robeson might have been a (scientific) socialist, that he might have been supportive of the labor movement in the United States and abroad, that he was at the very least a "fellow traveler," and an avid promoter of the Soviet Union in the West and elsewhere. The ad copy refers to "the creation of a non-person," while marginalizing important aspects of Robeson's work and commitments. The implicit suggestion seems to be that a heroic Robeson as usable text for the post–civil rights era would have to be stripped of his complexity and separated from the full scope of his ambitions and projects. In this light, it is useful to consider the significance of the fact that the signatories for the protest campaign were all black. More to the point, later the same year, the Executive Council of the Dramatists Guild would issue a press release criticizing group censorship and the campaign against the play *Paul Robeson*. Among the individuals signing this declaration were Paddy Chayefsky, Jules Feiffer, Terrence McNally, John Guare, Lillian Hellman, Arthur Miller, Stephen Sondheim, Jule Styne, and Betty Comden. None of the individuals supporting this position were of color.[147] The racial divide that characterized the debate about the play underscored in some respects the ways the articulations of broader political positions have inevitably been racialized and illustrated the distance traveled since the late 1940s with regard to the kinds of challenges the Popular Front posed to the American status quo and the sorts of constraints placed on the black artist-activist.

As mentioned earlier, Robeson emphasized the racial angle of his protest activities in the late 1950s as he sought to reestablish his credentials among African Americans. Those efforts, though, never erased his commitment to labor, the Left, and internationalism. In contrast, the late 1970s debate about his legacy suggested that it was really only as a race man that Robeson could be engaged, effectively completing the dismembering and disarticulation that had occurred during the Cold War. For instance, in his comments on the play in the *Afro-American*, Samuel F. Yette argues that the controversy around Robeson, the individual and the play, was a question of maintaining manhood:

> But the essence of this great and versatile man, and how his own society has sought to separate him from his manhood and manhood from his people are not—from the record—subject to honest and reasonable doubt. . . . [T]he conspiracy against Robeson was to separate him from his natural powers—from his manhood.[148]

If Robeson was to be retrieved and made useful, if he was to be revived and recuperated, it would have to be in terms that replicated the disarticulation of race and class, black politics and internationalism, while treading the safer waters of manhood rights. Robeson, then, as political infratext, would in the decades after his death function as a race man containable within the borders of a postage stamp and of discourses that, in many respects, avoided the political.[149]

[T]he space of the modern nation-people is never simply

horizontal. Their metaphoric movement requires a kind of

"doubleness" of writing; a temporality of representation

that moves between cultural formations and social

processes without a central causal logic.

—Homi Bhabha, *The Location of Culture*

3

NATION TIME

The formal achievement of legal equality represented by the passage of the Civil Rights Act of 1964 and the Voting Rights Act the following year raised the question of what shape black politics should assume in the wake of these victories. Especially with the possibility of significantly increased representation in the arenas of formal politics, what kinds of relationships would be established among actors in the realms of electoral politics; protest politics, by this point anchored more in the religious sphere than in leftist and labor movements; and the ritual spaces of black popular culture? Which territories and what forms would black political practices claim and assimilate? Moreover, what rhythms and temporalities would define the imagination, articulation, and translation of black desires and with what corresponding legitimacies and illegitimacies? If politics in the pre–civil rights era was marked by a certain randomness in terms of what sorts of actors—nationalists or integrationists, elected or protest, creative artists and/or others—would lead the way, and a certain skepticism regarding suggestions that any of the corresponding realms could be cleanly distinguished, what logic, if any, would dictate the arrangement of black politics afterward? Specifically, to what extent would the anarrangement characteristic of earlier modes of making politics be rejected in favor of a new poetics—an antidactylic metrical template perhaps—in which cultural and protest actors would each play, at most, an unstressed, preparatory role in the articulation of black politics with those in the electoral realm, focused on the state, emerging as the most emphasized and recognized?[1] Might a Rustinian model prevail, in which actor-activists and protest elements would be cast even more deeply into the shadows, reflecting the paths followed by Bayard Rustin himself, as he moved from Popular Front folksinger to civil rights organizer to champion of a vision of politics that excluded all but elected officials and those interest groups primarily concerned with, and licensed by, the state?

These conceptions of politics in which certain actors and sorts of practices are identified with the making of politics, and politics itself, while others are interpreted as peripolitical, prepolitical, or nonpolitical, because of the spaces in which they operate or are rooted, also suggest, in their desired hierarchies and deferential norms, the conflation of a range of binaries. In this matrix, for example, we can imagine the "political" assuming a masculine character that disavows any uncertainty with regard to questions of gender and sexuality. Indeed, politics in this mode must constantly delegitimize its competitors and mark them as other and outside the realm (a process that can be thought of as happening not only between spaces but also within spaces).[2] To be properly political requires, then, the constitution of a nonpolitical exterior and the refusal of those elements and categories of performance that might introduce undecidability and ambiguity into—contaminate, perhaps—its articulations. This is, at least, the operation—the aspiration—I will be seeking to identify and understand in this chapter: the extent to which antidactylic and Rustinian conceptions of black politics became hegemonic in the immediate post–civil rights era.

Related to the urge to manage politics by managing its definition was the issue of which concerns would ground black mobilizations. Implicit in any debates regarding where black politics should be seen as happening legitimately, and attempts to distinguish these spaces in terms of gender, sexuality, and class, are suggestions that certain issues should be accorded priority. In other words, commitments to bound black politics spatially and temporally would inevitably articulate with efforts to provide and delimit its proper substantive borders. Following a period—the 1950s and early 1960s—in which the problems of racial hierarchy had been scripted as civil rights deprivations, and largely a matter of domestic politics manageable within local jurisdictions, to what degree would black politics continue to respect national mores and boundaries? In the wake of the McCarthy era, and in the still-tight grip of the Cold War framework, and subsequent to the triumphalist moments that followed the successes of the mid-1960s, around which antagonisms, if any, would black politics be organized?[3]

THE LAST MINUTES OF NORMAL TIME

Arguably, the central character with regard to the rethinking and repackaging of black politics in the immediate post–civil rights moment was Amiri Baraka, formerly LeRoi Jones. "Baraka's work is in the break, in the scene, in the music," observes the poet–cultural studies scholar Fred Moten, and indeed there is a sense in which, in his ongoing redefinitions and reconstitutions, Baraka's work, and at times his body, are exactly in that place we might call "the break."[4] It was Baraka who, perhaps, most vividly illustrated the relationship between black radical politics understood in the traditional narrow sense, as delineated in the work of Cedric Robinson, and the sensibility that intersects with, but ultimately mocks and haunts, that tradition.[5] It is this second, doubly subaltern voice that must be denied and suppressed in order for a radical politics in the Robinsonian sense to be constituted and stabilized, and for a radical political order to be imagined and articulated. This is one of Moten's implicit theses: radical traditions that appear transgressive in their claims and textures often depend themselves on, and draw sustenance and derive definition from, a presence they must contain, refuse, and—ultimately—try and fail to extradite.[6]

Working roughly chronologically, the first scene that provides us with some sense of the ways Jones's/Baraka's journey is significant is his self-fashioning in the wake of the protests against the murder of Patrice Lumumba and his increasing identification of his own work as political in response to the events of that period. News that the first elected prime minister of the Congo had been murdered under mysterious circumstances in January 1961 provoked a number of protests against the government of Belgium, which had recognized its former colony's independence only six months earlier on June 30, 1960. The United Nations and the United States—under the administration of Dwight Eisenhower—were also criticized for failing to intercede. A planned silent demonstration by a group of about sixty individuals, among them the actor Maya Angelou, the vocalist/actor Abbey Lincoln, and her husband, drummer Max Roach, led to a disruption of the proceedings of the United Nations Security Council on February 15, 1961, and clashes with the organization's guards. The same day, roughly two hundred individuals were reported to be picketing outside the United Nations building on Forty-second and Forty-third streets. This crowd, which included Paul Robeson Jr.—"son of the singer who has been associated with pro-Communist causes," the *New York Times* would note—demanded the resignation of Dag Hammarskjold, the secretary general of the United Nations. Dispersed by the police when they tried to march on Times Square, many of the demonstrators reconvened that evening for a rally in Harlem on Seventh Avenue between 125th and 126th streets, a gathering that would be described in the mainstream press as "a call for unity among Negro nationalist groups." Asked to comment, Roy Wilkins of the NAACP suggested that Lumumba's assassination was an unfortunate development but contended, predictably, that the United Nations demonstrators "were not representative of the position of American Negroes."[7]

Among the demonstrators was LeRoi Jones, at that point a poet, novelist, and playwright based in the bohemian enclave of New York City's Greenwich Village who had only recently begun to think of his work and its function in political terms. "I'm a poet . . . what can I do?" he asked in an essay reflecting on a 1960 tour of Cuba that journalist Richard Gibson invited him to join. "I'm not even interested in politics."[8] The Cuban experience, though, provoked a reevaluation of his sense of himself, a reorientation that led to his participation in the protests outside the United Nations in the winter of 1961. Shortly afterward, Jones would try to articulate a sensibility that went beyond the practices and assumptions of the civil rights movement and argued—in his 1962 essay "Black Is a Country"—for the need for a more nationalist orientation in black politics. "To a growing list of 'dirty' words that make Americans squirm add the word *Nationalism*," he offered. "I would say that the word has gained almost as much infamy in some quarters of this country as that all-time anathema and ugliness, *Communism*. In fact, some journalists, commentators, and similar types use the words interchangeably." Defining nationalism rather loosely as "acting in one's own best interests," Jones posited that conditions called for "an extreme 'nationalism,' i.e., in the best interests of our country, the name of which the rest of America has pounded into our heads for four hundred years, *Black*."[9]

Jones's nationalism was developing at an interesting juncture and at a time when most of the American public, taking notice of the changes taking place in the South, was of the mind that what "the Negro" wanted most was integration. While it still was not clear that the campaigns against Jim Crow would ultimately be successful, the dominant axis of debate centered on the question whether integration would and should occur. Accordingly, in the eyes of many, nationalism appeared anachronistic; just simply odd (as evidenced by the tone of the media fascination with the Nation of Islam) or, in another light, useful (as a justification for rejecting the claims of the civil rights movement on the basis of the suspicion that behind every integrationist smile lay a nationalist boogeyman). Jones's politics, then, should be understood as a break from that assumption, a rupture whose stridency was correlated with the intensity of the wider American inability to recognize and engage nationalist sentiment among blacks on its own terms—as well as, in its early forms, partly a form of provocation.[10]

The coltish instability of black nationalist politics in this particular context was arguably reflected in the developments in LeRoi Jones's own life as he moved rapidly from one rhetorical commitment to another. As he would subsequently recollect, much of his thought in this period was influenced by his wanting to write himself back into "blackness." This entailed, for him, an abrupt departure from his white wife, family, and social scene in the Village for his new home in Harlem. There, along with Larry Neal and others, he established the short-lived Black Arts Repertory Theater/School (BARTS) the month after—and in response to—Malcolm X's murder. As he observes in his autobiography, he was compensating in certain respects for his own deeply rooted insecurities:

> The arrival uptown, Harlem, can only be summed up by the feelings
> jumping out of Césaire's *Return to My Native Land* or Fanon's *The
> Wretched of the Earth* or Cabral's *Return to the Source*. The middle-
> class native intellectual, having outintegrated the most integrated,
> now plunges headlong back into what he perceives as blackest,
> native-est. Having dug, finally, how white he has become, now,
> classically, comes back to his countrymen charged up with the desire
> to be black, uphold black, etc. . . . a fanatical patriot.[11]

In this spirit, Jones published two of the central documents of what became known as the Black Arts movement. In "The Revolutionary Theatre," first published in the *Liberator* in July 1965, he argued:

> The Revolutionary Theatre must EXPOSE! Show up the insides of
> these humans, look into black skulls. White men will cower before
> this theater because it hates them. Because they themselves have
> been trained to hate. The Revolutionary Theatre must hate them for
> hating. For presuming with their technology to deny the Supremacy
> of the Spirit. They will all die because of this.

Making reference to the protagonists in his own plays—*Dutchman, The Toilet,* and *The Slave*—as "victims," he cast this new theatre as "a theatre of Victims . . . [that] even if it is Western, must be anti-Western."[12] This essay, along with his poem "Black Art"—"We want 'poems that kill' / Assassin poems / Poems that shoot guns"—provided the template on which many of the black creative artists of the era, including Nikki Giovanni, Sonia Sanchez, and Don L. Lee (later Haki Madhubuti), June Jordan, Larry Neal, Rolland Snellings (later Askia Touré), and Stanley Crouch (later Stanley Crouch), among others, would elaborate in journals such as the *Liberator* (where "Black Art" first appeared in January 1966), *Black America, Soulbook, Black Dialogue,* the *Journal of Black Poetry, Black Theatre,* and *Black World.*[13]

One of the most striking developments of this period was the explicit fusion of culture and politics. Although creative artists had played a role in the making of the southern section of the civil rights movement, the vast majority of the labor in that endeavor was provided by rank-and-file activists in the field, with some collaboration with civil rights organizations in the region and elsewhere. In contrast, the late 1960s saw the roles almost reversed. In an argument that Addison Gayle Jr. would echo in his articulation of the black aesthetic, Larry Neal suggested,

> Black Art is the aesthetic and spiritual sister of the Black Power
> concept. . . . both relate broadly to the Afro-American's desire for
> self-determination and nationhood. Both concepts are nationalistic.
> One is concerned with the relationship between art and politics; the
> other with the art of politics.[14]

As Stokely Carmichael, the individual publicly associated with the emergence of the slogan "Black power," notes in his autobiography,

> I had expected—hoped for—the political response [from artists].
> But I must admit that the range and the *intensity* of the cultural
> aspect surprised me a little. I mean, the extent and the passion with
> which our artists and writers, and especially the musicians, just
> picked up the ball and ran with it.

In reference to the emergence of this new generation of black aestheticians, he adds,

> [T]here was the Black Arts movement, which just seemed to emerge
> in the North—as the cultural expression of Black Power—among

young writers and artists. Young brothers like Gil Scott-Heron, Amiri Baraka (LeRoi Jones), Larry Neal, Sonia Sanchez, and them. . . . Political consciousness moved into the popular arena.[15]

Of all the figures associated with the Black Arts movement, Jones most effectively converted his prominence in cultural circles into political capital. Having changed his name to Amiri Baraka, under the influence of Maulana Karenga and his particular take on black nationalist possibilities (i.e., his Kawaida theory), Jones was the pacesetter with regard to black cultural and political developments in the 1960s and early 1970s, and more specifically, he was responsible for the alignment of black politics and popular culture, for their synchronic engagement. If the 1960 trip to Cuba and the murders of Lumumba and Malcolm X triggered an increasingly explicit engagement with politics on Baraka's part, the 1967 riots in his hometown of Newark, New Jersey, to which he had relocated after the collapse of the BARTS effort, was his finishing school. Having just returned from teaching at San Francisco State College that spring and interacting with Eldridge Cleaver, Huey Newton, and Bobby Seale of the Black Panthers, Baraka had a template on the basis of which he might approach the situation in Newark. The police beating of a black taxi operator on July 12, 1967, led to a confrontation in the city's Central Ward district that lasted six days and claimed at least twenty victims. Among the more than seven hundred injured was Baraka himself. A *Jet* magazine photo of the artist bloody and handcuffed in a hospital wheelchair came to symbolize the conflict and elevated Baraka's status considerably.[16]

On the heels of the riot, a previously planned black power conference was held in Newark on July 20 and 21. The meeting, chaired by Nathan Wright— an Episcopalian minister, college professor, and civil rights advocate—was a follow-up to a similar conference Adam Clayton Powell Jr. had convened the year before in Washington, D.C. Among those present were Karenga, Jesse Jackson (representing the SCLC), H. Rap Brown of SNCC, James Farmer and Floyd McKissick of the Congress of Racial Equality (CORE), the *Liberator*'s Daniel Watts, Dick Gregory, and, still in bandages, Baraka.[17] The delegates, including representatives from the Urban League, the NAACP and SCLC as well as US, the Organization of Afro-American Unity, and the Nation of Islam, sought to identify some common strategy that could bring about increased political power for the constituencies they represented, in line with Karenga's "unity without uniformity" formulation.

Beyond contributing to the revival of the convention as a mechanism for organizing and mobilizing black activist sentiment on the national level,

Jones also began to get involved in electoral politics in Newark. After the riots and the Black Power conference, he organized the United Brothers with the purpose of increasing black participation in municipal politics. Reflecting a shift in focus that was occurring across the country in the wake of the Voting Rights Act of 1965, black power advocates and integrationists were in common aiming to have cities with majority or plurality black populations elect councils and mayors that were descriptively and hopefully substantively representative (e.g., the Black Panther Party's involvement in municipal politics in Oakland, California). Accordingly, while speaking in Newark in March 1968, Martin Luther King Jr. suggested that he might abandon his commitment to nonpartisanship. Characterizing Lyndon Johnson's politics as "dead-end," he offered that he was considering endorsing either Robert F. Kennedy or Eugene McCarthy for the Democratic presidential nomination. Moreover, after a private meeting with Baraka, he concluded, speaking before a capacity audience at Abyssinian Baptist Church, "The hour has come for Newark . . . to have a black mayor."[18]

SPEECH/ACTS

King's assassination in Memphis in early April 1968, little more than a week after the Newark speech, represented both a significant turning point and rupture in the orientation and imagination of black life and politics. "My whole world collapsed," recollects Isaac Hayes, who had participated in King's last march in Memphis featuring the now iconic "I AM A MAN!" picket signs. "I couldn't create or do anything. It took me a year to get back in full form."[19] That year saw the physical transformation of many of the nation's black communities (particularly outside the South) after the subsequent riots and, as one might expect, the grasp of the new consciousness, culture, and structure of feeling categorized as "soul" intensified. Evidence of this new sensibility first registered in Aretha Franklin's "Think," released in May 1968, and although its lyrics were addressed to a backsliding male suitor, its "freedom, freedom" chorus was inevitably read on a number of levels. The same year, even James Brown abandoned the process and let his natural grow—an act of solidarity, according to the Godfather—as he moved from the Booker T. Washington aesthetics of "America Is My Home," recorded in 1967 and released in May 1968, to "Say It Loud, I'm Black and I'm Proud," recorded and released in the summer of 1968.[20] Public spaces in black neighborhoods were turned inside out, and boundaries reconfigured, in a restructuring accelerated by the various urban renewal schemes under way at the time (and some of those neighborhoods—Washington's U and Seventh streets, and Baltimore's North and Pennsylvania Avenues come to mind—would take a very long time to recover). Also in this period, the quantity of black elected officials increased dramatically, the CBC was formed, and the number of "chocolate cities" multiplied: within two decades, Baltimore, Cleveland, Atlanta, Detroit, Newark, and St. Louis would join Washington as townships where (at least temporarily) the majority of the population was black. Finally, King's murder hastened the intensity of the efforts to constitute and consolidate a new black politics.

Speaking to the press shortly after King's death about the United Brothers initiative, Baraka proposed that, given the experience of the riots, electoral politics represented the most suitable response to the disempowerment of blacks in the United States: "We've come to the conclusion that the city [Newark] is ours anyway, that we can take it with ballots." In this spirit, his group distributed leaflets urging blacks to avoid engaging in any conflicts with the police: "Don't riot. Don't do what the man wants you to do. Come together as blacks and support blacks. Take this city by ballot. This is not punking out. This is being smart."[21] Accordingly, the United Brothers gave rise to the Committee for a Unified NewArk, which under Baraka's leadership organized black and Puerto Rican voters to unseat much of the predominantly white city council and elect Kenneth Gibson in 1970, to join Richard Hatcher of Gary, Indiana, and Carl Stokes of Cleveland as one of the few black mayors of a major American city. The Newark campaign also energized Baraka's activities at the national level. The Congress of African Peoples (CAP) emerged in 1970 as one of the primary vehicles geared toward the pursuit of a black, independent, and nationalistically oriented politics.[22]

What is perhaps most remarkable with regard to Baraka's role in the making of black politics in this period is the extent to which narration and instantiation were conflated. To a degree that distinguished him even from other poet-politicians such as Senegal's Léopold Senghor and Angola's Viriato da Cruz, Baraka was in this era increasingly both poetical orator and political organizer of black nation time, offering artistic representation as near political fact.[23] It is precisely this potential absence of an ablative disjunction between the word—understood broadly—and the act, this refusal of the antidactylic and Rustinian modes, which makes the artist-activist unique. Paul Robeson's increasingly radical renderings of "Ol' Man River"—first as *Showboat* feature, then as labor anthem, and subsequently as both an anti-imperialist gesture and a personal act of resistance to McCarthyism, in combination with his own active participation in the pursuit of an anti-imperialist, antifascist, and anti-racist transnational movement—represented a prior instance of this sort of confluidity: of the actively and formally political being embodied and organized through artistic performance. Baraka's roughly similar function within the politics of the post–civil rights era was distinguished, though, by the particular problem space in which he was operating.[24]

The intimacy, in this moment, of the poetic and the politic, of the imaginative and the institutional, must also be understood as a function of the nature of much of the art in question. Baraka's work, certainly by the time he left Greenwich Village for Harlem, was not regularly prone to nuance, ambiguity, deep irony, and humor or, frankly, to significant misinterpretation. One can safely characterize most of the work of the Black Arts movement in similar terms: subtlety was not a pressing consideration. The art worked in tandem with the politics of the era because both were quite comfortable with the earnest albeit flat, didactic, and banal slogan as a means of mobilizing sentiment and signifying attention.[25]

It is also interesting to contemplate the choices Baraka made, and that were made through and by means of his example and body, in order to achieve this particular alignment of cultural and political possibilities. The move from beatnik poet to political convention leader was accompanied by a series of marked shifts in the artist's self-representations. As a number of commentators have observed, in order to embody and represent the polity, and in particular a nationalist and self-professed radical vision of black possibilities, Baraka dispensed with the at times transgressive interiority that characterized his earlier work (e.g., *Preface to a Twenty Volume Suicide Note*, *The Toilet*, and *The System of Dante's Hell*) in favor of a sensibility that depended on the constitution of whites, women, and homosexuals as the necessary others to the realization of a black nationalist politics. In contrast, Hazel Carby notes, while "[Miles] Davis represses what [the gay novelist Samuel] Delany expresses . . . if we analyze Davis's innovations in jazz and assess the nature of his emotionally charged and passionate musical experiments, then we may find a more radical and, at times, revolutionary, challenge to the conventions of masculinity." It is in this context that we might understand Wynton Marsalis's suggestion, intended to be dismissive, that Davis's "sound [was] very, very tender to come out of a man," in tandem with Margo Jefferson's contention that he, Miles, seemed to need "to turn himself into his dramatic image of what a really tough street Negro would be." Committed to different performances before the studio microphone, backstage, and in public, Davis's arrangements of his sexualities varied according to place. As part of his comedy routines, Richard Pryor would offer a third model that regularly engaged the ironies and elasticities of black masculinity without regard to time or place. "I was the only dude in the neighborhood who'd fuck this faggot," he often noted as part of his stage routine. "A lot of dudes won't play that shit. In the daytime. But at night, they be knockin' on the door." Pryor also recalls an evening with Miles Davis—"When I entered [Davis's dressing room] he was kissing Dizzy Gillespie, with tongue and shit, which made me wonder what kind of shit he had planned for me"—and a separate exchange with Huey Newton in 1970 about Newton's fear of going to prison. In response to Newton's suggestion that he would "bite off" the penis of any inmate who tried to force himself on him, Pryor replied, "That's a plan. But right before you bite, you know, you're going to taste that dick in your mouth and wonder whether or not you like it." Pryor notes that "Newton shot up from his seat and punched" him. Whereas Miles Davis, in the relationship between his public persona and his trumpet playing, performed this suturing and resuturing of distinct conceptions of black masculinity throughout his career spatially, and Richard Pryor refused to cooperate with the pressures to aggregate and manage usable and impossibly durable notions of black manhood, Baraka negotiated this divide temporally by antiquating and rendering past tense and irretrievable the disruptive imaginings that had marked his early career.[26]

This refashioning, then, provided a model for the realization of a certain conception of the nation and endorsed the notion that for black communities to be mobilized, the artist must, if not step aside, at least disengage from discourses that might trouble the consolidation of a stable counterpublic. This dynamic—evident in the ways Baraka is employed and deployed, and ultimately refused, or, perhaps as accurately, negates and removes himself, as the focus of the articulation of black politics—is what is remarkable in this moment. In a sense, Baraka can be thought of as functioning as a sort of lawgiver: that presence offering terms on which the community might be constituted or reconstituted and revived who subsequently and necessarily is, if not banished, at least displaced on an ongoing basis.[27] Here again, given the idiosyncratic changes in Baraka's expressed politics in the early 1970s (i.e., his subsequent adoption of a relatively doctrinaire conception of Marxist-Leninism) and the difficulties associated with his personality (e.g., his efforts to "organize by insult," as one contemporary put it), I want to stress the possibility that he removed himself as much as he was removed, and denied himself as much as he was denied, at a number of levels. In other words, we might think of Baraka as being complicit in the desire to kill the poet (while retaining the poem). His location, then, on the cusp, in the break, to borrow again from Moten, and on the borders delineating art and formal politics, "radical" and substantively transgressive commitments, speaks to and reflects the nervous and unfixable boundaries of these formations and sensibilities.

GO UP MOSES

The National Black Political Assembly convention (NBPA) held in Gary, Indiana, in March 1972 and attended by roughly eight thousand individuals, including integrationists (with the exception of the NAACP), nationalists, protest elites, creative artists, and black elected officials, arguably represents the clearest moment and site of refusal with regard to the cipher that was Baraka.[28] Presided over by Baraka, Gary's mayor Richard Hatcher, and Charles Diggs, the longest-serving black member of Congress, the convention and the events surrounding it constituted a referendum of sorts, with the different potential templates for conceptualizing and dis/organizing black politics—the anarranged and anarranging fantastic, the antidactylic, and the Rustinian—in competition with each other.[29] It was, then, the logical outcome of the processes and contradictions the civil rights movement put into motion and brought to the surface: should struggle continue, and if so, on what basis, in which arenas, and according to whose terms?

The debate around which most of the conflict was organized was the question of whether an independent black political party should be established and more generally whether black nationalism should prevail as the dominant orientation within African American discourse. Black elected officials, for the most part, sought to use Gary to establish themselves as brokers within the system, and in particular the Democratic Party, in what was an election year. As a consequence, they hoped to establish control over the proceedings—for example, by performing accountability and even radical commitment if necessary—while remaining resistant to any language or decisions that might signal a break with their party's agenda. The most high-profile constituency among this cohort, the CBC, which had been recently established, was also seeking to play a leadership role in African American politics, given the growth in its membership, and the logics put in play by the Voting Rights Act.[30] By this point, Baraka himself had become more pragmatic and, as noted, had moved toward a deeper interest in electoral politics, while maintaining attachments to the convention mechanism, nationalism, and transnationality (primarily in the form of the African Liberation Day mobilizations). Accordingly, he was willing to work with the emerging cadres of black elected officials, though arguably, in the long term, he hoped—via a Trojan horse strategy—to convert the assembly into a means of achieving his own agenda.

Given the fluidity of the moment and the sense that control of black politics was up for grabs, though, it is not surprising that conflicts would erupt among and within the different constituencies. Regarding the latter category, and reflecting the disinterest in recognizing women as equals that characterized both nationalists and integrationists, elected and protest constituencies, Shirley Chisholm's candidacy for the Democratic nomination received little support at Gary. The Brooklyn congresswoman had announced her intention to seek the presidency with, as she has noted, little support from the women's movement (including the National Organization for Women [NOW], though she was a founding member of the New York branch) or the ranks of black elected officialdom.[31] Some, though not all, of the disinterest verging on animus expressed toward Chisholm was clearly related to her gender. She recollects:

What was really bothering the black males at the meeting [the Northlake, Illinois, planning session held in late 1971 before the Gary convention] was more directly hinted at by one who told a *Washington Post* reporter (anonymously—I don't know who he was), "In this first serious effort of blacks for high political office, it would be better if it were a man."[32]

Not surprisingly, at the convention, despite the presence of a number of prominent black women, including Betty Shabazz, Coretta Scott King, Barbara Jordan, and Queen Mother Moore, and the organizational role women had played, the assumption that politics was properly a masculine domain was not significantly challenged. Baraka, for his part, had recently equated feminist concerns with the Left and cast both—with a touch of anti-Semitism—as problematic:

Woman, learn the priorities of nation building and be an example of why we want a nation. . . . [Y]ou must complement us, complete us, so we are whole. . . . The Leftists have reintroduced the white woman for the precise purpose of stunting the nation, and changing the young Black would be "revolutionary" into a snarling attachment of Jewish political power.

Jesse Jackson, in his address, spoke of black "egos castrated," and used collective pronouns that were male-specific. Reflecting perhaps the difficulties and impossibilities associated with restricting politics to a particular gender—and the ways texts and narratives are energized by containment and denial—Jackson also stated with regard to the convention's potential achievements, "[W]e are pregnant . . . a new black baby [an independent black political party] is going to be born." Such intriguing possibilities aside, and consistent with a script that allowed few substantive roles for women, the keynote addresses were delivered uniformly by men—with Jackson's speech introduced by Betty Shabazz—while Coretta Scott King's only function was to stand and wave to the assembly. Both women were engaged, it appeared, as stand-ins for their deceased husbands rather than as independent and important thinkers and strategists (although King had played a significant role in the conceptualization of the conference).[33]

Baraka's persona itself also functioned as a dividing line at Gary, and Coleman Young, then a Michigan state senator very much committed to working within the Democratic Party, led most of his state's delegation (closely affiliated with the UAW) out of the convention in protest of Baraka's nationalist commitments and decision-making style. Operating firmly within the Rustinian mode, Young also implicitly questioned, as others had before, the propriety of artists providing political leadership:

> [T]he platform was completely off-target and unacceptable. It was
> a blatantly separatist document, the obvious work of Baraka, the
> misguided ramblings of a so-called artist who would be dictator. . . .
> I don't have much use for Baraka. . . . behind that fancy-ass name he
> was still LeRoi Jones to me, a half-assed poet in a flowing gown and
> patent-leather shoes.

In reference to Baraka's role within the NBPA, political scientist Robert C. Smith later wrote, "[I]t is probably wise that creative intellectuals . . . avoid overt leadership roles in political movements because . . . both their creative output and the movement are likely to suffer."[34]

One of the implicit subtexts that lent significance to the convention was the question of the relationship between black politics and the arts. Acknowledging this fact, Ossie Davis had suggested, in his keynote address at the first CBC dinner the previous summer, that as an actor-activist, he thought it was now time for black politicians to represent black interests and for "rhetoric," the gift of his own profession, "to take a back seat."[35] In this context, we can understand the struggle over Baraka's poem "Nation Time," which defined in many ways the extended moment in question:

> Time to get / together / time to be one strong fast black enrgy
> space / . . . the black man is the future of the world /. . . . [W]hen
> the brothers strike niggers come out / come out niggers / when the
> brothers take over the school / help niggers / come out niggers / all
> niggers negroes must change up.

A recording of the poem had been released by Motown's Black Forum label, and Baraka had recited it at the 1970 founding convention of the Congress of African Peoples in Atlanta, by which point it was already publicly identified with his personality and the Black Arts movement.[36]

At Gary, it was Jesse Jackson who performed Baraka's poem. Then activist Ben Chavis recalls,

> I think the most surprising thing about Jesse's speech was the
> end. No one would imagine that Reverend Jesse Jackson would
> affirm the nationalist call. . . . "It's Nationtime. It's Nationtime. . . ."
> [E]verybody expected Baraka to lead the chant . . . [but] Jackson
> became the keynote in terms of lifting the emotional level of the
> crowd to an all-time high. . . . [I]t was just not a hollow call. It was
> just not a rhetorical call. When people were repeating after Jesse, "It's
> Nationtime. It's Nationtime. It's Nationtime. Let the black nation
> rise," you could hear it reverberating Marcus Garvey.

For his part, Jackson states,

> I had drawn much of the strength of Nationtime from a poem
> written by LeRoi Jones, Amiri Baraka at that time. The sense of
> people saying, "What's happening? . . . It's Nationtime, it's time to
> come together. It's time to organize politically. . . . It's time for blacks
> to enter into the equation, it is indeed, whether you're in California
> or Mississippi, it is Nationtime."[37]

By this point, Jackson was recognized as one of the dominant personalities in African American politics, and his appropriation of Baraka's poem represented, one could argue, his attempt to usurp some of the rhetorical capital of one of his chief challengers. Given his connections to King, the SCLC, and the civil rights movement, his familiarity with black popular culture—he cowrote "Go Up Moses" with Roberta Flack for her 1971 album *Quiet Fire*, and his brother Chuck Jackson was a member of the R & B group the Independents and subsequently a successful songwriter—and his aspirations within the realm of formal politics, Jackson was in many respects at the center of an increasingly consolidated and arranged black politics.[38] Operation Breadbasket had been incorporated as the economic wing of the SCLC in 1965, and in a very short period, its young leader established himself at the vanguard of not only black politics in Chicago but the broader national community as well.

As a celebration of Jackson's achievements, the Cannonball Adderley Quintet had recorded the album *Country Preacher* live at the Operation Breadbasket headquarters in Chicago in 1969. In the album's liner notes, Adderley wrote:

> When Dr. Martin Luther King appointed Reverend Jesse Jackson . . . I am sure that he expected profound dynamic leadership. However, the success of Operation Breadbasket in just three short years must have exceeded his wildest dreams. . . . An unsuspecting visitor to a meeting of Breadbasket will witness powerful emotional exchanges between ministers, singers, musicians, sociologists, political figures, educators and the lay membership which often numbers eight thousand or more. Each Saturday morning the organization can expect to be visited by internationally celebrated people. Our memorable visits to these meetings have precipitated the inspirational composition, "Country Preacher," which is dedicated to Reverend Jackson (who often refers to himself that way) and the subsequent development of this album.[39]

The album itself was introduced with a speech by Jackson and was a major commercial success.

More broadly, Jackson's appropriation of Baraka's poem—and, to some degree, place—at the NBPA, and the ways his persona was rooted in a space and sensibility that engaged both the cultural and protest techniques and, increasingly, electoral politics, suggested that if black politics was shifting away, and being shifted away, from its pre–civil rights era anaformulation, antidactylic norms were becoming the hegemonic default mode rather than those endorsed by the Rustinian cohort. The preacher-politician might have displaced the poet, but the word in the end retained its power. Coleman Young's displeasure was directed toward Baraka at Gary, but it was Jackson with whom he—and other black elected officials—would battle in the future.[40]

The sense that the cultural realm, and the political significance of creative artists, could not be simply detached from electoral processes and policy-making procedures was reinforced at another event the same year. Wattstax, a concert organized by Al Bell of Stax Records to take place on August 20, 1972, to mark the seventh anniversary of the 1965 Watts riots in Los Angeles, would be the largest gathering of blacks since the March on Washington in 1963 (roughly ninety thousand attended the event).[41] Among the acts featured were the Bar-Kays, the Staple Singers, Rufus Thomas and his daughter Carla Thomas, Johnnie Taylor, and headliner Isaac "Black Moses" Hayes. In his introductory speech at the beginning of the concert, Jackson deployed many of the same lines he had used in March at the NBPA, including his signature exhortation "I am somebody!" and the call-and-response routine in which the question "What time is it?" is answered with "It's nation time!" "Something has happened to the black man in America. Nation time has come," he observed. "When we say nation time, what do we mean? It means that when dogs bite black people in Birmingham, black people bleed all over America." Extending the net further, he added, "It means that when black people cannot run [compete in track and field events] in Rhodesia, black people will not run for America."[42]

In contrast to the NBPA, at which Jackson was able to co-opt Baraka's message and to some extent his space and place, at the concert that August, it was Hayes who emerged as the dominant persona. Along with David Porter, Hayes had been a major contributor to the shaping of the southern soul sound that emerged from Memphis's Stax Studios and had established himself as one of the dominant black icons and public-spirited celebrities of the early 1970s. By this point, Hayes was at the peak of his popularity, having revolutionized rhythm and blues with his extended tracks, ambitious instrumentation and orchestration, and emphasis on albums (e.g., 1969's *Hot Buttered Soul*) as opposed to singles.[43] His transition from producer to artist and his dismissal of the recording norms associated with black pop music also marked him as a key figure in the reconstruction of the soul music industry. Moreover, his soundtrack for the film *Shaft* was a major crossover hit—he and the movie's lead, Richard Roundtree, were warmly greeted at Gary—and his musical significance was complimented by a personal style that combined a shaved head, dark glasses, and a vest of gold chains (signifying, in his view, the end of black subjugation).

A telling moment in the concert suggested, again, not only the confluidity of the cultural and political realms but also, I would argue, the extent to which there was a contest for supremacy among individuals representing these different arenas. Toward the end of the concert, as Jackson passed the microphone to Hayes after introducing him, there was an exchange of words between the two. It was unclear what was said, but what was apparent was that Hayes, this show's headliner, had the power, and Jackson looked a bit resentful that that was the case.

In this moment, one could detect a subtle negotiation taking place with regard to the issue of what the proper source of political legitimacy might be: the pulpit, the protest march, and the polling booth or the nightclub, dance floor, and festival stage? Jackson, who would claim and master many of these domains, has to concede to Hayes, at least at this juncture, the arena of popular culture and the political capital it might provide to its more talented representatives. If deeply ingrained gender codes dictated that Betty Shabazz could only introduce Jackson at Gary, similar understandings located the Reverend in relation to Hayes at Watts.

ALLUSWE

In tracing the Baraka/Jackson/Hayes exchanges, I do not mean to suggest that creative artists continued to provide political leadership after the civil rights movement. The dramatically increased opportunities for elected office, and the exercise of power, had an observable effect on the reconstruction of black politics in this period, an impact that was reflected in the changes in the location and orientation of black political discourse. Nevertheless, Rustinian notions of a proper black politics hardly prevailed—certainly not unchallenged—and the border between formal politics and popular culture remained fluid, if not quite porous, and uncertain.

It is important, too, to consider the relative salience of different cultural media and forms. The understandings that enabled Jackson to appropriate Baraka's work while casting the preacher as subservient in certain respects to the piano player, correlated with the perceived incompleteness and insufficiency of the poem in relation to the song, an assumption I would suggest was commonly shared by the Black Arts poets. In other words, music possessed a certain potency that poetry lacked and offered a sort of unfiltered expressiveness and audience that film and literature, respectively, could not quite match.[44] Accordingly, it was in the R & B music of the subsequent decade that most of the significant deliberations about black politics in the fullest sense occurred.

With regard to the changing currents within black politics, Marvin Gaye—whose willingness to break with R & B conventions was confirmed with the album *What's Going On*—recorded and released the single "You're the Man."[45] The different recorded versions of the song—his most explicit attempt to address political issues—suggest both a certain deference to the formal political arena and a recognition of the NBPA's impact. The latter is evident in the shift in the priority given to busing as a community concern. In the first version of the track—recorded in March and April of 1972 and addressed to the (male) candidates for the presidency—Gaye sings "Busing is *the* issue; c'mon with it, where's your plan mister?" In a second version completed on April 19 and released as a single one week later, the second line is "Do you have a plan with you?" (which Gaye sings as a backup line on the first version). An antibusing plank was a major part of the convention statement produced at the Gary conference, which had taken place over the weekend of March 10–12, and a third version of the track—recorded in May and intended to be included as part of the planned but never completed album *You're the Man*—asserts "Busing is just one issue, what about the rest of it, mister?"[46]

The failure of the single to cross over to the pop charts led Gaye to return to the mold—that of the singer of songs about male/female relationships—from which his 1960s hits were cast. The subsequent success of his next 45, "Let's Get It On"—originally conceived as "(Come On People) Let's Get It On"—reinforced his anxieties about recording "political" material (and he did not return in any sustained manner to such topics for the rest of his career).[47] Nevertheless, Gaye's work, regardless of its lyrical surfaces, in its blurring of the lines separating sex and formal politics, public and private, and the sacred and the profane and its characteristic multiple and often ecstatic vocalizations, would center on one basic concern: the location and character of substantive emancipation. In this sense, both despite and as a result of his many complexities, he would continue to function within black cultural politics as a troubling man, pushing to the surface many of the elements that an efficient politics—whether antidactylic or Rustinian in nature—required be repressed.

Indeed, while deliberations about gender, and its intersections with black politics, were largely pushed to the side at Gary, the same year saw the release of a number of songs by black male artists that probed the sorts of uncertainties formal politics must disavow. While Harold Melvin and the Blue Notes' "Be for Real," with its casting of black women as agents of community discord and class division, marked one end of the discursive spectrum, recordings by Bill Withers ("Use Me"), Stevie Wonder ("Superwoman"), and former Temptation Eddie Kendricks ("Girl, You Need a Change of Mind") suggested that the issues black women were raising were having a progressive effect at some level.[48] The centrality of the black male falsetto voice to many of this period's productions, building on precedents established by Curtis Mayfield, Smokey Robinson, and Eddie Kendricks, and evident in the work of William Hart of the Delphonics, Russell Tompkins Jr. of the Stylistics, and Phillipé Wynne of the Spinners, can also be read as a signifier of vulnerability and an attempt to not only resist but transcend symbolically the conventions of male performance.[49] These explicit and subliminal forms of reckoning contrast with the awkward, gendered metaphors featured in Jackson's Gary speech and the combination of visibility and inaudibility that encompassed black women's roles at the convention.

These negotiations around gender also seemed to depend, at this point, on a certain solidaristic stance on the part of black women and a willingness to defer, at least temporarily, a real engagement with issues of gender equality and the ramifications of a masculinist conception of the political, both at Gary—on the part of Betty Shabazz and Coretta Scott King—and in black popular culture. While an examination of the literature that Alice Walker and Toni Morrison, among others, were producing would offer a slightly different picture, few black women were explicitly challenging gender norms in the music business in any novel fashion in this period.[50] Among the exceptions one might count Laura Lee ("Women's Love Rights" and "Wedlock Is a Padlock"), although she distanced herself from feminism ("not really me at all") and argued that "a woman should basically be a woman [and] a man should . . . treat her right." The trio Labelle, which underwent a significant makeover in this period, offered a more clearly articulated alternative to masculinist expectations and, following in the footsteps of Nina Simone, the roles Aretha Franklin and Roberta Flack played as instrumentalists and composers should be counted as important achievements in a medium in which men typically wrote, played, and produced the songs.[51]

Other aspects of the structure of feeling that informed the Gary convention were observable in the black music of the early 1970s. In this context one can understand, for example, the wicker chair from the iconic photo of Huey Newton—staged and conceived by Eldridge Cleaver—that reappears in the cover art of Eddie Kendricks's *People . . . Hold On* and Al Green's *I'm Still in Love with You,* both released in 1972 (and later in the decade on Funkadelic's 1979 album *Uncle Jam Wants You*).[52] Similarly, the use of the community choir, with its implied solidarities and absence of pretension and concern with aesthetic precision and accomplishment, narrowly defined, in the work of Marvin Gaye (i.e., his friends the football players Lem Barney and Mel Farr provide backup vocals on "What's Going On"), Eddie Kendricks ("My People . . . Hold On"), War, and Gil Scott-Heron and Brian Jackson's Midnight Band suggests a commitment to a certain kind of (cultural) politics.[53] In this refusal to defer to specialists and professionals, one can detect traces again of a sort of politics that rejects the ambitions of those committed to the Rustinian mode and the notion that such matters need to be arranged, orchestrated, clearly defined, and managed by designated experts.

It was all new to me. I had never seen anything like it

before. —Frederick Douglass

One of the things I encountered in trying to pitch this story

[*Daughters of the Dust*] as a script was people kept saying,

"Well, what is it like? Is it like *Sounder*? Is it like *The Color*

Purple?" And I kept saying, "No, it's not like that." And

they kept saying, "We can't see it. Black people at the

turn of the century? What do they look like?" Because in

Hollywood they don't like to make a film that has not been

seen before. They kept saying that they couldn't see, they

just couldn't see it. —Julie Dash

4

LET THEM ONLY SEE US

The rejection of popular culture as a significant factor in the making of progressive politics is in many respects a welcome contrast to the overly celebra-
tory approach to these materials that some analysts promote. While the ways
younger constituencies choose to reproduce themselves culturally are certainly
intriguing in and of themselves, Adolph Reed is certainly correct to argue that
youthful resistance by itself is hardly enough to sustain a progressive politics. To contend that popular culture is relevant and necessarily integral to
an investigation of politics, black and otherwise, is not to argue that every
gesture, exchange, or triumph in the cultural realm is tantamount and equal
in value to the institutionalization of a comprehensive health care program, or

an income maintenance policy that allows real decommodificatory possibilities. In the introduction to *Race Rebels*, where Robin Kelley recalls his experiences as an employee at McDonald's as if he were a co-conspirator in a serious class revolt—"We fought . . . battles with amazing tenacity. . . . [and] even attempted to alter our ugly uniforms by opening buttons, wearing our hats tilted to the side, rolling up our sleeves a certain way, or adding a variety of different accessories"—he provides an inviting target for critics of the integration of cultural studies into a broader investigation of politics. His assertion that "the employees at the central Pasadena McDonald's were constantly inventing new ways to rebel" risks confusing adolescent discontent with guerrilla warfare.[1] The scenarios Kelley describes are imbued with class and political significance (and are indeed quite interesting). They also remind us that what appears to be merely compliance or complacency is usually more complicated and that resistance and contestation can take many different forms. In and of themselves, though, many of the transgressions Kelley catalogues might be too disconnected from formal arenas of political and economic decision-making to matter and, like many hidden transcripts, verge on the same understandable and stylized accommodationism characteristic of Ralph Ellison's blues, Maulana Karenga's New Africanism, Reed's own Old Leftism, and much of contemporary hip-hop.[2] Resistance, once it becomes routine and recognized, can be anticipated and welcomed by dominant authorities, and fetishized and folded into the broader process of institutionalizing dominant hegemonic understandings (e.g., the ability of anthropologists Edward Seaga and François Duvalier in the Jamaican and Haitian contexts, respectively, to use popular cultural forms and media of resistance to promote their own conservative objectives). This is particularly common in contexts in which few viable spaces for the formulation, expression, and transmission of specifically *hidden* transcripts exist.

The analysis of resistance also needs to be nuanced and precise. Formal and informal responses to attempted exploitation, and engagements with the dominant order, tend to be complicated, fragmented, and inconsistent, just as the exercise of power is rarely coherent, total, and omnipotent, especially if we understand power (and the possibility of resistance) as being widely dispersed. A movement that organizes on the racial front while ignoring or reinforcing problematic commitments with regard to the gender and class status quos might not in the aggregate represent a significant or substantive response to illegitimate power (for example, aspects of the Black Arts and black power movements). Otherwise progressive efforts that generate support by exploiting white supremacist sentiments—as was the case with the late nineteenth- and early twentieth-century suffragist, labor, and socialist movements—are not likely to transform understandings on any of the significant frontiers of social interaction and negotiation. In other words, it is important that we pay attention to the fissures within the movements of the marginalized and the multiple and distinct stages on which these negotiations proceed. Resistance on one front in isolation rarely represents a significant departure from or challenge to the dominant modes of being and production; the issues of sexuality, gender, class, race, and culture are conjoined; the dilemmas generated by the advent of the modern, and its successor structures of feeling, are many and connected. Transformative politics, accordingly, require that romantic—and limited—notions of resistance be dispensed with and that the problematic aspects of the dominant order not be reproduced under a faux-radical banner.

Furthermore, given that the terms and terrain of political contestation are fluid, progressive movements must constantly recalibrate. This ongoing process is complicated by the inevitable tar baby–like dimensions of political and social engagement. To the extent that resistance and transformative ambitions often rely on fixed notions of identity and clear distinctions between the optimal and the problematic, the reality that these conceptions are shifting—contaminated, one might suggest—in the process of making and envisioning change pushes temporal and contextual issues to the surface. The young become old, the culturally distinct hybridized and reconfigured, the subaltern comprador, and the migrant comprador—in moving from (post)colony to metropole—are repositioned as subaltern, in respects that make the construction and communication of coherent narratives of resistance and transformative strategies complicated, if not impossible. It is perhaps, in light of this inevitable and arguably irreversible transculturation, that we can recognize that the normative and empirical codes that shaped the northern civil rights movement would likely have limited applicability in the subsequent southern campaign. Similarly, the investments and assumptions that informed the late 1950s and most of the 1960s—for example, the integrationist/nationalist debate—might have reduced purchase on the politics of the next two decades, as the understandings developed in the immediate post–civil rights era, it can be argued, did not effectively and meaningfully correspond to the challenges and circumstances facing blacks in the years leading up to and following the end of the twentieth century.

In chapter 1, I identified the end of the civil rights movement and the beginning of significant African American direct engagement with electoral politics as important developments with regard to the conceptualization, making, and reframing of black politics. Here, I want to shift gears and focus on the changes taking place, particularly within the creative arena, that make the post–civil rights era a doubly different and, in many respects, difficult moment. More accurately, my goal is to clarify the relationship between the immediate post–civil rights era and the post-post-civil-rights era—the period marked by the emergence of the black superpublic—and the ways changes in the cultural realm marked this transition (or collision) and complicated efforts to achieve traction, and to imagine, manifest, and sustain a black progressive politics and, to some degree, a recognizable black counterpublic.

The untidy spectacles associated with late twentieth-century black popular culture became particularly politically significant for a number of distinct but overlapping reasons. At the most superficial level, the visual surplus associated with the emergence of hip-hop—the work of graffiti artists starting in the 1970s; the advent of videos and music video channels, videocassettes in the next decade; and later, video games, digital videodiscs (DVDs), dualdiscs (combining CD and DVD content), and the internet—simply overflowed the previously existing networks of intercommunity discourse. Black pop became suddenly, particularly, and violently public in a unique way in the late 1980s and 1990s—a development that, by itself, provoked a range of gatekeeping responses from those committed to restricting the circulation of certain kinds of information within black communities and maintaining "order." After opportunities for black actors—and to a significantly lesser extent, black writers and directors—increased in the blaxploitation era, a period of near invisibility in film and television followed that lasted from the late 1970s until the mid-1980s (with a couple of exceptions, including *The Cosby Show, The Color Purple*, the acting of Howard Rollins, and the "buddy" movies featuring Richard Pryor and subsequently Eddie Murphy). Even the early music video age, epitomized in the United States by the emergence of MTV, offered few openings for black artists. By the end of the 1980s, things had changed considerably, and black images circulated widely on television (particularly on the Fox, and later, WB, UPN and CW networks), on a number of video networks, in the straight-to-video market (which increased access to the film medium considerably), and in film itself, following Spike Lee's *She's Gotta Have It*. This increased exposure—and, in some eyes, vulnerability—triggered the same kinds of responses that surfaced in some quarters in reaction to the Harlem Renaissance. The appearance of the black folk voice—broadly understood and fully embodied—in the 1920s, in the newly technologically enabled realm of recorded music, in the pages of novels circulated by mainstream publishing houses, and in fine arts, often as raw material for the reiteration—and occasionally complication—of the primitive/modernist divide forced the arbiters of black respectability to retool. Similar dynamics unfolded with regard to the blaxploitation era. The major difference between the late 1980s' developments and the earlier eras' was the ubiquity, intensity, and pungent and florid, installation-like multimediality of these images.

Considering as well the proliferation of handheld and surveillance video cameras, camera phones, and awareness of these new technologies, one can suggest that the visual surplus would likely also produce a heightened performative sensibility—in other words, the internalization of the expectation that one is always potentially being watched. A related urge would be the conscious effort to always give one's best performance and encourage others to do the same, and indeed to perform even when one is not sure of one's audience (or whether there is in fact an audience). Prevailing notions of authenticity and sincerity would be troubled accordingly, as well (e.g., as in reality television) especially for those convinced that the ascriptive constraints characteristic of Jim Crow and pre-1965 black life might be challenged in the post-civil rights era through the nurturing of the evasive potential of the performative.[3] In other words, the increasing predominance of the visual in popular culture and elsewhere might enhance the belief that black bodies might escape sanction if they are committed to the presentation of nonblackness—or, more accurately, acceptable and assimilable forms of coloredness.

With regard to music specifically, the densification of the visual realm triggered a challenge to the performative norms that marked late 1960s and early 1970s black politics and popular culture. If the necessity of making videos encourages musicians to learn how to act, it is not surprising that late twentieth-century artists would argue that their audiences and critics should not conflate their on-screen personae and masks with their "true personalities" and that they should be given the same latitude as stage actors—for example, Jay-Z as opposed to Shawn Carter, Ice Cube as opposed to O'Shea Jackson—a trend enabled to some extent by the move away from proper names to monikers in hip-hop (a practice that has its roots in the minstrel, blues, radio, calypso, and Jamaican deejay traditions). In contrast, it would be difficult to imagine Aretha Franklin, Bob Marley, or even Marvin Gaye for that matter, making such claims with regard to their productions and self-representations in the early 1970s, a period characterized by studied and pronounced performances of black authenticity, by earnestness as opposed to modernist irony (an obvious example being the 1972 recording "Be Real Black for Me" by Roberta Flack and Donny Hathaway).[4]

The increased number of possible stages would also likely destabilize further the culture/politics equilibrium. If we think of the political, narrowly construed, as, among other things, an attempt or struggle to render empty, contain, or institutionalize the cultural, the changed nature and increased number of performative spaces—given formal politics' allergy to explicit performance—could only create anxiety among the bureaucratic classes. Moreover, if rational political behavior is marked as masculine, certain kinds of performances, and explicit performance in the aggregate, are coded as other. Accordingly, authorities in the realm of official politics and black participants in these arenas, to the degree that they are committed to assimilating these norms, would look on performative investments even more suspiciously. Generally, black politics would be particularly disturbed to the extent that black bodies are particularly subject to, or engaged and attracted by, this new visual apparatus and that black visibility and blackness—that fluid in/convenience—are read as being inherently unruly, surreal, outside the frame, and in need of discipline. Regarding this suggestion, Thelma Golden observes, in the context of a conversation with painter Kehinde Wiley about the representation of black males,

> You have to be ironic about it because it's so profoundly amazing to consider how historically loaded the image of the black male is. One cannot approach it objectively. . . . It's what makes black masculinity so fascinating as a subject in art and pop culture. There is no objective image. And there is no way to objectively view the image itself.[5]

A similar claim could be made with regard to the representation of all black subjects, regardless of gender, and black life in general.

It is worth noting as well that the heightened predominance of the visual as the primary mediator of communication might both enable potentially novel forms of political campaigning (e.g., in the way the Emmett Till photo mobilized constituencies that mere printed text could not reach) and impede attempts to transmit more nuanced and substantive sentiments, because of the crowding-out effect of the visual and the tendency of the camera to seek out spectacular and merely shocking, perhaps exciting images rather than provocative and paradigm-shifting ones. These new data can also, with time, as a consequence of their ubiquity and intensity, depress certain forms of citizen engagement (e.g., direct face-to-face conversation, conviviality, empathy, solidarity, and republican commitment). At the most mechanical level, the visual demands of the postsoul era—the requirement that one look—had an inca-pacitating effect. Films and videos, regardless of their content, compel their audiences to pay complete attention in a way that stand-alone sonic texts do not. Visual communication, in this sense, is detached from daily existence, in that it cannot be easily combined with other activities; it is distracting. The visual is in this context almost antisocial. Accordingly, art historian Michael Harris states, "Perhaps the onslaught of visual culture has numbed our sur-face sensibilities."[6] Although all representations—whether musical, literary, visual, or political—have the potential to short-circuit, depress, or displace (by replacing) more intimate forms of engagement and communication, visual forms are particularly effective in this regard.

Indeed, the commonsensical notion that the availability of visual images of previously invisible acts of violence—lynchings, murders, police beatings, torture, rape—are capable of generating durable political movements or even significant changes in popular consciousness needs to be questioned. "At issue here," observes Saidiya Hartman, "is the precariousness of empathy and the uncertain line between witness and spectator."[7] As Hartman contends, with reference to public displays of violence toward slaves, there is the possibil-ity that the sorts of empathy generated by certain spectacles and storytelling might stop at the borders of the nonwhite body. In other words, the transi-tive identifications put into play by these engagements might detach them-selves from the sufferer and become a means by which the spectator/witness becomes immersed in her/his own sentiment: my understanding of this other body's discomfort will go no further than my imagining myself in its place and working through the horror that I (imagine I would) feel. Reinforced in this context would be the notion that some bodies cannot be thought of, at least for long, as genuinely suffering or capable of substantive feeling: they are in the end just bodies, objects, things that at best enable others to feel more deeply within and about themselves while and by denying the nonwhite sufferer that sustained capacity.[8]

There is another, related tangent that might be pursued here. These nar-ratives, especially in visual form, might also function as a source of plea-sure—like pornography—and reinforce citizen attachments to the security state as a means through which to monitor, incapacitate, control, and disap-pear the highlighted and hypervisible. The visual accessibility of black life, then, rather than humanizing African Americans in the eyes of others (e.g., the assumptions underlying Paul Laurence Dunbar's "We Wear the Mask," Ellison's *Invisible Man,* and the hopes of many in the broader civil rights community) might simply underscore citizen expectations and imaginings regarding the proper disposition of these marginal constituencies (i.e., blacks). If we think of the visual as another form of narrative—of storytelling—we should expect that these sentimental appeals, rather than provoking others to rally in support of the subjected, might reinscribe the boundaries between the incorporated and the marginalized, the powerful and the powerless. In the same way slave narratives might have actually pleasured their audiences—as lynching postcards subsequently would—as much as they encouraged them toward an abolitionist position, by allowing their consumers to reinvest in the often absorbing details of their own power, visual evidence of black subjection should not be expected to automatically trigger audience identification.[9] Indeed, in their double effects and ambivalent impact, they are as likely to produce disidentification, in a manner that suggests the impossibility of blackness ever really being seen as separate from some larger narrative of disturbance, abnormality, or pathology and, in general, the futility of merely speaking—or showing—truth to power. Depictions and representations of the racialized might be read in the same way the efforts of the marginalized to call attention to their status—for example, by making explicit reference to the ways race and racism work—might be dismissed or deployed to reinforce racial hierarchy. If race, racism, and depictions of the raced are interpreted as lying outside of the significant, normal, and natural—and simply as signs of the unreasonable rather than the colonial—the thick meanings excluded populations assign to these references will be read by many in the intended audience as being outside of politics and the recognized and proper boundaries of the political (e.g., the supposition by some liberals and leftists that references to race are depoliticizing).[10] There might exist no evidence that could override the strength of these sorts of visceral commitments.

From a historical perspective, given the commonly public nature of many of these acts in earlier periods, the visual would simply be superfluous—pure excess—and provide that which had been *seen before*. In this sense, such images would rarely be genuinely surprising and consequently would be incapable of generating sustained progressive political activity, beyond mechanical performances of accountability, sensitivity, and regret (if even that), at least among those not directly affected by the violence in question (e.g., the Till photo, the Rodney King video, and the Abu Ghraib prison footage).[11] Beyond the defensive response of agents situated in the arenas of black formal politics, then, the heightened visibility of raced subjects in the post–civil rights era—in which Emmett Till becomes Rodney King becomes 50 Cent and Michael Jackson becomes Michael Jackson—arguably plays a confirming role and provides a rationale, as minstrelsy did in the nineteenth century, for the dismissal of the possibility of black humanity. On this point, we might also consider the unique forms of violence potentially embedded in the process of making pictures. As Edward Said argues,

> [T]he *act* of representing (and hence reducing) others, almost always
> involves violence of some sort to the *subject* of the representation,
> as well as a contrast between the violence of the act of representing
> something and the calm exterior of the representation itself, the
> *image*—verbal, visual, or otherwise—of the subject.[12]

Beyond the energies expended in the acts of containment and commodification common to all representative projects, there is a particular kind of subjection the visual entails. Moreover, given that the visual realm is that representative arena most thoroughly colonized and policed by others, it is necessary to remember that these texts often constitute for blacks, as both consumers and consumed, a unique form of alienation.

Questions of race, perspective, and visual representation are also not easily resolved through recourse to the language of simple antinomies, such as regressive or progressive, especially as our desires are so often at root committed to ambivalence and contradiction. As Kobena Mercer notes with regard to Robert Mapplethorpe's photographic representations of black male nudes, even when one is stereotyped and consumed by others, at times it is difficult to refuse to be attracted to those images that one finds at a certain visceral level disturbing, if not offensive.[13] This sentimental push-and-pull dynamic is perhaps even more acute when the gaze in question is nominally black, as in the case of Harold "Hype" Williams's 1998 feature *Belly,* in which Taral Hicks and Earl "DMX" Simmons are lit in a sex scene to appear as if their brown skins are an unnatural shade of blue. The segment both encourages us to dis-identify with the two characters because it portrays them as fundamentally other, while at the same moment drawing us in with its depiction of a charged and heated—and, we are supposed to think, animalistic—physical encounter between a black woman and man.

More broadly, we must also think of how the increased availability of these pictures troubles the relationship between citizen expectations and the narratives developed and communicated by the marginalized in terms beyond the narrowly racial. To what extent and how are members of the black middle and upper classes disturbed by images designed to (geo)graphically contain and specify, and naturalize supposed black lower income disorder? How do black elites respond to, and engage with, the specter of the nigger? Are they more likely to disidentify if they themselves aspire to be recognized as citizens who play by the "rules of the game"? Similarly, can we assume that ocular evidence of the subjection and exploitation of black women will trigger empathetic—as opposed to merely patriarchal—responses among African American men who themselves might be seeking to situate themselves securely among the ranks of the incorporated; a process that might entail a certain distancing from, or require a public expression of disdain with regard to, the very same peoples who are rendered as visual commodities that in certain private or semiprivate contexts bring such men pleasure? At another level, these developments raise a question (that I will return to later): how should we conceptualize the relationship between the black counterpublic remade and remodeled in the wake of the civil rights movement and the black superpublic that emerges in the mid-1980s?

The promotion of the visual, by raising the costs of production, also led to a reduction in the number and range of voices that could be heard as part of a process that has historical precedents. While the relationship between blacks and technology has always been ambivalent, it is striking that the release of *The Birth of a Nation* in 1915 marked not only a significant advance in terms of cinematic accomplishment but also one of the more significant public attacks on black citizenship rights in the post-Reconstruction era. By the mid-1920s, partly in response to *The Birth of a Nation*, blacks were able to establish and support a film industry—the "race" picture market—that featured not only black directors and producers but black-owned theatre and distribution networks as well. The subsequent major advance in film technology—the advent of the talking picture, with the release of Al Jolson's *Jazz Singer* in 1927—increased the costs of production to such an extent that the black market collapsed, along with the associated networks and institutions (with only Oscar Micheaux surviving the transition).[14] *The Jazz Singer*, of course, with its blackface aesthetics, did little to advance the social interests of African Americans, and in the absence of black filmmakers, Hollywood studios produced images of blacks that were unflattering or chose not to represent black life at all.

Similarly, in the late twentieth century, music artists who could not afford to make videos, or could not convince their recording companies to fund such productions, were at a competitive disadvantage in an era in which music was increasingly consumed visually (bear in mind here MTV's initial refusal to air any black artist's videos). In this context, seminal house music artist Larry

Heard (aka Fingers Inc.) refers to the prevideo era as a time of "making my decisions with my ears, not my eyes."[15] At the same time, performers whose visual appearances were not thought to be attractive, despite the quality of their musical output, would suffer in a context in which visual "competency" was a required skill. Not surprisingly, given that the vast majority of video directors were and continue to be men, women were more consistently subjected to these ocular interrogations. "I don't like videos, but they come with the territory," observes Miriam Makeba. "I don't like seeing men fully dressed while the women are in bathing suits or underwear. There's no respect for women. If a woman is in a bikini, I want to see a man in a swimsuit. Let's undress the boys and see how they like it."[16] Men, especially in the R & B genre, would not be completely exempt from these restrictions either. The video released for D'Angelo, "Untitled (How Does It Feel)" in 2000 was significant because of the way it drew attention to the singer's physicality.[17] As Ahmir Thompson, the drummer for the Roots and for D'Angelo's touring band, relates,

> Some nights on tour he'd look in the mirror and say, "I don't
> like the video. . . ." So, he'd say, lemme do two hundred more
> stomach crunches. . . . Some shows got cancelled because he didn't
> feel physically prepared. . . . [T]he first night of the . . . tour, the
> take-it-off [i.e., his shirt] chants started not ten minutes into the
> show. . . . That put too much pressure on him. . . . [B]y night four,
> he was angry and resentful. . . . [W]hat he wants [now] is to get fat.
> He doesn't want the pressure of being "Untitled" the video.[18]

In an era in which video networks replaced radio stations as the key gatekeepers or determinants of popular taste, the expectation that music should be consumed via video also affected what radio stations would play. This development would create, for example, the context for the career of rapper Trevor "Busta Rhymes" Smith, whose recordings by themselves, without the striking and capital-intensive visual associations, would otherwise likely not have proven very marketable in an earlier time. A song that did not have a video made to go with it would also, in the post-MTV era, be less likely to get airplay, given that the absence of the video would signify to radio programmers that the recording company in question was not committed to that particular track; such songs also would not benefit from listener requests the same way video-assisted tracks would, because they could not be heard and seen on the music video channels.[19]

The rise of videos would also affect collective memories. This causal relationship between preferred forms of text and the scope and reach of narrative retentions is obviously not new—another example is the effects of the promotion of the written word and later the printing press on our makings and understandings of the historically significant. The emphasis on the visual simply reinforced the often disarticulative impact of technological innovations. When video networks attempted to play "golden oldies," the available archives circumscribed their historical horizons. As a result, black music before the mid-1980s became almost invisible, and, in a sense, the notion that nothing happened before the video age would become naturalized and would complicate, if not completely undermine, processes of maintaining collective long-term memories.

While the visual turn might render those older musics inaudible, the same investments can be interpreted as having made previously lost data reaccessible. In other words, these technological changes and procedural options also offered other new substantive possibilities, new memories, and different ways to remember. Consider, for example, the ways the emergence of videocassettes—for example, the naturalization of the pimp aesthetic that is *The Mack* and the gangster romantic *Scarface*—allowed previously lost images and narratives to recirculate in a manner that disrupted the linear flow of memory, and the efforts to control and package collective memories. On the technological front, digital media and the internet enabled consumers to create their own scripts: to rearrange or anarrange recorded or video product as they saw fit to generate effects and forms of saturative impact that were not as easily achieved in the analog era (obviously, comparable developments—for example, sampling—occurred in terms of music consumption, too). Concurrently, the software produced as part of the digital revolution allowed filmmakers to underline their intentions by adding their own spoken narratives to DVD releases and enabled recording artists to specify preferred interpretations of their creations via DVD bonus material. Finally, reflecting the influence of the Dogma 95 school that emerged out of Denmark and its commitment to a "vow of chastity" with regard to the dominant technologies, and standard tropes and mechanisms deployed by mainstream film studios, digital film technology significantly reduced the generally prohibitive cost of making a movie (with Spike Lee being the first major American director to shoot a nondocumentary feature in this format: *Bamboozled,* in 2000). Reflecting the Adorno/Benjamin divide, while the overall impact of many of these technological changes was to restrict the articulative and rearticulative potentials of black popular culture, there were opportunities for resistance and to access and circulate information that would previously have been unavailable. Either way, these new visibilities, by broadening the terrain of engagement and, inevitably, contestation, compelled all constituencies to reconstitute and recalibrate their politics to speak to these rediscovered archives, restricted entry points, and asymmetrically thickened media.

SUTURING THE CUT

In this context, the pronounced contrapuntality of late twentieth-century popular culture is worth noting. A sampled loop might deliberately include static—the sonic impression of the record needle on vinyl—to register its temporal dissonance (and to summon nostalgic sentiment). Similarly, a recording could be based on a sample with a sentimental framework and implications that are at odds with the lyrics included in the new track (e.g., 50 Cent's appropriation of the Wailers' "Burnin' and Lootin'" for his 2005 release "Window Shopper"); be coupled with a video that seems to undermine initial readings of the song; or be remixed in a way that goes against the grain of the first draft of the text.[20]

One explanation for this development—the increased circulation of the explicitly bundled text—is the desire of artists, and the companies that own and distribute their work, to be present in every possible media or promotional venue. Consequently, despite the pronounced regionalism of early hip-hop, by the end of the 1990s, many artists would consciously seek to construct their songs, the remixes of their songs, and their albums in such a way as to tap into every regional fan base (e.g., by including rappers, producers, or rhythms from each region).[21] Another related motivation was to extend the shelf life of these products (by means of the remix, the recut video, the rereleased album or movie with new artwork and bonus tracks, possibly in a new format).[22] A third causal factor for this explicit contrapuntality was the potential multiplicity of authors involved: the writers, performers, musicians, and producers who created the track, the directors making the video or film, and the editors and remixers involved at various stages of the process. Finally, it should not be overlooked that these decision-makers and the audiences they sought to attract were increasingly diverse, though very few of the most powerful gatekeepers were nonwhites.[23]

The polyphonic character—phonic, understood broadly—of these productions is not unique to this era: in different respects, one can think of quilting, collage, bebop, the work of Andy Warhol, the potential disjunction between actor and script, and the gap separating James Brown's radical funk aesthetic and his generally conservative public political utterances as precedents. The striking normative tension observable between the film *Superfly* and its soundtrack, produced by Curtis Mayfield, is also relevant to this tradition. Mayfield, who agreed to record the soundtrack after reading the film's script, recalls, "[W]hen I saw it visually, I thought 'this is a cocaine infomercial.' That's all it was." Acknowledging the financial incentives and his own career ambitions, he continues, "I [had already] made the commitment and of course I wasn't going to let go of my chance to do a movie." In response to this dilemma, the Chicago native recollects, "[Given that] I didn't want to be part of that infomercial . . . it was important to me that I left the glitter [out] . . . and tried to go straight in the lyrics. I tried to tell the stories of the people in depth and not insult the intelligence of those who were spending their money," adding, "I did the music and lyrics to be a commentary as though someone was speaking as the movie was going." Indeed, the music provided by Mayfield operates as a critique of the film's narrative and moral economy and anticipated the negative responses the film's release would generate from the NAACP and Huey Newton, among others. Mayfield's contributions can also be read as a precursor of sorts of the director's commentaries commonly included on DVD releases (or perhaps more broadly as part of the tradition of actors and other "hired hands" resisting or elaborating on and reinterpreting the suggestions contained in scripts). The soundtrack itself was released two months before the film, thus providing a preexisting normative framework for its viewers, so that "by the time it came out," Mayfield stated, "the kids knew the songs . . . they had the depth of it already." The first hit single, "Freddie's Dead," referred and drew attention to a murder that received minimal attention in the final cut (indeed, the song was played only in instrumental form in the movie itself). Similarly, the second release, the title track "Superfly," in its emphasis on spiritual survival (with its interpolation of the familiar gospel standard "How I Got Over") was Mayfield's attempt to deflect attention from the materialism and hedonism the theatrical release celebrated. His performance of "Pusherman" in a club setting in the film itself underscored his critique of drug dealers. Overall, in the *Superfly* project, a certain discordance marks the relationship among the original script, written by Phillip Fenty, the final cut of the film, directed by Gordon Parks Jr., and Mayfield's counternarrative (all three of these individuals were African Americans; the film's producer, Sig Shore, was not). Specifically, the translation of the written text into its visual counterpart and the temptations and imperatives associated with performances in the visual medium—and Ron O'Neal's portrayal of Youngblood Priest, the main protagonist, must be factored in as well—generated a certain and inevitable contrapuntal effect.[24]

The ultratransparency of the joints and the collisions taking place in black cultural performances in the decades preceding the turn of the twentieth century, though, further marks the present era as a distinct epoch, as does the at times wilful circulation of imperfect and often almost accidentally surreal texts that mock, at various levels, political attempts to present coherent or unified intentional frameworks. Consequently, in my discussion in chapter 1 of the ways the intentions of creative artists can be ignored, displaced, or subverted by their audiences, the examples I cited were musical recordings—including Aretha Franklin's "Respect" and Martha and the Vandellas' "Dancing in the Street"—that predate the video and hip-hop eras and were productions in which one could reasonably seek and be able to identify authorial intent (albeit, on occasion, only after making an effort). This becomes more difficult when one moves into the realms of theatre—for example, Lorraine Hansberry's *Raisin in the Sun*—and film, as in the case of Mayfield's acts of resistance within and against the framing of *Superfly*.

Alice Walker's 1982 novel *The Color Purple* is a good illustration of this difference between realms and, beyond that, the transition that occurred as blacks gained access to creative roles—writing, directing, and producing, as opposed to just acting—within the mainstream theatrical and filmmaking worlds (it is worth noting that Gordon Parks Sr., father of the director of *Superfly*, would become the first black director employed by a Hollywood film studio with the making and release of *The Learning Tree* in 1969, reflecting the racial lag time and prohibitive economies of scale distinguishing the musical from the theatrical and filmmaking arenas). The different racial and gendered readings attributed to *The Color Purple* and the subsequent film spoke directly to the question of authorial intention and reflected the multiplicity of "writers" involved in the "final production." The attention paid to the roles Quincy Jones and Steven Spielberg played as producer and director, and Menno Meyjes played as the creator of the screenplay, in the making of the movie, and Walker's mixed feelings about the rendering of her novel when she first saw the film, mark the moment as a significant turning point not only in black gender relations, American racial discourse, and the intimately linked "dirty laundry" debate but also in the usefulness of the exercise of seeking to identify and fix artistic intent.[25]

The synchronic emergence of hip-hop and the video era reinforced and consolidated these changes. While the newer cultural commodities, in many respects, resembled party platforms and political campaign teams in their attempts to disguise their fault lines—just as blackness itself and the diasporic sensibility are constructs bounded by possibility and inevitability whose sutures are characteristically camouflaged—at times a certain willingness to reveal explicit struggle and tension between the constitutive elements of the final product was detectable. These performances of intratextual dissonance can be understood as being intended to register on both the cultural and political frequencies. In other words, they can be read as articulations of a disinterest in or disengagement from projects that require the maintenance or assume the existence of a certain functional blackness; as a dismissal of the certainties and conventional wisdoms that characterized an earlier era's publicly expressed sensibilities; and as an argument for the unrepresentability of the coherent black subject.

The aspiration for longevity that partly drove this polyphonicity also reflected changes in the racial frameworks underlying the culture industries. Following the late 1970s, and the temporary conflation of African American popular music with disco, and the disappearance of crossover opportunities for black artists in the wake of the backlash against dance music, the ability of these artists to reach white and wider audiences and be recognized *as artists* diminished considerably. As part of a process that became more apparent in the late 1980s with hip-hop, black artists' productions tended to be consumed as spectacular novelties in a manner that frustrated these performers' efforts to establish long-term relationships with broader audiences (and, as record companies codified these norms and artists internalized them, with black audiences too). In other words, the disco and particularly the hip-hop eras reintroduced the normalization of black music as devalued commodity that was common in the decades leading up to the civil rights and soul eras (e.g., the battles waged by Louis Armstrong, Duke Ellington, and the bebop generation to be accepted as creative artists rather than mere producers of ephemeral pop music).

In this period as well, outside the jazz idiom, instrumental skill—traditionally understood—would become superfluous, and bands would no longer be economically viable. If we think about the sensibilities and possibilities, albeit often masculinized, that connect jazz and funk (for instance, the horn phrasing courtesy of Pee Wee Ellis that links Miles Davis's "So What" and James Brown's "Cold Sweat") and the significance of the emergence of Sly and the Family Stone as a fundamentally diverse, self-contained group of composers and musicians, it can be posited that such collectives represent important and symbolic discursive formations in and of themselves (e.g., the

Parliament/Funkadelic family). Bands, both live and in the recording studio, and workshops more generally, then, might represent analogues for the kinds of deliberative potentials—or "breathing spaces," to borrow from Jacques Rancière—one can find in certain junctures in black politics (e.g., the convention movements, protest activities, transnational engagements) and alternately the sorts of interiority that are celebrated in the work of creative artists (e.g., James Baldwin, Aretha Franklin, Richard Pryor, and Me'Shell NdegéOcello). From this perspective, Ahmir "?uestlove" Thompson's observation that "The Roots are the only black band with a major recording label deal from the United States. *We're the only black band.* The only group of black musicians in pop music that has a major label recording deal" speaks to a development that is remarkable not only in terms of the cultural realm but politically as well.[26]

This transition can be operationalized by tracing the changes in software that occurred over the course of the last half of the twentieth century. The supplanting of relatively fragile, 78 revolutions-per-minute (rpm) recordings by more durable, long-playing albums, providing and justifying relatively large canvases for quality artwork, coincides with the emergence of black artistic autonomy in jazz. Consider, for example, the connection between the emergence of the persona of Miles Davis and the 33 rpm recording, as reflected in the 1957 release *The Birth of the Cool,* which had been originally released by Capitol as a series of 78 rpm recordings shortly after their recording in 1949 and 1950 and subsequently as a ten-inch record, *Jeru,* in 1954. The long-playing record would become hegemonic a decade later in R & B (e.g., the late 1960s and early 1970s recordings of Aretha Franklin, Donny Hathaway, Isaac Hayes, Roberta Flack, Stevie Wonder, and Marvin Gaye's *What's Going On* that followed the earlier examples of Ray Charles and James Brown) and subsequently in reggae (the Wailers' *Catch a Fire*). While 45 rpm recordings created new consumption opportunities for younger constituencies, it was the album—configured as vinyl, cassette, or eight-track and symbolizing permanence and archiveability—that epitomized artistic achievement in this period.

The twelve-inch single, which rose to prominence with the disco era and the disco mix, mark in this context a sort of compromise between the disposability and stand-alone track focus of the pop music industry and recording artists' and more often record producers' and remixers' desire to establish themselves as artists. Of course, many of these remixers were also deejays, and the twelve inch allowed them to establish their artistic and professional credentials in the clubs as well as on the radio, in the parks, and at block parties: the first commercially available twelve-inch single—Double Exposure's successful interpolation of the classic Philly soul sound, "Ten Percent"—was released by Salsoul Records in 1976 and featured a remix from club deejay Walter Gibbons.[27] That avenue of resistance aside, the broader ways the disco phenomenon transformed the industry and displaced artists in the classic sense (particularly black artists) combined with the new technological potentials associated with the increasing predominance of digital representations of creative activity—the compact disc, the post-tactile download and shared file, the possibility of ignoring artistic intentions by programming tracks according to one's own preferences—made the sustained communication of artistic intent and the establishment of artistic authority much more difficult.[28]

Similar tensions and restrictions would mark the film and television industries before and after the civil rights era (e.g., the reluctance to support black creative work outside of the comedic or situation comedy genres, the deletion of news programming from the schedule of BET) and contribute to a general reembedding of black art in a structure of disposability. This development would echo the broader displacement of black workers and the post-Fordist downgrading of the value of free and, particularly, organized labor in general (i.e., the reemergence of the globalized sweatshop economy) and the significantly increased and—from a comparative perspective—historically unprecedented rates of incarceration experienced by blacks, and Americans in general, in this period.[29] Black cultural productions in this new but familiar problem space would be markedly divorced from any relevant organic, auratic, or clear authorial context.[30] Artists themselves would struggle in this aesthetic economy to establish career longevity, and the latitude, audience loyalty, and company support, to innovate. Those able and willing to produce and circulate "political" texts (politics understood in a narrow and conventional sense here) would also diminish in number. Furthermore, if we read the video age as being in tension with collective efforts to remember practices and sentiments that predate the mid-1980s—that is, the earlier suggestion that music not appended to an easily consumable visual image might get lost or "written out of the script"—it would also be the case that the possibility of black artistry in the classic sense would cease to be re-memorable or retrievable.

These need not necessarily be characterized as negative developments if we consider the challenges anonymous art, genealogical ambiguity, and the easy reproducibility enabled by the digital era might pose to notions of the aesthetic and artistic authority and the suggestion that creative artists should be separated from, and elevated above, their audiences. It is in this spirit that Kodwo Eshun disparages the fetishization of "the live show, the proper album, the Real Song, the Real Voice, the musical, the pure, the true [and] the proper."[31] New technologies have the potential to liberate and democratize (a possibility anticipated by many of the participants in the Afro-futurist and speculative fiction movements), and accordingly, blacks have struggled for access to new technologies as well as the right to enjoy the benefits of their own innovations. The technological innovations of the late twentieth century—synthesizers, programmers, drum machines, and subsequently samplers—lowered the costs involved in making marketable music by rendering string sections, wind and brass instruments, and other musicians redundant; Prince with his substitution of synthesizers for horn sections stands as a key turning point in this regard. As a result, access to the industry was increased, and in many respects the skill barrier—traditionally defined—was lowered.

It is worth noting, though, that these new technologies were characteristically used to replace rather than supplement existing instruments (i.e., instead of using the synthesizer to create new textures and sounds, as Stevie Wonder and the Isley Brothers did in the mid-1970s, in the early 1980s the same artists and others began, unfortunately, using these devices to stand in for other instruments).[32] Certain forms of sociality were also lost as a result, such as the experience of musicians playing together in the studio and the expectation and desire to see live and spontaneous performances. Furthermore, while it is apparent that technology shapes behavior, the arrows also point in the opposite direction: the technological innovations that resonate anticipate desires and emerge in response to perceived needs. In other words, we might think of these changes as reflective of some broader forces and the ways they are typically interpreted as expressive of some drive to contain, avoid, or marginalize certain voices and perspectives. Not surprisingly, black creative artists and black creativity were particularly transformed—both enabled and disabled—by the emergence of these various new forms of hardware and the corresponding new frameworks that underpinned the culture industries in the post-post-civil-rights era.

More broadly, the ways technological innovations trouble the modernity/blackness relation are relevant here. At the most basic level, there is a question of race and political economy: to what extent do new technologies replicate and multiply the means by which black labor can be exploited? Black performances rendered as printed text, phonographic recordings, or visual matter create the possibility of the commodification and marketing of colored source materials not only for and to others but also, more significant, by others. While these reproductions might be celebrated for the ways they enable black presences and intentions in previously unavailable and inaccessible public spaces, the processes of making and distributing the translations, iterations, reiterations, and disiterations (e.g., the Canadian quartet the Crew-Cuts take on the Chords' "Sh-Boom" and Pat Boone's rendering of Little Richard's "Tutti Frutti") of these performances often involve the alienation of control, whether voluntary or involuntary, over one's own labors and the profits that these disembodied/reembodied works can generate.[33] Accordingly, one of the most obvious concerns of the post–civil rights era with regard to the popular culture/politics nexus is the degree of autonomy black creative artists are able to exercise individually and collectively. While all artists face these dilemmas, it is black artists—and one might want to consider for a moment the particular situation of black female creative artists—who, in an era in which a small number of film studios, broadcast networks, and record companies dominate the entertainment industry, are compelled to make uniquely difficult choices if they want free access to exploit the dominant technologies, even those of their own creation, and to see their work widely produced and promoted.

From another perspective, does the confidence expressed in the technological vis-à-vis the unmediated—or, more accurately, less mediated—black performance reproduce in some ways the notion that, absent these forms of transfiguration, blackness and the various folkish and performative manifestations of this sensibility stand outside the acceptable and recognized sphere of modern discourse? Does blackness only become acknowledged as being relevant to the unfolding of the modern if it is technologically whitened, reupholstered, remade and remodeled, improved, and distanced from certain roots? To the extent that it appears to displace or erase, or at least mock and denigrate, the worrisome possibility of the black subject? In other words, does emphasizing certain forms of technique and process reinforce the marginalization/spectaclization of the untreated, albeit already and constitutively modern, black presence and voice?

There is no obvious or satisfying answer to the latter set of questions, as these are tensions that resist—quite rightly—easy resolution.[34] To the extent that technology is flatly read as a solution to the supposed problem of the black subject by blacks themselves, it is apparent that the standard opposition of modernity against blackness is simply being rearticulated under the guise of celebrating black scientific genius. In contrast, there are the ambivalence and skepticism and often ironic engagements of the technological realm that run through the best speculative fiction—for example, the work of Octavia Butler and Samuel Delany—and the recorded efforts of artists such as King Tubby, Lee Perry, Herbie Hancock, Juan Atkins, Carl Craig, and 4 hero, among others. From this perspective, the technological is more terrain to be contested and negotiated, process *and* substance, much in the same way that the cultural engages the political. How do those marked as outside of the technological order, yet fully involved in its shaping and development, engage its implications? Tentatively and aggressively, suggestively and authoritatively, from both inside and outside.

TIME AND TIME AGAIN

The late twentieth century is also distinguished by its particular assimilations of time and temporal possibility. The post–civil rights era, and particularly the video era, would be characterized by the embrace of the accelerated, as expectations that the new would be available quickly, consumed, and dispensed with aggravated the normal generational gaps that occur within communities (e.g., those registered in changing normative and fashion commitments, slang, and body languages). As younger cohorts sought sounds, images, and sensations that arrived and passed ever more quickly, their ability to engage with older generations socialized in more stately rhythmic environments was attenuated. As a reflection of this shift, for example, younger deejays (on the radio, in clubs, and on mixtapes) would become even more attentive to rhythmic continuity than the substantive quality of the music they were playing as the beats-per-minute (bpm) sensibility became hegemonic. Accordingly, bad mixing rather than poor song selection would become the cardinal sin. Regional engagements and rejections of this new regime were audible—evidenced, for example, in the emergence of "screwed" remixes in the Southwest (dramatically slowed-down versions of songs partly designed to accommodate the intoxicated young consumers of cough medicine); the high-speed rhythms of the Miami-bass sound; sped-up altered-pitch samples (e.g., the "chipmunk soul" characteristic of the work of the Wu-Tang Clan and the rapper-producer Kanye West); and the almost anachronistic 4/4 commitments of classic New York–area hip-hop.[35]

As with the visual surplus, these accelerated rhythms—driven and reflected by the quick cut-and-paste tempo of film, and the rapidity of the internet and video game technologies, as well as the musical creations of the period—also outpaced and frustrated the organizing and regulatory mechanisms that older cohorts institutionalized and maintained. Observable in this context is a certain discordance between the political sensibilities formed in the midst of a particular moment—the "nation time" of the late 1960s and early 1970s—and a cultural aesthetic significantly reconfigured in the middle 1980s. In contrast to the high-velocity exchanges and instantaneous pleasures of the post-1980s cultural realm, the increased access to institutionalized electoral politics won as a result of the civil rights campaigns, in some respects, encouraged black formal politics to assimilate a slower and more regular tempo: specifically the "every four years" rhythm characteristic of the American system.[36] Indeed, one might suggest that, like younger deejays, the growing ranks of black elected officialdom were to some degree understandably preoccupied with establishing rhythmic continuity with mainstream actors and the temporal logics of brokerage politics (e.g., Bayard Rustin's arguments) rather than challenging and transforming the norms prevalent in these arenas, for example, by pursuing means of expression and change—the protest, the riot, and possibly irregular internal mobilization campaigns (e.g., the convention movement)—that might disregard or disrupt the dominant politico-temporal framework and its related ablative disjunctions.

The contemporary inclination to read the cultural realm as a primary political space, then, can be understood partly as a comment on the ability of the performers operating in these arenas to deliver quickly—on time and in between times—if not necessarily to satisfy substantively. Going further, we can identify which forms of popular culture would most effectively fulfil this immediacy function (with its inevitable partner ephemerality). In a hierarchy based on responsiveness, live comedy and music would come first, followed by their recorded forms (i.e., the bootleg, the mixtape, and subsequently the officially sanctioned product), music videos, vernacular theatre, televised situation comedies and dramas, and then film, literature, and dance. If we factor in impact, music emerges as the primary forum for political and symbolic exchange, given its accessibility to creative artists, producers, and consumers and to the relatively unfiltered expression of black intent; its ear-to-the-groundedness; and the shaping effect it has on many of the other forms (including film, comedy, theatre, and, in many respects, the fine arts). The plastic arts would not rank high on this list, if only because of their limited audiences; exemption from the processes of producing and marketing mass culture; and their general absence from black vernacular exchange spaces. "If black writers had had to rely on the kinds of people and developments that determine the value of art, if writing had to be accepted into rich white people's homes and into their investment portfolios in the manner of the prized art object," adds Michele Wallace, "I suspect that none of us would have ever heard of Langston

Hughes, Richard Wright [and] Zora Neale Hurston. . . . Indeed, we are lucky to have heard of Jacob Lawrence, Betye Saar, Romare Bearden . . . and Faith Ringgold."[37] As a result of their organic detachment from black spaces, conventionally defined, the fine arts have been limited in their ability to shape, if not register, African American political investments.

It will become apparent, though, that any assessment of the political efficacy of different artistic media should acknowledge the extent to which men control the dominant communicative venues. The realm of comedy, for example, while it has included a number of women practitioners, is largely an arena for masculine rhetoric. If we consider the influence songwriters, producers, and musicians have on a recorded product, even the significant number of women involved in black popular music is counterbalanced by their relative powerlessness in shaping the final product. This is even more the case in subgenres such as jazz, funk, and rap. In film and in video, the overwhelming majority of blacks behind the camera are men. One influential space in which black women's presences have been felt in the post–civil rights era is literature. Accordingly, the ranking of artistic genres on the basis of political impact, immediacy, and responsiveness provided here reflects the dominance of male discourse in the cultural sphere, and literature (and perhaps theatre) would be ranked just below or alongside music and comedy in a more gender-balanced analysis of the relationship between politics and distinct cultural arenas.[38]

Although the two sensibilities, the political and the cultural, are clearly related, as the realms themselves are connected, one can imagine that the two spaces might—at least briefly—operate under distinct temporal rules with correspondingly distinct sets of expectations. In the same matrix, the very definition and viability of black politics, traditionally understood, arguably are open to question, as a real contest over the meaning of that proverbial phrase "colored people's time" can be detected (especially if we read time as a suggestion rather than as an impenetrable, unalterable regime). There is a medical term, *hyperchronicity*, that refers to the loosening of the DNA double helix—the two strands on which a cell's genetic codes are inscripted—that occurs in response to stress and exposure to toxic environments and is associated with ageing, increased cancer markers, and mutation. Stripped of its morbid and structural-functionalist (i.e., homeostasis-fixated) implications, we can understand the unraveling of the formally political and cultural strands in the post–civil rights era as a reflection of hyperchronic activity—in the sense of a sharp articulation of temporal dissonance.[39] In this context, then, mutation would be inevitable, not necessarily problematic, and not quite unprecedented: the 1920s, 1940s, and mid-1960s might be conceived of as eras characterized to varying degrees by hyperchronicity, tied in many respects to geotemporal factors—north/south distinctions within the United States and local/national/diasporic/global dynamics—as well as strictly generational factors. We might also think of the cultural realm as being the exposed flank, the space most likely initially to register these dissonant temporal cues.

Finally, with regard to the ways technology, popular culture, and politics intersect, it is important to consider the particular forms of sound systemization that dramatically reconfigured the boundaries between black public and private spaces toward the end of the twentieth century. Loudspeakers dedicated to transmitting paradigm-shattering lower acoustic frequencies make their appearance in the late 1970s and 1980s in the form of portable cassette players, and the cohort socialized in that technological moment, not surprisingly, outfitted their cars with equipment capable of making similarly strong impressions on its environment. Although the walkman and later the MP3 player and iPod would allow for new means of consuming sound privately, the woofer revolution—the proliferation in number and expansion in size of the speaker cones designed to reproduce bass frequencies—physically demolished the line separating Saturday night from Sunday morning and transformed black spaces into arenas in which the radio was always on and quite audible. Herb Kent, a longtime radio personality in Chicago, remembers that when Sam Cooke's "You Send Me" was released in 1957, it could be heard virtually everywhere throughout the city's South Side; Aretha Franklin's "I Never Loved a Man (The Way I Love You)" would repeat the trick a decade later.[40] While the ubiquitous audibility of a particular recording is not completely new, the public airings of popular material in the later decades are distinguished by their intensity and organ-shaking inescapability. Accordingly, one did not have to purchase a copy of Public Enemy's "Don't Believe the Hype" in the summer of 1988, Naughty By Nature's "O.P.P." in 1991, the Fugees' "Killing Me Softly" in the spring of 1996, or 50 Cent's "In Da Club" in 2003 to hear them. These recordings could be heard on virtually every passing car's radio, and from the windows and doorways of many storefronts and households, in what constituted a well-wired multiblock party, particularly in the warmer seasons, and represented—along with the emergence of graffiti—a vivid example of masculine display and performance. In terms of political implications, given these sound investments, it was harder not to know what was going on in black popular culture in this context and consequently more likely that those forced into this awareness—perhaps in a Rousseauian sense—would feel compelled to react.

Associated with the visibility, omniaudibility, and speed addictions of late twentieth-century forms of popular culture was their tendency to arrive and be consumed as commodities. Those cultural practices and performances not engaged in or exploited in these ways—or at all—by the market and its related processes would consequently be marginalized to the point of near invisibility. Given the uniquely complicated relationship new world blacks have had with the process of commodification, and the consequently intricate struggles to make the transition from being modern objects to becoming postmodern subjects, a number of cultural artists' embrace of the market in the post–civil rights era provoked a range of responses. While I have compared the role of cultural politics to protest movements and religious practices and institutions, it is the inescapability of the market, and the inevitability of all political possibilities being offered through the market, that is arguably the appropriate starting point, at least in the period under study. If we think of black performances in the terms Fred Moten has suggested, as literally speaking and shrieking commodities, late twentieth-century black pop's thorough and conscious celebration of the market process marks it as a unique development in the broader history of the efforts to negotiate the object/subject divide that has underscored black politics since the Middle Passage.[41] This sensibility, it should be noted, characterizes not only the work of black musicians and hip-hop artists: consider, for example, the fusion of artist, performance, and commodity in the public offerings of Jean-Michel Basquiat, Spike Lee, Terry McMillan, and Kara Walker.

Broadcast analyst Drew Marcus observed in 2001, "The African-American niche is one of the fastest-growing segments in the economy in terms of income and population growth, and this is attractive to advertisers and investors," and indeed, one of the most important linkages between formal politics and cultural forces was the market's renewed attempts to penetrate black communities from the 1960s onward and the absorption of some forms of black popular culture into the processes of generating mass culture.[42] In particular, the active commercialization of black youths and black youth culture that began in the mid-1980s increased the market's access to black communities and, as it did elsewhere, left every assumed verity and value open to question: for example, the use of civil rights–style marchers and picket signs by Sean "Puffy" Combs's Bad Boy street/promotional teams to advertise the release of new product in the late 1990s to both invoke and mock the protest tradition. Reflecting the issues raised in the Benjamin/Adorno debate, the increased exposure of blacks, and black youth in particular, to the market theoretically created new opportunities, and the potential for progressive, transcendent coalitions, although the reality is that often these options were not being realized or exercised (thus explaining my previous references to black pop as representing a site of "vulnerability" and an "exposed flank"). Although one can read the extreme commodification of relationships evident in R. Kelly's seemingly banal but effectively surreal lyrics from his 1995 song "You Remind Me of Something"—"You remind me of my Jeep"—as an intentionally subversive effort to provoke a collective spiritual awakening, few popular artists were following the singer's example.[43]

THESE ARE THE BREAKS

The developments considered in this chapter regarding the shifting sensory intensities and refigured political economies associated with the emergence of the black superpublic need to be read in the context of the narrowing of the range of the discursive that occurred at the end of the 1980s and the corresponding reduction in the scope of the political. Although most alternatives to the status quo had been rendered unreasonable in the decades following the beginning of the Cold War, the displacement of the bipolar arrangements that had characterized international relations by a new paradigm in which the United States appeared as the obvious embodiment of the desirable in the eyes of its inhabitants—if not quite those of peoples elsewhere—inevitably influenced at some level the phrasing of the ambitions of black creative artists. On a superficial level, the removal of the Soviet Union and its global aspirations from the scene and, as important, the coincident peak of the antiapartheid campaign (i.e., the disiteration of the most explicit marker of colonialism and its associated racial order) affected states' ability to negotiate ways of being that might resist the dominance of the United States (e.g., in the Caribbean basin, continental Africa, and elsewhere) and publics' capacity to generate an agonistic politics in a world apparently postpolitical. The synchronic collapse of the institutional foundation of the Left/Right antagonisms that structured the post–World War II period and the publicly codified racial—the toppling of the Berlin Wall and Nelson Mandela's release from prison occurred within three months of each other—also reduced the nominally transgressive possibilities these other presences might suggest (e.g., Cuba).[44] The potency of the American example was only heightened then by the passing of its nearest competitor and the undoing of the institutionalized reiteration of its racial id (i.e., the degree to which apartheid-era South Africa was conveniently represented as a "colonial anachronism" while not coincidentally, to borrow from Sartre, constituting a "super-American monstrosity").[45]

The completion of the disarticulative cycle that had been initiated at the end of World War II—involving the construction of a convenient enemy in communism, the promotion of a narrative that equated complete liberation with civil rights victories and/or national independence narrowly defined, and the casting of the United States as a break with old Europe with its wars and racist hierarchies (including, on this view, apartheid)—marked the anti-apartheid campaign as the "last hurdle." For evidence of the potency of this discursive strategy, consider the changes in emphasis evident in Gil Scott-Heron's and Brian Jackson's 1975 album *From South Africa to South Carolina*, which implied, in the Robeson tradition, a comparability between the situations of blacks in the United States and South Africa and included the classic "Johannesburg," as opposed to Kashif's "Botha Botha (The Apartheid Song)" and Stevie Wonder's "It's Wrong (Apartheid)," both released in 1985; Jeffrey Osborne's "Soweto," issued the following year; and Maze featuring Frankie Beverly's 1989 release "Mandela," in which it is suggested that "We who are free are the first who should see your plight." The construction of the narrative in Spike Lee's 1992 film *Malcolm X*, which includes at its conclusion a clip featuring Nelson Mandela and Aretha Franklin's version of "Someday We'll All Be Free," in tandem with the R & B recordings of the mid- to late 1980s, suggests an underlying, aggregate sentimental structure supporting the notion that the "race problem" had been solved in the United States in some past time and would be resolved globally once apartheid was dismantled.[46] Not surprisingly, with the formal end of apartheid, even such nominal references to racial hierarchy and marginalization would largely disappear from the lyrics of R & B recordings.

Although one might celebrate the creative, new, thick socialisms that might emerge once the ubiquity of the Comintern model had been eclipsed—and the possibilities offered by the left-leaning antiapartheid movement engaged—in the immediate post-1989 moment, it would be difficult to imagine departures from the pervasive and intense American impulses to circumscribe the imaginary. It is also important to note the ways discourse interacts with the institutional through politics and the manner in which structure and agency are mutually constitutive. The post-1989 triumphalism and the associated disavowal of dissent occurred at the same time as the significant rearrangements in the culture industries: the emergence of oligopolies in the radio and television industries (despite the proliferation of channels) and the marked reduction in the number of major film and recording companies with the capacity to distribute product widely. African Americans and black popular culture would hardly be immune to these changes. It is as a result of these developments on the global scene that we can better understand the cultural turn that took place toward the end of the century and the disenchantment with—if not abandonment of—formal political engagements. Following this narrative, the mid-1980s/post-1989 emergence of a black superpublic can be thought of as a sign of the return of the colonial gaze—always present as a default setting and energized by the visual turn—as natural and hegemonic and unencumbered by anticolonial resistance. In the absence of a robust, transnational, and self-defining black counterpublic—or, more accurately, the overlapping cluster of formations that constitute "black politics"—black performances might increasingly bend and be bent to serve, and be read as seeking to engage, seemingly new but frankly familiar masters in the context of this different conjuncture.[47]

An equally important story relates not to what different creative artists do but rather what others make of their works and the questionable uses to which representations of black popular culture are put. In many respects, it is not the engagement with black popular culture's wide-ranging normative intentions that distinguishes the moment; it is the representation of a superpublic hip-hop with its hyperchronic potentials as grounds for disengagement and as a justification for the disarticulation of black possibilities. The forms of black popular culture—including hip-hop—that emerged in the late twentieth century as *the* dividing line in black life became important not only because of what was going on within these subgenres but also because of the reactions to the representations of these cultural developments.[48] Hip-hop, in particular, became, in so many interesting, and problematic, ways, one of the most crucial tests of—and a laboratory for the testing of—the linked fate hypothesis that Dawson developed in *Behind the Mule*. Although there are certainly other issues or developments that stretched the ligaments of the black counterpublic in more provocative ways—for example, the emergence of AIDS as described by Cohen, and the unfolding gender and class dynamics among blacks that contributed to the general nonresponse to the 1996 abolition of AFDC—even the dynamics particular to these situations were driven tangentially, if not directly, by the reactions to hip-hop, as much as the discourses within hip-hop, and popular culture in general. If blackness is the object that is called into being by, and gives shape to, the modern, black youth culture of the post–civil rights era is the other—much like the character Trueblood in *Invisible Man*—against which many define their notions of black politics and/or launch their arguments *against* black politics, agency, and autonomy. In both cases, the "real" substance of the object is in many respects irrelevant to its representation and counterrepresentations, akin perhaps to Sartre's reference to the possibility of anti-Semitism without the presence of Jews.[49] These representations then take on haunting, phantasmic functions within the discourses in question. Accordingly, most of the crises of black community that erupted toward the end of the twentieth century occurred against the backdrop of the omnipotent and spectacular but faceless and threatening b-boy.

It is in these ways, then, as a source of new commentaries and as the subject of communal discourses, that hip-hop—"the most amoral, resourceful and cannibalistic folk music in history" in Greg Tate's terms—rearranged the geography of black life in the late 1980s and 1990s much in the same way that the energies unleashed by Ella Baker's launching of the SNCC impacted black politics in the 1960s.[50] Like other more coherent, focused, and defined social movements (e.g., abolitionism, first wave feminism, populism, the Progressive movement, the New Deal and Popular Front coalitions, civil rights), hip-hop's influence was not evenly felt across the country. Indeed, its often hegemonic ambitions generated backlashes among different constituencies, and it was outflanked (sometimes only temporarily) in terms of its significance in certain areas and urban centers.[51] The church is commonly designated as the predominant social organization within black communities: Adolph Reed refers to it "as the principal linkage institution in Afro-American life." "We must go back to our roots, the black church," CBC member Elijah Cummings recently urged.[52] That assertion, though, is now open to question, given the diversity of the black churches in terms of their missions, the increasingly secular disposition of the various African American communities, and the emergence of other connective experiences, including the media, black-owned and otherwise, and popular culture, particularly the nominally secular but often Rasta, Muslim-inflected, or evangelical late 1980s and early 1990s genres of hip-hop. Indeed, the heightened contest between religious authorities and the agents of the secular world employed in the media of popular culture for supremacy over the definition of norms and symbols, while hardly new—and these camps are not exclusive—has represented one of the more intriguing subtexts of the post–civil rights era.[53] In common with most social movements (i.e., the early and enthusiastic uniquely southern reading of the New Deal as an attack on Yankee privilege), hip-hop's meaning also varied according to region. Despite the heterogeneous dynamics the phenomenon put into play and the absence of an identifiable agenda, its significance as a social and political moment deserves serious attention.

Reed's questioning of the applicability of the concept of resistance to contemporary black popular culture forces us to be careful in our deployment of the term and to consider the ways mere resistance does not always engender transformation, as well as the potential limits and inherent impossibilities of resistance. Moreover, performances of resistance can assist in the legitimation of the status quo and strengthen in some ways the hold of hegemonic formations over marginalized peoples. Nevertheless, when he equates cultural studies' integration into politics with the celebration of the empty gestures of adolescence, he is missing the very real ways the terrain changed in the late twentieth century because of developments in the cultural realm and between the political and cultural arenas, and the significance of these shifts. The extent to which blacks are engaged in a full-blown class war would not be easily detectable from the pronouncements of black elected officials, and as Dawson has written, "[S]ystematic manifestations of . . . class divisions [among blacks] in the political arena have been difficult to find."[54] Similarly, the discussions of issues related to gender, sexuality, and the (national) limits of black community, in the arenas of formal policy-making, were rarely explicit or public. Nevertheless, the challenging, rupturing, and recasting of black solidarities on these various fronts—as a result of the hyperchronic dissonance reflected in the renegotiation of the borders between formal politics and popular culture— were increasingly apparent in post–civil rights era popular culture and, as I will argue in the next chapter, largely in response to the hip-hop phenomenon.

We had all been in the rain together until yesterday. Then

a handful of us—the smart and the lucky and hardly ever

the best—had scrambled for one shelter our former rulers

left, and had taken it over and barricaded themselves in.

And from within they sought to persuade the rest through

numerous loudspeakers . . . that all argument should cease

and the whole people speak with one voice.

—Chinua Achebe, *A Man of the People*

[T]he Jester's role in the pursuit of human knowledge

alternates with the Priest's role—transforming heresies into

new orthodoxies, the contingent into the modes of the

Absolute. —Sylvia Wynter, "The Ceremony Must Be Found:

After Humanism"

5

VARIATIONS ON THE SOLIDARITY BLUES

The rules and understandings according to which communities are structured and defined typically do not make explicit reference to their exceptions. Accordingly, the violence that marks the borders between the welcome and the spurned is constitutively and constitutionally unremarkable. It is as a result of these kinds of commitments and practices that broad claims regarding rights and liberties, universalities and democracy, are sustainable. Similar processes can be observed at work in the ways public benefits are allocated and beneficiaries are identified. Public goods, by definition, are available to all citizens in theory. Obviously, the key word here is *citizen,* and the salient question is what value and limits we should assign to this term.

Toward this end, it is useful to identify the hegemonic conceptual field that is naturalized as part of the project of modernity and in which we might locate and trace the sign of the citizen. This field, or conceptual string, includes certain discourses and politics, and I am thinking particularly of Michel Foucault's governmentality and biopolitics: in other words, specific styles of engagement and interpellation, distinct and expansive agendas, and invasive, intensive, and ambitious orders of politics. Regarding governmentality, in an attempt to join his studies of the exercise of state power and the ways individuals govern themselves, and in contrast to the standard opposition of the Habermasian public sphere against the potentially oppressive activities of the Hobbesian state, Foucault asked us to conceive of a set of relationships, discourses, and projects that might bind together state and nonstate actors, the political narrowly defined and the personal, in the interpellation of subjects and the organization and management of the people. Foucault introduced this neologism in order to describe a turn, an "emergence," he observed in the history of European political practices and social development that was marked by a shift away from more explicitly disciplinary modes of statecraft. With this form of government, he suggested, "[I]t is not a question of imposing law on men but of disposing things . . . to arrange things in such a way that, through a certain number of means, such-and-such ends may be achieved." On the basis of this reading of European history, he then goes on to talk about the ways certain social, cultural, and political norms of governance deployed by and emanating from many different points within and outside the formal apparatus of the state operate on, and are internalized and reproduced by, what he refers to as "the population."[1]

Biopolitics, as Giorgio Agamben writes, elaborating on Foucault's conceptualization, marks the "politicization of bare life as such[;] constitutes the decisive event of modernity and signals a radical transformation of the political-philosophical categories of classical thought." Continuing, he adds,

> [o]ne of the most persistent features of Foucault's work is its decisive abandonment of the traditional approach to the problem of power, which is based on juridico-institutional models (the definition of sovereignty, the theory of the State), in favor of an unprejudiced analysis of the concrete ways in which power penetrates subjects' very bodies and forms of life.[2]

These new practices, priorities, and intensities are realized partly, I would suggest, through the construction and reconstructions of the prophylactic state, which inoculates, injects, protects, and secures through the provision of public goods and wards off those elements suspected of spreading various diseases and contagions, in order ideally to produce healthy, self-regulating, and self-fashioning citizens. The conceptual field I am trying to flesh out here, then, would include modernity, governmentality, biopolitics, the prophylactic state, and the fetishizing of the citizen.

There is another parallel conceptual string or field that is typically disavowed but functions as a constitutive outside or supplement and stands in relation to the first in much the same way that constitutions give life to states of exception, and archives produce silence. As Walter Mignolo observes, "[T]here is no modernity without coloniality . . . coloniality is constitutive of modernity. That is modernity/coloniality. . . . [W]hile modernity is presented as a rhetoric of salvation, it hides coloniality, which is the logic of oppression and exploitation."[3] Drawing from the logic of Mignolo's insight, we might imagine a set of subordinative discourses or subordinativities as counterparts of Foucault's governmentalities and a necropolitics, the latter term introduced by Achille Mbembe, as the necessary other of the biopolitics described by Foucault (and subsequently revised in the work of Agamben).[4] In the same way one can read Mignolo as a corrective to the sorts of narratives of modernity that thinkers such as Jürgen Habermas and Charles Taylor have put into circulation, Mbembe's work can be taken as a critique of the arguably provincial imaginations of Foucault and Agamben. I am referring to their conceptualizations of race and biopolitics and their efforts to assist in the whitening of the Western canon and the naturalization and reinscription of coloniality, even as they imagine—following Nietzsche and Heidegger—that they are mounting a thoroughly transgressive critique of the likes of Hegel, Taylor, and Habermas.[5]

For example, as others have noted, Foucault's writing in the aggregate tends to underplay the role of colonialism and the modern articulation of race as phenomena inextricably linked to the histories he is suggesting.[6] Passing references to colonialism in his analysis of biopolitics, for instance, are matched by equally undertheorized observations regarding the role of "mercantilism" in the movement from the disciplinary stage to that of governmentality.[7] Similarly, in his rendering of governmentality, "the population" is unmarked and never disaggregated (except as a collection of individuated subjects). Nevertheless, Foucault does provide us with enough information that we might conceive of this change in tactics, engagements, and concerns in this space, Europe, and time—the beginning of the eighteenth century—as intimately connected to the establishment of the racial and gender hierarchies associated with coloniality and the power imbalances and geographical displacements characteristic of colonialism. In other words, if we consider, as Homi Bhabha suggests, the ways "the postcolonial perspective is subversively working in his text," the historical turn from the disciplinary (i.e., power working against bodies) to governmentality (i.e., power flowing through citizens) within an emerging Europe in Foucault's narrative can be cast as dependent in a number of ways on the colonial and the displacement of the disciplinary to other spaces marked as the colonial.[8]

It is because of this tension—between the citizenship claims and possibilities that are recognized and nurtured under the umbrella of governmentality and those that are ritually denied—that I would resist the application of the concept of governmentality to subaltern populations not deemed worthy of being made subject or party to the various arts of government or to processes that engage and produce populations differently (i.e., that involve the instantiation or reinforcement of social bifurcations). Let me qualify this claim. The production and reproduction of any population involves some degree of bifurcation and subordination, in that these discourses and processes engage and position differently classed, gendered, and sexualized constituencies differently. As Foucault himself notes, disciplinary modes are never entirely displaced by the governmentalist "emergence." In other words, the governmentalist turn hardly marks the disappearance of coercive practices within the metropolitan imagination. Similarly, subordinativities have a consensual dimension. Indeed, the same patriarchal, heteronormative, and bourgeois norms that function coercively on certain constituencies in the modernist project often appear as consensual entanglements in the matrix of coloniality. That qualification aside, I would suggest that we should be careful in the way we engage Foucault's neologism. My point is not that we should dispense with governmentality as a concept, for it does some very useful work. Rather, I think we enhance its utility by reserving it to describe exactly those processes and their engagements with certain racialized and spatialized populations—for example, those captured by the evolving signifier "European"—that Foucault had in mind.[9]

It is here, again, that Achille Mbembe's casting of "race [as] the nocturnal side of the idea of the republic," and his discussion of commandement as a characteristic of both the colony and postcolony, are relevant.[10] In contrast to the mutual engagements and reciprocities that mark at least the surface of the governmentalist moment, Mbembe notes,

[T]he colonial potentate forms no bond with the object of *commandement*—that is, the native. In principle, there exists no mutual need between the parties. Nor is there hope of any eventual mutual benefit. On the contrary, colonial sovereignty is defined by the assurance of its omnipotence; its right to rule and command must in no case countenance any resistance on the part of the native. This form of government does not rest on a covenant since, in Hobbes's words, covenants "are made of such things only as fall under deliberation."[11]

It is in this context that Mbembe distinguishes between "citizens" and "subjects," providing a means by which we might differentiate the processes unfolding simultaneously in Europe and in the colonial world and understand the emergence of the citizen in the West as connected to the disciplines that defined the sphere of the other. Furthermore, we might consider the former process as requiring the geographical disarticulation of its colonial counterpart. Building on Mbembe's articulation of commandement and necropolitics, we can think of subordinative discourses as the unrecognized and suppressed other of the governmentalities that are the focus of Foucault's later writing.

Returning to the construction of these fields, and their relationality, in contrast to the service-providing, benefit-conferring, and risk-reducing prophylactic state, this second field or string does much of its work through the operations of the "duppy state." This instrument marks the potent afterlife, mocking persistence, and resurgence—rather than the remission—of coloniality: the state that is "there and not there" at the same time. The duppy, roughly translated from Jamaican patois, refers to the specter or the ghost that emerges when one has failed to properly bury or dispose of the deceased: therefore, emancipation is haunted by slavery, independence by colonialism, and apparent civil rights victories by Jim Crow. I should note here that the prophylactic state and duppy state are not geographically or spatially disarticulated, in contrast to the relationship between normative states and the cluster of metonymic instruments that go by the names "failed state" or "rogue state." The prophylactic/duppy difference is functional, and indeed these disarticulated formations typically occupy and claim the same geographical and temporal borders (e.g., separate schools, water fountains, and graveyards in the segregated South, and the Janus-faced police forces familiar to subaltern populations throughout the diaspora). The ideal, desired product, then, of this supplemental string—coloniality, subordinativity, necropolitics, and the duppy state—is the convenient and necessary other of the citizen: the exploitable, expendable, and disposable (and blackened) body (aka "the nigger").[12]

The question, then, is what happens when the geographical disarticulation that characterizes and sustains metropolitan/colonial relations—and renders a certain narrative of modernity hegemonic—comes under pressure? The citizen-shaping discourses of European nation-states and civil societies were transformed once a critical mass of formerly colonized populations landed on Western shores after World War II; peoples to whom significance and meanings were ascribed regardless of, and often despite, their actions or intentions but simply because of their mere (visible) presence. Not surprisingly, at this point, the viability of governmentality—in the classic, historically specific sense—came into question, and its status as the overriding paradigm of state rationality and social convenience, to use Foucault's wording, was denaturalized, given that the interpellation and self-fashioning of citizens through governmentality required the denial of any such relationship with nonwhites at home and abroad. If we follow Foucault in his historicization of the roots of governmentality and bring the colonial connections that trigger and enable this moment out of the shadows, it makes sense to imagine that the governmentalist movement has limits, that it is not a static, unending, inherently stable set of practices, contracts, and relationships. Recognizing the conditionality and contingency of these understandings, we can anticipate the possible horizons and disruption of the grasp of these norms (and perhaps the potential reemergence of the disciplinary as the dominant mode of state–subject interaction in the West).

It is also in this context that the political Left, with its own hubristic claims to represent the universal class, becomes increasingly marginalized, and diversity and multiculturalism correlate with receding redistributive ambitions, as previously ratified public policy commitments are revised or vitiated (e.g., the connection between Margaret Thatcher's observation that Britain was being "rather swamped" by nonwhite immigration and her subsequent suggestion that "there is no such thing as society"; the French government's proposals in 2006 to justify loosening job tenure as a means of opening up the labor market for marginalized nonwhite youth).[13] What benefits and protections exist for those not classified as citizens? What kinds of practices and speech acts, with fingers, tongues, and whole bodies, do prophylactic states and populations engage in so as to be able to disavow the citizenship claims of peoples within their borders? What happens when the shadows are foregrounded and those not normally seen as citizens with full rights—the disposable—are brought into the picture and the lines distinguishing nuanced processes of subjectification and raw mechanisms of subjection are blurred? These are the kinds of questions raised by developments in Canada and Europe with the demographic changes that have taken place in the last five decades.

The United States is significant in this regard, in that the modal/mondial disjunction that underpinned the governmentalist emergence in Europe could not be as easily finessed in the Americas. Or, to be more precise, it required far greater labor and of a slightly different sort. For instance, as Stuart Hall notes,

> [B]ecause Britain—unlike the United States—managed slavery and colonization at a safe distance, the migrations of the 1950s were the first time a black working class population in any significant numbers had come to live, work, and settle, in the white domestic space. These and other facts should make us wary of easy U.S./U.K. comparisons.[14]

In other words, the United States can be regarded as a formation that has long been struggling to reconcile republican governmentality with its investment in colonial subordinativity. As a result, not surprisingly, the colonial aspects of the American enterprise are even more heatedly denied (with the support at times, as noted in chapter 2, of blacks). The shapers of the nation's founding myths have insisted that the United States was born out of resistance against colonial ambition rather than forged through such sensibilities. Despite suggestions that questions of problematic ascription were solved with the Declaration of Independence—although the 1776 revolution actually reinforced the racial order and the grip of slavery on the republic—or perhaps Reconstruction, the riddle of thick citizenship continues to haunt, mock, and confound rhetorical representations of the nation's character. These discursive projects, understandably, become especially urgent following the southern outmigration of blacks and whites at the beginning of the twentieth century, and the end of Jim Crow in the 1960s. In many respects, then, the United States is arguably the most exemplary model of the embedded colonial/postcolonial structure; a polity lacking even the language—indeed resisting the language—required to speak to these dynamics and tensions.[15]

Consequently, there are few popular narratives that can explain the general pattern that has emerged over the course of American (public policy) history. In this matrix, significant extensions of recognition, rights, or services to nonwhites have thrown the gears of American public policy-making and citizen/subject interpellation into reverse. Accordingly, when voting rights were extended to black males in the wake of the first Reconstruction effort, states moved to limit access to the franchise by means of literacy tests and poll taxes and other devices that depressed voter turnout and reduced the value of the electoral process across the board. Once the programs Franklin Delano Roosevelt instituted—the Social Security Act and the National Labor Relations Act of 1935, and the legislation that established the Federal Housing Authority two years later—were reformed and reoriented three decades later to work for and include blacks, the New Deal was revised and subsequently eviscerated. Accordingly, income maintenance policies and pension programs become targets for reform, dismantling, and privatization, following the lifting of the barriers to black enrollment in the 1960s. Following their construction in the 1930s and 1940s, public housing developments became stigmatized as blacks started to move in. After the *Brown* decision, we saw a gradual disinvestment in public education across the country. The Democratic Party and the labor movement themselves were abandoned by a number of working-class and middle-class whites when they become identified (belatedly) with civil rights in the early and middle 1960s. Overall, one can observe a characteristic demonization of not only the prophylactic state, public policies, goods, and spaces but also the city as a site of liberation and transformation following attempts to include nonwhites as citizens.[16]

Given these developments, we might also consider the extent to which imprisonment functions as a form of deportation and the ways the hyperincarceration of black individuals—and the associated deprivations that typically follow release (beyond the restrictions associated with parole and probation)—in terms of voting rights, access to public housing and public benefits in general, stigmatization, and effective disqualification from participation in the mainstream economy—represent a form of denaturalization: the removal of citizenship status from those involved (and to some extent their families as well). Such a move would encourage us to stop fetishizing borders and literal sovereignty and reimagine the ways prisons, camps, and asylums might be geographically articulated (i.e., thereby allowing us to identify contemporary penal colonies and their varied boundaries). Overall, it does not require much imagination to suggest that the civil rights movement and the prison construction movement are causally related—given the broader historical tendency to read black agency as outside the political, as unnatural, improper, or simply criminal—or to identify the discursive retractions that have enabled and mirrored these new social geographies.

These racialized dynamics also help us understand more accurately why there is no American Left and how the United States has managed to avoid the degree of explicit, class-based social conflict that is characteristic of other Western societies' politics. Similarly, the uniquely American inability to sustain commitments to comprehensive health care, public transportation, education and housing, gun control, and inclusive voting procedures must be understood as a ramification of the nation's hyperarticulated racialization of the public and private spheres. As women, blacks, and other nonwhites, separately and together, press for full participation rights within the public realm or merely make their presence known, these spaces and processes are stigmatized and abandoned. It is on the basis of these sorts of developments that we might entertain the possibility that the neoliberal turn, which is the focus of much of the literature on governmentality—and energized by a genuine hostility toward the sign of the citizen—occurs partly as a result of these demographic pressures. Accordingly, neoliberal governmentalities might be seen as particularly precarious and tenuous, in comparison to their republican and Fordist predecessors. The nervous bimodality, with its instabilities, fragilities, and undecidabilities, then, that characterizes current discursive and institutional arrangements, and their always messy and absurd attempts to engage some while refusing others within the same theatre of activity, can be read as pointing toward the long-term unsustainability of governmentalist projects, not just in the United States but in the West as a whole.

While the broader norms that form the basis of a social order are rarely openly expressed, these codes do not become hegemonic without struggle. In periods of flux, uncertainty, or crisis, political ambitions and agendas become visible and audible (e.g., the recent open discussion regarding the legitimacy of torture and preemptive war as acceptable policies for "liberal democratic" states). The exclusions that defined earlier periods are denaturalized, and silences are broken. The exercise of power is most apparent at the times and in the spaces in which rules have been suspended, the law does not apply, and social relations are in a state of upheaval. It is in this context that I want to consider how blacks, the quintessential marginal population in the American polity, have responded to the changing macroeconomic and social developments that have defined the politics of the last four decades and how relations among the community's different and overlapping internal subconstituencies have been negotiated. Given the evolving framework of incentives and cues, what forms of subjectivity did blacks pursue, endorse, internalize, and reproduce in the transition from a Fordist to a neoliberal environment? How did African Americans engage the emerging discourses of performativity—that is, the notion, among other things, that the competitive norms of the private sphere should be extended into the public sphere—and the dissuasive campaigns that sought to persuade publics that the state could not and should not be depended on any longer, efforts that were largely energized by the countermobilizations that occurred in response to the civil rights movement?[17] How should we understand the promotion of respectability discourses among blacks that might resemble governmentalities in their temper and texture, and in the ways they are circulated and internalized, except that they are forged and reproduced in the awareness of marginalization and are consciously designed not to challenge bases of exclusion directly? In other words, if it is the specter of "the nigger" that provides the conveniences and makes the rationalities on which governmentalities depend, how do American blacks constitute and represent themselves?

In particular, this chapter's focus will be on welfare policy and the reform campaign that led to the abolition in the mid-1990s of the federal guarantee of income support for lower-income Americans. Moreover, I want to highlight the role deliberations in the arenas of popular culture played in shaping and affecting African American responses to this public policy debate and suggest that significant, highly gendered and classed developments took place within the cultural realm, and between the cultural and political arenas, regarding the impossibilities of black interiority and solidarity.

WOMEN AND CHILDREN FIRST

It was one of the more memorable promises made in the campaign leading up to the presidential elections of 1992. Bill Clinton, then governor of Arkansas, was pledging if elected to "end welfare as we know it." After assuming office in January 1993, he proposed a reform of the AFDC program, whose roots lay in the Social Security Act signed by Franklin Delano Roosevelt in August 1935, which involved spending an additional $10 billion to assist welfare recipients in making the transition to work (largely through increased support for job training, transportation, and child care). After the midterm elections of 1994, the Clinton administration, partly as a result of its inability to deliver on comprehensive health-care reform, found itself facing a Congress that was under the control of the Republican Party for the first time in forty years. By the summer of 1996, with Clinton seeking reelection, pressure was building on the White House to announce how it would respond to the welfare reform bills Congress was proposing. In contrast to Clinton's earlier suggestion that more funds would have to be spent, at least in the short term, to reform welfare, the legislation generated called for welfare budget cuts of $55 billion over six years.

The bill also called for legal immigrants to be denied access to welfare and provided little in the way of support for families seeking to move from the welfare rolls to the ranks of the employed. Nevertheless, political considerations weighed heavily on the president's mind: a failure to bring about significant welfare reform would be used against him in the Republicans' upcoming campaign, and polls suggested that a majority of Americans wanted to see some sort of welfare reform occur. On August 22, 1996, Clinton signed the reform legislation Congress had already passed.[18]

This "new social bargain for the poor," as Clinton termed it, involved the abolition of AFDC and the establishment of a new program, Temporary Assistance for Needy Families (TANF). Whereas the older program required the federal government to match state commitments to provide income maintenance support to poor Americans in programs administered by the states themselves, the new program would be funded through block grants—monies the federal government provided to the states for use on a range of related activities, with few strings attached or regulatory restrictions—with the stipulations that recipients could remain on the rolls for no more than two years at a time and five years over the course of a lifetime. In accordance with the new regime, welfare offices were reoriented from assisting clients (and supervising them) to facilitating their removal from public assistance (reflecting the abandonment of antipoverty concerns and the prioritization of budget cutting).[19]

Given the broader patterns that have emerged during the course of American public policy-making, that a promise to "end welfare as we know it" was acted on is hardly surprising. As the literature on the American welfare state has emphasized, income maintenance programs targeted toward the poor have always been relatively underdeveloped and underfunded from a comparative perspective. That income support for seniors—instituted as part of the same Social Security Act—was placed in the federal administrative domain rather than left to the states' control reflects, as many analysts have noted, the broader influence of race on the architecture of the American policy state: those programs most likely to challenge southern racial preferences were left to state powers to administer (i.e., Aid to Dependent Children [ADC], the predecessor of AFDC, and subsequently Medicaid).[20] The programs designed to benefit the deserving poor—pension programs and, later, Medicare—in an environment in which race, class, and virtue were conflated, were then prioritized as federal rather than as state or local (although even these programs were initially set up in such a way so as to exclude possible black recipients, i.e., the disqualification of domestic and agricultural workers as potential pension recipients).

Consistent with this narrative, once blacks are given or successfully demand access—and the prophylactic state/duppy state border is troubled—such programs are stigmatized, defunded, and, in the case of AFDC, abandoned.

When Clinton suggested that he intended to "end welfare as we know it," he was undoubtedly aware of the racial subtext undergirding this pledge. He had campaigned as a moderate Democrat from the South and as a representative of the Democratic Leadership Council and its efforts to reorient the party toward the center of the political spectrum (in effect, to the right). The welfare promise was only one part of a broader symbolic campaign designed to reassure working- and middle-class whites that a Clinton administration would not be operating at the beck and call of black voters. It was meant to articulate, as clearly as was possible in the post–civil rights era, that Clinton intended to have a different kind of relationship with black constituencies. This new relationship was negotiated publicly, more often than not, through the stigmatization or mistreatment of black women—author and rapper Lisa "Sister Souljah" Williamson, law professor Lani Guinier, and surgeon-general Jocelyn Elders—and Clinton's repeated disengagements from black women corresponded in a number of ways with the symbolic thrust of the welfare reform effort.[21]

In the wake of the abolition of AFDC, political scientist Katherine Tate lamented the relative silence among black leaders during the period leading up to it.[22] Beyond their votes—most of the CBC voted against the legislation—she suggested, the caucus members were not particularly active in opposing the proposals. This restraint, she contended, could be explained as a reflection of the demoralization of the CBC after the 1994 earthquake (i.e., the Republican takeover of both houses of Congress), and its dependence on the Clinton White House in the 1996 preelection season. Indeed, the black members of the House of Representatives were generally quite active in opposing the reform measures that constituted the Personal Responsibility and Work Opportunity Reconciliation Act of 1996 (PRWORA) as they passed through these members' chamber. While most believed that the welfare system needed to be revamped, the majority argued that more resources, rather than fewer, were necessary, at least in the short term, and only a small minority supported the abandonment of the federal safety net.[23] "Most welfare recipients want to be independent," observed California representative Maxine Waters, who had grown up in a family that had relied on public assistance, during the debate about the third reform bill in the summer of 1996. "They do not like being on welfare. We need to have credible child care, we need to have credible job training programs."

The current proposals, she stated, were little more than "welfare bashing." New Jersey's Donald Payne noted: "We had 100 jobs available in the city of Newark. Fourteen hundred people started to get in line at 6 a.m. for those 100 jobs." Pennsylvania's Chaka Fattah questioned whether AFDC really was a drain on the public treasury:

> [T]he biggest lie that has ever been told to the American people . . . is that we are spending too much as a country to help poor people. . . . The AFDC payments are about a little more than one penny out of every dollar that this Government spends to help poor children.

Jesse Jackson Jr., whose district was on the South Side of Chicago, raised the rhetorical stakes a little higher:

> I rise in strong opposition to this deadly and Draconian piece of garbage which will do nothing to reform the conditions of poverty and unemployment suffered by our Nation's most vulnerable. . . . Please know, Mr. Speaker, that I will not join demorepublicans and republicrats in this mean-spirited attack. . . . [L]et's apply "Two Years and You're Off" [i.e., the time limitations proposed for beneficiaries] to dependent corporations.[24]

Most black House members also rejected the proposal to deny legal immigrants access to welfare state benefits, partly out of solidarity with their Hispanic colleagues, because a number of the districts represented by African Americans were populated by black immigrant communities, and out of basic principle. "[D]o we reform the system by denying benefits to legal immigrants who, despite working hard and paying taxes, fall upon hard times?" asked Ohio's Louis Stokes. Sheila Jackson-Lee, a House member from Texas and daughter of Caribbean immigrants, remarked, "I do not believe in sending legal immigrants into war, but yet when they need a helping hand this Nation will say you can fight for us but we do not have any support for you and your children."[25]

Jackson-Lee also tried to get her colleagues to rethink their conceptions of the circumstances under which individuals became involved with the welfare system and made the connection between the abuse of women, who constituted 90 percent of AFDC recipients, and welfare dependency. "The victims of domestic violence and their children would still have no assurance that, if they escape violence, they could at least survive with cash assistance until they are able to find work," Lee noted. "This would cause many women and their children being forced by harsh economic realities back into the abusive environment they were attempting to escape." While the vast majority of black members of the House argued and voted against the abolition of AFDC, there was evident in their discourse a certain detachment from the adults involved, again overwhelmingly women, and a corresponding concern and engagement with the circumstances of the children (constructed in contrast to their parents as innocent and deserving of government support). This sentiment was clearly articulated by Maryland's Wynn when he stated,

> I agree the current welfare system does not work. . . . As a result of the . . . system, its recipients have lost self-respect. We have created a system of dependency and put welfare recipients outside the mainstream of American society. . . . Let's talk about the children. Children are going to be harmed by this bill.

New York's Charles Rangel sounded a similar note (in characteristic Rangellian fashion): "Someone has to be responsible for that child. . . . Do not ask the child whether, by choice, the mother is a bum." A number of members raised the issue of innocent children suffering as a result of the proposed legislation; few spoke as sympathetically about these children's parents.[26]

On the whole, black representatives in Congress were, at least on the public record, overwhelmingly opposed to the proposed abandonment of a national safety net. The story in the civil rights community was a bit different. Katherine Tate cites the remarkable absence of the civil rights community as a whole, with the noted exception of Marian Wright Edelman, who "attacked welfare reform early on." In an effort to put these developments in perspective, Tate writes that "one can't help but imagine that Dr. [Martin Luther] King would not have been silent on the subject of welfare reform" and suggests that the dissipation of support for these programs among black leaders in general was partly a function of class differences. "The big civil rights groups don't reflect well the interests of the black poor," she observes, "because they are not members." She adds, "[A]lthough welfare is closely linked with the public's attitude toward blacks, the welfare reform debate was carefully presented by those involved as a 'non-racial' issue."[27]

Clearly, among those in the civil rights community, there was some uncertainty as to how to proceed in terms of responding to the developments in Congress. For Hugh Price of the National Urban League, the appropriate response was evident, and his assessment resembled those black members of Congress offered: "We're deeply dismayed and keenly disappointed that Congress would pass this law and the President would sign it. It's almost as if Washington has decided to end the War on Poverty and begin a war on poor children." Others were not as confident that welfare reform was a civil rights issue. In response to a question about Congress's record in the 1995–96 term—"Have there been any votes in the 104th Congress that have been detrimental to the Civil Rights Movement?"—Wade Henderson, executive director of the Leadership Conference on Civil Rights, replied, "I don't know if I would characterize it as detrimental to the Civil Rights Movement, but . . . I think that this welfare vote was a disastrous vote that is going to have very pernicious consequences."[28]

Jesse Jackson Sr.'s response also reflected a certain disengagement from the issue. As Tate notes, he did, despite expressing some misgivings about the abolition of AFDC, campaign for Clinton rather actively in 1996, after making it clear to Clinton that, if he were to roll back affirmative action programs, he should expect a primary challenge: "There is no question about it. My position on [affirmative action] was quite public, and I stated it to him [i.e., Clinton]. I had no inclination to run. My choice was, rather, to support him. But if he had taken away that program for equal opportunity, he would have crossed the line." Implicit in this formulation is that Jackson did not perceive Clinton's signing the bill creating TANF as "crossing the line." By extension, Clinton knew that while a move to revise affirmative action practices would have generated a challenge from Jackson, he was safe on the welfare reform front. Indeed, in the mid-1970s, Jackson had encouraged a self-help approach as a solution to what he characterized as "a definite welfare mentality in many black communities that derives perhaps from slavery." He had also argued that the state was not the answer:

> [M]any black and white leaders demand Federal aid as the only
> solution. More Federal aid is certainly needed, but money alone,
> or in combination with minor reforms, will not significantly
> change the welfare system, reduce crime, build enough new houses,
> improve education, restore stable families or eliminate drug abuse.
> A multitude of Federal antipoverty and urban-renewal programs
> should have proved that by now.

Given Jackson's earlier disinterest in King's plans for a Poor People's March, it is not entirely surprising that he was not particularly disturbed by the abolition of the federal safety net that was AFDC.[29]

It is important to note, too, that while black members of Congress were vocally opposed to the reform initiatives when they were being discussed, little effort was made to categorize the issue as part of the civil rights agenda, and remarkably, no mention was made of race at all in the phrasing of their objections, although all concerned were undoubtedly fully aware of the racial subtexts in play. If welfare was cast as a program that black representatives were particularly concerned about because it disproportionately involved black families, it might be easier, given the broader climate, to stigmatize AFDC as a form of racial set-aside. On the other hand, by choosing not to invoke the racialized history and racial deficits associated with the operations of the American state as part of the public debate, black representatives allowed their opponents to gloss over the stakes involved and to speak in general terms that overlooked the dynamics at work.[30]

With regard to the black public, Tate notes "another surprise," that most blacks were "divided in their opinion" about the issue, a sentiment that was partly a reflection of their warm feelings toward Clinton himself. Echoing this observation, poll data from the mid-1990s indicates that majorities among black respondents felt that AFDC discouraged recipients from seeking employment (81 percent), favored work requirements for beneficiaries (73 percent) and five-year lifetime limits (66 percent). Nearly half of black respondents (48 percent) supported caps on recipient families, regardless of whether additional children were born. Finally, although 49 percent of black respondents favored increased welfare transfers in 1984, twelve years later this number had dropped by more than half to 21 percent. Black conservatives might not have been able to convince African Americans to question their allegiance to the Democratic Party, but maybe they had been able to affect the basic value orientations of key constituencies within the various black communities. Indeed, as Tate suggests, "When one examines . . . the congruency between Black public opinion and legislative votes on welfare reform, one finds that Republicans more than Black Democrats, or even White Democrats, represented more accurately Black opinion on this issue."[31]

Besides class issues, Tate and others have highlighted the ways gender-related factors and constructs might explain the responses and nonresponses of black publics and their representatives to the welfare reform process. Similarly, Angela Davis has offered,

> Media reports keep us painfully aware that African-American women
> are the most visible targets of the recent campaign to dismantle
> welfare. The demonization of welfare mothers, however, was met
> with overwhelming silence, even from successful African-American

women whose proximity was perhaps too great for them to imagine their sisters' fate.[32]

If we remember that 90 percent of adult AFDC recipients were women, it would make sense that gender would factor into any explanation of black responses to welfare reform.

One might argue that there is no valid reason to expect that blacks would see welfare reform as a "black" issue, except that by all accounts, African Americans were disproportionately represented on the welfare rolls. While making up roughly 12–13 percent of the total population, blacks composed almost a quarter (23 percent) of those receiving welfare benefits for less than two years, and roughly a third (34 percent) of those enrolled for five years or more.[33] In other words, it could not be pretended that a dramatic reconfiguration of income maintenance programs would not affect a large number of black families. It is, of course, at this point that we should begin to disaggregate the category black and attend to the particular intensities of domination and exclusion that attach to certain combinations of gender, class, and racial identities—in other words, to borrow from Kimberle Crenshaw, their intersectionality.[34] How should we understand the relationship between the increasing dissatisfaction with welfare programs as registered in poll data among blacks and the behavior of their representatives in Congress and in the realm of interest group politics (i.e., the civil rights community)? Why would members of the civil rights community be uncertain as to whether or not welfare reform should be a concern of theirs and why would black representatives in the legislature, even while relatively vigorously opposing the reform initiative, not engage the racial subtexts in play in their speeches? With respect to the broader themes underlying this book, where and how were these different decisions made?

To some extent, these actions and inactions, disengagements and reinterpellations, are easily explained. In the black responses to the welfare reform initiative, we can see the tension between Michael Dawson's conception of linked fate and Cathy Cohen's treatment of marginalization and specifically secondary marginalization (i.e., the boundary work that takes place among the already marginalized). Visible as well are the signs of new identities being calibrated and staked out; and the associated closures and exclusions inevitably associated with any process of social reformation. In this context, it is worth revisiting Dawson's observation from *Behind the Mule*: "[S]ystematic manifestations of . . . class divisions [among blacks] in the political arena have been difficult to find. The puzzle for researchers and political observers is why given the growing economic cleavage among black Americans, political unity among blacks appears to remain fairly strong." The key to responding to Dawson's legitimate question is fleshing out what it is we mean by "politics." This is exactly what Cohen's *Boundaries of Blackness* does so well and so thoroughly: forces us to identify and recognize political activity that we might overlook because it takes the form of (not easily quantified) silence and/or silencing outside the realms of formal political exchange and deliberation. As she observes, "[T]he framework of marginalization expands our understanding of the places we must look to identify and understand the use of power." Similarly, we might try to affix pronouns. Whose fates? Who decides when they should be linked and how?[35]

Borrowing from Cohen's insights, I want to attempt an answer to the questions Katherine Tate and Dawson raise, explicitly and implicitly, respectively, about black officialdom's response to the welfare reform initiatives of the mid-1990s. Specifically, I want to examine the arenas of black popular culture—in particular, literature, film, R & B, rap, and comedy—with a particular emphasis on certain texts, including the early films of Spike Lee, Public Enemy's *It Takes a Nation of Millions to Hold Us Back*, Chris Rock's *Bring the Pain*, and Erykah Badu's *Mama's Gun*. The focus throughout will be on the discursive strategies being pursued within and among these texts and spaces, and the domains of formal political activity, with a particular attention to those relating to issues of gender, class, and race and their interrelationships. An analysis of these discourses suggests that a significant amount of black deliberative energy is expended in the cultural arena and that the "decisions" reached as a result of these exchanges do register within the formal political realm. In other words, we cannot understand black politics and the ways black subjectivities are (differently) interpellated in the distinctive postcolonial geo-imaginary we call the post–civil rights era without examining the developments in the corners not traditionally considered politically significant, and the spaces, as Foucault usefully reminds us, not formally linked with the state.

THROUGH THICK AND THIN

In the previous chapter, I considered the changes in the cultural realm, particularly the densification of the visual channel, that coincided with and contributed to the emergence of a black superpublic distinct from the counterpublic, which itself had been reformatted in the late 1960s and early 1970s (i.e., nation time). Here I want to mark in more detail the impossibility, suggested by these developments, of representing a coherent black subject and to trace the workings of the respectability discourses that, albeit ambivalent at their margins, both disavow and depend on cultural politics.

In particular, the focus will be on the linkages between pursuits of black interiority and the forms of black solidarity that subsequently emerge. Specifically, two broad categories of solidarity can be distinguished in the post-1965 period. The first refers to those sensibilities that accord a strategic value to black solidarity while anticipating the transcendence of race and its supportive structures (i.e., the modernity/coloniality complex with its related hegemonic and suppressed conceptual fields). These projects also seek to challenge and disrupt conservative constructions of the relationship among the properties of race, sexuality, gender, class, and nationality. Performances of black interiority, according to this perspective, provide an opportunity for the articulation of solidaristic commitments that contain within them always the thickly cosmopolitan, aspirations toward the convivial, and means by which private spaces might be rendered usefully public. In contrast, thinner conceptions of black solidarity, operating as a sort of default position, are promoted in response to the realization that blacks continue to be marginalized on the basis of race and tend to be defensive (if not simply accommodationist or overtly opportunistic). For those committed to this second matrix of practices and performances, black solidarity entails the containment or exclusion of those invested in the substantively deliberative, and the suppression and derogation of black interiorities that reveal the possible means by which postcoloniality might be imagined, mapped, and realized. This second tendency correlates with the circulation and promotion of respectability discourses and attempts to represent black community as a closed, coherent and manageable text. Much of the interesting work in the post–civil rights era occurs on the borders distinguishing these two conceptions of black solidarity; it is this underlying tension between the thick and thin that constitutes the main fault line within contemporary black discourse and politics.[36]

To understand the patterns of these new contestabilities, it is worth revisiting the debate regarding the proper status of gender roles within black literature and thought that followed the publication of Alice Walker's *Color Purple* in 1982 and the release of the film based on the book three years later. In a remarkable article in the *New York Times*, Mel Watkins essentially cast Walker and other black women writers who highlighted gender discrimination within black communities as race traitors:

> [The] black women writers who have chosen black men as a target have set themselves outside a tradition that is nearly as old as black American literature itself. They have, in effect, put themselves at odds with what seems to be an unspoken but almost universally accepted covenant among black writers . . . the commitment to rectify the antiblack stereotypes and propagandastic images created by nonblack writers.

In contrast to the work of Walker, Gayl Jones, Toni Cade Bambara, Gloria Naylor, Ntozake Shange, and the essayist Michele Wallace, Watkins argued that "the primary concern in the fiction of their male predecessors was the oppressive nature of American society," a suggestion that overlooked the misogyny and homophobia in the work of Baraka and Eldridge Cleaver, among others, and the absence of developed female characters in the writings of Richard Wright, Ralph Ellison, and James Baldwin. Watkins added further that in highlighting gender issues, these authors were violating the basic principles of the aesthetic, asserting, "These writers have, in effect, shifted their priorities from the subtle evocation of art to the blunt demonstration of politics and propaganda." Finally, he suggested, "in deciding that sexism is more oppressive than racism," these writers faced the wrath of the wider (presumably ungendered) black community, as indicated by the "irate reaction by a large segment of the black population—readers as well as writers and critics." In Watkins's analysis, we can see an effort to mark feminist concerns as antagonistic to black solidarity and the promotion of a conception of community that seems to require the exclusion of women's voices and concerns.[37]

The year after the release of *The Color Purple*, a new wave of black filmmaking was launched with the arrival of Spike Lee's *She's Gotta Have It* in 1986, a film that would in a less explicit manner engage many of the same anxieties that marked Watkins's editorial. Loosely based on Zora Neale Hurston's novel *Their Eyes Were Watching God*, the script portrays a female protagonist who has established relationships with three men simultaneously. Shot in black and white and borrowing aesthetics from the independent genre, French *film noir*, and the work of Oscar Micheaux, the movie established an affective nostalgic bridge between the pre–World War II and post–civil rights eras. With regard to its significance, Clyde Taylor notes, "[C]inema history had changed. . . . It was like before *She's Gotta Have It* and after *She's Gotta Have It*."[38]

While the movie represents on the whole a crucial and welcome addition to the black film canon, its treatment of the main character (Nola, played by Tracy Camila Johns) and questions of gender in general are problematic. As Mark Reid observes, "Lee's construction of Nola resembles a patriarchal design: the sexually and mentally dispossessed woman whose body is a conquered terrain where men game, hunt, and create territorial boundaries through dating, marriage, and paternity.... If he intended Nola to embody a sexually independent attitude, then his film fails."[39] In the journal Lee kept during the writing and making of the screenplay, there is ample evidence that he was aware of the ways his work might be read, and was struggling to tell the story he was committed to without producing an antifeminist text: "It's important to me that I not exploit women in this film."[40]

Specifically, Lee was having trouble finding an appropriate resolution for the screenplay, a narrative device by which the text might be energized and its borders established. "Maybe for the end scene," he writes, "Nola is upset. She calls her man on the phone [Jamie, played by Tommy Hicks]. He shows up. She's all over him, but he's not bringing it. 'What do you want?' 'Ya know, fuck me.' 'What?' 'Fuck me.' He shakes his head and walks out the door." After having completed this draft, he acknowledges in a conversation he has with a friend, "I still don't know [how the movie ends]. I'm gonna really have to think about this one." The final draft would involve Jamie raping Nola. The scene itself is staged and shot in such a manner as to draw the viewer's attention away from what has actually happened. Besides an acknowledgment of her discomfort—"You're hurting me"—and her tears, Jamie and Nola barely recognize the assault. Indeed, when Nola refers to the incident in conversation with her best friend, she says, "I think I might have really fucked up this time," as if she is to blame for teasing Jamie and bringing about the end of their relationship. After the encounter between Nola and Jamie, Lee writes in the script, "[Nola] decides it's Jamie she truly loves. ... Now you know I'm playing [with] dynamite with this subject matter." This is followed by a restatement of his earlier concern, this time in capital letters: "IT'S IMPORTANT THAT THE CHARACTER OF NOLA DARLING NOT BE EXPLOITED."[41]

Despite Lee's remonstrations, given the nature of the story, it is hard not to read the intended message as being that women who deviate from the assumed codes of respectability should be punished. In this way, a protofeminist text like Hurston's is restaged in a manner that reasserts patriarchal privilege. In his journal, Lee states, "On the second draft, Jamie might have to apologize for the way he boned the hell out of her. He should feel sorry for it, and Nola should mention it also. It shouldn't be like she thought it was all right." More than a decade later, Lee would use different language to describe Jamie's transgression and express regret for including the scene. When asked if there were anything in his previous films he would change, the director replied,

> I would take the rape scene out of *She's Gotta Have It*. Rape is obviously a very violent act, and I just wish I hadn't put the scene in. It brought a lot of things into the picture that didn't belong there, and it just wasn't necessary. It was my ignorance at the time that put it there. . . . I'm 41 now. I was 24 [actually he was 27] when I wrote that script.[42]

As Toni Cade Bambara suggests, Lee's thick engagement of black life in Brooklyn undoubtedly led viewers to grant him some leeway, in terms of the messages he promoted:

> [W]itting and unwitting defenders of patriarchy champion Spike Lee films. . . . So do many progressives . . . because many extratextual elements figure into the response. Hunger for images is one element; pride in Lee's accomplishment is another. . . . Many spectators are willing to provide the interrogation missing in the representations on screen because of progressive features.

"[D]espite . . . Nola Darling's being raped into submission," argues Michele Wallace, "*She's Gotta Have It* became an instant black classic by default. There was no competition." Besides the linked fate solidarities that black firsts can usually depend on and the ways underserved markets will at least initially celebrate almost any product designed to satisfy their needs, two other (intratextual) factors help explain the film's warm acceptance: the film's abundant sense of humor (largely embodied in the persona of Mars Blackmon, the character Lee plays) and its saturation with visual images suggesting a certain unfiltered activist black consciousness at work (e.g., the pictures of King, Bob Marley, and Malcolm and references to the antiapartheid struggle, and the fact that Lee had final cut privileges, which few directors, regardless of race, can exercise). It is the combination of the latter factors and the way Nola Darling is scripted that makes *She's Gotta Have It* such an intriguing, significant, yet ambivalent and disturbing template with regard to the making of contemporary black film and, more generally, black popular culture.[43]

Corresponding developments occurred in black popular music, as the distinctions between rap and rhythm and blues were being reconfigured as a gendered divide, with hip-hop being cast as a space for men and authentic political debate and R & B as the proper space for women and private sphere negotiations. Whereas earlier generations of rap had featured women in creative roles, late second- and early third-generation hip-hop—that is, hip-hop produced after the release of the paradigm-shifting singles "Planet Rock" and "The Message" in 1982—was almost uniformly constructed by men. This regendering of black popular music was most obvious in the work of Public Enemy, an audio collective engaged in the same sentimental economy as Spike Lee.[44] The group's first album, *Yo! Bum Rush the Show* (1987), featured a track entitled "Sophisticated Bitch" that criticized upwardly mobile black women for failing to give sufficient attention to black men. Their second album, *It Takes a Nation of Millions to Hold Us Back* (1988), a brilliant, near genius, experiment in the relationship between noise and nationalist politics, was—simultaneously and not remarkably—a blueprint for the remasculinization of the texts of black politics and the community's public spaces. Carlton Douglas "Chuck D" Ridenhour notes, "We believe[d] in the concept 'hate at first love.' We *intentionally* made records that girls [would] hate and once they hated it, we knew we had some shit." Taken as a whole, Public Enemy and *Nation* sold an appealing, even thrilling, politics that required as the price of the ticket the banishment of women (and some men) from black deliberative arenas.[45]

While this gender-based discourse would play out within rap, it would be more obviously expressed in the tension between R & B and hip-hop, with hip-hop's resistance to the sorts of fluidity characteristic of R & B. In this matrix, Luther Vandross's recordings, connecting as they did the soul era, the disco period, and 1980s R & B, mark him as a bit of a soul rebel, as he insisted on maintaining a public space for the performance of black male vulnerability. As he observed, "The female singer who wants to be gruff and convincing, she will tend to go ahead and do that quicker than a male singer will soften up and become sensitive. That's society, that's rearing, that's the package. I *refuse* to buy into that." If the falsetto was read as an attempt to transcend existing expectations of gender performance, it is not surprising, then, that Prince, who had been a cutting-edge artist at the beginning of the 1980s, would find himself pushed against the ropes by the end of the decade.[46] The Atlanta-based group Cameo also explicitly engaged the issue of the relationship between gender and musical genre in this period. In 1985, the group released a video for its R & B success "Single Life" that featured the group's lead singer Larry Blackmon at the altar in church in a wedding dress preparing to marry a woman dressed in a tuxedo and then stripping down to a black leather outfit and abandoning the ceremony. In the song's lyrics, Blackmon offers, "I don't want anybody to get the wrong idea about me; I've got nothing to hide; I want the world to see." The video for the group's next single, "Word Up," featured Blackmon in a distinctive red codpiece that became with time the group's trademark. At the same time that the band sought to expand the range of available images of black masculinity, it also incorporated aspects of hip-hop culture, including, most prominently, rapping (e.g., its 1984 hit "She's Strange") and a drum and guitar sound that resembled early recordings by Run-DMC and LL Cool J. In the lyrics of "Word Up," though, Blackmon would disparage "sucker deejays" for "acting like fools." It can be assumed that, like Prince, the group's members recognized in the dominant forms of hip-hop a threat to the sorts of narrative and textual undecidability that were still possible in mid-1980s black music.

The singjay tradition—rappers singing, often off-key—then, emerged within hip-hop as a dissident practice and as a means for providing men within the genre an opportunity to signal interiority and display some degree of vulnerability (as well as rejecting technical expertise as a priority). Borrowing directly from the repertoire of Jamaican deejays, rappers such as Slick Rick, Biz Markie, Q-Tip and Phife of A Tribe Called Quest, and later the Wu-Tang Clan's Ol' Dirty Bastard sang lyrics—usually drawn from old or current R & B tunes—to signify a kind of openness that rapping generally prohibited. Another mode was the recorded tearful breakdown: a device commonly engaged by the Wu-Tang Clan's Dennis "Ghostface Killa" Coles.[47]

Beyond the resistance to singing, particularly falsetto vocalizing, and dancing—outside of the militarized rituals characteristic of hip-hop—the urgency associated with the genre as a whole and the impatience with R & B technique can be understood as a response to the substantive imprecision of mainstream black music. Where R & B was aspiring to timelessness (and "the classic"), hip-hop celebrated detail, precision, and ephemerality, in a manner that rendered melody and the aesthetic (traditionally understood) less important. The combination of these tensions between hip-hop and R & B became the symbol for a number of other polarities that became conflated in the late 1980s and early 1990s. Hip-hop logically, then, became linked with the preservation of masculine privilege, youth, heterosexuality, lower-income status, and to some extent Islam (whether of the Five Percent, Nation of Islam, or orthodox variety). Rhythm and blues would be seen as the locus for the formation of feminine identities, the articulation of a black bourgeois sensibility, and the practice of Christianity. In the context of these broader developments, younger black women who listened to rap and older black men who listened to R & B were rendered queer.[48]

Black radio initially resisted playing any rap (except for those R & B tracks that featured a rapper as ornamentation), and some stations went so far as to announce their intention to play "all the hits and no rap," a declaration that had overlapping gender, class, and generational subtexts. By the early 1990s, things changed dramatically, as a number of black radio stations shifted their attentions toward a markedly younger demographic that was engaged by rap and only listened to R & B that was filtered through a hip-hop sensibility (e.g., Teddy Riley's new jack swing and the general sound of Andre Harrell's Uptown label).[49] Although generational differences had long marked black radio programming—for instance in the distinctions between blues-oriented stations and jazz outlets and the (adult) hard soul versus (youth-oriented) soft soul splits of the early and mid-1960s—a relatively dramatic reconfiguration occurred in the early 1990s that correlated with the marginalization of the particular black cultural economy, often represented as "soul," that had been hegemonic since the late 1960s.[50]

Another major contributor to the explicitly gendered, and to a certain extent generational and classed, discourse within black popular culture in this period was the emergence of crack cocaine. Crack was the first drug that more women consumed than men. It would, as a result, produce a range of images and stereotypes that were sex specific—the crack whore, the crack mother, the crack baby—and provide, for some, a justification for writing off a cohort of women as insatiable, addicted, and beyond salvation. As Michele Wallace has noted, the female crack addict appears as a common trope in black film in the late 1980s and early 1990s and coincides with the emergence of young black male film directors (e.g., *Fresh*, *Sugar Hill*, *Menace II Society*, *Boyz 'n the Hood*, *New Jack City*, *Clockers*, *Jungle Fever*, and *Losing Isaiah*).[51] The black women who use narcotics in these movies (and offer sex in exchange for money) are uniformly undeveloped characters lacking histories or explanations. In contrast, the role Chris Rock plays in *New Jack City* (Pookie, who struggles with his addiction to crack) is understandable, multidimensional, and humanized. The effect of these gendered constructions was to naturalize the deviance of a certain class of black women and mark them as unworthy of our investment and attention; and to add the crack house as a specific geographical articulation to the list of the abnormal exceptional (e.g., the colony, the prison, the brothel, the ghetto, the asylum).[52] These developments registered in black popular music as well and triggered a critical response from a number of rappers. "Yo Chuck, they must be on the [crack] pipe," exclaims Public Enemy's Flavor Flav, in reference to the group's critics in "Don't Believe the Hype." Also featured on *It Takes a Nation of Millions to Hold Us Back* is "Night of the Living Baseheads," which was accompanied with a long-form video that featured the comedian Chris

Thomas and was partly set in a crack house. The lyrics contained an extended critique of crack abusers—the "comatose walking around"—and particularly dealers who "sell to their own."[53] In contrast to previous generations of artists' characteristic responses to the situation of the drug-addicted—for example, the Gil Scott-Heron and Brian Jackson recordings "Home Is Where the Hatred Is," "The Bottle," and "Angel Dust" and Richard Pryor's "The Wino and the Junkie"—there were few sympathetic portrayals of the crack addict (and even fewer of the female crack addict).[54]

The transgendered background these developments created provided the conditions of possibility for the class-coded recasting of black communities in film (and vice versa). In *She's Gotta Have It*, the treatment of Mars Blackmon—who represents hip-hop and its assumed lower-income origins—and the playful resistance to this character, as indicated by the tension between his sympathetic depiction and the jazz score and black classical aesthetics underpinning the project as a whole, presents a slightly ambivalent engagement of the contemporary black working class. A more explicit exploration of class differences takes place in Spike Lee's second film, *School Daze* (1988). In one scene, the "Fellas," the crew of lower-middle-class male students around whom the film is centered, go off campus to a fast food outlet. Inside the restaurant they encounter four male residents of the community surrounding Mission College, the fictional all-black institution (based on Lee's experiences at Morehouse) at which the movie is set. Whereas these Mission students are less wealthy than most of their antagonists on campus, off campus they are made aware of their relative class privilege. A minor dispute over access to a salt shaker leads to the local men baiting the college students (by suggesting that Mission men have a reputation for being homosexual), followed by a face-to-face confrontation outside the restaurant. Dap, played by Laurence Fishburne, asks one of the other group of men, "Brother, what do you want?" One of the group replies, "We ain't kin," while another, Leeds (played by Samuel L. Jackson), adds, "And we're not your brothers." At this point, Dap suggests that bigger forces are at play—"You got a legitimate beef, but it's not with us"—and tries to invoke a linked fate interpretation of their relationship. Rejecting this attempt at a form of solidarity, Leeds questions Dap's racial credentials, a move that provokes, for the first time in this scene, Dap to lose his temper: "Don't *ever* question whether I'm black. In fact, I was gonna ask your country, BAMA ass, why do you put those Jerri-curl, drip-drip chemicals in your black nappy hair? . . . And on top of that, come out in public with these plastic shower caps on your heads." "Just like a bitch," one of Dap's colleagues chimes in. Returning to his earlier thesis, Leeds states, "I betcha you niggers think y'all are white. College don't mean shit, you'll always be niggers, always, just like us!" "You're not niggers," responds Dap with a hint of sadness in his voice, and a silent pause follows, suggesting that some profound border has been crossed.[55]

In this scene, as with the treatment of Mars in *She's Gotta Have It*, it is apparent that Lee is committed to a form of solidaristic politics (that extends beyond just class differences) but at the same time is unable to identify wholeheartedly with the black working class. The restaurant scene is written and shot in such a way as to make it clear that both Dap and Lee consider class differences among blacks worrisome. That said, in both films, blacks outside of the middle class are cast as jokers (in the case of Mars) or clowns (in the case of Leeds and his colleagues). In the script notes, Lee describes the neighborhood residents as "a group of local yokels. . . . All six wear Jerri curls, some have those plastic caps on their heads to keep their curls moist. (Look like shower caps but in loud, bright colors)."[56] Besides the fact that Jerri curls were hardly a fashion statement unique to the black working classes, the scene is set up in such a way as to establish the Fellas as the sympathetic characters and to make the locals look unnatural. Overall, it is evident that Lee, by including this scene—given that it does not contribute significantly to the film's overall plot—wants to highlight class differences as a problem. Nevertheless, his attempt at solidarity is undermined by his inability to render the local residents as recognizable human beings (as opposed to caricatures). Furthermore, the class negotiations in Lee's early movies inevitably take place at the expense of women, gays, and lesbians (i.e., the ritualistic references to "bitches" and the gay-baiting that occurs in this scene).[57]

YESTERDAY WILL MAKE YOU VERY HAPPY

One of the primary means by which solidarity was facilitated and maintained within African American communities, and particularly within the arenas of formal political exchange, was a studied silence with regard to the issue of class, and nostalgia provided an important avenue for the imagining of a unified sepia polity. Specifically, in the second half of the 1980s, and arguably partly in response to the emergence of the black superpublic, an extended engagement with aspects of the past was initiated. Traces of this broader campaign were visible in the work of William Julius Wilson and his reconstruction of a functional black urban past in his 1987 publication *The Truly Disadvantaged*. "Blacks in Harlem," he wrote, and in other ghetto neighborhoods did not hesitate to sleep in parks, on fire escapes, and on rooftops during hot summer nights. . . . There was crime . . . but it had not reached the point where people were fearful of walking the streets at night. . . . There were single-parent families, but they were a small minority of all black families and tended to be incorporated within extended family networks. . . . [U]nlike the present period, inner-city communities prior to 1960 exhibited the features of social organization—including a sense of community, positive neighborhood identification, and explicit norms and sanctions against aberrant behavior. . . . The very presence [of the black middle and working classes] provided stability to inner-city neighborhoods and reinforced and perpetuated mainstream patterns of norms and behavior.[58]

Wilson's recollections were hardly unique. "While we were terribly poor," Jesse Jackson has stated with regard to his own childhood,

the black neighborhoods were economically integrated. Had to be, the better-off didn't have anywhere else they could go. So you could live in our class but have the benefits of being among all kinds of classes. Teachers down there [on the one hand, while over] in this alley, a whole other subculture—people back in here selling bootleg liquor, fight[ing] on the weekend, go[ing] to jail.

On the same theme, Coleman Young has written with regard to Detroit,

We never locked our doors when we lived in Black Bottom. . . . I loved that old neighborhood. Inevitably, the black neighborhoods . . . took in a vast range of social and economic types within the race. As one of the largest and boomingest black neighborhoods in the North, Black Bottom was a thrilling convergence of people, a wonderfully versatile and self-contained society. It was degenerate, but not without a lofty level of compassion. It was isolated, but sustained by its own passion. It was uneducated, but teeming with ideas. It was crowded, but clean. It was poor, for the most part, but it was fine.[59]

There is a certain inevitability regarding these kinds of narratives, given that every generation eventually looks backward for its golden age in search of innocence, reassurance, and clarity. Nostalgic sojourns are, in a sense, understandable efforts to touch base with one's roots. Sometimes, though, the motivations can be a bit more sinister—to introduce an idealized past into a much more complex and troubling future in order to establish a "history without guilt"—and as Homi Bhabha observes, "[D]enial is always a retroactive process."[60] There is, Gerald Early contends, "an intense sentimentality in American life, a yearning for a fantasized, idealized past of racial grandeur and simplicity. This sentimentality appeals powerfully to the black middle class, which yearns for a usable, untainted past." He adds, "A significant number of . . . blacks . . . want, strangely, to go back to an era of segregation, a fantasy time between 1920 and 1955, when . . . blacks felt unified and strong because black people were forced to live together." Similarly, Adolph Reed argues that much of this nostalgia is class-interested, and reflects a "wish for a world that is simpler and settled in ways that clarify and consolidate the status of the upper middle class as the social order's presumptive center." He also proposes—referring specifically to William Julius Wilson's sociology, Harold Cruse's *Plural but Equal*, Clifton Taulbert's novel *Once upon a Time When We Were Colored*, and Henry Louis Gates Jr.'s memoir *Colored People*—that in yearning for the communal arrangements of the pre–civil rights era, the proponents of this nostalgia might be promoting a politics that "serves reactionary and frankly racist interests in the present."[61]

Reed is correct to highlight the class-driven nature of much of this reminiscing. We might also consider the possibility that other desires might be at work: for example, a yearning for a "simpler" sexual order, a more hierarchical generational arrangement, and other factors that are not solely reducible to class analysis.[62] It should also be noted that individuals from lower-income backgrounds, and here one can include Jesse Jackson and William Julius Wilson, have also expressed such sentiments (perhaps because they were able to move on to enjoy more secure economic circumstances and may regret not having the opportunity to experience the status among blacks that earlier middle- and upper-class cohorts took for granted). Reed's second claim, that nostalgia for the pre–civil rights era might have inadvertent racist implications for African Americans in the present, also is convincing. On this point, though, one might be able to distinguish northern and southern experiences, and nostalgia for the pre–civil rights era from the yearning for the immediate post–civil rights era (the late sixties and early seventies). Regarding the gap between northern and southern experiences, nostalgia for the pre–civil rights era extends as well to northern black communities (e.g., the memories invoked by Wilson and Coleman Young), which were certainly not as constrained by explicit, formal racial codes as those in the South.

With respect to the second distinction, in *The Death of Rhythm and Blues*, Nelson George expresses sentiments similar to those of Wilson, Jesse Jackson, Kweisi Mfume, and the others, but his yardstick is the quality of black music, and his "golden era" extends into the 1970s: "As a musical genre, a definition of African American culture, and the code word for our national identity, soul has pretty much been dead since Nixon's reelection in 1972." Given that de jure segregation was largely absent throughout the country by this period, late 1960s–early 1970s nostalgia escapes the criticism that such indulgences might inadvertently inspire contemporary agents of racism and (re)segregation. In other words, while 1970s nostalgia has been energized by an older tradition of yearning (for the supposed cohesion of black communities in the pre–civil rights era), it is worth marking the difference between the two eras. The post–civil rights era, shaped by the white backlash of the mid-1960s and the ramifications of the Vietnam war, was clearly and consciously freer of the restrictions of explicit state-sponsored, institutionalized racism.[63]

The nostalgic turn that took place, then, in the late 1980s was also a reflection of a desire to return to "nation time." "Somebody brought the 70s back, damn it feels good to be black," suggested one mid-1990s R & B song, and the implication was clear: "blackness" twenty years later did not always "feel that good."[64] Prompted by the combination of the dislocating effects of the Reagan revolution, the transition from the seemingly pacific and heroin-saturated to the brutal calculations of the crack cocaine–energized, the real income stratification that was developing within African American communities, and the apparent inability of black leaders and communities to respond in any coordinated manner to these changes, the late 1960s and early 1970s looked like an attractive oasis. It is in this matrix that we might understand Spike Lee's *Crooklyn* (1994), Matty Rich's *Inkwell* (1994), the Hughes brothers' *Dead Presidents* (1995), and Mario Van Peebles's *Panther* (1995), which all represented, albeit in slightly different ways, a desire to revisit and reinhabit the early postcolonial.

In the musical arena, Public Enemy's work represents an accurate reflection of this nostalgic urge. The cover of *It Takes a Nation,* which features Chuck D and Flavor Flav behind prison bars, besides being a solidaristic gesture of sorts toward the increasing numbers of (mostly lower-income) black men who were incarcerated, also refers to the artwork for James Brown's 1971 release *Revolution of the Mind: Live at the Apollo Volume III* and to Brown's work, in general, in its thorough reliance on samples drawn from his archives. The project can also be seen as an homage to the Wattstax concert. The introduction to "Rebel without a Pause" is drawn from Jesse Jackson's speech at the show ("Brothers and sisters, I don't know what this world is coming to!"), and Rufus Thomas's utterance—"Now here's what I want y'all to do for me"—prefaces "Don't Believe the Hype." "Night of the Living Baseheads" includes another Thomas voicing ("Wait a minute"), as well as William Bell saying, "We're gonna get down now." Finally, the Bar-Kay's statement "Freedom is a road seldom traveled by the multitude" can be heard at the beginning of *It Takes a Nation*'s "Show 'Em What You Got." "It was the soul in the voices," suggests Chuck D, "that's what we were after. . . . Back when we made those first Public Enemy records . . . at that time Black music was hurtin' for soul. All the soul had been squeezed out. Everything had become smoothed out. It was all champagne and caviar, so you couldn't get any soul out of R & B." It is worth remarking that this attempt to reconstitute soul bypassed the singing voices in evidence at the 1972 concert in favor of the exhortative and excluded from consideration women as well.[65]

Late 1960s and 1970s jazz, funk, and soul samples also gave life to much of this period's rap and R & B. As Public Enemy recreated Wattstax—and *Wattstax*— in its construction of *It Takes a Nation*, Cannonball Adderley's album *Country Preacher,* recorded in 1969 at Operation Breadbasket's headquarters in Chicago, became a popular source of samples in the early 1990s. "Footprints," a track on A Tribe Called Quest's first album, *People's Instinctive Travels and the Paths of Rhythm,* included an extract from Jackson's introductory speech ("you got to walk tall, walk tall, walk tall"). The title track from the Adderley session, "Country Preacher," provided the introduction for Pete Rock and C. L. Smooth's "Return of The Mecca," with the rap duo translating the Christian texts of the original into an invocation of the Islamic. And Paul "the Large Professor" Mitchell would rerecord a third track from the quintet's set, the Adderley original "Hummin.'" That *Wattstax* and the *Country Preacher* recordings were referenced in this manner speaks to their significance as examples of the fusion of the political and the musical, and a more obvious solidaristic disposition. Other means by which nostalgic sentiment for nation time was communicated included the articulation of the neosoul movement within R & B; the recording of cover versions; making sartorial references (e.g., the reemergence of the Afro); and the intentional incorporation of background static and turntable noises on recordings in the post–analog era to signal resistance to the digital regime.[66]

The explicit struggle over gender roles in the early 1990s—that is, the issues and conflicts aired in the wake of the Clarence Thomas nomination— also contributed to the nostalgic urge, the longing for and romanticization of earlier periods among certain constituencies. As Angela Davis has written,

> [T]he televised confrontation between Clarence Thomas and
> Anita Hill symbolically represented the passing of a conception of
> community with which many [blacks had] lived. I experienced it
> both as a loss and as an emancipation. . . . This is why my mother,
> who politically identified with Anita Hill, also felt compelled to
> embrace and protect Clarence Thomas. . . . [S]he now finds herself
> in an untenable situation.

Consequently, it was not surprising that some of the retrospective considerations of black life in the immediate post–civil rights era read the earlier
relative silence on gender issues as a reflection of gender parity and harmony.
Consider the sentiments the recording artist Me'Shell NdegéOcello expresses
on "I'm Diggin You (Like an Old Soul Record)," from her first album, *Plantation
Lullabies* (1993), which offers a number of odes reminiscing about the supposedly healthier state of male-female relationships, and mind, in 1970s black
America:

> Remember back in the day, when everyone was black and down for
> the struggle. Love brought us together . . . cultivating a positive vibe,
> blue lights in the basement, freedom was at hand and you could just
> taste it! Everything was cool . . . and brothers were singing "Ain't No
> Woman (Like the One I Got)."

NdegéOcello's recollections—"Ain't No Woman (Like the One I've Got)" was
a hit for the Four Tops in 1973—are striking because they suggest a blissful
peace between the sexes while ignoring the clear-cut male orientation of the
politics and culture of the era (and because she was dubious about such claims
in some of her other work and in her public pronouncements). NdegéOcello
was hardly alone, though, in her attempts to retrieve simplicity out of the jaws
of complexity.[67]

SOCIAL WORK IN NEW TIMES

Beyond the investment in nostalgic maneuvers, there was a second way hip-
hop, in the aggregate, sought to maintain class solidarity—to manage class
differences—and avoid the fragmentation of the genre and, by extension, the
representations of the broader community. It is in this context that the work
of De La Soul is important. Up until the release of their first album, *Three Feet*

High and Rising, in 1989, it was assumed that hip-hop was largely the work of working-class black and Hispanic youth in the Bronx and Manhattan (i.e., specifically Harlem) first, and subsequently in the other boroughs, parts of the tristate area (including New Jersey and Connecticut), and Philadelphia. The references in the lyrics of the first two generations of rap were to urban spaces and concerns—"The Message" by Grandmaster Flash and the Furious Five being the most familiar example. "Potholes in My Lawn," the second single released from De La's first album, signaled a break from this tradition. "Being where we were," group member Kelvin Mercer observes, "there was just more room for you to try different things. . . . There wasn't the city congestion." Dave Jolicoeur adds, "Hip-hop was something that we had the opportunity to digest from afar. . . . If we had grown up in the Bronx, De La Soul definitely wouldn't have been the same."[68] Over the course of the two decades following the first indications of mainstream interest in rap music—that is, the crossover success of Run DMC, LL Cool J, and the (all-white) Beastie Boys—an interesting deliberation about the relationship between race and class unfolded. At the heart of these discussions was the question of authenticity: who could legitimately speak for the broader (imagined) black community? If class differentiation among blacks was increasing, could any one voice speak for the whole? Given these changes, would the assumptions underlying the linked fate identifications of earlier periods survive?

Given these norms, De La Soul's playing out, their deliberate performance, of suburban black authenticity—for example, by means of their black neobohemian aesthetic—was striking. This is not to suggest that the group's members were the first products of the black middle class to participate in the hip–hop genre. Many of the most prominent acts of the second and third generation were from the outer edges of Queens—for example, Run DMC and LL Cool J—or called Long Island home: Eric B and Rakim ("It ain't where you're from; it's where you're at"), Biz Markie, EPMD, Keith Murray, Craig Mack, Freddie Foxx, and Public Enemy.[69] The difference between De La, and most of the Native Tongues collective that emerged in the wake of their success (e.g., the Jungle Brothers and A Tribe Called Quest), and these other groups was the willingness to be specific about their class backgrounds.

It is important to note that class differences among blacks are rarely as clear and cut-and-dried as the terms *middle-class* and *working-class* might suggest. As Mary Pattillo illustrates in *Black Picket Fences*, the black middle classes often reside in neighborhoods that are mixed income and adjacent to lower-income constituencies, and "residents of black middle-class neighborhoods share schools, grocery stores, hospitals, nightclubs, and parks with their poorer neighbors, ensuring frequent interaction within and outside the neighborhood."[70] Furthermore, black families are more often economically heterogeneous, with the result that individuals in the middle-income classes often interact on a regular and personal basis with members of lower-income constituencies.[71] Even black suburban populations tend to be relatively segregated, economically heterogeneous, and less well off in comparison to their white counterparts. Accordingly, Bill Stephney, a Long Island native and production supervisor for Public Enemy's *It Takes a Nation*, states:

> Growing up in Long Island—Howard Stern, Eddie Murphy and
> Jerry Seinfeld grew up around the same time there—our experiences
> as black kids [were] probably far different than black kids growing
> up in the places where hip hop was birthed, like the Bronx and
> Manhattan. Those environments were pretty much all black
> and Latino, whereas we were growing up in a sort of segregated/
> integrated environment, by that I mean the so-called middle-class
> towns that we were growing up in were *sort* of segregated, but we
> were in the middle of this incredible white country. Once you left
> your specific villages you had to interact with white kids from other
> areas who were into all sorts of different music.

Any discussion of class differences within hip-hop, and for that matter among blacks generally, then, has to be sensitive to the fact that these boundaries are porous and the related identities are fluid, overlapping, and interlinked. It is in this context that Public Enemy's promise to "teach the bourgeoise [*sic*] and rock the boulevard" and the group's logo—featuring a silhouette figure framed by rifle sights that suggests that all black males are targets—make sense. The explicit nationalist framework the group espoused required that class differences be bridged rather than acknowledged, reinforced, or exploited.[72]

At the same time, one can read the cover of *It Takes a Nation* and the album as a whole as an attempt by the group's front men to position themselves not just as attentive to the situation of less well-off black males but as an example of the romantic engagements the middle classes can have with lower-income constituencies. Here we might consider the precedents established by Langston Hughes, Zora Neale Hurston, Chester Himes, Miles Davis, LeRoi Jones (aka Amiri Baraka), and Donald Goines as products of the middle class who seek to negotiate—by means of a particular set of performances, and playing under—a space for themselves within the ranks of the supposed black authentic by imagining, engaging, and constructing often extreme representations of black life. Consequently, Phillip Fenty, the author of the screenplay for *Superfly*, relates that he had "always been fascinated with street life . . . pimps and dealers . . . and a whole alternate lifestyle they'd created for themselves." Frederick Brathwaite, aka Fab Five Freddy, a Brooklyn native, the son of lawyers and one of the major players in the popularization of hip-hop during the first and second generations (and subsequently host of *Yo! MTV Raps*), explains his attraction to the Bronx and the early hip-hop venues: "I was a voyeur at the time hip hop was created. . . . You just wanted to be part of that world, hear that sound, just be in a cloud of angel dust smoke, all that energy, just funky perspiration odor, some stick-up kids that could rob you." Similarly, Todd "Too Short" Shaw asserts,

> I was always fascinated with pimps—from the big hats to the
> pimp walks. From an early age I wanted to make sure I was a cool
> muthafucka when I grew up. And I practiced that shit till I perfected
> it. It wasn't like I was doing this . . . because I was starving in the
> projects. I was getting money from my parents—both had good
> jobs and I was sent to private schools for most of my life—but I just
> wanted to be a pimp. The Too Short persona came about through
> a combination of reading Iceberg Slim . . . and from watching '70s
> movies like *The Mack*, *Superfly*, and *Dolemite*."[73]

The black film boom of the 1970s was also responsible for the emergence of another trope in black popular discourse: the cross-pressured black social worker. *The Spook Who Sat by the Door* (1973), *Claudine* (1974), Jamaa Fanaka's *Black Sister's Revenge* (1976), and *A Piece of the Action* (1977), directed by Sidney Poitier, all feature social workers in typically explicitly gendered contexts having to choose whether to identify with, exploit, abandon, or betray "the community." Accordingly, in Bill Gunn's visually arresting and thematically sophisticated *Ganja and Hess* (1973), the black middle classes are portrayed literally as vampires feeding on the blood of the black community. It is against this backdrop that many of the performances engaged by hip-hop artists raised in largely middle-class circumstances were staged. If blackness is defined against middle-class possibilities—or more broadly, if the nigger is constructed in opposition to the citizen—how will those closest to these borders identify, align, and constitute themselves? Indeed, the social worker represents more than an interesting metaphor for the position of the black middle classes, as some of the artists involved in the construction of hip-hop's most recognized mid-period templates were actually members of the guild.[74]

Scott Monroe Sterling, born in 1962 in South Ozone Park, Queens, and with an undergraduate degree from Castleton State College, worked in the mid-1980s in the Franklin Armory Men's Shelter in the Bronx (at 166th Street) supervising the residents of the facility. The young, black social worker also deejayed at the Broadway Repertoire Theatre on 145th Street. One evening he found himself arguing with one of the shelter residents about the subway tokens the shelter provided to its clients so that they might travel to job interviews; Sterling was convinced that some of the younger men were using the tokens for other purposes. Displeased by Sterling's questions, the resident called Sterling a "handkerchief-head house negro, tap-dancing for the white establishment" and a "sellout" who had "nothing to do with black folks." In response, Sterling stated, "You don't even know me. You don't know who I am! All you homeless blacks who want to sit on your ass, you're lazy and you're wasting your life." After a couple of rounds, the angry resident was removed by the shelter's security staff. Subsequently, Sterling ran into the same shelter resident at the apartment of rapper Cedric "Ced Gee" Miller (later of the Ultramagnetic MCs). After that encounter, the two—Sterling and the younger Lawrence "KRS-One" Parker—formed Boogie Down Productions and recorded and released *Criminal Minded,* one of the first gangster rap recordings and a response to what they saw as the increasing commercialism of rap (i.e., the success of Run-DMC). The gangster inflections were Sterling's idea. "The title *Criminal Minded,*" Chris Lighty, a friend of Sterling and later a music industry employee, remembers, "was really his plan. He was like, 'Let's talk about reality, and do what we have to do to get the money, *but not become criminals ourselves.*'" Sterling "gained a *freedom* hanging out with us," Parker recalls.[75]

Another social worker employed in New York was trying to put together a rap group at roughly the same time. Keith Elam, born in Boston in 1961, was the son of the city's first black judge and the chief librarian of the city's public schools. He himself graduated from a prestigious private school and received his undergraduate degree from Morehouse College in 1983 in business. In the late 1980s, he met Christopher Martin, whose parents were both teachers at Prairie View A & M University, and formed the group Gang Starr. With Elam as "Guru" (Gifted Unlimited Rhymes Universal) and Martin as "Premier," the group's deejay, they established a reputation for releasing some of the grimmest, most intense depictions of life on the streets of Brooklyn ("the planet," as Guru would put it). Describing his function, Martin would state,

[C]all me for the street record. That's what I like to represent, the streets is the birthplace [of hip-hop] and that's got to be a major element of the record. Some people can't keep it street and that's all good, but don't try to be street when you're not. It's going to show in your record or it's going to show in your personality when you get approached on the street.

In his own self-presentation and vocal delivery, Elam performed the role of the wizened and reflective street hustler. As his brother, a university professor, observes, "My brother claims not to be from middle class Boston. He's from the Bronx."[76]

Elam would, in fact, claim Brooklyn and Roxbury rhetorically as the spaces that shaped his consciousness and sense of being. This sort of identification is not uniquely his. It is a common practice for individuals, particularly under stress, to identify with a particular geographical space.[77] Hip-hop's geographical specifications, then, should be understood as both a response to the vagueness and generalities of disco and R & B and as an effort by many of its middle-class practitioners to link themselves with broader black communities and draw attention away from their economic origins. Accordingly, Lonnie Rashid "Common" Lynn made frequent reference to the city of Chicago, particularly the South Side, in his work. The son of an educator with a Ph.D. and the product of a private school education, Lynn's negotiations of class identity correlated with his engagements with the city of Chicago in which the "South Side" figured much in the way that "Harlemworld," as described by John Jackson, does: as an almost mythical, magic space in which authentic blackness is produced and maintained. "Chicago is really about the black experience— barbecues, witnessing gangbanging and such," he observed. "You may go to a party where there's preppies or whatever; you may go to a private school; I did. You get a balance of life there: I grew up in the middle-class area, but there was still niggaz doing they dirt." Lynn's assessment of Chicago bespeaks a certain desire for place, "realness," and a version of black community that is almost familial in its operation: "Chicago is where I get my base of people who work for the CTA [Chicago Transit Authority], who work for health clinics, teachers. It's an *authentic* place. If you try to be something other than yourself, Chicago people will let you know real quick that it's not working." At another point, he observes, Chicago "allowed me to grow up in a real place, a very authentic place where there were so many different mixtures of blackness, in a way. . . . Chicago is a blue-collar place. That just gave me a certain authentic vibe, an ordinary people connection." "Chicago," then, becomes the means by which Lynn resolves his own class dilemmas; it is the stage on which he can claim and perform black authenticity. As he notes, "I use a lot of street stuff when I rap 'cause that's how we've been groomed. That's what been put upon us. Sometimes I don't speak my own language. I want to stress this point. I grew up middle class. We was straight. I just had a lot of friends in that street shit." In his public appearances, Lynn characteristically not only performed in the voice of the other but also, in his physical gestures, could be seen trying to embody the other rather earnestly and awkwardly, like a new anthropologist in the field attempting to be both observer and participant (if not lawgiver).[78]

Striking in this context are the ways Lynn characterizes his relationship with the field and its inhabitants. In one interview, he states, "Our parents instilled spirituality as much as they could, but at the same time you still get the nigga element—some rawness in you that you grew up expressing." At another point, speaking of the pressure he feels to produce a certain kind of music, Lynn asserts, "I want the street niggas to respect my music but I can't ever limit what I'm feeling myself." In reference to his fellow Chicagoan and middle-class product Kanye West, and producer James "Jay Dee" Yancey, he says, "They're two soulful beings. Both of them are so creative and still in tune with the ghetto." In other words, in these statements Lynn implies that creativity, spirituality, and individuality are lacking outside of the black middle class and its habitus. Although his work is saturated with a familiar longing for "the ghetto," at the same time this space is seen as bereft of inspiration. These characterizations cohere with his overall sense of his role with regard to the "South Side" and the broader, imagined black community. "When I come home, I just see the response that I get when niggas see me at a store or something. I might go somewhere to get something for my mother, and they like, 'Damn, Common, you up in the hood, man!' *They just feel good.*" These geopolitical identifications, then, provide Lynn not only with a sense of place but a Du Boisian sense of purpose, as well as the materials for the imagining of a reciprocal relationship.[79]

This transfigured Talented Tenth sensibility was also evident in the performances of Sean Combs, one of the dominant personalities in 1990s hip-hop. Born in 1969 in Harlem, Combs articulated a persona that seemed to be rooted in that neighborhood's image. He would invoke the memory of his father, Melvin, a numbers runner and drug dealer who also worked for the Board of Education and drove a cab, who was killed before Combs had reached his third birthday, as evidence of his authenticity and his legitimacy as a product of "Harlemworld."[80] At the same time, "Puff Daddy," as he was known in the mid-

1990s, had been raised in Esplanade Gardens on Lenox Avenue, one of the more upscale parts of Harlem, and moved to suburban Mount Vernon at the age of twelve, where he attended private school (Mount St. Michael's Academy) and lived in a home with a swimming pool in the backyard. It was only after this relocation that he learned the details of his father's activities and the circumstances of his death. He would subsequently attend Howard University before getting involved in the music business as an intern at Uptown Records.

Like many other products of the black middle class, Combs was attracted to what he saw as the authentic black experience: "[I was] always attracted to motherfuckers who were real, niggas who really don't have a lot. . . . I like the sense of being in trouble." At Uptown, Combs groomed the label's most successful R & B acts, Mary J. Blige and Jodeci, to make them more palatable in a market in which hip-hop was becoming dominant and R & B was perceived as the preoccupation of an older, more middle-class-inclined market. After leaving Uptown, Combs established his own label in cooperation with Clive Davis's Arista, Bad Boy, to which he signed Brooklyn native and former drug dealer Christopher "Biggie Smalls" Wallace (who had been rejected by Uptown, which did not see itself as an appropriate home for a gangster rapper). Wallace, who changed his moniker to "the Notorious B.I.G." aka "Biggie Smalls," almost single-handedly reestablished New York as the cutting edge of rap by trading liberally in the gangster aesthetics that had made the West Coast artists the trailblazers (at least in sales records) at the beginning of the decade. As he had at Uptown, Combs sought to create an image for his act that represented the proverbial ghetto. As the photographer who shot one of Wallace's album covers (*Life after Death*, featuring the artist beside a hearse in a graveyard) remembers, "Puffy was in charge of that shoot for sure. He pretty much told Biggie what to do. He was *in control* of Biggie's image, I'd say, pretty much all the way."[81]

The image management worked. As Erick Sermon of EPMD explains,

I could tell . . . that I wasn't going to fit into the [hardcore] realm. Biggie Smalls was so prevalent. That was where the world was going to go to, and everybody followed him. That wasn't my life. I didn't do the stuff they did. I'm from Long Island, you know what I'm saying? I can't contend on that [hardcore] side.

Osten "Easy Mo Bee" Harvey Jr., who produced much of Wallace's first album, *Born to Die*, and was himself a former rap artist (with the group Rappin' Is Fundamental), recalls being intimidated by Biggie's material: "The first time I heard Biggie rhyme it kinda scared me a little. I thought he sounded like the roughest thing in New York. . . . To me, some of his stuff was almost a little too graphic." It is important to note that Wallace himself was the son of a school-teacher, and his upbringing could be described as lower middle class.[82]

Combs also coined the term "ghetto fabulous":

> Ghetto-fabulous! I'm the nigger who started it: I'm the one driving around in the Rolls Royce with his hat turned, goin' down Fifth Avenue with the system booming in the back. Walkin' into Gucci, shuttin' it down, buying everything at the motherfuckin' same time! Driving up to Harlem, out to 125th Street, and on my way back downtown goin' and givin' $100 bills to homeless people. No other nigger out there can say they're ghetto-fabulous; I'm ghetto-fabulous!

The linguistic reference to the communities of the black poor as "fabulous" effectively made economic disadvantage invisible and a matter of individual achievement (and excess) and represented a unique articulation of the linked fate sensibility. The political work Combs's various productions performed is interesting, too. On his own solo albums, as Puff Daddy, he covered one classic hip-hop track, Public Enemy's "Public Enemy No. 1," and sampled liberally from Grandmaster Flash and the Furious Five's "The Message" to create new tracks that replaced the particular political messages of the originals with celebrations of his own achievements and wealth. Similarly, he mounted fashion shows for his clothing line, Sean John, that featured clips of Martin Luther King Jr., Malcolm X, and civil rights demonstrators being attacked with fire-hoses while a black model with "revolution" painted on his back and a white model with "black power" inscribed on his chest worked the runways. Combs's Bad Boy street (i.e., promotional) teams staged mock demonstrations with picket signs to publicize new album releases. Albeit fascinating and at times amusing, the Bad Boy ethos drained black politics of much of its content and resembled the broader society's exploitation of, and fascination with, certain aspects of black culture.[83]

THE CARNIVAL

It was the summer of 1996. A thin, rather hyperactive, thirty-one-year-old black man was pacing back and forth across the stage, his fingers splayed in an awkward fashion, as if the words rushing from his mouth were sending electric charges through his body at the same time. "There's like, a civil war going on with black people, and there's two sides: there's black people . . . and there's niggas. And niggas have got to go!" he pronounced. "Everytime black people want to have a good time, ign'ant ass niggas fuck it up! . . . I love black people, but I hate niggas, brother! Oh, I hate niggas! Boy, I wish they'd let me join the Ku Klux Klan!"[84] This remarkable performance would be taped and rebroadcast on Home Box Office (HBO) repeatedly over the course of the summer. Videocassettes circulated, and excerpts from the show were heard at the proverbial water cooler throughout the subsequent months. It was hardly an unheard-of distinction—that there were different classes of blacks and tensions between them—but rarely had this position been enunciated with such clarity and vigor in public.

Against the broad history of black comedy, and black life for that matter, Chris Rock's articulation of intraracial warfare was groundbreaking. Going back as far as the minstrel shows of the nineteenth century (and undoubtedly before that), black performers were always aware of the demands associated with living life in public in the view of whites and the need to separate public from private transcripts. "[B]ehavioral adjustments forced many African-Americans to assume dual roles," writes Mel Watkins,

> one for a hostile white world, the other the natural demeanor they
> reserved for interactions among themselves. . . . In the privacy of
> completely black settings, black humor was more acerbic and more
> explicitly revealed that evasive, hidden black life . . . a life kept under
> tight wraps. . . . For much of America's past, the two faces of black
> humor could not be combined without serious risk.[85]

The circumstances associated with Jim Crow existence meant that the transgressive character of black comedy had to be restrained or expressed in a particularly clever fashion that would escape white audiences' detection and understanding. While the minstrel aesthetics that predominated in black comedic, and most filmic, performances in mainstream arenas—for example, Bert Williams, Butterfly McQueen, Mantan Moreland, Stepin Fetchit—up until the 1950s could be read (quite properly in some instances) as a mocking of American consumers' lack of self-awareness, they were at the same time so masked that they were unable in any deeply emancipatory fashion to speak to black aspirations. The next generation of black comedians, which included Pigmeat Markham, Moms Mabley, Nipsey Russell, George Kirby, Melvin "Slappy" White, and his one-time partner the blue extraordinaire Redd Foxx, were also hamstrung by the same prohibitions and were compelled to reproduce many of the minstrel conventions in their acts (right though the 1960s in some cases).

It was not until the civil rights era that black comedic efforts would approximate the explicitly carnivalesque. The emergence of Dick Gregory in the early 1960s marked a further development in the articulation of a black public transgressive, building on the examples offered by Andy Razaf and Louis Armstrong ("[What Did I Do to Be So] Black and Blue"), Billie Holiday with her performance of "Strange Fruit," Richard Wright in *Native Son*, and the bebop movement after World War II. "[N]ow I get five thousand dollars a week for saying the same things out loud, I used to say under my breath," Gregory would joke, acknowledging his ability to speak openly about Jim Crow in a way few earlier black comedians had dared (or could afford). Gregory quickly became an activist-comedian and made the absurdities of the American racial status quo his primary source of material.[86]

Gregory would move from performing in clubs on Chicago's South Side to the largely white establishments in the city's downtown Loop district. Unlike his predecessors, he spent very little time paying dues. As he notes with regard to Malcolm X's former colleague Redd Foxx, "As I reflect on Redd's career and compare it with mine I am illegitimate because I didn't have to work the chitterling circuit. I didn't have to stay on the segregated side of town." As Watkins notes, in delivering his social satires, Gregory also dispensed with many of the physical traits and behaviors that marked his predecessors' routines: "a passively slumped shoulder while delivering a punchline, an overly exaggerated widening of the eyes, or an apprehensive glance in search of approval from non-black crowds." While Gregory did not possess the aesthetic qualities or the extensive vaudeville experience the earlier generation of black comics had, his success opened many doors for black comics to perform in front of white audiences and earn the higher fees associated with mainstream venues. Part of a generation of comedians that included Mort Sahl and Lenny Bruce, Gregory used material that was topical and reflected a willingness to challenge the status quo and engage racial taboos. Gregory, who attended Southern Illinois University on a track scholarship, represented the public face of the emerging, increasingly formally educated, black middle class, and other college-educated black comedians emerged in his wake. Bill Cosby would develop a comic persona that avoided racial issues as well as the vaudevillian traditions that shaped the pre-Gregory era, and former premed student Godfrey Cambridge pursued a path in between the two.[87]

The joining of the hidden and public transcripts that had previously remained largely distinct in black life really occurred with the arrival of Richard Pryor on the scene. In contrast to Gregory, whose transgression involved the revelation of black frustration with regard to Jim Crow, Pryor added complexity, absent any explicit concerns about respectability, to the mix. Born in Peoria, Illinois, in 1940, Richard Franklin Lennox Thomas Pryor III was raised in a whorehouse but with middle-class-oriented values. After leaving school in the ninth grade, he eventually established himself as a comedian in the 1960s, working largely in the mode of Bill Cosby (at that time the most popular black comic in the country). Somewhere between 1967 and 1970, Pryor experienced a nervous breakdown of sorts and relocated to Berkeley to reorganize. There, in the company of Ishmael Reed, Cecil Brown, Al Young, Claude Brown, and David Henderson, he developed the material that would establish him as a top writer for Flip Wilson and Redd Foxx, as well as the tendency toward a deep interiority that would make him the best comedian of his (and arguably any) generation. In the wake of Pryor's critical and commercial success, a wave of younger black comedians emerged, including not only Eddie Murphy, who was the most prominent, but also Whoopi Goldberg, Paul Mooney, Chris Rock, and Dave Chappelle. While many of them assimilated the surface textures of Pryor's work, few replicated—and indeed most studiously avoided—his propensity for reflexivity: the ability to "open [himself] up for everybody," as Chappelle puts it, and make private space available to the public in a manner that exposed the modern/colonial relation.[88]

Paralleling these shifting norms in black performance, one of the significant developments over the course of the changes in the black comedic tradition of the post–civil rights era that linked Dick Gregory to Chris Rock was a shift that took place within the discourses related to black class identity. Gregory, whose family depended on public assistance while he was growing up, espoused a class politics that was explicitly solidaristic, at a time when black claims for citizenship relied on assumptions of intraracial unity and collaboration (albeit filtered through the lens of black respectability). At the outset of his autobiography, he writes: "Richard Claxton Gregory was born on Columbus Day, 1932. A welfare case. You've seen him on every street corner in America." In one of his classic routines, he developed a theme that opponents to the abolition of the federal safety net three decades later would pick up:

> The President is willing to give Lockheed $250 million. . . . When it comes to giving welfare layouts to black folks, so many legislators say, "They ought to learn to pull themselves up by their own bootstraps." So I sent the president of Lockheed Aircraft a telegram. . . . "Why don't you learn to pick yourself up by your own landing gear?" I just can't understand Lockheed asking for all that welfare money and they don't even have any illegitimate planes!'"[89]

The real break came with the post–civil rights generation of black comics, those who came of age after the struggle for voting rights and social equality. Edward Regan Murphy, who was born in Brooklyn in 1961 in the Bushwick projects, moved at the age of ten to Roosevelt, Long Island, where he grew up along with many members of Public Enemy's Bomb Squad. Aware of the distance blacks had traveled since the civil rights era, Murphy joked during a concert taping at Constitution Hall in Washington, D.C., that he was getting paid as a twenty-two-year-old black man to "hold his dick" in the same venue where Marian Anderson was barred from performing in 1939. In many respects, his biography reflects the neither-rich-nor-poor, always-one-or-two-checks-away-from-insolvency circumstances of the black middle classes. Murphy's performances in *Delirious* and subsequently *Raw* speak to these roots and are reflective of this in-between sensibility. A skit in the earlier concert film depicts a group of pre-adolescents mocking a child who does not have the money to buy anything from the ice cream man driving through the neighborhood ("You are on the welfare; you can't afford it"). When the protagonist, a young Eddie Murphy, drops his own ice cream in the process of dancing and singing and making fun of the child, his situation reflects that of the insecure black middle class. We are meant to wonder here if he has the money to buy another ice cream cone (he does not) and how different his family's economic circumstances are from those of the child who is "on the welfare." Young Eddie picks up the cone and starts to eat it again, remarking that if it had fallen in dog waste he still would have retrieved it (thereby underlining the kinds of choices children in his cohort have to make and their status anxiety). In *Raw*, his subsequent concert feature, there are skits referencing "welfare green pepper burgers"—the familiar, homemade sandwich one's mother makes with the grease turning the bread red and soggy—and a surreal skit about the poor circumstances in which his stepfather grew up (involving, remarkably, the need and capacity to eat children's toys).[90]

Murphy's most explicit engagement of class politics came in the form of *The PJs*, a half-hour "foamation" sitcom situated in a housing project ("the Hilton-Jacobs projects," alluding to actor Lawrence Hilton-Jacobs, who appeared in the movies *Claudine* and *Cooley High* and the sitcom *Welcome Back, Kotter*). The show featured the building's janitor, Thurgood Orenthal Stubbs (as in Thurgood Marshall and O. J. Simpson), a Haitian voodoo priestess, and Smokey, a crack addict living in a cardboard box (in effect, a claymation Pookie). George Clinton of Parliament/Funkadelic wrote the theme song, Murphy provided the voice of the janitor, and Ja'net Dubois of *Good*

Times did the same for a senior citizen character who was not immune to profanity and vulgarity. The show itself was a significant and visually striking technical achievement. The scripts were at points quite funny, especially in the ways the inefficiencies and irrationalities of the public sector were lampooned (as Thurgood says after he is tear-gassed by employees of the Department of Housing and Urban Development, "And then, like a public school, everything turned black"). At the same time, the show's effect was both to highlight the barriers facing the black poor and to naturalize those conditions (for example, by rendering the show's characters as laughable claymation figures rather than as human beings). Although the building's residents were portrayed as basically moral agents facing a rather inhumane system, the show depended heavily on caricature and stereotype (and in casting the show's characters as lazy and addicted to drugs, cigarettes, and food, implied that their circumstances might be a result of a broader culture of poverty). The show, like Murphy's work in the aggregate, displayed a certain ambivalence with regard to the question of black interclass relations.[91]

In contrast to Murphy's work, Chris Rock's commentary typically included an explicit critique of black lower-income constituencies. Rock, like Spike Lee and Eddie Murphy, grew up as part of the black middle class but in circumstances that correspond to the conditions Pattillo identifies in *Black Picket Fences*. Born in 1965, Rock recalls his immediate neighborhood in Bedford-Stuyvesant on Decatur Street as "the nicest block in the ghetto." At age seven, he was bused to school in Gerretson Beach, a white working-class neighborhood in Brooklyn, and subsequently attended a largely black high school. In common with many of the post–civil rights products of the black middle classes, Rock's comedy reveals an anxiety with regard to the situation of black lower-income cohorts. Moreover, in contrast to the more ambiguous and conflicted self-representations of the black middle class within hip-hop—including the inclination to engage in nostalgic maneuvers and solidaristic identifications—in Rock's work, the desire to distinguish oneself as much as possible from the hyperstigmatized black poor is more obviously detectable.[92]

In common with rap in general, the films of Spike Lee, and Murphy's work, Rock's comedy negotiated a solution to this tension through a rejection of the sorts of radical public introspection that marked Pryor's work—and the engagement of an explicit, unambiguous distrust of women. In *Delirious*, Murphy laments the passage of the "days when you could beat up a woman," and much of his recorded comedic work is saturated with misogyny and homophobia. Regarding his own personal beliefs in this area, Rock states, "Look, men and women are equal. I believe that. But my grandfather and my father treated their women like their daughters. Not quite, but you know, close. And they were happier, I think, because the roles were defined." During his first (and only) appearance on the *Arsenio Hall Show* in 1989, Rock made an extended joke about the improbability of date rape, a routine that compelled Hall to apologize for Rock's appearance during the opening monologue of his next broadcast. In *Bring the Pain*, Rock refers to the O. J. Simpson case and indicates that while he thought murder was inappropriate, he could relate to the former football star's frustration ("I'm not saying he shoulda killed her, but I understand") and observes that though he would never hit a woman, grabbing one's partner and shaking her rather vigorously would be acceptable. Rock's contributions to the war of the sexes are in and of themselves hardly novel and simply represent new twists on routines written and performed by Redd Foxx, Jackie Gleason, Pigmeat Markham, and Murphy, among others; but they represented a sort of foundational work that was necessary for the making of his novel formulations and representations of class politics.[93]

In his extended dissertation on black interclass relations, Rock moved beyond the blacks-versus-niggas metanarrative toward a discussion of the specific issue of welfare. Significant in this context was the timing. Rock was talking on June 1, 1996, at the same time the most recent debates regarding the abolition of welfare reform were taking place in Washington D.C. (where his show was being taped). After castigating those who take, in his view, "credit for some shit they're *supposed* to do," like holding a job, providing for their children, and not going to prison, he asserts, "Black people don't give a fuck about welfare: niggas are shaking in their boots!" He went on to identify with what he imagined to be the frustrations of the average working black man and woman. "Shit, a black man that's got two jobs going to work everyday hates a nigger on welfare. Nigga, get a job, I've got two, you can't get one?" he remonstrated, adding that this man's female counterpart would be no more sympathetic: "A black woman that's got two kids going to work everyday bustin' her ass hates a bitch with nine kids getting welfare. 'Bitch, stop fucking. Put the dick down. Get a job!'" It was also apparent that Rock was aware that he was breaking a taboo and, as a consequence, anticipated some criticism:

> I see some black people looking at me, "Man, why you got to say that? It's the media. . . ." Please cut the fuckin' shit, okay? When I go to the money machine tonight, I ain't looking over my back for the media; I'm looking for niggas! Ted Koppel ain't never took shit from me.

Overall, the obvious interpolation of Ronald Reagan's welfare queen rhetoric could not be any less subtle. We see, then, in Rock's work a version of the carnival that, rather than mocking the pretensions and hypocrisies of the powerful, substitutes a spectacle that turns its attention to the relatively powerless.[94]

In the wake of the show's repeated broadcasts on HBO, Rock would get his own talk show, increased acting opportunities (*Lethal Weapon 4* [1998], *Nurse Betty* [2000], *Down to Earth* [2001], and *Head of State* [2003], among others), spots on *Oprah* and *60 Minutes*, and an offer to host the MTV Awards (and subsequently the Oscars in 2005). His popularity created the same crossover dilemmas that black creative artists (and African Americans in general) had been facing for decades: what did it mean to be celebrated by white audiences and was it possible to satisfy the expectations of both blacks and whites? Quite aware of these challenges, Rock would make reference to the need to "speak two languages . . . and to perform for people who don't look anything like you." That said, Rock deliberately tried to get a black audience for his next concert taping, *Bigger and Blacker*, by performing at the Apollo (the recently reopened entertainment center in the nation's black capital) and not having tickets available for purchase until just before the show (on the assumption that blacks are prone to buying tickets at the last minute).[95]

Rock was also aware that the *Bring the Pain* show might have been his last chance to revive his stalled career and that it was the blacks-versus-niggas/welfare skit that transformed his career ("the skit really helped my career like nothing else") though he feared becoming a "one hit wonder [or] a one joke wonder." The routine crossed over and become popular with white audiences nationally, and in some of the interviews in this period, one can sense that Rock was not completely comfortable with aspects of his popularity. While suggesting "If I had done this same routine in the 1950s, I probably couldn't walk through Harlem because it would be all misconstrued," he argued that the references he made to tensions among blacks were popular among other ethnic groups because they captured a universal sentiment: "Everyone has their own version of it. Italians have their own version of it. Jewish people have their own version of it." The other universal sentiment that might better explain the popularity of this material—the widespread appetite for disparaging tales of the nigger—was overlooked in favor of a much less convincing rationalization.[96]

One of the most significant and telling offers Rock received after the success of *Bring the Pain* was to act as one of *Politically Incorrect*'s commentators for the

1996 conventions (broadcast on Comedy Central). Although he accepted the opportunity, Rock consistently denied that his work was political. "I never think about this stuff in political terms," he stated in one interview, adding, "[P]eople politicized it maybe more than it should have been. It's just jokes man."[97] These claims aside, in *Bring the Pain* and afterward, one can indeed easily detect a certain consciousness—an obvious politics—at work. Consider, for example, his intervention in the debate regarding the meanings of the words "nigger" (and "nigga"). Dick Gregory prefaced his autobiography *Nigger* with the dedication "Dear Momma—Wherever you are, if you hear the word 'nigger' again, remember they are advertising my book." Jokes aside, the word was not one he embraced, as evidenced by his suggestion that when a "white man. . . . calls us a nigger, he's calling us something we are not, something that exists only in his mind. So if nigger exists only in his mind, who's the nigger?" At the beginning of the book, Gregory writes,

> This is a revolution. . . . You didn't die a slave for nothing, Momma.
> . . . Those of us who weren't destroyed got stronger, got calluses on
> our souls. And now we're ready to change a system, a system where a
> white man can destroy a black man with a single word. Nigger. When
> we're through, momma, there won't be any niggers any more.

Indeed, while he used the term as the title of his autobiography and refers to it in the text itself, it did not figure as part of his onstage routines.[98]

It was Richard Pryor who made the word a staple in virtually every black comedic routine and moreover initiated its deployment in front of mixed audiences. Characteristic of his plain-speaking and truth-telling inclinations, for most of his career he uttered "nigger" quite freely and frequently, used it interchangeably with "black," and invoked it as a solidaristic term, an implied signifier of the depressed conditions blacks commonly faced, and a legitimate anthropological category (as in "white folks fuck quiet; niggers make noise"). He famously renounced use of the term in his *Live on the Sunset Strip* concert. With regard to an epiphany—"magic"—he experienced in a hotel lobby during a trip to Kenya in 1979, he recalled:

> It hit me like a shot. Man, I started crying and shit. . . . I've been
> there three weeks and I haven't even said it, I haven't even thought it
> and it made me say, "Oh, my God, I've been wrong, I've been wrong.
> I got to regroup my shit. I ain't never gonna call another black
> man nigger." [applause] Y'know cause we never was no niggers.

That's a word that's used to describe our own wretchedness and we perpetuate it now cause it's dead; that word is dead.

Pryor suggested that his intentions in using the word had been misinterpreted and that it had taken him a long time to recognize that his efforts were in vain. "Yeah, I told myself all those lies," he admitted, and expressed regret for "ever having uttered the word 'nigger' on a stage or off it." "Its connotations weren't funny, even when people laughed," he added. "I felt its lameness. It was misunderstood by people. They didn't get what I was talking about. Neither did I." In his reversal on this issue, one could also see the effects of the collision of the public and private transcripts that take place in his performance and through his popularity.[99]

Rock's contemporaries, including Eddie Murphy (and later Dave Chappelle and particularly Eddie Griffin), used the word rather freely. "[T]he more you say shit," contends Eddie Griffin, "the less power it has. . . . Richard [Pryor] went to Africa and said there was no niggas. I seen nothing but niggas over there." Paul Mooney, who cowrote a lot of material with Pryor (and subsequently appeared in Spike Lee's *Bamboozled* and on *The Chappelle Show*), dismissed most of the criticisms launched against those who used the word:

I'm not bothered by it. The word is going nowhere, it's not leaving
this planet. I'm going to use it because it conjures up demons and I
like that. It comes from the word Negro, Negroid—it all means black.
When it was powerful and offensive, people called me "nigga" enough,
so much so that I feel like I own it. I was born in the South, y'know?

In this context, Rock's contrasting of the term "nigger" with the term "black" is interesting, and given his obvious identification with the latter as opposed to the former, it is apparent that he was not endorsing "nigga" as a term of affection or using it in the manner Murphy, Griffin, or the early Pryor used it. When Rock referred to "niggers," he intended the pronoun to mean what it has meant for centuries. Whereas Gregory made reference to a revolution that would make the word unusable, Rock in his rearticulation of the term sought to distinguish himself from the people with whom he felt the word was properly associated and urged other "respectable" black folk to do the same.[100]

There is a related distancing from hip-hop in Rock's comedy, though his disengagement often assumes playful forms. This is most evident in his deployment of another native of Bedford-Stuyvesant, the late Russell Jones, aka Ol' Dirty Bastard (ODB). At first glance, the impression one gets from Rock's interactions with Jones is that they are partners engaged in a comic venture together, although on closer inspection—and it is the ambiguity here that lends this public engagement power—it becomes obvious that Rock is also using Jones as comic fodder. Jones functions as an effective trope in Rock's project, largely because of the way he was first introduced to the public. On the cover of his first release, *Return to the 36 Chambers* (1995), there is an authentic-looking mock-up of Jones's welfare identification card ("for food coupons or public assistance"), including his picture and date of birth, thereby identifying him as a welfare recipient. Picking up on that theme, in a segment he recorded for *MTV News* in March 1995, a camera crew followed the rapper as he went to pick up his monthly allotment of food stamps from a check-cashing outlet with his still-valid welfare card (in a limousine). Given his references in the broadcast to the benefits as "free money" and his contention that he was "owe[d] 40 acres and a mule anyways," we are supposed to be amused, because by that point Wu-Tang Clan, the group in which he first made his breakthrough—less than twenty-four months earlier—had been quite successful, and he had just received a $45,000 advance from Elektra Records (to whom he was signed as a solo artist). The segment showing the welfare system still providing support to a recording artist was meant to demonstrate that the system could easily be abused, welfare recipients really did not need support, and claims for racial reparations were unjustified. (Another possible implication was overlooked: recording artists are rarely fairly compensated.) In combination with Jones's reference to having twice been "burned by gonorrhea," his various arrests for driving without a valid license, possessing crack cocaine, and failure to maintain child support, among other things, the overall impression was established that he was an accurate representative of the problems of the welfare system and that structural responses to cultural deficiencies were misguided. It was this framing that rendered him suitable for Rock's narrative.

Rock's intentions aside, it is apparent that Jones himself was quite aware of the uses to which "ODB" was being put and was a willing participant in aspects of the broader performance. As Dante Ross, who was working for Elektra Records at the time Jones's solo career was launched, remembers, "Dirty designed the cover [of the album *Return*] basically. . . . The photographer, Danny Clinch, and the rest of us didn't have a clue what the remaining part of the package would be, so we just followed Dirty's lead." He also agreed to future television features for MTV ("Everybody Loves Dirty") and VH1 ("ODB on Parole"), underscoring the role visual media played in the making of black popular culture in this period. In his press interviews and television appearances, then, it is apparent that Jones was consciously performing a character he sensed would be appealing to certain constituencies. "Whatever suits the needs of the public, that's what I'll put out," he offered during an interview. It is also important to interpret Jones's work from behind the mask of ODB as part of a broader comic tradition that has always been present in hip-hop and contributed to the contrapuntal quality of many of its texts: the Fat Boys, Biz Markie (who received lyrical assistance from Big Daddy Kane), the repartee between Chuck D and Flavor Flav (who would subsequently expand on Jones's template) that in some ways anticipates the Rock/ODB duo, and the combination of De La Soul and their producer "Prince Paul" Huston (who initiated the practice of including comedic skits on rap albums).[101]

Beyond questions of agency, the Ol' Dirty Bastard character provided Chris Rock with a living embodiment of the case he was trying to make in *Bring the Pain*. In the interactions between the two Bed-Stuy natives, Rock played "black" against Jones's niggerality. Although the visceral distaste that marks his performance in the original routine is absent, and despite the comedic and at times almost affectionate ways Rock engages Jones, and vice versa, the effect over time is to reinforce the original script, in which the nigger, the other, must be identified, isolated, and deployed in such a manner as to sustain a viable, marketable, assimilable, and respectable blackness. On *Bigger and Blacker*, the first comedy album Rock released after the success of *Bring the Pain*, there are a number of skits titled "Wisdom from the O.D.B." (e.g., "if a brick didn't know how to sit on walls no more, what would you ask it?"). The other "words of wisdom from the ODB" included "If a dick don't get hard offa cocaine, what would you ask it?" and "If a pussy had the power to shrink itself, what would you ask it?" When Rock guest-edited an issue of *Vibe*, he employed Jones's public image as a frequent reminder of the sources of black middle-class anxiety and despair. Among the references were the following:

> On this day in Hip Hop: August 19, 1999 by Chris Rock: Russell
> Jones a.k.a. Ol' Dirty Bastard, was *not* under arrest. For a period of
> at least 24 hours, the Wu-Tang rapper didn't break a single law. On
> this historical day in hip hop, Ol' Dirty (who has since made a name
> for himself by getting arrested in rapid succession on an increasingly
> bizarre array of charges) walked the streets a free man. People
> rejoiced in Harlem. Even Mayor David Dinkins got into the act by
> proclaiming August 19 Ol' Dirty Bastard Not Arrested Today Day.[102]

In Rock's representations, then, of "the nigger," and hip-hop, largely through his interactions with the Ol' Dirty Bastard persona, a certain form of politics is observable that could be broadly termed anti–welfare statist. In *Bigger and Blacker*, in a skit entitled "Taxes," Rock observes that, despite his general admiration for then President Clinton, the "one thing Clinton did I didn't like . . . [was] raise taxes," in the context of suggestions that "Uncle Sam's on the [crack] pipe [i.e., always asking for more money for taxes]" and "black people should get social security at twenty-nine." In his subsequent concert recording, *Never Scared*, Rock states, "I've got some things I'm conservative about; I've got some shit I'm liberal about. Crime I'm conservative about; prostitution, I'm liberal." More broadly, the routines in the performance seemed designed to negotiate a space inside the American project for respectable African Americans in ways that almost echo black speech acts during the Cold War (absent, though, the explicitly restrictive context that compelled those earlier testimonies). While acknowledging the unpleasant aspects of the country's racial history, Rock appears determined to domesticate black aspirations. "America is like the uncle who paid your way through college but molested you," he offers at one juncture. Following this particularly striking reiteration of the family metaphor, he contemplates the legitimacy of nativism (with regard to the French, foreigners, Arabs, and illegal aliens), talks about the war in Iraq, and proclaims, flatly without any apparent irony, "America is the greatest country in the world." At this point, the monitors at the top of the stage, which have been showing the "CR" logo, cut to an American flag, rippling as if in a breeze. At the end of the show, red, white, and blue balloons and confetti drop from the ceiling.[103]

FRIED ICE CREAM IS A REALITY

Shortly after the broadcast of *Bring the Pain*, Bill Stephney, coproducer of Public Enemy's classic recordings, wrote an essay for the *New Republic* entitled "The Welfare Rap: Why Black Men Hate It." In the article, Stephney cited Chris Rock's concert film as evidence of black frustration with the welfare system: "[Rock's] monologue and the exuberant 'hoot's and 'teach, brother's it elicits from an all-black crowd reflect what polling data from within the African-American community has said for years: the silent majority of black folk don't want welfare and its destructive effects." The Long Island native went on to assert that the welfare system was responsible for the antifeminist sentiment in black communities:

The misogyny articulated by the hip hop generation comes from its marginalization by a welfare system that defines "family" as a woman with children and a check from AFDC or child support. It's not just the demise of work in America that has alienated black men from the family-supporting and child-rearing positions they used to occupy with pride, it's a welfare/child support system that has substituted for them. It's thirty years of black male dislocation that's moved us from the R & B of twenty-five years ago—"Ain't No Woman Like the One I've Got"—to such lyrics as "Bitches Ain't Nuthin but Hoes and Tricks."

Following criticisms of *Roe v. Wade* and the incentive structure that supposedly underlies the "child-industrial complex," Stephney concludes,

> Welfare: blow it up. Get rid of it. Americans deserve safety nets if the family is struck by unforeseen tragedy, not if the tragedy is by choice. . . . The civil rights/big government coalition may spend the coming years fighting to restore the welfare/child support system that this Congress and this president have taken apart. But in other parts of the African American community, we've moved on.[104]

Within black film, a similar mobilization took place with regard to whose preferences and agenda should be dominant in the visual marketplace. In response to the popularity of movies such as *Boyz'N the Hood*, the Hughes brothers' *Menace II Society* and *Dead Presidents*, a new genre of films emerged. These releases focused on the black middle class, in contrast to the earlier wave of films that were predominantly located in inner-city neighborhoods. What was most striking about the films that were made in this moment, in the aggregate, was their studied collective effort to render the black working class and poor invisible. In *Waiting to Exhale*, set, remarkably, in Arizona, all of the scenes were located in middle- and upper-middle-class spaces, and the characters were uniformly economically secure. The one exception to that pattern is the mother of Whitney Houston's character (Savannah), who, we are told at one point, is living in relatively depressed circumstances and dependent on the occasional subsidies she receives from her daughter. The reference to her circumstances is brief and is not developed any further as the plot returns to the efforts of the film's four female protagonists to find a good man. The mating habits of the black bourgeoisie were the main theme of subsequent releases such as *The Wood, The Best Man, The Brothers,* and *Love and Basketball*. Omar Epps, one of the leads in *Love and Basketball*, stated in reference to the film,

It's a new slice of American life, with basketball as a backdrop. It's refreshing in that it's part of that new movement in black films, looking at the middle class, both the kids [Epps and his costar, Sanaa Lathan] come from two-parent household[s], so it's not against all odds, or basketball or die.[105]

The promotional campaign for Malcolm Lee's *Best Man*, with its signifying title and focus on a world in which class nuances and complexities do not obtain, most clearly articulated the sensibilities of this new cohort. Word-of-mouth and email exchanges were deployed to spread the word about the film's opening to the connected black middle class. The advertisements boasted "Everyone you love will be there!" Lee observed, with regard to the film's success and appeal, "In particular, we had a lot of good response from the African American audience. And it really showed me that they're starving for other forms of entertainment and stories about the African American experience that don't involve drugs or despair or living in the ghetto." Lee also appeared on *The Newshour with Jim Lehrer* on PBS, along with Stacey Spikes, the founder of the Urbanworld Group (which organized a black film festival in New York, among other activities). Spikes offered perhaps the most remarkable explanation of the film's crossover commercial success and broader social significance:

> [It] is a wonderful film that you want to see. When you leave, you're very happy that you went and saw it. . . . One of the most unique things about this movie is no one was carrying a gun. No one was robbing a liquor store. Everybody was really happy, *upper* middle class prosperous, you know, married and everyone was what I know in America as Black Americans.

This articulation of a notion of black community—the happy, the prosperous, the married—not surprisingly, excluded mention and any representation of certain constituencies.[106]

In terms of African American politics, perhaps the most significant legacy of the Clinton era was the naturalization of the bifurcation of the black body politic and the related incorporation of the black middle classes. This was possible partly because Clinton represented in some respects a sympathetic figure whose policy choices might be overlooked. It is in this context that Toni Morrison's reference to Clinton, during the height of the Monica Lewinsky affair, as the nation's first "black president" makes sense (especially given his ability to perform blackness as effectively as any experienced black elected official). Political scientist Ronald Walters noted, as Clinton was leaving office, "There's a cultural symbolism in his whole approach to black people. He has found out, like a lot of politicians, that you can use that to real advantage. In fact, if you're good with that, you don't have to give public policy." Clinton's ability to establish a certain playful insider status within certain circles of the African American community provided him with (black) political capital he could expend elsewhere (and against the interests of other black constituencies). With his frequent visits to black churches, his enthusiasm for the saxophone, his strong record of appointing blacks to positions in the civil service, and his sponsoring of an investigation of race and race relations under the leadership of John Hope Franklin, in combination with his facility with black folkways, the anthropologist-cum-president was able to curry favor among those classes of blacks who generally prospered during his administration. "A lot of this was just personal," Clinton acknowledged as he prepared to leave office. With his support for the continuation of affirmative action, and personalized relationship with blacks, Clinton was given a certain latitude in his dealings with, and representations of, the black poor (e.g., the crime bill and welfare reform).[107]

The relative silence among black elected officials—their unwillingness to refer directly to the racial and gender antipathies that were driving the reform impulse and their subsequent support for Clinton's reelection, despite their vocal opposition to reform in Congress itself—was striking. Similarly, the absence of any significant dissent by the various black publics engaged in the realms of formal political activity is remarkable. Whether or not such opposition would have made a difference in the long run is hard to determine (and requires imagining a completely different set of background circumstances).[108] While one should not underestimate the potential impact of a mobilized black electorate, American orientations toward welfare policy, and public policy in general, have been determined by the choices made by nonblack constituencies and have usually been energized by antiblack animus.

The extent to which blacks struggled with these stereotypes and undoubtedly in some cases internalized them, though, was not apparent in the discourses in the arenas of formal political, protest, and even antistatist/nationalist activity, where a certain unity of expressed preferences prevailed and, failing that, silence obtained. In contrast, in popular culture an explicit consideration of the relationship among class, gender, and race was apparent. It might be useful, though, if we read the silence and evasions in the formal realm and the explicit deliberations in the arenas of popular culture together as part of the same larger discourse that assumes different forms in different spaces but works in all junctures—public, semipublic, and private—to produce the same results and subjectivities and encourage the same sorts of performances.

The outlines of this new paradigm became even clearer in the decade following the abolition of AFDC. In the spring of 2001, as further evidence of the increasing hegemony of thin conceptions of black community solidarity, a full-page advertisement appeared simultaneously in the *New York Times* and *Washington Post*. Published on April 4, 2001—the thirty-third anniversary of the murder of Martin Luther King Jr.—the ad was entitled: "African American Business Leaders Call for an End to the Estate Tax." Among the signatories to the appeal were Clarence Avant, a recording industry executive; Dave Bing, former Detroit Piston and head of the Bing Group (a group of businesses that supply materials to the automotive companies, among others); Thomas J. Burrell, chairman of Burrell Communications Group; Keith Clinkscales, then chairman of Vanguarde Media; Kenny "Babyface" Edmonds; Earl G. Graves Sr., publisher and CEO of *Black Enterprise* magazine; Debra Lee, president and COO of BET Holdings, Inc.; Butch Lewis of Butch Lewis Productions; Byron Lewis of Uniworld Group, Inc.; Ed Lewis, chairman and CEO of Essence Communications Partners; and Alfred Liggins, CEO of Radio One, Inc. The key signatory and organizer of this effort was Robert L. Johnson, chairman and CEO of BET Holdings, Inc.[109]

In the advertisement, it was argued that the estate tax unfairly punished black business owners and that the broader black community's interests lay in having a strong business sector:

> The Estate Tax will cause many of the more than 1 million black-
> owned family businesses to fail or be sold when the 55 percent
> Estate Tax is imposed on already undercapitalized minority-owned
> enterprises. . . . In addition, the *entire* Black community suffers
> when these minority-and-family-run businesses that provide
> jobs and services in underserved communities are forced to shut
> down and pay the Estate Tax. . . . Unlike most White Americans,
> many African Americans who accumulated wealth did so facing
> race discrimination in education, employment, access to capital,
> and equal access to government resources. In many cases, race
> discrimination was supported by governmental policies and
> failure to enforce equal rights law. It is unfair and unjust for the
> government through the Estate Tax to seize a portion of the estate of
> the individuals [to whom] it failed to provide equal opportunity.

The argument was also made that most of the black businesspeople affected by the Estate Tax had accumulated their wealth themselves, not through inheritance, and should have the right to pass their assets on "to the next generation and beyond." Finally, the signatories observed:

> Elimination of the Estate Tax will help close the wealth gap in this nation between African American families and White families. The net worth of an average African American family is $20,000 or 10 percent of the $200,000 net worth of the average White family. Repealing the Estate Tax will permit wealth to grow in the Black community through investment in minority businesses that will stimulate the economic well-being of the Black community and allow African American families to participate fully in the American Dream.[110]

On a number of levels, this was a remarkable development. As a simple matter of fact, very few blacks were wealthy enough to pay the so-called death tax (blacks constituted less than half of 1 percent of all those required to pay estate taxes, while forming roughly 12 percent of the general population). The abolition of the estate tax would deprive the federal government (and state governments) of a significant amount of revenue ($75 billion a year between 2014 and 2024) and, to the extent that public expenditures benefit nonwhites, any reduction in those monies would restrict the state's ability to provide social services and would actually increase the black/white income gap. If we consider the racial aspects and implications of this appeal, the picture becomes even more intriguing. Johnson and his associates, in asking that the estate tax be abolished because of the burdens it places on their heirs, were also—as they very well understood—supporting the abolition of estate taxes for all Americans, not just African Americans (indeed, a number of prominent wealthy whites, including Warren Buffett, George Soros, Paul Newman, William Gates Sr., and William H. "Bill" Gates III, came out against the abolition of the estate tax). Furthermore, the reference to the suffering of "the entire Black community" is evidence of the linked fate phenomenon at its most absurd. Johnson, who had never displayed any great concern for the broader black community and consistently dismissed suggestions that he should have any special social obligations that his white counterparts did not, was an odd mouthpiece for such communitarian passion.[111]

Johnson, one of the country's two black billionaires (the other being Oprah Winfrey), had made his money by serving as the black representative of largely white business ventures (e.g., BET's founding, which was funded by

TeleCommunications Inc.). He sought to prevent the formation of any unions within the network's employees and had made profit the primary consideration with regard to the network's programming. Considering BET's dependence on music videos, and particularly those featuring unclothed women and representations of urban gangsters, the solidaristic rhetoric underlying the advertisement stands as a rather bizarre reiteration of a familiar pattern: a constricted notion of community solidarity is invoked and subsidized by means of the exploitation of women and distorted images of black inner-city life. It was also striking that the vast majority of the signatories for the advertisement came from the entertainment and media sectors and that, not entirely surprisingly, this community position paper was published in the *New York Times* and *Washington Post*, as opposed to *Essence, Savoy*, the *Atlanta Daily World, Black Enterprise*, or any of the other media, radio, and television outlets at the disposal of these self-designated community spokespersons.

Congress passed legislation that would phase out the estate tax by 2010. Johnson, who was nominally considered a Democrat, joined a commission at the request of the Bush administration—the Commission to Strengthen Social Security—whose purpose was to examine the possibility of privatizing the federal pension program that had been established in 1935 as the foundation of Franklin Roosevelt's New Deal. Sitting as a Democrat on what was supposedly a bipartisan committee, Johnson argued for the privatization of Social Security—through private investment accounts—partly on the grounds that African Americans would benefit as a result of such an alteration: "Private accounts go directly to the problems that many Americans face, particularly minority Americans, women, who need a greater retirement security umbrella or a blanket they don't have now." Echoing Chris Rock, Johnson also asserted, "African Americans who contribute to the Social Security system and payroll taxes also have one of the highest mortality rates, so in the end, they may not receive the full benefits of what they put in Social Security." While American blacks do die younger, Social Security benefits include payments made to the spouses and children of beneficiaries who have passed, as well as disability payments for injured workers (which disproportionately benefit blacks), and are progressive, in that they redistribute income toward the least wealthy seniors (who are also disproportionately black).[112]

By this point, it was quite apparent that the absence of an economic critique during the classic phase of the civil rights movement and its aftermath, followed by a period in which the church's influence completely eclipsed that of labor unions, and the South emerged as a locus for black liberationist aspirations, had created the possibility of an African American politics that was either silent on class issues or antagonistic to the interests of lower-income constituencies (e.g., the arguments made by comedian Bill Cosby and the class perspectives a number of black clergy promoted).[113] In the realm of formal politics, the willingness and ability of the CBC to speak with one voice was restricted by developments on the class and gender fronts as well. The membership of the conservative "blue dog" caucus within the CBC would grow to three (Sanford Bishop, Harold Ford Jr., and Georgia's David Scott), as would the influence on the CBC's deliberations of the centrist Democratic Leadership Council (as Ford, Artur Davis, Gregory Meeks, and Albert Wynn would maintain affiliations with both the Council and the CBC).[114] The diverging economic interests represented within the CBC meant that it became less and less able to take a position on issues where a consensus was necessary. As a result, there was no coordinated response from the black members of Congress to the 2005 effort to repeal the estate tax permanently or to the tightening of the bankruptcy laws that passed the House in that same period. Indeed, eight members of the CBC voted in favor of the estate tax repeal and ten in favor of tougher bankruptcy regulation.[115] By this point, it was apparent that the CBC was not able to speak, even in the relatively tentative manner it had nearly a decade earlier with regard to welfare reform, on behalf of black lower-income (and middle-income) constituencies.

PACK LIGHT

There were attempts to disrupt the hegemony of these discourses. An accurate depiction of the deliberations taking place in the years preceding and following the passage of welfare reform legislation in 1996 would have to reflect the ways what was becoming the dominant narrative was contested—and the efforts to identify and promote thicker and more progressive notions of black community. In the area of film, for example, following in the tradition established by the individuals trained at the University of California at Los Angeles (UCLA) in the 1970s—including Julie Dash, Charles Burnett, Haile Geraima, and Jamaa Fanaka—there was the 1989 release *Sidewalk Stories*. Directed by Charles Lane, the feature was a silent movie shot in black and white depicting the situation of the homeless in New York City with Lane playing "the Artist," the film's protagonist. The absence of a soundtrack encouraged viewers to engage more directly with the visual cues and the characters themselves and allowed more room for contemplation and imagination than a standard talking picture. It might be argued that if Al Jolson's move into the talking film via blackface in *The Jazz Singer* silenced blacks and simultaneously disabled the black film industry, Lane's aesthetic decisions in *Sidewalk Stories* represented an effort to disrupt that history and render blacks visible as subjects rather than simply as ciphers.

In the film, the homeless Artist, modeled in many respects on the work of Charlie Chaplin, finds himself as the custodian of a small girl, a development that forces us to envision him as a fellow human being rather than a legitimate target of abuse and disrespect. When the little girl's crayon drawings become valuable as modern art, we are encouraged to lament the affectations of the New York art world (undoubtedly a reference to the experience of Jean-Michel Basquiat). In the Artist's various encounters with potential wealthy patrons and apartment-building doormen, a critique of the absurdities of the class system is developed. At the movie's conclusion, sound returns for a moment as the camera focuses on a group of panhandlers and their voices are heard urging "Remember the homeless" and asking "Can you spare a quarter?" Given its aesthetic commitments, it is not entirely surprising that the film was not a commercial success or that it failed to alter significantly the direction of black discourse around issues of class in the cultural realm.[116]

In the musical arena, Tracy Chapman espoused a similarly encompassing notion of community. With her eponymous debut album in 1988 and its successor, *Crossroads*, the following year, Chapman's music promoted a politics and an aesthetic that drew in many respects from the traditions established during the Popular Front and predecessors such as Josh White, Odetta, and the black British singer-songwriter Joan Armatrading. "Talkin' bout a Revolution," from the first album, would make reference to those "standing in the welfare lines" and "wasting time in the unemployment lines" at a time when few artists in any genre were paying attention to these constituencies. Other songs made references to economic marginalization ("Subcity"), interracial tension ("Across the Lines"), domestic abuse ("Behind the Wall"), materialism ("Mountain o' Things," "Material World"), apartheid ("Freedom Now"), as well as more conventional concerns such as romance. Chapman's music would receive virtually no airplay on mainstream black radio stations and in those media spaces designed to identify, commodify, and market black product (narrowly understood). Nevertheless, it is apparent that she was heard by black audiences (Richard Pryor was an early fan, and Spike Lee shot the video for "Born to Fight," which sought to place her squarely in the black music and activist tradition), and her aesthetic influenced subsequent developments in black popular music. Kenny "Babyface" Edmonds reintroduced the acoustic guitar to the R & B menu as a result of her work ("When Can I See You Again" on his album *For the Cool in You* [1993]), an example a number of other artists took up. Jamaican vocalist Foxy Brown recorded popular reggae cover versions of "Baby Can I Hold You" and "Fast Car" (also recorded by Wayne Wonder), and Chapman proved to be quite popular throughout the Caribbean. The most interesting indication that black music consumers were not simply contained by the playlists of R & B stations was the 1991 release and commercial success of "Sometimes I Rhyme Slow" by the rap duo Nice and Smooth, which referred directly to Chapman's "Fast Car." That said, explicit acknowledgment of Chapman's work and example rarely registered within the dominant circles of black popular culture.[117]

Finally, and my aim here is to be suggestive rather than comprehensive, the artistic efforts of Erica "Erykah Badu" Wright are worth consideration. The background: in a scene in the original *Shaft*, Bumpy Jonas, an uptown drug dealer (played by Moses Gunn), asks the detective played by Richard Roundtree to help him find his missing daughter. In making the request, he breaks down and cries, revealing a vulnerability and near tenderness we would not expect from a gangster (at least not *this* gangster in public). Shaft observes, though, that it is remarkable that Jonas is concerned about his daughter's safety yet quite willing to profit from the misery and exploitation of other women. Playing in the background is an Isaac Hayes composition ("Bumpy's Lament") featuring an organ and bass combination with strings, suggesting the despair of the Jonas character. Almost three decades later, Andre "Dr. Dre" Young would record "Xxplosive," based on the same instrumental motif but at a quicker tempo and with a repeated guitar figure reproducing the melody the organ carried in the Hayes original. Along with vocalist Nate Dogg, the featured rappers on the track included Hittman, Six-Two, and Rocardo "Kurupt" Brown, formerly of Tha Dogg Pound. Brown's lyrics were more venomous and seemingly heated and personal than the misogyny that had become standard in some parts of the rap music industry, and in an interview he explained that his sense that some women had forgotten their place motivated his lyrics.[118]

One year after the album *2001* was released, Erykah Badu released *Mama's Gun*, a collection anchored in hip-hop culture but reaching outward for its influences. On the album's cover, Badu looks directly into the camera lens, her face suggesting both a certain resistance as well as a degree of world-weariness, and a simultaneous matching and mocking of the standard gangster countenance.

Indeed, regarding this last possibility, Badu—along with artists such as Jill Scott, Patti Labelle, Grace Jones, Suzan-Lori Parks, and Kara Walker—would establish with her work a space for black female engagements with the absurd and the surreal outside of the overwhelmingly male-dominated arena of mainstream comedy. The first song on the album, "Penitentiary Philosophy," anchored in a rock and soul aesthetic that referenced early Rufus and Mother's Finest records, linked the circumstances of folks on both sides of the prison bars (and made an indirect reference to her own father's imprisonment), an embracing of those so many others preferred to forget. "Cleva" celebrated a woman's mental skills over her transient physical attributes ("gotta little pot in my belly . . . but I'm clever when I bust a rhyme") and, like the album as a whole, bespoke a willingness to engage conflict directly if necessary. "Green Eyes" invoked the spirit of the blueswoman and channeled Bessie Smith to describe the tribulations associated with the end of a relationship. Other tracks included a tribute to Amadou Diallo ("A.D. 2000") and a duet with Bob Marley's son Stephen ("In Love with You"). The lead single, "Bag Lady," was based on the same guitar lick Dr. Dre had drawn from Isaac Hayes for "Xxplosive," but slowed (back) down to the tempo of the *Shaft* original. The sentiments espoused in the lyrics were also of a distinctly different tenor. Speaking to an unidentified woman carrying the burdens associated with a problematic relationship, she advises, "One day all them bags gone get in your way, so pack light. . . . [O]ne day he gone say, 'You crowding my space,' so pack light." In the video released for the single, and directed by Badu, she is featured along with four other women. The five women are costumed in different colors—yellow, blue, purple, green, and red—in a manner that brings to mind Ntozake Shange's play *For Colored Girls Who Have Considered Suicide/When the Rainbow Is Enuf*, and each has a name: the nickel bag lady, the punching bag lady, the booty bag lady, the paper bag lady, and the baby bag mama (i.e., Badu herself dressed in red and, at one point in the clip, in a Che Guevara T-shirt against a red background). Here she presents a spectrum of black womanhood that rejects the gendered bifurcations evident in the pronouncements of both Bumpy Jonas and Kurupt. Furthermore, in what can only be imagined as a comment on the constrained space in which black women have been encouraged to operate, the clip opens with a shot of Badu literally pushing the boundaries of the frame of the picture outward.[119]

Lane, Chapman, and Badu—along with individuals such as Richard Pryor, the Wu-Tang's Ghostface, Me'Shell NdegéOcello, the filmmakers Julie Dash and Charles Burnett, Luther Vandross, Kara Walker, and a number of novelists (Morrison, Walker, Randall Kenan, among others)—would in different ways and to varying degrees provide templates for the engagement of black interiority in opposition to the dominant disinterest in such fluidity and ambiguity, undecidability and uncertainty.[120] In the battle regarding which ways the texts of blackness might be made to lean, these artists offered, individually and in the aggregate, examples of, and arguments for, a more encompassing and expansive notion of solidarity. Again, as I hinted in the last chapter with regard to the fate of bands in black music, we might think of the resistance these artists have offered to the dominant flow, and the opposition to their works, as an analogue to the debate about whether black politics can afford to incorporate deliberation and free and frank exchange. In all of these cases, interiority, discursivity, and deliberation are associated with the potential for (undesirable) vulnerability; exposure that in the racialized environment that is the black superpublic is understood as only capable of working against black interests; hence the relative silences of the CBC and the efforts to manage and contain black class differences (including, if necessary, the spectaclization and elimination of "the nigger" and her progeny).

More broadly, we might understand these dynamics as characteristic of the thinner sorts of solidarity I identified earlier in this chapter. Replaying the tensions that distinguish W. E. B. Du Bois's *Philadelphia Negro* and *The Souls of Black Folk*, the difference between the thin and thick conceptions of solidarity can also be interpreted as contesting responses to the problem of coloniality.[121] While thick conceptions correspond to a sensibility according to which the dominant tendency is to seek and construct narratives of the self that foster a sense of autonomy, potential, and capacity, and a history of that capacity (i.e., to self-narrativize), thinner approaches to the conceptualization of black possibility are typically devoted to the disarticulative and the collapsing or problematizing of the space between the representations and aspirations of the denizens of the colonial and metropolitan spheres. It is in this latter context that speculative deliberations and interior investigations of the moments around "freedom" are stigmatized and abandoned; the discourses of respectability are reupholstered and rendered hegemonic; and the colonial gaze—once again—becomes dispositive. Thinking across spaces, if the decisions by Claude McKay, Zora Neale Hurston, Langston Hughes, Aimé Césaire, and, subsequently, Frantz Fanon to reject the *noir* and identify with the *nègre* symbolize an important turning point in the anticolonial imaginary, Chris Rock's re/organization and representation of the nigger as a freestanding, self-generating commodity signposts the late—or second stage—postcolonial abandonment of such projects. In Rock's work we also see the naturalized deference to the dominant codes of post–Berlin Wall, postapartheid modern public discourse: the resistance to being categorized as "political"—that is, his attempt to cast his work as remaining within the aesthetic—and his awkward embrace of the trope of the American family and the national as the most significant interpellative frames. Despite his claims of fearlessness—*Never Scared*—it is an Ellisonian disengagement from a substantively agonistic conception of politics that defines Rock's efforts (with the former enabled by constructing and rejecting a convenient foreign blackness, the latter a locally available minstrel stereotype). Furthermore, we can see in these postcolonial respectabilities the absence of the sorts of reflexivity a transgressive politics would require, despite the occasional signs of ambivalence and opportunities for counter-interpretation. Accordingly, the sorts of maneuvers around solidarity that are attempted in this period—against the gendered other, by means of nostalgic constructions, through the management of class difference, and the mocking and excommunication of the nigger—are not surprising. Nevertheless, it is impossible to miss—and Rock's invocation of the family metaphor again speaks clearly to this reality—the gap between these respectabilities and the governmentalities they seek to mimic and assimilate. Every effort on the part of blacks to distinguish themselves from "those people," as the comedian Bill Cosby would put it in 2004, without disrupting the citizen-versus-nigger frame itself, also reinscribed the distance between the citizen and the black body and bound, quite oddly and inevitably, Br'er Rabbit even closer to the tar baby in the bordered and disciplined otherworld of subaltern existence.

Long ago I was a real Trinidadian; I used to boast of my

native land. But now to go near to Cumato I am afraid.

And a Teteron Bay I'm forbidden to bathe. So don't bother

me with nationality, for that's all abound in hypocrisy. . . .

Long ago who remember know, to any part of Trinidad

you could go. To Arima, Sangre Grande, or Tamboo

Laytay, Siparia to Los Iros Bay. But today if below Carenage

you venture, you'll find yourself in a prohibited area. The

Yankee sentry will shoot you and then declare, you had no

right in America. —Atilla the Hun, "No Nationality"

6

ROUND TRIPS ON THE BLACK STAR LINE

"Nationality doubtful . . . with no place to go" is the description Claude McKay offers regarding the situation of one of the characters in his novel *Banjo,* and in a sense it could be applied to most of the individuals whose paths we cross in his fiction (and perhaps McKay himself).[1] I want to use McKay's phrasing as a point of departure for the purpose of explicating an aspect of the normative framework underlying this chapter. Specifically, I would like to extend his reference, which is made in the context of summarizing British immigration policies and their application to nonwhites, in the direction of a firmer, empirical statement. Accordingly, beyond doubtful, we might assert that for nonwhites—and for all others, *nous sommes tous des sans-papiers*—nationality is not only doubtful and improbable but indeed impossible and, furthermore, that these impossibilities themselves might be seen as desirable and appealing.

Consistent with the broader themes of this book, this chapter's emphasis will be on the ways black artists as space traitors painting outside the lines might contribute, through the pursuit of diasporic conviviality and by means of often serious play, if not to the disorganization of the signs of the nation and the citizen, at least to their recontextualization. In other words, the focus will be on the patterns, causes, and consequences of black creative activities that overflow, undermine, and dislocate national boundaries and the kinds of politics that can be derived from the commitment to avoid settlement or perhaps, more accurately, the recognition of the impermanence approaching unavailability of such contentments. Toward this end, it might be argued that the nation itself, as a modern emergence, cannot sustain nonwhite aspirations for emancipation and that such projects require the decentering of the nation-state and the decoupling of colored subjectivities and the limiting framework of the national.

Some support for this claim can be derived by considering the ways the language of the nation itself can be deployed to deflect attention from the norms and mechanisms that underwrite coloniality. As Saidiya Hartman observes with regard to a prior moment of apparent liberation, and the relationship between slavery and freedom in the American context, "[T]he failures of Reconstruction cannot be recounted solely as a series of legal reverses or troop withdrawals; they also need to be located in the very language of persons, rights, and liberties." Elaborating, she asserts that there is a need to "examine the forms of violence and domination enabled by the recognition of humanity, licensed by the invocation of rights, and justified on the grounds of liberty and freedom." In this light, she contends that "the enduring legacy of slavery was readily discernible in the travestied liberation, castigated agency, and blameworthiness of the free individual." Hartman's rendering of "subjection in the context of freedom" can be applied to the "very language" of nation, sovereignty, and fiscal independence. Indeed, the short six-month gap between the declaration of the end of Belgian rule in the Congo and Patrice Lumumba's removal made it quite clear that colonial understandings would continue to haunt, constrain, and mock the grammatical and substantive options available to blacks throughout the diaspora. It is in this spirit that Trinidad and Tobago's prime minister, Eric Williams, keenly aware of the limits of political sovereignty in the context of the postcolonial, asserted,

> It is one thing to get rid of colonialism. There will be joy before
> the angels of heaven for every imperialist sinner that repents but

if . . . colonial nationalists think that it is as easy as that, I am afraid they have another thought coming to them. . . . A lot of the colonial attitudes are not dead at all.

Furthermore, the expectations that the formerly colonized would continue to "behave according to a code of regulations and . . . feel certain things and not others," to borrow from Edward Said, would not evaporate with the recognition of formal independence.[2]

The projects envisioned, nationalisms pursued, and nation-states established in the latter half of the twentieth century, then, were of a fundamentally different nature from those institutionalized in earlier epochs. In other words, while it was not often acknowledged publicly, those states newly recognized in the post–World War II era rarely presented any substantive threat to the colonial frameworks in which they were realized or to coloniality in the aggregate. It is in this sense that the "postcolonial state" construction verged and verges on the oxymoronic and the attempts to manifest and institutionalize black nation-states would represent, to borrow again from Hartman, scenes of (re)subjection and exercises in futility.

This is not, furthermore, a simple matter either of chronology. The Palmares in seventeenth-century Brazil, and the experiences of Haiti, Liberia, and Ethiopia all suggest that the model of the nation-state was not designed to apply to these entities constituted by nonwhites, regardless of the temporal setting, and despite, as Michael Hanchard has noted, the implicitly transnational dispositions and potentials of these formations. Indeed, there were transnational movements and actors committed to the nonexistence or perpetual instability and vulnerability of these projects (e.g., the trans-imperial cooperation generated by the threat of the Haitian revolution; the League of Nation's silence about the Italian invasion of Ethiopia). The nation-state as an organizational mechanism, then, from this vantage point, might be best understood as intrinsically antiblack. In this matrix, in which white nationalisms (and transnationalisms) appear natural and unremarkable, black nationalisms are cast as egregious, schizophrenic, constitutively absurd, tragic, deterritorialized, and to some extent performative, given the real impossibility of black autonomous states along the classical lines of the modern projects that were unveiled in the eighteenth and nineteenth centuries. In other words, there is a need to question the assumption that there is a *natural* progression from the passing of colonialism to the end of coloniality. In fact, we might best read the embrace of the culture of the state, in combination with the persistence of racial subtexts and overtexts, and the fetishization of the modern, as real, albeit generally unintentional, investments in the long-term viability of coloniality. The characteristically anticolonial teleologies that equate formal emancipation with thick freedom, and the independence of states with substantive postcoloniality, would then have to be queried. Indeed, it is these various teleoillogica that define subaltern existence in the postcolonial glass garden, and these tar baby phenomena that signal autonomy but suggest immersion, that both make the contemporary language of "failed states" and "rogue states" predictable and circumscribe the political by narrowing the terrain of the imaginable and debatable. More broadly, we might think of these conveniently lapsed and imperfect states as necessary supplements to the project of rendering reasonable and appropriate the status of, and exercise of power by, the Western nation-state.[3]

In this context, what is more remarkable perhaps, from a historical perspective, is not the end of colonialism but rather the antiquation and abandonment of anticolonial struggle. It is against this background that a substantive postcoloniality would seem to require if not a committed resistance to the existence of the state, at least an anarchist-inflected imagination, a pragmatic understanding of the constraints and limitations of this category of institutions, and a disinvestment in the conception of the state—whether developed or newly established—as the proverbial final frontier: not a replacement or a displacement but, again, a recontextualization of the national and the nation-state. Such a move would underline not only the de facto unavailability of the sorts of thick citizenship naturally conferred on whites to their darker counterparts in *both* privileged and marginalized, Western and non-Western locales, but also the limited value of such inclusions. This repositioning would mark the difference between lamenting one's not being recognized by a nation-state—for example, Louis Armstrong's comment in the context of the Little Rock crisis that "It's getting so bad, a colored man hasn't got any country"— and refusing to fetishize a particular national citizenship. It would also encourage those for whom nation and state signify overlapping, verging-on-identical mechanisms of exclusion to distinguish between readings of statelessness as a punishment—or, to borrow from Orlando Patterson, a form of social death—and interpretations of this sort of marginalization as an opportunity, as an intriguing form of provocation.[4]

As part of the commitment to approaching the state as one frame of meaning among others, we might reconsider the status, and sense of closure and security, accorded to national citizenship, to the passport, to the social insurance card. If the resistance to nonwhites as citizens that has been characteristic of the histories of metropolitan spaces is read as evidence of the impossibility of such identifications and confidences, a politics aligned with postcoloniality would underwrite not only the recontextualization of the state but render citizenship itself as less than the ultimate recognition of an individual's value and other than the only recognized marker of meaningful membership.

What remains to be troubled, then, is the gap between the end of colonialism, the direct rule of Western states over peoples and spaces cast as constitutively non-Western, marked by the rhetorical availability of citizenship within autonomous nations—and that which is still repressed and reproduced by modern ceremonies. We can conceive of this gap—coloniality—in a number of ways: as the global meta-understandings that prevail beyond the end of empire such as the race/gender matrix, hierarchical labor relations, and the panics and ensuing competition justified by narratives suggesting the inevitability of scarcity and the state as the most reliable procurer, defender, and organizer; as the means by which "Europe" imagines, makes, and manages itself and its others; or, more broadly, as the shifting processes through and by which identities are ascribed, hierarchically and spatially arranged, and consequently options, choices, and life-chances, are determined and dictated. The question then would be by what means might these prerogatives, assumptions, and projects be disrupted.

A crucial element of any response, conceptually, is the notion of diaspora and how we might understand the relations and potentials embedded within this culture of dislocation. Two paths can be pursued with regard to where we might place emphasis in our definition of the term. A familiar set of narratives centers on the ruptures associated with the Atlantic slave trade and the Middle Passage, notions of dispersal and discontinuity, and the cycle of retaining, redeeming, refusing, and retrieving "Africa." This framework, then, tends to suggest that diaspora happens only outside of an "Africa" that is figured as a home that does not allow easy return. Disowning and desiring "Africa" are not entirely dissimilar positions, in that they depend on an often static homeland whether cast as magical or in need of quarantine. I will argue in the next chapter that both of these stances, despite their seeming normative incompatibility, reinforce colonial scripts in their common refusal to disarticulate place, gender, sexuality, and function (and engage "Africa" without quotation marks).

For my purposes here, I want to suggest a different starting point or first principle: the impossibility of settlement that correlates throughout the modern period with the cluster of disturbances that trouble not only the physically dispersed but those moved without traveling. This approach to diaspora compels us to resist conceptual templates and metaphors that subsidize thinking in terms of seeds and stems, roots and routes, origins and elsewheres and that promote the problematic reification and detemporalization of "Africa." Given the connections among modernity, coloniality, race, and diaspora, it is crucial that we remain skeptical with regard to claims that the last of these formations can be understood without or outside an engagement with the "Africa" that is produced and reproduced by colonialist and postcolonialist structures and discourses. The forces that both make and disrupt the virtual Africa, and encourage blacks elsewhere to internalize stigmatized notions of the "African," are the same pressures that make settlement unavailable elsewhere and diasporize all within and without the continent. It is in this modern matrix of strange spaces—outside the state but within empire—that naturalization and citizenship are substantively unavailable, regardless of geographical position.

Approaching diaspora as anaformative impulse, in other words, that which resists hierarchy, hegemony, and administration, suggests a different orientation toward this category of politics. From this perspective, which might be thought of as a temporally distinct stage from that characterized by the denial and desiring of "Africa," the primary focus is on deconstructing colonial sites and narratives and rearticulating them in ways that delink geography and power. This would require a politics not reducible to the language of citizenship and governance, and, accordingly, allergic to the sensibilities underlying the national (and, to some extent, the inter*national* and trans*national* to the degree that they depend on or reinscribe the nation-state). Moreover, it would mean being suspicious of homeland narratives and indeed any authenticating geographies that demand fixity, hierarchy, and hegemony. Conceiving of diaspora as anaform, we are encouraged, then, to put (all) space into play.[5]

As well as a culture of dislocation, then, we might conceive of diaspora as an alternative culture of location and identification to the state, which would encourage a deemphasis on the circulation and primacy of national blacknesses and suggest different and dissident maps and geographies. Accordingly, instead of considering simply how African Americans interact with Ghanaians or blacks in Canada or in the United Kingdom, we might also focus on the ways Charleston, Halifax, Accra, Marseilles, and Liverpool articulate with each other, and more generally the ways the local can function as a site of diasporic rediffusion. More to the point, we would be required to think of Montreal's relationship to Toronto, or Santiago's with Havana, Handsworth's with Brixton and Toxteth, Cape Town's with Johannesburg, and, working within the framework of the failed West Indian Federation, Laventille's with Tivoli. This is not to suggest that the aggregated national blacknesses to which we accord meaning and which circulate with impact—the Afro-Brazilian, the UK black, the Kenyan—should be dismissed or disregarded. Rather, the implication is that in recognizing the flows and interactions of sepia nationalisms we should not lose sight of the way diaspora also works across, within, and against, states. Moreover, we must be mindful of the cultural heterogeneity of black sensibilities that cannot be simply subsumed under racial categories or rendered as proxies for the national.[6]

Given these realities, we are compelled as well to consider what sort of instrumentality, or political project, diaspora represents. These potentials can be thought of as not just structure—a product of unsettlement and ritual exclusion—but also as a rediscursive albeit agonistic field of play that might denaturalize the hegemonic representations of modernity as unencumbered and self-generating and bring into clearer view its repressed, colonial subscript. As a result, a number of possible pressure points are made available: the commitments that sustain biopolitics and necropolitics but render them as unrelated, the temporal heritage shared by governmentalities and subordinativities, the symbiotic connections between the prophylactic and duppy states, and the coproductions of the citizen and the nigger. Furthermore, in contrast to the range of operations that power these disarticulations, diasporic breathing spaces enable critical engagement with the conveniences and false happy endings—slavery giving way to emancipation, colonialism to postcolonial independence, racism to colorblindness, forced to voluntary labor and movement—that explain the persistence of these hegemonies reconstituted on an ongoing basis by modern appetites.[7]

By which means might these disjuncted realms—broadly speaking, the consensual and the coercive—be brought together into a single, unified discursive field and some, if not all, of these mod cons troubled? There is the potential of making visible, or perhaps more accurately legible and audible, the modernity/coloniality matrix by putting into conversation a range of discourses that separated from each other, disarticulated, and experienced, and read, and struggled against in isolation, cannot be recognized, contested, and transcended. Here I am referring to the tendency to represent coloniality in the United States in the thinner grammars of race, Jim Crow, segregation, racism, and "race relations"; in Brazil as the benign operations of racial democracy; in the United Kingdom and France as a matter of a colonial past; in South Africa as apartheid and in India as caste; to varying degrees in parts of Africa, Latin America, and the Caribbean as colonialism and neocolonialism; and in

Canada as those things that only happen elsewhere. The potential that might disrupt this tendency can be described as juxtapositivity: the ability of individuals and movements operating within the spatial register that is the diaspora to put together the scattered pieces of the puzzle in order that we might read modernity and coloniality together and develop our critiques accordingly. As a result of engaging with and recognizing these different but similar practices, diaspora has the potential to denaturalize or declassify coloniality.[8]

A second possibility offered by diaspora is a way of rethinking the dominance of nation-state discourses and their attendant governmentalities and geoörthodoxies. If the prophylactic state depends on the exclusion of certain groups, their nonrecognition as citizens, and the impossibility of their ever being members, diaspora provides a means by which these marginalizations and theographies can be recognized, contested, and profaned. The term geoheterodoxy can be used to describe this diasporic potential: the capacity to imagine and operate simultaneously within, against, and outside the nation-state. It is this ethical lack of commitment—this anarchist-inflected imagination—that enables subaltern subjects to push for inclusion among those protected by the prophylactic state while at the same time recognizing the limitations of this recognition.

A third form of insubordination imaginable by means of diaspora is energized by the relationship among the nation-state, diaspora, and art and popular culture. What I want to suggest is that there is an autodiasporic quality to black life (and I would suggest life in general) that results from the impossibility of aligning culture and the borders of nation-states. The governmentalities and subordinativities that, respectively, desire and demand that identities beyond the state be abandoned and that art and politics remain separate—that is, the aesthetic—work against the visceral commitments of black bodies and communities to performative arenas and audiences that exceed the national and that in their productive tensions with the aesthetic invoke transgressive sensibilities prone to the reactivation of the political.[9]

Given the embedded potential challenges diaspora presents to the mock secularity of the European project, and efforts to occlude the colonial relation—for example, the juxtapositive, geoheterodox, and autodiasporic—there is still the issue of intensity of commitment. Diasporic identifications can be used as default mechanisms by which subjects bargain with empire or apply pressure and mobilize resources in order to achieve—again, an always elusive—recognition as citizens within existing or desired states. A second level of intentionality casts diasporic investments as exactly that: an effort to establish, sustain, and institutionalize a forum for deliberation, and the interpellation of subjects, and the representation of a community that might claim priority over or alongside state identifications. Diaspora appears, in this light, as a long-term, as opposed to purely instrumental, commitment to a form of resistance: an attempt to forge and maintain connections among those disconnected, disturbed, and unsettled in a particular fashion by the intersection of coloniality and race. We can also glean from Claude McKay's work evidence in support of a third option. In his illustration of the "poetical enthusiasm of the vagabond [sensibility]" in *Home to Harlem*, and more clearly in *Banjo* and his autobiography *A Long Way from Home*, there is a framework, albeit masculinized, as Michelle Ann Stephens and Brent Hayes Edwards have noted, that would deploy diaspora as a means toward a sort of substantive postcolonialism and a postracial cosmopolitanism that avoids the hubris and hierarchical inscriptions characteristic of the significantly thinner global normatives we are usually offered. In McKay's "bad nationalism" we see the roots of a perspective that might, in his own words, contain such "radical implications."[10] While these three positions are distinguishable—that of the frustrated, desiring but marginalized citizen; the committed diasporic activist; and the aspiring thick cosmopolitan—they also can be bundled in various combinations. Furthermore, it can be suggested that there is an easy slippage between the different gears, depending on the circumstances (e.g., Martin Delany, Mary Ann Shadd, and later W. E. B. Du Bois, Claudia Jones, and Bob Marley). It is in this context that we can think of diaspora as both mapping onto and contesting racial hegemonies, and as containing traces and suggesting potential ways of being beyond the extended problem spaces of coloniality and modernity.

One of the more striking developments over the course of the last half century has been the increasing predominance of the nation-state as frame in the making of black politics in the Americas, Europe, Africa, and Asia and the corresponding disengagement—across the board—from diasporic channels, from tales as tape loops imagined but not composed, playing but not heard, or spinning but unseen. As a consequence of the transformation of early twentieth-century Pan-Africanism after the independence movements in Africa and the Caribbean, as evident at the 1945 Pan-African Congress in Manchester; the collapse of the international left and labor movements, which were closely linked with midcentury Pan-Africanism; the triumphalism that followed the civil rights movements in the United States and, to a lesser degree, the United Kingdom and Canada; and more recently the end of a certain history with the toppling of apartheid in South Africa; black diasporic politics have struggled to engage and place in substantive conversation the increasingly isolated movements that have emerged in these seemingly posthistorical, postpolitical, and antagonism-free domestic contexts.

Developments in the United States are particularly significant in this regard simply because the United States emerged after World War II (and clearly after the Suez crisis in 1956) as the dominant superpower and the successor to those European nations that were actively engaged in colonial endeavors before the war. In this context, American power represented both a disiteration and a reinscription and reinforcement of coloniality. The coincidence of the American moment and the persistence of the problem of coloniality reflected the unique ways the United States had been able to bring center and periphery into intimate contact with each other, a phenomenon whose significance only grew in the post-Bandung context. The rise of the United States contributed to the elision of anticolonial discourse and the perceived impropriety of agonistic forms of global antiracist mobilization in the second half of the twentieth century. The unavailability of appropriate terminology for the engagement of the problematics associated with coloniality would hamper and confound the imagination and organization of things diasporic.[11]

As a consequence, the possible willingness on the part of some African Americans to renounce diasporic membership also should be understood in light of the broader American disengagement from Europe and the rest of the world. These almost cyclical estrangements, reflecting the degree to which blacks have felt optimistic or been compelled to perform satisfaction with regard to their circumstances in the United States, can be traced back to the Jacksonian era, and earlier, but were particularly energized by the events of the first half of the twentieth century. The extent to which American blacks have engaged with these pressures to disarticulate and domesticate their politics has in turn had a further, significant effect on the ability of those committed to uprooting coloniality to achieve their goals.

It is in this matrix that the relationships established between blacks in the United States and Jamaica, and the Caribbean in general, and the developments within the realm of popular culture as a point of exchange, are interesting. This chapter's primary purpose, then, is to investigate the "foreign policy" implications of the changes in these relationships as mediated through the cultural arena. In particular, I want to examine the ways creative artists have negotiated and affected the potentially conflicting national and transnational attachments that define and circumscribe diasporic discourse. Have their various projects contributed to the reactivation of a black politics not bound by the state or to the sedimentation of understandings that cast black national sensibilities as representing a firm empirical and normative limit? Given the possibility of putting blackness into play in such a way that its geographies become contingent, shifting, and fundamentally and profitably undecidable, have new approaches to the conjunction of the local, transnational, and international—new ways of going above, below, and beyond the nation-state—been realized in the autodiasporic realm of popular culture?"[12]

GARVEY'S GHOST

One of the first significant developments in the relationship between blacks in the United States and the Caribbean in the twentieth century was the emergence of Marcus Garvey and the Universal Negro Improvement Association (UNIA) in the late 1910s. Garvey, a Jamaican by birth, came to the United States in 1916, originally to meet Booker T. Washington and return home. Shortly after his arrival, though, he decided to relocate permanently to Harlem (Washington died before Garvey could meet him). As is well known, within five years Garvey attracted a readership of between sixty thousand and two hundred thousand for his newspaper the *Negro World* and established the UNIA as the largest, mass-based organization in African American history. Elaborating on the "Back to Africa" idea that had been popular throughout the nineteenth century among whites and blacks—Edward Blyden, Henry Highland Garnet, Martin Delany, Alexander Crummell, and later Henry McNeal Turner—Garvey mobilized support in the United States, the Caribbean, South and Central America, the African continent, Canada, Europe, and even Australia by advocating a form of Pan-Africanism consistent with the kinds of ethnic nationalism that were flourishing throughout the world during the Versailles era. Garveyism also incorporated appeals to racial purity, a rejection of the possibility—and indeed the desirability—of integration, and a version of the self-help perspective Booker T. Washington had promoted in his 1895 Atlanta Exposition address. Popular enough to fill New York City's Madison Square Garden to capacity at its first international convention in the late summer of 1920, the Garveyists were able to persuade a significant number of blacks throughout the diaspora to contribute funds toward the UNIA's Black Star Line shipping business, a venture that, their leader argued, "would be respected in the mercantile and commercial world, thereby adding appreciative dignity to our downtrodden people."[13]

Garvey's organizational successes did not occur without opposition. His nationalism was a challenge to the integrationist commitments of other organizations, including the NAACP, and of W. E. B. Du Bois, the editor of its magazine, the *Crisis*. Similarly, the UNIA's adherence to the antiunionism of Washington, Garvey's spiritual mentor, particularly after the post–World War I Red Scare, and belief that racial concerns were a more important priority than class concerns eventually alienated black socialists such as A. Philip Randolph, Chandler Owen, and Wilfred Adolphus (W. A.) Domingo, as well as those blacks even further to the left, for example, the membership of the African Blood Brotherhood (ABB), which included, among others, Cyril Briggs, Harry Haywood, Claude McKay, Otto Huiswoud, Grace Campbell, and Richard B. Moore. Given these differences, it is not surprising that the communication between Garvey and his opponents during the early years of the Harlem Renaissance also pushed the envelope, in terms of the degree of rancor black leaders were willing to express toward each other. Perhaps most significantly for Garvey, the poorly organized activities and finances of the Black Star Line project exposed the UNIA and its leader to charges of fraud. The company, whose few ships only sailed between the United States and the Caribbean basin, despite the "Back to Africa" sentiments underlying the Garveyist movement, ran aground partly because what was sold to subscribers as a viable and profitable commercial enterprise was, according to Hugh Mulzac, captain of one of the Black Star vessels, "simply being used as a propaganda device for recruiting new members." Garvey was imprisoned in 1925 after being convicted of fraud by federal authorities and in December 1927 was deported from the United States after Calvin Coolidge signed a pardon freeing him from the federal penitentiary in Atlanta.[14]

The spectacular rise and sudden collapse of the UNIA also brought to the surface tensions between West Indian immigrants and blacks in the United States and challenged the assumption that there was some natural affinity among all those of African descent. At the most basic level, questions were raised as to whether immigrants from the Caribbean were really interested in, or understood, the particular struggles facing African Americans, and many suggested that the racial radicalism expressed by the Garveyites and other West Indian activists was really directed at the British Crown, and rooted in the historical relationship between England and its Caribbean territories. In this spirit, Chandler Owen characterized the UNIA as a "British West Indian Association," and Du Bois accused Garvey of "trying to solve the West Indies' problems with Britain in the United States."[15]

West Indian immigrants, and Garvey in particular, were also seen as responsible for making an issue of color distinctions and concerns about racial purity and "introduc[ing] a new element into Afro-American politics." Despite the fact that color distinctions had long had social and political significance among African Americans and Garvey's suggestions that it was his success as a leader that provoked opposition from light-skinned blacks—"Being black, I have committed an unpardonable offense against the very light colored negroes in America and the West Indies by making myself famous as a negro leader of millions"—his explicit and public references to his opponents and ambitions in color-coded terms were certainly, from a historical perspective, a new development. Du Bois was always "the mulatto" or "the cross-bred Dutch-French-Negro editor of the *Crisis*," in Garvey's speeches, which also frequently commented on the importance of maintaining racial purity.[16]

There were also suggestions that Afro-Caribbean immigrants did not identify with their African American peers, attempted to exploit black communities in the United States for their own purposes, and saw themselves as superior. Among Caribbean Americans, references to the notion that growing up in the West Indies gave immigrants a greater sense of confidence than their African American counterparts were not uncommon. W. A. Domingo suggested, "Forming a majority in their own countries and not being accustomed to discrimination expressly felt as racial, they [West Indians] rebel against the 'color line' as they find it in America." Historian Clarence Walker contends, "American blacks found the islanders pushy, aggressive, clannish, insensitive, and self-seeking. Underlying their hostility was the fact that the Americans were less well educated than many of the West Indians, a number of whom were skilled artisans, business people, and professionals."[17]

In light of some of Garvey's actions, some commentators' attempts to characterize his movement as alien to African American values, and distinct from, and possibly antagonistic to, African American traditions and concerns, is understandable. The pomp and circumstance associated with the UNIA, as evidenced in the honorary titles it bestowed on some of its officers (e.g., supreme deputy potentate, provisional president, high chancellor) distinguished the Garveyites from the more somber and buttoned-down aesthetics of Garvey's contemporaries and predecessors among African American leaders (with the exception of the various Masonic organizations, of which Garvey was apparently a member).[18] There were other signs—for example, Garvey's infamous meeting with the Ku Klux Klan in the summer of 1922—that his politics represented a clear departure from the norms and practices of

African American leadership. Despite his subsequent rationalization that the Klan was the most honest representative of white American racial opinion, it can be legitimately argued that only someone substantially divorced—alienated—from an understanding of the specificities of American racial dynamics could imagine participating in such a meeting. Furthermore, after his deportation, as his politics became increasingly reactionary, Garvey continued to offer support to white racists. With his promotion of a bill introduced by Mississippi's Theodore G. Bilbo (entitled the Greater Liberia Act) in the Senate, in 1938, he sought to secure American support for the emigration of five to eight million American blacks to Liberia, even though Bilbo's motives were explicitly racist.[19]

Nevertheless, some of Garvey's fiercest opponents advocated many of the basic principles associated with Garveyism after his deportation. "Shorn of its bombast," W. E. B. Du Bois wrote in the *Crisis* in 1928,

> the main lines of the Garvey plan are perfectly feasible . . . American
> Negroes can, by accumulating and administering their own
> capital, organize industry, join the black centers of the Atlantic by
> commercial enterprise, and in this way, ultimately redeem Africa as a
> free and fit home for black men.

Five years later, writing just before he would leave the NAACP over its resistance to his proposals that blacks, at least in the short term, develop their own institutions, he noted, "[A]s consumers, [Negroes] must at the very lowest estimate spend ten billion dollars a year. . . . We furnish such capital today to the white industrial world. There is no reason on earth why it should not be spent to establish a black industrial world." He reiterated this point in a *Crisis* article the same year:

> Pan-Africa means intellectual understanding and co-operation
> among all groups of Negro descent in order to bring about at the
> earliest possible time the industrial and spiritual emancipation of
> the Negro peoples. Such a movement must begin with a certain
> spiritual housecleaning. American Negroes, West Indians, West
> Africans and South Africans must proceed immediately to wipe
> from their minds the preconcepts of each other which they have
> gained through white newspapers.

In terms that can be understood as referring directly to the debates about Garveyism, he added that blacks must "cease to think of Liberia and Haiti as failures in government; of American Negroes as being engaged principally in frequenting Harlem cabarets and Southern lynching parties; of West Indians as ineffective talkers; and of West Africans as parading around in breech-clouts."[20]

Regardless of the UNIA leader's obvious shortcomings, the debates about him and his particular anticolonial project that took place, for example, in the pages of the *Messenger,* involving Chandler Owen, A. Philip Randolph, and W. A. Domingo, also revealed a significant degree of intraracial animosity. Owen and Randolph referred to Garvey as "a Jamaican Negro of unmixed stock" and "a supreme Negro Jamaican Jackass," and added that "no American Negro would have stooped to [the] depths" Garvey did. The slogan that was used to mobilize the anti-Garvey movement, "Garvey Must Go," implied that an effective solution required his physical removal and deportation—in other words, that he was a foreign agent who did not belong in the United States. Accordingly, in one *Messenger* editorial, Owen and Randolph wrote of the need to "drive the menace of Garveyism out of this country." Domingo, a Jamaican immigrant and friend of Garvey since childhood who had left the UNIA because of its failure to incorporate socialist principles, and up to that point a close ally of Owen and Randolph, objected to the emphasis on Garvey's Jamaican background and noted that among Garvey's harshest critics were other immigrants from the Caribbean (including himself). For instance, Claude McKay criticized Garvey for speaking "of Africa as if it were a little island in the Caribbean Sea," and Cyril Briggs characterized Garvey as a "demagogue" and a "reactionary" and dismissed his movement as "a tool of the imperialists." Nevertheless, in defending West Indians, Domingo made arguments that in some ways contributed to the conflicts between the two groups, for instance, suggesting that without West Indians, "the genuinely radical movement among New York Negroes would be unworthy of attention," and that American blacks were "inclined to indulge in displays of emotionalism that border on hysteria," in contrast to "the punctilious emotional restraint characteristic" of immigrants from the British West Indies. For her part, Amy Jacques Garvey, the UNIA leader's partner, contended that "Randolph and others . . . in their hey-day regarded American Negroes as Americans, Africans as savages, and West Indians as Monkey-Chasers." Randolph, in response to these suggestions, stated that he personally "had nothing against West Indians" but that he could not see how he "could have avoided mentioning Garvey's nationality," given that Garvey's tendency to make color differences an issue was, in his view, a reflection of his Jamaican background.[21]

MASKING, MINSTRELSY, AND DIASPORIC DISCOURSE:
PLAYING OUT, UNDER, AND AGAINST

Houston Baker's characterizations of the origins and nature of black modernism provide another context in which we might place and assess Garvey's example and legacy. In *Modernism and the Harlem Renaissance*, Baker seeks to understand "the meaning of speaking (or *sounding*) 'modern' in Afro-America" and identifies "the mastery of the minstrel mask by blacks [as] constitut[ing] a primary move in Afro-American discursive modernism." In a subsequent publication, *Turning South Again*, black modernism is fundamentally recast as "coextensive with a black citizenship that entails documented mobility (driver's license, passport, green card, social security card) and access to a decent job at a decent rate of pay." To this revised conception he adds, "A central right and incumbency of black modernism, as well, is the vote."[22]

The primary figure linking both of Baker's texts and his rather dissonant discussions of black modernism is that of Booker T. Washington. Specifically, in the earlier discussion, Baker cites Washington's ability to inhabit the minstrel mask in his 1895 Atlanta Exposition address as time zero in the history of African American modernism. Among the signs he points out as evidence of Washington's minstrel talents are the Wizard's reference to his mother's stealing of chickens, his willingness to "set forth a dim view of black Reconstruction politics," and his commitment to issuing "reassuring sounds" in the presence of white audiences (albeit without the burnt cork). On this basis, Baker concludes, Washington in his speech "achieves an effective modernity." In contrast, in *Turning South Again*, working with a different conception of black modernism, he reads Washington as rather closely tied to the plantation as symbol and fact of American southern life in ways that constitute an effective antimodernism. In this revision he argues, "Washington, literally and publicly, worked within the framing mind of the South to produce not a utopia of black modernism at Tuskegee, but a retrograde and imperialist plantation." Later, he elaborates that he "believe[s] the reason there have been only few and brief windows of black modernism is denoted and connoted in the United States by the single word *plantation*."[23]

My interest in Baker's treatments of black modernism and Washington runs in two directions. Consistent with the arguments made earlier, I would suggest that—however cast—attempts to reconcile black signifying prefixes with the modern, whether suffixed or not, need at the very least to acknowledge the deep, constitutive tension that exists between the two terms in theory and in practice. Both of Baker's takes on black modernism underscore this problematic. In his suggestion that the minstrel mask marks the instantiation of black modernism in a theatrical space that bridges the political and the artistic, and the modern and the modernist, in ways that trouble the paradigm of the aesthetic, he reveals the limitations and difficulties, if not the inherent impossibilities, of the sort of sensibility he seems at this point to be celebrating.[24] We can attribute all sorts of complexity and ambiguity to the blackface mask—and its receptions—but that should not lead us to overlook the fact that certain dominant and hardly liberating or subversive interpretations would prevail in the mix. The mask destabilizes but hardly obliterates racial subordination.

In his second pass at the concept, made despite evidence that the term might best be simply abandoned, Baker implies that efforts to achieve black citizenship are in tension with the plantation and its legacies, and that a black modernism that seeks such recognition must reject, or at least problematize, approaches—among them Washington's—that institutionalize the plantation. The problem here, and this goes to the heart of the question of the utility of the black modernism frame, is that the plantation is a modern emergence and indeed one of the central institutional innovations of the modern era, just as an ironic engagement with blackness is a familiar modernist trope. One might add that Baker's inclination toward regional and national frames and their interrelationships suggests that he has missed the ways the hauntings of the plantation in its various geographical and temporal incarnations exceed southern and indeed American borders. Similarly, his promotion of a rather hermetic, flat, and hollowly triumphalist notion of citizenship raises the possibility that he has accepted unthinkingly Habermasian representations of the modern and the public sphere and overlooked the constitutive bifurcations embedded in the modern/colonial relation as expressed in asymmetrical and differential access to the benefits of citizenship.

More to the point, though, given the concerns of this chapter, is the issue of how we might resituate Washington's supposedly modernist grasp of the minstrel mask and the arts of performance. Here I want to join Baker's reading of Washington with his comments regarding the comedian Bert Williams. "Like Billy Kersands stretching the minstrel face to a successful black excess," Baker writes, "or Bert Williams and [his stage partner] George Walker converting nonsense sounds and awkwardly demeaning minstrel steps into pure kinesthetics and masterful black artistry, so Washington takes up types and tones of nonsense to earn a national reputation and its corollary benefits for the

Afro-American masses." Williams, a Caribbean immigrant, achieved theatrical fame for his blackface performances at the turn of the century with Walker in productions such as *Sons of Ham* and *In Dahomey*, and later for his successful integration of the Ziegfeld Follies. Significantly, as Louis Chude-Sokei has noted, Washington was also an admirer of Williams's accomplishments both on and off the stage. Besides an engagement with minstrel theatrics, it is worth noting, Washington and Williams shared a commitment to the sorts of self-help, accommodationist program Washington sought to institutionalize at Tuskegee. "[I]t seems to me," suggested Washington writing in *American Magazine* in the fall of 1910,

> that Bert Williams has done for one side of the Negro life and character just what the old plantation Negroes did for another— given expression and put into a form which everyone can understand and appreciate something of the inner life and peculiar genius, if I may say so, of the Negro.

Regarding Williams's performance of self, Washington added,

> Bert Williams is a tremendous asset of the Negro race. He is an asset because he has succeeded in actually doing something, and, because he has succeeded, the fact of his success helps the Negro many times more than he could help the Negro by merely contenting himself to whine and complain about racial difficulties and racial discriminations.[25]

Although the two shared an appreciation of the trickster possibilities contained within minstrelsy and the medium's capacity to render blacks palatable for mainstream consumption, it is worth noting the different directions in which they deployed their respective masks. An aspect of Washington's program was to emphasize American blacks' loyalty to the nation, and particularly the South, and to urge southern and northern whites to accord a certain priority to employing African Americans because of their supposed fidelity and shared cultural commitments. In this spirit, he would contrast "the incoming of those of foreign birth and strange tongue and habits" with "the eight millions of Negroes whose habits you know," capable of "a devotion that no foreigner can approach." The familiar and familial refrain—"Cast down your buckets where you are"—also was meant to encourage blacks to see their best chances as depending on remaining within the United States (and specifically the South). Accordingly, despite his involvement in turn-of-the-century Pan-Africanism, and the influence of the Tuskegee model in various corners of the diaspora throughout Africa and the Caribbean, nativism figured as an important element in his politics. The particular minstrel mask, then, that Washington assimilated was combined with the performance of a certain visceral disengagement from substantive, multilateral diasporic exchange and cooperation, and indeed cosmopolitanism of any form.[26]

Williams, for his part, can be read as using the minstrel mask, and explicit blackface, to not only make a career in an environment in which employment options for nonwhites were few and far between, and to create a space through his obvious comedic genius and productive excess for the partial humanization of the black image in the white mind, but also to engage in what Chude-Sokei categorizes as "black-on-black minstrelsy." Born in 1874 in Nassau in what would later become the Bahamas, Williams immigrated as an adolescent to the United States, where he eventually found his way to celebrity by the beginning of the twentieth century. His blackface theatrics can then be understood, Chude-Sokei argues, not just as "a black man who came to fame masquerading as a white racist caricature of a 'black man'" but also as "a West Indian immigrant, self-consciously performing not as a 'black man' but as the white racist representation of an *African American*, which he may have phenotypically resembled, but which—as he emphasized—was also culturally other to him."[27]

Putting this last possibility aside for a moment, we can still classify Williams's burnt cork gymnastics as, among other things, a sort of solidaristic gesture, and as an effort to commit his comedic skill to the "uplift of the race," and specifically African Americans, by gaining through minstrelsy the respect of a broader American audience. Indeed, this is how Washington characterizes the actor's contributions; and Williams's African American partner, George Walker, also saw the duo's work as consistent with promoting the community's interests: "We want *our folks* to like us. Not for the sake of the box office, but because over and behind all the money and prestige which move Williams and Walker, is a love for the race. . . . Williams and Walker are a race institution." Moreover, Williams's efforts can be considered at points as evidence of diasporic conviviality. His partners in his success in the first part of his career, George and Ada Overton Walker, before and after he began blacking up, were African Americans. Furthermore, Williams certainly at times spoke in explicitly solidaristic terms. "Our race has taken root upon this soil," he observed in 1910, "after two hundred years of struggle upward, we may be apart here, but not alien." Finally, we might imagine Williams's often-remarked-on personal unease—for example, W. C. Fields's comment that he was "the saddest man I ever knew"—as the result of the burden he carried as a blackface performer.

He knew all too well that his success with mainstream American audiences came, to some extent, at the expense of his soul and dignity and that the acclaim he received possibly neither troubled nor disconfirmed to any significant degree the racial status quo in the United States.[28]

At the same time, beyond tweaking African American sensibilities by marking them as local, particular, and potentially worrisomely hegemonic, we might consider Williams's work as also an act of disidentification. In other words, it is possible that Williams was able to inhabit the minstrel's role with the burnt cork, which the darker-skinned Walker did not employ, because he did not to some crucial degree personally perceive himself as being represented onstage in his performances. From this perspective, he could be as easily grouped with other white blackface performers as with African Americans who made the difficult decision to black up. Perhaps, more accurately, it can be argued that he belongs in neither group. In a 1918 article in *American Magazine,* he suggested, "The sight of other people in trouble is nearly always funny. This is human nature. If you will observe your own conduct whenever you see a friend falling down in the street, you will find that nine times out of ten your first impulse is to laugh and your second is to run and help him get up." Later in the same piece, he contended, almost in the guise of an anthropologist and in a manner that supports the notion, that he saw American blacks to some degree as "other people":

> For among the American colored men and negroes there is the greatest source of simple amusement you can find anywhere in the world. . . . But Americans for the most part know little about the unconscious humor of the colored people and negroes, because they do not come in contact with *them.*

While the unmarked reference to "Americans" is intriguing, in that it implicitly excludes "colored people and negroes," it is the choice of pronouns—"them" as opposed to "us"—at the end of the assertion addressed to a reading audience that would have been overwhelmingly white that further indicates Williams's detachment from blacks in the United States. As he remarks with regard to the unfamiliarity of his source material, "I took to studying the dialect of the American negro, which to me was just as much a foreign dialect as that of the Italian."[29]

That Williams was an immigrant from the Caribbean was no secret; Washington notes this fact in his commentary. Blues singer Alberta Hunter, who was an acquaintance of Williams's niece, also recalls, "He was a West Indian. They're full of baloney, a lot of them. Thought they were better than God made little apples. Forgive me for saying it, because so many of my friends are West Indians and I love 'em so. But they've always been big shots." Furthermore, it was observed that offstage Williams spoke with a relatively pronounced Caribbean accent.[30] Given that Williams moved to the United States as a young boy, it can be speculated that a sharp and clearly detectable accent evident in his adulthood might have had, to some degree, a performative function: to signal difference from African Americans and to make a claim for inclusion within the communities of more recent arrivals forming in the New York area in this period. When we recognize further that, with one exception—late in his career during a performance with the Ziegfeld Follies—Williams never represented himself on stage as a West Indian, it becomes more plausible that his "black-on-black minstrelsy" had an expedient dimension to it. Furthermore, he might have negotiated the move from working with the Walkers into the otherwise all-white Ziegfeld Follies company—during a period of increasing Caribbean immigration—by casting himself increasingly in the mold, at least offstage, of the black other.

Evidence of black-on-black minstrelsy, and the desire to flesh out the Caribbean self while and by emptying out the black American other, can be detected in Claude McKay's work as well. As with Williams, a range of engagements and strategies are apparent in McKay's performances of self, especially if we consider the changes in his politics that occur over time. "If We Must Die," his famous sonnet written in response to the "Red summers" following World War I, stands in this context as one example within his repertoire of his willingness to identify in a solidaristic fashion with African Americans. In contrast, despite the considerable and valuable juxtapositive labor his texts perform, we might cite the ways African Americans are cast in *Home to Harlem* and *Banjo*: sympathetically, to be sure, but at points lacking interiority and with minstrel overtones (e.g., "Jake" and "Banjo," respectively, in contrast to the Haitian migrant "Ray"). It is important to recognize that in common with Washington, and arguably Williams as well, McKay perceived in black minstrelsy an effective means of troubling the racial status quo. As he observes with regard to a feature he wrote in the left-leaning *Liberator* on the groundbreaking 1921 musical *Shuffle Along*, featuring the creations of Eubie Blake and Noble Sissle, and the talents of Josephine Baker and Paul Robeson,

> I wanted especially to do this [piece] because the Negro radicals of
> those days were always hard on Negro comedy. They were against
> the trifling, ridiculous and common side of Negro life presented in
> artistic form. Radical Negroes take this attitude because Negroes have

traditionally been represented on the stage as a clowning race. But I felt that if Negroes can lift clowning to artistry, they can thumb their noses at superior people who rate them as a clowning race.[31]

In much the same way that McKay put words such as "primitive" into comic and subversive play, he would identify the stage as a useful space for the unsettling of the assumptions of the self-identified "superior." Nevertheless, there are moments in his novels when his ironic investments appear to play not only under but against more developed and empathetic representations of African American life, and the pursuit of diasporic conviviality.

Moving into a slightly later time period, we can arguably include the comic actor Lincoln "Stepin Fetchit" Perry as part of this tradition. Perry, the Florida-born son of a Bahamian mother and a Jamaican father, would proclaim himself a proud "descendant of the West Indies" decades after the peak of his fame portraying "the world's laziest man" in the 1930s. Reading between the lines, we might speculate that Perry's willingness—like Williams's—to deploy minstrel aesthetics was energized not simply by Hollywood's appetite for such performances but also by his sense of himself as not quite African American. As others did with regard to his predecessor, Perry also emphasized what he perceived as his ability to make whites more open to blacks: "I made the Negro as innocent and acceptable as the most innocent white child." While I am engaging in supposition here, it is possible to imagine that Perry's ability to perform "Stepin Fetchit"—his obvious sense of professional achievement and detachment from the coon he was bringing to life—combined with his dissonant public, offstage persona, by means of which he promoted an image of himself as anything but shrinking and servile, was made manageable by means of a deep-rooted disassociation from the peoples he was interpreted as representing on film. Again, as with Washington, Williams, and McKay, we can see in the excessive quality of his minstrelsy a certain marking and mocking of his audience. "The whole country laughed when old Step's pictures came to town, especially the good white citizens of Waycross, Georgia, where I grew up as a boy," Ossie Davis recalls.

> There they'd be, downstairs at the Saturday night movie looking up at that dumb stupid darkey up on the silver screen and laughing to split their sides. And me and my buddies, we'd be up in the balcony where all the black folks had to sit according to the law, and we'd be laughing just as loud as they did, but we weren't laughing at Stepin Fetchit; we were laughing at them.[32]

At the same time, the wink caught by some arguably did little to balance the confirmation of more entrenched prejudices in the hearts and minds of others, and it can be supposed that that imbalance was possibly acceptable to Perry because he did not feel as if he had all that much at stake.

Marcus Garvey's displays stand in some contrast to those of Williams, McKay, and Perry. We can read Garveyism as not just a solemn attempt to approximate the trappings of empire but also, in sotto voce, in its pageantry, a sort of playing out. "Social satire," historian Robert Hill argues, "seems not to have been beyond Garvey." Furthermore, Hill contends that the spirit of carnival was evidently at work in the UNIA and apparent in its faithful reproduction of "the ensemble of monarchical elements that go to make up West Indian masquerade." Garveyism, in this light, can be understood as a mocking of the pretensions of the colonial; in other words, as an explicitly Caribbean performance of engagement with power, albeit staged in a seemingly, formally, perhaps in transition African American space to produce new sorts of black diasporic intratext, hybrid spectacles, and examples of what Hill calls "cultural reworking and adaptation." Other signs of syncretic labor were observable in the annual UNIA convention parades on the first day of August that coincided with the commemoration of emancipation in the British Empire; a date that was also celebrated by blacks in the United States in the nineteenth century as a means of underlining the relative limitations of American commitments to racial equality before and after the 1863 Emancipation Proclamation. Similarly, as Mary Ryan notes, the parade itself as ritual was also "the characteristic genre of American ceremony." Garvey's occasionally playful relationship with African Americans and familiarity with black popular culture were also suggested by his interpolation of the lyrics of "West Indies Blues," a well-known and frequently performed composition that made light of the aspiration of a Jamaican immigrant's desire to return home. In a speech delivered at Liberty Hall in 1924, Garvey referenced the song's chorus—"I am goin' home, won't be long"—to register the potentially multiple meanings of home. While acknowledging at one level the frustration of some Caribbean immigrants with American life, as well as the legitimate comic material the homesickness of these migrants provided, his suggestion to his audience—"We are going home"—also spoke to the UNIA's determination to enable the repatriation of blacks living outside the African continent.[33]

What is important to recognize here is the distinction between this sort of playing out and the kinds of playing under and the subtle sorts of disidentification, the playing against, we can detect in the work being done in the shadows by Williams, McKay, and perhaps Perry. While Garvey can certainly be charged with misunderstanding, and arguably overlooking, the realities and experiences that shaped black American politics and culture, and a certain clumsiness, he never achieved or seemed to attempt the composite forms of masking and mocking others did in this extended era. Moreover, Garvey's primary intended audience, blacks in the diaspora, would have rendered superfluous the exploration of the sorts of minstrel complexities that other audiences would have demanded. Washington, Williams, Perry, and, to a lesser degree and only at certain junctures, McKay, given their different aspirations, positioning, respective market dictates, and national as opposed to diasporic foci, were undoubtedly under greater pressure to develop these kinds of skills.

Finally, regarding masks, nationality, and performances of self, it is worth remembering that one of Garvey's primary nemeses during the 1920s, W. E. B. Du Bois, was also capable of shifting shapes on the question of identity. "Once and for all, let us realize that we are Americans," he would urge at one point with regard to one of the dilemmas associated with double consciousness, "that there is nothing so indigenous, so completely 'made in America' as we are." Indeed, Du Bois usually represented himself as an African American and was read that way by others, especially in the context of his public debates with Garvey. At the same time, he would assert, somewhat disingenuously, in a letter addressed to former Garvey associate W. A. Domingo in January 1923 at the height of the anti-Garvey mobilization, that "the object of the [attack on Garvey] should be the opinions of the man and not the man himself or his birthplace," adding that "American Negroes, to a much larger extent than they realize, are not only blood relatives to the West Indians but under deep obligations to them for many things. For instance without the Haitian Revolt, there would have been no emancipation in America as early as 1863." He added, making reference to his Haitian father and grandmother and Bahamian grandfather and great-grandmother, "I, myself, am of West Indian descent and am proud of the fact."[34]

NEGOTIATING THE BOUNDARIES OF THE AMERICAN NEGRO IN A COLD WAR SETTING

The migration of foreign blacks was reduced substantially with the imposition of national origins quotas as part of the Immigration Act of 1924, and as a result of the depression. At the same time, Garvey's imprisonment in 1925, his deportation two years later, and the subsequent collapse of the UNIA contributed to a diminution of conflicts between United States–born blacks and Caribbean immigrants in the 1930s and 1940s. Although the number of immigrants began to increase again in the late 1930s, the launching of the Cold War disciplined and circumscribed any negotiations around the possibility of diasporic solidarity, as the freedom struggle within the United States was reconfigured and became increasingly and consciously domesticated. This turning inward was reinforced, despite the objections raised by Harlem's representative, Adam Clayton Powell, by the passage of the Smith and McCarran acts in the early 1950s. The acts added new, specific restrictions on Caribbean immigration, in addition to the national origins quotas institutionalized in 1924. This legislation and the identification of immigrants with dangerous others led to the deportations of Trinidadian red feminist Claudia Jones, her compatriot C. L. R. James, and Jamaican trade unionist Ferdinand Smith, among others. Consequently, the kinds of discourse that had characterized black intramural discourse in the 1920s and 1930s around the issues of race, class, and nationality were less affordable, as the example of Paul Robeson suggests, and most of the deliberations that took place in the 1950s transpired within the psyches of the second and third generations, those of West Indian background born in the United States, as much as they were staged between native-born blacks and first-generation immigrants.[35]

The syncretic possibilities that might develop with the emergence of a significant second-generation immigrant cohort were rarely publicly explored in the period leading up to and including the civil rights era. Indeed, those who immigrated at an earlier age, and the children of older immigrants, played an integral role in the evolution of African American politics and culture, largely as "African Americans" in the post-Garvey era. Kenneth Clarke, William Patterson, Lester Granger, Constance Baker Motley, Roi Ottley, and St. Clair Drake; and later, SNCC's Robert Moses, Michael Thelwell, Ivanhoe Donaldson, Courtland Cox, and Stokely Carmichael; CORE's Roy Innis; and Shirley Chisholm, among others, would fall to varying degrees into this category. So would both Malcolm X and Louis Farrakhan, although Farrakhan would at different points throughout his career make reference to his West Indian background. "Since my parents were from the Caribbean," Farrakhan, who started his career as a calypsonian—"the Charmer"—before he joined the Nation of Islam, has observed, "I learned to sing calypso from some of the great calypsonians of that time." The novelist Paule Marshall, whose work has been claimed by both Caribbean and African American literature scholars, and established a model—for example, in *Brown Girl, Brownstones* (1959)—that situated developments in the United

States firmly within the broader diaspora, cited the influence of Garveyism on her own development. Growing up with a Barbadian mother who was involved in the UNIA's Nurse's Brigade, she notes,

> Because of [her mother's friends'] constant reference to [Garvey],
> he became a living legend for me, so that although, when I was a
> little girl, he had been stripped of his power and was an old man
> living out his days in obscurity in England, he was still an impressive
> figure, a Black radical and freedom fighter whose life and example
> had more than a little to do with moving me toward what I see as an
> essentially political perspective in my work.[36]

In the musical arena, Hazel Scott, Duke Ellington's longtime trombonist Joe Nanton, the Canadian native Oscar Peterson, Carmen McCrae, Wynton Kelly (after whom Wynton Marsalis was named), Alphonso "Dizzy" Reece, the drummers Roy Haynes and Andrew Cyrille, and Eric Dolphy played a prominent role in the making and remaking of jazz; Kelly and Reece were both immigrants from Jamaica (Reece having traveled to the United Kingdom on the SS *Empire Windrush* before migrating to the United States).[37] Rarely, if ever, did these artists make explicit reference to their West Indian connections (although the drummer Jimmy Cobb has suggested that the pianist Kelly "got his spirit and flavor from his West Indian background"). Pianist Randy Weston, born in Brooklyn in 1926, would trace his interest in North African music and the diaspora in general (e.g., his involvement in the jazz ambassador tours, his 1960 recording "Uhuru Africa," and his cover of Duke Ellington's calypso-inspired "Limbo Jazz") to having been raised by a Caribbean immigrant father, who was a Garvey supporter, and an African American mother. "I've always been interested in the history of myself and my people, wherever they may be," Weston observed in a 1968 interview, adding, "I guess it's because I'm sort of half-breed in the black community. My father was from Panama and my mother came from Virginia. At that time black people were going through their own bit. Divide and conquer had gotten to them. They put each other down." Continuing, he suggests that he personally resolved the tensions between these groupings by seeking "similarit[ies]" and "certain basic things which were very much alike," and through his engagement with "Africa." Saxophonist Sonny Rollins, like Weston another prominent exception to the general pattern of the second-generation immigrants in the bebop cohort, would record calypsos throughout his career—for example, "Don't Stop the Carnival" and "St. Thomas"—establishing the form as a staple in the jazz repertoire. "Sometimes in Harlem we had to play

Caribbean-type tunes for dancing only," noted Rollins, the son of immigrants from the Virgin Islands, years later. "[B]ut a certain musical element was foremost—that's why I still play those Caribbean tunes." Highlighting the uncertain space the second generation occupied, he added, "I always did my own variations, tried to change things around a bit. I play a style of calypso that is different from the authentic stuff I hear when I go to the Caribbean, and Caribbean people may think I'm not really playing calypso."[38] One intriguing example of the sorts of play going on in this particular moment was the pianist Andrew Hill, born and raised by African American parents on the South Side of Chicago. Hill's music, for example, the classic Blue Note releases *Judgment!* and *Point of Departure*, often containing Caribbean motifs as the titles of some of his compositions—"Le Serpent Qui Danse" and "Les Noirs Marchant"—lent support to the perception that he was an immigrant from Haiti (as he himself often suggested). He would later reveal that that assumption was partly made as a result of his friendship with Andrew Cyrille, who was a native of Haiti, and because he simply never bothered to deny the assertion (and, indeed, after awhile embraced the immigrant persona).[39]

Among actors of this generation, the pattern was generally the same. Given the limited roles available to black actors, and the broader imperatives that linked the representation of blacks in film to the concerns of the civil rights movement, it is not surprising that those actors of Caribbean background who were working in the 1950s and early 1960s, including Canada Lee, Brock Peters, William Greaves, and later, Cicely Tyson, Calvin Lockhart, Percy Rodrigues, Antonio Fargas, and Billy Dee Williams, did not bring any demonstrably visible Caribbean element to their work. The one partial exception to this tendency was, of course, Harry Belafonte. As the figurehead associated with the calypso craze of the 1950s, Belafonte is one example of an individual of West Indian background who achieved significant mainstream success in the United States as a visible product of the Caribbean, albeit in ways that often reinforced the suggestion that Afro-Caribbeans were foreign, exotic others.

Although Belafonte was actually born in the United States, his mother was a Jamaican Garveyite, his father was from Martinique, and between the ages of one and twelve he was raised in St. Ann's, Jamaica. Significantly, he initially launched his career as a jazz singer, playing with Al Haig, Charlie Parker, and Dizzy Gillespie at the Red Rooster in Manhattan in the late 1940s. He subsequently moved into the Caribbean folk idiom popularized in the U.S. by Trinidadian calypsonians Atilla the Hun, Roaring Lion, Lord Beginner, Lord Invader, and Tiger; Trinidadian immigrant Wilmoth Houdini; Ella Fitzgerald and Louis Jordan ("Stone Cold Dead in the Market"); and the Andrews Sisters (their hit recording of Lord Invader's "Rum and Coca-Cola").[40]

Reflecting the same kind of in-between space in which Sonny Rollins negotiated the calypso into the jazz tradition, it is also worth noting that Belafonte received a fair deal of criticism on account of the title attributed to him—the "King of Calypso"—from Trinidadians, for whom such titles are a serious matter. In response to these challenges, Belafonte offered a remarkable characterization—perhaps more accurately mischaracterization—of the art form:

> I find that most of the culture coming out of Trinidad among
> calypso singers is not in the best interests of the Caribbean
> community. . . . [They] sing about our sexual power, and our gift
> of drinking, and rape, and all the things we do to which I have, and
> want, no particular claim. What I have sought to do with my art is
> take my understanding of the region and put it before people in a
> positive way. And doing these songs gives people another impression
> than the mythology they have that we're all lazy, living out of a
> banana tree, fucking each other to death.

While this assessment overlooked the effects of censorship in the British colony, and the preference among tourists, gatekeepers, and consumers abroad for certain sorts of material, he later expressed greater respect for Trinidadian practitioners of the idiom and sensitivity to the ways his popularity displaced "real" calypsonians, noting,

> I resisted and disliked intensely . . . the callous, indifferent, almost
> racist way in which marketing people defined me as the "King of
> Calypso," with very little reverence for the fact that there was a
> place called Trinidad, a tradition called Carnival, and a history of
> great poets coming together and writing these very witty songs.
> Consequently there was a sense in the Caribbean that I was
> somehow complicit in the pirating of a culture.[41]

As cultural studies historian Lisa McGill argues, we should think of Belafonte's work—and she emphasizes in particular the increasing deployment of his body and physicality in this context—as establishing a beachhead for the consideration of black male sexuality as well as civil rights aspirations, and their conjunctions. Although interventions could not be explicitly and directly made in the American imaginary, the readings of Belafonte's foreign body had to and inevitably did have some effect on domestic American racial discourse. In this context, Belafonte's role in *Island in the Sun*, a film that spoke rather directly to racial inequalities and the forces driving anticolonial politics, is worth considering, if only for the effects it had that his music alone never quite achieved. In the 1957 release, he is featured singing twice, and the impact of the associated visuals gives even greater political import to the lyrics, written by Irving Burgie. The composer of many of Belafonte's hits in this period, including "Day-O" and "Jamaica Farewell," Burgie notes that his own background, being "a person of West Indian and American descent," influenced the songs he wrote for the film: "I was keenly interested in the move toward independence in the Caribbean in the mid-1950s as well as the civil rights movement in the US. To me they were definitely related, so I approached the movie assignment with as much passion as I could muster." A large part of the film's power derives precisely from its joining of Belafonte the singer representative, at least until that point, of a tropical, and benign albeit sensual Caribbean, and Belafonte the actor-approaching-activist signifying a firmer, although again provocatively sexualized resistance, to colonial practices abroad and, by implicit extension, in the United States.[42]

Set in the fictional British Caribbean colony of Santa Marta, which is about to achieve some degree of autonomy, the film features Belafonte as David Boyeur, a native seeking a seat in the legislature and a leadership role on the island. In *Island*, issues of racial purity and interracial relationships provided most of the plot structure against a backdrop of electoral politics and carnival. "Grudges get paid off at carnival," notes a character played by Joan Collins, and indeed it would have been hard for American audiences to miss the implicit references to domestic racial arrangements and the ways the (carnival) mask might be misread as purely playful and accommodationist. Significantly, though, the predominant imperial power in the film is England, and the United States, in the character of an American journalist, functions as a social leveler of sorts by investigating and revealing the island's fragile hierarchies and hypocrisies.[43]

Belafonte's character was located and constrained by many of the same forces and understandings that bound his own career. On the one hand, the movie emphasizes his physicality and appeal, as well as his popularity with the island's black population. At the same time, he is marked as separate from this community by his color—being visibly lighter than the vast majority of the blacks on the island—and his existence above and apart from the laboring classes, a distinction captured most clearly in a scene where he sings "Lead Man Holler" while the fishermen surrounding him work drawing in their nets.

While Boyeur is distinguished visually and by his relation to the means of production from the island's black population, he is also, despite the attention paid to his physical charms, involved in a relationship with a character (played by Joan Fontaine) that does not allow for much in the way of fireworks. Although the film was marketed to exploit the popularity of Belafonte's calypsonian persona, scenes scripted and in some cases shot were deleted in order not to provoke American sensibilities too much. As a result, a palpable tension underscores the film between Belafonte's/Boyeur's amplified sexuality—and the sensuality often attributed to the Caribbean itself—and the inability of the movie to engage and acknowledge these possibilities fully. Although the film did reasonably well on release in the United States, it met with a cooler reception in the South (and indeed at one point the South Carolina legislature threatened theaters considering screening the feature with fines of $5,000).[44]

The sorts of triangulation Belafonte was engaged in during this period, then, were not easily finessed or entirely successful. As McGill emphasizes, his efforts were

> severely hampered by white America's inability in the late 1950s
> to finally translate its adoration of the King of Calypso into an
> acceptance of African American male citizenship. America's flirtation
> with Belafonte really said as much about the uncertainties of the times
> and the mood of mainstream America as it did about Belafonte's
> talent itself.[45]

Moreover, Belafonte's increasing identification as a Caribbean American icon in the late 1950s can be interpreted as an attempt to escape not only the racial impasse of the mid-1950s (even post-*Brown*) but also the pressures associated with the Red Scare. If he was being blacklisted as a result of his leftist affiliations and his clear commitments to Paul Robeson, the calypso reinvention allowed him to renegotiate, if not escape completely, that constrained and limiting space, while still remaining a politically viable contributor to the more narrowly defined post–Red Scare civil rights movement (i.e., his simultaneous public involvement with Martin Luther King Jr., the SCLC, and SNCC).

On the other hand, Belafonte in *Island in the Sun*, and more generally, can be seen as functioning as a sort of semicolon, not only because of his positioning in the film and in popular culture or his complexion but also because he is both an African American from a supposedly noncolonized space and a subaltern at least partly subsumed within colonial borders. His presence, then, disrupts the narratives that might distinguish these places by revealing crucial entanglements and juxtaposing the intimacies of the (Caribbean) colonial with the (American) modern. As the semicolon allows the joining of two thoughts that might otherwise have to be separated—or remain disarticulated—Belafonte's text draws our attention to that which comes after, to the possible elaborations that might otherwise be censored or silenced.[46]

It is in the same context that the emergence of Sidney Poitier as the cinematic symbol of black American respectability and upward mobility in the late 1950s and 1960s was intriguing and, in some ways, ironic. Growing up without the experience of American racism, the American-born and Caribbean-raised Poitier has argued, gave him and Harry Belafonte an "opportunity to arrive at the formation of a sense of ourselves without having it fucked with by racism as it existed in the United States" and a sense of "pride and entitlement."[47] At the same time, it is fascinating to compare and contrast the ways these two West Indian disciples of Robeson performed self in this period, with one—the brown and sensual Belafonte—playing out and the other, black and asexual, effectively playing under. This contrasting should be qualified: Belafonte, whose film career was rather limited in comparison to his friend's, played under as an African American in the two films he appeared in after *Island*—*Odds against Tomorrow* and *The World, the Flesh, and the Devil* (both 1959)—and Poitier did portray Africans abroad in *Cry, the Beloved Country* (1951) and *The Mark of the Hawk* (1958). In other words, while Belafonte's recordings and acting in *Island* marked him as a black other, it was an alterity apparently tied to a distinct geographical imagination situated largely outside the United States. In the roles he played set firmly within the nation's borders, he was cast as a native son. Poitier's own foreign adventures in acting, at least in this period, did not put into question his credentials as an authentic American black or, more broadly, trouble the association of a certain way of being with black life in the United States and assumptions regarding how cultures correlate with national frameworks.

Accordingly, one of the more amusing passages in Poitier's first biography refers to his attempts to free himself of his Bahamian intonation—Frederick O'Neal of the Harlem-based American Negro Theatre had told him, "[Y]ou can't be an actor with an accent like that"—and assimilate an American accent (by listening to the radio). Regarding the effectiveness of Poitier's masking, Nelson George writes,

> I'd never known Sidney was what we ignorantly called West Indian
> when I'd first seen his work and, very likely, it would have negatively
> affected my view of him. . . . The very qualities I admired in Sidney

were the things that made me resent the West Indians I knew. The irony is that a lot of the regal bearing he projected could, *in another context*, have been seen as insufferable superiority.⁴⁸

Poitier's engagement of the African American mask, then, never featured the playing against aspect, at least throughout the late stages of the civil rights campaign.

Cold War–era American efforts to improve the country's image abroad lent support to the passage of not only the Civil Rights Act of 1964 and the Voting Rights Act of 1965 but also the immigration law reforms of 1965 that lifted the national origins quotas, including the restrictions specifically placed on Caribbean migration. With the relaxation of barriers to West Indian migrants in the United States and Canada (at the same time, nevertheless, that new restrictions on Caribbean immigration to England were being imposed), a broader space would emerge for sorts of play not directly connected to the concerns of "the movement."⁴⁹ In this new context, the comedian and actor Godfrey Cambridge (*Watermelon Man*) would make occasional use of a West Indian accent in *Come Back, Charleston Blue*. At one point in the film, he breaks into patois when his character, a detective, goes undercover as a woman being threatened by her drunken partner. Later on, Cambridge, a Harlem native of Caribbean parentage, largely raised by his grandparents in the Canadian province of Nova Scotia, assumes the character of a West Indian cab driver in New York: "Back home in the islands we don't do nothing unless we want to. And you know something? We live longer!" Significantly though, this film, including what were undoubtedly Cambridge's own improvisations, was made and released post-1965. Poitier, for his part, would play a Caribbean immigrant in London in the 1967 production *To Sir, with Love*. In *For Love of Ivy*, released the following year and one of the first films Poitier had a hand in conceiving, and part of his effort to free himself from the civil-rights-era icon straitjacket, he is a West Indian immigrant to the United States who is labeled by his love interest Ivy (Abbey Lincoln), in a moment of anger, as a "lowlife, rotten West Indian." In the last line of the film, after the protagonists have reconciled, Poitier asks Lincoln, with a smile on his face, "What have you got against West Indians?" This question posed in *For Love of Ivy* presents an interesting analogue to one he asks of a racist "psychopath" played by Bobby Darin in his earlier feature *Pressure Point* (1962) in which Poitier plays a psychiatrist: "What have you got against us Negroes?" Both queries probe for some explanation of what is seen as the unreasonable exclusion of a particular group and, given the extratext that is Poitier—and in particular, his embodiment of the cool, rational gaze—it is intriguing to read the two utterances together for evidence not only of changes in Poitier's persona but also the shifts in black intramural discourse that might follow the civil rights moment.[50]

SOUL REBELS AND THE CIA

By the late 1960s, the backlash against Poitier as a symbol of the integrationist movement persuaded him to step out of the limelight temporarily and "into a kind of retirement," as he later suggested. "I didn't announce it formally, but [I] went on down to the Caribbean and just cooled it." Returning to the Bahamas, his childhood home, Poitier became involved in Bahamian politics, and specifically the 1967 campaign of the Progressive Liberal Party (PLP) and its leader, Lynden O. Pindling. The PLP, the Bahamas' first formal party, had been established in 1953 as an outgrowth of the Citizen's Committee, formed to protest the all-white ruling elite's disengagement from efforts to form a West Indian Federation; the racial segregation practiced in many businesses, clubs, schools, hotels, and cinemas; and the actions of the government's Censorship Board, which had recently banned three films perceived to be "racially sensitive." Ironically, one of the movies in question—the others were *Pinky* and *Lost Boundaries*—was Poitier's 1950 film debut *No Way Out*, a rather provocative feature in which he played a black doctor trying to negotiate racial tensions in the context of the riots that took place after World War II. This movie, which established the role Poitier would play with slight variations for the next two decades—the intelligent and capable black man who keeps his cool and dignity in the face of white irrationality—was also banned in parts of the United States (as it featured a black doctor treating white patients). By the late 1960s, the PLP was challenging the United Bahamian Party (UBP)—which had formed to represent the white elite, in response to the emergence of the Liberals—for control of the government and a mandate to push for Bahamian independence. Besides the credibility Poitier's appearances on the stump generated for the PLP, he was also a key contributor, with further support coming from Adam Clayton Powell Jr., Martin Luther King Jr., Kwame Nkrumah, and Jamaica's Norman Manley. After Pindling's victory in a tight race, Poitier became involved in the cultural arena, which he saw as crucial to the nation's future. Ultimately, though, he was frustrated by the effects of tourism, which in his view "contaminated, diluted [and] debased . . . any real semblance of a

Bahamian cultural identity"; the efforts of the "middle-class black community . . . to differentiate themselves from the grass-roots black population"; and tensions between himself and Pindling. "Mr. Poitier is a wonderful actor," Pindling would contend, "but he's no politician," an assessment the actor later suggested contained "a great deal of truth." By 1974, the Poitier-Pindling collaboration had run aground, and the actor relocated to Beverly Hills.[51]

The soul revolution that triggered Poitier's marginalization in the late 1960s was having an impact in other parts of the diaspora as well. Brazilian popular culture was affected by the black power movement, particularly in Bahia; black British politics reflected the influence of Malcolm X and the Black Panther Party; James Brown's sonic theories registered in the transformation of Nigerian high-life into Afro-beat—for example, the work of Wole Soyinka's cousin, Fela Anikulapo-Kuti, which was in turn absorbed by JB's band; and the Caribbean was being remade through its incorporation of African American aesthetics. Jimmy Cliff recollects,

> America had long since had Malcolm X, civil rights, the Black
> Panthers and all their movements. And while that had an effect on
> Jamaica insofar as we could see it was possible to do something about
> it, it also made us think we had to get our own thing going. People
> would investigate anything to do with black movements in the United
> States, as people would go backwards and forwards to there and bring
> back news or publications about what was going on there.[52]

Jamaican music had been drawing inspiration from the United States long before the 1960s and particularly since the advent of radio (particularly shortwave radio), which allowed Caribbean listeners to access broadcasts from stations in New Orleans (WNOE), Miami (WINZ), Nashville (WLAC), Schenectady (KDKA), and southern Texas. As a consequence, American R & B artists, including Rosco Gordon, the Tams, the Moonglows, and later the Impressions, provided the models much of Jamaican pop was based on in the late 1950s and 1960s.[53] As Prince Buster (aka Cecil Campbell), ska pioneer and one of the chief architects of Jamaican sound system culture, puts it, "The minds of the Jamaican people were colonized by America's rhythm and blues."[54] The transition from mento to ska, the soundtrack for Jamaican independence, to rock steady and finally reggae, in Jamaican popular music, reflected the changes that took place in African American pop during the decade of the 1960s—filtered, though, through a particular sensibility: the ska productions of Clement "Coxsone" Dodd, a former cane cutter and carpenter in the United States who brought R & B records back home after his trips, were reportedly inspired by "national pride"; and Prince Buster contends that he made "Jamaican records ... [to] push out that American thing." "[C]ultural independence from the USA was every bit as important as political independence from the UK," suggests musicologist Lloyd Bradley. Nevertheless, the imprint of soul (e.g., Aretha Franklin, Otis Redding, and James Brown) would be quite evident in the work of Jamaica's two most popular bands by the end of the decade, the Maytals, led by Frederick "Toots" Hibbert (e.g., "54–46 That's My Number," "Funky Kingston") and the Wailers, who had hits such as "Soul Shakedown Party" and "Soul Rebel," featuring Neville O'Riley "Bunny Wailer" Livingstone, Winston Hubert McIntosh, aka "Peter Tosh," and Robert Nesta ("Bob") Marley.[55]

American influences were increasingly felt in another area as well. As Britain was adjusting to its junior partner relationship with the United States and its reduced status after World War II, the former British colonies and soon-to-be independent nations of the Caribbean found themselves under the sway of American foreign policy concerns. Although there certainly were beneficial aspects of this development, in terms of trade and technology, the heightened interest of the United States in the Caribbean, especially given the United States' Cold War preoccupations, particularly with regard to Cuba, placed limits on the kinds of experiments the Caribbean islands could pursue without incurring resistance from their dominant neighbor to the north. In this regard, the United States' role in removing Cheddi Jagan from power in Guyana in 1964 was, as Cary Fraser notes, "a signal to the rest of the Commonwealth Caribbean of the limits of American tolerance."[56]

Against this backdrop, the Jamaican People's National Party (PNP), established in 1938, struggled to negotiate some leeway with regard to instituting redistributive mechanisms that might tackle some of the problems facing postindependence Jamaica, especially after the failure of the effort to join the anglophone Caribbean in a West Indian Federation. Two years before his 1972 election, PNP leader Michael Manley—a graduate of the London School of Economics and son of the party's founder, Norman Manley—had written in *Foreign Affairs* in reference to the situation in Jamaica, "Where gross disparities in wealth, massive unemployment, showpiece industries, and conspicuous consumption coexist in one overpopulated island, violence and even revolution must lurk in the wings." Consequently, after assuming power, Manley instituted socialist policies that worried American foreign policy–makers and increased the interactions between the island and its neighbor to the north,

Cuba. The response from the Jamaican establishment was not surprising. An editorial in the conservative *Gleaner* suggested:

> Government ministers can laugh if they want but many Jamaicans are very worried about the sudden interest in relations with socialist countries. . . . Jamaica has always been very firmly on the side of the West. Any sudden departure from this . . . has to upset some people. And those who are most easily upset are those who have . . . money to invest.

In response to the criticisms in the *Gleaner* and elsewhere, the PNP's policies were outlined in the following statement issued by Manley in 1974:

> We believe that the mixed economy has a permanent place and relevance in Jamaican economic affairs. The government is committed to the concept of a mixed economy within . . . the Socialist organization planned for Jamaica. The role of the government within this type of economic organization is to ensure that all development takes place in accordance with the needs and goals of the society.

Speaking to a reporter in 1976, Manley elaborated,

> We believe in the free political system—free institutions, the right of dissent, the rule of law, parliamentary democracy, the right of people to form their own political organizations, and the obligation of Socialists to hold on to power by being so effective that they outcompete in the marketplace of the political system.

It was also Manley who would identify Jamaica as part of the "Third World," a perception of the island that, one commentator suggests, "was without precedent among its inhabitants."[57]

Not surprisingly, reggae music and musicians played a role in this transition. The PNP's theme song during the 1972 election campaign was Delroy Wilson's "Better Must Come" (although Wilson would later deny that the song had anything to do with politics), and songs by other artists, including Max Romeo ("Let the Power Fall on I"), Junior Byles, and Ken Lazarus, offered implicit support for the PNP in its competition with the governing Jamaican Labour Party (JLP). In response, the JLP banned a number of reggae songs from the airwaves. Perhaps the closest symbolic connection was the "rod of correction," given to him by Ethiopia's Haile Selassie, that Manley carried with him throughout the campaign. The rod, and Manley's acceptance of the support of the largely Rastafarian reggae community—a constituency that had been ignored, and indeed avoided and stigmatized, in previous campaigns— brought him the support of class and generational groups that might not otherwise have supported the PNP. Accordingly, Clancy Eccles, who served as Manley's musical consultant and advisor, recorded "Rod of Correction" as part of the 1972 campaign and—along with former Skatalites manager Percival "P. J." Patterson—organized the PNP Bandwagon, which featured, among others, Dennis Brown, Alton Ellis, Inner Circle, Judy Mowatt, Scotty, and Bob and Rita Marley. The caravan was also filmed by Perry Henzell, who helped produce ads for the PNP (and was responsible for the release of the film classic *The Harder They Come* the same year).[58]

The closest connection between the realms of music and formal politics was the bond that connected Manley and Marley, the lead singer of the Wailers. Marley, who had initially adopted Rastafarianism in the mid-1960s, had become by the early 1970s the most prominent artist in Jamaican reggae, at least in the international market. In common with the other major acts of the era (e.g., Burning Spear, the Maytals, Culture, Third World), and Rastafarians in general, Marley's music promoted the ideas of Marcus Garvey filtered through a form of Ethiopianism that the UNIA's leader undoubtedly would not have recognized, or likely endorsed (indeed, Garvey's relations with the Rastafarian movement, as with Selassie, in the 1930s were hardly warm). The element of resistance common to Rastafarianism and Manley's leftism— "a brand of Socialism" he claimed was "unique to Jamaica"—made the subtle collaboration between the two feasible (a commonality reflected in what Paul Gilroy would later refer to as "Marley's inherent socialism").[59]

Certainly up until 1976 and Manley's reelection campaign that year, it is apparent that Marley was offering, at the very least, implicit support for the PNP and its policies. "Money is like water in the sea," he observed in late 1976. "People work for money, den dem don't want to split it. . . . So much guys have so much—too much—while so many have nothing at all. We don't feel that is right, because it don't take a guy a hundred million dollars to keep him satisfied. Everybody has to live." Making the connection to the ruling PNP, he continued, "Michael Manley say 'im wan help poor people. . . . You *have* to share. I don't care if it sounds political or whatever it is, but people have to *share*." This relationship reached its apex at the end of that year when Manley called an election on November 22 (for December 15), shortly after Marley agreed to the PNP's request that he play a free concert—the "Smile Jamaica" festival—in Kingston on December 5, 1976. At Manley's suggestion, Marley also wrote and recorded a single, also entitled "Smile Jamaica," that was as close to a PNP advertisement as one could imagine, given the circumstances ("Smile, natty dread, smile, you're in Jamaica; get it together right now in Jamaica"); as the poet-intellectual Linton Kwesi Johnson suggests, the song "was quite clearly propagandist." The partisan implications of Marley's work were also clear in the lyrics on the Wailers' album that year, *Rastaman Vibration*, most obviously on the track "Rat Race," in which Marley sang, "Rasta don't work for the CIA," a double-edged reference to the United States' clear support for the JLP and its leader, Edward ("CIAga") Seaga.[60]

This cross-identification was heightened by the events that took place on December 3, 1976, at Marley's headquarters at 56 Hope Road, in one of the more upscale neighborhoods in Kingston (a setup that resembled in some ways Fela Kuti's Kalakuta compound in Lagos). That evening armed intruders invaded the Marley homestead and shot Marley, his wife Rita, a friend of his, Lewis Griffith, and his manager Don Taylor. While Griffith and Taylor were critically wounded, no one died, and it is still not clear whether the gunmen were acting on orders from supporters of the JLP or independent operators seeking to settle an unrelated score. A CIA memo circulated after the incident suggested that the concert "was scheduled to coincide with the Jamaica Labour Party's . . . release of its long-awaited manifesto—to the detriment of news time and public attention for the latter" and that the shooting might have been "an attempt by JLP gunmen to halt the concert which would feature the 'politically progressive' music of Marley and other reggae stars." Regardless, the response by Manley and the PNP underscored the political significance of the attack. Manley met the cars carrying the wounded at Kingston's University College Hospital and urged Marley to go ahead with the "Smile Jamaica" concert scheduled for two days later. The PNP's housing minister (and one of the party's so-called Gang of Four), Anthony Spaulding, who had given Marley's wife Rita a house in 1972, similarly pressured the Wailer to keep his commitment to appear at the festival ("Never make a politician grant you a favor; they will always want to control you forever," noted Marley in the song "Revolution"). Offers of support and words of encouragement from Stephen ("Cat") Coore, a member of the popular reggae band Third World and the son of PNP Finance minister David Coore, reinforced these efforts. Marley, and most of the Wailers, did eventually agree to do the show, with Roberta Flack in attendance, after spending the period between the shooting and the show under armed guard provided by the PNP. Manley won the subsequent election, taking forty-seven of the sixty seats in the legislature, under the slogans "We are not for sale" and "We know where we're going." A state of emergency was in force throughout the campaign. Support also came again from Clancy Eccles, who produced Neville "Struggle" Martin's popular PNP theme song entitled "My Leader Born Ya."[61]

The shooting, though, marked a clear turning point in Marley's involvement, implicit or explicit, in Jamaican politics. His subsequent statement "When I decided to do [the] . . . concert . . . *there was no politics*; I just wanted to play for the love of the people" can be read as both an understandable attempt to get out of the line of fire by denying his clear affiliation with Manley, as well as a dismissal of politics, narrowly conceived, as implicitly corrupt. Stepping away from any clear partisan affiliation, he would add, "It's hard not to get involved, but them can't get me involved in politics. I'm a Rastaman, not a politician. At Smile Jamaica, I hadn't done a concert for years and wanted to do a concert. It looked as if I supported politics, but it wasn't like that."[62] Immediately after the concert, Marley left Jamaica for almost a year and a half, going first to the Bahamas, and then, more permanently, to Miami. (The customs officials in Nassau reportedly asked him—appropriately, given the circumstances—if he was entering an application for political asylum.) When he did return to Jamaica in the spring of 1978, it was to investigate the possibility, along with fellow Rastafarians Claudie Massop and Bucky Marshall, of forming a third party to represent the marginalized constituencies in the garrison districts in downtown Kingston (a plan that never came to fruition) and to headline a "Peace Concert" at Kingston's National Stadium, at which he brought Manley and Seaga on stage to embrace, in what was clearly an awkward moment for both party leaders. The concert would mark Marley's final estrangement from the intricacies of Jamaican domestic politics: "I neither go right or left. I go straight ahead, seen? I can't unite the JLP or the PNP because these are two organizations set up to fight against each other. That is called politics and I'm not into those things. We are talking about *Rasta*." Like Fela, who lived in exile in Ghana for a period after his Kalakuta compound was raided in 1977 (as described in "Unknown Soldier") and struggled against the backdrop of a roughly comparable contest between African American–inspired black power politics and American government–supported reaction, Marley's experience (as recorded in the first song he wrote after the shooting incident, "Ambush in the Night") forced him to spend most of the remainder of his career abroad.[63]

Although Manley won the 1976 election, the island's economy was weakened by the events that took place during the eight years the PNP was in power (including disputes with the International Monetary Fund, currency devaluations, and the imposition of austerity measures). His association with Fidel Castro and openness to relations with communist Cuba disturbed American authorities, as well as some members of the Jamaican middle and upper classes (in response to the complaints of the latter, Manley noted, "We have five flights to Miami every day"). Even within the musical community, displeasure was evident. In response to the United States–supported anti-ganja program (Operation Buccaneer), Peter Tosh released "Legalize It," challenging the PNP to follow through on what some felt it had implicitly promised in the 1972 campaign. Junior Murvin released the classic "Police and Thieves" in 1976, and Max Romeo, who had participated in the PNP Bandwagon during the previous election season—and released "Socialism Is Love" in 1974—recorded "One Step Forward" ("and two steps backward"), "Uptown Babies Don't Cry," and "No Joshua No," with its warning "Rasta is watching you and blaming you." The Heptones echoed these sentiments in "Mr. President" and "Sufferah Time." "It was getting too much to bear," suggests toaster Big Youth, with regard to this period and relations between the PNP and the Rastafarian and musical communities, "so we feel we have to hit back with something. Which is our music."[64]

While the complete story remains to be written, there were also possibly efforts by American authorities to destabilize Jamaica and bring about the reelection of a JLP government. Evelyne Huber Stephens and John D. Stephens wrote in 1986,

> Initially, we believed that the allegations of CIA involvement were probably true . . . [but subsequent] investigation raised serious questions as to whether the CIA was conducting a covert action operation in Jamaica. . . . [Although] it is unlikely that there was any CIA-directed covert action operation. . . . our evidence is not conclusive.

Writing eight years later, Anthony J. Payne suggests,

> the involvement of the CIA has not been proven, which is to say it has not been admitted by official US government spokesmen. On the other hand, the circumstantial evidence that its agents were active in Jamaica is strong—too strong, finally, to be ignored. . . . [and] makes it likely the CIA was at work.

It has also been suggested, as Timothy White notes, that "CIA operatives . . . threatened . . . [Marley's] life if he dared come home before the [subsequent 1980] election was over." Either way, a significant increase in guns and drugs flowing into the island contributed to a massive increase in the level of random violence, political tension, and vulnerability of the crucial tourist industry. While there may or may not have been covert action by the CIA, certainly the State Department's overt policy to disseminate negative and frequently false information about the Manley government's policies, and conditions in Jamaica in general (and probably to channel funds into the coffers of the PNP's opponents), illustrate the processes by which nonwhite nation-states are rendered unstable and the relationship between normative, modern democracies and their postcolonial counterparts. Partly as a result of these developments, the JLP and Seaga were returned to power in the 1980 elections, the same year Ronald Reagan was elected president in the United States.[65]

"PLAY I ON THE R & B"

In an attempt to develop an export market for Jamaican culture, and to encourage tourism, Edward Seaga, as Jamaica's minister of development and welfare, had organized a presentation of ska musicians for the 1964 World's Fair in New York City. The Boston-born, Harvard-trained anthropologist had previously collected tapes of early Jamaican folksingers as part of his research; he owned a record label, W.I.R.L. (West Indies Records Limited), which he sold—to Byron Lee, who renamed it Dynamic Records—after he entered politics as a JLP member of parliament in 1959 (representing West Kingston). In other words, he was hardly a stranger to Jamaican music or the intricacies of Caribbean culture. There was some debate, though, about Seaga's choices to represent ska and Jamaica at the 1964 exposition. Millie Small, who had had an international hit with "My Boy Lollipop," was featured, as were Prince Buster (who knew Seaga from his days as a music producer) and Jimmy Cliff. The Wailers, who were by that point Jamaica's most popular singing group, were rejected as inappropriate for the mission. In particular, Seaga's choice of Byron Lee's Dragonaires as the backing band for the show, instead of the more proficient and representative Skatalites, was criticized. "Seaga was thinking like a businessman," suggests Jimmy Cliff, "not an artistic person. If he wanted to promote the music, he should have got the people who were creating it. The singers were good, but Byron Lee's backing didn't work. Seaga wanted up-town guys who looked good, but he should have had people from the roots." Elaborating further, he adds, "It was probably a big factor that the Byron Lee band didn't smoke ganja like all the other musicians. . . . Lee's band were just a calypso band really, playing dance music for people in the hotels, up on the north coast [of Jamaica]." Almost a decade later, though, with the release of Perry Henzell's interpolation of the western genre in the form of *The Harder They Come*, featuring Cliff as the lead actor—and on the soundtrack along with Desmond Dekker, and Toots and the Maytals—the international profile of Jamaican music, which by this time had mutated into reggae, was raised substantially.[66]

The major focus of this heightened attention in the United States would prove to be Bob Marley and the Wailers. The Wailers' ability to establish a certain profile in the American rock music market owed much to the promotional strategies devised by their label, Island Records—named after the 1957 Belafonte movie. The artwork for the group's first U.S. release, *Catch a Fire*, involved an expensive sleeve that opened up like a lighter, reflecting both the project's title and its connection to the emerging weed culture, the latter angle being one of the major selling points for the Wailers, reggae, and Rastafarianism among rock music audiences. Similarly, advertisements for the Wailers' albums, certainly up until the late 1970s, by which point Peter Tosh and Bunny Wailer had left the group, were slanted toward a rock audience ("reggae at its sinuously, sexily, rocking best" as one rock trade advertisement put it). Even though Island Records' founder, Chris Blackwell, Jamaican-born of English background, had first established himself by serving the British ska and rock steady music markets during the 1960s (as coowner of the Trojan label), he had grown accustomed to the tastes of the rock market, and it is not surprising that he promoted the Wailers in the United States via the same media his label used for its other acts (e.g., bands such as King Crimson, Roxy Music, Jethro Tull, and Traffic) and spoke of making Marley "as big as [Jimi] Hendrix." He later elaborated, "[M]y concept was always that Bob was a black rock act, not R & B; forget about R & B, later for that. . . . The audience I felt he could really reach, apart from Jamaica, was the rock audience: college kids, liberal kids interested in culture, people's lives, and what was going on."[67]

Blackwell, who played a significant role in constructing the Wailers' sound and image in foreign markets, Marley, and the Wailer's bassist, Aston "Family Man" Barrett, also considered it important to add a rock guitar element to the Wailers' music to make it more palatable. Consequently, lead guitarists with a blues-rock background were a consistent element in the Wailers' lineup throughout the 1970s. Perhaps ironically, these guitarists were usually African Americans. The first musician to fill this role, Al Anderson, a native of Montclair, New Jersey, recollects, "I was in a funny position with the Wailers.

I was the 'white' cat in the band, the Yank, the American guy fuckin' up the music by playing loud rock and roll." "American guitarists, white guitarists," Marley suggested in a 1976 interview, "don't understand the beat of reggae. But Al, man, he's black and he knows the feeling; he's an exception." After Anderson's temporary departure from the group, he was replaced by blues-rock guitarist Donald Kinsey, who in turn left the band immediately after the "Smile Jamaica" incident in 1976 (the shooting, which he witnessed, happened during his first visit to Jamaica). Kinsey was replaced by another blues-rock guitarist, Julian "Junior" Marvin, a native of Jamaica who had been raised in the United Kingdom and the United States.[68]

Marley, for his part, was hardly a stranger to the United States. Aside from the Wailers' borrowings from African American soul, Marley's mother had moved to Wilmington, Delaware, in the early 1960s, and Marley lived with her for periods throughout the latter half of the decade, working at different points as a waiter, a DuPont lab assistant, a forklift driver on the night shift (an experience recalled in the song "Night Shift" from the album *Rastaman Vibration*), a bellboy at the DuPont Hotel, under the pseudonym "Donald Marley," and a Chrysler assembly-line worker. His wife, Rita, worked as a nurse's aid and as a housemaid in Wilmington. Indeed, it has been suggested that he returned to Jamaica primarily to avoid a draft notice from the Selective Service after being laid off by Chrysler.[69]

Texas native Johnny Nash, a pop and R & B singer, had also scored a hit with Marley's "Stir It Up" in 1973 (from the same album that featured Nash's most popular recording, "I Can See Clearly Now") thus providing an opening for Marley and his music in the American market.[70] Nevertheless, in the early and mid-1970s, the Wailers and reggae music never made the inroads into the black American consciousness that Marley and others expected they would, on the basis of the assumption that blacks in the United States would welcome the soul-revolution-inspired Wailers into the broader black American music community. In this period, Marley's then manager, Danny Sims, tried to persuade prominent R & B disc jockeys Hal Jackson and Frankie Crocker to play recordings Marley had made with his wife Rita, and Peter Tosh, to no avail—with Crocker suggesting that Sims needed to "bring a translator" along with the records. Perhaps symbolically, after signing to Island, in 1973 the group was thrown off its first American tour, as the opening act for Sly and the Family Stone, because they were apparently making too strong an impression on the audiences and consequently creating problems for the headliners. "Sly don't dig that," noted Sly's manager, and the Family Stone's drummer exclaimed, in response to the Wailer's dreadlocks and general presentation, "Holy shit! What country are these guys *from*? They look like they're from something out of the Old Testament."[71]

Reggae in general did offer a distinctly new image of West Indians for African American consumers, as it emerged as the dominant modal Caribbean culture in the West Indies and abroad, in contrast to that presented during the reign of calypso. "Before Bob Marley and ganja and Rastafarianism put an Afrocentric, rootsy spin on the American view of Caribbean culture," writes Nelson George, "I'd always viewed its transplanted natives as snobby, snotty, and uppity." Up until the early 1970s, West Indians were still, as George notes, associated with anglophilia, arrogance, and in some circles, bourgeois affectations. Orde Coombs, himself an immigrant to New York City from St. Vincent, argued in a gendered fashion that, given the developments associated with the soul revolution and the black power movement, West Indians could benefit from African American leadership:

> This is 1970 and it is imperative now that the West Indian and
> the American black move toward each other. They need each
> other, not so much out of love, but because of the realities of
> the age. The liberation of the black psyche is going to be one of
> the struggles of the seventies; the American black must lead this
> struggle. It is his experience of flexibility, of energy, of vitality that
> would not die that must be the West Indian's guiding light. . . .
> West Indians [can find] . . . a viable identity. . . . in that continuum
> of sensibility that stretches through the Caribbean and Africa and
> North and South America. They can find it in a community of
> black men with a not dissimilar past, an agonizing present, and a
> fantastic future.[72]

In other words, before the paradigm shift provoked by the emergence of Rastafarianism and reggae as the public representations of Caribbean possibilities on the American scene in the early 1970s, West Indians were not seen as likely agents of cultural change or particularly in tune with the spirit of the times. The new politics and black power aesthetics associated with reggae's appearance offered an opportunity for African Americans and West Indians to interact on potentially radically different terms, and in this context it is interesting to think of the Island logo, with its slightly dissonant references to the Belafonte film and an idyllic West Indies, anticipating this transition while at the same time remaining in some tension with the distinctly new Caribbean imaginary that 1970s reggae embodied.

Reggae-influenced sounds did have some discernible influence on a number of drummers during the soul era. The music of the instrumental recording group Booker T. and the MG's reveals some of the earliest examples of the influence of Jamaican pop on American R & B (e.g., "Booker-Loo," "Soul Limbo," and "Melting Pot"). As the group's guitarist, Steve Cropper, recalls, "Soul Limbo" began "as a reggae kind of thing that [MG's drummer] Al [Jackson] had been toying with, since he was into the Jamaican sound really early." The MG's sound clearly had an impact on the evolution of Jamaican pop as well (e.g., Jackie Mittoo). Teddy Pendergrass, who drummed with Harold Melvin and the Blue Notes before he became their lead singer and later a solo star, recollects: "All the traveling we did to the Caribbean and South America exposed me to rhythms and sounds I'd never heard before. I began combining my basic, straight-ahead, heavy backbeat grooves with the full spectrum of exotic syncopated Caribbean styles." Bernard ("Pretty") Purdie, one of the most influential drummers of the 1960s and 1970s, played on sessions in Jamaica in the late 1960s (primarily for JAD records), and has noted that his subsequent playing was influenced by reggae:

> I played and recorded with Bob in Jamaica. . . . The musicians
> there taught me the real authentic reggae music, which usually has
> percussion played by five different people. . . . Because of what I
> learned with Bob Marley's musicians, I incorporated so much of
> the reggae feel into my music over the years. For example, listen to
> Aretha Franklin's "Daydreaming" and "Rocksteady," [and] Donny
> Hathaway and Roberta Flack's "Where Is the Love?" to name a few.[73]

Accordingly, given these subliminal borrowings and possibilities for more explicit diasporic interaction, and seeking to secure more direct access to black American audiences, Marley contemplated signing with Berry Gordy's Motown Records during a 1974 dispute with Island.[74] Despite his outreach efforts, though, R & B disc jockeys reportedly "dismissed reggae as 'jungle music'"—using a term that had been applied to Duke Ellington (during his Cotton Club period) and Miles Davis (with regard to *Bitches Brew*) previously—and were unresponsive, Arnold Shaw suggests, because of the music's "not easily understood patois." Furthermore, Shaw contends that Marley's efforts in particular were rejected because of "the social and political protest that [underlay his work] . . . and characterized him as a revolutionary [as well as] . . . his denunciation of colonialism, which . . . made him so attractive to the Third World nations." To some extent, reggae was coming from a place that many contemporary 1970s R & B

people were fleeing. Gil Scott-Heron, the Chicago-born son of a Jamaican football player raised in Canada, and one of the few "political" artists remaining in
this period—he referred to his music as "Third World music"—recollects that,
given the prevailing trends, continuing to focus on broader social themes "was
like being the only guy in an all-girls school. We always thought we were out
there by ourselves, even when we weren't. It was as if I was a gorilla driving a car."
Reggae musicians also felt alienated by what they perceived to be the dominant
trends in mid-1970s African American culture. The Wailers' keyboard player,
Tyrone Downie, remarked, "The blacks in America are into glitter; they're into
platform shoes, fur coats and Cadillacs. They're tame, man, and they're not
about to let their pretty Afros down. All that talk of revolution—it *vex* 'em, it
vex 'em bad." "Death to disco," stated former Wailer Peter Tosh, now pursuing
a solo career, "I am here to make reggae the international music, because disco
doesn't have the spiritual potential of reggae. The devil created disco, telling
black people to get down get down all the time. But I-man seh to black people,
'Get up stand up for your rights.'"[75]

By this point, the latter half of the 1970s, Marley had established a significant profile in the United Kingdom. A natural additional site for Marley's
operations, London had functioned as a launching pad and refuge for exiles
such as Haile Selassie, Garvey, Padmore, and James in the 1930s, and Claudia
Jones. Jones, who was deported from the United States in 1955, initiated the first
carnival in London in response to the Notting Hill riots of 1958. An earlier generation of African and Caribbean musicians had also migrated to the United
Kingdom, including the Trinidadian calypsonians Aldwyn "Lord Kitchener"
Roberts and Egbert "Lord Beginner" Moore. After popularizing their music
in Jamaica, Roberts and Moore traveled in 1948 on the SS *Empire Windrush* to
England, where along with subsequent migrants—Hubert Raphael "Roaring
Lion" Charles and, for a brief period, Rupert Westmore "Lord Invader"
Grant—they contributed significantly to the midcentury reformation of black
British culture. As noted earlier, Moore, Charles, and Grant had also played an
important role, along with Raymond "Attila the Hun" Quevedo and Wilmoth
Houdini, in raising the profile of calypso in the United States in the late 1930s
and 1940s.[76]

Building on the available base of support that the various Caribbean expatriate communities provided, the Wailers had been able to make significant
inroads into the British market by the early 1970s (where the pre-Island albums
Soul Rebel and *African Herbsman* made an impact). While a number of Jamaican
artists emigrated to Canada, Toronto in particular, in this period—including

Jackie Mittoo, Alton Ellis, and Leroy Sibbles of the Heptones—London, with its relatively sizeable West Indian population and the increasing appeal of Rastafari to the younger generations of black youth throughout England, proved an especially attractive home for Marley. After the attempted assassination forced him to leave Jamaica, the ties he had established in black London made the city a convenient second headquarters; his colleague Neville Garrick recalls, "Bob felt safe in London. He liked the fact that the police didn't carry guns."[77]

Black Britons of Caribbean descent were themselves trying to negotiate a path between the various immigrant backgrounds that informed their parents' upbringings and the pop and rock cultures promoted on British airwaves and television channels. These labors were further energized and complicated by the availability, influence, and hegemonic appeal of African American culture, which provided a relatively accessible means by which to articulate nonwhite identities and unsettle racist hegemonies. Regarding an encounter with Paul Mooney, Richard Pryor's most prominent collaborator, the British comedian Lenny Henry recollects:

> I'm sitting with him and we were doing this routine about blackface, and we were talking about the history of blackface and everything. And *as I was looking at myself in the mirror* suddenly I realised that I'd worked with people in blackface too [i.e., the popular UK television program *The Black and White Minstrel Show,* which was on the air from 1958 until 1978]. And then suddenly there was this big "bing," this bell ringing inside me. I told [Mooney] and he said something like, "Well, it's something you had to go through."

In other words, it was only after engaging with an African American comedian, coming from a context in which blackface performances had stopped being acceptable or necessary half a century earlier, that Henry realized that participating in the television production, ironically, perhaps, based on an American cultural form—well into the 1970s—was problematic, and that with regard to questions of race, Britain left to its own devices was to some significant degree a unique and anachronistic geotemporal formation.[78]

As a consequence of these various presences and pressures, and reflecting the racial bifurcations that underwrite modern citizenship practices, as Barnor Hesse observes, "Black Britishness...retain[ed] the resonance of an oxymoron." Regarding the U.S./UK entanglement, bassist-producer Dennis "Blackbeard" Bovell makes reference to the difficulties aspiring British reggae bands faced in the 1960s and 1970s—such as his own Matumbi, the London outfits Aswad, the Cimarons, and Black Slate, and Birmingham's Steel Pulse—in struggling to establish themselves financially. "[O]nce we decided to just play reggae," he recalls, "it was considered professional suicide, because at the time the most work black musicians could get was at the bases playing for [American] black servicemen who, while they liked the idea of a black group *from the islands*, wanted to hear Wilson Pickett [and] Otis Redding." On another cultural front, Bovell, a native of Barbados who arrived in London as a young child with his parents, also spoke of the code-switching required for many black Londoners as they moved between "cockney accent[s]" and "some kind of Jamaican tone" in a context in which Jamaican patois and reggae were emerging as the modal black cultural forms.[79]

The appetite for "authentic" Jamaican musical product, and the sense that an indigenous black Britishness was to some degree impossible, even among the second and third generations, compelled Bovell and others to present their work as if it originated in Jamaica, a ruse facilitated by a number of means. Beyond attempting sartorial and phonic fidelity through the assimilation of Jamaican patois, these aspirations toward the "authentic" included having records pressed in Ireland, "where the finished product didn't come out as sophisticated" or in Jamaica, "so they *felt* Jamaican," as Jamaican singles and albums tended to be of a rougher quality, with irregular grooves and rough edges. Another means of masking black British origins involved acquiring the machines used to make seven-inch singles in the United States and Jamaica to punch the larger, 3.75-centimeter holes standard in those national markets— and accordingly requiring a record adapter—in contrast to the 0.75-centimeter, spindle-wide holes typical of British product. Not surprisingly, similar pressures registered in the Canadian context as well, where records recorded and pressed in Toronto would be stamped "Made in Jamaica" because of the perception that Canadian reggae could not be marketed at home or abroad on its own terms. Indeed, reflecting the hierarchies that existed among Caribbean expatriate communities, British reggae product was granted a certain legitimacy over Canadian product in this period in Canada and elsewhere, with Jamaican releases remaining, as always, the most respected and "authentic."[80]

Despite the pressures to reproduce authentic Jamaican sounds and textures imposed on and internalized by black British reggae artists, and the expectation that they should play under rather than play out, this cohort made innovations that arguably impacted Marley's own stylistic choices in this period. Specifically, the lovers' rock idiom emphasizing romantic lyrics rather than the "cultural" concerns characteristic of most Jamaican reggae—that is, rockers—would be shaped and take root in England. Representing an attempt to conjoin reggae and the appeal of American R & B, the new form marked the first significant contribution of black British artists to the reggae international. "Because the majority of the crowds that made lovers' rock such a big scene were born in the UK, and maybe not even to Jamaican parents," notes Bovell, "lovers dub was always about matching the *Jamaicanicity* necessary for the best reggae with sounds and arrangements that made it palatable to the British ear." Regarding the latter concern, in contrast to the characteristic structure of reggae compositions that involved only verses and choruses, bridges were commonly added to lovers' rock recordings and indeed were a regular feature in most British reggae product—constituting as Bovell notes, "a very American way of writing," similar to, in his view, the templates popularized by Isaac Hayes and David Porter at Stax, and Motown's Holland-Dozier-Holland writing team. Further, suggests Bovell, who played a pioneering role in the emergence of these recordings, which usually featured female vocalists, including Janet Kay (the classic "Silly Games") and Brown Sugar—featuring future Soul II Soul member Caron Wheeler—lovers' rock was also seen as being more likely to draw women and their admirers into spaces they would otherwise not enter. "[T]he sounds [DJ crews] that played the best lovers' attracted the prettiest gal," he contends, "and that meant the guys would go there looking fi' capture, so you always got a good crowd."[81]

In this milieu in 1977 Marley and the Wailers completed two albums: *Exodus,* released that June, and *Kaya,* released the following March. The former release, which would prove to be Marley's most popular if not highest charting album, was recorded at two studios in London, the Fallout Shelter, in the basement of Island Records' headquarters in Chiswick, and Basing Street, located in the Caribbean immigrant neighborhood of Ladbroke Grove (adjacent to the similarly populated Notting Hill district). The first half of the album itself focused on political matters, in the narrow sense, and spoke directly to Marley's reorientation following the assassination attempt in Jamaica. Through the opener "Natural Mystic" and "So Much Things to Say," "Guiltiness," and "The Heathen," the Wailers' front man pronounced his ability to rise above and survive the attacks of his enemies and his identification with the Garveyist legacy.

The album's title track, "Exodus," most clearly marked Marley's new sensibility. In contrast to "Smile Jamaica" and its implicit celebration of the PNP and the island's possibilities ("Get it together in Jamaica"), "Exodus" with its biblical references recontextualized the slogan the PNP used in the 1976 election, "We know where we're going," by appending the line, "We're leaving

Babylon [which would now include Jamaica]; we're going to the fatherland." Musically, the song incorporated elements from the soundtrack for the film *Exodus* (1960), at the suggestion of Wailers' bassist and bandleader Family Man Barrett, and a charging 4/4 rhythm more compatible with the disco music of the late seventies. "Exodus" received its first public hearing courtesy of Dennis Bovell's Sufferers Sound System at a party in London's Westbourne Park. Provided with a white label test pressing, and with Marley unobserved but present along with Family Man and Neville Garrick, Bovell was able to garner instant feedback for the Wailers' crew, who subsequently returned to the studio to finish the recording.[82]

The second side of the album *Exodus*, and indeed most of *Kaya*, which was recorded at the same time, tended toward more romantic and mellower themes. "Waiting in Vain" and "Turn Your Lights Down Low" in the first collection represented the first straightforward love songs of Marley's Island career, and one can consider these tracks, along with the similarly oriented tracks on *Kaya*—many of them rerecordings of compositions from the late 1960s and early 1970s—as partly inspired by the popularity of the British lovers' rock genre in the United Kingdom and elsewhere. A second factor was, arguably, the understandable desire to step out of the political arena and the kinds of engagements that might have brought about the assault on the Tuff Gong complex on Hope Road (a possibility directly addressed in the lyrics of *Kaya*'s "Running Away"). Another consideration was evidently how best to appeal to the American R & B market. *Kaya* in this context was, from Marley's perspective, "sweet bait" to hook African American listeners: "Dem call reggae jungle music. If I sweeten it with some R & B flavour, it will make them [in the U.S. market] listen." Extending the metaphor, Neville Garrick, the art director for Marley's albums during this period, contends:

> Being the clever artist he was is why Bob did "Exodus" [and] "Waiting
> in Vain" . . . [and] all those kinda songs, because he realized that
> there was a fight. We wanted that drive time [afternoon and evening
> radio airplay], and we wanted black America; so by having the
> "foreign musicians," the Al Andersons, the Donald Kinseys, the Junior
> Marvins to add that blues and R & B texture, Bob was being a clever
> fisherman.[83]

Seeing it as his mission to build on and complete the efforts initiated by the UNIA in the 1920s, Marley noted, "Marcus Garvey said, 'When the black people in America get ready, the Jamaican must get ready.' It's working in a different way, in a sense, but still, it's gonna work like Marcus Garvey said."[84] In the same spirit he had released "Roots, Rock, Reggae," the first single from the album *Rastaman Vibration*, in which he proclaimed, "Play I on the R & B, want all my people to see," and in the song's fadeout added, in a possible explicit reference to Garvey, "I feel like preaching on the streets of Harlem, want all my people to see."[85] His desire to succeed with African American music consumers only became that much more apparent after the shooting, as his attention shifted from Jamaican developments and politics toward broader diasporic and Pan-Africanist concerns. In 1978, he made his first trip to Africa, visiting Gabon and Ethiopia, and began to see himself as a contributor to greater cohesion among the different diasporic communities, in some ways like Malcolm X after his initial trips to the African continent. With regard to African Americans, he came across an article W. E. B. Du Bois had published in the *Crisis* in 1933, urging diasporic unity, which convinced him of the importance of getting his music played and accepted on black radio stations in the United States.[86] "I feel communication will be good," he replied in response to an interviewer's question in 1979 about the likelihood of African Americans warming to his music, "Because people are starting to pay attention. And that is the thing, we want black people to *look*. 'Cause we don't have anything against the white man in the sense of color prejudice, but black is right!"[87]

The Wailers' album releases were, it should be noted, reaching the R & B charts as well as the rock and pop charts (at least after the album *Natty Dread* in 1974). Indeed, the album *Rastaman Vibration* reached the number eleven position on *Billboard*'s "Soul" charts in 1976 (only slighter lower than the number eight ranking it achieved on the pop charts the same year). The releases that followed, though, fared less well with the black American buying public, even though Marley's efforts to reach these listeners in particular were increased with each subsequent single and album: *Exodus* reached number sixteen, *Survival* number thirty-two, and *Uprising* number forty-one on *Billboard*'s "Soul" charts.[88]

The tour to promote the album *Survival* was launched with a four-night, seven-concert stop at the Apollo in Harlem, which reportedly buzzed as it had not "since the days of Garvey," although even that symbolic attempt to reach African Americans did not work out exactly as planned. As Lloyd Bradley notes, "When the curtains went up . . . Bob found himself looking out at the same faces that would have been there if the show had been at a club in [largely white] Greenwich Village." The album's lead single, "Wake Up and Live," did not do very well either, at a point when artists such as the Commodores ("Still"),

Prince ("I Want to Be Your Lover"), Kool and the Gang ("Ladies Night"), Funkadelic ("[Not Just] Knee Deep"), and Michael Jackson ("Rock with You") were topping the R & B charts. The album *Survival* itself, Marley's most explicit Pan-Africanist document—featuring "Africa Unite" and "Babylon System" and a cover designed by Garrick composed of the flags of the independent black nations and an image of the lower deck of a slave ship—and arguably his most compelling effort musically, also did not sell in great numbers.[89]

For his subsequent release, *Uprising*, the campaign to break the album on black radio was stepped up. A meeting was held in May 1980, at the headquarters of Inner City Broadcasting (ICB), the corporation that owned WBLS-FM and WLIB-FM, two of the major black music and news outlets in the New York area, regarding strategies for increasing Marley's profile in the rhythm and blues community. In attendance were Frankie Crocker, Island's Chris Blackwell, ICB's chief Percy Sutton (who was also Malcolm X's former attorney, future mayor David Dinkins's close advisor, and a prominent Manhattan politician), Marley himself, and more than a dozen executives from the black radio and music industries. Sutton expressed his commitment to the promotional campaign and reportedly told Marley, "I'm happy to be working with you, Bob, because you've just come back from Europe and Africa, where you're bigger than Christ and Muhammad combined. We want to promote shows in most major U.S. cities [and] . . . get you three nights headlining at Madison Square Garden!" Also at the meeting was Danny Sims, by then the owner of the company that published Marley's music, who, it has been suggested, "was always trying to dissuade Bob from actually recording reggae—and 'message' reggae at that . . . [but rather] saw . . . Marley being a money-maker, in [Sims's] . . . own words, 'in a rhythm-and-blues, Top Forty style.'" After an extended debate about the merits of attempting to stage a tour with the Wailers as headliners and the reasons for R & B radio's resistance to reggae music—in which Marley did not participate, even though he was in the room—it was eventually decided that the Wailers would be the opening act for the Commodores.[90]

The most obvious gesture Marley made in his efforts to reach African Americans was to record and release (as the album's first single) "Could You Be Loved," in the autumn of 1980. While the twelve-inch extended mix reached the low forties on *Billboard*'s disco charts, it peaked at number fifty-six on the "Hot Soul" charts, far below, ironically, Tom Browne's "Funkin' for Jamaica" (which referred to Jamaica, Queens, not the Caribbean island). The song's bass line was designed to mix easily with the rhythms popular on R & B radio, but despite the suggestions from Sims that Marley tone down the social commentary in his lyrics—"I discouraged Bob from doing the revolutionary stuff. I'm a commercial guy. I want to sell songs to thirteen-year-old girls, not to guys throwing spears"—"Could You Be Loved" was hardly an unambitious or unambiguous celebration of the material or romantic realms. Like Belafonte's work in *Island in the Sun*, the recording merged the sensual Caribbean with an explicit political challenge ("Don't let them fool you, or even try to school you, oh no; we've got a mind of our own") and juxtaposed disco, reggae, and West African rhythms and textures.[91]

Despite these efforts to make reggae music more palatable to the African American market, the Wailers still did not receive the degree of support they received elsewhere. "America is pure deviltry, dem t'ings dat go on there," lamented Marley during this period, "Dem just work with force and brutality. Dem lock out the punk thing because they see something is happening. [Marley had recorded and released "Punky Reggae Party" in 1977 as a gesture of his respect for the British punk music scene.] So the oppressors bring another man to blind the youth to the truth, and dem call him—John Tra-vol-ta." "It took so long for them [African Americans] just to hear the message, to turn on to the music," claimed Marley's wife, Rita: "Even at our concerts we would have a majority of white people coming to see us, more so than blacks in those days—even toward the end of his life."[92] One of the factors that contributed to Marley's sense of urgency in the last part of the 1970s was his awareness that he was dying, a realization poignantly communicated in the sparse "Redemption Song," the last track on the last album the Wailers recorded. A tour that was launched in the fall of 1980 was cut short when Marley collapsed after a concert in Pittsburgh as a result of the weakness brought on by cancer. On May 11, the following spring, he died in Miami.

COME AGAIN, SELECTOR

Partly as a result of Marley's popularity, and the spread of reggae and sound system culture, and the intersecting patterns of Caribbean outmigration, a deliberative forum of exchange had developed by the beginning of the 1980s that engaged blacks in the United States, United Kingdom, Canada, and the Caribbean and to varying degrees those located elsewhere.[93] It is in this space that Linton Kwesi Johnson's 1979 recording "Reality Poem"—"This is the age of science and technology and some a we a-deal with mythology. . . . This is the age of decision, make we leggo religion"—widely interpreted as a criticism of Rastafarianism, received a response within the year—on the title track of the Wailers' 1979 release *Survival*: "We're the survivors . . . in this age of technological inhumanity . . . scientific atrocity . . . atomic mis-philosophy; we're the survivors. . . . in the eyes of the Almighty."[94] Marley's invitations to play at Zimbabwe's independence celebration and serve as grand marshal at the Labor Day weekend West Indian Carnival Parade in Brooklyn in the last year of his life also illustrate black popular culture's diasporic tendencies, and its role in circulating data among communities engaged simultaneously with the local, national, and transnational.

Reggae music also made some inroads into the American R & B charts during the soul era. Cat Coore's band, Third World, reached the number eleven slot on the "Hot Soul" charts with their discofied remake of the O'Jays' "Now That We Found Love" in 1979, and Jimmy Cliff received some attention in the early 1980s with releases such as "Reggae Night" and "We Are All One." The prime architects of a reggae/funk hybrid that dominated dance floors at the beginning of the 1980s, Robbie Shakespeare and Sly Dunbar, in tandem with the Compass Point All-Stars, headquartered at Chris Blackwell's studio in the Bahamas, contributed to the hits attributed to Jamaican native and model Grace Jones, and Black Uhuru, a vocal trio that included Jamaican vocalists Duckie Simpson and Michael Rose and Sandra "Puma" Jones, a native of South Carolina and graduate of Columbia University. Island promoted Black Uhuru as candidates to fill the void left by Marley's passing, and their releases in this period, for example "Chill Out" and particularly "Sponji Reggae," gained some support from black radio; indeed, WBLS's Frankie Crocker was the first disc jockey to get behind "Sponji Reggae" (just as he had been instrumental in breaking Manu Dibango's 1974 Afro-funk recording "Soul Makossa"). The group's 1981 recording "Youths of Eglinton" made reference to black communities in Toronto (Eglinton Avenue), Brooklyn (Utica Avenue), and London (Brixton), again indicating the autodiasporic commitments of the cultural arenas.[95]

Other reggae-influenced songs also turned up on albums by rhythm and blues artists such as Gil Scott-Heron, the O'Jays, Dexter Wansel, and Cameo (e.g., "Tribute to Bob Marley"). A War recording, "Just Because," engaged a mock Caribbean patois in order to suggest that the turn to disco by R & B artists was driven by mercenary concerns—"Just because I want lots of money, mi no play no disco, mi no crazy"—and to question the distinctions drawn between black cultural communities: "Just because I come from the islands, doesn't mean that I ain't got no soul." Marvin Gaye included "Third World Girl" on the last album he recorded before his death (*Midnight Love*), a collection that was clearly influenced by his exposure to North African and Caribbean sounds while he was in tax exile in Belgium, England, and France. The harmonica playing on "Third World Girl" appears to be a reference to Marley's own "Three O'clock Roadblock" (a connection that is more obvious on the unreleased, original version of this track), and the initial focus of the lyrics is a rather vague testimonial to Marley's accomplishments, before the song shifts to Marvin's more carnal concerns ("My first, my second, my third world girl"). The song was reportedly inspired by a séance Marvin participated in while living in Ostend, Belgium. The most significant example of the influence of reggae on the work of African American musicians was Stevie Wonder's 1980 single "Master Blaster," clearly inspired by Marley in its lyrical references ("From the park I hear rhythms; Marley's hot on the box"), and melody (with its interpolation of the Wailer's "Jammin'"). Third World's 1982 hit "Try Jah Love" was also cowritten and produced by Wonder, and he wrote and produced "You're Playing Us Too Close" for the band, a track whose lyrics contained themes both Wonder and Marley had addressed throughout the 1970s.[96]

Nevertheless, until the "death of rhythm and blues," to borrow from Nelson George's book of the same title, reggae, and Caribbean musics in general, remained largely locked outside of the community of black musics in the United States. Moreover, the majority of the first- and second-generation Caribbean Americans involved in the articulation of 1970s soul, funk, and disco—for example, Philadelphia-based producer Thom Bell, the Main Ingredient's Cuba Gooding Sr., Chic's Nile Rodgers and Tony Thompson, Luther Vandross, and Randy Muller, and many of the other musicians associated with the Brooklyn-based groups Brass Construction, B.T. Express, and Skyy, among others—did not explicitly play out in the manner of Belafonte (or even Sonny Rollins and Poitier and Cambridge in the post–civil rights era).[97] In other words, the hegemony and fixity of R & B was such that—like their British counterparts operating in the face of a dominant and imported Jamaicanicity and an easily available American soul culture—few of these individuals perceived that there might be local occasion for the pursuit of substantive innovation or syncretic transgression.

In 1979, when Marley's "Wake Up and Live" was stuck at the bottom of *Billboard*'s "Hot Soul" singles chart, sitting at the top was a song that borrowed its rhythm from Chic's disco anthem "Good Times" and featured rapped lyrics. The Sugarhill Gang's "Rapper's Delight" was the first chart success for a genre of music that had been developing in the Bronx since the mid-1970s. The new music, which usually featured disc jockeys playing the role of musicians, and spoken lyrics rather than singing, also drew much of its inspiration from the bass fixations of Jamaican sound system culture. The *toasting* technique, which had come to prominence in the early seventies in reggae music (e.g., U-Roy, I-Roy, and Big Youth) and was itself an outgrowth of the influence of American R & B personality deejays, was applied to disco rhythms by the pioneers in the rap movement, who were disproportionately immigrants from the Caribbean or the children of Caribbean immigrants. The early habit of removing the labels from records so that competitors would be unable to find out where a deejay got her or his beats was another carryover from sound system practices. Finally, the roots of the broader remix culture of which rap is a part could be traced to the work of Lee Perry, King Tubby, and Augustus Pablo in launching the dub subgenre in the early 1970s.[98]

As a consequence of the increased number of West Indians in cities such as Miami, Atlanta, Houston, Washington, Baltimore, Philadelphia, Chicago, Detroit, Boston, the San Francisco Bay Area, and particularly the tri-state area (New York, Connecticut, and New Jersey), largely as a result of the changes in American immigration law in 1965, a new generation was faced with the question of how it would define itself in relation to black America in the post–civil rights era. Rap would emerge as one of the primary ways Caribbean immigrants and their children negotiated their identities as both African Americans and West Indians. "Well, what Kool Herc—the father—and myself and Grandmaster Flash did," Afrika Bambaataa, one of hip-hop's founding trinity, recalls, "was exactly what they were doing in Jamaica, where a lot of the deejays—or toasters, as they were called—would be rapping whatever came into their head on the 'versions,' the instrumental B-sides. We all have a West Indian background."[99] Indeed Herc (Clive Campbell) was Jamaican, Grandmaster Flash (Joseph Saddler) had immigrated from Barbados, and Bambaataa (Kevin Donovan) was the American-born descendant of immigrants from Barbados and Jamaica. All three came of age at a time when the various anglophone West Indian identities were becoming fused in the various immigrant outposts, including Britain, the United States, and Canada, as well as in the Caribbean, and reconfigured in the form of a hegemonic albeit syncretized Jamaican modality. These new hybrids reflecting the strong influence of dancehall culture and its means of reproduction, the sound system, adapted themselves to their particular environments.

For the first and second generations in the United States post-1965, explicit choices and calculations had to be made. As Kool Herc observes, "I moved to New York in '67 or '68. I was twelve or thirteen. Coming from Kingston, Jamaica, it was cold. I didn't expect tenements. I thought I was going to be in suburbia. I got picked on. I didn't have the right clothes. . . . So I started changing up, wearing Converse sneakers, sharkskin pants, cashmere coats." Herc, then, facing different cues and constraints from his British contemporaries, responded to this new environment by "changing up," playing under, and assimilating African American culture, in contrast to the Barbadian immigrant Dennis Bovell's approximations of Jamaicanicity in the British context.[100] Accordingly, Herc decided to move from playing primarily reggae to pumping R & B and Latin breaks while maintaining many of the aesthetic commitments of sound system culture: bass, a tendency to read technologies as both substantive and procedural devices (and consequently blurring the distinction between playing someone else's music—deejaying—and making your own), and the power of the spoken word. Bambaataa suggests, Herc "knew a lot of American blacks were not getting into the reggae of his country. He took the same thing that they were doing—toasting—and did it with American records, Latin or records with beats." Adds Herc himself, "People wasn't feelin' reggae at the time. I played a few but it wasn't catching. I'm in Rome, I got to do what the Romans do. I'm here [in the Bronx]. I got to get with the groove that's here." Employing the echo chambers then popular in reggae, and using emcees, including Clark Kent and Coke La Rock, who rapped in a style much closer to the Jamaican toaster model (in contrast to the more orthodox personality jock style displayed by DJ Hollywood), Herc fused dancehall aesthetics with American R & B culture.[101]

The resistance to reggae that Herc and others perceived in the 1970s would give way to a slightly different modal cultural sensibility, particularly in the New York area, by the midpoint of the subsequent decade. As New York–based rapper Dana Dane recollects of the Kangol Crew, of which he was a member, "[Slick] Rick, Lance Brown and Omega the Heartbreaker all had British or West Indian accents. Rick always wanted to sound American, and I was like, 'You're buggin,' I want to sound more like you guys. Rick couldn't escape using it, but I just ran with it." In other words, in hip-hop's second generation, of which Slick Rick and Dana Dane were a part, while there was still some reluctance to playing out—in this case by Ricky Walters, aka Slick Rick, an immigrant from England of Caribbean parentage—there were signs of an openness and curiosity on the part of African Americans regarding these black others (at least, again, in the New York area). Working in a slightly later moment, in the mid- to late 1980s, Fred "Kool DJ Red Alert" Krute, who emigrated to the Bronx as a child from Antigua, notes that he incorporated Jamaica culture, and specifically dancehall, into his hip-hop shows, both live and on the radio, because of the popularity of the genre with his audience. "When I was on tour with Boogie Down Productions in '88," he recollects,

> KRS-One had the idea to come out on stage to the version of "Telephone Love" [a popular dancehall tune] by JC Lodge.... It seemed that all the audience that was into hip-hop had Caribbean background[s] like me. So they felt proud. And what starts taking forth is the dancehall. I said, "You know what? When I come back, I'm gonna start playing some dancehall."

Upon his return to the airwaves at WRKS (KISS-FM), Red Alert suggests,

> So I did the first twenty minutes of my set with some of the popular dancehall records like "Telephone Love," "Sorry" [a dancehall version of a Tracy Chapman recording], and a few hip-hop records that had some Caribbean samples like Special Ed ["I'm the Magnificent"]; then I went into my regular set. It developed so much that . . . they extended my time to seven PM to twelve.... You could hear me playing some R & B, some uplifting hip-hop, some house music. Then I broke out from nine to ten and got to hit them on the head with the dancehall.

Also in this period the "singjay" tradition (i.e., moving back and forth between toasting and singing), which emerged in 1970s reggae, and particularly 1980s dancehall, was engaged by hip-hop artists such as Slick Rick, Brand Nubian's Grand Puba, and Phife (the self-identified "Trini gladiator") of A Tribe Called Quest, among others. In the same moment, Busta Rhymes, born Trevor Smith and a member of Leaders of the New School, would launch his career on dancehall-inspired intonations and exhortations. The Caribbean-descended, Brooklyn-born, and Long Island–raised Rhymes notes, "That whole upbringing influenced the rhythm I['ve] got, as far as lyrics are concerned, how I figure out flow patterns and the way to play with beats.... [T]hat's [Jamaican toaster] Papa San!"[102]

Grappling with the same dilemmas regarding identity and community that artists such as Belafonte, Poitier, Paule Marshall, Sonny Rollins, and Godfrey Cambridge faced before and after the civil rights movement, the Caribbean American artists involved in hip-hop did not respond in a uniform fashion to the various cues and incentive structures in place at the end of the twentieth century. We might also pay attention to the ways local geography and cultural sensibilities intersected within the genre. Reflecting the relocation of the city's carnival parade from Harlem to Brooklyn in 1964, in contrast to earlier cohorts that were more often drawn from Harlem and the Bronx, the members of the third generation within rap emerged from spaces more clearly marked in terms of storefronts, public discourse, and cuisine, and their general cultural modalities by recent Caribbean immigration—Brooklyn and, to a lesser degree, Queens—explaining perhaps their greater willingness to play out. Some would still continue to avoid identifying themselves explicitly as products of black immigrant cultures. "Wyclef Jean always teases me, saying, 'You [were] one of the original Haitians in hip-hop and nobody ever knew,'" notes Herby "Luv Bug" Azor, who came of age in East Elmhurst, Queens, and produced Salt-n-Pepa, Kwame, and Kid 'N Play, among others. "It's not like I'm not proud of my heritage, it's just I'm not really into separating race and culture. I'm just Herby." Azor's assumption that the demands of racial membership might preclude acknowledging cultural distinctions, and require the hegemony of national frames, undoubtedly was shared by others, and it is in this light that we might understand the relative silence in the work of artists such as Q-Tip (and later the Notorious B.I.G.) regarding their Caribbean backgrounds. Given, furthermore, that rap itself was already imbued with Caribbean aesthetics, an explicit playing out could be read as redundant or superfluous, particularly again in the New York area. To some extent, rapping was already a form of Caribbean immigrant signifying; one did not need to explicitly perform these identities lyrically. Finally, and here it is important to underscore the significance of the local not only across diasporic formations but also within national borders, to the extent that artists working in jurisdictions with a high degree of immigration, such as the New York area, were concerned with marketing their product to other markets within the United States, there might have been incentives to downplay or avoid explicit Caribbeanisms.[103]

Despite the factors that might restrict a certain form of explicit playing out, in this period a number of artists would signify and highlight their Jamaicanicity—and here I mean, as Bovell suggests, an engagement with a certain hegemonic Caribbean sensibility accessible to and endorsed by many who themselves were not "Jamaican." Among this cohort would be KRS-One, A Tribe Called Quest's Phife, Busta Rhymes, Heavy D (originally of Heavy D and the Boyz), and, as noted, DJ Red Alert, who emerged as a prominent radio personality in the late 1980s after a decade behind the scenes within the genre (starting as a deejay in Afrika Bambaataa's crew). In this broader context, a number of African American artists, not all of Caribbean background, made reference to or engaged with reggae and dancehall sounds and West Indian artists. Among the signs of this connectivity were KRS-One's incorporation of reggae as a regular source of inspiration for his own beats, and recordings with dancehall artists Shelly Thunder, Mad Lion, and Shabba Ranks; Phife's name-checking of the calypsonian the Mighty Sparrow, references to Grenada and "oversize mampies," verses in patois ("Jazz [We Got]," "Award Tour," "Oh My God," and "Stressed Out"), and dancehall recordings ("His Name Is Mutty Ranks"); and Heavy D's dancehall records made specifically for the Jamaican market. It is as a result of these developments that we might understand A Tribe Called Quest's "Steve Biko (Stir It Up)"—which manages to bring Marley, the antiapartheid struggle, and local conditions in New York City's outer boroughs into conversation—and the success of the British group Soul II Soul on both sides of the Atlantic in the late 1980s. Soul II Soul's recordings "Keep on Moving" and "Back to Life" articulated reggae, soul, and hip-hop influences with a fashion sensibility (i.e., the Funki Dreds) that dominated global black aesthetics for a period of time.[104]

The most obvious examples of hip-hop's relative openness to reggae and Caribbean motifs and aesthetics were albums released in the late 1990s, albeit based on templates generated in the earlier part of the decade and in many respects in response to the increased popularity of the gangster aesthetic in West Coast hip-hop and subsequently East Coast recordings (made by artists such as the Notorious B.I.G. and Jay-Z). Many of these recordings were released, as a collective or individually, by a group with a signifying name, the Fugees, whose membership resembled the classic Black Uhuru: two West Indian males (Jamaican in the case of Black Uhuru, and Haitian in the case of the Fugees) and a Columbia University–educated African American female (Black Uhuru's Sandra "Puma" Jones and the Fugees' Lauryn Hill). The group's albums, *Blunted on Reality* and the chart-topping *The Score*, made frequent references to reggae, and indeed the latter album included a Sly and Robbie remix ("Fu-Gee-La") as well as a remake of Marley's "No Woman No Cry." *The Carnival*, the first solo album released by group member Wyclef Jean, who emigrated to the United States at age nine in 1979, featured R & B, Jamaican, Cuban, and Haitian influences (among others), quite often in the same song. His second release, *The Ecleftic*, included an intriguing dubplate featuring pop country singer Kenny Rogers. A second dubplate he recorded with Michael Jackson, interpolating aspects of his own "Human Nature"—"Looking out in Jamaica, no one can touch Kingston City, the Refugee sound will kill a soundboy"—was reportedly played to great effect in a deejay competition in Jamaica; initially Jackson was hesitant to accede to Wyclef's request that he help him "kill a soundboy" (i.e., win a deejay competition), stating quite reasonably that he could not "talk about murdering."[105]

The most stunning appropriation of Bob Marley's aesthetics and legacy was undoubtedly Fugee Lauryn Hill's first solo venture, *The Miseducation of Lauryn Hill*. The chart-topping album, which was released in the fall of 1998, was partly recorded in the same studio in Kingston where Marley was shot, and where he did much of his own work (the Tuff Gong studios at 56 Hope Road); the album incorporated reggae rhythms on a number of tracks, including explicit references to the Maytals' "Bam Bam," which won the 1966 Jamaican Song Festival ("Lost Ones"), and the Wailer's "Concrete Jungle" ("Forgive Them Father"). The cover referred to the artwork from the Wailer's second Island release, *Burnin'*, with Hill cast, in effect, in the role of Bob Marley. Finally, with regard to the salience of Jamaican cultural references in African American pop, two of the most highly regarded rappers in what had become by this juncture the "underground," Mos Def and Talib Kweli, combined for the album *Mos Def and Talib Kweli Are Black Star;* the album's liner notes include comments from Makeda Garvey, the UNIA founder's great-granddaughter, information about the Marcus Garvey and Universal Negro Improvement Association Papers Project at UCLA, and the shout out (in Kweli's credits) "I'm feeling you Robert Nesta [Marley]."[106]

EDGES

The negotiations about the value of extranational linkages and the seamlessness of global blacknesses marked local politics within the United States as well. For instance, in the spring of 2000, a conflict developed between New York City municipal councilor Una Clarke (representing the Crown Heights and Flatbush districts in Brooklyn) and Major Owens (part of the borough's congressional delegation—Democrat, Eleventh District) over whether it was proper for Clarke to challenge Owens for his seat. Despite their history of mutual endorsements and cooperation (and even shared office space) and the fact that the candidates "agree[d] on just about every issue," the contest soon began to focus on a supposed rift between West Indians and African Americans. Clarke, who was born in Jamaica, had rejected the term African American to describe herself, asserting: "I am not an African-American. I identify as a black person, but you cannot take my identity and tell me I'm somebody else." Another historical linkage was made when Clarke asserted,

"I'd be like Shirley Chisholm. I am reclaiming her seat to do as well as she did and even better. She tells me that I have the right to run." Clarke's announcement that she would seek Owens's seat in the party's September primary was followed by a letter from the borough's Democratic machine (written by state assemblyman Albert Vann and signed by others) urging her to reconsider and contending that her campaign would aggravate tensions among blacks. The communiqué also implied that Clarke devoted more of her energies to representing immigrant constituents than other black Brooklynites (a charge she rejected) and was "push[ing] the ethnic card." When it became clearer that Clarke would not withdraw, Memphis native Owens asserted that her candidacy was mobilized by a worrisome ethnic nationalism: "What this candidate [Clarke] represents is a whole new kind of evil being introduced into the community. Whether it's [Joerg] Haider in Austria or Adolf Hitler, when you appeal to ethnic loyalties as a way to ascend to power it is the worst possible way to come to power." This comparison obviously had implications in a district with a significant Jewish population (as it was probably meant to, although Clarke's support among Jewish voters appeared to be strong). Owens also, at one point, sued to get Clarke dropped from the ballot, on the grounds that she had registered to vote before she had become a naturalized citizen, a charge he eventually dropped for lack of evidence. After the suit was dropped, Clarke stated, "He was trying to make me out to be a criminal and have me deported." Although the clash between the two was to a large extent a reflection of careerism, more mundane concerns, and the ugly side of local politics, the fact that it revealed the (U.S.) African American-versus-Caribbean fault lines as it did indicated that the distinction still resonated in certain circles under certain circumstances.[107]

At the same time, it is worth noting the degree to which Brooklyn and much of the tri-state area had become by this point a hybrid and hyperarticulated diasporic breathing space that was as Afro-Latin as it was anglophone and francophone Caribbean, continental African, or "African American." In common with other nodal points—for example, Paris, Montreal, Toronto, and London—and despite attempts to rid these spaces of nonwhites and nonnormative political possibility, the site refused reduction to, or characterization as, simply the sum of its elements.[108] It is in this context that we can think of these sites, and the diaspora itself, as means of contesting the tendency to erase and collapse locations in which deliberative activity—black thoughts—might occur, analogous to the potentials offered by smaller-scale counterpublics, transgressive interiorities, workshops and collectives, and mechanisms such as the band, the live performance, the long-playing record, and the various expatriate carnivals.

With regard to diaspora, the ability of actors in the cultural realm, intentionally and at times inadvertently, to resist the definition of politics as solely that which happens within state borders, or in the name of the nation, represents a significant means by which these norms might be denaturalized. In that illusory but meaningful space between the national and the imperial, where black subjects understood broadly are made, are to be found those most likely to recognize the convenient disarticulation of liberal and colonial regimes and their representation as benign and past tense, respectively. It is here, especially after the making of the mid-twentieth-century consensus that anticolonial struggle was no longer necessary, that cultural actors are particularly well positioned to act: to disassemble, re/present, and reimagine. Against this backdrop, black artists' and their audiences' simple inability and various refusals, then, to reproduce national grammars can be interpreted as evidence, at some fundamental level, of anticolonial labor.

Besides the individuals mentioned here such as Marcus Garvey, Claude McKay, Sonny Rollins, and Lauryn Hill, a number of others might be categorized as engaged in juxtapositive labor, in bringing together that which is disarticulated and rendered incomprehensible: Paulette Nardal, Aimé Césaire, Wifredo Lam, Ousmane Sembène, Mahatma Gandhi, Claudia Jones, Lorraine Hansberry, Paul Robeson, Grace Jones, Gil Scott-Heron, and a number of hip-hop artists. In the works of Bob Marley, like C. L. R. James, anarrangements of modern hegemonies and a willingness to imagine and commit simultaneously within, against, and outside the nation-state—that is, both juxtapositive and geoheterodox play—are discernible. Marley's late 1970s recordings, along with his engagements in Jamaican politics, African independence, and the maintenance of a viable diasporic counterpublic—in common with the various iterations and intentions of *The Black Jacobins*, James's earlier collaborations with George Padmore regarding anticolonial activity, his subsequent efforts to engender a stable postcolonial Trinidad as well as a functional West Indian Federation, and left cosmopolitanism—are evidence of diaspora's capacity to reveal and trouble the operations of the modernity/coloniality matrix.

These references to extranational linkages and decisions to identify and remember past the margins—Marley recalls Garvey and is, in turn, reinscibed by Lauryn Hill—become especially important, given the capacity of the American project to both expose and export racial hierarchies, to destabilize while recalibrating and reinscribing coloniality. Much of the appealing either/or ambiguity and powerful ambivalence of the American example can be attributed to the ways official policies and black preferences have been alternately entangled and coordinated, disentangled and operating at crosspurposes. The absence of clear distinctions between the resistant and the accommodationist, the emancipatory and the constraining, in American popular culture and the intriguing ways the aesthetic is both reproduced and exceeded in African American popular culture (e.g., the work of Ralph Ellison and James Brown) have contributed to the dissipation of anticolonial commitments over the course of the last century. In other words, it is American prerogative that would increasingly be marked as the public face of the colonial and the West, as the personification of all things Babylonian. While the postcolonial moment, with its false disruptions, apparent reversals, and convenient concessions, accompanied by performances of deep regret, has discouraged diasporic identifications among blacks worldwide, it has generated especially attractive incentives for African American communities—for example, the triumphalist grammars and discourses associated with the post–civil rights era—to turn inward and invest in the available benefits of American citizenship.[109] For an anaformative politics committed to putting all space into play, the constitution and reconstitutions of "America" would represent, then, a powerful geopolitical presence—like "Africa" albeit in a different manner—and a significant challenge to the anticolonial project.

You are the woman and mi a the man, but you look so

strong. —Nigger Kojak and Liza, "Fist to Fist (Rub a Dub)"

7

NOT AS OTHERS

If we think of politics as being as much the name we give to a certain category of processes and behaviors as the way we identify the place where certain things happen, we can imagine the procedural and substantive implications of the articulation of the black diaspora. More precisely, we can begin to think through the ways process and substance are intimately connected and space and politics are mutually constitutive. An important dimension of that entanglement is the question of how diasporic sensibilities are generated and gendered, the mechanisms through which diasporic identities are marked and made in relation to each other, the resultant hierarchies and hegemonies, and the consequences of the efforts to manage the diasporic erotic within the cultural realm in order to produce certain sorts of subjects, certain patterns of politics, and conceptions of the political.

The previous chapter emphasized the potential anticolonial implications of diasporic sensibilities sustained through discourses situated in and around the politics/culture nexus. Indeed, I have suggested that there is an autodiasporic dimension to all cultural expressions, given their resistance to simply reproducing national frames. These transgressions aside, diasporic circuits offer no specific guarantee of a progressive politics. Transnational and postnational configurations are not exempt from the masculinist and heterosexist impulses that energize modern arrangements and categories and much of our understanding of the political. Accordingly, it is not surprising that early twentieth-century Pan-Africanism often coexisted with, and in fact thrived on, a range of approaches to the importance of maintaining masculinity, and manhood rights. For example, despite his support of feminist causes throughout his career, W. E. B. Du Bois's writings, Joy James suggests, reveal that he was "influenced by a masculinist worldview which de-radicalized his gender progressivism. . . . [and presented] the male as normative." In Du Bois's politics and activities, Hazel Carby detects "a conceptual framework that is gender-specific . . . [that applies] exclusively to men . . . [and] only those men who enact narrowly and rigidly determined codes of masculinity." Similarly, although Tony Martin contends that "women . . . were fairly well integrated at all levels of the UNIA," he does admit that Garveyism certainly did not include "a specific feminist rhetoric in the modern sense." Despite Amy Jacques Garvey's prominent role in the UNIA, especially during the period of her husband's imprisonment, rarely did her duties involve challenging the era's gender norms.[1]

Beyond gender hierarchies within the UNIA is the issue of the tendency for hegemonies within diasporas to be registered and asserted in the languages of gender and sexuality. This possibility was evident in Garvey's conceptions of "racial progress" and the return to Africa, which were thoroughly imbued with these sorts of grammars. "No more fear, no more cringing, no more syncophantic begging and pleading; but the Negro must strike straight from the shoulder for manhood rights and for full liberty," he suggested at one juncture.

> Africa calls now more than ever. She calls because the attempt is
> now being made by the combined Caucasian forces of Europe to
> subjugate her, to overrun her and to reduce her to that state of alien
> control that will mean in another one hundred years the complete
> extermination of the native African. . . . This convention [has]
> left us full-fledged men; men charged to do our duty, and by the
> God Divine, and by the Heavens that shelter all humanity, we have
> pledged ourselves to bring the manhood of our race to the highest
> plane of achievement. We cannot, and we must not, falter.[2]

In Garvey's words we can detect a sense that relations between blacks outside of the continent and those based there required that the former assume a leadership role while the feminized spaces of the latter and their associated constituencies naturally followed.

Indeed, moving along the Afro-continuum from the "outposts" of the diaspora to its "original" centers, two distinct—yet generally compatible and problematic—visions and narratives are available and apparent. The first, which absorbs much of the sentimental packaging of the colonial project, envisions Africa as fallen and in need of the assistance of blacks based elsewhere. This is basically the blackface reenactment of the pith helmet fantasy, based on assumptions about science, reason, and access to economic and technological resources underpinned by the arrogance of, and aspiration to, power.

Accordingly, historian Harvey Neptune writes with regard to the role played by African American soldiers abroad, "Ever since the [United States] earnestly embraced an imperialist mission in the 1890s, black men have shouldered part of a national undertaking immortalized as the 'white man's burden,' hoping to be rewarded with effective American citizenship for their martial efforts." The second vision, which also has its own, albeit subterranean, colonialist underpinnings, reads distance from symbolic Africa as correlated with a different kind of descent. Masculinity in this tradition maps on to the phantasmic and impossible purity associated with the continent's constructions. This conception is efficiently captured in the lyrics of the Neville Brothers recording "Africa": "Take me on back to Africa . . . where a woman is a woman, and a man is a man." The implication here is that, outside of the continent, normative, natural, and desirable masculinities and femininities are in short supply. Both perspectives share the view that women, and those whose sexualities refuse accepted and privileged categories, should remain outside of decision-making spaces and external to the making of politics.[3]

In this light, following from Hazel Carby's *Race Men* and Michelle Stephens's *Black Empire*, it is useful to think through C. L. R. James's engagements with the hegemonic colonial scripts regarding appropriate gender aspirations. As Carby reveals on the basis of readings of *Minty Alley*, *The Black Jacobins*, and *Beyond a Boundary*, in much of James's classic work a certain masculinism is often detectable: an emphasis on men as agents and women, if visible, as passive (and often associated with "the masses"). Accordingly, we might suggest that these gendered commitments were reproduced in at least his early diasporic thinking and practice (e.g., his reading of Toussaint L'Ouverture, and his excitement about Paul Robeson as a political leader, following his casting of Robeson as Toussaint in the early theatrical rendering of *The Black Jacobins* in London). We also see in the early James a vacillation between the two different narratives mentioned earlier: one that associates normative masculinity with intellectual work and middle-class status—thus explaining his decision to join the middle-class Maple cricket club rather than the lower-middle-class Shannon or the working class Stingo in his youth in Trinidad, as described retrospectively in *Beyond a Boundary*—and a distinct but complimentary narrative that links masculinity with the physical and aesthetic work of the body. In other words, there is an internal debate regarding what kind of man should be on top.[4]

Moreover, moving beyond James's example, one could argue, that these two narratives—one upholding an imagined civilization, the other an uncontaminated and doubly tropic hypermasculinity—shifted in relation to each other over the course of the twentieth century. Specifically, as the century pro-gressed, new world blacks' willingness and capacity to identify the continent as a female space in need of guidance, custodianship, protection, or domination diminished. While such discourses certainly persisted at the end of this period, the propensity to think of these diasporic engagements in straightforwardly hierarchical and gendered terms, with blacks outside of Africa in the dominant position, lessened significantly after the confluence of events that preceded and followed the 1945 Pan-African Conference in Manchester. At this meet-ing Du Bois, as the father figure of the movement, realized that Africans did not need or seek the tutelage his cohort had assumed up to that point—a fact that had become even more pronounced by the time Ghana achieved indepen-dence in 1957. Against this backdrop, drawing on Harvey Neptune's account of the encounters between black American soldiers and Afro-Trinidadian men in Trinidad during the World War II–era American occupation, it is important to remember that the relatively easy power the former exercised over the latter did its work just before the tides would change in terms of the balance of the competing narratives of masculine domination. This assumption that African American men, as Americans, would naturally rule over Caribbean males was registered, as Neptune observes, in changing fashions and dance styles, the var-ious performances and receptions of calypso lyrics, and more obviously in the form of the 1943 Basilon Street riots, in the Laventille district bordering Port of Spain, which resulted in "serious property damage. . . . [including] broken windows and dented walls" and "twenty-four local men" in need of medical attention. Such claims, I would argue, would not have been asserted or as easily made in a later period. To be sure, the standard conflation of the civilizationist narrative with specific conceptions of gender roles and normative sexualities certainly prevails beyond the midpoint of the twentieth century, and the read-ing of the convenient African as a source of trepidation and anxiety—as more than "capable"—precedes 1945. Nevertheless, I would suggest that the relative salience of these mythologies changes over time, with World War II—and here one might think of the diasporic negotiations in the area of comparative mas-culinities depicted in Ousmane Sembène's *Camp de Thiaroye*—the Manchester Pan-African Congress, and the leadership role played by continental Africans and West Indians in the movement toward independence in the postwar period. It is interesting, in this context, to rethink the nègre/noir and African/Antillean negotiations within the Négritude movement—and black franco-phone discourse more generally—as reflecting changing notions regarding the location of dispositive/normative black masculinity.[5]

Focusing, then, on the latter half of the twentieth century, we can expect that blacks in the Americas and Europe would sing different songs to the "African woman" than they would to, and about, the "African man," and indeed if the "African woman" is being sung to, the "African man" must be rendered invisible to make the "seduction" work, and vice versa, with the overall result, of course, to paraphrase a popular calypso, that "they ain't see Africa at all."[6] With regard to the issue of how African American/Afro-Caribbean relations have developed over the course of this period, the discursive articulations of interactions between black males in the United States and the West Indies can be seen as paralleling those between new world blacks in general and continental Africans. Again, in this tradition, "masculinity" is correlated with one's closeness to "Africa," and the degree to which one's blackness remains "unadulterated." Desirable conceptions of femininity and masculinity, in this tradition, are related to the extent that one's sexual and gender identity can be extricated from the public history and effects of coloniality and slavery. Those most clearly "dominated" and transformed by "Western" ways, then, are those most divorced from their "natural essence." The patriarchal assumptions and homophobia generated in these discourses are particularly strident because of the conflation of standard sexist and heterosexist understandings, and certain strains of anticolonial and postcolonial rhetoric (e.g., Mugabe's Zimbabwe, much of the anglophone Caribbean postindependence). Accordingly, at the root of much of this fear of the real complexities of human sexuality is a deep and flexible antiwhite rhetoric: that is, our women are out of control because they have been contaminated by their exposure to European ways or to the arguments promoted by white feminists; black gays have been diverted from their true nature because they have been polluted by foreign ideas (or, more graphically, been sexually exploited by white men).

Given these overlapping logics, Afro–West Indian males are lacking in comparison to their counterparts from the continent, and African American manhood is limited, defined, and circumscribed by, and found wanting in relation to, the models provided by black men from the Caribbean. (Of course, as reflected in the work of Norman Mailer, LeRoi Jones, and Eldridge Cleaver, a roughly similar dynamic has informed discursive representations of relations between black and white men in the United States.) This transference is visible in contemporary popular culture. Consider, for example, Eddie Murphy's riff on "Dexter St. Jacques," in his 1987 concert film *Raw*, about the Caribbean man African American women seek satisfaction from while on vacation. "Dexter," with his generous phallus hanging over his shoulder, and singing Bob Marley songs ("Could You Be Loved"), functions in Murphy's skit as a diasporic "Jody" of sorts—to make reference to the archetype identified by Michael Hanchard—the economically marginalized but otherwise quite powerful black man imagined to be preying on the "property" of other black men while they are otherwise occupied, usually (far) away at work. Notes Hanchard,

> Ever watchful of errant desires, Jody represents a particular type of male gaze, one that must also acknowledge the gazes of reproachful, jealous, and potential lovers in turn. He is at his best when other men are not watching him; their public preoccupations with work, paying the rent, and being a man often obscure their vision. Indeed, it is often a man's idea of black manhood and masculinity as being individuated, separate from other members of his community, as well as his wife or companion, that undermines the very sand castle of masculinity he aims to construct. Jody is the liminal figure in the blind spots of that perspective.

The same suggestion that the foreign and often Caribbean black man represents a particularly potent catalyst for those seeking a certain form of restoration is developed in Terry McMillan's novel *How Stella Got Her Groove Back* (and the film of the same name) and the assumptions that inform Grace Jones's 1982 release "My Jamaican Guy" (sampled appropriately on LL Cool J's "Doin' It"), Me'Shell NdegéOcello's "Dred Loc," and, arguably, the significance of the Nigerian suitor, Asagai, in Lorraine Hansberry's *Raisin in the Sun* (in contrast to the college student George Murchison, played by Lou Gossett Jr., who is cast as queer by Walter Lee Younger Jr., Sidney Poitier's character).[7]

Underlying these depictions is the tendency (usually on the part of the male subject) to emphasize the feminine when the objective is to exploit or plunder, even if the mission is cloaked in the language of protective paternalism. Examples of this pattern would include Garvey's gendered foreign policy and Murphy's reinforcement of the most ignorant and troubling conceptions of "Africa," and the continent's women, with his character Mphuphu, in *Raw* (conceptions that are repeated verbatim in Jay-Z's 2001 release "Girls, Girls, Girls"). Garvey's "Africa," as well as Murphy's, is conveniently feminized, and depicted as lacking in capable men, to justify the continent's colonization by the UNIA's adherents, in Garvey's case, and the right to be abusive, in Murphy's case. In contrast—and it is this other narrative I am suggesting becomes increasingly hegemonic with time—when the issue is male insecurity expressed as confusion, respect, and/or fear, for example, Murphy's "Dexter," the relevant rituals necessitate the hypermasculinization of the other. To do otherwise, to seek relations with the "woman" while disregarding the obvious presence of the "man," or vice versa, would seem somewhat rude or improper (as even Jody knows good manners require that one waits until the man has left for work).[8]

In this tradition, I would add that the "Africa" that convinces Richard Pryor to stop using the word "nigger" in his act, as voiced and alluded to in his 1982 concert film *Live on the Sunset Strip*, is presented as masculine. Moreover, a similar dynamic arguably informs Sly and the Family Stone's restaging of "Thank You (Falettinme Be Mice Elf Agin)" as "Thank You for Talking to Me, Africa" on the 1971 release *There's a Riot Goin' On*, as well as the circumstances that provoked the comedian Dave Chappelle to leave his Comedy Central television show. Explaining his decision to go to South Africa—figured simply as "Africa" in most of the discussion about his actions—Chappelle cited his feeling "incredibly stressed out" and "like some kind of prostitute," and the attempts, he perceived, to "put every black man in the movies in a dress." Regarding the trip itself, he offered, "I feel like it was a place I could really reflect." Recounting his thinking at the time, he told one interviewer, "I'm going to go to Africa; I'm going to find a way to be myself." Like Pryor, he would return contemplating abandoning the use of the word "nigger" (except, he suggested, in personal conversation and perhaps in clubs).[9] In common, the continent typically figures as a restorative, gender "normalizing," and, in a certain sense, disciplinary presence in these sorts of discourses.

TIL SHILOH

Within this broader, fluid rhetorical field, I want to focus for a moment on the developments within Jamaican popular culture and politics, and their imbrication with questions of gender and sexuality, before moving back explicitly to the diasporic plane. To begin, I want to consider some of the ways reggae and its associated sound system culture naturalized a certain conception of gender relations while at the same time providing a foundation for the disarticulation of a number of colonial assumptions. In this context, although Rastafarianism enabled some of the most potent forms of resistance available in the second half of the twentieth century, both inside and outside Jamaica, it was often underpinned by a familiar Old Testament misogyny. Writes Maureen Rowe:

For the Rastafari male, it was significant that the first female
mentioned in the Bible was unfavourably mentioned. This was
interpreted as a clear warning against the potential evil in the
female. . . . It argues that the female is impure and must be kept
from corrupting the male. It is also implied wherever this attitude
is manifested that females should not get together because of the
potential for sinful thinking and practices. The female then must be
guided, instructed and restricted by the male.

Similarly, Carolyn Cooper refers to the "ambivalent response to woman that
is characteristic of Rastafarian fundamentalism . . . [and Bob] Marley's songs
and . . . his statements about his work." Indeed, although Marley's references to women in his music were often sympathetic (e.g., "No Woman No
Cry" and "Johnny Was") and revealed a certain romantic sensibility at times
(e.g., "Waiting in Vain" and "Is This Love?"), they never really transcended
the dichotomous (queen/whore) dynamic characteristic of most nationalist
movements (e.g., "Pimper's Paridise," which Cooper cites as "a good example
of Marley's ambivalent response to 'fallen' woman"). It is not surprising, then,
that *Survival* and *Uprising*, the most explicit expressions of his Pan-Africanism
and diasporic commitments, contain the fewest love songs.[10]

Regarding Marley's personal conduct, Grant Farred observes, "Throughout
his adulthood, Marley's treatment of women was highly problematic, mir-
roring much of the misogyny of Rastafarianism (and Jamaican society). In
his fifteen-year marriage to Rita . . . Marley claimed as his sexual prerogative the right to have very public relationships with other women." Although
Marley fathered a number of children outside of his marriage, he apparently
was resentful when his wife Rita gave birth to a daughter that was not his,
and reportedly "roughed up Rita one night" as a result (his mother, Cedella,
excused this hypocrisy in the following terms: "Nesta was a man, and a man
will always be a man . . . just because a man does something doesn't mean that
the woman should do it too").[11]

Rastafarianism's influence on Jamaican popular music declined in the
1980s with the emergence of dancehall, which itself reflected a shift in some
quarters from ganja to cocaine as the stimulant of choice; a local rejection
of reggae's increasing internationalism (e.g., Marley, Third World, Jimmy
Cliff) and perceived detachment from "Jamaicanness"; and the aftereffects of
the JLP's return to power in 1980. "Dancehall music . . . [was] the most pro-
establishment culture ever come inna Jamaica. It [was] dealing with exactly

what the society [was] dealing with. The lewdness, the downgrading of women, the slackness, materialism, gun violence. The establishment is not against any of these things that dancehall personifies," contended artist Mutabaruka regarding the transition, adding that he saw the subgenre as "the worst thing that ever happen[ed] to Jamaican culture." Maxine Stowe suggests that after Seaga's victory "the Rastafarian culture and Afrocentric talk started dispersing. Kids became less Afrocentric" and, she asserts, "more New York–centric."[12]

The new genre was hardly more open to more progressive conceptions of gender roles and relations. The recordings of artists such as pioneer Yellowman, General Echo, and Lovindeer would prove to be more sexually explicit, while dispensing with the obligatory references to "queens" characteristic of 1970s' reggae (symbolically represented by the I-Threes, the Wailers' female backup singers Judy Mowatt, Marcia Griffiths, and Rita Marley). With regard to the status of women in dancehall, Elena Oumano suggests that women do have some influence, and can exercise a certain power:

> Many of the women who pack . . . dancehalls [in Jamaica] see little
> hope of achieving real power in their lives. But while they're young,
> they do wield the power of their sexuality. So they preen in skimpy
> outfits while male deejays chant rhythmic, X-rated praises to their
> bodies. In that way, at least, even dancehall "ghetto gals," at least as a
> group, are a force to be reckoned with in the reggae world.[13]

Although women certainly had more input as creative artists, in the broadest sense of the term, in urban dancehalls in the 1990s than they did during the era of 1970s reggae, it was still an extremely limited influence. This was evident in the mid-1990s efforts to censor Lady Saw for being too sexually explicit—although male artists were not similarly chastised for making the same kinds of references—in her effort to move women (and female sexuality) from the realm of the objective into the subjective.

The *slackness*, as it has been characterized, associated with dancehall became the subject of much debate in the 1980s and 1990s. For instance, in response to Paul Gilroy's linkage of deejay slackness to the post-1980 conservative reorientation of Jamaican politics, Carolyn Cooper argues:

> It can be seen to represent in part a radical, underground
> confrontation with the patriarchal gender ideology and the pious
> morality of fundamentalist Jamaican society. In its invariant
> coupling with Culture [i.e., music that concerned itself with broader

social issues and uplift—e.g., Marley's work and his successors in the 1980s and 1990s, including Garnett Silk, Luciano, and Tony Rebel], Slackness is potentially a politics of subversion. For Slackness is not mere sexual looseness—though it certainly is that. Slackness is a metaphorical revolt against law and order, an undermining of consensual standards of decency. It is the antithesis of Culture.

At another point, Cooper argues, "The Culture/Slackness antithesis that is mediated in the dancehall is one manifestation of a fundamental antagonism in Jamaican society between up-town and down-town, between high culture and low, between literacy and oracy."[14]

Despite Cooper's claims, it is not clear that the gap between the concerns of the slackness crew and the advocates of culture was all that great, despite the protestations of the Jamaican upper classes. (In this context, it is also important to note that dancehall has been consumed, and in some cases produced—e.g., Sean Paul—by middle-class Jamaican youth as well.) Indeed, it might be more accurate to suggest that throughout Jamaican society (and elsewhere), there are adherents of both perspectives, and that they represent flipside expressions of what is essentially the same philosophical orientation toward gender issues and roles. Culture assumes that issues regarding gender are settled and, more specifically, that the natural equilibrium point involves male dominance of the public realm. Slackness, while reflecting a greater degree of insecurity regarding relations between women and men, and despite its obviously greater concern with female sexuality, is, among other things, a response to male uncertainty about the place of women, and therefore an attempt to police, actively and publicly, women's, and implicitly men's, possibilities. Accordingly, in response to criticisms of his own slackness lyrics, the dancehall artist Lovindeer recorded the song "Bump Up," arguing that his critics' priorities were incorrect, given that a homosexual beauty contest had been allowed to proceed:

Now mi did hol up a panty on TV, an half a Jamaica come down
upon mi. De write letter to newspaper daily, de call radio an
complain bout mi, se mi corruptin di youts of di country, an
all because of a red panty. Now dese same people se nutin to di
press about di dyam batty man [homosexual] contes. De will fin
demselves in a hell ev a mess, if dem support dis kin of slackness.

The implication is that there is "slackness" and there is *slackness*, and that the former is playful and harmless while the latter threatens the basic foundations of the social order. In contrast, it would appear that both culture and slackness are rooted in the same sentimental economy, with culture simply assuming what slackness attempts to restore.[15]

Ossie Davis's description of what he saw as the remarkable ability of West Indian students at Howard University in the 1930s to focus on other subjects besides women captures the naturalized paternalism that culture incorporates, a paternalism that easily transcends class lines:

> The West Indian bull session was nowhere as sex-obsessed as ours was. . . . Women were discussed, but girlfriends, mothers, sisters, and prospective wives were all expected to find their places somewhere near the bottom of a man's list of interests, and to stay there. The men expected to marry, and to marry well, to have children and also to have a mistress, almost as a matter of course. Sex and women were seldom subjects worthy of serious discussion among gentlemen.
> That seemed to be the West Indian attitude.

Culture then assumes that the male's responsibility to control women is not threatened and therefore that there is no need to discuss the issue, and to police boundaries. But clearly underlying this confidence is the willingness to engage the mechanisms of slackness should any doubts or instability arise on the home front. "Women are displacing men in this country in a real way," suggested Barbara Gloudon, the host of a popular Jamaican talk show, in an attempt to explain the increasing rates of suicide among the island's men. "Not every man is prepared to take that." The changes taking place in gender relations throughout the Caribbean and certainly elsewhere can be linked, to some extent, with the late twentieth-century upsurge in slackness lyrics (to which the advocates of culture are unable, and for the most part, probably unwilling, to provide a response). In the context of Jamaican dancehall culture, the ability of deejays, including Beenie Man, Buju Banton, and Sizzla, to move easily from one camp to the other is further evidence of the basic compatibility between the culture and slackness postures.[16]

The basic consensus, underlying the slackness/culture debate within Jamaica, that certain normative masculinities should be promoted was differently received in the international market, and indeed a dynamic emerged whereby the types of sentimental commitments Jamaican artists felt compelled to perform at home were the subject of much controversy abroad. It was not surprising, then, that dancehall artist Buju Banton's "Boom Bye Bye," which called for the execution of homosexuals, caused a furor in Britain and the United States, among whites and to a lesser degree blacks, around the issue of homophobia in 1993.[17] Banton had already generated controversy in Jamaica with his song "Love Mi Browning," which expressed a preference for light-skinned women (Buju's equation of women and property—"Me love me car, me love me bike, me love me money and 'ting, but most of all me love me browning"—was not remarked on). While the "Boom Bye Bye" fracas was a news item in Jamaica, it was in the United States and England that Banton (born Mark Anthony Myrie) was criticized, and it was to international audiences that he offered an explanation of his views on the issue: "I do not advocate violence against anyone and it was never my intention to incite violent acts with 'Boom Bye Bye.' However, I must state unequivocally that I do not condone homosexuality, as this lifestyle runs contrary to my religious beliefs."[18] The controversy indicated the degree to which coloniality continued to provide the boundaries of interracial and international discourse: Banton's ironic invocation of religious commitments and values derived from the historical exercise of civilizing, colonial, and missionary knowledge/power systems; the popular and convenient contention that the attempt to challenge homophobia in Jamaica on the part of largely white British and American audiences was itself evidence of neocolonial arrogance; and the equally convenient tendency on the part of these international audiences to be particularly attentive to homophobic utterances made by blacks while overlooking similar transgressions made in whiteface (e.g., Eminem).[19] In other words, sincere commitments to challenging homophobic practices would prove to be difficult to sustain free and outside of the colonial structures that underpinned these transnational and allegedly intercultural exchanges.

Banton's subsequent American releases, *Til Shiloh* (1995), *Inna Heights* (1998), and *Unchained Spirit* (2000), represented a remarkable shift in emphasis. His previous album, *Voice of Jamaica*, had been a standard, although quite popular, collection of "slackness" productions. *Til Shiloh*, in contrast, featured a newly dreadlocked Banton, professing Rastafarianism; a map of Africa on the back cover; and a focus on "cultural" lyrics that made reference to Marcus Garvey, Ethiopia, and other predictable Pan-Africanist markers. This transition was also a reflection of the broader resurgence of culture in the dancehall in the 1993–94 period, evidenced in the work of Garnett Silk, Tony Rebel, and Capleton; and a reaction to the murders of deejays Panhead and Dirtsman. By the time of *Unchained Spirit*, Banton's lyrics were focused solely on spiritual matters. Again, given the compatibility of slackness and culture, it made sense for Banton to respond to the criticisms he received in the United States, and the crosspressures he faced at home (where he had broken the sales records established by John Holt and Marley), by "retreating," in effect, to the security a Rastafarian-cum-Pan-Africanist foundation could offer. Seeking to shield himself from scrutiny, in terms resembling those Marley used after the 1976 shooting, Banton stated in an interview with a British publication, "Rasta is not an ism. You have tour-ism, social-ism and terror-ism. Rasta cannot ism." Endorsing the gendered sentiments that link his work to Garvey (and, to a lesser extent, Marley), Banton continued,

> The black man doesn't belong in London, neither does he belong in America. We are just passing through these places. We need to get together and go back to whence we came. We can build empires here [in London] but as black people you should have in mind to take that empire elsewhere. . . . It is not a bad thing I'm saying, man. The Arabs do it, the Chinese do it. We need to start building stock and stop going off and multi-marrying in multiracial marriages: that cannot save us neither. We're looked down upon as being weak.[20]

That said, it should be noted that *Til Shiloh* is compelling listening and—along with Marley's *Survival*, Fela's *Expensive Shit*, and Public Enemy's *It Takes a Nation*—represents one of the most effective and sure-footed musical renderings of black inter/nationalism. It is the ways these texts manifest convenient and appealing conceptions of community and resistance to illegitimate authority by drawing tight boundaries around the political that both give them their power and mark their normative limitations.

The supposed differences between Jamaican customs and American values came to the surface again in 2001 after the video for a song ("Hey Baby") recorded by the Californian ska/rock group No Doubt, featuring the popular dancehall deejay Bounty Killer (aka Rodney Price), was released. In the video, one of Bounty Killer's lines ("The way you rock your hips, you know that it amaze me") is followed by a clip of No Doubt's drummer Adrian Young dancing unclothed (with his private parts blurred out). Bounty Killer was criticized by his longtime nemesis Beenie Man, born Moses Davis, who suggested that "the video portray[ed] Bounty as a gay. That is a Jamaican artist, and that can't gwan in a dancehall, no way. No man can dance naked in a dance—white, black, pink, Syrian, anybody." Beenie Man himself had had his sexuality questioned by Bounty Killer and others three years earlier because of the lyrics in his 1998 international hit "Who Am I," in which he had, with indeterminate punctuation, observed, "How could I make love to a fella in a rush; pass me the keys to the truck." Bounty Killer, for his part, initially refused to appear in promotions for the recording with No Doubt and explained the video as a cultural misunderstanding: "They [No Doubt] did not understand because they are from America and they accept gay people. Jamaica was upset. And I'm upset if Jamaica was upset. I ain't gonna accept no success that my culture is not proud of. I can't do it." This personal identification with a particular conception of the island's preferences, and the island itself, was underlined in a separate interview: "[E]verything I do I feel like Jamaica. So long as you booked Bounty Killer, you just put a piece of Jamaica on your record. That's what I'm doing—travelling like a piece of Jamaica. Anywhere I be, you're supposed to feel Jamaica." Missing, not surprisingly, from the deejay's comments is any reference to the ambivalent feelings he and his cohort felt toward the United States. On the one hand, Price recognized that the No Doubt recording and video substantially raised his profile abroad and would likely increase sales of his own records, and consequently he decided to rejoin the promotional campaign for the song. At the same time, he perceived that maintaining credibility in Jamaica—which was tied in some respects to his long-term credibility elsewhere as an authentic representative of the island's culture—required that he not be seen as watering down his music or risking the integrity of Jamaican culture or music: "Everybody has been doin' music (in Jamaica) but it has been more Americanised and toned down to get the record sales. We no in fe dat, we jus' do our music fe suit the dancehall community and the whole Jamaican heritage." At some level, Price must have recognized that he was playing both ends of the field.[21] The ritualistic condemnation of homosexuality that became a staple of dancehall culture in the 1990s (with deejays Sizzla and Capleton perhaps the most strident ideologues in this respect), not surprisingly, spilled over into the realm of formal politics. During the campaign leading up to the 2002 national elections, Edward Seaga selected as one of his unofficial campaign songs T.O.K.'s "Chi Chi Man," a song whose chorus ("Fire mek we burn them") implicitly called for the incineration of homosexuals (for the public record, a group member suggested that a "chi-chi man is a person who represents the negative and also corruption"). In the spirit of the lyrics, Seaga took to holding a lighter in the air during his rallies, exploiting the allegations and rumors that his opponent, then prime minister P. J. Patterson, was homosexual. This implicit gay-baiting provoked Patterson, a divorced father, to state publicly that his "credentials as a lifelong heterosexual person [were] . . . impeccable."[22]

Deejays' ability to define the acceptable limits of masculinity was also correlated with a certain agenda-setting power in the realm of formal politics.

A summit was called by the prime minister, himself a former manager of the Skatalites, in August 1999 in response to the concerns about the promotion of violence in dancehall lyrics at a time when it was perceived that dancehall artists exercised as much if not more influence over the public agenda than the island's politicians. (Hence Marjorie Stair's observation in a column in the *Gleaner:* "In the 1990s it is the music and the media which now hold the power [that the] political and intellectual leadership [exercised] in the 1970s and the 1980s.")[23] Specifically, rioters had closed down Kingston for four days that spring protesting gas price increases, with a soundtrack that included recordings such as "Fed Up" and "Anytime" ("We do what we do so we stay alive") by Bounty Killer. The suggestion in "Anytime" that "nines" (9-millimeter guns) were effective means of dealing with hunger upset the island's middle and upper classes, and both songs were banned from the nation's airwaves (as was Anthony B's similarly pointed "Fire Pon Rome") yet did very well on the charts. Although some of the musicians in attendance at the summit argued that the influence of American video broadcasts explained much of the violence in Jamaican popular culture, Patterson emphasized the responsibility of Jamaican artists: "I want to voice some concerns and to say to the entertainment industry, and the music industry in particular, that they have to make some contribution to help us quell crime and violence in the society."[24] Furthermore, the PNP's leader sought to draw a distinction between what he saw as legitimate protest and music that incited violence. In a direct reference to the work of Bounty Killer (who was present), Patterson stated: "There's nothing wrong with singing about poor people being fed up, but singing about guns is out of line." The summit concluded with an offering, a plastic bag of ganja, to the prime minister from deejay Jesse Jendau and the suggestion that legalization would ease the country's economic troubles, and Patterson's expression of appreciation in return: "Thank you very much, you've certainly introduced a new and exciting dimension to the discussions."[25]

PLAY WITHIN THE CHANGES

On the American front, one of the more interesting instances of the interaction of African Americans and Caribbeanisms occurred a decade earlier in the aftermath of the Clarence Thomas/Anita Hill controversy in 1991. In a *New York Times* editorial, the Harvard University sociologist and Jamaican immigrant Orlando Patterson argued in defense of George Bush's nominee to the

Supreme Court that "with his mainstream cultural guard down, Judge Thomas . . . may have done something completely out of the cultural frame of his white, upper-middle-class work world, but immediately recognizable to Professor Hill and most women of Southern working-class backgrounds, white or black, especially the latter." On this basis, Patterson suggested, "Thomas was justified in denying making the remarks [i.e., the subject of Hill's harassment allegations], even if he had in fact made them, not only because the deliberate displacement of his remarks made them something else but on the utilitarian moral grounds that any admission would have immediately incurred a self-destructive and grossly unfair punishment."[26]

In response to criticisms of his characterization of Thomas's actions, and specifically a letter from Rhonda Datcher that the *Times* declined to publish, Patterson invoked an intriguing explanation for his earlier reading of the situation:

> In the West Indies the war of the sexes is no joke; it is a pervasive
> and deeply embedded aspect of life that goes back to plantation
> days and the succeeding peasant communities. Humor, sometimes
> playful, sometimes caustic, and always sexual, is an essential aspect
> of this interaction. . . . No one who grew up with Calypso, as I
> did, or dance-hall reggae, as my friends' and relatives' children do,
> could take seriously the squeals of outrage over Clarence's alleged
> "bacchanalian" humor (to use the Trinidadian term for it).

In other words, Patterson contended that his own Jamaican background led him to overlook the specific implications of Thomas's actions in an African American context. This claim was then appended to an even more remarkable allegation regarding class differences and the relationship between Jamaican pop and African American cultural politics:

> I had been reflecting on the differences between the lyrics of dance-
> hall—which is quite lewd, but happily wholly unintelligible to
> Americans—and rap music, which is an African-American derivation
> of reggae dub. These two proletarian musical forms from the
> diaspora now mutually influence each other (to the dismay of folks
> back home). But before rap, dance-hall lyrics were harmlessly erotic,
> something I could listen and dance to with my daughters. Rap lyrics,
> as you know, are incredibly brutal, expressing the "rage and revenge"
> you speak of. There is a horrible sickness here, and I agree with you
> that it has nothing to do with any acceptable form of humor.

Patterson concluded by offering: "The question you [Datcher] raise is perhaps the most important in our attempt to understand what is going on *in the underclass*."[27]

Over the course of his arguments, then, Patterson, a university professor of Jamaican background who characterizes himself as "a father of two African American women," moves from a defense of Clarence Thomas's misogyny to the suggestion that the real problem lay with the combined cultural inclinations of the African American and Jamaican lower-income classes. As Belinda Edmondson has argued,

> The redefinition of the "bad" carnality of dancehall to the "joyful" carnality of soca and carnival reroutes the middle class's discomfort with the social and racial meaning of dancehall into an easy division between violence (associated with dancehall and ghetto dwellers) and order . . .; the immorality of "slackness" lyrics versus the playful erotic suggestiveness of soca lyrics; the vulgarity of ostentatious ghetto gold chains versus the "colorful" carnival pageantry.

In other words, Patterson's representation of calypso maps quite neatly onto the Caribbean middle classes' broader efforts to distinguish themselves culturally and economically from other economic groupings.[28]

Besides underscoring the intimate terms on which slackness and culture articulate, and illustrating the capacity of elites to self-identify and congregate across national borders, Patterson's rhetorical arrangement of the temporal dimensions of diasporic geography is also telling. His contrasting of mid-twentieth-century calypso and subsequent developments within the genres of reggae and dancehall also speaks to the changes in the relationship between blacks in the United States and the Caribbean. In this context, we can think of the differences between the receptions and perceptions of calypso-era Caribbean immigrants to the United States and those arriving post-1965, or more broadly, the kind of break Marley and Rastafarianism represent from the more staid earlier representations of West Indian immigrant life (i.e., "Afro-British" rather than "African"; drinking rum versus smoking ganja). In other words, if the Manchester Pan-African Congress and World War II are the turning points I am suggesting they represent, it is not surprising that calypso would constitute in Patterson's nostalgic narrative an appealing cultural formation, with its distinct, attendant masculinities and openness to performative ambiguities, bacchanalian humors, and transnational hegemonies not observable or available in Jamaican sound system culture. In his desire for the "harmlessly erotic," we can see the continued viability of the civilizationist narrative of appropriate masculinity and distaste for its constructed and impossibly black other.

The particular classed and temporalized form of diasporic masculinity Patterson articulates can be mapped onto a broader field of play that in its hegemonic representations and dynamics tends to encourage and reproduce a certain gendered geography (and by this reference, I do not mean to suggest that cartographic exercises can ever easily escape preexisting commitments to certain arrangements of gender, race, class, and sexuality).[29] I proposed at the outset of this chapter that we might think of diasporic exchanges throughout the American century as being structured by these two narratives—the civilizationist and the hypermasculine—both of which depend in slightly different ways on the marginalization of the figure of the woman and the suppression, extradition, or disappearance of the sign of the lesbian or gay other. Furthermore, it is the second narrative that, post-Manchester, begins to dominate, although as Patterson's comments reveal, the first hardly disappears. It is in this postwar matrix that the intradiasporic characteristically involves the alignment of place with the hypermasculinist narrative and, accordingly, that the new world is increasingly cast as lacking in relation to the continent, with the Caribbean and Latin America functioning as floating, undecidable midpoints.[30]

With regard to the effect of these developments on the relationship between African Americans and Afro-Caribbeans, it is apparent that Jamaicanisms have contributed to, or perhaps more accurately, been employed to aggravate, the gender tensions evident in African American popular culture, and politics in general. As a result of the gendered and classed transition from soul to disco to hip-hop, R & B has come to be seen increasingly as the music of women and hip-hop as a male-only domain, given their respective concerns: "love songs" in the case of the former, and "everything else but" in the case of rap. The distinction of private realm (female) versus public realm (male), then, has been reinforced in contemporary African American popular culture with hip-hop—or, more accurately, some of the "political" subgenres of hip-hop—assuming that issues involving gender relations are not worthy of discussion and indeed that effective politics requires the exclusion of women.

Given these dynamics, the individual and often existentialist expressiveness characteristic of the blues tradition has collided with the typically collectivist and impersonal pronoun preferences of sound system (and Rastafarian) culture (i.e., "we" and "I and I" as opposed to the explicitly first person singular).[31] For example, in Marley's "Redemption Song," even the singer's knowledge that he is near the end of his life does not lead him to engage in any degree of introspection or self-absorption but rather to submerge his very real personal concerns in the interest of summoning and representing broader communal sentiments. In the following quotation, Linton Johnson captures some of the spirit of this sound system sensibility and resistance to interiority: "[M]y impetus to write was political—from the very beginning—it wasn't a need to clear things off my chest or to, in any way, express any profound, deep inner emotion or anything like that. From the very beginning I saw myself as giving voice to, and documenting, the experiences of my generation."[32] As is evident in Johnson's work (with the very significant exception of the 1980 recording "Lorraine"), as well as 1970s reggae and 1990s drum and bass, this emphasis on the political, cultural, and implicitly collective, and on emotional sobriety, has also generally been linked with an absence of sensuality, sexuality, and female creative agency (despite the use of women's voices, for example, the Wailers' I-Threes, in some instances), if not necessarily outright misogyny. "Reggae was more tied up with black nationalism and certain rigidities of sex and race," writes film director Isaac Julien, with regard to the options available to black British youth in the late 1970s. "Soul, on the other hand . . . challenged some of the structures of black masculinity. It opened up a less fixed and more fluid space." In a roughly similar fashion, it might be observed, Fela Kuti, with his increasing commitment to the performance of a hypertropic "African" masculinity, moved away from performing love songs after he returned to Nigeria in 1970, and adopted what he called "blackism" and a properly "political"—in the narrow and problematic sense—stance.[33]

Jamaicanisms have functioned in this environment increasingly as signifiers of "hardness," a stripped-down, antiseptic sexuality, and an adherence to a relatively inflexible conception of gender roles. The version of the island received through the work of Harry Belafonte, Stevie Wonder's "Boogie on Reggae Woman," or (most of) Marvin Gaye's "Third World Girl" is quite different from the image promoted in Hype Williams's 1998 movie *Belly* and the way Jamaica is more often seen now by African Americans. Although *How Stella Got Her Groove Back* was released in the same year as *Belly*, it is *Belly*'s take on Jamaican life that arguably has become dispositive and increasingly representative of the Caribbean in the eyes of others. It is from this perspective that the film's opening, with Soul II Soul's "Back to Life" playing in the background as the main characters prepare to commit mayhem, makes sense: the song read as a marker of sound system culture enables the imagination and articulation of a certain sense of dread and inherent danger. This is a reading, I would suggest, that runs partly against the grain of the song's powerful and provocative fusion of R & B/lover's rock feminism and sound system masculinism, but much—if not all—of the original structure of feeling underlying the original and undecidable text slides under the power of the particular set of visual images Williams uses to introduce the film.[34]

Grace Jones's border-straddling persona, perceived androgyny, and gender-transcendent box top haircut in the early 1980s (in 1981's "Walking in the Rain" she speaks of "feeling like a woman, looking like a man") stood in partial contrast to the images African American pop culture has imported from the Caribbean and exposed some of the sexual ambivalence, homophobia, and homoeroticism at the heart of contemporary African American popular culture (e.g., her 1981 hit "Pull Up to the Bumper"). Her productions, though, with time, also contributed to—or, more accurately, were appropriated and recontextualized by—another tradition, centered on the notion of an almost mechanical and rather sterile, antisensual Caribbean hypersexuality. In a sense, if Jones's sensual labors threatened to disrupt a certain project and sexual order, the restoration and reinforcement of that hegemony required that she specifically be interpolated, recast, and localized, in order to diminish any residual effects, and uproot possibly encoded traces, of her example. This at times intriguing and engaging reconstruction of the archetypal Caribbean woman as omnivorous sexual machine became, of course, one of the building blocks of late 1980s/early 1990s dancehall culture, for example, Patra's "Worker Man"—"I need a man with five furlongs"—and Lady Saw's "Stab Up the Meat" (and would be reflected to lesser effect in the subsequent work of rap artists such as L'il Kim, Foxy Brown, and Trina). The centrality of some of Jones's personae to late twentieth-century dancehall was evidenced by the inclusion of a remake of "My Jamaican Guy" on the soundtrack to the 1997 film *Dancehall Queen,* featuring Jones (in tandem with deejay Bounty Killer), as her relevance to hip-hop was underscored by her guest appearance on L'il Kim's "Revolution" on Kim's 2000 release *The Notorious Kim.* Most of these interpolations would involve flattening or domesticating Jones's potentials as either simply a convenient icon for nationalist productions (i.e., *Dancehall Queen*) or a somewhat imaginative sex worker (e.g., L'il Kim).[35] Each of these attempts failed, of course, to contain the threatening extratext in question, as each strategic recontextualization, to some crucial degree, reinscribed the template being resisted.

The impact of Jamaicanisms on contemporary African American hip-hop culture has also been particularly evident in the efforts to define the permissible limits of black masculinity. The shift toward the spoken or rapped or toasted male voice in both reggae and hip-hop, as the signifier of "authenticity," spoke in clearly problematic ways to the issues of changing gender relations and sexuality. Accordingly, KRS-One, a child of Caribbean immigrants, and one of the most prominent forces behind the blurring of the African American/ Afro-Caribbean border, used a strained patois to attack Queensbridge's hip-hop representatives, MC Shan and Marley Marl, in the classic "The Bridge Is Over," in the following fashion: "Rhyming like they're gay . . . they don't know what to say." Three years later, on the procultural, nationalist "Ya Strugglin'," from his 1990 album *Edutainment*, he would wonder whether "there [were] any straight singers in R & B," a song that featured the late Kwame Ture (aka Stokely Carmichael) and implied that if his suspicions were correct, then there must have been something wrong with R & B. Not entirely surprisingly, Peter Tosh made the same argument in the 1970s, complaining, "Me hear them things [R & B love songs] too much and them not saying nothing more than 'Darling I love you. I swim the ocean and climb the mountains!' Madness! Them things make American man wear pantie."[36]

Against this backdrop, Jamaicanisms would be imported into African American cultural discourses to serve a range of distinct but arguably compatible functions: to restore biblical and specifically Old Testament order, as in Tupac's "Blasphemy" and throughout Lauryn Hill's album *The Miseducation of Lauryn Hill*—even as she seeks to resignify Marley's masculine template— or again to legitimize the adoption of misogynistic and homophobic perspectives, evidenced, for example, in Method Man's 1998 recording "Cradle Rock," on which a Jamaican toaster is brought in to intone "cock a gun and unload it on a battybwoy." That said, it is interesting to contrast the use of patois by Method Man and by KRS-One in the "The Bridge Is Over" to reinforce homophobic—and in Method Man's case, homicidal—sentiments with the deployment of the same inflections by Hill ("Lost Ones"), Queen Latifah ("U.N.I.T.Y."), and Jill Scott ("Watching Me") to challenge sexism, in the first two cases, and to suggest that black American men are wanting in a way that does not reinforce hypermasculinist norms and racial profiling, in Scott's case. Although these cases hardly constitute an exhaustive sample, they suggest that there is the possibility that, in the aggregate, women and men characteristically seek different things when they engage the Caribbean, and the more broadly diasporic.[37]

A more recent example of the deployment of Caribbean motifs to signify a certain masculinist status or order is the film *Get Rich or Die Tryin'*, roughly based on the biography of Curtis "50 Cent" Jackson. One interesting revision introduced in the film that is not true to Jackson's own life story is the suggestion that his mother's family and, by extension, he and his mother are of Caribbean extraction. Although one of his uncles by marriage is in fact West Indian, and plays a mentoring role of sorts in his life, according to his written biography, in the film version, his grandparents and extended family are represented as Caribbean American. Moreover, his grandfather, played by the Trinidadian American actor Sullivan Walker, has the strongest most pronounced West Indian accent and functions as the movie's normative masculine figure. Given the general commitment on Jackson's part to promote himself as the epitome of hypermasculine possibilities—muscles, bullet holes, and homicidal tendencies all in play—it is interesting and telling that the film script, written by Terence Winter, adds the element of the Caribbean background.[38]

FREE EXCHANGE

Beyond the ways the import-export symbolic trade between black communities in the United States and the Caribbean might map onto the larger, increasingly hegemonic narrative I am suggesting, there is the question of how other places populated by blacks are registered. In particular, I am thinking of the way a fourth category of place—besides the United States, the Caribbean and Latin America, and the African continent—is produced and more generally the mechanisms and discourses by which this queer space is constructed and engaged, raced, and sexed.[39]

Focusing on music exclusively, it can be suggested that the hip-hop/reggae axis demands the exclusion or denial of musical genres that might embody sensibilities that are more fluid, not only rhythmically but also in terms of their gender orders and structures. According to this thesis, then, disco and its successor form, house music, Latin-derived sounds in general (including calypso), and the various forms of techno and electronica would be cast as problematic and as sponsoring and subsidizing unappealing, unfixed, and indeterminate conceptions of sexual identity. It is in this tradition that we can interpret hip-hop's increasingly antagonistic relationship with disco, despite its partial roots in the genre (e.g., the Sugarhill Gang's borrowing of Chic's "Good Times" and the disco aesthetic that dominated first-generation rap) and the brevity of the hip house movement in the late 1980s, during which attempts were made to fuse house music and hip-hop, for example, the Jungle Brothers' "I'll House You" and Queen Latifah's "Come into My House," with its lyrical references to "children" (which can be read as an acknowledgment of the gay ballroom scene). Accordingly, Nathaniel "Kool G Rap" Wilson argues in a 2003 interview about "The Polo Club," a hip house track he released in 1990 with his recording partner DJ Polo, "That wasn't my idea! That was Polo's. Me and Polo were never a match made in heaven. That's why it's at the end [of the album *Wanted: Dead or Alive*]. I haven't seen Polo in ten years." The intensity of his disavowal—of the track and his former musical partner—speaks to his discomfort with being associated with a recording that is linked too closely, in his view, to the nonheteronormative house scene.[40]

The resistance to this anxiety that is evident in Osten "Easy Mo Bee" Harvey Jr.'s production of the Notorious B.I.G.'s "Friend of Mine" is what gives the recording its subversive effect. As he explains,

> The thing about that record is [the hook I sampled]. . . . That's Black Mambo. I might've been working with hard-ass Big but I was gonna pull in a whole other crowd because of that Black Mambo. Black Mambo was from the Paradise Garage. DJ Larry Levan would throw that on . . . and you would hear people stomping and going crazy. So I knew that anybody who heard that song was gonna think about the Paradise Garage—a disco, dance-music type of club from back in the day.

Harvey's decision to slide a sample drawn from a club popular with black and Latino homosexuals under the rap of an individual who "kinda scared [him] a little" produced an interesting tension and contrapuntal effect that acknowledged while troubling the expected norms of late twentieth-century black male performance. Harvey's transgression aside, house music, along with the various offshoots of hip-hop such as techno and its British analogues, with time became "white" and/or queer, and suspect, according to the narratives that sought to institutionalize and render hegemonic an impossibly authentic conception of masculinity (with an accompanying and naturally complimentary notion of the feminine). As I suggested earlier, it is in this light that we might understand Prince's early distaste for and mocking of hip-hop, Cameo's arm's-length engagement with rap, and Public Enemy's search for, and celebration of, beats women would resist.[41]

What is remarkable is the way this queering of musics becomes conflated with race and geography. In other words, music produced by blacks outside the rap/dancehall continuum or outside the United States and Jamaica (and, of course, in theory the "Africa" that is frequently deployed but rarely substantively engaged) is rendered strange and problematic—almost incomprehensible and indigestible—as well. On one level, there is American hip-hop's disavowal of genres closely related to it, including techno, drum and bass (or jungle), and later broken beat, garage, grime, dubstep, and bassline. These subgenres, largely British in their immediate origins, are perceived as fundamentally outside the market of black American popular culture exchange.[42] Accordingly, OutKast's Andre "Andre 3000" Benjamin observes, "To the average player on the street, house music is kind of connected with the gay community, and drum 'n' bass is connected with house music. In the 'hood, they think you're gay or that you're 'white.'" In response to these sorts of perceptions, the group's first attempt at integrating jungle rhythms ("B.O.B.," released in 2000) would be constructed in order to avoid being read as suspect by submerging the drum and bass elements in a more familiar, palatable, and "harder"—to quote Benjamin—musical setting.[43]

One of the most remarkable anarrangements of the dominant diasporic discourses in this period is the recalibration by Adrian "Tricky" Thaw of Public Enemy's "Black Steel in the Hour of Chaos" (from the album *It Takes a Nation*). The original recording, which is a vague but compelling retelling and recasting of the Attica prison riot story, draws links between the draft, the situation of black prisoners, slavery, and the implications of "not [being] a citizen." The plot involves Chuck D leading a group of prisoners to freedom after having taken a gun from a male corrections officer. In terms of its gender commitments, there are repeated reference to the number of brothers Chuck is leading, and the only corrections officer who is shot or killed is a woman—"I popped her twice"— after she tries to escape. "Black Steel" is also a typical representation of Public Enemy's work in this period, during which the collective was trying to reorient its music so as to make it more acceptable to a black audience, as defined by the market, by downplaying the rock elements prominently displayed on the group's first album. Finally, just before "Black Steel" begins, Flavor Flav can be heard telling a live audience "Bass for your face, London," and indeed, English audiences were early supporters of the group, in fact signing on before black American listeners expressed significant interest. "We always respected the British audience from London to Birmingham. Blacks there are either from the Caribbean or African roots, they were very receptive," recalls Chuck D. "It was actually harder to crack it here [in the United States] because people were still in the slave-like mentality. It still exists in England too, but they have their Caribbean roots and it's in the back of their minds."[44]

Given this sentimental structure, Tricky's cover version constitutes an almost perfect supplement, and arguably a response, to Public Enemy's trans-Atlantic call. A former member of the Bristol collective Massive Attack, Tricky had launched his solo career in tandem with his partner, and subsequently coparent, Martina Topley-Bird. In early promotional photos, the duo would restage the scene from Cameo's "Single Life" video with Thaws wearing a wedding dress (but with smudged lipstick and makeup carelessly applied) and Topley-Bird wearing a tuxedo. On the album *Maxinquaye*, named after Thaws's deceased mother, Martina's voice would be mixed slightly higher in the mix than Tricky's, and as Alexander Weheliye has observed, "the vocal interplay between [the two] worries the distinction between lead/background and female/male singer in several significant ways." Moreover, Weheliye notes that in its contrast to Chuck D's particular stentorian inflections, Topley-Bird's "voice unearths the Americanness of the original." Musically, the Thaws/Topley-Bird rendition draws on a rock/punk energy, in contrast to the R & B foundation that supports the Public Enemy recording, and one can speculate that Tricky's intention is to let loose precisely that which the American rap group felt compelled to suppress between its first and second albums. In other words, one can read Tricky's choice of aesthetic genres as an act of restoration, of scraping away the coats of paint that were obscuring the original piece of art, and of opening up space previously abandoned.[45]

Besides revealing the particularity of Chuck's geographic location, Topley-Bird's resignifying of a text as male-identified as "Black Steel" is deeply disruptive. While the Public Enemy version is anchored and sexed by Chuck's lyrical attention to his murder of a female officer who tries to run away, and the pleasure he seems to derive from the act—that is, his shooting her twice—in this second version of "Black Steel," Topley-Bird can be heard singing and repeating "they cannot understand that I am a black man" and in general assuming the position and identifying with the anxieties to which Chuck D gives voice. In this gesture, Topley-Bird and Thaws (who can be heard on the track as well, but in the background for the most part) mark politics, oppression, marginalization, and the attempts at emancipation as a matter engaging women and men, as a concern that exceeds local and national borders, and indeed all bordering projects.[46] If Public Enemy's "Black Steel" can be read as reinforcing certain aspects of the modernity/coloniality matrix, and seeking to fix and locate normative community—femininity, masculinity, and sexuality—the reply offered by Martina and Tricky destabilizes these same assumptions by arguing for a delinking of space, race, gender, and sexuality and an anaformative geography that resists sedimentation as it refuses hegemony.

8

SPACE IS THE PLACE

While a number of more important issues were raised by the flooding of New Orleans that happened in the wake of Hurricane Katrina in the late summer of 2005, and by the series of earlier decisions that made the disaster possible and predictable, one of the more remarkable processes associated with the crisis was the search for language to characterize the situation. In this context, certain potent and always available narratives were engaged and references were made to armed gangs supposedly shooting at helicopters, looting, rape, and renegade buses (i.e., allegations that vehicles were being highjacked to convey those escaping the devastation), creating the sense that these peoples now spilling out onto the nation's roads were suspect, dangerous, of dubious origins, and undeserving. Particularly intriguing was the effort to identify an appropriate term to describe those forced to flee their homes. Specifically, a CNN reporter's reference to "refugees" provoked much uproar. "The image I have in my mind is people in a Third World country, the babies in Africa that have all the flies and are starving to death," one victim of the storm suggested with regard to the classification. "That's not me. I'm a law-abiding citizen who's working every day and paying taxes. . . . We're everyday working people that own our own homes. *We didn't ask for this.*" Black elected officials were quick to react to the appellation as well. "These people are not refugees," congresswoman Caroline Kirkpatrick asserted, speaking at a press conference held by the CBC. "[T]hey are American citizens." Her colleague Diane Watson echoed, "Refugee calls up to mind people that come from different lands and have to be taken care of. These are American citizens." Maryland's Elijah Cummings added, "They are not refugees. I hate that word." Jesse Jackson Sr. would later contend, "It is racist to call American citizens refugees."[1]

The rhetorics deployed in response to media impulses to render the overwhelmingly black victims of the flooding as something other than human, as possibly beyond anyone's proper concern, and consequently as not just outside but inconvenient and disposable were understandable. The horror suggested by the images broadcast by the networks was incomprehensible, despite the attempts to mitigate the impact of this visual data by means of dissuasive commentary and an editing logic that sought out and looped images suggesting inherent black tendencies toward disorder—for example the camera's obsession with a young black girl protesting along with a dreadlocked man, presumably her father, outside the city's convention center, which was meant to signify that certain folk are (genetically) prone to be angry (about anything). How could this be happening? Here. Humans abandoned on rooftops, on highways, in overcrowded, decaying stadia, and left to die on the street or floating in the bad waters that had come to reclaim the city, bringing to mind Foucault's description of indirect murder: "exposing someone to death, increasing the risk of death for some people, or quite simply, political death, expulsion, and so on." Talk of refugees, looters, and renegade buses was meant as a challenge, as a provocation, as a means of naturalizing quickly—if such an operation makes sense—the violence, old and new, being visited on the heads of these human beings and the boundaries distinguishing the prophylactic and duppy states. The message was clear: these peoples must be from somewhere else. And the answer was even clearer: We are from here. And nowhere else. That was the choice; that was the implication of the assertions of residence and relevance. The only actionable claim, it seemed, was one that called on the familiar tropes of American, and more broadly modern, identity. Not from Africa, but law-abiding and tax-paying. We didn't ask for this. Perhaps those others did.[2]

After some public debate, it would be decided that "refugees" was not the correct term but rather "displaced persons." But by that time it did not matter, as the positions had been staked out. Who are they, where do they belong, where did they come from, on the one side. From here, and only here, on the other. Not a thickly cosmopolitan "we are from here *and* there" or an existentialist "from nowhere *just like you*" but "from here and only here." It is the narrow scope of this debate to which I wish to draw attention: the visceral congruence at the intersection of black respectability discourses and citizen-centered governmentalities, and the speed and ease with which the refugee and implicitly colored other was constructed, denied, and stigmatized by both sides through discourse as less worthy or undeserving of compassion.[3] "We are from here and only here," with its appeals to the rights of citizens falling flat because of the generic instabilities of such identifications, and the specific impossibilities that obtain when such discourses are engaged by nonwhites, and the price of these particular tickets, to borrow again from James Baldwin:

what other resources were available by this point, in this place, under these circumstances, to refuse and contest this sort of marginalization?[4]

There was, of course, another development related to the flooding and the response to the crisis that drew attention to the same constricted norms of discourse that had been internalized and were being reproduced by all. "I hate the way they portray us in the media," stated Kanye West, a successful recording artist and producer, as part of NBC's *Concert for Hurricane Relief*, broadcast in the days following the rupture of the levees. He also made reference to his own sense of guilt for not responding more quickly with financial support; the class dynamics in play; the attribution of criminal intentions to blacks (i.e., their being cast as looters) for engaging in the same behavior for which whites escaped critique; and the ways race is, among other things, the marker dividing valued citizens from those whose lives, by definition, do not matter: "They've given them [the National Guard] permission to go down there and shoot us." Finally, he asserted, "George Bush doesn't care about black people," a comment that captured in many respects what the federal response in all its absences and shortcomings seemed to underscore.

Of all the public statements made by blacks in the wake of the flood, West's drew the most attention. This is partly because of its nature: it was literally unscripted, as West decided to ignore the words being fed to him. Moreover, there was a deeply felt and raw texture to his performance; he was clearly nervous and uncertain whether he was making the right decision by speaking in the manner that he was. There was also a comic aspect, with the actor Mike Myers standing beside West looking rather stunned and checking to see if the words coming out of this rapper-without-a-stage-name's mouth were indeed scrolling across the teleprompter screen while trying to pretend unsuccessfully as if nothing out of the ordinary was happening. In this respect, he was joined by the comedian Chris Tucker, to whom the camera cut rather quickly, and apparently unexpectedly, after West's critical assessment of Bush's presidency. West, also, as a creative artist was exercising his influence in a manner few of his black contemporaries were willing to do up to that point. He was able to speak as frankly as he did because he was not bound, to some crucial degree, by the same rules of the game as those in the realms of formal politics (though he was hardly free of constraints).[5]

What is ultimately most revealing about West's statements is not so much their content but that he was seen as breaking some unwritten rule and that he was as obviously tentative as he was in the presentation of his views. "[T]he thing I want to stress is I'm not into politics," he would state predictably afterward with regard to his comments about Bush. "I don't know that much about politics."[6] As commendable as West's willingness to dispense with the prevailing protocols was, it was the fact of his being alone in speaking in the way he did, in combination with the apparently broad consensus that Katrina would and could be discussed and contained only within the parameters of the discourses of American citizenship, that stands out. The various exchanges, then, brought to the surface evidence of how creole New Orleans—a major nodal point within the Caribbean basin and diasporic geography—and the African American imagination had been thoroughly domesticated. Moreover, the postflood dynamics confirmed the absence of spaces for frank deliberation and the articulation of differing viewpoints outside those permitted and encouraged by mainstream arbiters, and the inverse correlation between increased black visibility and the ability of African Americans to influence public discourse and policy-making.

It is, again, the perceived unavailability of a more expansive rhetorical terrain, the absence of space within language, that I want to emphasize here as an example of the ways process and substance, structure and agency, and speculative geographies and the representation of the culture/politics nexus are mutually constitutive. In other words, if we conceive of black fantastic sensibilities as pursuing and working through specific sorts of spaces, for example, the extension of the public enabled by transgressive interiorities and the anticolonial and substantively postmodern diasporic, and as suggesting certain kinds of practices and disruptive articulations—for example, the conjunctions made possible by the artist-activist, and efforts to sustain infrastructures that might support more extended and intensive forms of creative expression such as the band, the collective, workshops, and live performances—the struggle for room within language itself constitutes a natural analogue. It is in this matrix that the shift that occurred within black politics and its relationship to popular culture—particularly in the post–civil rights era, as evidenced in the efforts to generate and render hegemonic a notion of the political that disavows connections to the cultural realm, and the intimately related compulsion to establish national borders as the limits of political imagination—becomes significant. It is this co/operation of the aesthetic and the national in the disarticulation of black politics, I have argued, that helps explain the persistence and apparently strengthened grip of colonial norms and hierarchies on the constructions and expressions of contemporary black politics.

As intriguing as this drift in the imagination of the supposedly postcolonial is the apparent consensus—the decision—within academic discourse that modernity should function as the master signifier within global black discourse. We are merely conscripts of modernity, striving to be black and modern, and perhaps, in our better moments, capable of Afro-modernisms. By implication, we no longer think in terms of a lingering, perhaps deeply entrenched, shape-shifting coloniality or in terms of race—as Barnor Hesse has argued—as a metastructure that escapes national boundaries and exceeds the mundane fetishization of skin tones. These signifiers have dropped off the page, and we are supposed to assume that the resulting silence about coloniality means that colonial orders have been eclipsed and transcended rather than reupholstered and internalized. Instead, we aspire to be modern, as if this were somehow a new position and as if blacks and nonwhites were not already clearly *and uncomfortably* modern, as if modernity were sustainable without the nigger and the fluid in/convenience that is blackness lying, albeit differently, both outside and inside its borders.[7]

In a powerful set of arguments, the theorist and anthropologist David Scott contends that we are operating now within a new and different problem space and that this requires that we ask new questions that entail new and different answers. "The old languages of moral-political vision and hope are no longer in sync with the world they were meant to describe and normatively criticize," he suggests. In a subsequent passage he offers, "[I]t is our postcolonial *questions* and not our answers that demand our critical attention. . . . [A]n adequate interrogation of the present (postcolonial or otherwise) depends upon identifying the *difference* between the questions that animated former presents and those that animate our own." These are appealing claims. Times have changed, no? Is it not logical that our thinking would too? Indeed, I have made use of his interpolation of Quentin Skinner's concept of problem spaces throughout this book to distinguish the immediate post–civil rights era from the post-post period I have associated with the emergence of a black superpublic in the United States and, in a broader sense, to demarcate the American moment. But there is a case to be made for not carrying this attention to periodization too far. What might these new questions be exactly and to what extent have the larger, longstanding concerns that framed subaltern discourse been transcended? What is emancipation and what does it entail? What does it mean to be free? What is the value and status of the human? These questions might not admit of easy or definitive answers, and their particular textures and intensities might wax and wane, but can we really believe that these concerns do not transcend problem spaces or at least the pre- and post-Bandung divide, the post–civil rights moment, and the times we find ourselves in now after the supposed end of history, politics, and antagonism? Is it the dominant interpretations of the reconfiguration brought on by the synchronic release of Nelson Mandela and the toppling of the Berlin Wall that should structure our interpretations of our current priorities and possibilities? In other words, can we safely assume that the bifurcating impulses implicated with the black borders of the "enlightenment" have been eclipsed, that we are thickly and meaningfully past the colonial? The humility of the careful historian is always appreciated, as is the skepticism of the poststructuralist regarding overarching narratives. Bold declarations that the pressing questions of our time can be read backward into the past, or conversely that the past can be read without constraint, and without attention to context and flux, into the present and future invite doubt (even as we might admit that our constructions of the past are inevitably married to our present concerns). At the same time, the same reluctance to assert continuity and imagine seemingly implacable structures should lead us to be wary of positing radical discontinuity and to consider the possibility that our impulses to distinguish eras might be shaped by the same forces that make our politics. In other words, the notion that we are in a new problem space maps quite conveniently onto the claim that we have moved— progressed as some would have it—beyond politics. This eagerness to draw boundaries in and around time should lead us to investigate what it is that is being discounted and marginalized in order to make these borders hold.[8]

FADE TO BLACK

Pushing back the frame. This is how the video for "Bag Lady" begins. Pushing back the frame past the standard margins with her hands. She needs more space and imagines, perhaps knows, that it is available. This gesture by the recording artist, actor, and director Erykah Badu captures, in a certain respect, the sensibility I am trying to articulate: that willingness to engage time, space, and other modalities outside of the given parameters. It is in these ways that popular culture troubles formal and institutionalized politics—by rendering the assumed and rehearsed into the vernacular of the contingent and the carnivalesque. In its hyperchronic frequencies, and its less mediated discursive articulations of gender, sexuality, and class, audible, tangible, and visible, are not simply the rearrangement of the political but its an anarrangement and random disordering.[9]

If we think of the fantastic as a genre that destabilizes, at least momentarily, our understandings of the distinctions between the reasonable and the unreasonable, and reason itself, the proper and improper, and propriety itself, by bringing into the field of play those potentials we have forgotten, or did not believe accessible or feasible, I would suggest its effects are not all that dissimilar from those of blackness, with its compulsive externalities and unintended consequences. The latter presence's commitment to probing the excesses and challenging the mythologies associated with the constructions and reconstructions of the modern, and disrespect of the governmentalities that structure modern discourse, including the conjoined aesthetic and national, resembles the ways the fantastic functions in relation to foundational thinking. In other words, my reference to a black fantastic is to some degree a pleonasm or, to borrow from Zora Neale Hurston's anthropologies of negro syntax, a double descriptive: separately and in tandem, blackness and the fantastic work to disrupt the bodily imperialisms of the colonial and corrupt the related, innocent representations of the modern.[10] It is in this spirit that I might suggest that analyses of black politics, and by necessary extension the "generic" political, require that the exhaustion with politics itself that structures so much of contemporary discourse not delimit our own investigations of the ways certain things are kept together and others kept apart, and the capacity of the substances and processes associated with the cultural realm to deepen our understanding of these operations.

NOTES

Chapter 1

1. If we understand culture, without a prefix, as a broad matrix of beliefs with corresponding signs, grammars, and practices, popular culture would be further marked as a form of sociality that is made, remade, and exchanged, as experience translated into communicable and marketable form. Specifically, "popular" culture would assume a certain freedom of discourse—or at least aspirations to such freedoms—and accessibility, and can be read as implicitly political. It would also connote a resistance or challenge to unratified, elitist, and universalist conceptions of the cultural and the aesthetic. Stuart Hall suggests: "The role of the 'popular' in popular culture is to fix the authenticity of popular forms, rooting them in the experiences of popular communities from which they draw strength, allowing us to see them as expressive of a particular subordinate social life that resists its being constantly made over as low and outside." See Stuart Hall, "What Is This 'Black' in Black Popular Culture?" in *Stuart Hall: Critical Dialogues in Cultural Studies*, David Morley and Kuan-Hsing Chen, eds. (London: Routledge, 1996), p. 469. We might also think of popular culture as the name of the site where these exchanges take place, as a particular space or arena where a certain kind of political work is done.

2. I will use the terms "formal politics" and "formally political" to distinguish and highlight exactly that which is often excluded when the term *politics* is deployed. *Politics* is often invoked as a reference to everything except for electoral processes, policy-making, and institutionalized practices that have a fundamental bearing on our daily existences. By using this terminology, I do not mean to imply that cultural politics does not constitute a significant form of political activity or to privilege one form of politics over another. In other words, I also want to avoid reinforcing the notion that electoral processes, policy-making, and institutionalized practices constitute the whole of "real" politics, when it can be argued convincingly that the fetishization of exactly these procedures and arenas marks the absence and disavowal of politics and the political in a certain sense (including the significant activities taking place in cultural spaces). Rather, I want to focus on the relationship between these two things—popular culture and formal politics—and avoid the elision of certain forms of politics under the rubric of a broad, undefined, and selectively applied and investigated cultural politics.

3. Regarding the expectation that the protest activities associated with the civil rights movement would diminish as electoral possibilities opened up, see Bayard Rustin, "From Protest to Politics," *Commentary* 39 (February 1965), pp. 25–31; Charles V. Hamilton, "Black Americans and the Modern Political Struggle," *Black World*, May 1970, pp. 5–9, 77–79; Coretta Scott King, "The Transformation of the Civil Rights Movement into a Political Movement," paper presented at one of the meetings leading up to the 1972 National Black Political Convention in Gary, Washington, D.C., November 18–20, 1971; Martin Kilson, "From Civil Rights to Party Politics: The Black Political Transition," *Current History* 67, no. 399 (November 1974), pp. 193–99; and Robert C. Smith, "Black Power and the Transformation from Protest to Politics," *Political Science Quarterly* 96, no. 3 (fall 1981), pp. 431–43.

4. See Rustin, "From Protest to Politics," pp. 25, 28–30. Although the AFL-CIO had not endorsed the 1963 March on Washington, Rustin characterized the labor movement as a key partner in the effort to bring about an improvement in the socioeconomic status of blacks and as the "largest single organized force . . . pushing for progressive social legislation."

5. Rustin, "From Protest to Politics," p. 28.

6. Donald Bogle, *Toms, Coons, Mulattoes, Mammies, and Bucks: An Interpretive History of Blacks in American Films*, 3rd ed. (New York: Continuum, 1997), p. xxiv.

7. See Ossie Davis and Ruby Dee, *With Ossie and Ruby: In This Life Together* (New York: Morrow, 1998), pp. 86–87; and *I'll Make Me a World* (Blackside 1999).

8. Regarding *The Souls of Black Folk*'s "literary and political grip," see Robert Gooding-Williams, "Du Bois, Politics, Aesthetics: An Introduction," *Public Culture* 17, no. 2 (2005), pp. 203–15.

9. See Marcus Garvey, "Editorial," *Negro World*, September 11, 1928, p. 1; Robert G. Weisbord, "Marcus Garvey, Pan-Negroist: The View from Whitehall," in *Marcus Garvey and the Vision of Africa*, John Henrik Clarke, ed. (New York: Vintage, 1974), p. 433; and Martin Bauml Duberman, *Paul Robeson* (New York: Ballantine Books, 1989), p. 203.

10. See Wayne Cooper, *Claude McKay: Rebel Sojourner in the Harlem Renaissance* (New York: Schocken, 1987), p. 244; and W. E. B. Du Bois, "The Browsing Reader," *Crisis*, June 1928, p. 202.

11. See W. E. B. Du Bois, "Criteria of Negro Art," in *The Portable Harlem Renaissance Reader*, David Levering Lewis, ed. (New York: Penguin, 1994), p. 103. In this light, the negative response in the late 1990s to the work of cutout artist Kara Walker (e.g., fellow artist Betye Saar's characterization of her younger colleague's work as "revolting [and] negative [and] a form of betrayal") flows from a longstanding tradition. See the transcript of the documentary *I'll Make Me a World*. Regarding the Walker controversy, see "Extreme Times Call for Extreme Heroes," *International Review of African American Art* 14, no. 3, and 15, no. 2 (1998), pp. 3–16; "Kara Walker Speaks: A Public Conversation on Racism, Art, and Politics with Tommy Lott," *Black Renaissance* 3, no. 1 (fall 2000), pp. 69–91; Holland Cotter, "A Nightmare View of Antebellum Life That Sets Off Sparks," *New York Times*, May 9, 2003, p. E36; Gwendolyn DuBois Shaw, *Seeing the Unspeakable: The Art of Kara Walker*

(Durham, N.C.: Duke University Press, 2004); and Hilton Als, "The Shadow Act: Kara Walker's Vision," *New Yorker*, October 8, 2007, pp. 70–79.

12. The Vandross quotation is from Omo, "Album of the Month: I Know, Luther Vandross," *Pride*, September 1998, p. 27. Similarly, Smokey Robinson has suggested, "Love is a never-ending subject. You can write about politics, cars, and dances, but somewhere down the line, those are going to become passé," as Kenneth "Babyface" Edmonds has argued, "I don't think people want another 'We Are the World' song. I think Marvin Gaye's 'What's Going On' was a hit because it had a catchy melody.... [M]usic is an escape and people just don't want to be preached to. They don't want to be schooled. They want to forget about the pain that life brings." See Gail Mitchell, "Smokey Robinson's 'Intimate' New Set Finds Home at Motown," *Billboard*, September 4, 1999, p. 14; and *allhiphop.com*, September 15, 2005. Vandross's claim is a bit disingenuous. His lyrics and presentation, at least on his later albums, suggested a certain agenda with regard to black male sexuality (e.g., "Killing Me Softly," *Songs*, Sony 1994, and "Religion," *I Know*, Virgin 1998) and, in certain respects, Vandross was a bit of a conscious soul rebel.

13. Similarly, rapper Talib Kweli Green contends, "Politics is not the truth to me; it's an illusion," and Haile Gerima, a filmmaker (of the UCLA school of black independent cinema), argues, "[P]olitics is an art of lying. When art becomes politics, it deceives" (although he contends at another point that "everything is political"). See Brett Johnson, "Mama Africa," *Vibe*, September 2000, p. 104; Jeff Chang, "Selling the Political Soul of Hip Hop," *alternet.com*, posted January 8, 2003; and Pamela Woolford, "Filming Slavery: A Conversation with Haile Gerima," *Transition* 64 (1994), pp. 92, 96 (italics in original).

14. See Arlene Croce, "Discussing the Undiscussable," *New Yorker*, December 26, 1994–January 2, 1995, pp. 54–60.

15. On this point, see Walter Benjamin, "The Author as Producer," in *Art in Theory, 1900–1990: An Anthology of Changing Ideas*, Charles Harrison and Paul Wood, eds. (Oxford: Blackwell, 1992), pp. 484–88.

16. For a useful discussion of the relationship between race and the aesthetic, see Clyde Taylor, *The Mask of Art: Breaking the Aesthetic Contract—Film and Literature* (Bloomington: Indiana University Press, 1998). As Taylor observes, it is important to recognize the notion of the aesthetic as a product of a particular moment and space—eighteenth-century Europe, to be precise—despite its universalist pretensions.

17. Regarding the question of whether popular culture actually addresses "political" realities, see Robin D. G. Kelley, *Race Rebels: Culture, Politics, and the Black Working Class* (New York: Free Press, 1994), pp. 8–10; Adolph Reed Jr., "Posing as Politics," in *Class Notes: Posing as Politics and Other Thoughts on the American Scene* (New York: New Press, 2000), pp. 167–70; and Todd Gitlin, "The Anti-political Populism of Cultural Studies," in *Cultural Studies in Question*, Marjorie Ferguson and Peter Golding, eds. (London: Sage, 1997). Legitimate concerns have also been raised regarding the wisdom of reading popular culture as politics, given the absence of formal mechanisms of accountability in the former realm, though it is worth

noting that creative artists' livelihoods do depend on maintaining some connection with their audiences. Also worth considering is popular culture's ability to cross barriers and engender broader solidarities. To varying degrees, the surrealist movement of the interwar years; the cultural front of the pre–Cold War Popular Front; the rock 'n' roll movement of the mid- and late 1950s; the Third Cinema movement of the 1960s; the feminist literature of the post–civil rights era; Latin rock in the early 1970s; and disco in the late 1970s presented opportunities for the promotion of convivial norms, to borrow a term from Paul Gilroy. See Paul Gilroy, *After Empire: Melancholia or Convivial Culture* (Abingdon, England: Routledge, 2004); and Michael Denning, *The Cultural Front: The Laboring of American Culture in the Twentieth Century* (New York: Verso, 1997), and "The Novelists' International," in *Culture in the Age of Three Worlds* (London: Verso, 2004), pp. 51–72. For conflicting assessments of the degree of interracial dialogue within the surrealist movement—narrowly defined—see Brent Hayes Edwards, "The Ethnics of Surrealism," *Transition* 78 (1998), pp. 84–135; and Robin D. G. Kelley's preface, "A Poetics of Anticolonialism," in Aimé Césaire, *Discourse on Colonialism*, Joan Pinkham, trans. (New York: Monthly Review Press, 2000), pp. 7–28, 97 n. 13; and "Keeping It (Sur)real: Dreams of the Marvelous," in *Freedom Dreams: The Black Radical Imagination* (Boston: Beacon Press, 2002), pp. 157–94.

18. "The reason the 'negro vote' has rarely decided the outcome of an election is because of its political ignorance and blind, single-party loyalty," Chuck Stone argued in 1969. See "Black Politics: Third Force, Third Party or Third-Class Influence?" *Black Scholar*, December 1969, p. 9. Regarding the role of violence as a political strategy, see Richard C. Fording, "A Political Response to Black Insurgency: A Critical Test of Competing Theories of the State," *American Political Science Review* 95, no. 1 (March 2001), pp. 115–30. In the documentary *Wattstax* (filmed in the summer of 1972 and released at the beginning of 1973), one commentator suggests that the Watts riots in 1965 brought a positive change in the community's circumstances. Specifically, the speaker refers to the opening of the Martin Luther King Jr. General Hospital in the area. Construction began on the hospital on April 10, 1968 (four days after King's assassination), and the facility officially opened on March 27, 1972 (it was renamed the Martin Luther King Jr. / Drew Medical Center in 1982 and lost its accreditation in early 2005). Similarly, after the June 2003 riots in Benton Harbor, Michigan, Reverend Edward Pinkney, of the Bethel Christian Restoration Center, and the Black Autonomy Network Community Organization, observed: "I hate to see this happen, but sometimes you have to get your message across. . . . There's never change without conflict." Later that summer he added, "Things are really moving; the window's open now. Nobody got killed. A few houses burned down, but we're going to get fifty new ones [as a result of a commitment made after the riots]. That may not be a bad exchange at all." Quoted in Jodi Wilgoren, "Fatal Police Chase Ignites Rampage in Michigan Town," *New York Times*, June 19, 2003, p. A16; and Jodi Wilgoren, "Help Comes to a Riot-Stricken City, but Its Problems Remain," *New York Times*, August 26, 2003, p. A12.

19. See Fredrick C. Harris, *Something Within: Religion in African-American Activism* (New York: Oxford University Press, 1999), p. 4. See also Ralph Bunche, *A World View of Race* (Washington, D.C.: Associates in Negro Folk Education, 1936); E. Franklin Frazier, *The Negro Church in America* (New York: Knopf, 1963); and Manning Marable, "Religion and Black Protest in African American History," in *African American Religious Studies*, Gayraud S. Wilmore, ed. (Durham, N.C.: Duke University Press, 1989).

20. See Du Bois, "Criteria of Negro Art," p. 104; and David Levering Lewis, *W. E. B. Du Bois: The Fight for Equality and the American Century, 1919–1963* (New York: Holt, 2000), p. 306. Observes Lewis, "Du Bois's distaste for the vibrant evangelism of black religious observance was so palpable that he might well have invented the tag line about religion being the opiate of the people had not Marx supplied it," adding that "an informed reading of Du Bois's *oeuvre* discloses virtually no modern role assigned to the Negro church." For a different view, see Edward J. Blum, *W. E. B. Du Bois: American Prophet* (Philadelphia: University of Pennsylvania Press, 2007).

21. Houston A. Baker Jr., "Critical Memory and the Black Public Sphere," in *The Black Public Sphere*, Black Public Sphere Collective, ed. (Chicago: University of Chicago Press, 1995), p. 20. The apparent willingness of a number of black clergy (e.g., T. D. Jakes, Boston's Eugene Rivers) to consider supporting George W. Bush's "faith-based initiative" and school voucher plans (e.g., New York's Floyd Flake and a number of Detroit's black clergy during a 2000 Michigan referendum on the issue) is consistent with this reading of the aggregate political inclinations of the black churches.

22. Adolph Reed Jr., *The Jesse Jackson Phenomenon: The Crisis of Purpose in Afro-American Politics* (New Haven, Conn.: Yale University Press, 1986), pp. 41, 56–57.

23. See Hortense Spillers, "Who Cuts the Borders? Some Readings on 'America,'" in *Comparative American Identities: Race, Sex, and Nationality in the Modern Text*, Hortense Spillers, ed. (New York: Routledge, 1991), p. 12; and Valentin Y. Mudimbe, *The Idea of Africa* (Bloomington: Indiana University Press, 1994), p. xii.

24. Adolph Reed Jr., "'What Are the Drums Saying, Booker?': The Curious Role of the Black Public Intellectual," in *Class Notes*, pp. 88–89.

25. Toni Morrison, "The Site of Memory," in *Out There: Marginalization and Contemporary Culture*, Russell Ferguson, Martha Gever, Trinh T. Minh-Ha, and Cornel West, eds. (Cambridge, Mass.: MIT Press, 1990), p. 302.

26. Quoted in Richard Kostelanetz, "Ralph Ellison: Novelist as Brown Skinned Aristocrat," *Shenandoah* 20 (summer 1969), p. 74.

27. Relevant in this context is Milton Nascimento's wordless vocalizing that emerged in the 1970s in response to the efforts of Brazilian censors during the country's years of military rule. Not surprisingly, as Michelle Mercer notes, "censors then became suspicious of Milton's voice itself." See Michelle Mercer, *Footprints: The Life and Work of Wayne Shorter* (New York: Penguin, 2004), p. 171. With regard to the Temptations' recording "Cloud Nine," Dennis Edwards, the group's lead singer

at the time, remembers, "We were a little nervous about it. . . . That song can be taken a lot of ways, and *we* weren't sure what it was saying. . . . It was border-line—it could go either way—and what we found out was that some of the best songs work like that." The song is often read as a reference to the experience of using drugs (and encouragement to do the same). Quoted in Ben Edmonds, "Final Frontier," *Mojo*, August 2001, p. 64.

28. Quoted in Robert G. O'Meally, introduction to Ralph Ellison, *Living with Music: Ralph Ellison's Jazz Writings*, Robert G. O'Meally, ed. (New York: Modern Library, 2001), p. xi (italics in original). See also Ralph Ellison, *Shadow and Act* (New York: Vintage, 1964), p. 263; *Going to the Territory* (New York: Random House, 1986), p. 108; and *Juneteenth*, John Callahan, ed. (New York: Vintage, 1999). The Ellisonian tradition would include the work of Albert Murray, Stanley Crouch, Charles Johnson, and Wynton Marsalis. Regarding Ellison's politics, see Richard Kostelanetz, *Politics in the African-American Novel: James Weldon Johnson, W. E. B. Du Bois, Richard Wright, and Ralph Ellison* (Westport, Conn.: Greenwood Press, 1991); Jerry Gafio Watts, *Heroism and the Black Intellectual: Ralph Ellison, Politics, and Afro-American Intellectual Life* (Chapel Hill: University of North Carolina Press, 1994); Lawrence Jackson, *Ralph Ellison: Emergence of Genius* (New York: Wiley, 2002); Kenneth W. Warren, *So Black and Blue: Ralph Ellison and the Occasion of Criticism* (Chicago: University of Chicago Press, 2003); and Arnold Rampersad, *Ralph Ellison: A Biography* (New York: Knopf, 2007).

29. Ellison writes in "Harlem Is Nowhere" almost—ironically—in the spirit of Theodor Adorno: "[T]he lyrical ritual elements of folk jazz—that artistic projection of the only real individuality possible for him in the South, that embodiment of a superior democracy in which each individual cultivated his uniqueness and yet did not clash with his neighbors—have given way to the near-themeless technical virtuosity of bebop a further triumph of technology over humanism." See "Harlem Is Nowhere," in *Shadow and Act*, p. 300.

30. This refusal is remarkable, given that both *Invisible Man* and *Juneteenth* are about politics and politicians. With regard to A. Z. Hickman, the hero in *Juneteenth*, Ellison notes, "One of the implicit themes at work here [in the book] is Hickman's *refusal* to act politically, his refusal to use politics as an agency for effecting change." See *Juneteenth*, p. 360. In "Harlem Is Nowhere," he implies that there is necessarily a tension between "creating works of art" and "overcom[ing] the frustrations of social discrimination." See "Harlem Is Nowhere," p. 297. For a more grounded and useful engagement of the blues as political theory, see Clyde Woods, *Development Arrested: Race, Power, and the Blues in the Mississippi Delta* (London: Verso, 1998). It is important to note that Ellison's writing and his normative commitments shift over time (explaining, for example, the tonal differences that distinguish "Harlem Is Nowhere" [1948] and the posthumous *Juneteenth*) though traces of many of the arguments that are stated in a rather trite manner in his later work can be found in the earliest writings. For more generous interpretations of Ellison's theoretical commitments—in response to arguments made by Theodor Adorno and Hannah Arendt, respectively—see Lorenzo

C. Simpson, "Musical Interlude: Adorno on Jazz, or How Not to Fuse Horizons," in *The Unfinished Project: Toward a Postmetaphysical Humanism* (New York: Routledge, 2001), pp. 42–59; and Danielle S. Allen, *Talking to Strangers: Anxieties of Citizenship since Brown v. Board of Education* (Chicago: University of Chicago Press, 2004). See also Ellison's response to "Black Boys and Native Sons," by Irving Howe, *Dissent*, autumn 1963, in "The World and the Jug," *New Leader* 46, no. 25 (December 9, 1963), pp. 22–26.

31. Regarding the discourse on respectability, see Evelyn Brooks Higginbotham, *Righteous Discontent: The Women's Movement in the Black Baptist Church, 1880–1920* (Cambridge, Mass.: Harvard University Press, 1993); Kevin G. Gaines, *Uplifting the Race: Black Leadership, Politics, and Culture in the Twentieth Century* (Chapel Hill: University of North Carolina Press, 1996); Randall Kennedy, *Race, Crime, and the Law* (New York: Pantheon, 1997); and Dwight A. McBride, *Why I Hate Abercrombie and Fitch: Essays on Race and Sexuality in the U.S.* (New York: New York University Press, 2005).

32. See C. L. R. James, *The Black Jacobins: Toussaint L'Ouverture and the San Domingo Revolution*, 2nd rev. ed. (New York: Vintage, 1989); Eric E. Williams, *Capitalism and Slavery* (Chapel Hill: University of North Carolina Press, 1994); Partha Chatterjee, *Nationalist Thought and the Colonial World: A Derivative Discourse?* (London: Zed, 1986); Homi Bhabha, "Race and the Humanities: The 'Ends' of Modernity?" *Public Culture* 4, no. 2 (1992), pp. 81–85; Paul Gilroy, *The Black Atlantic: Modernity and Double Consciousness* (Cambridge, Mass.: Harvard University Press, 1993); and Michael Hanchard, "Afro-modernity: Temporality, Politics, and the African Diaspora," *Public Culture* 11, no. 1 (1999), pp. 245–68. Ellison recognized the problematic relationship between on the one hand prevailing conceptions of Western civilization, modernity, and humanism and on the other the characterization of black life. As an African American character notes in an early draft of his *Invisible Man*, the "humanist tradition . . . has flourished through our own dehumanization, debasement, through our being ruled out of bounds." See Barbara Foley, "From Communism to Brotherhood: The Drafts of *Invisible Man*," in *Left of the Color Line: Race, Radicalism, and Twentieth-Century Literature of the United States*, Bill V. Mullen and James Smethurst, eds. (Chapel Hill: University of North Carolina Press, 2003), p. 175.

33. At another point, Trouillot adds, "As part of the geography of imagination that constantly recreates the West, modernity always required an Other and an Elsewhere. It was always plural, just like the West was always plural. This plurality is inherent in modernity itself, both structurally and historically. Modernity as a structure requires an other, an alter, a native—indeed, an alter-native." Michel-Rolph Trouillot, "The Otherwise Modern: Caribbean Lessons from the Savage Slot," in *Critically Modern: Alternatives, Alterities, Anthropologies*, Bruce M. Knauft, ed. (Bloomington: Indiana University Press, 2002), pp. 222, 224. For a genealogy of "the nigger," see Ronald A. T. Judy, "On the Question of Nigga Authenticity," *Boundary 2* 21, no. 3, Autumn 1994, pp. 211–30.

34. For discussions of Hegel's treatment of questions of race and modernity, see James A. Snead, "On Repetition in Black Culture," in *Racist Traces and Other Writings: European Pedigrees/African Contagions*, Kara Keeling, Colin McCabe, and Cornel West, eds. (London: Palgrave Macmillan, 2003), pp. 11–33; and Michelle M. Wright, *Becoming Black: Creating Identity in the African Diaspora* (Durham, N.C.: Duke University Press, 2004), pp. 27–65. For discussions of the relationship between blacks and modernity, see among others, Gilroy, *The Black Atlantic*; Hanchard, "Afro-Modernity"; Houston A. Baker Jr., *Modernism and the Harlem Renaissance* (Chicago: University of Chicago Press, 1987); and *Turning South Again: Re-thinking Modernism/Re-reading Booker T.* (Durham, N.C.: Duke University Press, 2001); Guthrie P. Ramsey Jr., *Race Music: Black Cultures from Bebop to Hip Hop* (Berkeley: University of California Press, 2003); Wright, *Becoming Black*; Deborah A. Thomas, *Modern Blackness: Nationalism, Globalization, and the Politics of Culture in Jamaica* (Durham, N.C.: Duke University Press, 2004); Alexander G. Weheliye, *Phonographies: Grooves in Sonic Afro-Modernity* (Durham, N.C.: Duke University Press, 2005); Kevin K. Gaines, *American Africans in Ghana: Black Expatriates and the Civil Rights Era* (Chapel Hill: University of North Carolina Press, 2006); Louis O. Chude-Sokei, *The Last "Darky": Bert Williams, Black-on-Black Minstrelsy, and the African Diaspora* (Durham, N.C.: Duke University Press, 2006); and Adam Green, *Selling the Race: Culture, Community, and Black Chicago, 1940–1955* (Chicago: University of Chicago Press, 2006).

35. See Achille Mbembe, "On the Postcolony: A Brief Response to Critics," *Qui Parle* 15, no. 2 (2005), p. 3. Regarding the continuities between modern and postmodern discourses, see Achille Mbembe, *On the Postcolony* (Berkeley: University of California Press, 2001); David Harvey, *The Condition of Postmodernity: An Enquiry into the Origins of Cultural Change* (Oxford: Blackwell, 1989); Frank Kermode, "Modernism, Postmodernism, and Explanation," in *Prehistories of the Future: The Primitivist Project and the Culture of Modernism*, Elazar Barkan and Ronald Bush, eds. (Stanford, Calif.: Stanford University Press, 1995); Hall, "What Is This 'Black' in Black Popular Culture?"; James A. Snead, "Racist Traces in Postmodernist Theory and Literature," in Keeling et al., *Racist Traces and Other Writings*; Kwame Anthony Appiah, *In My Father's House: Africa in the Philosophy of Culture* (New York: Oxford University Press, 1992); Gilroy, *The Black Atlantic*; and Bhabha, "Race and the Humanities."

36. Building on Timothy Mitchell's interpolation of Michel Foucault's work, the casting of the modern national state as distinct from (civil) society should be seen as a creative effort to naturalize the desires of certain emerging dominant constituencies, as an effort to place certain practices and norms above and beyond partisan or ideological challenge. This distinction, then, between the state and civil society is meant to deflect or mask the continuities of power and interest that link the two realms and the common exclusionary efforts and commitments emanating from both essentially falsely disjuncted spaces. Not surprisingly, this masking is characteristically less developed and apparent where state power has yet to achieve a natural form (and here I would include the United States). "Power

here is more naked than in any other part of the world," C. L. R. James noted in 1963 in reference to the Caribbean. See Timothy Mitchell, "The Limits of the State: Beyond Statist Approaches and Their Critics," *American Political Science Review* 85, no. 1 (March 1991), pp. 77–96 (the quotation in the text is from p. 94); Michel Foucault, "Governmentality," *Ideology and Consciousness* 6 (summer 1986), pp. 5–21; David Scott, *Refashioning Futures: Criticism after Postcoloniality* (Princeton, N.J.: Princeton University Press, 1999); and "Political Rationalities of the Jamaican Modern," *Small Axe* 14 (September 2003), pp. 1–22; and James, *The Black Jacobins*, p. 408. Regarding the relationship between aesthetics and politics, see Jacques Rancière's discussion of "the police order" and its role in determining "the distribution of the sensible," in *The Politics of Aesthetics*, Gabriel Rockhill, trans. (New York: Continuum, 2004).

37. For a useful consideration of the ways traditions might be identified and constituted through discourse, see David Scott, "'An Obscure Miracle of Connection,'" in *Refashioning Futures*, pp. 106–27.

38. Italics in original. See Wendy Brown, *Politics out of History* (Princeton, N.J.: Princeton University Press, 2001), p. 6; and Frederick Cooper, "Modernity," in *Colonialism in Question: Theory, Knowledge, History* (Berkeley: University of California Press, 2005), pp. 113–49. It is in this broader context, for example, that Jerry Seinfeld's comment in his documentary *Comedian* (Bridgnorth/Miramax 2002)—that *even* Hutu tribespeople know to wait until after the beep before leaving a message with an answering service—makes its meaning.

39. As Aimé Césaire observes, "[A]fter all we are dealing with the only race which is denied even the notion of humanity." Michael Hanchard's observation "People of African descent have often been depicted as the antithesis of western modernity and modern subjectivity" is also relevant here. See Morrison quoted in Paul Gilroy, *Small Acts: Thoughts on the Politics of Black Cultures* (London: Serpent's Tail, 1993), p. 178; Gilroy, *The Black Atlantic*; Césaire, *Discourse on Colonialism*, Joan Pinkham, trans. (New York: Monthly Review Press, 2000), p. 94; and Hanchard, "Afro-Modernity," p. 245. On this point, see also Oliver C. Cox, *Caste, Class and Race: A Study in Social Dynamics* (1948; reprint, New York: Modern Reader, 1970). Cox writes "Probably a realization of no single fact is of such significance for an understanding of racial antagonism as that the phenomenon had its rise only in modern times" (p. 322).

40. See Walter J. Ong, *Orality and Literacy: The Technologization of the Word* (London: Routledge, 1982), p. 12. If modernity is really simply a meaningless, empty signifier or benign temporal marker, there is no reason to make it such a focus of black and postcolonial aspirations.

41. This sense of being more than one place at the same time (or being in many times while standing in the same place) is effectively captured in the following quotation from Ellison's 1948 essay "Harlem Is Nowhere": "Historically, American Negroes are caught in a vast process of change that has swept them from slavery to the condition of industrial man in a space of time so telescoped (a bare eighty-five years) that it is possible literally for them to step from feudalism into the vortex of

industrialism simply by moving across the Mason-Dixon line." Ellison, "Harlem Is Nowhere," p. 296.

42. Regarding strategic and pragmatic essentialisms, see Gayatri Chakravarty Spivak with Elizabeth Grosz, "Criticism, Feminism, and Institution," in *Postcolonial Critic: Interviews, Strategies, Dialogues*, Sarah Harasyn, ed. (New York: Routledge, 1990); Judith Butler, *Bodies That Matter: On the Discursive Limits of "Sex"* (New York: Routledge, 1993); and Tommy Lott, "Du Bois's Anthropological Notion of Race," in *Race*, Robert Bernasconi, ed. (Oxford: Blackwell, 2001), pp. 59–84.

43. See Taylor, *The Mask of Art*; Sylvia Wynter, "Rethinking 'Aesthetics': Notes towards a Deciphering Practice," in *Ex-iles: Essays on Caribbean Cinema*, Mbye B. Cham, ed. (Trenton, N.J.: Africa World Press, 1992), pp. 237–79; and Julio García Espinosa, "For an Imperfect Cinema," in *Twenty-five Years of the New Latin American Cinema*, Michael Chanan, ed. (London: British Film Institute, 1984), p. 30; and "Meditations on Imperfect Cinema . . . Fifteen Years Later," *Screen* 26, nos. 3–4 (May–August 1985), pp. 93–94. More broadly, regarding the issues the work of Wynter, Taylor, and Espinosa raises in relation to questions of the aesthetic, imperfection, composition, and improvisation, see Manthia Diawara, "Black British Cinema: Spectatorship and Identity Formation in *Territories*," in *Black British Cultural Studies: A Reader*, Houston A. Baker Jr., Manthia Diawara, and Ruth H. Lindeborg, eds. (Chicago: University of Chicago Press, 1996); Ted Gioia, *The Imperfect Art: Reflections on Jazz and Modern Culture* (New York: Oxford University Press, 1988); Eric Porter, "Writing 'Creative Music': Theorizing the Art and Politics of Improvisation," in *What Is This Thing Called Jazz? African American Musicians as Artists, Critics and Activists* (Berkeley: University of California Press, 2002), pp. 240–86; Vijay Iyer, "Exploding the Narrative in Jazz Improvisation," in *Uptown Conversation: The New Jazz Studies*, Robert G. O'Meally, Brent Hayes Edwards, and Farah Jasmine Griffin, eds. (New York: Columbia University Press, 2004), pp. 393–403; and Howard Mandel, "Chasing Their Muse: Ben Allison, Matthew Shipp, Vijay Iyer, and Stefon Harris Discuss the Art of Modern Jazz Composition," *Down Beat*, April 2005, pp. 44–49.

44. The argument I am making here resists the claims of the "alternative modernities" school (energized by the work of Charles Taylor). Like David Scott, I am arguing for the centrality of a modernity that does not allow for significant variations or multipolar authority. "Modernity" in this sense is intimately linked to race, colonialism, and slavery in ways that would not permit any alternatives as such. Again, in common with Scott, I am assuming the need to grapple with and work through this dominant and singular phenomenon. In contrast to Scott, I do not see blacks' engagement with modernity as a matter of mere "conscription." Blacks, and other nonwhites, have been crucial participants in the framing, making, and negotiation of this thing called modernity, and unlike Scott, I do not see modernity as a finished product (certainly not in the way he depicts it in his discussion of Toussaint L'Ouverture) or, as he seems to suggest at points, as an uncomplicated blessing (e.g., the absence of any significant discussion of race in his book). In general, I do not share Scott's apparent unwillingness to trouble the traditional

Enlightenment narrative. See David Scott, *Conscripts of Modernity: The Tragedy of Colonial Enlightenment* (Durham, N.C.: Duke University Press, 2004); Charles Taylor, *Modern Social Imaginaries* (Durham, N.C.: Duke University Press, 2004); James Tully, "Diverse Enlightenments," *Economy and Society* 32, no. 3 (August 2003), pp. 485–505; and Chantal Mouffe, *On the Political* (London: Routledge, 2005), pp. 123–30.

45. Regarding the potential political rewards of placing deviance at the center of normative political theory and practice, see Cathy J. Cohen, "Deviance as Resistance: A New Research Agenda for the Study of Black Politics," *Du Bois Review* 1, no. 1 (2004), pp. 27–45.

46. I am thinking of race in the way Barnor Hesse has conceptualized it: as more than simply a matter of identifying, making, and remaking black and other bodies—a broad, global phenomenon, a marker of the divide between "Europe" and "non-Europe," with intimate connections to the colonial order and cultural, epistemological, and governmental implications that far exceed historical, localized, and corporeal boundaries. "Race," as we commonly understand it, is in this perspective fundamentally part and parcel of the conjoined projects of modernity and colonialism. Accordingly, race, racism, and antiracist discourse approach the paradoxical, untranscendable, and insoluble (i.e., $x = -x$) if we hold modernity (y) constant and leave its dominant (self) representations free and untroubled. See Barnor Hesse, "Racialized Modernity: An Analytics of White Mythologies," *Ethnic and Racial Studies* 30, no. 4 (2007), pp. 643–63; and *Creolizing the Political: A Genealogy of the African Diaspora* (Durham, N.C.: Duke University Press, 2009). On the same point, see Homi Bhabha, "Conclusion: 'Race,' Time and the Revision of Modernity," in *The Location of Culture* (London: Routledge, 1994), pp. 338–67; and Thomas C. Holt, "Racial Identity and the Project of Modernity," in *The Problem of Race in the Twenty-first Century* (Cambridge, Mass.: Harvard University Press, 2000), pp. 27–56. As I will explain in greater detail in chapter 5, I am using "post-colonial" to refer to that which occurs after or works against coloniality. "Postcolonial"—i.e., without the hyphen—should be understood to refer to that which occurs after or operates more narrowly against colonialism, given colonialism's status as one convenience—among others—within the broader matrix of coloniality. "Always there" is meant to refer (ironically) to both Hegel's readings of Africa's relation to history and the work of Ronnie Laws.

47. Regarding these hidden imperialisms and their relation to public rhetoric or, as Giorgio Agamben puts it, "this no-man's-land between public law and political fact," see Carl Schmitt, *Political Theology: Four Chapters on the Concept of Sovereignty*, George Schwab, trans. (Cambridge, Mass.: MIT Press, 1985); Agamben's *Homo Sacer: Sovereign Power and Bare Life*, Daniel Heller-Roazen, trans. (Stanford, Calif.: Stanford University Press, 1998) and *State of Exception*, Kevin Atwell, trans. (Chicago: University of Chicago Press, 2005), p. 1; and Ousmane Sembène's film *Camp de Thiaroye* (1985; New Yorker Films Video, 1992). It is important to note that Agamben cites Nazism and the Holocaust as crucial markers of modernity's "hidden matrix" (Agamben, *Homo Sacer*, p. 166)

while paying little attention to the broader phenomenon of colonialism. In contrast, in common with the earlier work of Du Bois, Oliver Cox, George Padmore, Aimé Césaire, and C. L. R. James (and, writing from a different normative perspective, Schmitt), Sembène's film foregrounds the colonial factor and makes the connections between this history and the events that took place in Europe leading up to and during World War II. In other words, Sembène's work suggests the possibility of a fuller, more informed history of the "camp."

48. Waldo E. Martin Jr., *No Coward Soldiers: Black Cultural Politics and Postwar America* (Cambridge, Mass.: Harvard University Press, 2005), p. 3.

49. Regarding the black smile, as is well known, and still the case, black laughter and glee have always been symbolically loaded, especially in public spaces open to the gaze of others: e.g., the minstrel show; Zora Neale Hurston; Louis Armstrong and the different responses to his legacy attempted by Dizzy Gillespie, Charlie Parker, and Miles Davis; MC Hammer; and Clarence Thomas's 1991 nomination ceremony smile. For contrasting readings of the black smile, see Ellison, *Shadow and Act*, pp. 225–26; and Toni Morrison, "Introduction: Friday on the Potomac," in *Race-ing Justice, En-gendering Power: Essays on Anita Hill, Clarence Thomas, and the Construction of Social Reality* (New York: Pantheon, 1992), pp. xii–xiii. Among the recent Hollywood films that have used black bodies as punctuation, often in ways that echo lynching photos, one can cite *The Green Mile, Swordfish, Any Given Sunday, Pulp Fiction,* and *Traffic.*

50. Reed, "Posing as Politics," p. 167.

51. Ellison notes, "[M]usic is heard and seldom seen, except by musicians." See Ralph Ellison, *Invisible Man* (New York: Random House, 1952), p. 13; and Fred Moten, *In the Break: The Aesthetics of the Black Radical Tradition* (Minneapolis: University of Minnesota Press, 2003), pp. 85–102.

52. The emergence of salsa music in the 1970s, as a reporter with *Billboard* recognized, "helped give Latinos a sense of national identity and political unity [and specifically represented] a musical vehicle . . . [through which Puerto Ricans could make] a political statement to the world . . . [and] especially to the broad anglo community in the New York metropolitan area." See David Medina, "A View from New York: Salsa Is Also a Political Force," *Billboard*, June 12, 1976, p. S-6; and various artists, *El Barrio: Gangsters, Latin Soul and the Birth of Salsa, 1967–75* (Fania/V2 2006). Three decades later, the reggaeton phenomenon would perform the same function, on a larger scale.

53. Examples of popular culture's ability to focus attention on a specific issue would include, in the American context, Harriet Beecher Stowe's *Uncle Tom's Cabin*, Stevie Wonder's "Happy Birthday," and Spike Lee's *4 Little Girls*. More broadly, one might consider the work of Baaba Maal, Ousmane Sembène (*Moolaade*), and Alice Walker (*Warrior Marks* and *Possessing the Secret of Joy*) that has raised awareness regarding the topic of female genital mutilation.

54. The term "public sphere" is often used to describe what I refer to here as "location." While the public sphere construction has some utility, I do not want to

endorse its problematic aspects and implications. Much of the discussion to follow relates to the limitations of the term "public sphere" as it has been traditionally defined (building on critiques made by others). My references to "location" and, more often, "counterpublics," then, should be taken to mean forms of activity and discourse at odds with, and hopefully transcending, the norms and practices of traditional nominally public spheres. In other words, given the oxymoronic tensions embedded in the "black public sphere" construction, and my unease with regard to the Enlightenment optimism embedded in Jürgen Habermas's formulation of the concept, I am resistant to using it here: the qualifier "black" cannot be unthinkingly attached to the concept of the public sphere, given that nonwhites, like women, have lived much of their lives on the fault lines separating the public and private spheres as conventionally defined. One can make similar arguments regarding terms such as "black civil society," "black popular culture," and "Afro-modernity": public spheres, civil societies, popular culture, and modernity are not blank slates and are in fact in antagonism with prefixes such as "black" and "Afro," a tension that needs to be acknowledged. On this point, see Thomas C. Holt, "Afterword: Mapping the Black Public Sphere," in Black Public Sphere Collective, *The Black Public Sphere*, pp. 325–28; and Michael Warner, "Publics and Counterpublics," *Public Culture* 14, no. 1 (winter 2002), pp. 49–90.

55. Michael C. Dawson, "A Black Counterpublic? Economic Earthquakes, Racial Agenda(s), and Black Politics," in Black Public Sphere Collective, *The Black Public Sphere*, p. 201; and *Black Visions: The Roots of Contemporary African-American Political Ideologies* (Chicago: University of Chicago Press, 2001), pp. 36, 40.

56. Thanks to Todd C. Shaw and Mary Pattillo for encouraging me to rethink my acceptance of the standard "collapse" narrative. For evidence of support for this narrative, see Dawson, "A Black Counterpublic"; Adolph Reed Jr., "Black Particularity Reconsidered," *Telos* 39 (spring 1979), p. 72; Robert C. Smith, *We Have No Leaders: African Americans in the Post–Civil Rights Era* (Albany: State University of New York Press, 1996); Nelson George, *The Death of Rhythm and Blues* (New York: Pantheon, 1988); and Greg Tate, "Cult-Nats Meet Freaky-Deke," in *Flyboy in the Buttermilk: Essays on Contemporary America* (New York: Simon and Schuster, 1992), p. 198. There is, of course, a comparable literature that suggests that the "wheels came off" in the late 1960s, when integrationism ceased to be the dominant determinant of black ideological discourse (and, not coincidentally, after the "white backlash" was in full effect). With regard to popular culture, the relevant literature would include Peter Guralnick, *Sweet Soul Music: Rhythm and Blues and the Southern Dream of Freedom* (New York: HarperPerennial, 1986); Brian Ward, *Just My Soul Responding: Rhythm and Blues, Black Consciousness, and Race Relations* (Berkeley: University of California Press, 1998); and Craig Werner, *A Change Is Gonna Come: Music, Race, and the Soul of America* (New York: Plume, 1998). In common, these texts imply that very little of significance or value happens within black popular culture, and by extension the black counterpublic, once "race relations" and the concerns of white audiences cease to be the defining elements of the black agenda. For a discussion of black women's mobilization

in the context of second wave feminism, see Belinda Robnett, *How Long? How Long? African American Women in the Struggle for Civil Rights* (New York: Oxford University Press, 1997); and Kimberly Springer, *Living for the Revolution: Black Feminist Organizations, 1968–1980* (Durham, N.C.: Duke University Press, 2005).

57. Combining the two narratives, one might ask a third question of the analysts lamenting the supposed disappearance of American communal public spaces: what does it mean that American civil society and social capital are seen as being diminished at the same time that nonwhites, women, lesbians, and gays are starting to mobilize? For one of the more popular versions of this particular lament, see Robert D. Putnam, "Bowling Alone: America's Declining Social Capital," *Journal of Democracy* 6, no. 1 (1995), pp. 65–78. With regard to a similar dynamic in the humanities, Alexander Weheliye refers to "the irony in the dissolution, and perhaps even abandonment, of the subject as a category of critical thinking just as minorities are being recognized as subjects within academic discourse." See *Phonographies*, p. 47. Linking all these dynamics is the question of whether the particular, and specifically the marginalized particular, can ever speak in the vernacular of the general and the universal and be recognized as legitimately entitled and capable of doing so. Evident as well are the kinds of processes—the sorts of work—involved in the formation of an identity or political project. What gets dropped—or, more accurately, repressed on an ongoing basis—in order that the subject can be tidily packaged, promoted, and naturalized into the commonsensical?

58. Quoted in Janny Scott, Charles S. Dutton, and David Simon, "Who Gets to Tell a Black Story?" *New York Times*, June 11, 2000, p. A17.

59. Quoted in Monica Corcoran, "That's a (W)rap!" *New York Times Magazine*, November 9, 2003, p. 27. After being disinvited to speak at Coretta Scott King's funeral in February of 2006, Harry Belafonte declined to challenge his exclusion, arguing, "[L]et us try to repair it [the breach between himself and some of King's children] rather than to go into public discourse." See "After Criticizing Bush, Harry Belafonte Says He Was Disinvited from Delivering Eulogy at the Coretta Scott King Funeral," *democracynow.org*, posted March 20, 2006.

60. With regard to what he calls "Aesopian utterance," Taylor adds, "texts are precariously balanced so their ironies or registrations of difference in meaning typically fall on both sides of the discursive barrier between power and the lack of power, but may be finely calculated in retrospect (or later historical reconsideration) to have served one better than the other." *The Mask of Art*, p. 166.

61. For an indication of how much the axis of black political discourse has changed, consider the centrality of Harold Cruse's book *The Crisis of the Negro Intellectual* to the debates of the late 1960s and early 1970s and how it might be received if it were published today. I would argue that Du Bois, Aimé Césaire, and Eric Williams, among others, in their shifting readings of "independence," and commitments to working both within and outside the state without significant regard for the integrationist–nationalist line, recognized that regardless of orientation, the same basic problems associated with coloniality obtained. On a separate point, it is not my intention to suggest that geographically oriented and genealogical scholarship

is not important or that the study of cultural retentions is not useful. Much of the discussion in this book will address precisely these sorts of questions.

62. This is not to suggest that black elected officials have not concerned themselves with many of the issues facing their constituents or that they have not considered policy alternatives (especially as there has been increasing differentiation among black representatives in the formal realm and geographically within the CBC itself, which now has southern, conservative, "blue dogs" among its membership). Sources of controversy that have emerged within the CBC include debates regarding endorsement strategies for presidential campaigns (e.g., Shirley Chisholm, Jesse Jackson, and Barack Obama); and the CBC's relationship to the National Black Political Assembly. Other issues that have generated debate within the CBC include the merits of Jimmy Carter's administration; tobacco subsidies and the B-2 bomber proposals of the 1980s; gun control; the death penalty; and proposals regarding campaign finance reform. The CBC has also divided over internal organizational matters (often related to personality differences): the propriety of accepting funding from Coors for the CBC legislative weekend (given the connections between the corporation and right-wing causes), the status of the political action committee set up by the CBC (CBCPAC), whether whites could become members, and the distribution of perks associated with the various offices within the CBC. To date, though, there has been little substantive public dialogue among the representatives of black communities in the formal realm about the "black agenda," and the different strategies available to black voting constituencies. The absence of meaningful discourse in this realm can be confirmed by examining the primary contests for congressional seats (usually having no incumbent) in districts likely to elect a black representative. The issues that generate attention are usually mundane or personality-related and/or scandal-driven: e.g., Shirley Chisholm's first congressional campaign against James Farmer in 1968; Charles Rangel's defeat of Adam Clayton Powell Jr. in 1970; the 1986 contests between John Lewis and Julian Bond in Georgia's Fifth District in Atlanta, and Kweisi Mfume and St. George Crosse in Maryland's Seventh District in Baltimore; the challenge incumbent Major Owen faced in the 2000 Democratic primary in New York's Eleventh District from city councillor Una Clarke (and the contest for his seat after his retirement in 2006); and the competition for the open seat in California's Thirty-second District in December 2000. The major focus of debate in the 2002 primary contests in Alabama's Seventh District between incumbent Democrat Earl Hilliard and eventual victor Artur Davis, and in Georgia's Fourth District between incumbent Cynthia McKinney and eventual victor Denise Majette, was the Palestinian/Israeli conflict (although there were other issues in both races). There have been, on occasion, instances when substantive issues have been raised in races for congressional seats likely to produce a black office holder (e.g., the ultimately successful challenges from the Left centering on the Iraq war, mounted by Donna Edwards against incumbent Albert R. Wynn in 2006 and 2008 in the Democratic primaries in Maryland's Fourth District). Generational tensions were also evident in the Davis–Hilliard contest and marked the mayoral

campaigns that led to the election and reelection of Kwame Kilpatrick in Detroit in 2001 and 2005, respectively, and the reelection of Sharpe James in Newark in 2002. In the Newark race, James's opponent, Cory Booker, would also have his sexuality and "blackness" questioned. Regarding the latter, James would suggest, "It takes more to be black than just skin color. It's your experience, it's what you've been through. Booker says he's a Democrat, but he's really a Republican inside. He says he's proud to be black, but he hasn't had any of the experiences *we've* had." (italics added). Booker would win Newark's mayoralty race in 2006. In the two congressional races and the 2002 mayoral contest in Newark, funds for the challengers also apparently came from organizations such as the right-wing Bradley Foundation, which sought to generate appearances of conflict among black voters and specifically youth and middle-class dissatisfaction with existing black elected representatives. The 2004 Illinois senatorial contest, as a result of some unusual circumstances, featured two black candidates, Alan Keyes of the GOP and the eventual victor, Barack Obama, representing the Democrats, and to a minor degree provided a public forum for the discussion of different possible agendas for blacks. On these points, see Ron Dellums and H. Lee Halterman, *Lying Down with the Lions* (Boston: Beacon Press, 2000), pp. 117, 120; William L. Clay, *Just Permanent Interests: Black Americans in Congress, 1870–1991* (New York: Amistad Press, 1992); Kweisi Mfume with Ron Stodghill II, *No Free Ride: From the Mean Streets to the Mainstream* (New York: One World, 1996), p. 336; Steven Mikulan, "Some Came Running," *Los Angeles Weekly*, April 6–12, 2001, pp. 18–19; K. Terrell Reed and Sonia Alleyne, "What It Takes to Win," *Black Enterprise*, November 2002, p. 90; Glen Ford, "Hip Hop and the Hard Right: Media-Made Illusions of Power," *ColorLines* 5, no. 4 (winter 2003), pp. 4–7; Todd Steven Burroughs, "Is Booker Black Enough for Newark?" *africana.com*, May 13, 2002; and Richard Lezin Jones, "Race, Writ Large," *New York Times*, May 5, 2006.

63. With regard to "Respect," Franklin adds, "It is still my biggest song in concert today. So many people identified with and related to 'Respect.' It was the need of a nation, the need of the average man and woman on the street, the businessman, the mother, the fireman, the teacher—everyone wanted respect. It was one of the battle cries of the civil rights movement. The song took on monumental significance." See Aretha Franklin and David Ritz, *Aretha: From These Roots* (New York: Villard, 1999), p. 112. Famously, Franklin offered to post bail for Angela Davis, when she was being tried as a conspirator to kidnapping and murder charges in 1971, arguing, "I have the money. I got it from black people and I want to use it in ways that will help our people." See Gary Younge, "We Used to Think There Was a Black Community," *Guardian*, November 8, 2007.

64. In his classic essay "The Changing Same," LeRoi Jones writes, "[The song] provided a core of legitimate social feeling, though mainly metaphorical and allegorical for Black people." See Gerald Early, *One Nation under a Groove: Motown and American Culture* (Ann Arbor: University of Michigan Press, 2004), p. 104; and LeRoi Jones, "The Changing Same (R & B and New Black Music)," in *Black Music* (New York: Morrow, 1967), p. 208.

65. Earlier that year, Snellings wrote: "[A]ll over this sullen planet, the multi-colored 'hordes' of undernourished millions are on the move like never before in human history. They are moving to the rhythms of a New Song, a New Sound; dancing in the streets to a Universal Dream that haunts their wretched nights: they dream of Freedom! From the steaming jungles of Viet Nam to the drought-ridden plains of India: Dancing in the streets! From the great African savannahs to the peasant-ridden mountains of Guatemala: Dancing in the streets!" See Rolland Snellings, "Afro American Youth and the Bandung World," *Liberator* 5, no. 2 (February 1965), p. 4; and "Keep On Pushin': Rhythm and Blues as a Weapon," *Liberator* 5, no. 10 (October 1965), pp. 6–8. The reference to "Patterson" should be, of course, to "Paterson."

66. The Martha Reeves quotation is from David Cole, "Come and Get These Memories!" *In the Basement* 37 (February–April 2005), p. 27. On this point, see also Suzanne E. Smith, *Dancing in the Street: Motown and the Cultural Politics of Detroit* (Cambridge, Mass.: Harvard University Press, 1999). Reeves ran for a seat on Detroit's city council in 2005 and proposed an improved rapid transit system, the construction of a downtown mall, more support for arts programs in the public schools, and the placing of statues honoring Motown stars to attract tourists. "My heart is in Detroit," she stated, "[but] I'm not making promises like many politicians." Her campaign was successful, and after taking office she reiterated, "I'm not going to ever be like a politician. In fact, I don't think I even like politicians." See "News Round-Up," *In the Basement* 40 (November 2005–January 2006), p. 5; and Jeremy W. Peters, "In Detroit, Motown Singer Is Trying a Brand New Beat," *New York Times*, January 19, 2006.

67. The Vandellas' "Live Wire" (1964) and "Tear It on Down" (1972) can be added to Gaye's list. "Dancing in the Streets" was written by Gaye, William "Mickey" Stevenson, and Ivy Joe Hunter. Gaye quoted in David Ritz, *Divided Soul: The Life of Marvin Gaye* (New York: Da Capo, 1985), p. 107. On a separate note, it is tempting to contemplate the possibility that creative efforts associated with women artists are either more likely to be recontextualized or reinscribed by audiences and/or conceptualized—phrased, written, drafted—in such a way as to have more universal appeal (and, consequently, more likely to be appropriated, reappropriated or "misappropriated," as the case may be). Consider, in this light, the gendered controversies surrounding Lorraine Hansberry's play *A Raisin in the Sun* and Alice Walker's novel *The Color Purple*.

68. The South Shore Commission's 1975 release "Free Man" was read by many as an explicit celebration of gay liberation within a black cultural context ("one of the great gay proclamations of self-determined freedom"). Nevertheless, what appears to be a vocal exchange between two men—with the declaration "All I need is a man like you," and the question "Are you a free man?" receiving the response "I'm a free man and talking 'bout it"—was apparently an effect created by Tom Moulton's remix of the original studio tapes that slowed the track's tempo to such an extent that group member Sheryl Henry's voice achieved a masculine effect. See Tim Lawrence, *Love Saves the Day: A History of American Dance Music Culture, 1970–1979* (Durham, N.C.: Duke University Press, 2003), p. 193; and Gary Jardim,

liner notes for *Give Your Body Up: Club Classics and House Foundations* (Rhino 1995). For examples of songs that appear to be about romantic relationships but actually refer to political issues, narrowly defined, see Chic, "At Last I Am Free" (*C'est Chic*, Atlantic 1978); and Phyllis Hyman, "Gonna Make Changes" (*Sing a Song*, Buddah 1978).

69. Regarding the importance of opportunities to deliberate, see Jürgen Habermas, *The Structural Transformation of the Public Sphere: An Inquiry into a Category of Bourgeois Society*, Thomas Burger, trans. (Cambridge, Mass.: MIT Press, 1989); Nancy Fraser, "Rethinking the Public Sphere: A Contribution to the Critique of Actually Existing Democracy," in *Habermas and the Public Sphere*, Craig Calhoun, ed. (Cambridge, Mass.: MIT Press, 1989); Lani Guinier, *The Tyranny of the Majority: Fundamental Fairness in Representative Democracy* (New York: Free Press, 1994); Melissa S. Williams, *Voice, Trust, and Memory: Marginalized Groups and the Failings of Liberal Representation* (Princeton, N.J.: Princeton University Press, 1998); Jon Elster, ed., *Deliberative Democracy* (New York: Cambridge University Press, 1998); and John S. Dryzek, *Deliberative Democracy and Beyond: Liberals, Critics, Contestations* (New York: Oxford University Press, 2000).

70. The one exception to this pattern among the newer media might be the Internet, although this space is not equally accessible to all.

71. Another factor that reduces the pressure on black Democratic members of Congress to respond to the concerns of their constituents is their high rate of incumbency. Districts that are majority black (and Hispanic) tend to be less competitive.

72. Hamilton, "Black Americans and the Modern Political Struggle," p. 77.

73. Regarding the political orientations of CBC members, see Carol Swain, *Black Faces, Black Interests: The Representation of African Americans in Congress* (Cambridge, Mass.: Harvard University Press, 1995); and Katherine Tate, *Black Faces in the Mirror: African Americans and Their Representatives in the U.S. Congress* (Princeton, N.J.: Princeton University Press, 2003). Currently, 43 of the 535 members of Congress are black.

74. See Michael C. Dawson, *Behind the Mule: Race and Class in African-American Politics* (Princeton, N.J.: Princeton University Press, 1994), pp. 76–88; and Cathy J. Cohen, *The Boundaries of Blackness: AIDS and the Breakdown of Black Politics* (Chicago: University of Chicago Press, 1999), pp. 24–27, 33–77.

75. Among the recorded responses to the murder of Diallo, a Guinean immigrant, are the following: Weldon Irvine, *The Price of Freedom* (Nodlew Music 1999); various artists, *Hip Hop for Respect* (Rawkus 2000); Wyclef Jean, "Diallo" (*The Ecleftic: 2 Sides II a Book*, Sony 2000); Erykah Badu, "A.D. 2000" (*Mama's Gun*, Motown/Universal 2000); Roni Size/Reprazent featuring Zack de la Rocha, "Centre of the Storm" (*In the Mode*, Talkin' Loud/Mercury/Universal 2000); Antonio Hart, "For Amadou" (*Ama Tu Sonrisa*, Enja 2001); Terry Callier, "Lament for the Late A.D." (*Alive*, Mr. Bongo 2001); Bruce Springsteen and the E Street Band, "American Skin (41 Shots)" (*Live in New York City*, Sony/Columbia 2001); David Rudder, "Forty-One Bullets" (*The Autobiography of the Now*, Lypsoland 2001); and Lauryn Hill, "I Find It Hard to Say (Rebel)" (*MTV Unplugged, 2.0* Sony/Columbia 2002).

76. The CBC has been active, suggests Ron Dellums, and "remained unified as long as . . . [it] focused on the issues of race: affirmative action, minority business set-asides, treatment of minorities by government agencies, government appointments." See Dellums and Halterman, *Lying Down with the Lions*, p. 117.

Chapter 2

1. This "reluctance manifested as a hegemonic bundle of inclinations and efforts to render the already said unsaid and unimaginable" can be conceptualized as a *disarticulative cycle*. On the academic front, I would include the turn toward (narrow) empiricism—and the positivist obsession with survey data results—in the study of black politics as aspects of this disarticulative process.

2. Adam Clayton Powell was prevented from taking his seat after the 1966 midterm elections as a result of House Resolution 278 (February 28, 1967), which concerned his alleged misappropriation of funds. He was subsequently expelled (a move the Supreme Court later found unconstitutional in *Powell v. McCormack* [395 U.S. 486 1969]). Powell was reelected in a special election but was not available to be sworn in. On his return to the chamber, he was stripped of his seniority. In the 1970 midterm elections, he was defeated in the Democratic primary by Charles B. Rangel, and would fail to meet the deadlines for a campaign as an independent candidate.

3. A number of blacks would become alienated from the communist movement in this period. On this point, see Richard Wright, "I Tried to Be a Communist," 2 pts., *Atlantic Monthly*, August 1994, pp. 61–70, and September 1944, pp. 48–56; George Padmore, *Pan-Africanism or Communism* (Garden City, N.Y.: Doubleday, 1971); Horace R. Cayton, *Long Old Road: An Autobiography* (Seattle: University of Washington Press, 1970); Chester Himes, *If He Hollers Let Him Go* (Garden City, N.Y.: Doubleday, 1945); Ralph Ellison, *Invisible Man* (New York: Random House, 1952); and Wilson Record, *Race and Radicalism: The NAACP and the Communist Party in Conflict* (Ithaca, N.Y.: Cornell University Press, 1964). Regarding the experience of Pan-Africanists in the context of the French Popular Front, see Gary Wilder, *The French Imperial Nation-State: Negritude and Colonial Humanism between the Two World Wars* (Chicago: University of Chicago Press, 2005).

4. See Coleman Young and Lonnie Wheeler, *Hard Stuff: The Autobiography of Coleman Young* (New York: Viking, 1994), pp. 95, 128–29.

5. For the details of Canada Lee's life and experiences with the Red Scare, see Mona Z. Smith, *Becoming Something: The Story of Canada Lee* (New York: Faber and Faber, 2004).

6. On this point, see Richard Iton, *Solidarity Blues: Race, Culture, and the American Left* (Chapel Hill: University of North Carolina Press, 2000).

7. See Clara Bryant, Buddy Collette, William Green, Steven Isoardi, Jack Kelson, Horace Tapscott, Gerald Wilson, and Marl Young, eds., *Central Avenue Sounds: Jazz in Los Angeles* (Berkeley: University of California Press, 1998), p. 399.

8. C. L. R. James, "Paul Robeson Black Star," in *Spheres of Existence: Selected Writings* (London: Allison and Busby, 1980), p. 262.

9. James adds, "This is a part of the history of the United States which everybody in the United States should know. What was here, what was possible, what was missed, and why." Appropriately, Robeson played Toussaint L'Ouverture in James's theatrical rendering of the Haitian revolution when both were based in London in the 1930s. "Paul Robeson Black Star," pp. 262–63.

10. For a more detailed discussion of Robeson's work and career in this period, and the relationship between race and the Popular Front in general, see Hazel Carby, *Race Men: The W. E. B. Du Bois Lectures* (Cambridge, Mass.: Harvard University Press, 1998); Jeffrey C. Stewart, ed., *Paul Robeson: Artist and Citizen* (New Brunswick, N.J.: Rutgers University Press, 1998); Michael Denning, *The Cultural Front: The Laboring of American Culture in the Twentieth Century* (New York: Verso, 1997); Martin Duberman, *Paul Robeson* (New York: Knopf, 1988); and Iton, *Solidarity Blues.*

11. See Duberman, *Paul Robeson*, p. 342.

12. Duberman, *Paul Robeson*, p. 342.

13. Walter White, "The Strange Case of Paul Robeson," *Ebony*, February 1951, pp. 78, 80–83.

14. See, for instance, Roy Wilkins, "Robeson Speaks for Robeson," *Crisis* 56, no. 5, May 1949, p. 137.

15. The interview was with Martin Duberman in 1983. See Duberman, *Paul Robeson*, p. 344.

16. Walter White, "Paul Robeson: Wrong," *Negro Digest*, March 1950, p. 17 (italics in original).

17. As Martin Duberman notes, when Rustin sent greetings to Robeson on his return to the United States in 1963, Robeson would have nothing to do with him and characterized him as "a stooge for American foreign policy." See Duberman, *Paul Robeson*, pp. 344, 761 n. 13; and John D'Emilio, *Lost Prophet: The Life and Times of Bayard Rustin* (New York: Free Press, 2003), p. 179.

18. For Robeson's responses "to the Walter Whites, the Lester Grangers, [and] the Adam Powells," see Paul Robeson, "Here's My Story," *Freedom* 1, no. 2 (February 1951), p. 2. Martin Duberman suggests that Robeson's columns in *Freedom* were largely the work of Lloyd Brown. See Duberman, *Paul Robeson*, p. 393.

19. Robinson apparently later regretted his role in the affair. See the documentary *Scandalize My Name: Stories from the Blacklist* (Ventura 2005). For Robeson's response, see *Freedom* 3, no. 4 (April 1953), pp. 1, 3.

20. For an indication of the differences between Du Bois and White with regard to the Soviet Union and the Communist Party, see W. E. B. Du Bois, "Paul Robeson: Right," *Negro Digest*, March 1950, pp. 8, 10–14; and White, "Paul Robeson: Wrong," *Negro Digest*, March 1950, pp. 9, 14–18.

21. See Josh White, "I Was a Sucker for the Communists," *Negro Digest*, December 1950, pp. 26–31. In Martin Duberman's *Paul Robeson*, White is quoted as saying, "They've got me in a vise. I'm going to have to talk." Robeson replies, "Do what you have to but don't name names." See Duberman, *Paul Robeson*, p. 391. In general, Robeson proved to be quite understanding and forgiving of those who felt

compelled to clear their names in this period (with the apparent exception of Bayard Rustin). Facing similar pressures, Duke Ellington offered that "movements of a political nature . . . any kind but orchestral movements—have never been part of my life." The "only communism" he claimed to be familiar with, echoing Josh White's suggestion and with wit obviously intact, was "that of Jesus Christ." See Denning, *Cultural Front*, pp. 317–18.

22. See Langston Hughes, *Famous American Negroes* (New York: Dodd, Mead, 1954), and *Famous Negro Music Makers* (New York: Dodd, Mead, 1955).

23. Ossie Davis and Ruby Dee, *With Ossie and Ruby: In This Life Together* (New York: Morrow, 1998), p. 234.

24. See Roi Ottley, *No Green Pastures* (New York: Scribner, 1951), pp. 1, 9–10.

25. Intriguing in this context is Lamming's description of a Long Island party as "Negro society at its very highest level of colonial achievement." George Lamming, *The Pleasures of Exile* (London: Michael Joseph, 1960), pp. 187–88, 202, 206. Blacks outside the United States, particularly those in the Caribbean looking to remain in the good graces of British and American authorities, also sought to separate themselves from perceived communist taint. Accordingly, in 1952, Norman Manley, leader of the anticolonial People's National Party (PNP) in Jamaica called for the expulsion of Party members Richard Hart, Arthur Henry, and brothers Frank and Ken Hill in order, as Hart suggests, to "make safe that the British and American weren't turned against the PNP's demands for self-governance." Despite his removal, Hart later contended that Manley's actions were understandable, as pragmatically he "had to be anti-communist." Quoted in "'No Hard Feelings'—Richard Hart Forgives Manley for Throwing Him Out of the PNP" *Jamaica Gleaner*, June 12, 2006. For more background on these developments, and Ferdinand Smith's involvement in the Jamaican case, see Gerald Horne, *Red Seas: Ferdinand Smith and Radical Black Sailors in the United States and Jamaica* (New York: New York University Press, 2005). One prominent exception to this pattern would be the antiapartheid movement in South Africa, which would maintain close linkages with the communist Left. On this point, and some of the connections between developments in the United States and South Africa, see David H. Anthony, "Max Yergan and South Africa: A Transatlantic Interaction," in *Imagining Home: Class, Culture and Nationalism in the African Diaspora*, Sidney J. Lemelle and Robin D. G. Kelley, eds. (London: Verso, 1994), pp. 185–206.

26. Twenty-nine countries, including India, Ceylon (now Sri Lanka), Burma, Pakistan, Indonesia, Ethiopia, China, Egypt, the Philippines, Sudan, Libya, Turkey, Iraq, Iran, Saudi Arabia, Jordan, Afghanistan, Cambodia, the Gold Coast, Nepal, Laos, Lebanon, Liberia, Syria, Thailand, North Vietnam, South Vietnam, and Yemen, were in attendance at Bandung. The conference ran from April 18 to April 24, 1955.

27. Charles V. Hamilton, *Adam Clayton Powell, Jr.: The Political Biography of an American Dilemma* (New York: Collier, 1991), p. 239. In the original letter, Powell misspelled "Indonisia."

28. See Marguerite Cartwright, "What Did Cong. Powell Really Do at Bandung?" *New York Amsterdam News*, May 14, 1955, pp. 1–2.

29. See Homer Bigart, "Powell Tells Asia About U.S. Negro; Red Newsmen Find Him Off the 'Line,'" *New York Herald Tribune*, April 18, 1955.

30. Back in the United States, Powell criticized India's Jawaharlal Nehru and suggested that he was "through" as an effective leader in the Asian world. In the *Afro-American*, columnist James L. Hicks asked, "Why should a colored man of the stature of Mr. Powell take it upon himself to try to politically slay another colored man who stands upright on the highest rostrum with other leaders in the forums of the world?" See A. M. Rosenthal, "Nehru Condemns the West, Says Alliances Hurt Peace," *New York Times*, April 1, 1955, pp. 1, 3; Robert Alden, "Powell Bids U.S. Bar Colonialism," *New York Times*, April 23, 1955, p. 2; "Laud Powell's Role in Asia," *Chicago Defender*, May 7, 1955, p. 5; James L. Hicks, "Voters' Vineyard," *Afro-American*, May 14, 1955, p. 4; and "Powell: Congressman Praised by Sen. Lehman," *Afro-American*, May 14, 1955, p. 6.

31. Richard Wright, "Racial Shame at Bandung," in *The Color Curtain: A Report on the Bandung Conference* (Cleveland: World, 1956), p. 178 (ellipses in original).

32. Wright, "Racial Shame at Bandung," pp. 178–79 (ellipses and italics in original).

33. Continuing, Prattis proposes, "Of course, Adam, I agree it is a distinction to be Adam Clayton Powell, even though a Negro," and in reference to Powell's rather fair complexion, "I guess you just plain baffled some of those Asians when you started talking about 'we black men.'" See "Horizon: Letter to Adam Powell," *Pittsburgh Courier*, May 21, 1955, p. 6. For other assessments of Powell's performance, see "Powell Protests," *Afro-American*, May 14, 1955, p. 2; "People, Places and Things," *Chicago Defender*, May 7, 1955, p. 11; "Powell's Asia Reports Are Criticized," *New York Amsterdam News*, May 14, 1955, p. 2; and Abner W. Berry, "On the Way: The Blessings of Liberty," *Daily Worker*, April 7, 1955.

34. "The New Cong. Powell," *Pittsburgh Courier*, June 4, 1955, p. 6.

35. Horace R. Cayton, "World at Large," *Pittsburgh Courier*, May 14, 1955, p. 7. Max Yergan and Powell also wrote columns for the *Courier* on the Bandung conference. See Max Yergan, "History Made in Bandung: Africans, Asians Begin Big Confab," *Pittsburgh Courier*, April 23, 1955, pp. 1, 4; and Adam Clayton Powell Jr., "Afro-Asian Meet Puts U.S. on Spot," *Pittsburgh Courier*, April 30, 1955, pp. 1, 4.

36. Felix Belair Jr., "United States Has Secret Sonic Weapon—Jazz," *New York Times*, November 6, 1955, pp. 1, 42.

37. See "U.S. Government to Send Jazz As Its Ambassador," *Down Beat*, December 28, 1955, p. 6; and "Remote Lands to Hear Old Democracy Boogie," *New York Times*, November 18, 1955, p. 16.

38. Quincy Jones, *Q: The Autobiography of Quincy Jones* (New York: Doubleday, 2001), p. 110.

39. Penny M. Von Eschen, *Satchmo Blows Up the World: Jazz Ambassadors Play the Cold War* (Cambridge, Mass.: Harvard University Press, 2004), p. 31. On the general topic of race and American foreign policy, see Brenda Gale Plummer, *Rising Wind: Black Americans and U.S. Foreign Affairs, 1935–1960* (Chapel Hill: University of North Carolina Press, 1996); Penny M. Von Eschen, *Race against Empire: Black Americans and Anticolonialism, 1937–1957* (Ithaca, N.Y.: Cornell University Press, 1997); Mary L. Dudziak, *Cold War Civil Rights: Race and the Image of American Democracy* (Princeton, N.J.: Princeton University Press, 2000);

Thomas Borstelmann, *The Cold War and the Color Line: American Race Relations in the Global Era* (Cambridge, Mass.: Harvard University Press, 2001); and Carol Anderson, *Eyes off the Prize: The United Nations and the African American Struggle for Human Rights, 1944–1955* (New York: Cambridge University Press, 2003).

40. Robeson was a regular patron of jazz shows at the Savoy Ballroom and the Apollo in Harlem, and at Café Society Downtown and the Manhattan Casino in the 1940s and 1950s, and formed friendships with a number of the younger jazz artists. In 1940, Robeson recorded "King Joe" in honor of Joe Louis (another Café Society regular), a track with lyrics by Richard Wright and music provided by Count Basie. The blues and swing inflections demanded by the material proved to be too much for the folk- and spiritual-oriented Robeson. Basie observed, "It certainly is an honor to be with Mr. Robeson, but the man certainly can't sing the blues." In 1958, Robeson said, in contrast to his much earlier dismissals of the jazz genre for being inauthentic, "For my money, modern jazz is one of the most important musical things there is in the world." See Duberman, *Paul Robeson*, p. 177. After attending a Miles Davis concert in Finsbury Park (London) in 1960, Robeson told Davis, "I like the way your band sounds—the modal music." See John Szwed, *So What: The Life of Miles Davis* (New York: Simon and Schuster, 2002), p. 215. Regarding Gillespie's admiration for Robeson, see Dizzy Gillespie with Al Fraser, *To Be or Not to Bop: Memoirs* (Garden City, N.Y.: Doubleday, 1979), pp. 288, 462.

41. Bruce Cook, "Singer/Activist Paul Robeson Dies: A Tragic Hero," *Rolling Stone*, March 11, 1976, p. 15; and Gillespie with Fraser, *To Be or Not to Bop*, p. 80.

42. "Dizzy Urges Ike to Back Jazz Tours," *Pittsburgh Courier*, August 4, 1956, p. 21.

43. "Our tour was limited to countries which had treaties with the United States or where you had military bases: Persia, Lebanon, Syria, Pakistan, Turkey, and Greece. . . . Wherever we went, the political question was definitely involved," stated Gillespie. See Gillespie with Fraser, *To Be or Not to Bop*, pp. 414, 417.

44. This was a fallow period for big bands in general in the United States. Benny Goodman, another jazz ambassador like Gillespie, got an opportunity to work in a big band setting again because of the support from the State Department.

45. "Louis Armstrong, Barring Soviet Tour, Denounces Eisenhower and Gov. Faubus," *New York Times*, September 19, 1957, p. 23; "Armstrong May Tour: U.S. Hopes He'll Visit Soviet Despite Segregation Issue," *New York Times*, September 20, 1957, p. 15; and "Musician Backs Move: Armstrong Lauds Eisenhower for Little Rock Action," *New York Times*, September 26, 1957, p. 12. Armstrong and his All-Stars released a live album drawn largely from shows recorded in Amsterdam and Milan, featuring Armstrong on the cover in a vest and knee-length formal jacket with a traveling bag in his right hand and his trumpet in the crook of his left arm. Additional tracks for *Ambassador Satch* (Columbia 1955; reissue, 2000) were recorded in the studio, presumably because of the subpar quality of some of the live tapes. It was this European tour that inspired Felix Belair's *Times* feature.

46. See Leonard Ingalls, "Armstrong Horn Wins Nairobi, Too," *New York Times*, November 7, 1960, p. 5; and Nat Hentoff, "Jazz in Africa," *Nation*, January 4, 1958, pp. 16–17.

47. See Ossie Davis, "Louis Armstrong," in *Life Lit by Some Large Vision: Selected Speeches and Writings*, Ruby Dee, ed. (New York: Atria Books, 2006), p. 162. The political subtexts were made more obvious in a 1962 project, *The Real Ambassadors*, involving Armstrong, fellow jazz ambassador Dave Brubeck, Brubeck's partner Iola, who composed the lyrics, and others. In "Remember Who You Are," Armstrong sings, "Always be a credit to your government. No matter what you say or do, the eyes of the world are watching you." His trombonist, Trummy Young, adds, "Remember who you are and what you represent. Never face a problem, always circumvent. Stay away from issues. Be discreet—when controversy enters, you retreat." See Louis Armstrong, Dave Brubeck, Lambert Hendricks and Ross, *The Real Ambassadors* (Columbia 1962; reissue, 1994), and Von Eschen, *Satchmo Blows Up the World*, pp. 79–91. For a sense of the uncomplicated ways Armstrong was understood and deployed in the mainstream American media in this period, see Gilbert Millstein, "Africa Harks to Satch's Horn," *New York Times Magazine*, November 20, 1960, pp. 24, 64–76.

48. Quoted in Reinhold Wagnleitner, *Coca-Colonization and the Cold War: The Cultural Mission of the United States in Austria after the Second World War* (Chapel Hill: University of North Carolina Press, 1994), p. 212. In response to Ellender's efforts, Gillespie wrote to Eisenhower, "Shocked and discouraged by the decision of the Senate in the Supplementary Appropriations bill to outlaw American jazz music as a way of making millions of friends for the USA abroad." See "Dizzy Urges Ike to Back Jazz Tours," *Pittsburgh Courier*, August 4, 1956, p. 21.

49. "Louis Armstrong, Barring Soviet Tour, Denounces Eisenhower and Gov. Faubus," *New York Times*, September 19, 1957, p. 23.

50. The Ghanaian government provided accommodations and funding for the Provisional Government of the Republic of Algeria, the official representatives of the Armée de la Libération Nationale, to which Fanon was committed. While in Accra, he interacted with Kwame Nkrumah, Patrice Lumumba of the Congo, the Kenyan Tom M'Boye, and Felix Moumié of Cameroon, among others.

51. Frantz Fanon, *Toward the African Revolution*, Haakon Chevalier, trans. (London: Writers and Readers Publishing Cooperative, 1980), p. 178. Fanon also mentions Armstrong in *Black Skin, White Masks* when he is mocking the Négritude sensibility. See *Black Skin, White Masks*, Charles Lam Markmann, trans. (New York: Grove Press, 1967), p. 45.

52. Pianist Horace Tapscott remembers being invited by Lionel Hampton to meet Armstrong. During that visit, Armstrong reportedly shared his thoughts about the Congolese adventure, including the quality of the marijuana he was given during his sojourn. Indeed, Armstrong generously shared some of his Congolese reefer with Hampton and Tapscott. With regard to Armstrong's tour, a United Press International wire notes: "The Moscow radio charged tonight that Louis Armstrong was sent to the Congo to 'distract' the Congolese from the crisis there." See Horace Tapscott, *Songs of the Unsung: The Musical and Social Journey of Horace Tapscott* (Durham, N.C.: Duke University Press, 2001), pp. 77–78; Paul Hofmann, "Satchmo Plays for Congo Cats: Trumpeter Arrives on Red Throne and

Crew of Bearers," *New York Times*, October 29, 1960, p. 8; and Ludo De Witte, *The Assassination of Lumumba* (London: Verso, 2001).

53. Aimé Césaire, "Culture et Colonisation," *Présence Africaine*, June–November 1956, p. 190.

54. See John A. Davis, "Débats," *Présence Africaine*, June–November 1956, pp. 213–15; and James Ivy, "The NAACP as an Instrument of Social Change," *Présence Africaine*, June–November 1956, p. 331. Davis helped organize the American Society of African Culture (AMSAC) following the conference to heighten awareness of African culture among American blacks. The society's other cofounders included James Ivy, Horace Mann Bond, William T. Fontaine, and Mercer Cook. Brenda Gale Plummer observes, "AMSAC shared headquarters with the Council on Race and Caste in World Affairs, a CIA front with which it merged in 1957. Selected private foundations became channels for CIA funding to AMSAC, unbeknownst to most of its members and participants." See Plummer, *Rising Wind*, p. 254. The society's CIA connections became public in 1967.

55. See *Présence Africaine*, June–November, 1956; and Hazel Rowley, *Richard Wright: The Life and Times* (New York: Holt, 2001), pp. 477–78.

56. See *Présence Africaine*, June–November 1956; and Rowley, *Richard Wright*, p. 478. Specifically, Wright had suggested that Horace Mann Bond, the president of Lincoln University, and Mercer Cook, a professor in the French department at Howard University, be invited to the Paris meetings. In his comments, Wright also lamented the absence of women at the congress. He later expressed his frustration with Senghor's explication of Négritude and was eager to promote what he saw as a more rational and scientific approach to the situation of nonwhites. See Richard Wright, "Tradition and Industrialization," in *White Man, Listen!* (1957; reprint, Westport, Conn.: Greenwood Press, 1978), pp. 78–79, 94. A similar degree of dissonance marked the All African People's Conference, held in Accra, Ghana, in December of 1958. Here, as with Bandung, the American government declined to participate officially. Others in attendance at the Paris conference included Alioune Diop, the editor of *Présence Africaine*, Cheikh Anta Diop, Fanon, and Léopold Senghor.

57. See James Baldwin, *Nobody Knows My Name: More Notes of a Native Son* (New York: Dell, 1961), pp. 28–29, 40; and "Encounter on the Seine: Black Meets Brown," in *Notes of a Native Son* (Boston: Beacon Press, 1955), p. 123. Baldwin, despite his cosmopolitanism, was never deeply engaged in diasporic currents, and his deployments of "Africa" and the diaspora tended to be instrumentalist in nature. For evidence of this tendency, see James Baldwin, "A Negro Assays the Negro Mood," *New York Times Magazine*, March 12, 1961.

58. Hannah Arendt, "Reflections on Little Rock," *Dissent* 6, no. 1 (1959), pp. 45–56. For an extended discussion of the significance of this exchange, see Danielle S. Allen, *Talking to Strangers: Anxieties of Citizenship after Brown v. Board of Education* (Chicago: University of Chicago Press, 2004).

59. Ellison argued that Arendt had "absolutely no conception of what goes on in the minds of Negro parents when they send their kids through those lines of hostile

people. . . . [I]n the outlook of many of these parents (who wish that the problem didn't exist), the child is expected to face the terror and contain his fear and anger *precisely* because he is a Negro American." Quoted in Robert Penn Warren, *Who Speaks for the Negro?* (New York: Random House, 1965), p. 344.

60. Arendt, "Reflections on Little Rock," pp. 46–47.

61. See Ralph Ellison, "Some Questions and Some Answers," in *Shadow and Act* (New York: Vintage, 1964), pp. 262–64. In the fall of 1958, *Time* published an article entitled "Amid the Alien Corn," suggesting that both Wright and Ellison were living in Europe in exile from the United States (and arguably intended to mark the two as having abandoned their native country). Wright contended that the quotations attributed to him were entirely fabricated (although some of the comments corresponded to his views regarding the relative freedom life in France offered from the racial exigencies of the U.S.). Ellison wrote a letter, which the magazine published, noting that he was not in exile per se, as he had received a fellowship from the American Academy of Arts and Letters, which explained his being in Rome. "Exile," he would add, "is, fortunately (and even for Negro Americans) largely a state of mind." See "Amid the Alien Corn," *Time*, November 17, 1958, p. 28; "Letters," *Time*, February 9, 1959, p. 2; and Michel Fabre, *The Unfinished Quest of Richard Wright* (New York: Morrow, 1973), pp. 471–72.

62. Jerry Gafio Watts, *Heroism and the Black Intellectual: Ralph Ellison, Politics, and Afro-American Intellectual Life* (Chapel Hill: University of North Carolina Press, 1994), p. 61. Ellison's lampooning of a Garvey-like character ("Ras the Exhorter") in *Invisible Man*, his expression of disinterest in any possible African sources for the trickster figure in "Change the Joke and Slip the Yoke"—"[A]djustment to the contours of 'white' symbolic needs is far more intriguing than [the trickster's] alleged [African] origins"—and his comments regarding Haitian culture, are consistent with this interpretation. See Ellison, *Invisible Man*; and *Shadow and Act*, pp. 51, 263.

63. See Ralph Ellison, *Living with Music: Ralph Ellison's Jazz Writings*, Robert G. O'Meally, ed. (New York: Modern Library, 2001), pp. 243, 286; and Albert Murray and John F. Callahan, eds., *Trading Twelves: The Selected Letters of Ralph Ellison and Albert Murray* (New York: Vintage, 2000), pp. 166–67.

64. Carl T. Rowan, *Breaking Barriers: A Memoir* (New York: HarperPerennial, 1991), p. 156.

65. Rowan subsequently wrote with regard to the Robeson feature, "I felt proud that I had given the marvelous man a fair hearing, a decent break." See Rowan, *Breaking Barriers*, p. 157.

66. There were questions Robeson avoided answering directly, including whether he was a member of the Communist Party (though he implied that the answer was no) and his views regarding the Soviet Union, given Khrushchev's "denunciations of Stalin as a murderer and a tyrant." See Carl Rowan, "Has Paul Robeson Betrayed the Negro?" *Ebony*, October 1957, pp. 41–42.

67. Rowan, "Has Paul Robeson Betrayed the Negro?" p. 34.

68. Rowan, "Has Paul Robeson Betrayed the Negro?" p. 40.

69. See W. E. B. Du Bois, *In Battle for Peace: The Story of My 83rd Birthday* (New York: Masses and Mainstream, 1952), pp. 75–76; and E. Franklin Frazier, *Black Bourgeoisie* (Glencoe, Ill.: Free Press, 1957). For evidence of a different assessment of the Talented Tenth on Du Bois's part, see David Levering Lewis, *W. E. B. Du Bois: The Fight for Equality and the American Century, 1919–1963* (New York: Holt, 2000), p. 264.

70. Forced by the attorney general to register with the U.S. government in 1953 as a communist front organization under the Subversive Activities Control Act of 1950, the National Negro Labor Council dissolved in April 1956.

71. The CPUSA was also involved in organizing sharecroppers' unions and black farmers in the South and rent strikes in the northern cities. See Nell Irvin Painter, *The Narrative of Hosea Hudson: His Life as a Negro Communist in the South* (Cambridge, Mass.: Harvard University Press, 1979); Mark Naison, *Communists in Harlem during the Depression* (Urbana: University of Illinois Press, 1983); Robin D. G. Kelley, *Hammer and Hoe: Alabama Communists during the Great Depression* (Chapel Hill: University of North Carolina Press, 1990), and "'Afric's Sons with Banner Red': African American Communists and the Politics of Culture, 1919–1934," in *Race Rebels: Culture, Politics, and the Black Working Class* (New York: Free Press, 1994), pp. 103–21. Symbolically, the CPUSA moved its headquarters to 125th Street in Harlem in 1951.

72. Martin Duberman argues that Robeson's "retreat [in early 1958] from a high level of *open* commitment to the Soviet Union was a reflection not of disillusion but, rather, of a conscious determination to restore his reputation as a spokesman for black people." See Duberman, *Paul Robeson*, p. 453.

73. Paul Robeson, *Here I Stand* (Boston: Beacon Press, 1988), p. 1.

74. Robeson, *Here I Stand*, pp. 28, 64, 70–71. Carl Rowan also asked the State Department to explain its rationale for denying Robeson a passport. He wrote, "The State Department argues that technically a state of emergency exists, as declared by the president, and that 'In the present world situation it also seems clear that, in administering such emergency controls designed to safeguard the national security, the Secretary of State may decline to issue a passport to a present member of the Communist Party.'" See Rowan, "Has Paul Robeson Betrayed the Negro?" p. 35.

75. See Young and Wheeler, *Hard Stuff*, p. 111; Rowan, "Has Paul Robeson Betrayed the Negro," p. 32; and Victor S. Navasky, *Naming Names* (New York: Viking, 1980).

76. See *Kent et al. v. Dulles* 357 U.S. 116 (1958).

77. Quoted in Duberman, *Paul Robeson*, p. 391.

78. Young and Wheeler, *Hard Stuff*, p. 133.

79. Sidney Poitier, *The Measure of a Man: A Spiritual Autobiography* (San Francisco: HarperSanFrancisco, 2000), pp. 88, 91; and Henry Louis Gates Jr., *Thirteen Ways of Looking at a Black Man* (New York: Random House, 1997), p. 161.

80. Davis and Dee, *With Ossie and Ruby*, pp. 177–78.

81. Sidney Poitier, *This Life* (New York: Knopf, 1980), pp. 172, 178–79.

82. *Counterattack*, January 8, 1954; and February 12, 1954.

83. In the same piece, Paul Robeson Jr. is quoted as saying with regard to whether he believed Belafonte testified: "I just have to leave it as an open question." I refer here

to the "blacklist" simply as a matter of stylistic economy; there were in fact multiple, overlapping blacklists. See Gates, *Thirteen Ways of Looking at a Black Man*, p. 164; and Navasky, *Naming Names*, p. 193.

84. It is obvious that while Belafonte and Poitier can be quite critical of each other (especially Belafonte of Poitier), they at the same time are obviously quite close and relate to each other as brothers with all the dynamics unique to sibling relationships. Belafonte turned down the role Poitier subsequently accepted (and for which he won an Academy Award) in *Lilies of the Field* because he found the lead character lacking in a credible backstory. Poitier's appearance in *To Sir with Love* (1967) also came about because Belafonte declined the part, viewing the lead role as insufficiently realized and humanized and lacking sexuality ("neutered," as he put it). See Gates, *Thirteen Ways of Looking at a Black Man*, pp. 161, 170; and David Montgomery, "Tally Man Come, Name Belafonte," *Washington Post*, April 2, 2006, p. D1.

85. Belafonte recollects, "I didn't think the organization should be killed. I think the NAACP served a very important purpose. I just thought that the leadership should be swiftly annihilated. Nonviolently!" See Brian Ward, *Just My Soul Responding: Rhythm and Blues, Black Consciousness, and Race Relations* (Berkeley: University of California Press, 1998), p. 318; and D'Emilio, *Lost Prophet*, pp. 295–96.

86. Gillespie with Fraser, *To Be or Not to Bop*, p. 288. Jazz musicians in this period in the titling of their recordings often made reference to developments in the American struggle and signified their attentiveness to the Continent: e.g., Miles Davis, "Airegin" (*Cookin'*, Prestige 1956); Art Blakey and the Jazz Messengers, *Drum Suite* (Columbia 1957); Max Roach, *We Insist! Max Roach's Freedom Now Suite* (Candid 1960); Grant Green, "Freedom March" (*Sunday Morning*, Blue Note 1962); Lee Morgan, "Mr. Kenyatta" (*Search for the New Land*, Blue Note 1964); and Wayne Shorter, "Juju" (*Juju*, Blue Note 1964).

87. Davis and Dee, *With Ossie and Ruby*, p. 117. One does need to be cautious of retrospective analyses, as it is inevitable that, given the opportunity, recollections can involve obfuscation and mismemory.

88. Stokely Carmichael would later make the same strategic decision as Randolph. See Stokely Carmichael with Ekwueme Michael Thelwell, *Ready for Revolution: The Life and Struggles of Stokely Carmichael (Kwame Ture)* (New York: Scribner, 2003), p. 94.

89. In the Davis and Dee biography, there are some hints. While Davis refers in the text to socialism as often as to communism to describe the 1940s and 1950s—e.g.: "A Socialist, as far as we understand it, Paul believed that black people would never get their freedom under capitalism"—at a later point in the book, Dee says to Davis, "[I]t's strange the way you make them [your grandchildren] think about the glories of the market and the free enterprise system—capitalism—when I know deep down you believe in a system that could be closer to socialism." See Davis and Dee, *With Ossie and Ruby*, pp. 178, 420. Lena Horne suggests that while she certainly was acquainted with a number of leftists, she was hardly active in a substantive sense: "My association with Paul Robeson was used against me later, when the political witch hunts were on, when I was actually banned from radio and television for a time. Oh, yes, I did benefits, and the old left-wing newspaper, *PM*, was

very fond of me as it was of most of the people who played Barney's [Josephson, owner of Café Society] clubs, and I was friendly with all kinds of people who were active in left-wing politics. But I had a kind of ingrained suspicion about all the promises that were made." The cabaret scene was even freer of McCarthyism than Broadway; as a result, Horne was not overly affected by the Red Scare. See Lena Horne and Richard Schickel, *Lena* (Garden City, N.Y.: Doubleday, 1965), pp. 118–19. Poitier's two biographies, while they are quite revealing in other respects, in contrast to the public silence he generally maintained, offer nothing to explain how he managed these changes in the dominant discursive and rhetorical paradigms. Interesting in this context are Poitier's supposed statements at the Moscow International Film Festival in 1963, where Sidney Kramer's *The Defiant Ones*, starring Poitier and Tony Curtis, was shown. Speaking afterward, in response to what was reportedly an extremely enthusiastic audience, Kramer observed that the film addressed "some of our faults," that the United States had "quite a few of them" but that Americans were willing and able to discuss these issues openly. Regarding the reception accorded *The Defiant Ones*, Poitier stated that the audience "caught not only the picture's statement about race relations but also the idea that such a picture could only be made in a free country, unafraid of self-criticism." See Henry Tanner, "Moscow Film Fete: Ideas in Motion," *New York Times*, July 28, 1963, p. 75; Howard Thompson, "Closer Film Ties with Soviet Seen: U. S. Delegates to Moscow Festival Report on Trip," *New York Times*, August 3, 1963, p. 8; Richard L. Coe, "Poitier Heading to Berlin As Diplomat," *Washington Post*, June 21, 1964, p. G1; and Aram Goudsouzian, *Sidney Poitier: Man, Actor, Icon* (Chapel Hill: University of North Carolina Press, 2004), p. 209. Dizzy Gillespie's biography is the most explicit in terms of its description of this transition, though the tension between his words and his actions (i.e., his lifelong devotion to Robeson) raises questions about the sincerity of his sometimes glib dismissals of the significance of his "fellow-traveling." Harry Belafonte has not yet published an autobiography (though his interview in Gates's *Thirteen Ways of Looking at a Black Man* does feature a frank discussion of the Red Scare era).

90. See Claudia Jones, "An End to the Neglect of the Problems of Negro Women!" in Buzz Johnson, *"I Think of My Mother": Notes on the Life and Times of Claudia Jones* (London: Karia Press, 1985), pp. 103–20. Regarding the treatment of gender issues within the CPUSA, see Kate Weigand, *Red Feminism: American Communism and the Making of Women's Liberation* (Baltimore: Johns Hopkins University Press, 2001); Gerald Horne, "The Reddening of the Women," *Science and Society* 66, no. 4 (winter 2002–3), pp. 506–10; Van Gosse, "Red Feminism: A Conversation with Dorothy Healey," *Science and Society* 66, no. 4 (winter 2002–3), pp. 511–18; Bettina Apthetker, "Red Feminism: A Personal and Historical Reflection," *Science and Society* 66, no. 4 (winter 2002–3), pp. 519–26; and Kate Weigand, "Reply to Critics," *Science and Society* 66, no. 4 (winter 2002–3), pp. 527–35.

91. See Elizabeth Shepley Sergent, "The Man with His Home in a Rock: Paul Robeson," *New Republic*, March 3, 1926, pp. 40–44; Carby, "The Body and Soul of Modernism," in *Race Men*, pp. 45–83; and Sheila Tully Boyle and Andrew Bunie, *Paul Robeson:*

The Years of Promise and Achievement (Amherst: University of Massachusetts Press, 2001).

92. Quoted in the documentary *Scandalize My Name* (Encore Media 1999).

93. Ossie Davis, "Purlie Told Me," *Freedomways* 2, no. 2 (1962), pp. 155–56 (italics in original).

94. See Malcolm X and Alex Haley, *The Autobiography of Malcolm X* (New York: Grove, 1965), pp. 454, 457–458. Similar ruminations on race and masculinity can be found in Max Roach, "Jazz," *Freedomways* 2, no. 2 (1962), p. 174; and Michael Roemer's *Nothing but a Man* (1964), particularly in the roles played by Ivan Dixon (whose costar is Abbey Lincoln), Julius Harris, and Yaphet Kotto.

95. While my phrasing here implies that Poitier was somehow able to make himself, it is important to recognize that as much as he was chosen, he also chose. Reading his biographies, it is quite evident that—especially after he was able to exercise some discretion in the late 1950s and early 1960s—Poitier only took those parts he felt comfortable with. The one major exception to that pattern was *Porgy and Bess* (1959), in which he appeared as a result of considerable pressure. He was criticized (privately) by Belafonte and, if one reads in between the lines, Harold Cruse for appearing in this feature. See Poitier, *This Life*, pp. 205–14; and Harold Cruse, *The Crisis of the Negro Intellectual: From Its Origins to the Present* (New York: Morrow, 1967), p. 429.

96. Lorraine Hansberry, *To Be Young, Gifted and Black* (New York: Signet, 1970), p. 63. Carl A. Hansberry, Hansberry's father, had won a case in the Supreme Court challenging a racially restrictive covenant in the Chicago area. See *Hansberry v. Lee* 311 U.S. 32 (1940). The Hansberrys owned rental properties in Chicago. During *Raisin*'s run on Broadway, a *New York Post* article (July 1, 1959, p. 3) described the family as "slumlords."

97. At another point, Hansberry refers to herself as a "serious odd-talking kid who could neither jump double dutch nor understand . . . [the] games [of the children of my youth], but who—classically—envied them. And their costumes. And the things that, somehow, gave them joy: quarters, fights, and their fascination to come into the carpeted quiet of our apartment. They, understandably, never understood (or believed) my envy—and they never will." Hansberry, *To Be Young, Gifted and Black*, pp. 63, 66.

98. See Lorraine Hansberry, "'Gold Coast's' Rulers Go, Ghana Moves to Freedom," *Freedom* 1, no. 12 (December 1951), p. 2; "Noted Lawyer Goes to Jail; Says Negroes' Fight for Rights Menaced," *Freedom* 2, no. 5 (May 1952), p. 3; and "Women Voice Demands in Capital Sojourn," *Freedom* 1, no. 10 (October 1951), p. 6. The reference to her duties with the newspaper is from *Freedom* 1, no. 9 (September 1951), p. 2.

99. Poitier, *This Life*, p. 233.

100. Poitier, *This Life*, pp. 233, 235; and *The Measure of a Man*, pp. 155–56, 158, 161.

101. Davis and Dee, *With Ossie and Ruby*, p. 282.

102. It is, of course, interesting that Davis is the one who speaks for the couple on this issue. See Davis and Dee, *With Ossie and Ruby*, p. 283; and for an earlier version of this argument Ossie Davis, "The Significance of Lorraine Hansberry (1965)," in *Life Lit by Some Large Vision*, pp. 95–103.

103. Beneatha was, by Hansberry's admission, supposed to be a younger version of herself. See Davis and Dee, *With Ossie and Ruby*, p. 285. McNeil filed a complaint with Actor's Equity against Dee for "unprofessional behavior." Indeed, the character of the mother seemed to attract a significant amount of negative attention from the other cast members and from the play's director, Lloyd Richards. Ossie Davis, who stepped into the role of Walter Lee Younger when Poitier left the production in August 1959, remembers Richards pulling him aside and telling him, "Ossie, do me a favor. I want you to go out there on that stage; I want you to confront Claudia McNeil. Forget the lines, forget the character, forget how Lorraine has written the scene, forget the rest of the play." See Davis and Dee, *With Ossie and Ruby*, p. 284. McNeil also got into conflict with Glynn Turman, her onstage grandson, offstage (a conflict rooted in a longstanding enmity between McNeil and Turman's mother that predated the play). "Seen today," Donald Bogle suggests, "McNeil seems grossly like the mammy of Hattie McDaniel vintage, but without the humor and spontaneity." See *Toms, Coons, Mulattoes, Mammies, and Bucks: An Interpretive History of Blacks in American Films*, 3rd ed. (New York: Continuum, 1997), p. 198.

104. Poitier remembers that for much of the production, the two were "not on speaking terms," adding that Hansberry, "who was understandably happy because her play was doing so well . . . couldn't grasp why I was dissatisfied." See Poitier, *This Life*, p. 234. See Lorraine Hansberry, "An Author's Reflections: Willie Loman, Walter Younger, and He Who Must Live," *Village Voice*, August 12, 1959; and Philip Rose, *You Can't Do That on Broadway! A Raisin in the Sun and Other Theatrical Improbabilities* (New York: Limelight Editions, 2001), pp. 107–9, 144–49.

105. For a characteristically scathing critique of Hansberry's work, see Harold Cruse, "Lorraine Hansberry," in *The Crisis of the Negro Intellectual*, pp. 267–84.

106. The play was not performed until 1970, after Hansberry's death. Her husband, Robert Nemiroff, was responsible for the final revisions. See Robert Nemiroff, ed., *Les Blancs: The Collected Last Plays of Lorraine Hansberry* (New York: Random House, 1972), p. 97.

107. See Nina Simone with Stephen Cleary, *I Put a Spell on You: The Autobiography of Nina Simone* (New York: Da Capo Press, 1993), pp. 86–87; and Andy Stroud, "Nina Simone," *Fader*, May–June 2006, p. 100.

108. In *Les Blancs*, Hansberry attempted to establish the linkages among the conditions blacks faced in different parts of the world. The central character in *Les Blancs*, Tshembe Matoseh, an African who has traveled to the United States and lived in England, mirrors in certain respects *Raisin*'s Asagai. See Nemiroff, *Les Blancs*, pp. 121–22; David Susskind letters to Sam Briskin, March 13, 1959, March 16, 1959, and December 30, 1959, David Susskind Papers, Wisconsin State Historical Society, Madison; and Mark A. Reid, *Redefining Black Film* (Los Angeles: University of California Press, 1993), pp. 58–59.

109. For a comprehensive examination of northern civil rights activism in New York City, see Martha Biondi, *To Stand and Fight: The Struggle for Civil Rights in Postwar New York City* (Cambridge, Mass.: Harvard University Press, 2003).

110. "The people of Birmingham don't need me, or Dick Gregory, or Nat 'King' Cole, or Sammy Davis, Jr.," contended comedian Nipsey Russell. "They need only one man, and that's Martin Luther King. It's the six-year-olds who are going to jail who are doing the job." See Bill Lane, "Nat Cole Defends Stars Who Shun Dixie Racial Picket Lines," *Chicago Defender*, national ed., May 11–17, 1963, p. 10; and Morris Duff and Blaik Kirby, "'We'll All Follow Martin Luther King': U.S. Negro Stars," *Toronto Daily Star*, May 11, 1963, p. 26. In the late 1950s, Belafonte and Cole had considered coproducing films and stage shows, a plan that did not come to fruition and led to some tension between the two. See Leslie Gourse, *Unforgettable: The Life and Mystique of Nat King Cole* (New York: St. Martin's Press, 1991), p. 203. The visually impaired Al Hibbler led pickets in Birmingham, but the police, under the control of Eugene "Bull" Connor, refused to send him to jail, despite his efforts and wishes. "You can't work and anyone who goes to jail has to earn his food," Connor told the vocalist responsible for many of the classic Ellington recordings (e.g., "Don't Get Around Much Anymore"); "You can't do anything, [not] even entertain." In response, Hibbler lamented, "The police are trying to segregate me from my own people." There were apparently plans at one point for Hibbler and Ray Charles to coheadline a civil rights benefit. See Foster Hailey, "Alabama Police Jail Blind Singer: Al Hibbler Later Freed in Birmingham Racial Unrest," *New York Times*, April 10, 1963, p. 29; Foster Hailey, "Negroes Uniting in Birmingham: Anti-Segregation Picketing Again Led by Blind Singer," *New York Times*, April 11, 1963, p. 21; and "Ray Charles, Al Hibbler to Aid Fight Against B'ham Jim Crow," *Afro-American*, April 13, 1963, pp. 1, 11.

111. Lane, "Nat Cole Defends Stars Who Shun Dixie Racial Picket Lines," *Chicago Defender*, national ed., May 11–17, 1963, p. 10.

112. "I don't like to mix politics with my art," stated the "West Indian Negro dancer" Geoffrey Holder. "I know how I'm going to fight it [segregation], however. Not by going to Birmingham, but by very hard work, to be accepted as an artist without reference to my color." See Lane, "Nat Cole Defends Stars Who Shun Dixie Racial Picket Lines," *Chicago Defender*, national ed., May 11–17, 1963, p. 10 (italics added); and Duff and Kirby, "'We'll All Follow Martin Luther King': U.S. Negro Stars," *Toronto Daily Star*, May 11, 1963, p. 26.

113. "Grapevine News," *Afro-American*, May 28, 1963, p. 11.

114. See Hanes Walton Jr., *Black Politics: A Theoretical and Structural Analysis* (Philadelphia: Lippincott, 1972), p. 171; and Lucius J. Barker and Mack H. Jones, *African Americans and the American Political System*, 3rd ed. (Englewood Cliffs, N.J.: Prentice Hall, 1994), p. 251. In *The Spook Who Sat by the Door*, Sam Greenlee gave the black police lieutenant in Chicago who seeks to stop the "revolution" by arresting the protagonist ("Dan Freeman") the surname "Dawson."

115. See Barbara Reynolds, *Jesse Jackson: The Man, the Movement, the Myth* (Chicago: Nelson-Hall, 1975), pp. 283–84.

116. Reynolds, *Jesse Jackson*, p. 46.

117. Regarding Powell's battles with the NAACP, see "Integration: Irritant and Needle," *Newsweek*, April 1, 1963, p. 21; and "N.A.A.C.P. Hails Biracial Board In Rebuttal

to Powell's Attack," *New York Times*, April 20, 1963, p. 12. In response to Powell's criticisms, Roy Wilkins distributed a pamphlet, *The N.A.A.C.P. and Adam Clayton Powell*, challenging his "separatism." There were also rumors at the time that Malcolm X might run against Powell. Accordingly, Powell's increasingly nationalist rhetoric was seen as an attempt to draw support away from any such campaign.

118. "Diggs Turns Fire Fighter in Miss." *Afro-American*, April 20, 1963, pp. 1–2.

119. Indeed, Gregory subsequently launched an independent write-in campaign against Richard Daley for the city's mayoralty, and later the presidency.

120. See Lane, "Nat Cole Defends Stars Who Shun Dixie Racial Picket Lines," *Chicago Defender*, May 11–17, 1963, p. 10; and Lorraine Hansberry, "A Challenge to Artists," *Freedomways* 3, no. 1 (winter 1963), pp. 31–35.

121. See "Fats Domino Abandons Freedom Push: Will Take Segregated Dates," *Kansas City Call*, January 11, 1963; and "Fats Domino Denies Break with NAACP," *Kansas City Call*, January 18, 1963.

122. Lane, "Nat Cole Defends Stars Who Shun Dixie Racial Picket Lines," *Chicago Defender*, May 11–17, 1963, p. 10.

123. Quoted in Gourse, *Unforgettable*, p. 177; "Nat King Cole Attacked by Whites in Birmingham," *New York Amsterdam News*, April 14, 1956, p. 1; "A King Is Uncrowned: An Editorial," *New York Amsterdam News*, April 21, 1956, pp. 1, 8; "Cole Leaves Us Cold! His Discs Face Huge Sales Drop," *New York Amsterdam News*, pp. 1, 25; "King Cole Now NAACP Life Member," *New York Amsterdam News*, April 28, 1956, pp. 1, 26; Clyde Reid, "Mrs. Nat Says King 'Appeased' NAACP with $500," *New York Amsterdam News*, May 5, 1956, pp. 1, 24; and "Too Little—Very Late," *New York Amsterdam News*, May 5, 1956, p. 10.

124. "Firing of Dick Gregory Protested," *Afro-American*, April 27, 1963, p. 1; "Gregory Tells Beating in Birmingham Jail," *Chicago Defender*, May 11–17, 1963, p. 2; "Reds Bitterly Hits [sic] U.S. Racism," *Chicago Defender*, May 11-17, 1963, p. 2; "NAACP Kicks About Dick," *Pittsburgh Courier*, May 4, 1963, p. 13; "Belafonte in Birm'ham," *Pittsburgh Courier*, May 4, 1963, p. 13; "Gregory Says: 'They Kick You Hard,'" *Pittsburgh Courier*, May 18, 1963, pp. 1, 4; and Dick Gregory with Robert Lipsyte, *Nigger: An Autobiography* (New York: Simon and Schuster, 1964), p. 156.

125. Quoted in Morton Cooper, "Brook Benton Afraid He Can't Be Non-Violent," *Chicago Defender*, May 25–31, 1963, p. 15.

126. In the *Pittsburgh Courier*, it was noted that Charles's manager had announced that the singer would not get involved in the "politics [of the] anti-segregation fight." Sam Cooke's "A Change Is Gonna Come," one of the few R & B songs to explicitly address civil rights concerns in this period, was partly inspired by Bob Dylan's "Blowin' in the Wind." At a roundtable (on November 10, 2005, at Chicago's Du Sable Museum), L. C. Cooke stated in response to a question from the audience that if his brother were still alive, "I think he'd be in politics." Cooke's biographer, Peter Guralnick, subsequently added that Cooke's contemporary Solomon Burke had told him the same thing. Regarding the relative involvement of the rhythm and blues and gospel communities, see "Clyde McPhatter in NAACP's Spotlight," *New York Amsterdam News*, July 9, 1960, p. 15; "Belafonte in Birm'ham," *Pittsburgh*

Courier, May 4, 1963, p. 13; Duff and Kirby, "'We'll All Follow Martin Luther King': U.S. Negro Stars," *Toronto Daily Star*, May 11, 1963, p. 26; Bob Hunter, "Mahalia Begs Chicago Negroes to Aid Dixie," *Chicago Defender*, May 9, 1963, p. 24; "Gregory to Highlight Chicago Protest Rally," *Chicago Defender*, May 13, 1963, p. 2; "Eartha Kitt to Star at $50,000 Benefit Show," *Chicago Defender*, May 21, 1963, p. 16; Bob Hunter, "Staple Singers' Pop Finds Montgomery a Changed Place, Credits Rev. King," *Chicago Defender,* weekly ed., May 11–17, 1963, p. 15; Ray Charles and David Ritz, *Brother Ray: Ray Charles' Own Story* (New York: Warner Books, 1978), pp. 297–98; Daniel Wolff, S. R. Crain, Clifton White, and G. David Tenenbaum, *You Send Me: The Life and Times of Sam Cooke* (New York: Morrow, 1995), p. 238; Ward, *Just My Soul Responding*, p. 291; and Peter Guralnick, *Dream Boogie: The Triumph of Sam Cooke* (Boston: Little, Brown, 2005).

127. At Hansberry's funeral, where Paul Robeson Sr. gave a eulogy, Malcolm X asked Paul Robeson Jr. if he could arrange a meeting with his father for him. Despite his misgivings with regard to his affiliation with the Nation of Islam, Robeson was impressed with Malcolm's increasing internationalism and was willing to talk. Before they could arrange a time to meet, Malcolm was dead. See Duberman, *Paul Robeson*, pp. 527–28, 755–56. Indeed, a number of prominent activists associated with various phases of the northern civil rights movement (defined broadly) would pass in the 1963–65 period; besides Hansberry and Malcolm X, Eslanda Robeson, Claudia Jones, Benjamin Davis, and W. E. B. Du Bois all died in these years.

128. See Simone with Cleary, *I Put a Spell on You*, p. 89; and Al Schackman, "Nina Simone," *Fader*, May–June 2006, p. 92.

129. Regarding his own role in the movement, Poitier writes, "As a supporter of the civil rights struggle, I found myself participating most frequently by making appearances on behalf of those on the firing line. I went from street corner rallies to picket lines to fund-raising events in the homes of wealthy white sympathizers to light arm-twisting of studio heads in Hollywood for financial support for Martin Luther King." See Poitier, *This Life*, pp. 278–79; and Ward, *Just My Soul Responding*, pp. 319–20.

130. See Duff and Kirby, "'We'll All Follow Martin Luther King': U.S. Negro Stars," *Toronto Daily Star*, May 11, 1963, p. 26; and Ralph Ellison, *Going to the Territory* (New York: Random House, 1986), p. 292. For a more detailed discussion of Ellison's politics in this period, see Watts, *Heroism and the Black Intellectual*; and Arnold Rampersad, *Ralph Ellison: A Biography* (New York: Knopf, 2007).

131. See LeRoi Jones, *Blues People: The Negro Experience in White America and the Music that Developed From It* (New York: Morrow, 1963); and Ellison, "Blues People," in *Shadow and Act*, p. 248.

132. Quoted in Duff and Kirby, "'We'll All Follow Martin Luther King': U.S. Negro Stars," *Toronto Daily Star*, May 11, 1963, p. 26.

133. Ellison, *Blues People*, p. 253.

134. While Robeson was alive, attempts were made to shoot a television movie based on his life. One proposal that would have involved James Earl Jones was rejected

because he was not seen as a capable enough singer. A plan was in the works to create a one-man show featuring Brock Peters, of the script of which Robeson would have final approval. Robeson died before that project could be realized. One week after Robeson died, NBC contacted Jones regarding his interest in doing a television drama based on Robeson's life. Jones indicated interest, but NBC pulled out, partly out of dissatisfaction with the script Phillip Hayes Dean had written. Charles Nelson Reilly was involved, for a period, in the redrafting of Dean's theatrical script, before Dean was brought in again to write the version with which Jones toured. See Richard L. Coe, "An Inspiring 'Paul Robeson,'" *Washington Post*, December 6, 1977, pp. B1, B11; Judith Martin, "Robeson," *Washington Post*, December 9, 1977, weekend sec., p. 15; Townsend Brewster, "'Robeson' Play Is a Mixed Bag," *New York Amsterdam News*, January 28, 1978, p. D11; Samuel F. Yette, "Washington Viewpoint: They're Still Trying to 'Tackle' Robeson," *Afro-American*, December 13–17, 1977, p. 5; Erika Munk, "Pale Red," *Village Voice*, February 6, 1978, p. 75; Richard Goldstein, "For Colored Folks Who Have Considered Censorship," *Village Voice*, March 13, 1978, p. 44; and Phillip Hayes Dean, *Paul Robeson* (New York: Dramatists Play Service, 1997).

135. *Variety*, January 11, 1978, pp. 133–34.

136. *Variety*, January 11, 1978, p. 133 (italics in original).

137. The address given was that of the Black Theology Project, Interchurch Center, Room 349, 475 Riverside Drive, New York, N.Y., 10027.

138. In *Washington Post*, Marion Barry was quoted as stating that he believed Jones gave a "splendid performance." He would add, though, "I'm not so sure this play is as deep and serious as it should be." See Jean M. White, "Applause and Protest on Opening Night," *Washington Post*, December 6, 1977, p. B11.

139. Regarding the connection between Baldwin's experiences with the Malcolm X script and his response to *Paul Robeson*, see David Leeming, *James Baldwin: A Biography* (New York: Holt, 1994), pp. 338–39.

140. See "A Statement by James Baldwin," *Village Voice*, March 27, 1978, p. 6.

141. Years later, Jones checked to see if he had been investigated by federal authorities: "In 1991, when I sought my FBI file under the Freedom of Information Act, I was told that the government does not have a file on me." See James Earl Jones and Penelope Niven, *James Earl Jones: Voices and Silences* (New York: Touchstone, 1993), p. 95. Although Robert Earl Jones (1910–2006) was blacklisted on Broadway, he did do some off-Broadway work, including *Moon on a Rainbow Shawl* (1962), in which he appeared with his son. He later appeared in Broadway productions such as *All God's Chillun Got Wings* (1975), *The Gospel at Colonus* (1988), and *Mule Bone* (1991); and films such as *The Sting* (1973), *Cockfighter* (1974), *The Cotton Club* (1984), and *Witness* (1985).

142. Jones had also been through the process before of being involved with performances and productions that civil rights organizations criticized. He observed in an interview published in the *Washington Post* during the controversy, "The first time I ever tried 'Emperor Jones' it came under attack by the NAACP. Then I did a production on TV with Gene Hackman called 'Neighbors' and it came under siege by the

NAACP and was killed. It was knocked off the air. . . . But I'm not a missionary, I'm a mercenary." The last suggestion was cited prominently in subsequent protests against the play. Jones and Niven, *James Earl Jones*, p. 227; and Dorothy Gilliam, "James Earl Jones, Nearly Content," *Washington Post*, December 4, 1977, p. F5.

143. Paul Robeson, "Reflections on O'Neill's Plays," *Opportunity*, December 1924, p. 369.

144. This is a possibility Baldwin, for one, acknowledges in his *Village Voice* editorial: "We must say [that the play's portrayal of Robeson is not accurate] so that our children's children's children will know *better than we did* how to honor and protect him when they meet him in their own lives." Jones and Niven, *James Earl Jones*, p. 261; and "A Statement by James Baldwin," *Village Voice*, p. 6.

145. Davis had led an earlier protest against plans to make a movie based on William Styron's *Confessions of Nat Turner* (New York: Random House, 1967) in which Jones was scheduled to appear. See Jones and Niven, *James Earl Jones*, pp. 228–29, 261–62. Davis was not one of the signatories to the advertisement protesting the play, although he did speak at the Hunter College forum in opposition to the play. Interestingly, neither Sidney Poitier nor Harry Belafonte seems to have been, at least publicly, involved in the debate. Both, though, worked with Jones (e.g., Poitier's direction of *A Piece of the Action*) and might have been disinclined to endorse a campaign against a colleague (despite their obvious affection for Robeson).

146. See Goldstein, "For Colored Folks Who Have Considered Censorship," p. 44.

147. Ntozake Shange, though, whose play *For Colored Girls Who Have Considered Suicide When the Rainbow Is Enuf* was to be paired with *Paul Robeson* for a run at Joe Papp's New York Shakespeare Festival at the Booth Theatre, would criticize the campaign against the play as well and argue that "poetic people should have poetic license." Goldstein, "For Colored Folks Who Have Considered Censorship," p. 44.

148. See Yette, "Washington Viewpoint," *Afro-American*, December 13–17, 1977, p. 5. The individuals who participated or sent notes of acknowledgment for Robeson's seventy-fifth birthday celebration at Carnegie Hall provides some sense of his reach, influence and significance. Among the participants were Odetta, Sidney Poitier, James Earl Jones, Roscoe Lee Browne, Ruby Dee, Ossie Davis, Leon Bibb, Gary mayor Richard Hatcher, and Harry Belafonte (who also produced the show). Coretta Scott King would speak of Robeson having been "buried alive" because, like Martin Luther King Jr., he "tapped the same wells of latent militancy." Notes of acknowledgment were sent by Andrew Young, Michael Manley (Jamaica), Cheddi Jagan (Guyana), Forbes Burnham (Guyana), Lynden Pindling (Bahamas), Errol Barrow (Barbados), Indira Gandhi (India), and Kenneth Kaunda (Zambia), among others. See Duberman, *Paul Robeson*, p. 547.

149. In 2004, the United States Postal Service issued a stamp in commemoration of Robeson's legacy (as part of its Black Heritage series) after a campaign initiated in 1997. While the press release announcing the stamp noted his accomplishments as an athlete, singer, actor, and "activist," his opposition to "racism" and "colonialism in Africa" and support for the "labor and peace movements" and the Allied effort during World War II, predictably, no mention was made of his battles with the

State Department or leftist affiliations. At the unveiling of the stamp's artwork, though, Jarvis Tyner, vice-chair of the CPUSA, was present—along with former New York mayor David Dinkins and Manning Marable—and identified Robeson as the embodiment of the Party's ideals. See www.usps.com/communications/news/stamps/2004/sr04_005.htm.

Chapter 3

1. I have drawn the reference to "anarrangement" from Fred Moten, *In the Break: The Aesthetics of the Black Radical Tradition* (Minneapolis: University of Minnesota Press, 2003). In terms of poetic feet, the dactyl is composed of one long or stressed syllable followed by two short, or unstressed, syllables. Accordingly, the antidactylus (or anapaest) refers to a metrical foot composed of two short, unstressed syllables followed by a long or stressed syllable.

2. There are many examples of status, power, and recognition being distributed in ways that replicate gender and class hierarchies within black popular culture and black protest circles that could be cited here, and indeed, I will discuss instances from the cultural arena in this chapter. Regarding the other realms, the predominance of male preachers over congregations largely constituted of women that disavow lesbians and gays from the pulpit while depending on their regular attendance and performance of church ceremonies is evidence of the promotion of social hierarchies within spaces outside formal politics, as is the marginalization of local political mobilizations within black communities, which are overwhelmingly maintained by black women, in relation to the national campaigns, typically fronted by men. Regarding the latter, see Andrea Y. Simpson, *Controlling Women: Race, Class, Gender, and Political Activism* (New York: Oxford University Press, forthcoming).

3. For a useful discussion of the relationship between "antagonism" and "the political," albeit framed within a democratic horizon that renders the state and its modern/racial/colonial implications invisible, see Chantal Mouffe, *On the Political* (New York: Routledge, 2005). For considerations of the agonistic properties of the concept of democracy and democratic theory, see Bonnie Honig, *Political Theory and the Displacement of Politics* (Ithaca, N.Y.: Cornell University Press, 1993); Jacques Derrida, "The Last of the Rogue States: The 'Democracy to Come,' Opening in Two Turns," *South Atlantic Quarterly* 103, nos. 2–3 (spring–summer 2004), pp. 323–41; and Grant Farred, "Argentine Chronometrics: The Time of the Constitution," *South Atlantic Quarterly* 106, no. 1 (winter 2007), pp. 183–202.

4. See Moten, *In the Break*, p. 85.

5. Cedric J. Robinson, *Black Marxism: The Making of the Black Radical Tradition* (1983; reprint, Chapel Hill: University of North Carolina Press, 2000).

6. This suggestion implicit in Moten, *In the Break,* dovetails quite neatly with the central claims made in Cathy Cohen, *The Boundaries of Blackness: AIDS and the Breakdown of Black Politics* (Chicago: University of Chicago Press, 1999). In a sense, this chapter and chapter 5 can be characterized as attempts to read these two texts together.

7. For the details of these events, and the vigorously contested claims by "United States officials, who declined to let themselves be identified . . . that Communist agitators had stirred up . . . pro-Lumumba demonstrations around the world," see "Riot in Gallery Halts U.N. Debate: American Negroes Ejected After Invading Session—Midtown March Balked," *New York Times*, February 16, 1961, p. 10; "U.N. Rioting Laid to Pro-Africans: Observers Blame Backers of Nationalists—Communist Agitation Is Doubted," *New York Times*, February 16, 1961, p. 11; "Protests in Several Nations," *New York Times*, February 17, 1961, p. 3; and Philip Benjamin, "400 Picket U.N. in Salute to Castro and Lumumba," *New York Times*, February 19, 1961, pp. 1, 18; James Baldwin, "A Negro Assays the Negro Mood," *New York Times Magazine*, March 12, 1961, p. 25; and Maya Angelou, *The Heart of a Woman* (New York: Random House, 1981), pp. 143–70.

8. LeRoi Jones, "Cuba Libre," in *Home: Social Essays* (1966; reprint, New York: Ecco Press, 1998), p. 42. Sarah Wright, John Henrik Clarke, Robert Williams, and Harold Cruse were also in Cuba with Jones at Gibson's invitation. James Baldwin, John O. Killens, and Langston Hughes were invited to participate in the Cuban trip but declined.

9. Jones, "'Black' Is a Country," in *Home*, pp. 82–83, 86.

10. For evidence of the mutability of the nationalist frameworks that were being espoused in this period, see Ossie Davis, "Anti-Semitism and Black Power," *Freedomways* 7, no. 1 (1967), p. 78; and Milton Esterow, "New Role of Negroes in Theater Reflects Ferment of Integration," *New York Times*, June 15, 1964, p. 35.

11. Amiri Baraka, *The Autobiography of LeRoi Jones* (Chicago: Lawrence Hill Books, 1997), p. 295. Regarding Baraka's evolution in this period, see Harold Cruse, "The Harlem Black Arts Theater—New Dialogue with the Lost Black Generation," in *The Crisis of the Negro Intellectual: From Its Origins to the Present* (New York: Morrow, 1967), pp. 533–43; Komozi Woodard, *A Nation within a Nation: Amiri Baraka (LeRoi Jones) and Black Power Politics* (Chapel Hill: University of North Carolina Press, 1999); and Jerry Gafio Watts, *Amiri Baraka: The Politics and Art of a Black Intellectual* (New York: New York University Press, 2001).

12. Jones, "The Revolutionary Theatre," in *Home*, pp. 210–11.

13. LeRoi Jones, *Black Magic Poetry: 1961–1967* (Indianapolis: Bobbs-Merrill, 1969), p. 116. While Stanley Crouch was clearly, like Baraka, a committed nationalist within the Black Arts movement, he later would become identified with the Ellisonian camp—indeed, arguably, the most outspoken, if not insightful, representative of that tradition. On this point, see Celia McGee, "A Return to Rage, Played Out in Black and White," *New York Times*, January 14, 2007, Arts and Leisure sec., p. 4.

14. Larry Neal, "The Black Arts Movement," in *The Black Aesthetic*, Addison Gayle Jr., ed. (Garden City, N.Y.: Doubleday, 1971).

15. Stokely Carmichael with Ekwueme Michael Thelwell, *Ready for Revolution: The Life and Struggles of Stokely Carmichael (Kwame Ture)* (New York: Scribner, 2003), pp. 528–29.

16. The *Jet* photo was somewhat similar, in terms of its iconic qualities, to the photo of Miles Davis in August 1957 showing him wearing a white jacket splattered with

his own blood after having been beaten by the police outside Birdland in New York City. The Davis photo circulated widely within the United States and abroad. Herbie Hancock composed "Riot" and recorded it with Miles Davis on July 19, 1967, in Columbia Records' Thirtieth Street Studios in New York City, one week after Newark and four days before the beginning of the Detroit riots (which started on July 23, 1967). The track was first released on Davis's album *Nefertiti* (Columbia 1968).

17. The *New York Times* reassured its readership that the conference "could do much to bring a constructive meaning to the phrase ['black power']." Adam Clayton Powell did not attend, as he was living in Bimini by this point, to avoid being arrested on a criminal contempt citation. Karenga is described in the *Times* as "the squat, bald chief of a militant black-nationalist culture organization in Watts called US. He was wearing an orange kimono-like jacket. His organization is said to recruit and train Negroes for a revolution which, according to one timetable, will take place in 1972." See Martin Arnold, "Newark Meeting on Black Power Attended by 400," *New York Times*, July 21, 1967, p. 34; Homer Bigart, "Powell Remains in Island Exile," *New York Times*, July 22, 1967, p. 10, and "Black Phoenix," *New York Times*, July 22, 1967, p. 24.

18. During an afternoon address at a local high school, King also asserted that blacks "must develop and maintain a continuing sense of somebodyness" and argued that for "too long black people had been ashamed of themselves." "Now, I'm black," he stated, "but I'm black and beautiful." See Walter H. Waggoner, "Shift in Position Is Hinted By King," *New York Times*, March 28, 1968, p. 40.

19. The riots in Detroit the year before also impacted Hayes: "I saw blacks running around the streets [on television] with their fists clenched in rage and screaming, 'Yeah, soul brother, yeah!' Whether it's right or wrong, they are united and they are taking pride in the word soul. I thought, Soul Man, that's it. So I called David [Porter, his writing partner] and we got together in the studio and I started playing the intro riff. It came really fast." See Bill DeMain, "10 Questions for Isaac Hayes," *Mojo*, February 2004, p. 35. For other accounts of the effects of King's murder, see Andria Lisle, "I Know a Place," *Waxpoetics* 11 (2005), p. 105; Michael Eric Dyson, *Reflecting Black: African-American Cultural Criticism* (Minneapolis: University of Minnesota Press, 1993), p. xxvi; Charles Waring, liner notes for Eugene McDaniels, *Headless Heroes of the Apocalypse/Outlaw* (Warner Strategic Marketing 2002), p. 8; and Quincy Jones, *Q: The Autobiography of Quincy Jones* (New York: Doubleday, 2001), pp. 216–17.

20. To pursue the James Brown/Booker T. Washington parallel a little further, the Godfather's 1968 was in some respects the equivalent of the Wizard of Tuskegee's 1912: the year the Democrats regained control of the White House and Washington's patronage powers were significantly reduced. Clearly by the late 1960s, Mr. "Please, Please, Please" was reacting to the changing currents rather than anticipating them, though by the early 1970s he had returned to the hot combs and curlers and, along with Elvis Presley, Frank Sinatra, Jim Brown, Sammy Davis Jr., Wilt Chamberlain, and others, become a Nixon supporter. Al Sharpton explains his own processed

hair as a sign of his allegiance to Brown, his mentor, who took him to get his first perm before a meeting Brown had with Ronald Reagan in 1981 at the White House. Brown insisted that those who wanted to prove their loyalty to him get their hair permed. Fred Wesley Jr., Brown's long-serving trombonist, writes, "I finally had to wear his hairstyle to convince Mr. Brown that I was on his side. You see, Mr. Brown has an innate mistrust of people who don't wear the hairdos." Nevertheless, that a man as taken with his follicles as Brown was at least temporarily consented to an Afro was undoubtedly significant, and a sign that at some fundamental level, the game had changed. See James Brown, "America Is My Home" (King 1968), and "Say It Loud, I'm Black and I'm Proud" (King 1968); James Brown with Bruce Tucker, *James Brown: The Godfather of Soul* (New York: Macmillan, 1986), pp. 199–200; Al Sharpton and Anthony Walton, *Go and Tell Pharaoh: The Autobiography of the Reverend Al Sharpton* (New York: Doubleday, 1996), pp. 71–72; Will Dana, "The Messenger," *Rolling Stone*, November 27, 2003, p. 45; and Fred Wesley Jr., *Hit Me Fred: Recollections of a Sideman* (Durham, N.C.: Duke University Press, 2002), p. 163.

21. See Michael T. Kaufman, "Jones Asks Votes, Not Rioting, to 'Take' Newark" *New York Times*, April 14, 1968, p. 60.

22. Ruby Dee, Ossie Davis, Sammy Davis Jr., the Temptations, Herbie Hancock, Chuck Jackson, Max Roach, Stevie Wonder, Dustin Hoffman, and James Brown also lent support to the Gibson campaign. By this point, the alliance between Karenga and Baraka had collapsed, and indeed US (especially after its armed conflicts with the Panthers) had dropped off the scene (with Karenga soon to imprisoned). For the details of this parting of the ways, and a more comprehensive discussion of Baraka's political evolution, see Woodard, *A Nation within a Nation*.

23. See Léopold Sédar Senghor, *The Collected Poetry*, Melvin Dixon, trans. (Charlottesville: University Press of Virginia, 1991); and Viriato da Cruz, *Poemas* (Lobito, Angola: Capricórnio, 1974).

24. Regarding the concept of "problem spaces," drawn from the work of Quentin Skinner, see David Scott, *Conscripts of Modernity: The Tragedy of Colonial Enlightenment* (Durham, N.C.: Duke University Press, 2004).

25. The "satire, parody, and slapstick humor" characteristic of the Mexican American El Teatro movement of the same period, as Harry Elam notes, was lacking in Baraka's Black Revolutionary Theatre. See *Taking It to the Streets: The Social Protest Theater of Luis Valdez and Amiri Baraka* (Ann Arbor: University of Michigan Press, 1997), p. 5.

26. See Amiri Baraka, *Preface to a Twenty Volume Suicide Note* (New York: Totem Press, 1961); *The System of Dante's Hell* (New York: Grove, 1965); *The Baptism and The Toilet* (New York: Grove, 1967); and *The Autobiography of LeRoi Jones*; and Hettie Jones, *How I Became Hettie Jones* (New York: Dutton, 1990); Ron Simmons, "Baraka's Dilemma: To Be or Not to Be?" in *Black Men on Race, Gender, and Sexuality: A Critical Reader*, Devon W. Carbado, ed. (New York: New York University Press, 1999), pp. 317–23; Watts, *Amiri Baraka*; and Moten, *In the Break*. With respect to Davis and Pryor, and the broader questions of black masculinities

in pre-hip-hop black popular culture, see Miles Davis with Quincy Troupe, *Miles* (New York: Simon and Schuster, 1990); Richard Pryor with Todd Gold, *Pryor Convictions: And Other Life Sentences* (New York: Pantheon, 1995), pp. 100, 120, 219; Hazel Carby, *Race Men: The W.E.B. Du Bois Lectures* (Cambridge, Mass.: Harvard University Press, 1998), p. 149; Hilton Als, "A Pryor Love: The Life and Times of America's Comic Prophet of Race," *New Yorker*, September 13, 1999; Quincy Troupe, *Miles and Me* (Berkeley: University of California Press, 2000); James Gavin, "Homophobia in Jazz," *Jazztimes*, December 2001, pp. 64–70; *Jazz: A Film by Ken Burns* (PBS Paramount 2004); Donald L. Maggin, "Cubop: Dizzy Gillespie, Chano Pozo and the Afro-Cuban Jazz Revolution," *Jazztimes*, April 2005, p. 40; and "Under the Influence," *Fader*, May–June 2005, p. 95. I use the term "transgressive interiority" in order to distinguish interiorities that challenge existing exterior arrangements and those that simply reproduce and reinforce these structures (for example, in the way performances of [persona] drama—e.g., Tupac Shakur, Mary J. Blige—might).

27. Regarding the possible derivations and functions of the lawgiver, see Jean-Jacques Rousseau, *On the Social Contract*, Donald A. Cress, trans. and ed. (Indianapolis: Hackett, 1987); and Bonnie Honig, *Democracy and the Foreigner* (Princeton, N.J.: Princeton University Press, 2001). Baraka, and arguably Miles Davis, represent significant examples of the practice of prominent lawgivers energizing "politics" and defining and enabling "community" by denying and sacrificing, on a recurring basis, the gay black male body. The contemporary work of the gospel singer Donnie McClurkin and the playwright Tyler Perry can also be seen as falling, albeit somewhat differently, in this tradition.

28. Regarding the NAACP's decision not to endorse the NBPA's proposed text, see Henry Hampton and Steve Fayer with Sarah Flynn, *Voices of Freedom: An Oral History of the Civil Rights Movement from the 1950s through the 1980s* (New York: Bantam, 1990), p. 571; William Greider, "Discord Is the Keynote for Black Convention," *Washington Post*, March 11, 1972, p. A2; and Austin Scott, "NAACP Pullout Bares Schism Among Blacks," *Washington Post*, May 18, 1972, p. A2.

29. Diggs, who was particularly engaged with issues relating to the African continent and U.S. foreign policy and whose former aide Randall Robinson would later organize the lobbying group TransAfrica, was elected to represent Michigan's Thirteenth District in Detroit as a Democrat in 1954 and remained in office until 1980.

30. After the 1970 midterm elections, there were twelve black members of Congress (all Democrats): Charles Diggs (Michigan), Robert Nix (Pennsylvania), Augustus Hawkins (California), John Conyers Jr. (Michigan), Shirley Chisholm (New York), William L. Clay (Missouri), Louis Stokes (Ohio), Ralph Metcalfe (Illinois), Charles B. Rangel (New York), Ronald V. Dellums (California), George W. Collins (Illinois), and Parren J. Mitchell (Maryland). After the 1974 midterm elections, this number would increase to sixteen with the addition of Yvonne B. Burke (California), Barbara C. Jordan (Texas), Andrew Young (Georgia), and Harold E. Ford (Tennessee). Cardiss Collins (Illinois) replaced her deceased husband George

W. Collins after a special election (in June 1973). See Jeffrey L. Katz, "Growing Black Caucus May Have New Voice," *Congressional Quarterly Weekly Report* 51: 1, January 2, 1993, p. 10.

31. For an extended discussion of the Chisholm campaign and its significance in the broader histories of the civil rights movement and second wave feminism, see Paula Giddings, *When and Where I Enter: The Impact of Black Women on Race and Sex in America* (New York: Bantam Books, 1984); and the documentary *Chisholm '72—Unbought and Unbossed* (Twentieth-Century Fox, 2003). NOW would eventually, albeit halfheartedly, endorse Chisholm. Chisholm has acknowledged that her chances of winning were quite slim, that her organization was severely underfinanced, and that she made few attempts to coordinate her efforts with the ongoing political activities of other black elected officials and the women's movement.

32. Continuing, Chisholm contended, "[I]f anyone thinks white men are sexists, let them check out black men sometime. Representative Ronald Dellums . . . was . . . one of the few who were able to transcend those feelings." At the Chicago Operation Breadbasket/Black Expo, Chisholm would overhear "There she is—that little black matriarch who goes around messing things up." Besides Dellums, Maryland's Parren Mitchell (1970–86), Manhattan borough president Percy Sutton, and the Black Panthers also supported Chisholm's campaign at various stages. With regard to Chisholm's conflicts with Missouri House member William Clay and conference cochair Richard Hatcher, see Shirley Chisholm, *The Good Fight* (New York: Harper and Row, 1973), p. 31; William L. Clay, *Just Permanent Interests: Black Americans in Congress, 1870–1991* (New York: Amistad Press, 1992), pp. 197–98; and Hampton et al., *Voices of Freedom*, pp. 579–80.

33. See Imamu Amiri Baraka, "Black Woman," *Black World*, July 1970, p. 11; *Nationtime—Gary* (1972; William Greaves, dir.); and Coretta Scott King, "The Transformation of the Civil Rights Movement into a Political Movement," paper presented at one of the meetings leading up to the 1972 National Black Political Convention in Gary, Washington, D.C., November 18–20, 1971.

34. Shirley Chisholm raised similar concerns in the same period, positing, "Imamu [Baraka] is a separatist. . . . [T]o be consistent, [he] should work outside the existing political structure. . . . [H]e has for some reason never submitted himself to the test of running for office." There are reports that Baraka's supporters (i.e., in the Congress of African Peoples) tried to block the Michigan delegation from leaving and that with a display of arms, of some unspecified sort, Young's supporters "convinced" Baraka's people to let them pass. See Coleman Young and Lonnie Wheeler, *Hard Stuff: The Autobiography of Coleman Young* (New York: Viking, 1994), p. 190; Watts, *Amiri Baraka*, p. 407; Chisholm, *The Good Fight*, pp. 36–37; and Robert C. Smith, *We Have No Leaders: African Americans in the Post–Civil Rights Era* (Albany: State University of New York Press, 1996), p. 308 n. 131. For a good indication of Baraka's views regarding black elected officials, see Amiri Baraka, "Statement on the National Black Assembly," *Black World*, October 1975, pp. 42–43.

Although subsequent NBPA meetings occurred in 1974 (Little Rock, Arkansas) and 1976 (Cincinnati), the tensions between black elected officials and Baraka would render the convention mechanism unworkable. For further details of what happened at Gary, see Hampton et al., *Voices of Freedom*, pp. 565–86; Smith, "The National Black Political Convention, 1972–84," in *We Have No Leaders*, pp. 29–85; Woodard, *A Nation within a Nation*; and *Nationtime—Gary*.

35. See Clay, *Just Permanent Interests*, p. 166.

36. Imamu Amiri Baraka, *It's Nation Time* (Chicago: Third World Press, 1970), pp. 21–22. Regarding Black Forum, a project spearheaded by Junius Griffin, a journalist who had worked as King's assistant for two years with the SCLC, see Berry Gordy, *To Be Loved: The Music, the Magic, the Memories of Motown: An Autobiography* (New York: Warner Books, 1994), pp. 249–50; and Suzanne E. Smith, *Dancing in the Street: Motown and the Cultural Politics of Detroit* (Cambridge, Mass.: Harvard University Press, 1999). In 1971, the Ebonys, a trio from Camden, New Jersey, best known for their hit "It's Forever," recorded a track written by Leon Huff and his musical partner Kenny Gamble at Philadelphia International Records using the same title as Baraka's poem and with similar lyrical emphasis. See "Nation Time" (*The Ebonys*, Philadelphia International/Epic 1971).

37. Quoted in Hampton et al., *Voices of Freedom*, pp. 576–77.

38. See Roberta Flack, "Go Up Moses" (*Quiet Fire*, Atlantic 1971); and the Independents, *The First Time We Met* (Wand 1972). "Go Up Moses," a rousing uptempo composition with the widely applicable refrain "You've been down too long," was produced by Flack and Joel Dorn. His half-brother, Charles Henry "Chuck" Jackson (not the singer of "Any Day Now" fame), coproduced and cowrote, along with Marvin Yancy, most of Natalie Cole's mid-1970s hits (e.g., "Inseparable" and "Our Love").

39. Adderley, one of the most successful artists working in the soul-jazz idiom, recorded (and in one instance rerecorded) some of his most popular hits at the Chicago session, including "Walk Tall" and "Country Preacher." Among the visitors to the regular Saturday morning Breadbasket services were Nancy Wilson, Dionne Warwick, Isaac Hayes, Redd Foxx, the Jackson 5, Muhammad Ali, Richard Roundtree, and Chicago native Quincy Jones. When Operation PUSH (People United to Save/Serve Humanity) was launched, Chicago native and former Impressions lead vocalist Jerry Butler would serve as chair of its board of directors. Among the other board members were Isaac Hayes, Cannonball Adderley, Nate Adderley, Roberta Flack, and Donny Hathaway. See Cannonball Adderley, liner notes, Cannonball Adderley Quintet, *Country Preacher* (Capitol 1969); and Marshall Frady, *Jesse: The Life and Pilgrimage of Jesse Jackson* (New York: Random House, 1996), pp. 259–60.

40. Indeed, Young and Jackson were already at odds with each other before Gary. Regarding their relationship, see Young and Wheeler, *Hard Stuff*; Barbara A. Reynolds, *Jesse Jackson: The Man, the Movement, the Myth* (Chicago: Nelson-Hall, 1975); Adolph Reed Jr., *The Jesse Jackson Phenomenon: The Crisis of Purpose in Afro-American Politics* (New Haven, Conn.: Yale University Press, 1986); and Lucius J. Barker and Ronald

W. Walters, eds., *Jesse Jackson's 1984 Presidential Campaign: Challenge and Change in American Politics* (Urbana: University of Illinois Press, 1989).

41. Admission to the concert was $1. Stax and the Schlitz Brewing Company picked up most of the expenses for the show. Its profits went to the Sickle Cell Anemia Foundation, Operation PUSH, and the Martin Luther King Jr. General Hospital (which had opened officially in March of the same year).

42. See the documentary *Wattstax*, thirtieth anniversary ed. (Warner Home Video 2004; Mel Stuart, dir.); and "introduction by Reverend Jesse Jackson," *Music from the Wattstax Festival and Film* (Stax 2003).

43. *Hot Buttered Soul* contained only four tracks: a twelve-minute version of "Walk On By," the almost ten-minute "Hyperbolicsyllabicsesquedalymistic," "One Woman" (five minutes, eight seconds), and a cover of Jim Webb's "By the Time I Get to Phoenix" that clocked in at almost nineteen minutes.

44. The performative commitments of the Black Arts poets—and their predecessors (including LeRoi Jones) in the New American Poetry movement—and the Last Poets, as well as Gil Scott-Heron's migration from poetry and literature to music and singing, make sense in this context.

45. Regarding the genesis of *What's Going On* and Gaye's battles with his brother-in-law and Motown owner Berry Gordy Jr., see David Ritz, *Divided Soul: The Life of Marvin Gaye* (New York: Da Capo, 1985); Steve Turner, *Trouble Man: The Life and Death of Marvin Gaye* (London: Michael Joseph, 1998); Ben Edmonds, *What's Going On? Marvin Gaye and the Last Days of the Motown Sound* (Edinburgh: Canongate, 2001); and Ben Edmonds, liner notes, Marvin Gaye, *What's Going On* (reissue, Motown 1994), pp. 7–9.

46. Italics added. All three versions feature the same chorus: "If you've got the plan . . . I've got to vote for you because you're the man." Gaye also cites taxation, economics, and achieving "peace and freedom" as pressing concerns in the song. He briefly considered rerecording "You're the Man" in the lead-up to the 1984 presidential election (just before his murder that year). See Marvin Gaye, "You're the Man" (Tamla Motown 1972) and the previously unreleased versions included on the remastered and expanded edition of *Let's Get It On* (Motown 2001), and Ritz, *Divided Soul*, pp. 162, 326. Regarding Gaye's public views on women—which were not quite progressive and revealed a great deal of anxiety and insecurity—see Patrick William Salvo, "What's Really Going On With Marvin Gaye?" *Sepia* 4 (April 1978), p. 14.

47. An earlier version of "Let's Get It On," cowritten by Gaye and Ed Townsend, does indeed make references to "peace and love," "understanding and brotherhood," suggests that "everybody ought to do some good," and is directed toward the general public ("Come on people," "Come on everybody"). The final version, in which carnal intentions are much more explicit, was reportedly inspired by the appearance of sixteen-year-old Janis Hunter in the studio (who would later become Gaye's second wife). See Marvin Gaye, "Let's Get It On (Demo Version)" (*Let's Get It On*, Motown 2001).

48. For an insightful, extended discussion of Harold Melvin and the Blue Notes' "Be for Real," featuring Theodore "Teddy" Pendergrass on lead vocals, see Mark

Anthony Neal, *What the Music Said: Black Popular Music and Black Public Culture* (New York: Routledge, 1999), pp. 118–19.

49. Other groups featuring male falsetto leads in this period include Blue Magic, Enchantment, the Moments, Black Ivory, the Chi-Lites, the Whatnauts, and Earth Wind & Fire (i.e., Philip Bailey). The jazz singer "Little" Jimmy Scott stands as a significant pioneer with regard to the troubling of assumptions regarding appropriate modes of expression on the part of black men.

50. See Toni Morrison, *The Bluest Eye* (New York: Washington Square Press, 1970); Alice Walker, *The Third Life of Grange Copeland* (New York: Harcourt, Brace and Jovanovitch, 1970); and Toni Cade Bambara, *The Black Woman: An Anthology* (New York: Random House, 1970).

51. Another significant female artist in this period was Betty Davis, who released a number of groundbreaking—though commercially unsuccessful—albums after her divorce from Miles Davis. Millie Jackson has also stated that she "never considered [herself] a feminist and never wanted to be involved in politics." At the same time, she expressed support for "independence," and her lyrics, with their frank discussions of gender relations—in the tradition of the blues women—were in many respects quite consistent with the goal of challenging gender inequalities. See Lee Hildebrand, liner notes, Laura Lee, *Greatest Hits* (HDH Records 2002); Al Green, *Take Me to the River* (New York: HarperEntertainment, 2000), pp. 279–80; Alexandra Phanor, "Sexaholic," *Vibe*, July 2002, p. 52; and Jean-Claude Moriot, "Caught Up with Millie Jackson," *In the Basement* 39 (August–November 2005), p. 20. Regarding pioneering black women instrumentalists, Sister Rosetta Tharpe, Mary Lou Williams, and Melba Liston, should also be acknowledged. On the resistance to women functioning as decision-makers and producers in R & B, see David Nathan, "Just the Music: The Diana Ross Interview," *Billboard*, October 23, 1993, pp. 62–76; and Gerald Early, *One Nation under a Groove: Motown and American Culture* (Ann Arbor: University of Michigan Press, 2004), p. 116.

52. The Newton shot is also restaged in the inner-sleeve photos of Missy Elliott's *This Is Not a Test!* (Elektra 2003).

53. One can read Marvin Gaye's recordings with the Originals ("The Bells" and "Baby I'm For Real") and his own multitracked vocals in his solo work as falling in roughly the same tradition. Motown insisted that Gaye rerecord "What's Going On" with professional backup singers; nonetheless, the version with Detroit Lions Farr and Barney was ultimately the official release.

Chapter 4

1. Robin D. G. Kelley, *Race Rebels: Culture, Politics, and the Black Working Class* (New York: Free Press, 1994), pp. 2–3.

2. Adults can certainly engage in battles over uniforms in a similar manner, and on the basis of personal experience, I would suggest that this resistance rarely presents a substantive challenge to the status quo. Such issues often become flashpoints because more significant battles have been conceded: control of the workplace and the allocation of the benefits, profits, and leisure opportunities derived from the process of production.

3. Regarding the question of the relationship between race and performance, it might be useful to consider the cases of Homer Plessy, Takao Ozawa, Bhagat Singh Thind, Hidemitsu Toyota, and Toyosaburo "Fred" Korematsu, among others, and their attempts to perform acceptability and American respectability—i.e., near whiteness—as a means of gaining recognition as citizens before the Supreme Court in *Plessy v. Ferguson* 163 U.S. 537 (1896), *Ozawa v. United States* 260 U.S. 178 (1922), *Thind v. United States* 261 U.S. 204 (1923), *Toyota v. United States* 268 U.S. 402 (1925), and *Korematsu v. United States* 323 U.S. 214 (1944), respectively. These efforts would be uniformly unsuccessful.

4. Music videos, of course, blur the line between the intentions and expectations artists and audiences, respectively, might have, in contrast to music and film. Andre "Dr. Dre" Young and Jason "Jadakiss" Phillips, among others, have argued that rappers should be extended the same degree of latitude as stage actors. Rapperactors O'Shea "Ice Cube" Jackson and Clifford Joseph "T.I." Harris Jr. have argued otherwise. Harris contends, "The thing about rapping is what you say is supposed to be the truth." On this point, see Jon Pareles, "The Street Talk, He Says, Is a Bum Rap" *New York Times*, November 14, 1999, sec. 2, p. 18; Monica Corcoran, "That's a (W)rap!" *New York Times Magazine*, November 9, 2003, p. 27; Rashaun Hall, "Street's Disciple," *Source*, June 2005, p. 105; "King of the World," *Redeye*, March 27, 2006, p. 21; and Richard Harrington, "Ice Cube's Welcome Return to Rap," *Washington Post*, May 12, 2006, p. WE6. It is also important that these claims be placed in context. When rap artists argue that their performances should be judged in the same manner as screen actors' efforts, they are responding to challenges from a community that wants them to act like "respectable, responsible and concerned citizens." Accordingly, Shawn Carter suggests in the 2001 "Girls, Girls, Girls" video that Jay-Z is just a character by concluding the clip with a shot in which he enters a dressing room with his given name posted on it. His attempt to mix irony with the demands for a "real" gangster—and highlight the border separating the genuine and the assumed—undoubtedly raised questions about his authenticity in certain circles. Many consumers are engaged by these personalities precisely because they feel they can legitimately expect a certain genuine quality that they do not associate with television and film actors. As a result, performing someone else's lyrics—whether ghostwritten, credited, or "bitten" (as in plagiarized)—is seen as a problem in hip-hop, as it is in rock as opposed to pop. In the face of these pressures, Carter, a well-known ghostwriter, tried in his later work to negotiate a space between these two camps. His decision to retire (at least temporarily) with *The Black Album* in 2003, then, can be read as his recognition (e.g., "What More Can I Say?") that he could no longer coherently articulate a way of being and play both sides of the fence. The clearest support for this interpretation would be the video released for "99 Problems," which concludes with the shooting of Jay-Z (a scene intended, he suggests, to "put the whole Jay-Z thing to rest" and mark the rebirth of Shawn Carter). On the questions of race and authenticity, see John L. Jackson, *Real Black: Adventures in Racial Sincerity* (Chicago: University of Chicago Press, 2005).

5. Quoted in Thelma Golden, "Kehinde Wiley: The Painter Who Is Doing for Hip-hop Culture What Artists Once Did for the Aristocracy," *Interview*, October 2005, p. 162. With regard to the inevitably surreal quality of representations of blackness, the "natural" tonal setting for cameras—i.e., the point at which one has established the proper "white balance"—tends to reproduce colored skin tones inaccurately (much in the same way that makeup artists have trouble working with black skin because of the normative biases embedded in the cosmetics they characteristically use). The impossibility of seeing objectively, *through race*, runs in both directions to some degree. In *Native Son*, for instance, Richard Wright notes, "To Bigger and his kind white people were not really people; they were a sort of great natural force, like a stormy sky looming overhead, or like a deep swirling river stretching suddenly at one's feet in the dark." See *Native Son* (1940; reprint, New York: HarperPerennial, 1998), p. 114.

6. See Michael D. Harris, *Colored Pictures: Race and Visual Representation* (Chapel Hill: University of North Carolina Press, 2003), p. 251. For an elaboration on the potentials of spectatorship that is not inconsistent with the claims made here, except in emphasis, see Jacques Rancière, "The Emancipated Spectator," *Artforum*, March 2007, pp. 271–80. Regarding the modern relationship between distraction and reception, see Walter Benjamin, *Illuminations*, Hannah Arendt, ed., Harry Zohn, trans. (New York: Schocken, 1969); Theodor Adorno, "On the Fetish-Character in Music and the Regression of Listening," in *The Essential Frankfurt School Reader*, Andrew Arato and Eike Gebhardt, eds. (New York: Urizen, 1978), pp. 270–99; Martin Jay, *Downcast Eyes: The Denigration of Vision in Twentieth Century French Thought* (Berkeley: University of California Press, 1993); and Jonathan Crary, *Suspensions of Perception: Attention, Spectacle and Modern Culture* (Cambridge, Mass.: MIT Press, 1999). On the colonial aspects and potentially pernicious impact of the gaze, see Frantz Fanon, *Black Skin, White Masks*, Charles Lam Markmann, trans. (New York: Grove Press, 1967).

7. See Saidiya V. Hartman, *Scenes of Subjection: Terror, Slavery, and Self-Making in Nineteenth-Century America* (New York: Oxford University Press, 1997), pp. 3–4.

8. For an example of this tendency, see the film *Amazing Grace* (IDP/Samuel Goldwyn Films 2006) regarding the campaign to abolish the slave trade in the British Empire. It is against this backdrop that Fred Moten makes his arguments about black performances as constituting, among other things, a phonic resistance to being objectified. See "Resistance of the Object: Aunt Hester's Scream," in *In the Break: The Aesthetics of the Black Radical Tradition* (Minneapolis: University of Minnesota Press, 2003), pp. 1–24.

9. On this point, also see Anthony Paul Farley, "The Black Body as Fetish Object," *Oregon Law Review* 76 (fall 1997), pp. 457–535; and Fanon's contrasting of humanizing and racializing processes in *Black Skin, White Masks* (which renders both projects as linked and accordingly normatively problematic).

10. See, for instance, the arguments made by Robert Miles in *Race after "Race Relations"* (London: Routledge, 1993), and Robert Miles and Malcolm Brown in *Racism* (London: Routledge, 2003). While blacks might be trying to make salient broad

and intersectional phenomena when they make reference to "race" and "racism," others—because of the structural hierarchies and power imbalances that provide the context in which such exchanges take place—might be inclined to interpret the same terms narrowly: so narrowly that, by definition, they seem extraneous to the significant and the embedded that constitute the familiar and safer terrain of the quotidian and the political.

11. Regarding the murder of Emmett Till, it is worth noting that his mother, Mamie Till Bradley, sought to have the photographs of his disfigured visage published in an era after lynching photographs moved freely without sanction. In other words, she sought to make public and widely visible again that which had previously been commonly available (and that which was still privately practiced) but had been discouraged and made invisible in the public arena (e.g., the move by southern congressmen in 1908 to pass legislation that would prohibit the U.S. Post Office from handling lynching postcards because they felt the circulation of such images would be bad for business). Clearly, the constituencies directly affected and targeted by such violence have an interest in having these kinds of images circulate, if only to raise their own collective awareness and mobilize among themselves. On this point, see Elizabeth Alexander, "'Can You Be BLACK and Look at This?': Reading the Rodney King Video(s)," in *The Black Public Sphere: A Public Culture Book*, Black Public Sphere Collective, ed. (Chicago: University of Chicago Press, 1995), p. 82; and George H. Roeder Jr., *The Censored War: American Visual Experience during World War Two* (New Haven, Conn.: Yale University Press, 1993), pp. 44–57.

12. Edward Said, *Power, Politics, and Culture: Interviews with Edward S. Said*, Gauri Viswanathan, ed. (New York: Pantheon, 2001), p. 40.

13. Kobena Mercer, "Reading Racial Fetishism: The Photographs of Robert Mapplethorpe," *Welcome to the Jungle: New Positions in Black Cultural Studies* (London: Routledge, 1994), pp. 171–219.

14. Mark Reid suggests that Micheaux's post-1929 films should not be categorized as black independent productions, as they were not "produced by black controlled film production companies." See *Redefining Black Film* (Los Angeles: University of California Press, 1993), pp. 16–17.

15. See Andy Greenman, ""Larry Heard: The Original Speaks," *Keep On* 1, no. 4 (2004), p. 27; and Tom Barlow, "Dark Side of the Sun," *Jazzwise* 99 (July 2006), p. 38. The increasingly popular youtube.com does offer, among other things, the possibility of viewing pre–video era footage of classic soul and jazz artists. The website also compensates for the marginalization of musicians who could not or cannot afford to make videos, as songs are often posted accompanied by still images selected by the individuals submitting the material to the website (i.e., thus creating an [at least rudimentary] visual image as required by the medium so that otherwise ineligible audio tracks might be retrieved and enjoyed by others). If, in the aggregate, the advent of the superpublic privileges certain sorts of archives and produces new, politically significant silences at the same time, we should not overlook the ways these tendencies might be contested or subverted.

16. Quoted in *Pulse*, July 2000, p. 87. In one priceless episode of the TV show *Pump It Up*, host Dee Barnes flipped the standard script and taped an interview with the rap duo Nice and Smooth sitting relatively unclothed in a hot tub while she sat fully dressed at the side asking them questions. With respect to the particular constraints placed on black female film and video directors, see Carla Hay, "The Billboard Report: Female Video Directors Remain Rare in Industry," *Billboard*, November 11, 2000, pp. 1, 103; and Ernest Hardy, "I, Too, Sing Hollywood: Four Women on Race, Art and Making Movies," in *Bloodbeats*, vol. 1, *Demos, Remixes and Extended Versions* (Washington: Redbone Press, 2006), pp. 153–71.

17. In an era of increasingly expensive videos, the clip for D'Angelo's "How Does It Feel" (*Voodoo*, EMI 2000) was also quite cheap to shoot.

18. Quoted in Touré, *Never Drank the Kool-Aid* (New York: Picador, 2006), pp. 307–9.

19. It should be noted that while radio station programmers were the most influential forces behind the shaping of American popular tastes throughout the four decades following World War II, in the United Kingdom, the music press—e.g., the *New Musical Express* and *Melody Maker*—played a more prominent role (with television emerging as a major player in the 1960s). Videos themselves were commonly made in the British context, and as a result, the emergence of MTV in the early 1980s coincided with a second British invasion of sorts of the American pop charts, as British bands were more likely to have videos made (and to be correspondingly image-conscious) than their American counterparts. On a related point, the emergence of satellite radio (e.g., XM and Sirius Satellite Radio) might provide an alternative to the tightly scripted playlists of conventional, "terrestrial" radio and video networks, though one might expect that there would be a demographic skew in terms of the medium's listenership (i.e., it would tend to attract older listeners less dependent on visual stimulation). There are signs also, as one might expect, that some commercial stations are moving to lengthen and diversify their playlists in response (e.g., increasing their rotation from one or two hundred songs to twelve or fifteen hundred different tracks). "Urban" formats—R & B and hip-hop—have traditionally tended toward tighter rotations and shorter playlists (i.e., closer to the one-hundred-song rotation end of the spectrum).

20. Other examples of clashing structures of feeling made intimate include Notorious B.I.G.'s use of the Isley Brothers' "Between the Sheets" on "Big Poppa"; Blackstreet's interpolation of Bill Withers's "Grandma's Hands" in "No Diggity"; Donnell Jones's "When I Was Down" (*Where I Wanna Be*, La Face 1999), a song about the breakup of a romantic relationship that uses a sample from Curtis Mayfield's "Freddie's Dead" (*Superfly*, Curtom 1972); Akon's "Don't Matter" (*Konvicted*, Universal 2006), which makes absurd use of Bob Marley's "Zimbabwe"; and Mary J. Blige's "PMS" (*No More Drama*, MCA 2001), a song whose title is self-explanatory ("Today I'm not feeling pretty; I'm feeling quite ugly") and that borrows from one of Al Green's most transcendent vocal performances, his classic turntable hit "Simply Beautiful" (*I'm Still in Love with You*, Hi 1972). Kanye West's "Diamonds Are Forever" is a recent example of a song substantially revised via remix.

21. Accordingly, in reference to the remix of a recording by Milwaukee resident Coo Coo Cal entitled "My Projects" and featuring Trick Daddy (identified with Miami) and Kurupt (linked to the West Coast and Philadelphia), the general manager of his label stated, "We have been doing great with the single, but we think a remix will help us go to the next level in rotation. Where we are getting played is spreading, but it isn't national." See Colin Finan, "Coo Coo Cal Calls Out Milwaukee," *Billboard*, September 8, 2001, p. 38.

22. Regarding these cultural bundles, one might also add songs included on movie soundtracks that do not actually appear in the film in question (an increasingly common phenomenon, dating back to the 1990s move toward using movie soundtracks as promotional devices for launching the careers of new artists), and those songs whose videos are composed of film clips that often do not correspond to the song's lyrics. With regard to the role of regionalism, while there is clear evidence of regional difference and the existence of regional markets, there are at the same time forces working against the expression of regional distinctions. Consider the Top 10 Charts for the Chicago area and the nation as a whole for the week of January 24–31, 2005. The top ten songs in the Chicago area were (in descending order): Mario, "Let Me Love You"; The Game featuring 50 Cent, "How We Do"; Ludacris, "Get Back"; Eminem, "Toy Soldiers"; Jennifer Lopez, "Get Right"; Ashanti, "Only U"; Destiny's Child featuring T. I. and L'il Wayne, "Soldier"; Nelly featuring Tim McGraw, "Over and Over"; Twista, "Hope"; and Usher and Alicia Keys, "My Boo." On the national charts, the top four songs were the same (and in the same order), followed by Destiny's Child featuring T. I. and L'il Wayne, "Soldier"; Ashanti, "Only U"; Jennifer Lopez, "Get Right"; Nelly featuring Tim McGraw, "Over and Over"; Usher and Alicia Keys, "My Boo"; and Green Day, "Boulevard of Broken Dreams." Twista, the one artist who appears on the Chicago charts but not the national charts, is from Chicago's West Side. Evident in these charts as well is the bundling referred to earlier: the East and West coasts are joined in the 50 Cent/ Game collaboration; New York and Atlanta in the Usher/Alicia Keys duet; and hip-hop and country in the recording made by Nelly and Tim McGraw. See "charts," *Redeye*, February 2, 2005, p. 27.

23. On this point, see Gail Mitchell, "Black Execs Downsized," *Billboard*, July 30, 2005, pp. 24–25. As Mitchell observes (p. 24), "Almost one-quarter of the total album sales for 2005 are R & B, rap or hip-hop releases. . . . [T]here are only a handful of African-American execs in key major-label roles." The nationalist upsurge of the 1960s generated a number of attempts in the artistic realm to establish black-owned businesses, including The East, a nightclub that was established in 1969 in Bedford-Stuyvesant as a space for the "new thing"; and the Ak-ba, Survival, Strata-East, and Anima record labels (and Haki Hadhubuti's Third World Press). In mainstream R & B, similar convictions led to the formation of the Soul Clan (a group of soul artists including Otis Redding, Don Covay, Wilson Pickett, future Nation of Islam member Joe Tex, and Solomon Burke) and Curtis Mayfield and Eddie Thomas's Curtom Records. For more background on these other attempts at establishing black independent corporations and institutions in the

artistic arena, see Horace Tapscott, *Songs of the Unsung: The Musical and Social Journey of Horace Tapscott* (Durham, N.C.: Duke University Press, 2001); Kwasi Konadu, *Truth Crushed to the Earth Will Rise Again! The East Organization and the Principles and Practice of Black Nationalist Development* (Trenton, N.J.: Africa World Press, 2005); Andrew Schrock, "Return to the East: Brooklyn Reclaims the Black Art Form Known as Jazz," *Waxpoetics* 14 (fall 2005), pp. 64–72; and Robert Pruter, *Chicago Soul* (Urbana: University of Illinois Press, 1991), p. 142. With regard to the ways the mainstream film industry characteristically defines and treats (i.e., underfunds and underpromotes) "black" films, see George Alexander, "Fade to Black," *Black Enterprise*, December 2000, pp. 107–15. Alexander suggests that "black" films are by definition films with small budgets. Films featuring black characters with bigger budgets (e.g., *Beloved*, *Big Momma's House*, and *Hurricane*) are, according to this definition, "not black," as the studios involved see them as having crossover potential and international box office possibilities and consequently fund and market them differently. It is worth noting that blacks constitute roughly 20 percent of the American moviegoing public (while representing around 12 percent of the population). African Americans also watch about 42 percent more television [1999 figures]—73 hours versus 51 hours per week—than the rest of the population. See Bevolyn Williams-Harold, "Not All Channels Are in Color," *Black Enterprise*, December 2000, p. 38. For a more developed and nuanced discussion of the significance of black aesthetics, autonomy, control, and decision-making ability within the film industry, see Tommy L. Lott, "A No-Theory Theory of Contemporary Black Cinema," *Black American Literature Forum* 25, no. 2 (summer 1991), pp. 221–36; Reid, *Redefining Black Film*; and S. Craig Watkins, *Representing: Hip Hop Culture and the Production of Black Cinema* (Chicago: University of Chicago Press, 1998). Finally, with regard to radio, it is important to consider the impact of monies dispensed to influence airplay—i.e., payola—as well. On this point, see Fredric Dannen, *Hit Men: Power Brokers and Fast Money inside the Music Business* (1991; reprint, London: Helter Skelter, 2002).

24. I have combined statements Mayfield made in two separate interviews. Ironically, perhaps, Mayfield later convinced Pop Staples of the gospel group the Staple Singers to participate in the recording "Let's Do It Again" (for the soundtrack of the movie of the same name) despite his, i.e., Staples's, resistance to contributing to a song that was so clearly secular and salacious. Notes Bill Withers regarding his refusal to do movie soundtracks during this period, "Offers were popping up left and right but my attitude was that the last thing the world needs is another *Mack*." See Craig Werner, "Curtis Mayfield," *Goldmine*, July 4, 1997, pp. 129–30; Anthony DeCurtis, "The Soul of Soul—1942–1999," *Rolling Stone*, February 3, 2000, p. 52; "Criticism Mounts over Superfly," *Jet*, September 28, 1972, p. 55; and David Ritz, liner notes, *The Best of Bill Withers* (Columbia/Legacy 2000).

25. Regarding some of these controversies, see Alice Walker, *The Same River Twice: Honoring the Difficult: A Meditation on Life, Spirit, Art, and the Making of the Film "The Color Purple," Ten Years Later* (New York: Scribner, 1996). The first African American woman to helm a studio film was Darnell Martin, who directed *I Like

It Like That (Columbia TriStar 1994). It is worth noting that one of the recordings commonly cited as evidence of hip-hop's political potential, Grandmaster Flash and the Furious Five's 1982 release "The Message," was resisted by the group's members. As Melle Mel, one of the group's main rappers, recalls, "The Sugarhill Gang was supposed to do 'The Message.' They didn't want to do it. I didn't want to do it. Nobody wanted to do it." Similarly, Billy Paul and the O'Jays often resisted recording the songs written for them by Leon Huff and Kenny Gamble. See William Shaw, "A Bronx Tale," *Details*, November 1998, p. 195; John A. Jackson, *House on Fire: The Rise and Fall of Philadelphia Soul* (New York: Oxford University Press, 2004), p. 127; and interview with Kenny Gamble, *BET Tonight with Ed Gordon*, April 8, 2002.

26. See Sally A. Edwards, "The Roots," *Blag* 2, no. 2 (spring 2005), p. 74; and Bettina Funcke, "Displaced Struggles," *Artforum*, March 2007, p. 285. Regarding workshops, I am thinking of musical examples such as Horace Tapscott's Pan Afrikan Peoples Orchestra, and the soul- and hip-hop-oriented Soulquarians led by ?uestlove; Robin Harris's Los Angeles–based Comedy Act Theater; and film collectives such as the UCLA School of the 1970s (including Julie Dash, Charles Burnett, Haile Geraima, and Jamaa Fanaka) and the United Kingdom–based Black Audio Film Collective, Sankofa, Retake, and Ceddo. Regarding live performances, it is interesting to note that the rise and fall of the black band—again, outside the jazz idiom—corresponds to the advent of the extended concert as a forum for expression, digression, and exploration for the self-contained musical collective. In other words, the package tour format, featuring a large number of acts playing short sets on the chitlin' circuit (e.g., the Apollo, Howard, Royal, and Regal theatres) was displaced during the late sixties and early seventies as the rock concert and jazz models became hegemonic and bands such as Earth, Wind & Fire, Parliament Funkadelic, War, Rufus, Santana, and the Isley Brothers, began playing extended sets (with perhaps one or two opening acts). The eclipse of the black band can be traced to the reemergence during the disco era—with Chic standing in this respect as a significant transitional presence—of the track date (solo vocalists singing over prerecorded tracks) and the package tour concept characteristic of 1980s hip-hop and R & B (e.g., the Fresh Fest tours). With regard to the question of the relationship between technology and artistry, the advent of commercial radio playing recorded music was interpreted as a threat by live musicians (and their unions, which organized strikes to increase royalty payments as a means of compensating for income lost from live radio sessions) and sheet music publishers, as consumers shifted their focus from playing the top hits at home on the piano to listening to others play them (at first live and then in a recorded form) on the radio.

27. The original seven-inch release of Double Exposure's "Ten Percent" had a running time of three minutes and five seconds; Walter Gibbons's twelve-inch remix was nine minutes and forty-two seconds long. Before "Ten Percent," the only available twelve-inch records were made for promotional purposes, not for retail. Twelve-inch singles, because of their wider grooves, also allowed for better sound quality and reproduction (they did cost, though, roughly three times the price of a seven-

inch single). Another dimension of this struggle was the question of packaging: would twelve-inch singles have artwork, including representations or photos of the artist featured? In this regard, it is important to note that in the United Kingdom, in contrast to the United States, seven-inch/45 rpm records often featured artist-specific artwork (and b-sides recorded specifically for the single and unavailable on any long-playing album; indeed, both sides of British singles were often unavailable on 33 rpm releases, except for subsequent compilations). Regarding album artwork, see Paul Gilroy, "Wearing Your Art on Your Sleeve: Notes towards a Diaspora History of Black Ephemera," in *Small Acts: Thoughts on the Politics of Black Cultures* (London: Serpent's Tail, 1993), pp. 239–40; and Pablo Yglesias, "Cookin' with Heat," *Waxpoetics* 12 (spring 2005), pp. 132–40. In this context, the brand loyalty a (visible) record label might enable and nurture—e.g., the visceral, affective response one might develop over time in response to seeing the Motown, Hi, Philadelphia International, Island/Mango, or Joe Gibbs labels spinning on a turntable—would be reduced by cassettes' and then compact discs' supplanting of vinyl. With the advent of iPods and MP3s, of course, this artwork has become even more insignificant and, in many cases, nonexistent.

28. The advent of downloads has further transformed the music industry. The Atlanta-based group D4L reached the top of the popular music charts in early 2006 with the "snap" music–influenced "Laffy Taffy." The song set the record for the number of sales via download in a week (175,000). D4L's album, though, *Down 4 Life* (Dee Money/Asylum/Atlantic 2005) would sell at a much slower pace (230,000 by January 2006). See Kelefa Sanneh, "'Laffy Taffy': So Light, So Sugary, So Downloadable," *New York Times*, January 12, 2006.

29. On this point, see Angela Y. Davis, *Abolition Democracy: Beyond Empire, Prisons, and Torture* (New York: Seven Stories, 2005); and Ruth Wilson Gilmore, *Golden Gulag: Prisons, Surplus, Crisis, and Opposition in Globalizing California* (Berkeley: University of California Press, 2007). For further ruminations on the perceived disposability and dispensability of African Americans, see Derrick Bell, "The Space Traders," in *Faces at the Bottom of the Well: The Permanence of Racism* (New York: Basic Books, 1992), pp. 158–94; and Trey Ellis's rendering of Bell's speculative fiction, as directed by Reginald Hudlin, in *Cosmic Slop* (HBO 1994).

30. See Quentin Skinner, "A Reply to My Critics," in *Meaning and Context: Quentin Skinner and His Critics*, James Tully, ed. (Princeton, N.J.: Princeton University Press, 1988); and *Visions of Politics* (Cambridge: Cambridge University Press, 2002), for a discussion of the concept of "problem space."

31. Kodwo Eshun, *More Brilliant Than the Sun: Adventures in Sonic Fiction* (London: Quartet Books, 1998), p. ii. Indeed, following Eshun's lead, the sonic adventures pursued by groups such as Public Enemy (i.e., the Bomb Squad) and later many of the artists in the drum and bass, garage, grime, and broken beat genres have fruitfully disrespected the purist aesthetics that defined earlier eras concerning the proper definition of a "musician."

32. Pro Tools technology, for instance, allows musicians to record their tracks at home and send them elsewhere to be mixed with other separately recorded tracks. It also

reduces the need for large recording studios and the associated costs. Regarding the shifting approach to the use of synthesizers in the work of the Ìsleys and Stevie Wonder, it is worth noting that their respective sounds began to change after they stopped working with programmers and producers Malcolm Cecil and Robert Margouleff. In the same period, Carlton Barrett, the drummer for Bob Marley and the Wailers, would object to the first known use of a drum machine in the reggae idiom for the recording "Waiting in Vain." As one participant in the studio sessions taking place in London in 1977 recalls, on learning that his drum track had been replaced, Barrett exclaimed, "I hope this fucking machine isn't taking my place. Why will I come and play live if a machine comes to play for me?" The reliance on the drum machine would, of course, be one of the signature markers of the turn to "dancehall" music in the early 1980s. Quoted in Vivien Goldman, *The Book of Exodus: The Making and Meaning of Bob Marley and the Wailers' Album of the Century* (New York: Three Rivers Press, 2006), p. 238. For one of the earliest uses of the drum machine in R & B, see Sly and the Family Stone, "Family Affair" (*There's a Riot Goin' On*, Epic 1971).

33. The Toronto-based Crew-Cuts earned the first rock 'n' roll number one in 1954 with their version of a record by the South Bronx natives the Chords that was reportedly inspired by the possibility of nuclear war between the United States and the Soviet Union. "Coming out of Canada," Pat Barrett of the Crew-Cuts suggests, "we weren't aware of racial problems." See Fred Dellar, "Time Machine: This Month in 1954," *Mojo*, September 2004, pp. 36–37. For an engaging consideration of the legal and commercial possibilities enabled by the deployment of slavery as a metaphor, see Stephen M. Best, *The Fugitive's Properties: Law and the Poetics of Possession* (Chicago: University of Chicago Press, 2004).

34. For a more informed and comprehensive discussion of these issues, see Alexander G. Weheliye, *Phonographies: Grooves in Sonic Afro-Modernity* (Durham, N.C.: Duke University Press, 2005), pp. 19–45.

35. Regarding the origins of the use of sped-up samples, Mathematics, the Wu-Tang Clan's deejay and occasional coproducer, explains, "Well, originally, sampling machines only had but so much time, so you had to speed it [the sampled clip] up to get it in there." See Oliver Wang, "Wrath of the Math: Soul Talk with Wu-Tang Clan's Mathematics," *Waxpoetics* 13 (summer 2005), p. 24. It is interesting in this context to consider the changing speeds of Jamaican music in the postindependence period: the slower rhythms of 1970s reggae in comparison to the ska and rock steady of the early and mid-1960s, and the quicker paces of post-1980 dancehall.

36. By "every four years" rhythm I mean not just the literal predominance of presidential elections in the United States but also the naturalization of an African American political sensibility that focuses primarily on electoral politics and disengages from the political "rhythms" of grassroots mobilizations, other nations and geographical spaces, and political communities (e.g., the black diaspora). One might suggest that given the fact that forty-two of the current forty-three members of the Congressional Black Caucus are members of the House of

Representatives—and consequently up for election every two years—should dictate an "every two years" rhythm. In response, it should be remembered that the rates of incumbency among black House members are particularly high.

37. Michele Wallace, "Modernism, Postmodernism and the Problem of the Visual in Afro-American Culture," in *Out There: Marginalization and Contemporary Culture*, Russell Ferguson, Martha Grever, Trinh T. Minh-Ha, and Cornel West, eds. (Cambridge, Mass.: MIT Press, 1990), p. 41. With regard to the contemporary accessibility of mainstream theatre to nonwhites, see Margo Jefferson, "Will Theatre in Los Angeles Fade to White?" *New York Times*, August 7, 2005, sec. 2, pp. 5, 7.

38. "I purposely people my plays with fast-talking, quick-thinking black women," notes Pearl Cleage, "since the theatre is, for me, one of the few places where we have a chance to get an uninterrupted word in edgewise." See "Fast-Talking, Quick-Thinking Black Women," in Helen Krich Chinoy and Linda Walsh Jenkins, eds., *Women in American Theatre*, 3rd ed. (New York: Theatre Communications Group, 2006), p. 381.

39. Of course, the two strands of the DNA double helix are identical (except in their positioning); in my use of the term, they are related but not identical (i.e., related in the way the cultural and formally political realms are interlinked but distinct). "Hypochronicity" is the term for the opposite process: the tightening of the strands of the DNA double helix. There is of course another meaning that could be attributed to "hyperchronicity" related to the nickname given to a strain of marijuana ("the chronic").

40. Muddy Waters's "I Can't Be Satisfied," released in 1948, should also be cited in this context (especially for residents of Chicago's South Side). Kent was speaking at Chicago's Du Sable Museum on November 10, 2005.

41. Moten, *In The Break*, pp. 1–24.

42. Quoted in Carla Hay, "BET Announces Genre-Specific Spinoffs: Channels for Soul, Gospel, Hip-Hop May Lead to Increase in Video Production," *Billboard*, May 5, 2001, p. 4. See also Avis Thomas-Lester, "Black History and Ads Don't Mix, Activists Say," *Washington Post*, February 24, 2005, p. A1.

43. See R. Kelly, "You Remind Me of Something" (*R. Kelly*, Zomba/BMG 1995); Walter Benjamin, *Illuminations*; and Theodor Adorno, *Prisms* (London: Spearman, 1967). In 2004, 40 percent of the recordings in the top 20 charts made references to commercial products—cars, clothing, alcohol, etc.—and, with one exception, all of these songs were from the genres of rhythm and blues or hip-hop. See "McPimpin': Burger Giant Wants to Pay Rappers to Plug Big Macs," *Redeye*, April 1, 2005, pp. 12–13. Moreover, advertisers have often sought to employ those artists known precisely for their integrity and "authenticity." Accordingly, Mos Def, KRS-One, and Common have appeared in campaigns for Levi's, Sprite, Coca-Cola, Nike, and the Gap, which to varying degrees have espoused progressive values and blurred the line distinguishing commercialism and the promotion of an anti–status quo politics (e.g., making reference to the murder of Amadou Diallo, quoting Gil Scott-Heron's song "The Revolution Will Not Be Televised," and interpolating Eugene McDaniel's antiwar classic "Compared to What?"). On this point, and the resulting

complexities associated with the attempts to translate hip-hop's popularity into hard currency in the arenas of formal politics, see Felicia Williams, "Mos Def: From Here (Down Under) to Eternity," *Source*, November 1999, p. 180, and "Ear to the Street: Culture Shock," *Source*, March 2002, p. 63; Tony Ware, "Club Culture," *Urb*, October 2001, p. 161; Bakari Kitwana, *The Hip Hop Generation: Young Blacks and the Crisis in African-American Culture* (New York: Basic Books, 2002); and S. Craig Watkins, *Hip Hop Matters: Politics, Pop Culture, and the Struggle for the Soul of a Movement* (Boston: Beacon, 2005).

44. Although the most celebrated events took place virtually at the same time (i.e., Berlin and Mandela's release), it might be argued that the processes that led to the collapse of the Soviet Union helped set the boundaries for the discursive ending of apartheid. Regarding Cuba and the changes in its racial politics and significance, see Mark Sawyer, *Racial Politics in Post-revolutionary Cuba* (New York: Cambridge University Press, 2005); and consider the symbolic role the island plays in Perry Henzell's 1972 classic *The Harder They Come* starring Jimmy Cliff.

45. It is worth remembering that South African apartheid was modeled on American Jim Crow and the Canadian reservation system designed for the containment of indigenous peoples. In other words, apartheid is interesting, given the way that it conjoins colonialism and the specific characteristics of the American century.

46. See Gil Scott-Heron and Brian Jackson, *From South Africa to South Carolina* (Arista 1975); Kashif, "Botha Botha (The Apartheid Song)" (*Condition of the Heart*, Arista 1985); Stevie Wonder, "It's Wrong (Apartheid)" (*In Square Circle*, Motown 1985); Jeffrey Osborne, "Soweto" (*Emotional*, A&M 1986); Maze featuring Frankie Beverly, "Mandela" (*Silky Soul*, Warner Brothers 1989); *Malcolm X* (Warner Brothers 1992); and *Music from the Motion Picture Soundtrack Malcolm X* (40 Acres and a Mule/ Qwest/Reprise, 1992); as well as James Ingram, "Someday We'll All Be Free" (*It's Real*, Warner Brothers 1989), at the end of which he intones "South Africa," and Will Downing, "Come Together as One" (*Come Together as One*, Island 1989).

47. Generally speaking, the state-like institutions—the mechanisms developed in and by a state of exclusion—that existed within African American communities before the mid-1960s and that restricted the "airing of dirty laundry" were challenged by the possibility of integration and its potential to undermine their legitimacy, thus creating a context in which racial solidarities could be renegotiated and cultural actors might feel freer to express themselves with regard to previously taboo subjects. One can imagine that the process of decolonization in the Caribbean and the African continent involved a slightly different tendency: "civil society," its related counterpublics, and the outspokenness on the part of cultural actors came to be seen as normatively redundant and vulnerable to sanction by black majority governments, as they were during colonial rule. In this context, one might consider C. L. R. James's experiences in postcolonial Trinidad; Léopold Senghor's decision to ban Ousmane Sembène's 1976 film *Ceddo* because it might offend Senegal's Muslim population (as well as the problems Joseph Rai Ramaka faced with his 2001 release *Karmen*); Wole Soyinka's dealings with Nigeria's postindependence regimes; the imprisonment and attacks on Ngugi wa Thiong'o in Kenya; and

Thomas Mapfumo's experiences with both Ian Smith's government in the former Rhodesia and Robert Mugabe's administration in postcolonial Zimbabwe. In all instances, state authorities would be inclined to be suspicious of attempts to locate legitimacy in, or accord significance to, spaces outside the reach and control of the formal arenas of political exchange. On this point, see Grant Farred, "The Ellisonian Injunction: Discourse on a Lower Frequency," *Small Axe* 16 (September 2004), pp. 205–13.

48. "A lot of us are scared about this hip hop generation," media personality Tavis Smiley has observed. See "Tavis Talks," *africana.com*, April 25, 2001.

49. See Jean-Paul Sartre, *Anti-Semite and Jew* (New York: Schocken, 1948). Comparable to the panic and crises provoked by the arrival of hip-hop is perhaps the effect of the *ruud bwai* (ragamuffin) on Jamaican social discourse. On this point, see David Scott, *Refashioning Futures: Criticism after Postcoloniality* (Princeton, N.J.: Princeton University Press, 1999), pp. 219–20; and Deborah A. Thomas, *Modern Blackness: Nationalism, Globalization, and the Politics of Culture in Jamaica* (Durham, N.C.: Duke University Press, 2004).

50. Quoted in Greg Tate, "The King of Coonology: Spike Lee Mounts His Revenge on Black Hollywood," *Village Voice*, November 7, 2000, p. 57.

51. "The term 'hip-hop generation' [can be] used interchangeably with Black youth culture," suggests Bakari Kitwana. "No other term better defines this generation of Black youth, as the entire spectrum of Black youth (including college students and young professionals, as well as the urban masses) has come to identify with hip-hop's cadence." While there is a certain validity to Kitwana's claim, there is the risk of erasing other cultural practices and identities that cannot be collapsed into the category of hip-hop. See Kitwana, *The Hip Hop Generation*, p. xiii.

52. See Adolph Reed, *The Jesse Jackson Phenomenon: The Crisis of Purpose in Afro-American Politics* (New Haven, Conn.: Yale University Press, 1986), p. 44. The Elijah Cummings quotation is from Hamil Harris, "Upfront: Mel Watt Sets New Agenda as Chair of the CBC," *Crisis*, January–February 2005, p. 8.

53. Regarding this last point, the tensions that would develop between the worlds of hip-hop and gospel were rooted to some extent in the different religious orientations of the genres: the different normative and social trajectories implied by gospel's Christianity and the more overt Islamicities existent in hip-hop, whether of the Sunni, or Five Percent traditions (for example, consider the religious, cultural, and political trajectories of Benjamin Muhammad, formerly Chavis, and Conrad Tillard, formerly Muhammad). This tension, verging on hostility, was further aggravated by the relative amenability of the black churches—primarily the Baptist, Methodist, and Pentacostal faiths—to female participation, in comparison to the Muslim-affiliated faiths. In some respects, jazz has been separated from gospel by similar differences rooted in aggregate religious orientation and gender politics. On a separate point, it is interesting to note that increasingly political office seekers campaigning for support in black communities target not only churches, as is the tradition, but also the identifiable arenas associated with the "hip-hop generation."

54. Adolph Reed argues in response that Dawson's contrasting of the alternatives—a class-divided black polity versus the persistence of the linked fate phenomenon—overlooks the possibility that the latter's survival "may reflect not a mitigation of class consciousness but its expression as an ideology through which those very petit bourgeois strata enact the dominance of a particular definition of the scope and content of black political activity." See Michael Dawson, *Behind the Mule: Race and Class in African-American Politics* (Princeton, N.J.: Princeton University Press, 1994), p. 45; and Adolph Reed Jr., "The Jug and Its Content: A Perspective on Black American Political Development," in *Stirrings in the Jug: Black Politics in the Post-segregation Era* (Minneapolis: University of Minnesota Press, 1999), p. 46.

Chapter 5

1. Michel Foucault, "Governmentality," in *Power*, James D. Faubion, ed., Robert Hurley et al., trans. (New York: New Press, 1994), pp. 201, 211.
2. See Giorgio Agamben, *Homo Sacer: Sovereign Power and Bare Life*, Daniel Heller-Roazen, trans. (Stanford, Calif.: Stanford University Press, 1998), pp. 4–5; and *The State of Exception*, Kevin Atwell, trans. (Chicago: University of Chicago Press, 2005). For discussions of Agamben's revisions of Foucault's concept of biopolitics, see Matthew Calarco and Steven DeCaroli, eds., *Giorgio Agamben: Sovereignty and Life* (Stanford, Calif.: Stanford University Press, 2007).
3. Walter Mignolo, "Introduction: Coloniality of Power and Decolonial Thinking," *Cultural Studies* 21, nos. 2–3 (March–May 2007), p. 162.
4. "All manifestations of war and hostility that had been marginalized by a European imaginary," Mbembe observes, "find a place to reemerge in the colonies." See Achille Mbembe, "Necropolitics," *Public Culture* 15, no. 1 (2003), pp. 12, 25; Foucault, "Governmentality"; and *The History of Sexuality: An Introduction*, vol. 1, Robert Hurley, trans. (New York: Random House, 1978); and *Society Must Be Defended: Lectures at the Collège de France, 1975–76*, Mauro Bertani and Alessandro Fontana, eds., David Macey, trans. (New York: Picador, 2003); and Agamben, *Homo Sacer*.
5. I am not arguing that Mbembe means to criticize Foucault, and I might be treating him here as a bit of a hostile witness. Arguably, he is—in the earlier work—more interested in extending rather than critiquing Foucault. See Achille Mbembe, "The Banality of Power and the Aesthetics of Vulgarity in the Postcolony," *Public Culture* 4, no. 2 (spring 1992), pp. 1–30; and *On the Postcolony* (Berkeley: University of California Press, 2001). Regarding the repression of colonialism within modernity's hegemonic narratives, see Barnor Hesse, "Racialized Modernity: An Analytics of White Mythologies," *Ethnic and Racial Studies* 30, no. 4 (July 2007), pp. 643–63; and Michelle M. Wright, *Becoming Black: Creating Identity in the African Diaspora* (Durham, N.C.: Duke University Press, 2004).
6. On this point, see Mitchell Dean, "Foucault's Obsession with Western Modernity," *Thesis Eleven* 14 (1986); Homi Bhabha, *The Location of Culture* (London: Routledge, 1994), pp. 278–82, 352–67; Ann Laura Stoler, *Race and the Education of Desire: Foucault's History of Sexuality and the Colonial Order of Things* (Durham, N.C.: Duke University Press, 1995); and Walter D. Mignolo, "Post-occidental Reason: The Crisis

of Occidentalism and the Emergenc(y)e of Border Thinking," in *Local Histories/ Global Designs: Coloniality, Subaltern Knowledges, and Border Thinking* (Princeton, N.J.: Princeton University Press, 2000), pp. 93–126.

7. See Foucault, "Governmentality," pp. 212–14; *The History of Sexuality: An Introduction*, vol. 1; and *Society Must Be Defended*. For traces of Foucault's resistance to engaging coloniality substantively in the work of theorists who take up his concepts, see Andrew Barry, Thomas Osborne and Nikolas Rose, eds., *Foucault and Political Reason: Liberalism, Neo-liberalism and Governmentality* (London: UCL Press, 1996); Nikolas Rose, *Powers of Freedom: Reframing Political Thought* (New York: Cambridge University Press, 1999); Mitchell Dean, *Governmentality: Power and Rule in Modern Society* (London: Sage, 1999); and Thomas Lemke, "'The Birth of Bio-Politics': Michel Foucault's Lecture at the Collège de France on Neo-liberal Governmentality," *Economy and Society* 30, no. 2 (May 2001), pp. 190–207.

8. Bhabha, *The Location of Culture*, p. 281.

9. All governmentalities, then, are racial. For a range of approaches to this concept, see David Scott, "Colonial Governmentality," *Social Text* 43 (autumn 1995), p. 204; *Refashioning Futures: Criticism after Postcoloniality* (Princeton, N.J.: Princeton University Press, 1999); and "Political Rationalities of the Jamaican Modern," *Small Axe* 14 (September 2003), pp. 1–22; Roderick Ferguson, "Of Our Normative Strivings: African American Studies and the Histories of Sexuality," *Social Text* 84–85, nos. 3–4 (fall–winter 2005), pp. 85–100; and "'W. E. B. Du Bois': Biography of a Discourse," in *Next to the Color Line: Gender, Sexuality, and W. E. B. Du Bois*, Susan Gillman and Alys Eve Weinbaum, eds. (Minneapolis: University of Minnesota Press, 2007), pp. 269–68; Wendy Brown, *Regulating Aversion: Tolerance in the Age of Identity and Empire* (Princeton, N.J.: Princeton University Press, 2006); David Theo Goldberg, *The Racial State* (London: Blackwell, 2002); Lisa Lowe, "The Intimacies of Four Continents," in *Haunted by Empire: Geographies of Intimacy in North American History*, Ann Laura Stoler, ed. (Durham, N.C.: Duke University Press, 2006), pp. 191–212; and David Kazanjian, "Racial Governmentality: The African Colonization Movement," in *The Colonizing Trick: National Culture and Imperial Citizenship* (Minneapolis: University of Minnesota Press, 2003), pp. 89–138.

10. See Achilles Mbembe, "On the Postcolony: A Brief Response to Critics," *Qui Parle* 15, no. 2 (2005), p. 4; and *On the Postcolony*, pp. 24, 35–36.

11. Mbembe, *On the Postcolony*, p. 34. Drawing the distinction between the status of settler and native, Major Rice, a character in Lorraine Hansberry's *Les Blancs*, observes, "[A]uthority in this colony has always depended on the sacredness of a white life." See *Les Blancs: The Collected Last Plays of Lorraine Hansberry*, Robert Nemiroff, ed. (New York: Random House, 1972), p. 133.

12. Regarding failed states and rogue states, see Gerald B. Helman and Steven R. Ratner, "Anarchy Rules: Saving Failed States," *Foreign Policy* 89 (winter 1992–93), pp. 3–21; and Jacques Derrida, "The Last of the Rogue States: The 'Democracy to Come,' Opening in Two Turns," *South Atlantic Quarterly* 103, nos. 2–3 (spring–summer 2004), pp. 323–41. To this list one might add Loïc Wacquant's "carceral state." See

"Deadly Symbiosis: When Ghetto and Prison Meet and Mesh," *Punishment and Society* 3, no. 1 (2001), pp. 95–133. For a discussion of the duppy state's workings, see Public Enemy, "911 Is a Joke" (*Fear of a Black Planet,* Def Jam 1990); and the Wailers, "Duppy Conqueror" (*Burnin',* Island 1973).

13. Margaret Thatcher, of course, was tapping into an older tradition of coded and not-so-coded racist discourse in England with regard to nonwhite immigration. On this point, see Paul Gilroy, "'The Whisper Wakes, the Shudder Plays': 'Race,' Nation and Ethnic Absolutism," in *There Ain't No Black in the Union Jack: The Cultural Politics of Race and Nation* (1987; reprint, Chicago: University of Chicago Press, 1991), pp. 43–71; Stuart Hall, *Hard Road to Renewal: Thatcherism and the Crisis of the Left* (London: Verso, 1988); and E. H. H. Green, *Thatcher* (London: Hodder Arnold, 2006), pp. 131–38. With respect to the Left, it is worth noting the role delegates from the British, Canadian, South African, and American labor movements played at each other's conventions, exchanging tales about the threats posed by nonwhite labor (e.g., black, South Asian, East Asian, Mexican) and reinforcing the alignment of the international labor movement with white supremacist commitments. On this point, see Richard Iton, *Solidarity Blues: Race, Culture, and the American Left* (Chapel Hill: University of North Carolina Press, 2000), pp. 51–58.

14. "Western Europe did not have, until recently, any ethnicity at all," Hall suggests in a separate piece. "Or didn't recognize it had any. America has always had a series of ethnicities." See Stuart Hall, "Assembling the 1980s: The Deluge and After," in *Shades of Black: Assembling Black Arts in 1980s Britain*, David A. Bailey, Ian Baucom, and Sonia Boyce, eds. (Durham, N.C.: Duke University Press, 2005), p. 3; and "What Is This 'Black' in Black Popular Culture?" in *Stuart Hall: Critical Dialogues in Cultural Studies*, David Morley and Kuan-Hsing Chen, eds. (London: Routledge, 1996), p. 466; and, for a similar assessment, Claudia Jones, "The Caribbean Community in Britain," *Freedomways* 4, no. 3 (1964), p. 343. For a recontextualization of Britain's nonwhiteness, and the efforts to displace a domestic history of race, see Barnor Hesse, "Diasporicity: Black Britain's Post-colonial Formations," in *Un/settled Multiculturalisms: Diasporas, Entanglements, Transruptions* (New York: Zed, 2000), pp. 96–120.

15. To introduce race into American discourse is to risk apparently being labeled unpatriotic. At the Chicago staging in 2005 of the exhibit *Without Sanctuary: Lynching Photography in America*, there was a sign at the entrance to the hall stating: "We interpret difficult, unpleasant, or controversial issues not to embarrass, cause pain, or be unpatriotic but out of a responsibility to convey a fuller, more inclusive history."

16. Margaret Thatcher's abolition of the Greater London Council, after an election campaign in which she and her party had co-opted the xenophobic vote, and the late 1970s abandonment of New York City and its subsequent remaking—or, more accurately, Manhattan's remaking and the marginalization of the Bronx, Brooklyn, and the other boroughs—as an oasis for capital and Disney, reflected the broader stigmatization of cities and were in part responses to their potential to operate as spaces for crossracial, and possibly postracial, forms of politics and citizenship.

17. See Janine Brodie, "The Great Undoing: State Formation, Gender Politics, and Social Policy in Canada," in *Western Welfare in Decline: Globalization and Women's Poverty*, Catherine Kingfisher, ed. (Philadelphia: University of Pennsylvania Press, 2002), pp. 97–98.

18. On Clinton's misgivings about the legislation, see William Jefferson Clinton, *My Life* (New York: Knopf, 2004), pp. 720–21. For the background story on the deliberations within the Clinton administration, see Robert Pear, "Millions Affected: After the President Acts, More in Party Back Measure in House," *New York Times*, August 1, 1996, pp. A1, 8–11; and George Stephanopoulos, *All Too Human: A Political Education* (Boston: Little, Brown and Company, 1999), pp. 419–22. Regarding the role race played vis-à-vis Clinton's health care reform efforts, see Iton, "Beyond the Left II: Making the Public Good," in *Solidarity Blues*, pp. 146–82.

19. See Jason DeParle and Steven A. Holmes, "A War on Poverty Subtly Linked to Race," *New York Times*, December 26, 2000, p. A1. The legislation stipulated that in the future, legal immigrants would be denied access not only to TANF benefits but also food stamps and other Supplementary Security Income (SSI) programs (while giving states the option of denying these benefits to legal immigrants already in the recipient pool). Adults under the age of fifty were also prohibited from receiving food stamps for more than three months out of every year. With the abandonment of the national eligibility standards, states were empowered to determine for themselves who would be entitled to benefits (and their duration) as long as they did not exceed the two-years-at-a-time restriction (and the lifetime limits of five years total). States would be allowed to keep some recipients on the rolls for longer than two years (i.e., those falling in the "hardship" category).

20. Regarding the role racial considerations might have played in the design of American welfare state policy, see Michael K. Brown, *Race, Money, and the American Welfare State* (Ithaca, N.Y.: Cornell University Press, 1999); Michael Goldfield, *The Color of Politics: Race and the Mainsprings of American Politics* (New York: New Press, 1997); Iton, *Solidarity Blues*; Robert C. Lieberman, *Shifting the Color Line: Race and the American Welfare State* (Cambridge, Mass.: Harvard University Press, 1998); Gwendolyn Mink, *Welfare's End* (Ithaca, N.Y.: Cornell University Press, 1998); and Jill Quadagno, *The Color of Welfare: How Racism Undermined the War on Poverty* (New York: Oxford University Press, 1994).

21. Williamson had spoken sympathetically about the actions of black youths during the Rodney King riots, and Elders was dismissed because of hardly radical comments she made about the functional utility of masturbation. Regarding Clinton's actions with regard to Lani Guinier's nomination as assistant attorney general, see Steven A. Holmes, "Clinton's Record," *New York Times*, October 20, 1996, sec. 1, p. 16; and Jason DeParle and Steven A. Holmes, "A War on Poverty Subtly Linked to Race," *New York Times*, December 26, 2000, p. A25; Lani Guinier, *The Tyranny of the Majority: Fundamental Fairness in Representative Democracy* (New York: Free Press, 1994); and Clinton, *My Life*, pp. 523–24.

22. Katherine Tate, "Welfare Reform: Scrapping the System and Our Ideals," in *African Americans and the American Political System*, Lucius Barker, Mack H. Jones, and Katherine Tate, eds. (Upper Saddle River, N.J.: Prentice Hall, 1999), pp. 350–59.

23. The picture might be different at the state level, where smaller districts allow the possibility of majority black middle-class constituencies electing black representatives. That said, there is thus far no evidence of such dynamics. On this point, see Kerry L. Haynie, *African American Legislators in the American States* (New York: Columbia University Press, 2001), pp. 21–26. Regarding earlier responses by black elected officials to welfare reform proposals, see William L. Clay, *Just Permanent Interests: Black Americans in Congress, 1870–1991* (New York: Amistad Press, 1992), p. 291; and Ralph David Abernathy, *And the Walls Came Tumbling Down: An Autobiography* (New York: HarperPerennial, 1989), pp. 589–603.

24. The House legislation in question was HR 3734. See *Congressional Record*, July 17, 1996, pp. H7749–H7750; and July 31, 1996, pp. H9398, H9407–H9408, H9411–H9412.

25. See *Congressional Record*, July 17, 1996, p. H7755; July 31, 1996, pp. H9400, H9423.

26. Linking the issues of immigration and deservingness, Rangel stated, "Do not ask the child for its identification, and ask whether or not it is a citizen." Florida's Carrie Meek raised the issue of welfare fraud. See *Congressional Record*, July 17, 1996, pp. H7748, H7755; and July 31, 1996, pp. H9395–H9396. Two black Democrats in the House were missing in action during this debate: Tennessee's Harold Ford Jr. and New York's Floyd H. Flake. Ford, who had leadership ambitions and was seeking to establish himself as a moderate Democrat, would not likely have wanted to have to publicly oppose the position staked out by his CBC colleagues. Flake, a pastor in the African Methodist Episcopal church, similarly, tended to take centrist positions. The only black Democratic member of the House who voted in favor of the reform package was Sanford Bishop of Georgia, a "blue dog" (i.e., centrist) whose district was majority white. Ford's and Flake's reticence and the relatively mild support Bishop offered for the welfare proposals speak to black elected officials' understandable unwillingness to work out their differences in public. The two blacks in the Republican Party's caucus, Oklahoma's JC Watts and Gary Franks, who both represented white majority districts and did not feel any such restraints, both supported the changes. See Floyd H. Flake, "Gore's Achilles' Heel," *New York Times*, March 12, 2000, sec. 4, p. 15; and *Congressional Record*, July 31, 1996, p. H9421. The debate in the Senate, where again the Republicans constituted the majority, was not all that different. The arguments made by the one black member of the chamber, Illinois Democrat Carole Mosely-Braun, were quite similar to those of her counterparts in the House. Remarkably, New York's Daniel Patrick Moynihan, the author of the infamous Moynihan Report, was one of the leaders of the opposition to what would become PRWORA. See *Congressional Record*, August 1, 1996, pp. S9363–9364, S9366, S9380, S9383. For content analysis of the welfare reform debate, see Ange-Marie Hancock, *The Politics of Disgust: The Public Identity of the Welfare Queen* (New York: New York University Press, 2004). The final vote in the House was 328 to 101; the Democrats in the chamber split their votes evenly, 98 in favor and 98 against.

27. Michael Eric Dyson makes similar claims in *I May Not Get There with You: The True Martin Luther King Jr.* (New York: Free Press, 1999). See Tate, "Welfare Reform," pp. 353–54; and Marian Wright Edelman, "Taking a Stand," *Emerge*, June 1996, pp. 59–63.

28. Henderson's concern about welfare reform is clear—"Welfare is one of the most significant civil rights issues facing the nation today"; his uncertainty relates to whether the civil rights movement would see AFDC as one of its concerns. See Robert Pear, "Millions Affected: After the President Acts, More in Party Back Measure in House," *New York Times*, August 1, 1996, p. A9; and Wade Henderson, "Contract on Black America," *Emerge*, March 1995, pp. 50–51; and Alayna A. Gaines, "Coalition Politics," *Emerge*, October 1996, pp. 33, 36.

29. See Jesse Jackson, "Give the People a Vision," *New York Times Magazine*, March 18, 1976, p. 13; and Steven A. Holmes, "Clinton's Record," *New York Times*, October 20, 1996, sec. 1, p. 16. It is interesting to compare and contrast Jackson and King's respective class origins, trajectories, and identifications. Jackson, who was born to an unwed mother, in relative poverty, grew up to become the primary voice of the aspiring black middle class; King, who was born and raised among the old black middle class, would, as the civil rights movement unfolded, become explicitly engaged with the situation of the black poor, the poor in general, and the working classes (e.g., his involvement in the strike of the sanitation workers in Memphis). As late as 1977, Jackson equated abortion with slaveholding.

30. For a discussion of the ways American welfare programs have featured built-in racial discrimination, see Sanford F. Schram, "Contextualizing Racial Disparities in American Welfare Reform: Toward a New Poverty Research," *Perspectives on Politics* 3, no. 2 (June 2005), pp. 253–68.

31. See Tate, *Black Faces in the Mirror: African Americans and Their Representatives in the U.S. Congress* (Princeton, N.J.: Princeton University Press, 2003), pp. 94, 167; Tate, "Welfare Reform," p. 355; and Karlyn H. Bowman and Everett Carll Ladd, "Reforming Welfare," *Public Perspective* 4, no. 6 (September–October 1993), pp. 86–87.

32. See Angela Y. Davis, "Women in Prison," *Essence*, September 2000, p. 216. For a useful examination of the changing intersections of gender and race in the making of economic inequality see Michael B. Katz, Mark J. Stern, and Jamie J. Fader, "The New African American Inequality," *Journal of American History* 92, no. 1 (June 2005), pp. 75–108.

33. See Robert Pear, "Millions Affected: After the President Acts, More in Party Back Measure in House," *New York Times*, August 1, 1996, p. A9.

34. Kimberle Crenshaw, "Mapping the Margins: Intersectionality, Identity Politics, and Violence against Women of Color," *Stanford Law Review* 43 (July 1991), pp. 1241–99.

35. See Michael C. Dawson, *Behind the Mule: Race and Class in African-American Politics* (Princeton, N.J.: Princeton University Press, 1994), p. 45; Cathy J. Cohen, *The Boundaries of Blackness: AIDS and the Breakdown of Black Politics* (Chicago: University of Chicago Press, 1999), p. 36; and regarding the concept of boundary

work, Michèle Lamont, *Money, Morals, and Manners: The Culture of the French and the American Upper-Middle Class* (Chicago: University of Chicago Press, 1992).

36. Regarding the issue of black solidarity, see Tommie Shelby, *We Who Are Dark: The Philosophical Foundations of Black Solidarity* (Cambridge, Mass.: Harvard University Press, 2005); Eddie S. Glaude Jr., *Exodus! Religion, Race, and Nation in Early Nineteenth-Century Black America* (Chicago: University of Chicago Press, 2000); and Robert Gooding-Williams, "Politics, Racial Solidarity, *Exodus!*" *Journal of Speculative Philosophy* 18, no. 2 (2004), pp. 118–28.

37. See Mel Watkins, "Sexism, Racism and Black Women Writers," *New York Times Book Review*, June 15, 1986, pp. 35–37; and Robert Fleming, "John A. Williams: A Writer Beyond 'isms," *Black Issues Book Review*, July–August 2002, p. 48. For other readings of the gender politics underlying these changes in black literature, see Michele Wallace, *Black Macho and the Myth of the Superwoman* (New York: Dial, 1979); Ishmael Reed, *Reckless Eyeballing* (New York: St. Martin's Press, 1986); Darryl Pinckney, "Black Victims, Black Villains," *New York Review of Books*, January 29, 1987, pp. 17–20; Calvin C. Hernton, *The Sexual Mountain and Black Women Writers: Adventures in Sex, Literature and Real Life* (New York: Anchor, 1987); Stanley Crouch, "Aunt Medea: *Beloved* by Toni Morrison," *New Republic*, October 1987, pp. 38–43; and Alice Walker, *The Same River Twice: Honoring the Difficult: A Meditation on Life, Spirit, Art, and the Making of the Film "The Color Purple," Ten Years Later* (New York: Scribner, 1996).

38. See Spike Lee, *Spike Lee's Gotta Have It: Inside Guerrilla Filmmaking* (New York: Simon and Schuster, 1987), pp. 110, 114. The Taylor quotation is from the documentary *I'll Make Me a World* (Blackside 1999).

39. Mark A. Reid, *Redefining Black Film* (Berkeley: University of California Press, 1993), pp. 97–98.

40. Indeed, Lee was told by a representative of a potential funding source (the Film Fund) that his script was "sexist and problematic" before he began shooting, to which he responded: "I won't compromise my script. The film will not be sexist. . . . Their problem is that a MALE is doing a film like this." See Lee, *Spike Lee's Gotta Have It*, pp. 79, 137–38.

41. Clyde Taylor cites Lee's plot irresolutions as evidence of his deliberate engagement with "imperfect cinema." Suggests Lee, "There are certain things that I want the audience to do when it comes to the endings of my films. More often than not, I let the audience do some work." Clyde Taylor, *The Mask of Art: Breaking the Aesthetic Contract—Film and Literature* (Bloomington: Indiana University Press, 1998), pp. 267–70; Lee, *Spike Lee's Gotta Have It*, pp. 79, 86–87; and Spike Lee and Kaleem Aftab, *That's My Story and I'm Sticking to It* (New York: Norton, 2005), p. 298.

42. Contrary to Lee's intimation, one of the consistent traits in his work has been an inability to craft multidimensional, fully developed female characters (e.g., the flat female presences in *School Daze*, *Do the Right Thing*, *Mo' Better Blues*, *Girl 6*, and *She Hate Me*). Island Pictures, which distributed the completed film, asked Lee to rewrite the scene, but he refused. See Gary Dauphin, "(He Got) Game Plan,"

Village Voice, May 5, 1998, p. 51; Lee, *Spike Lee's Gotta Have It*, p. 132; and Lee and Aftab, *That's My Story*, pp. 40, 47–48.

43. Toni Cade Bambara, "Programming with School Daze," *Five for Five: The Films of Spike Lee* (New York: Stewart, Tabori and Chang, 1991), p. 50; Michele Wallace, "Doin' the Right Thing: Ten Years after *She's Gotta Have It*," in *Dark Designs and Visual Culture* (Durham, N.C.: Duke University Press, 2004), p. 402; and Terry McMillan, "Thoughts on She's Gotta Have It," *Five for Five: The Films of Spike Lee* (New York: Stewart, Tabori and Chang, 1991), pp. 19–29. In the spirit of full disclosure: when I first saw the film it had to be pointed out to me that a rape had occurred.

44. On this point, see Lee and Aftab, *That's My Story*, p. 90. On the degree of continuity between the disco and hip-hop aesthetics, see Jean Williams, "Soul Sauce: Quick Nat'l Reaction to Sugarhillers," *Billboard*, October 13, 1979, pp. 50, 52; and Fred Goodman, "The Adventures of Frankie Crocker on the Wheels of Steel," *Village Voice Rock & Roll Quarterly*, winter 1990, p. 17.

45. "She Watch Channel Zero," which criticized a female protagonist for watching too many soap operas on television, also reflected the broader gender animus underlying Public Enemy's project. If we consider the association between driving and masculinity, dancing and femininity, the following quotation from Ridenhour establishes further the gendered ambitions of Public Enemy: "We believed there were dance records, but there were also driving records. We knew that. . . . *Nation* would be more of a driving record. And beyond that a fighting record." Public Enemy recordings did create a bit of a conundrum when they were played in clubs: was one supposed to dance and, if so, with whom exactly? In this light, Rosie Perez's performance in the introduction to Spike Lee's *Do the Right Thing*, dancing and boxing to Public Enemy's "Fight the Power" was an ironic and powerful statement with significant gender subtexts. It is also worth noting that hip-hop artists, beginning with Run-DMC, but even more clearly Public Enemy, were less likely to be seen dancing in their promotional videos (the implication being that such movements, particularly in the area of the waist, were improper). See Oscar Cabarcas, "Hip Hop 101" *Source*, June 1997, p. 45; Brian Coleman, "Classic Material: Public Enemy's *It Takes a Nation of Millions to Hold Us Back* (Pt. 1)," *XXL*, April 2001, p. 172; Brian Coleman, "Classic Material: Public Enemy's *It Takes a Nation of Millions to Hold Us Back* (Pt. 2)," May 2001, p. 170; Chuck D, "Soul 2004: Feeding Them or Feeding Off Them?" *Elemental Magazine* 59, 2004, p. 82; Jesse Serwer, "Bomb the Suburbs," *Waxpoetics* 17 (June–July 2006), pp. 62–63; and Dzana Tsomondo, "Bum Rush the Show," *Cool'ehmag.com* 3 (July 2007).

46. Similarly, Byron Stingily, formerly of the Chicago house music trio Ten City, suggests, "Back when a lotta people sang falsetto it seemed to give a sensitivity and soulfulness to the songs—but nowadays people aren't into sensitivity. The attitude is 'I wanna take you and do it to you'—that real macho thing—and I guess falsetto doesn't really come across right—you know, 'Come here woman!' [in squeaky self-parody voice]." The depictions of rappers in the movie *Graffiti Bridge* reflect some of Prince's resentment toward the genre. *The Black Album*, which was recorded

in the late 1980s (but not released until 1994), most clearly reflected his bitterness (e.g., "2 Nigs United 4 West Compton"). See Pete Lewis, "High Intencity," *Soul CD* 1 (1992), p. 67; Richard Harrington, "Luther Vandross: Putting the Class in Classic Soul," *Washington Post*, July 3, 2005, p. D1 (italics added); and Ernest Hardy, "Home of the Brave: P.M. Dawn," in *Bloodbeats*, vol. 1, *Demos, Remixes and Extended Versions* (Washington, D.C.: Redbone Press, 2006), pp. 79–82.

47. See, for example, "I Can't Go to Sleep," on the Wu-Tang Clan's *The W* (Sony 2000), on which Isaac Hayes tells Coles/Ghostface, "Stop all this crying and be a man." The toneless insertions of West Coast hip-hop vocalist Nathaniel Dawayne "Nate Dogg" Hale are an appropriate signifier of the constraints under which vocalists must operate within rap. His voice allows no inflections, no melisma, and no possibility of emotional vulnerability. He in effect (and in reality) cannot sing.

48. It is in this broader system of meanings that Shahrazad Ali's 1989 publication *The Blackman's Guide to Understanding the Blackwoman*, advocating that black men were entitled to slap black women if they stepped out of line, found its mark, and that Naughty By Nature's Anthony "Treach" Criss memorably queered his patriarchal line in "Ghetto Bastard"—in reference to his missing-in-action father, he states, "[M]otherfuck the fag"—while highlighting class boundaries: "If you ain't been to the ghetto, don't ever come to the ghetto! Cause you wouldn't understand the ghetto, so stay the fuck out of the ghetto!" See Shahrazad Ali, *The Blackman's Guide to Understanding the Blackwoman* (Philadelphia: Civilized Publications, 1989); and Naughty by Nature, "Ghetto Bastard (aka Everything's Gonna Be Alright)" (*Naughty by Nature*, Tommy Boy 1991).

49. The fusion of hip-hop's genetic code with an R & B recording that is Aaron Hall's "Don't Be Afraid" replicates much of the casual misogyny characteristic of the rap genre. The track, produced by Public Enemy's Bomb Squad, originally appeared on the soundtrack for the film *Juice*, and while it is musically appealing, Hall's lyrics, when closely examined, sound like a rape narrative. See Aaron Hall, "Don't Be Afraid" (*Juice*, MCA 1992). Russell Simmons launched the OBR (Original Black Recordings) label (under the Def Jam umbrella) in the mid-1980s (as a precursor to the success of the Uptown label) featuring artists such as Alyson Williams, Chuck Stanley, Oran "Juice" Jones, the Black Flames, Tashan, Newkirk, and a revived Blue Magic. Although these artists produced a number of solid albums, the hip-hop aesthetics Simmons drew from were largely first- and second-generation rather than the third-generation sounds Harrell and his producers engaged toward the end of the decade. See, for instance, Oran "Juice" Jones, *Oran "Juice" Jones* (Def Jam 1986); Tashan, *Chasin' a Dream* (Def Jam 1986); Blue Magic, *From out of the Blue* (OBR/Def Jam 1989); and Alyson Williams, *Raw* (Def Jam 1989). Another important group with regard to the early makings of a rap/R & B divide is the Force MDs.

50. Paralleling developments in pop radio, adult-oriented R & B stations would appear (and, subsequently, R & B oldies formats). The most obvious example of this broader trend was the launching in 1994 of the nationally syndicated *Tom Joyner Show*, carried nationally by the ABC radio network. By the early 1990s, the vast majority of the R & B artists who had been popular in the 1970s and 1980s were

dropped by their record labels. Among the acts affected were Teddy Pendergrass, Ashford and Simpson, Stephanie Mills, Deniece Williams, Howard Hewitt (formerly of Shalamar), Patrice Rushen, Angela Bofill, Freddie Jackson, Gerald Alston (formerly of the Manhattans), Michael Cooper (of Confunkshun), Peabo Bryson, Earth, Wind & Fire, Jennifer Holliday, Shirley Murdock, James Ingram, Teena Marie, Alexander O'Neal, Cherrelle, and Jeffrey Osbourne (formerly of L.T.D.). A number of these acts reestablished their careers on independent labels, where they had to work with substantially smaller recording budgets (e.g., Cooper, Ingram, Jackson, O'Neal), as contemporary jazz singers (e.g., Osbourne, Bofill), or as gospel artists (e.g., Mills, Hewitt, Holliday, Murdock) as those domains became home for older R & B artists in exile. As a result of these trends, when the Temptations released the single "I'm Here," in 2000, they sent it anonymously to radio stations so as to circumvent the resistance they might receive at contemporary hip-hop/urban stations that would automatically reject a record by the name of the group (on account of their age). The song got significant airplay. See Sean Ross, "R & B Oldies Stations Grow Fast," *Billboard*, December 4, 1999, pp. 130, 132; Kristal Brent Zook, "It's His World," *Savoy*, February 2002, p. 82; Ashante Infantry, "United They Funk, Again," *Toronto Star*, June 20, 2000, p. D5; and the Temptations, "I'm Here" (*Ear-Resistable*, Motown 2000).

51. See Lisa Maher, "Reconstructing the Female Criminal: Women and Crack Cocaine," *Southern California Review of Law and Women's Studies* 2, no. 1 (1992), pp. 140–41; James Inciardi, "Kingrats, Chicken Heads, Slow Necks, Freaks, and Blood Suckers: A Glimpse at the Miami Sex for Crack Market," in *Crack Pipe as Pimp*, Mitchell S. Ratner, ed. (New York: Lexington Books, 1993); Michele Wallace, "*Boyz N the Hood* and *Jungle Fever*," in *Dark Designs and Visual Culture*, pp. 215–19; and Jamal Shabazz, *A Time before Crack* (New York: Powerhouse Books, 2005).

52. It is, of course, in Spike Lee's *Jungle Fever* that this spatial representation of the horrible is most apparent. In general in these films, the willingness to perform oral sex represents the line between "good" and "fallen" women. A second consequence of these developments was the displacement and reconfiguration of the pimp. The availability and influence of crack are seen as having dramatically transformed the sex trade, as the supply of services went up and the costs went down. In this context, the middle "man," the pimp, was cut out. Never one to remain idle, the pimp figure reemerged in black popular culture as a mythological presence (e.g., Bishop Don Magic Juan's roles in music videos and films). "Crack and the VCR and the public recorder came at the same time," notes Chris Rock (*In the Actor's Studio*, March 12, 2007). The advent of the crack trade also represented a change in the nature of street life in black communities where the public ramifications of this sort of drug use were most evident. "The people who used heroin," a respondent in a study of crack's effects recollects, "we'd be sitting there in the shooting galleries, nodding, talking politics, talking about music, the paper under our arms, and then all of [a] sudden these twitchy crackheads showed up, *and they looked dangerous*." Quoted in "Getting Better Amid Despair," *New York Times*, September 19, 1999, sec. 1, p. 46 (italics added).

53. Public Enemy, "Night of the Living Baseheads" (*It Takes a Nation of Millions to Hold Us Back,* Def Jam 1988). One of Chuck D's favorite groups, De La Soul, recorded the similarly themed "My Brother's a Basehead" (*De La Soul Is Dead,* Tommy Boy 1991). The emerging West Coast rap scene responded differently to these developments. Groups such as Niggaz Wit' Attitude (N.W.A.) celebrated aspects of the crack economy and their ability as hustlers and dealers to control the game and the women involved, and ward off any challengers. Within a decade, in certain circles, one's credibility as a hip-hop artist would be enhanced by having been a drug dealer (e.g., the Notorious B.I.G., Jay-Z, 50 Cent, the Clipse, and Rick Ross).

54. In the comic work of Dave Chappelle (*Killin' Them Softly,* HBO 2000), through the lens of the crack epidemic, the "ghetto" almost becomes another planet and addicts alien creatures.

55. I am quoting throughout from the text of the screenplay included in Spike Lee with Lisa Jones, *Uplift the Race: The Construction of School Daze* (New York: Simon and Schuster, 1988), pp. 273–78. In that draft, the Laurence Fishburne character is named Slice. In the actual film, the name is changed to Dap.

56. Lee with Jones, *Uplift the Race,* pp. 275–78. Amiri Baraka launched a protest campaign against Lee's *Malcolm X* project—in the form of the United Front to Preserve the Memory of Malcolm X and the Cultural Revolution—and suggested that Lee's middle-class aesthetic made him an inappropriate choice to helm the production. Baraka submitted a critical essay for Lee's *Five for Five* collection, which was refused (and subsequently published as "Spike Lee and the Commerce of Culture," in *Black American Cinema,* ed. Manthia Diawara [New York: Routledge, 1993]). These developments caused tensions, understandably, between Lee and Baraka's daughter, Lisa Jones (his "collaborator and sometime girlfriend"). See Lee and Aftab, *That's My Story,* pp. 142–44.

57. This scene echoes an exchange between Walter Lee Younger Jr. (Sidney Poitier) and "college boy" George Murchison (Louis Gossett Jr.) in *Raisin in the Sun* with regard to Murchison's supposedly "faggoty white shoes." A somewhat different moral economy is observable in John Singleton's 1991 directorial debut *Boyz 'n the Hood.* Laurence Fishburne appears in this film as Jason "Furious" Styles, the father of Tre (played by Cuba Gooding Jr.), and the moral authority the film accords him suggests an intertextual linkage to Fishburne's role in *School Daze* (the previous "black" movie in which he was featured). Here, Tre's mother is portrayed as incapable of raising her son and decides to hand him over to his father. Juxtaposed against Styles's parenting of his son is the situation of Tre's friends across the street, who are raised by a single mother, and the household in which a drug-addicted mother is too preoccupied to pay attention to her infant child wandering into the street. In a particularly disturbing exchange, Styles tells his son that he sees it as his job to watch out for him and that he, Tre, is lucky in contrast to his friends (Doughboy and Ricky, played by O'Shea "Ice Cube" Jackson and Morris Chestnut). The scene is remarkable because it features the supposed moral anchor of the picture stating that he believes he can logically and morally watch over his son yet not be concerned for the welfare of his son's friends (who are fatherless), a calculation that

even the movie's ending suggests is not the safest of bets (i.e., Tre's near involvement in a revenge shooting). The difference between the worlds created by Lee and Singleton is that while Lee tries to imagine a black community that is inclusive while ultimately failing, Singleton for the most part rejects solidarity as a worthwhile investment.

58. William Julius Wilson, *The Truly Disadvantaged: The Inner City, the Underclass, and Public Policy* (Chicago: University of Chicago Press, 1987), pp. 3, 7.

59. On this general theme, see Marshall Frady, *Jesse: The Life and Pilgrimage of Jesse Jackson* (New York: Random House, 1996), p. 83; Kweisi Mfume with Ron Stodghill II, *No Free Ride: From the Mean Streets to the Mainstream* (New York: Ballantine, 1996), p. 56; Coleman Young with Lonnie Wheeler, *Hard Stuff: The Autobiography of Coleman Young* (New York: Viking, 1994), pp. 143–44; Felicia R. Lee, "Lost and Found in Lackawanna," *New York Times*, February 6, 2005, sec. 13, p. 15; and Randall Kenan, *Walking on Water: Black American Lives at the Turn of the Twenty-first Century* (New York: Knopf, 1999), p. 364.

60. See Bhabha, *The Location of Culture*, p. 88; and Michael Kammen, *Mystic Chords of Memory* (New York: Vintage, 1991), p. 688. Svetlana Boym writes, "Nostalgia (from *nostos*—return home, and *algia*—longing) is a longing for a home that no longer exists or has ever existed." See Svetlana Boym, *The Future of Nostalgia* (New York: Basic Books, 2001), p. xiii. In this light, we might want to consider the various African socialist reconstructions of the postcolonial era that sought to establish a past for the newly independent countries of the continent that was both "African" and compatible with the "modern" demands of socialism (and, in most cases, Soviet patronage) in an attempt to reassure constituencies that the future would not be all that foreign. With time, of course, the scenarios offered by Léopold Senghor, Julius Nyerere, Amilcar Cabral, and others—that traditional "Africa" was naturally and originally socialist—were rendered less useful by the real challenges facing those societies. See Julius K. Nyerere, *Ujamaa—The Basis of African Socialism* (Newark: Jihad Productions, 1962); Léopold Senghor, *On African Socialism* (New York: Praeger, 1964); Amilcar Cabral, *Return to the Source* (New York: Monthly Review Press, 1974); and Marina and David Ottaway, *Afro-Communism* (New York: Africana, 1986), p. 19.

61. See Gerald Early, "Understanding Afrocentrism," *Civilization*, July–August 1995, pp. 33, 39; Adolph Reed Jr., "Dangerous Dreams: Black Boomers Wax Nostalgic for the Days of Jim Crow," *Village Voice*, April 16, 1996, pp. 24, 27; Harold Cruse, *Plural but Equal: A Critical Study of Blacks and Minorities and America's Plural Society* (New York: Morrow, 1987); Clifton Taulbert, *Once upon a Time When We Were Colored* (Tulsa: Council Oak Books, 1989); and Henry Louis Gates Jr., *Colored People: A Memoir* (New York: Vintage, 1994); the 1997 film *Eve's Bayou*; and the 1998 television movie *The Wedding*. *Idlewild*, the 2006 release starring the members of OutKast, named after a popular black middle-class resort in Michigan but set in Prohibition-era Georgia, offered no hint that Jim Crow existed (an impression underlined by the ability of one of the lead characters to book a first-class train ticket from Georgia to Chicago without having to ride in the segregated section).

For a distinctly different sort of memory work, see Richard Pryor's "Bicentennial Nigger" and Gil Scott-Heron's "Bicentennial Blues," both released in 1976.

62. For the record, Henry Louis Gates Jr. suggests, "What hurts me most about the glorious black awakening of the late sixties and early seventies is that we lost our sense of humor." See Gates, *Colored People*, p. xvi; Adolph Reed Jr., ed., "What's Left: An Exchange," in *Race, Politics and Culture: Critical Essays on the Radicalism of the 1960's* (Westport, Conn.: Greenwood Press, 1986), p. 246.

63. See Nelson George, *The Death of Rhythm and Blues* (New York: Pantheon, 1988), pp. xii, 2; Henry Louis Gates Jr., "The Two Nations of Black America; Interview: Cornel West," www-c.pbs.org/wgbh/pages/frontline/shows/race/interviews/west.html, posted in February 1998; Robert C. Smith, *We Have No Leaders: African Americans in the Post–Civil Rights Era* (Albany: State University of New York Press, 1996), p. 32; Mfume with Stodghill, *No Free Ride*, p. 147. Regarding the general impact of the Vietnam War on black communities, see Clyde Taylor, *Vietnam and Black America: An Anthology of Protest and Resistance* (Garden City, N.Y.: Anchor Press, 1973); Wallace Terry, ed., *Bloods: An Oral History of the Vietnam War* (New York: Random House, 1984); Marvin Gaye, *What's Going On* (Motown 1971); Curtis Mayfield, *Back to the World* (Curtom/Buddah 1973); Stevie Wonder, "Frontline" (*Original Musiquarium I*, Motown 1982); the music compilations *Soldier's Sad Story: Vietnam through the Eyes of Black America, 1966 to 1973* (Kent 2004); and *Does Anyone Know I'm Here? Vietnam through the Eyes of Black America, 1962 to 1972* (Kent 2005); and the Hughes Brothers' movie *Dead Presidents* (Buena Vista 1995).

64. Art n' Soul, "Touch of Soul" (*Touch of Soul*, Big Beat/Atlantic 1996). Levert's "Good Ol' Days" (*For Real Tho'*, Atlantic 1993) trades on the same sentiments.

65. See *Waxpoetics* 10 (fall 2004), p. 59; and James Brown, *Revolution of the Mind: Live at the Apollo Volume III* (Polydor 1971). The cover photo was taken, of course, during the period when Brown was not processing his hair.

66. See A Tribe Called Quest, "Footprints" (*People's Instinctive Travels and the Paths of Rhythm*, Jive/RCA 1990); Pete Rock and C. L. Smooth, "Return of the Mecca" (*Mecca and the Soul Brother*, Elektra 1992); and Large Professor, "Hummin'" (*The New Groove: The Blue Note Remix Project*, Blue Note 1996). Allstate Insurance would use Adderley's "Walk Tall" (in an advertisement featuring the actor Dennis Haysbert and a black multigenerational family playing softball). Another familiar nostalgic touchstone was Gladys Knight and the Pips' "Try to Remember / The Way We Were," which was sampled by the Wu-Tang Clan and later Lauryn Hill. See Gladys Knight and the Pips, "Try to Remember / The Way We Were" (*Soul Survivors: The Best of Gladys Knight and the Pips, 1973–1988*, Rhino 1990); *Anthology* (Motown 1995); the Wu-Tang Clan, "Can It Be All So Simple" (*Enter the Wu-Tang [36 Chambers]*, Loud RCA 1993); Lauryn Hill, "Ex-Factor" (*The Miseducation of Lauryn Hill*, Ruffhouse/Columbia 1998); Raekwon, "Can It Be All So Simple (Remix)" (*Only Built 4 Cuban Linx*, Loud 1995); and Sylvia Patterson, "Clan of the Titans," *New Musical Express*, November 11, 2000, p. 25. The introduction to the Knight recording was itself drawn from "Try to Remember" from the musical *The Fantasticks*; "The Way We Were" was a hit for Barbra Streisand from the

soundtrack for the 1973 movie of the same name. Other Knight references include Lyfe Jennings's "Goodbye" (*The Phoenix,* Sony Urban/Columbia 2006). Angie Stone has based most of her solo career on 1970s references: "No More Rain (In This Cloud)," "The Making of You," "Soul Insurance," and "I Wish I Didn't Miss You Anymore." With regard to the function of the cover record as a nostalgic strategy, see Angie Stone, *Black Diamond* (Arista 1999); Mary J. Blige, *My Life* (Uptown 1994), *Share My World* (MCA 1997), and *Mary* (MCA 1999); Faith, *Faith* (Bad Boy 1995), and *Keep the Faith* (Bad Boy 1998); the Fugees, *The Score* (Ruffhouse/Sony 1996); Aaliyah, *Age Ain't Nothing but a Number* (Blackground/Jive/BMG 1994); D'Angelo, *Brown Sugar* (EMI 1995), and *Voodoo* (Virgin 2000); Chico DeBarge, *Long Time No See* (Kedar/Universal 1997); Dru Hill, *Enter the Dru* (Island 1998); Big Bub, *Timeless* (Kedar/Universal 1997); and K-Ci and JoJo, *Love Always* (MCA 1997). Among the recordings that make explicit use of static are Black Star's "Thieves in the Night," Lauryn Hill's "The Miseducation of Lauryn Hill," Erykah Badu's "Tyrone" and "Green Eyes," and the Isley Brothers' "Speechless."

67. See Angela Davis quoted in "Discussion," in *Black Popular Culture,* Gina Dent, ed. (Seattle: Bay Press, 1992), p. 328; Me'Shell NdegéOcello, "I'm Digging You (Like an Old Soul Record)" (*Plantation Lullabies,* Maverick/Warners 1993); Greg Tate, "Future of the Funk," *Vibe,* December 1993–January 1994, p. 133; Ray Rogers, "The Passion of Me'Shell," *Out,* July 1996, pp. 56–59, 97–101; Joshua Redman, "Me and Me'Shell," *Jazziz,* April 1997, pp. 47–49, 76; Rebecca Walker, "Have No Fear," *Vibe,* May 1997, pp. 80–83; and Ernest Hardy, "Darkness Audible: An Interview with Me'Shell NdegéOcello," *Los Angeles Weekly,* September 10–16, 1999, pp. 24–32; and "No Fear: Me'Shell NdegéOcello's *Peace* by Pieces," *Bloodbeats,* vol. 1, pp. 1–6. The Four Tops song NdegéOcello refers to was reconfigured by Jay-Z and Foxy Brown as "Ain't No Nigga" in 1996, and by Todd "Too Short" Shaw as "Ain't No Bitches" in 1999. In Mario Van Peebles's film *Panther* (1995), achieving gender equality within the Panther organization was cast as a simple matter of asking (with "the brothers" acceding immediately). The retroconstructions offered by organizations such as the Nation of Islam (perhaps most obviously at the Million Man March, with its attempt to "restore" black gender relations to their "proper" place) and the slightly milder versions found, for example, in the lyrics of Babyface's "Simple Days"—"Bring back those simple times of yesterday when a man was a man"— represented some of the sentiments underlying 1990s nostalgia for the 1970s. See Babyface, "Simple Days" (*The Day,* Epic 1996). Intriguing in this same context is Sandra St. Victor's romantic celebration of the Million Man March, "Chocolate" (*Mack Diva Saves the World,* Warner Brothers 1996), which sounds like a standard love song on first hearing (before the lyrics register).

68. See Brian Coleman, *Rakim Told Me: Hip-Hop Wax Facts, Straight from the Original Artists: The '80s* (Somerville, Mass.: Wax Facts Press, 2005), p. 79; and *Waxpoetics* 13 (summer 2005), p. 33.

69. See Mary Huhn, "Fresh As a Daisy: De La Soul from Three Feet Up," *Village Voice Rock & Roll Quarterly,* winter 1988, p. 15; "Watch Out" (*A.O.I.: Bionix,* Tommy Boy 2001); and *Now* [published in Toronto], October 19–25, 2000, p. 46.

70. Mary Pattillo, *Black Picket Fences: Privilege and Peril among the Black Middle Class* (Chicago: University of Chicago Press, 1999), p. 6.

71. On this point, see Colleen M. Heflin and Mary Pattillo, "Poverty in the Family: Race, Siblings, and Socioeconomic Heterogeneity," *Social Science Research* 35 (December 2006), pp. 804–22.

72. See Lloyd Bradley, "Pride and Prejudice," *Mojo*, November 1999, pp. 70–71; and Public Enemy, "Don't Believe the Hype" (*It Takes a Nation of Millions to Hold Us Back*).

73. See David Toop, *Rap Attack 2: African Rap to Global Hip Hop* (London: Serpent's Tail, 1992), p. 140; Bill Brewster and Frank Broughton, *Last Night a DJ Saved My Life: The History of the Disc Jockey* (New York: Grove Press, 2000), p. 234; Graham Bent, "Too Short," *Hip Hop Connection*, March 2001, pp. 33–34; Bonsu Thompson, "Born Again," *XXL*, July 2000, p. 120; Nelson George, *Buppies, B-Boys, Baps, and Bohoes* (New York: HarperPerennial, 1994), p. 95; Pattillo, *Black Picket Fences*, pp. 93, 119–20; and Sister Souljah, "Mary's World," *New Yorker*, October 11, 1999, p. 57. British grime MC Dylan Mills, aka Dizzee Rascal, observes, "Everybody wants to be ghetto but nobody wants to be poor." See Dizzee Rascal, "Fickle" (*Showtime*, XL Recordings/Beggars Group 2004). "I always hated the way [Dizzy Gillespie and Louis Armstrong] used to laugh and grin for the audiences. . . . I came from a different social and class background than both of them, and I'm from the Midwest, while both of them are from the South. So we look at white people a little differently," Miles Davis contends in *Miles: The Autobiography* (New York: Simon and Schuster, 1990), p. 83.

74. In John Sayles's 1984 release *Brother from Another Planet*, Tom Wright plays Sam, a black social worker employed in Harlem. At one point, one of the other characters finds out that Sam lives in suburban Englewood, New Jersey, chides him—"You let people know that?"—and implicitly questions his allegiances and authenticity. Similar dynamics are at play in Joe Brewster's film *The Keeper* (1996), in which Giancarlo Esposito plays a conflicted prison guard, alternately despising and identifying with the clientele he is paid to supervise. On this point, see Helen Williams, "The Black Social Workers' Dilemma," in *The Black Woman: An Anthology*, Toni Cade Bambara, ed. (1970; reprint, New York: Washington Square Press, 2005). Regarding the tensions embodied by the "middle man" as a signifier of the cross-pressured black middle class, see Mary Pattillo, *Black on the Block: The Politics of Race and Class in the City* (Chicago: University of Chicago Press, 2007).

75. See Coleman, *Rakim Told Me*, pp. 225, 234; and *Check the Technique: Liner Notes for Hip-Hop Junkies* (New York: Villard, 2007), pp. 73–91; and Noah Callahan-Bever, "Black Clouds," *XXL*, September 2002, pp. 166–67 (italics added).

76. Quoted in *Waxpoetics* 8 (spring 2004), p. 73. The statement was made at the Association for Theatre in Higher Education (ATHE) conference in Toronto, July 31, 2004. George "Sweet G" Godfrey, whose biggest hit would come in 1983 with "Games People Play," was also a social worker (as well as a deejay and manager at the pioneering hip-hop club Disco Fever).

77. Consider, for example, Paul Robeson's references to Harlem during the McCarthy era, when he was being criticized for lacking an organic connection to African

Americans: "I've got a home in that rock! . . . [I]t's so good to be back. For this is my community." See *Here I Stand* (Boston: Beacon Press, 1958), pp. 1–2.

78. See William "Upski" Wimsatt, "Upgrading Self," *Rap Pages*, December 1997, p. 60; Omar Dubois, "Surround Sound," *Trace* 54 (March–April 2005), p. 60; "Common Ground," *Chicago Tribune*, April 17, 2005, sec. 7, p. 5 (italics added); and Michael Cusenza, "Common: Rap for Real, Something You Feel," *Elemental Magazine* 6, no. 67 (2005), p. 60. Lynn's moniker was originally "Common Sense," but after another recording act claimed it had chosen the name first, he shortened his tag to "Common." For evidence of similar negotiations by other hip-hop artists, see Lola Ogunnaike, "West World: How Kanye West Went from Being a Nerdy Midwestern Kid with Braces to Become the Most Provocative Popstar in America," *Rolling Stone*, February 9, 2006, p. 44; Claude Grunitsky, "The Prophet," *Trace* 56 (July–August 2005), p. 94; and Lauryn Hill, "Every Ghetto, Every City" (*The Miseducation of Lauryn Hill*, Columbia/Ruffhouse 1998). The mothers of Lynn, Kanye West, and Talib Kweli Green have Ph.D.s.

79. "When I see them struggling, I think how I'm touchin' them," offers Common in "The People" (*Finding Forever*, Geffen 2007). See Dubois, "Surround Sound," p. 60; Kevin Le Gendre, "Sense and Sensitivity," *Echoes*, March 25–April 7, 2000, p. 28; Cusenza, "Common: Rap for Real, Something You Feel," p. 63; and Brendan Frederick, "Bridging the Gap," *Mass Appeal* 33, 2005, p. 47 (italics added). Regarding the political subtexts underlying Common's renegotiations of class and gender identity on his adventurous *Electric Circus* (MCA 2002) and the subsequent *BE* (MCA 2005), see Jonah Weiner, "Relationships: Thug Love," *New York Times*, February 20, 2005, sec. 2, p. 2; Jesús Triviño, "Common Ground," *Scratch*, May–June 2005, p. 60; Anslem Samuel, "Production Credit," *XXL*, June 2005, p. 144; and "Second Coming," *Redeye*, June 1, 2005, pp. 10–11.

80. Combs's mother, Janice, relates, "He [Melvin] was a man that was in the street— things like that happen. This [life on the street] was a new thing, maybe a few months. He worked for the Board of Ed and he drove a cab. He was a gambling man. Used to play pool and cards—he would go out to the Rhythm Club on 133rd Street. I never knew about the drugs stuff, because he always worked—he did it in between times." See Steven Daly, "The Player King," *Vanity Fair*, August 2000, p. 137.

81. See Scott Poulson-Bryant, "Puff Daddy," *Vibe*, September 1993, p. 96; Danyel Smith, "Tuff Love," *Vibe*, August 1995, p. 66; and Amy Linden, "Deep Cover," *Vibe*, June 2005, p. 132 (italics added). The photographer in question is Michael Lavine.

82. See Neil Drumming, "Get In Where You Fit In," *XXL*, November 2001, p. 68; "25 Years of Hip Hop on Wax," *Blues and Soul*, December 14–27, 2004, p. 37; and Voletta Wallace with Tremell MacKenzie, *Biggie: Voletta Wallace Remembers Her Son* (New York: Atria, 2005).

83. As John Jackson suggests, the "Harlemworld" created by Combs "represents everyday realities that few of the people in Harlem ever see or experience . . . [and] argues for a blackness based on a high class position, fancy cars, expensive clothes, and lush scenery." See David Kamp, "Puffy in Hot Water," *GQ*, August 1999, p. 142;

and John L. Jackson, *Harlemworld: Doing Race and Class in Contemporary Black America* (Chicago: University of Chicago Press, 2001), pp. 220–21. It is also worth noting that many of the black men who would manage record labels and artists' careers, and the marketing of hip-hop in general—for example, Fab Five Freddy, Russell Simmons, Damon Dash, Steve Stoute, Sean Combs—were products of the black middle classes, often educated in private schools with college degrees. The same was true for a number of the artists involved. Simmons and Dash have both—in an awkward fashion—sought to present themselves as true products of the proverbial ghetto. See Ed Gordon, "Phat Cat," *Savoy*, April 2003, p. 76; Craig Werner, *A Change Is Gonna Come: Music, Race, and the Soul of America* (New York: Plume, 1998), p. 260; Rashaun Hall, "The Last Word: A Q & A with Damon Dash," *Billboard*, November 8, 2003, p. 64; *Backstage* (Alliance/Atlantis 2000); *CB4* (Universal 1993); and Peter Stallybrass and Allon White, *The Politics and Poetics of Transgression* (Ithaca, N.Y.: Cornell University Press, 1993), pp. 5–6.

84. Chris Rock, *Bring the Pain* (Dreamworks 1996).

85. Mel Watkins, *On the Real Side: Laughing, Lying, and Signifying: The Underground Tradition of African-American Humor That Transformed American Culture, from Slavery to Richard Pryor* (New York: Touchstone, 1994), p. 35.

86. See Watkins, *On the Real Side*, pp. 480, 497; and Mikhail Bakhtin, *Rabelais and His World*, Helene Iswolsky, trans. (Cambridge, Mass.: MIT Press, 1968).

87. "If I really want to scare the hell out of my white friends," Cambridge joked in an effort to identify the limits of white liberalism, "I drive out to the suburb they live in and walk down their street slowly, carrying the real estate section of the *New York Times*." See Dempsey J. Travis, *The Life and Times of Redd Foxx* (Chicago: Urban Research Press, 1999), p. viii; Watkins, *On the Real Side*, p. 501; and Watkins, ed., *African American Humor: The Best Black Comedy from Slavery to Today* (Chicago: Lawrence Hill Books, 2002), p. 268. Malcolm Little, aka Malcolm X (aka "Detroit Red") and Jon Elroy Sanford, aka Redd Foxx (aka "Chicago Red"), were coworkers at Jimmy's Chicken Shack on Seventh Avenue in New York (waiter and busboy-dishwasher, respectively) and social acquaintances in the 1940s. It is interesting to consider Dave Chappelle's physical self-representations, given that in person—with regard to the ways he communicates with his eyes and contorts his body—he seems to be channeling the "coon" (Lincoln "Stepin Fetchit" Perry comes to mind). For the record, Chappelle claims his inspiration is Bugs Bunny; if we read the Warner Brothers rabbit as a darkie presence, though, the end result is the same.

88. Other descendants of Pryor would include Garrett Morris, Franklin Ajaye, Marsha Warfield, the Wayans brothers, Charlie Barnett, Martin Lawrence, Robin Harris, Bernie Mac, Thea Vidale, Steve Harvey, Eddie Griffin, Chris Tucker, Wanda Sykes, Cedric the Entertainer, and Mo'nique. See Dave Chappelle, interview with James Lipton, *In the Actor's Studio*, February 12, 2006. Of Pryor's successors, Martin Lawrence and Chappelle came the closest to Pryor in terms of their willingness to make themselves, and their personal lives, the subject of their material.

89. Regarding humor about welfare policy, see Dick Gregory with Robert Lipsyte, *Nigger: An Autobiography* (New York: Bantam, 1964), p. xi; Watkins, *African*

American Humor, p. 241; Watkins, *On the Real Side*, p. 502; and Jesse Jackson Jr.'s comments, *Congressional Record*, July 31, 1996, pp. H9407–9408.

90. Members of Public Enemy's Bomb Squad were also scheduled to work with Murphy on his musical efforts at one point. See Jason Lopeyre, "Louder Than Bombs: An Oral History of the Bomb Squad, Public Enemy's Production Machine," *Waxpoetics* 17 (June–July 2006), pp. 120–136; *Delirious* (Paramount 1983); and *Raw* (Paramount 1987). More broadly, in *Delirious*, Murphy tentatively engages formal politics in his response to a shout from the audience suggesting that "Reagonomics sucks"—"Now tell us something we don't know"—and celebrates the election of Harold Washington as mayor of Chicago but follows this brief digression with the comment "[R]acism isn't as bad as it used to be."

91. Spike Lee characterized the program as "very demeaning" and questioned Murphy's intentions: "I kind of scratch my head why Eddie Murphy's doing this because it shows no love for black people." Stanley Crouch called it "a third rate update of *Amos'n Andy*." Quoted in Jeff Z. Klein, "A New Neighborhood for the Black Sitcom," *New York Times*, August 27, 2000, sec. 2, p. 21.

92. See Chris Rock, *Rock This!* (New York: Hyperion, 1997), p. 34. The television show *Everybody Hates Chris* launched in the fall of 2005 provided some insight into Rock's childhood circumstances. Rock's discussions of his childhood home recall C. L. R. James's description of his grandfather in *Beyond a Boundary* (London: Stanley Paul, 1963), p. 17, as having "raised himself above the mass of poverty, dirt, ignorance and vice which in those far-off days surrounded the islands of black middle-class respectability like a sea ever threatening to engulf them."

93. See Eugene Robinson, "Classic Rock," *Code*, November 2000, p. 71. In a scene in *Head of State* (2003), Rock almost punches Robin Givens in the face, a gesture that makes its meaning by referring sympathetically to her troubled relationship with Mike Tyson.

94. As Peter Stallybrass and Allon White suggest, "[C]arnival often violently abuses and demonizes *weaker*, not stronger, social groups—women, ethnic and religious minorities, those who 'don't belong'—in a process of *displaced abjection*." Similarly, Victor Vich observes, with regard to Peruvian street performers, that while comedians have the potential to transgress, they can also "stress the acceptance of the modern project (and reproduce some of its discourses)." See Stallybrass and White, *The Politics and Poetics of Transgression*, p. 19; and Victor Vich, "Popular Capitalism and Subalternity: Street Comedians in Lima," *Social Text* 22, no. 4 (winter 2004), p. 48. Rock has characterized the 1996 audience as "a working class black crowd," but there are reasons to doubt that, given his decision to tape his next show at the Apollo in order to seek a blacker audience. See the interview with Chris Rock by his close friend Nelson George that is included as part of the bonus material in the 2002 DVD rerelease of *Bring the Pain* (Dream Works 1996 and 2002). Rock, *Rock This!* p. 18 (italics in original).

95. See Lynn Hirschberg, "How Black Comedy Got the Last Laugh," *New York Times Magazine*, September 3, 2000, p. 65; and Josh Wolk, "Chris Rock on Fire," *Entertainment Weekly*, March 19, 2004, p. 26.

96. In his conversation with Nelson George, Rock candidly admits that his career was not in the best of shape and that the HBO taping was perhaps his last chance to break through. See *Bring the Pain,* bonus material. "You ever hear Chris Rock?" a white policeman asks a *New York Times* reporter doing a story on racial profiling. "He does this thing: 'Guy says, I got a job, man!' Like he's proud. Well, [expletive], you supposed to have a job." Quoted in Jeffrey Goldberg, "The Color of Suspicion: How Cops Talk About Race," *New York Times Magazine,* June 20, 1999, p. 64. In the American version of *The Office,* broadcast in the spring of 2005, Rock's skit is similarly cited and mangled. In *First Time Felon* (HBO 1997) Delroy Lindo in the role of a boot camp officer delivers Rock's blacks-versus-niggers skit virtually verbatim to an inmate (played by Omar Epps).

97. Congressman Jesse Jackson Jr. proposes that, despite Rock's denials, inevitably Rock's performances had political ramifications: "Chris may claim that his comedy is not political, but certainly his comedy has political overtones and political implications. His comedy shows an astute awareness of contemporary political issues that one would not necessarily expect from a comedian." The bonus material on the *Bring the Pain* DVD features an endorsement of Rock's work by Stanley Crouch. See *Bring the Pain* bonus material (interview of Chris Rock by Nelson George); Jamie Malanowski, "Film: 'Not to Say This Is a Better Movie' than Beatty's . . ." *New York Times,* February 11, 2001, sec. 2, p. 27; and Jay A. Fernandez, "President Rock," *Savoy,* April 2003, p. 48. Rock appeared at a rally in Washington, D.C., on April 30, 2006, to call for American intervention in the Darfur region in the Sudan. It was the first time he participated in that sort of event.

98. Gregory with Lipsyte, *Nigger,* pp. i, v, 201.

99. One indicator of Pryor's politics was his insistence that he would only appear on *Saturday Night Live* if Gil Scott-Heron, his ex-wife Shelley, and the actor Thalmus Rasulala were invited as well. He hosted the December 13, 1975, broadcast of the show, and Scott-Heron performed his soon-to-be classic "Johannesburg" (and "A Lovely Day"). See *That Nigger's Crazy* (Reprise 1974); *Richard Pryor Live on the Sunset Strip* (Columbia 1983); John A. Williams and Dennis A. Williams, *If I Stop I'll Die: The Comedy and Tragedy of Richard Pryor* (New York: Thunder's Mouth Press, 1991), pp. 95–96; and Richard Pryor with Todd Gold, *Pryor Convictions and Other Life Sentences* (New York: Pantheon, 1995), p. 175. Dave Chappelle faced a similar dilemma some twenty-five years later and resolved it by withdrawing from his highly rated television show.

100. On *It Takes a Nation,* the members of Public Enemy use the word only once to characterize the attempts by prison guards to kill black inmates (the reference in "Black Steel in the Hour of Chaos" to an "anti-nigger machine"). See "Black Steel in the Hour of Chaos" (*It Takes a Nation of Millions to Hold Us Back*); Tracy Grant, "Eddie Griffin Takes on His Family's DysFunktion," *africana.com,* April 3, 2003; Regina R. Robertson, "The Africana Q&A: Paul Mooney," *africana.com,* February 12, 2004; Rock, *Rock This!* p. 20; and "I Loved the Show" (*Roll with the New,* Dreamworks 1997); Lola Ogunnaike, "The Comic-Strip Revolution Will Be Televised," *New York Times,* October 30, 2005, sec. 2, p. 29; Carl Van Vechten, *Nigger*

Heaven (New York: Grosset and Dunlap, 1926); *Pulp Fiction* (Miramax 1994); *Coach Carter* (Paramount 2005); Randall Kennedy, *Nigger: The Strange Career of a Troublesome Word* (New York: Pantheon, 2002); "Epithet 'Has Many Meanings,' A Harvard Professor Testifies," *New York Times*, June 8, 2006, sec. B, p. 1; Jabari Asim, *The N Word: Who Can Say It, Who Shouldn't, and Why* (Boston: Houghton Mifflin, 2007); A Tribe Called Quest, "Sucka Nigga" (*Midnight Marauders*, Jive/Zomba/BMG 1993); Mos Def featuring Q-Tip, "Mr. Nigga" (*Black on Both Sides*, Rawkus/Virgin/EMI 1999); and Donnie, "Beautiful Me" (*The Colored Section*, Giant Step 2002). Mooney suggests, "Richard [Pryor] said he would stop saying it because he didn't see any 'niggas' when he was in Africa. He did stop using it on stage, but he said it in private." Mooney decided, in November 2006, that he, too, would no longer use the word in his performances, after former *Seinfeld* star Michael Richards was taped using the word, celebrating the power of white male authority in public and reminiscing fondly about the practice of lynching.

101. While the ODB persona—"the insane court jester" as one magazine put it—was in many respects a creation staged by Jones, there were also signs that he was not quite at peace with the requirements of the job. In the fall of 1996, he attended a Day of Atonement ceremony led by Conrad Muhammad at the Nation of Islam's Mosque No. 7 in Harlem and declared "Ol' Dirty Bastard is dead, Osirus [a new name] lives!" After a two-year stay in prison on drug charges, Jones was diagnosed as schizophrenic at the Manhattan Psychiatric Center, an assessment that would explain his propensity for self-medicating and some of his more intriguing behavior in the period before he was found unconscious in a recording studio in midtown Manhattan in November 2004. See Valerie Burgher, "It Takes a Nation," *Village Voice*, October 1, 1996, p. 43; The Blackspot, "Shaolin Shadowboxing," *XXL*, August 1999, p. 108; and *XXL*, January–February 2004, pp. 129–30; Jaime Lowe, "Digging in the Dirt," *villagevoice.com*, March 21, 2005; and Linden, "Deep Cover," *Vibe*, June 2005, p. 138.

102. At another point in the issue, Rock writes, "How about Ol' Dirty Bastard . . . renaming himself 'Evil Ka-Nigger?'" Rock also appeared on ODB's second album, *Nigga Please* ("I'm in the wrong place at the wrong muthafuckin' time with the wrong muthafuckin' man!"). See Chris Rock, *Bigger and Blacker* (Dream Works/Universal 1999); Ol' Dirty Bastard featuring Chris Rock, "Recognize" (*Nigga Please*, Elektra 1999); Chris Rock, "On This Day in Hip Hop," *Vibe*, November 1999, p. 86; and Chris Rock, Jeff Stilson, and Ali LeRoi, "17 Questions," *Vibe*, November 1999, p. 200. In the film *Talk to Me* (2007), the relationship struck between the two leads—played by Don Cheadle and Chiwetel Ejiofor—advertised as a friendship seems, at points, closer to a form of classed exploitation.

103. Chris Rock, *Bigger and Blacker*. The same sentiments were expressed on another skit entitled "Taxes" on a previous album, *Born Suspect* (Atlantic 1991), which represents Rock at his most conservative (e.g., "Prisons"). In the interview with concert attendees that is included at the beginning of the *Never Scared* DVD, a black woman is recorded as saying, "As he [Rock] says, there's black folks and there's niggers. I think he's a very *progressive* black man" (italics added). It is hard to imagine a comedian who sincerely

does not consider himself as political including such a statement in his own DVD release. It is equally difficult to imagine any of Rock's peers (e.g., Dave Chappelle, Eddie Griffin, or Jerry Seinfeld for that matter) or predecessors (such as Pryor) choosing to include such material. To be fair, in *Head of State* (2003), which Rock cowrote, he plays a presidential candidate who proclaims at one point "God bless America and everyone else" and makes explicit reference to Haiti, "Africa," and Jamaica, in response to his opponent's line "God Bless America and no place else." He also mocks his own nativism in "The Ugly African American," *Vanity Fair*, July 2007, p. 152.

104. See Bill Stephney, "The Welfare Rap: Why Black Men Hate It," *New Republic*, September 16 and 23, 1996, pp. 11–12. Stephney had opposed the inclusion of Flavor Flav in Public Enemy because he thought he would distract from the group's mission. If we consider Flav's role as a comic foil and a source of ambiguity and undecidability within the group, it is not surprising that Stephney would seek to have him excluded. Chuck D insisted on his inclusion. It is hard in light of Rock and Stephney's rhetoric not to be reminded of the line Adolph Caesar's character made famous in Charles Fuller's *A Soldier's Play*: "The black race can't afford you no more. . . . One less fool for the race to be ashamed of." For evidence of hostility to welfare on the part of rap artists, see Beanie Sigel, "These United States," *Fader*, November 2004, p. 119; and Brendan Frederick, "Ghetto Tax Advocate," *Vibe*, April 2005, p. 76. In contrast, on "The Grain," Ghostface Killah rhymes, "Ghetto poodles, fingers sticky with cheese doodles, starving for a fifty cent bag of Oodles of Noodles. Neighborhood sick with it, Clinton 'bout to cut W.I.C., maybe one y'all rich rap niggas need to politic." W.I.C. is the acronym for the federal government's Special Supplemental Nutrition Program for Women, Infants and Children. See "The Grain" (*Supreme Clientele*, Sony 2000).

105. *Soul Food* (1997) represented a partial break from this pattern, as it managed to portray black economic diversity in a relatively inclusive manner. Mario Van Peebles recalls, "I had a dinner a couple of years ago [he is speaking in 2004] at my house. I called up John Singleton, Vondie Curtis-Hall, F. Gary Gray, Reginald Hudlin, all the directors du jour who could make it. And we talked till four in the morning. At a certain point, I said, 'Look around. Most of us knew our fathers, went to college, very few of us were in a gang—maybe one or two of us might want to front a little bit—but we don't get to make movies about folks like us. We're being told that we had to direct films about the dominant culture—which is great—or if we wanted to make films with folks of color, they had to pretty much be hip-hop comedies or shoot-'em-ups.'" See J. Hoberman, "Who's Your Daddy?" *villagevoice.com*, May 24, 2004; Emory Holmes III, "Honorable Mention," *Code*, November 2000, p. 31; Cynthia Fuchs, "Baadasssss!" *popmatters.com*, May, 28, 2004; Veronica Chambers, "Playing for Keeps," *Savoy*, October 2001, p. 51; and *BET Tonight with Tavis Smiley*, March 21, 2001.

106. Italics added. Asked to compare his work to that of his cousin Spike, Malcolm Lee contended, "I think our sensibility is similar—especially in his earlier films, with images of black people and how we're portraying like a black middle class with careers and such." See Akiba Solomon, "Who's the Man?" *One World* 5, no. 3 (1999), pp. 61–62; and *The Newshour with Jim Lehrer*, November 5, 1999, transcript.

107. George Curry, in an editorial in *Emerge*, argued for the importance of the struggle to maintain affirmative action: "This is the moral equivalent of the Selma-to-Montgomery, Ala., voting rights drive." See Toni Morrison, "The Talk of the Town," *New Yorker*, October 5, 1998, p. 32; Deborah Mathis, "The Clinton Legacy and Black America," *Savoy*, February 2001, p. 73; Steven A. Holmes, "Clinton's Record," *New York Times*, October 20, 1996, sec. 1, p. 16; Jason DeParle and Steven A. Holmes, "A War on Poverty Subtly Linked to Race," December 26, 2000, p. A25; Lynn Hirschberg, "How Black Comedy Got the Last Laugh," *New York Times Magazine*, September 3, 2000, p. 36; Charles Whitaker, "Affirmative Action's Last Stand," *Ebony*, July 2001, pp. 110–11, 114; George E. Curry, "The Real Conservative Agenda," *Emerge*, November 1999, p. 8; and Stephanopoulos, *All Too Human*, pp. 361–75. With regard to income maintenance policies, the actual effects of the abolition of AFDC are still being assessed. On this point, see William Julius Wilson and Andrew J. Cherlin, "The Real Test of Welfare Reform Still Lies Ahead," *New York Times*, July 13, 2001, p. A21; and Sanford F. Schram, "Contextualizing Racial Disparities in American Welfare Reform: Toward a New Poverty Research," *Perspectives on Politics* 3, no. 2 (June 2005), pp. 253, 263. For a global perspective on the roots and routes of welfare reform, see Catherine Kingfisher, "The Big Picture: Globalization, Neoliberalism, and the Feminization of Poverty," in *Western Welfare in Decline: Globalization and Women's Poverty*, Catherine Kingfisher, ed. (Philadelphia: University of Pennsylvania Press, 2002), p. 58; and Petrina Francis, "Gov't Developing 'Welfare to Work' Programme," *Jamaica Gleaner*, July 7, 2005, p. 1.

108. Subsequently, during the Bush administration, funds were devoted to the promotion of "healthy marriages" as part of the renewal of PRWORA. The combination of amendments introduced by Congress in the process of renewing PRWORA, and the Bush administration's additional requirements in 2006, mandated stricter work or work-training regulations. States failing to reduce their percentages of nonworking recipients, according to the new codes, would lose federal funding. The definition of "work" was also narrowed, and recipients' access to job training, mental health support, drug rehabilitation programs, and university education was limited. See Robert Pear, "New Rules Will Require States to Move Welfare Recipients to Work," *New York Times*, June 28, 2006, p. A14; and Amy Goldstein, "Welfare Changes a Burden to States," *Washington Post*, August 7, 2006, p. A1.

109. *New York Times*, April 4, 2001, p. C3. The address at the bottom of the advertisement was BET Holdings, Inc., One BET Plaza, 1990 W Place NW, Washington, DC 20018. With the support of a number of black surrogates including Johnson and former Atlanta mayor Andrew Young, Bill Clinton invoked his insider status to challenge the racial credentials of Barack Obama during the 2008 Democratic primary contests on behalf of his wife, Hillary Clinton.

110. *New York Times*, April 4, 2001, p. C3 (italics added).

111. See Jeffrey H. Birnbaum and Jonathan Weisman, "The 1% Split Over Estate Taxes," *Washington Post*, August 12, 2005, p. D1; and Carey Goldberg, "Working Hard, Doing Well, Less Than Excited About Bush's Tax Plan," *New York Times*, April

8, 2001, p. A16. Regarding Robert Johnson's background and racial politics, see Brett Pulley, *The Billion Dollar BET: Robert Johnson and the Inside Story of Black Entertainment Television* (New York: Wiley, 2004). During this period Johnson got involved in a public exchange with Aaron McGruder, the cartoonist responsible for *The Boondocks,* with McGruder arguing that Johnson did not "serve the interests of black people." Johnson, in response, stated, "[T]he 500 dedicated employees of BET do more in one day to serve the interests of African-Americans than this young man has done in his entire life." See John Simpkins, "The Equal-Opportunity Offender; Aaron McGruder's 'Boondocks' Is the Anti-'Family Circus,'" *New York Times Magazine,* June 24, 2001, p. 42. Johnson, along with Earl Graves and Jesse Jackson, did rise up against the possibility that federal set-aside programs might be abolished during the Clinton administration following the Adarand decision (*Adarand Constructors v. Pena* [93–1841], 515 U.S. 200 [1995]). On this point, see Stephanopoulos, *All Too Human,* pp. 367–73.

112. The estate tax is currently scheduled to decrease until 2010, when it will be abolished for one year and then restored to its original level. George Bush, in a July 2006 speech at the NAACP convention, made reference to Johnson and his support for the abolition of the estate tax: "One of my friends is Bob Johnson, founder of BET. He's an interesting man. He believes strongly in ownership. He has been a successful owner. He believes strongly, for example, that the death tax will prevent future African-American entrepreneurs from being able to pass their assets from one generation to the next. He and I also understand that the investor class shouldn't be just confined to the old definition of the investor class." Thus far, Congress has not voted for a permanent repeal of (or further reduction in) the estate tax. See Birnbaum and Weisman, "The 1% Split Over Estate Taxes," *Washington Post,* August 12, 2005, p. D1; and the full transcript of Bush's NAACP speech, www.whitehouse. gov; transcripts of the meeting of the President's Commission to Strengthen Social Security, Park Hyatt Washington, Washington, D.C., December 11, 2001, www.csss. gov, pp. 20, 23; Jonathan Chait, "Painted Black: Robert Johnson, W.'s Favorite Race Baiter," *New Republic,* August 27, 2001, p. 33; Paul Krugman, "Little Black Lies," *New York Times,* January 28, 2005, sec. 1, p. 23; and Edmund L. Andrews, "G.O.P. Courts Blacks and Hispanics on Social Security," *New York Times,* March 20, 2005, p. 21.

113. Cosby's most intriguing elaboration on Chris Rock's script was likely the odd, presumably anti-Muslim, reference to "Mohammed and all that crap." Regarding Cosby's intervention and the new prosperity gospel—e.g., Creflo Dollar—see "Black Education: The Cosby Debate," special issue, *Black Scholar* 34, no. 3 (winter 2004); Michael Eric Dyson, *Is Bill Cosby Right? Or Has the Black Middle Class Lost Its Mind?* (New York: Basic Civitas Books, 2005); Adam Nagourney, "The Post-Sharpton Sharpton," *New York Times Magazine,* March 18, 2001, p. 47; Kevin Gray, "Bring It On," *Details,* May 2001, p. 127; Jack Newfield, "Rev. Vs. Rev.," *New York,* January 7, 2002, p. 48; Tracy Grant, "Fire and Brimstone," *Black Issues Book Review,* September–October 2002, p. 35; *New York Times,* February 3, 2002, sec. 9, pp. 1–2; and Kevin Merida, "Bill Cosby Sparked a Debate: Will His Own Troubles Snuff It Out?" *Washington Post,* February 20, 2005, p. D1. Following from the kinds of his-

tories invoked by Robin D. G. Kelley in *Hammer and Hoe: Alabama Communists during the Great Depression* (Chapel Hill: University of North Carolina Press, 1990), I do not mean to suggest that religious commitments are inherently antagonistic to a class-engaged or radical politics.

114. Corporations also provided funds for individual CBC members and the organization as a whole, creating at least the appearance of a conflict of interest. For example, Tyson Foods, the meat-processing business, made a contribution to the Congressional Black Caucus Foundation at the same time a group of black maintenance workers was accusing it of discrimination at its operation in Ashland, Alabama. See Aina Hunter, "Chicken Money," *Village Voice*, September 23, 2005.

115. The CBC members who voted in favor of the estate tax repeal on April 13, 2005, were Sheila Jackson-Lee, Sanford Bishop, William Lacy Clay, Edolphus Towns, David Scott, G. K. Butterfield, Albert Wynn, and William Jefferson. Jefferson, Bishop, Scott, Harold Ford, Albert Wynn, Al Green, Artur Davis, Emanuel Cleaver, Gregory Meeks, and Kendrick Meek, voted in favor of raising the threshold for those seeking to declare bankruptcy. Members of the CBC individually spoke out against this proposal. Michigan's John Conyers argued the bill was "the most special interest-vested" measure he had ever encountered and contended that it would "tilt the playing field in favor of banks and credit card companies and against working people and their families." Melvin Watt (North Carolina) called the bill "irresponsible legislating at its worst." Los Angeles's Maxine Waters concurred: "[T]he passing of this bill would be a complete detriment to the American people.... [T]he main reasons Americans file for bankruptcy is not to abuse the system and avoid paying their bills. Americans file for bankruptcy usually due to catastrophic medical expenses, divorce, or the loss of their jobs." Sheila Jackson-Lee, who voted in favor of repealing the estate tax but against tightening the bankruptcy laws, suggested that the bill would "close the door to working and middle class persons." See *Congressional Record*, April 13, 2005, pp. H1925, H1931; and April 14, 2005, pp. H2049, H2052, H2054, H2060. Maryland's Wynn would almost lose his seat in 2006 in a Democratic primary challenge from the Left mounted by Donna Edwards, who would cite his support for the estate tax repeal and the bankruptcy law reform, as well as his environmental record and vote authorizing the war on Iraq, among other things, as evidence that he was not a "real Democrat." She defeated him two years later.

116. *Sidewalk Stories* (Island Pictures 1989) was written, directed, and produced by Charles Lane. The movie did not open widely and has yet to resurface in either video or DVD form. Lane subsequently directed *True Identity* (1991), featuring the British comic Lenny Henry and himself, and appeared as an actor in Mario Van Peebles's film *Posse* (1993).

117. See Babyface, "When Can I See You" (*For the Cool in You*, Epic 1993); the recordings by Tony Rich, Joe, Dakota Moon, Donnell Jones, and Intrigue, among others; and Nice and Smooth, "Sometimes I Rhyme Slow" (*Ain't a Damn Thing Changed*, Def Jam 1991).

118. See Isaac Hayes, "Bumpy's Lament" (*Shaft*, Stax 1971); Dr. Dre featuring Hittman, Kurupt, Nate Dogg and Six-Two, "Xxplosive" (*2001*, Interscope 1999); and *XXL*,

January–February 2001, p. 115. In his lyrics, Brown offers, "Gobble and swallow a nut up, shut up and get my cash." Asked if his rage was directed at his ex-fiancée (and rapper) Inga "Foxy Brown" Marchand, Brown replied, "It wasn't towards her, but she was a part of the spark off. It wasn't like, 'This is for you,' but she sparked it."

119. I am thinking here, for example, of Badu's playing with her image and particularly her hairstyles—the dreadlocks followed by the shaved head followed by the extreme Afro wig donned and doffed at random on stage—and the consistent engagement of the comedic in her recorded work and her videos. See Erykah Badu, "Bag Lady" and "Cleva" (*Mama's Gun*, Motown 2000). The CD single included two mixes, the "main version" and the "cheebah sac mix." The latter version featured a tempo similar to "Xxplosive." In an earlier exchange, Funkadelic's classic "Cosmic Slop" (*Cosmic Slop*, Westbound 1973), a surreal song about a welfare mother of five forced by circumstances to labor in the devil's employ would be revised in subsequent versions (e.g., on *Hardcore Jollies*, Warner Brothers 1976) with the interpolation of a line—"space children, universal love"—from Labelle's recording "Space Children" (*Nightbirds*, Epic 1975), a Nona Hendryx composition.

120. NdegéOcello's openness about her sexuality apparently made a number of artists nervous about working with her. She suggests that she asked Erykah Badu, Jill Scott, Maxwell, D'Angelo, and Musiq Soulchild to appear on her album *Cookie: The Anthropological Mixtape* (Maverick 2002), and they all declined. "Unfortunately," she would state, "a lot of people don't want to have a relationship with me cause I'm real." Taalib "Musiq Soulchild" Johnson would offer in his defense, "It was a decision that was made. I don't know who made it." Talib Kweli, Lalah Hathaway, Caron Wheeler, Rockwilder, Missy Elliott, Redman, and Tweet are featured on the disc. See Asali Solomon, "A Different World," *Vibe*, May 2002, p. 124.

121. The editorial "Close Ranks," published in the *Crisis* in July 1918 to encourage African American support for World War I, might be classified as falling in the tradition established by Du Bois's work in *The Philadelphia Negro*. See W. E. B. Du Bois, *The Philadelphia Negro* (Philadelphia: University of Pennsylvania Press, 1899); *The Souls of Black Folk* (Chicago: A. C. McClurg, 1903); and "Close Ranks," in *W. E. B. Du Bois: A Reader*, David Levering Lewis, ed. (New York: Holt, 1995), p. 697.

Chapter 6

1. Claude McKay, *Banjo: A Story without a Plot* (New York: Harper, 1929), p. 313. One significant exception to this pattern might be *Banana Bottom* (New York: Harper, 1933).

2. See Saidiya V. Hartman, *Scenes of Subjection: Terror, Slavery, and Self-Making in Nineteenth-Century America* (New York: Oxford University Press, 1997), pp. 6–7; Colin Palmer, *Eric Williams and the Making of the Modern Caribbean* (Chapel Hill: University of North Carolina Press, 2006), pp. 18, 33; Gerald Horne, *Red Sea: Ferdinand Smith and Radical Black Sailors in the United States and Jamaica* (New York: New York University Press, 2005), p. 235; Edward Said, *Orientalism* (London: Routledge and Kegan Paul, 1978), p. 227; and "Edward Said in Conversation with

Neeladri Bhattacharya, Suvir Kaul, and Ania Loomba," in *Relocating Postcolonialism*, David Theo Goldberg and Ato Quayson, eds. (Oxford: Blackwell, 2002), p. 2; and Ato Quayson, *Postcolonialism: Theory, Practice or Process?* (Cambridge: Polity Press, 2000), p. 9. Regarding the desirability and possibility of postnationality, see Iain Chambers, *Migrancy, Culture, Identity* (London: Routledge, 1994); Linda Basch, Nina Glick Schiller, and Cristina Szanton Blanc, *Nations Unbound* (Langhorne, Penn.: Gordon and Breach, 1994); and James Holston and Arjun Appadurai, "Cities and Citizenship," *Public Culture* 8 (1996), pp. 187–204.

3. See Michael George Hanchard, "Afro-modernity: Temporality, Politics, and the African Diaspora," *Public Culture* 11, no. 1 (1999), pp. 245–68. Regarding the false discontinuities of the postcolonial and the limits of national independence, see C. L. R. James, *Party Politics in the West Indies* (San Juan, Trinidad: Verdic Enterprises, 1962), p. 163; Partha Chatterjee, *Nationalist Thought in the Colonial World: A Derivative Discourse* (Minneapolis: University of Minnesota Press, 1993); and R. Radhakrishnan, "Globalization, Desire, and the Politics of Representation," *Comparative Literature* 53, no. 4 (autumn 2001), pp. 315–32. In this light, it is interesting to consider the United Kingdom's suggestion in response to legal claims raised by Mau Mau detainees against it in 2006 that any responsibility for state-sponsored atrocities during the "emergency" period (1952–61) shifted to Kenya when colonial rule formally ended and Kenya was granted independence.

4. See "Louis Armstrong, Barring Soviet Tour, Denounces Eisenhower and Gov. Faubus," *New York Times*, September 19, 1957, p. 23; Orlando Patterson, *Slavery and Social Death: A Comparative Study* (Cambridge, Mass.: Harvard University Press, 2005); and regarding the relationship between anarchism and anticolonialism, Benedict Anderson, *Under Three Flags: Anarchism and the Anti-colonial Imagination* (London: Verso, 2005).

5. As the term "diaspora" has become hegemonic, I am reluctant to propose an alternate referent at this point, despite the ways the metaphor does suggest and reinforce certain assumptions and conceptual shorthands. While physical dispersion and dislocation (i.e., from the "homeland") are often read as key markers of the diasporized, it is important to note, as Souleymane Bachir Diagne has observed, that dislocation—for instance in the form of alienation—need not involve physical displacement (i.e., one can be "moved" and "removed" without "traveling"). On this basis, continental Africans—and "Africa" itself, often cast as natural and static and consequently outside the diaspora—remain crucial to examinations of the diasporic. This is obviously the case if we also remember that the continent's populations have always been and continue to be externally and internally mobile (i.e., it is the continent of Africa that has the largest proportion of displaced peoples within its borders) and that forms of slavery displaced and traumatized millions who did not cross the Atlantic (particularly in western Africa). We might also think not only of the impossibility of settlement but more broadly of the illegitimacy of settlement, especially with regard to environmental concerns and the ways attempts to settle and any attendant land claims might contribute to the marginalization and erasure of indigenous peoples (for example, in the Americas).

6. In this context, it might be more accurate to suggest that a diaspora politics subsidizes not so much a "new maps" as much as a "no maps" perspective. For an excellent demonstration of the ways diaspora might work within a nation-state, see Jacqueline Nassy Brown, *Dropping Anchor, Setting Sail: Geographies of Race in Black Liverpool* (Princeton, N.J.: Princeton University Press, 2005). While my comments here focus on the importance of the local in the way we approach diasporic formations, it is also possible to think of the temporal dimensions of these geographical networks: old Liverpool versus new London; Salvador and Brasilia; Halifax and its relationship to black Montreal and Toronto; Kumasi and Accra; Detroit and Atlanta; Memphis and Los Angeles. We can also think of these linkages as not only classed but gendered, a point I will develop in the next chapter.

7. Similarly open to question would be the supposition that there are multiple or alternative modernities. There are a number of factors we might imagine as functioning to keep the colonized subject in her/his place: violence, acculturation, zombification (as Achille Mbembe has offered), laughter, isolation and an inability to imagine subaltern community, décalage (following Brent Hayes Edwards), and the various effects of the divide-and-conquer ethos (e.g., the inability to think across categories). As Ann Laura Stoler's work indicates, underscoring coloniality's conveniences, at times colonial missions favored miscegenation and at others sought to preserve and protect the sanctity of the white settler family. These changes in tactics and preferences should not be conflated with the eclipse of, or diminishing commitment to, coloniality but rather should be considered as illustrative of its anxieties and undecidabilities. See *Race and the Education of Desire: Foucault's History of Sexuality and the Colonial Order of Things* (Durham, N.C.: Duke University Press, 1995).

8. "Juxtapositivity" does not, in and of itself, require that critical theorizing follow. I should make clear here that it is not my intention to suggest that discrete colonial practices map cleanly onto national borders. A range of subordinative projects, traveling under different names, can be imagined as operating within the same national boundaries (and within the same temporal frame). The United States is a good example of this possibility, given its combination of Jim Crow, reservations, and de facto segregations.

9. I have emphasized here just three of the opportunities diaspora makes available or salient. There are others. For example, we might think of diaspora's capacity to retrieve, make, or constitute memory; its forging of common cultures; and its function as a mechanism, to borrow from Bob Marley, to enable (black) survival. There is also, obviously, diaspora's availability as an instrument by which discrete national practices might be challenged and undone: for example, abolition, Jim Crow, colonialism, apartheid.

10. See Claude McKay, *Home to Harlem* (New York: Harper, 1928); *Banjo*, pp. 153–54, 202; and *A Long Way from Home* (1937; reprint, New York: Harcourt, Brace and World, 1970), p. 300; Brent Hayes Edwards, *The Practice of Diaspora: Literature, Translation, and the Rise of Black Internationalism* (Cambridge, Mass.: Harvard

University Press, 2003); and Michelle Ann Stephens, *Black Empire: The Masculine Global Imaginary of Caribbean Intellectuals in the United States, 1914–1962* (Durham, N.C.: Duke University Press, 2005). For other examples of this masculinized vagabond sensibility, see Langston Hughes, *The Big Sea: An Autobiography* (New York: Knopf, 1940); Hugh Mulzac, *A Star to Steer By* (New York: International, 1963); Horne, *Red Seas*; and Christopher John Farley's discussion of Bob Marley's father, Norval St. Claire Marley, and his travels to and experiences in the United Kingdom, Nigeria, and South Africa, as well as Jamaica, in *Before the Legend: The Rise of Bob Marley* (New York: Amistad, 2006). The Senegalese filmmaker Ousmane Sembène, whose work was influenced by McKay's writings, was also at one point a dockworker in Marseilles. With regard to the possibilities offered by cosmopolitanism, see Kwame Anthony Appiah, *Cosmopolitanism: Ethics in a World of Strangers* (New York: Norton, 2006); and Homi Bhabha's discussion of W. E. B. Du Bois, Mahatma Gandhi, Frantz Fanon, Bhimrao Ramji Ambedkar, and Toni Morrison with regard to "vernacular cosmopolitanism" in Homi Bhabha and John Comoroff, "Speaking of Postcoloniality, in the Continuous Present: A Conversation," in *Relocating Postcolonialism*, David Theo Goldberg and Ato Quayson, eds. (Oxford: Blackwell, 2002), pp. 15–46.

11. In this light, consider Michael Dawson's decision not to consider the "African diaspora" or Pan-Africanism in *Black Visions*. See *Black Visions: The Roots of Contemporary African-American Political Ideologies* (Chicago: University of Chicago Press, 2001), pp. xiii–xiv. Finally, as became clear at the 1974 Pan-African Congress in Dar Es Salaam in Tanzania, after the decolonization movement, Pan-Africanism would become inextricably and problematically implicated with the concerns and imperatives of states and their leaders, as opposed to "African peoples" (hence C. L. R. James's decision to boycott the 1974 gathering). On this point, see C. L. R. James, "Towards the Seventh Pan-African Congress—Past, Present and Future," in *At the Rendezvous of Victory: Selected Writings* (London: Allison and Busby, 1984), pp. 236–50; Malcolm X, "Not Just an American Problem, but a World Problem," in *Malcolm X: The Last Speeches* (New York: Pathfinder Press, 1989), p. 173; Martin Luther King Jr., "A Time to Break Silence," *Freedomways* 7, no. 2 (1967), pp. 107, 109; Palmer, *Eric Williams and the Making of the Modern Caribbean*; and David Slater, *Geopolitics and the Post-colonial: Rethinking North-South Relations* (Oxford: Blackwell, 2004), pp. 10–17.

12. For discussions of the concepts of "reactivation," "sedimentation," and "undecidability," see Edmund Husserl, *The Crisis of European Sciences and Transcendental Phenomenology*, David Carr, trans. (Evanston: Northwestern Illinois Press, 1970); Jacques Derrida, *Politics of Friendship*, George Collins, trans. (London: Verso, 1997); and Ernesto Laclau and Chantal Mouffe, *Hegemony and Socialist Strategy: Towards a Radical Democratic Politics*, 2nd ed. (London: Verso, 2001), pp. vii–xix.

13. See Marcus Garvey, "Why the Black Star Line Failed," in *Marcus Garvey and the Vision of Africa*, John Henrik Clarke, ed. (New York: Vintage, 1974), p. 139.

14. See Hugh Mulzac, "Memoirs of a Captain of the Black Star Line," in Clarke, *Marcus Garvey and the Vision of Africa*, p. 135, and Marcus Garvey and UNIA Papers

Project, UCLA, American Series, sample documents, vol. 2, August 1919–August 1920, www.isop.ucla.edu/africa/mgpp.

15. Quoted in Harold Cruse, *The Crisis of the Negro Intellectual* (New York: Morrow, 1967), pp. 119 and 123; and W. A. Domingo and Chandler Owen, "Open Forum: The Policy of the Messenger on West Indian and American Negroes," *Messenger*, January 1923, pp. 639–45.

16. See Jervis Anderson, *A. Philip Randolph: A Biographical Portrait* (New York: Harcourt Brace Jovanovich, 1973), p. 137; Clarence Walker, *Deromanticizing Black History: Critical Essays and Reappraisals* (Knoxville: University of Tennessee Press, 1991), p. 51; Amy Jacques Garvey, ed., *Philosophy and Opinions of Marcus Garvey* (London: Frank Cass, 1967), p. 132; and "An Answer to His Many Critics," *Marcus Garvey and the Vision of Africa*, John Henrik Clarke, ed. (New York: Vintage, 1974), pp. 249–50.

17. See W. A. Domingo, "Gift of the Black Tropics," in *The Portable Harlem Renaissance Reader*, David Levering Lewis, ed. (New York: Penguin, 1994), pp. 14–15; and E. Franklin Frazier, "Garvey: A Mass Leader," *Nation*, August 18, 1926, p. 147. Indeed, Clarence Walker argues that because of the tensions that existed between Afro-Caribbean immigrants and other African Americans, the claim that Garvey was "the leader of the largest mass movement of blacks in American history . . . needs to be qualified." See Walker, *Deromanticizing Black History*, pp. 41, 43.

18. These aesthetic flourishes combined with the masculinist tendencies characteristic of the era, a clear indifference to democratic norms, and an at times explicit anti-Semitism, produced a movement compatible in certain respects with the fascism that was developing in Europe at the same time. Regarding the relationship between Garveyism and fascism, see James Weldon Johnson, *Black Manhattan* (1930; reprint, New York: Atheneum, 1968), p. 256; J. A. Rogers, *The World's Greatest Men of Color* (New York n.p.: J. A. Rogers, 1947), p. 420; C. L. R. James, *A History of Negro Revolt*, Fact monograph no. 18 (London: Fact, September 1938; reprint, New York: Haskell House, 1969), p. 69; Marcus Garvey, "Editorial," *Black Man*, July–August 1936, p. 1; and Paul Gilroy, *Against Race: Imagining Political Culture beyond the Color Line* (Cambridge, Mass.: Harvard University Press, 2000).

19. See Garvey, *Philosophy and Opinions of Marcus Garvey*, vol. 2, p. 71; Tony Martin, *Race First: The Ideological and Organizational Struggles of Marcus Garvey and the Universal Negro Improvement Association* (Westport, Conn.: Greenwood Press, 1976), p. 351, and Marcus Garvey, "The World As It Is," *Black Man*, November 1938, p. 19. The bill did not pass.

20. A. Philip Randolph would also allow, years later, that Garvey "was an organizational genius. He organized more Negroes than any other single Negro in the history of this country. His impact upon black pride and consciousness . . . was tremendous. . . . Against the emotional power of Garveyism, what I was preaching didn't stand a chance." See W. E. B. Du Bois, "Pan-Africa and New Racial Philosophy," *Crisis*, November 1933, p. 247; Carol Cooper, "Tuff Gong: Bob Marley's Unsung Story," *Village Voice*, September 10, 1980, p. 33; and Anderson, *A. Philip Randolph*, p. 137.

21. Indeed, Domingo took credit for encouraging federal authorities to investigate the Black Star Line operations. McKay was also, at one point, a member of the ABB. See

Wayne F. Cooper, *Claude McKay: Rebel Sojourner in the Harlem Renaissance* (New York: Schocken, 1987), p. 155; Cyril Briggs, "The Decline of the Garvey Movement," in *Marcus Garvey and the Vision of Africa*, John Henrik Clarke, ed. (New York: Vintage, 1974), pp. 175, 177; Domingo, "Gift of the Black Tropics," pp. 14–15; and Anderson, *A. Philip Randolph*, p. 137. James and Padmore reportedly took pleasure in heckling Garvey during his Hyde Park speeches in London during the last years of his life. George Padmore, famously, wrote Garvey's obituary in May 1940 for the *Chicago Defender,* suggesting, among other things, he had been "deserted by his followers" and was "broke and unpopular," before concluding "Garvey's end was a tragic one." Garvey actually was not yet dead when the article was published, and it is suggested that upon reading it he did indeed pass (on June 10, 1940). For other accounts of the relations between American blacks and West Indians in this period, see Langston Hughes, "Brothers," *Crisis*, February 1924, p. 160; Orde Coombs, "On Being West Indian in New York," in *The Black Seventies*, Floyd B. Barbour, ed. (Boston: Porter Sargent, 1970); Gilbert Osofsky, *Harlem: The Making of a Ghetto—Negro New York, 1890–1930*, 2nd ed. (New York: Harper and Row, 1971); Theodore Vincent, *Black Power and the Garvey Movement* (Berkeley: Ramparts Press, 1972), pp. 212–14; Theodore Kornweibel, *No Crystal Stair: Black Life and the "Messenger," 1917–1928* (Westport, Conn.: Greenwood Press, 1975), pp. 132–75; David J. Hellwig, "Black Meets Black: Afro-American Reactions to West Indian Immigrants in the 1920s," *South Atlantic Quarterly* 77, no. 2 (spring 1978), pp. 206–24; John C. Walter, "West Indian Immigrants: Those Arrogant Bastards," *New England Journal of Black Studies* 2, (1981–82), pp. 17–27; and Winston James, *Holding Aloft the Banner of Ethiopia: Caribbean Radicalism in Early Twentieth-Century America* (London: Verso, 1998).

22. See Houston A. Baker Jr., *Modernism and the Harlem Renaissance* (Chicago: University of Chicago Press, 1987), pp. xvi, 17; and *Turning South Again: Re-thinking Modernism/Re-reading Booker T.* (Durham, N.C.: Duke University Press, 2001), pp. 33–34, 83 (italics in original).

23. See Baker, *Modernism and the Harlem Renaissance*, pp. 28, 30, 36; and *Turning South Again*, pp. 64, 83–84 (italics in original).

24. Regarding the modernity/modernism connection, see Michel-Rolph Trouillot, "The Otherwise Modern: Caribbean Lessons from the Savage Slot," in *Critically Modern: Alternatives, Alterities, Anthropologies*, Bruce M. Knauft, ed. (Bloomington: Indiana University Press, 2002), p. 225.

25. See Baker, *Modernism and the Harlem Renaissance*, p. 33; Louis Chude-Sokei, *The Last "Darky": Bert Williams, Black-on-Black Minstrelsy, and the African Diaspora* (Durham, N.C.: Duke University Press, 2006); and Booker T. Washington, "Bert Williams," *American Magazine*, September 1910, pp. 600–604. Besides Billy Kersands, other early African American blackface successes included Ernest Hogan and James Bland.

26. See Booker T. Washington, *Up from Slavery* (1901; reprint, New York: Gramercy Books, 1993), pp. 161–62. Regarding Washington's nativism, see Fred H. Matthews, *Quest for an American Sociology: Robert E. Park and the Chicago School* (Montreal: McGill-Queen's University Press, 1977), p. 66; and Booker T. Washington, *The Man*

Furthest Down: A Record of Observation and Study in Europe (Garden City, N.Y.: Doubleday, Page, 1912).

27. For Chude-Sokei, Williams's work "should be read as a corrective to the growing nationalistic chauvinism of an African American cultural politics that, despite its resistance and marginalization, veered too often toward an exceptionalism that severely limited the transnational borders of race and culture." Chude-Sokei, *The Last "Darky,"* pp. 5–6. Despite the tenor of Chude-Sokei's analysis, in the term "black-on-black minstrelsy" it is hard not to hear echoes of the contemporary references to "black-on-black crime."

28. Quoted in Ann Charters, *Nobody: The Story of Bert Williams* (London: Macmillan, 1970), pp. 11, 96; and Eric Ledell Smith, *Bert Williams: A Biography of the Pioneer Black Comedian* (Jefferson, N.C.: McFarland, 1992), p. 146 (italics added).

29. Bert Williams, "The Comic Side of Trouble," *American Magazine*, January 1918, pp. 33, 60 (italics added).

30. See Frank C. Taylor with Gerald Cook, *Alberta Hunter: A Celebration in Blues* (New York: McGraw-Hill, 1987), p. 44; and Chude-Sokei, *The Last "Darky"*, p. 49. For more recent analyses of Williams's work (with and without his African American partners George and Ada Overton Walker), see Caryl Phillips, *Dancing in the Dark: A Novel* (New York: Knopf, 2005); and Daphne A. Brooks, "Alien Nation: Re-imagining the Black Body (Politic) in Williams and Walker's *In Dahomey*," in *Bodies in Dissent: Spectacular Performances of Race and Freedom, 1850–1910* (Durham, N.C.: Duke University Press, 2006), pp. 207–80.

31. McKay, *A Long Way from Home*, p. 141.

32. See Joseph McBride, "Stepin Fetchit Talks Back," *Film Quarterly*, summer 1971, pp. 22, 25; Ossie Davis, "Stepin Fetchit," in *Life Lit by Some Large Vision: Selected Speeches and Writings*, Ruby Dee, ed. (New York: Atria Books, 2006), p. 163; Charles Bowen, "Bert Williams or Stepin Fetchit: Which Was the Greatest Comedian?" *Afro-American*, January 27, 1934, p. 21; and Mel Watkins, *Stepin Fetchit: The Life and Times of Lincoln Perry* (New York: Pantheon, 2005).

33. See Robert Hill, "Making Noise: Marcus Garvey Dada, August 1922," in *Picturing Us: African American Identity in Photography*, Deborah Willis, ed. (New York: New Press, 1994), pp. 198–99; Veerle Poupeye-Rammelaere, "Garveyism and Garvey Iconography in the Visual Arts of Jamaica," *Jamaica Journal* 24, June 1991; John R. McKivigan and Jason H. Silverman, "Monarchical Liberty and Republican Slavery: West Indian Emancipation Celebrations in Upstate New York and Canada," *Afro-Americans in New York Life and History* 10 (January 1986), pp. 10–12; Mary Ryan, "The American Parade: Representations of the Nineteenth-Century Social Order," in *The New Cultural History*, Lynn Hunt, ed. (Berkeley: University of California Press, 1989), p. 132; and Ted Vincent, *Keep Cool: The Black Activists Who Built the Jazz Age* (London: Pluto Press, 1995), pp. 129–30.

34. See Elliott M. Rudwick, *W. E. B. Du Bois: Propagandist of the Negro Revolt* (Philadelphia: University of Pennsylvania Press, 1968), p. 216; and *The Correspondence of W. E. B. Du Bois*, vol. 1, *Selections 1877–1934* (Amherst: University of Massachusetts Press, 1973), p. 263.

35. The McCarran-Walter Act of 1952 blocked West Indians from traveling to the United States on their British passports (in the period before independence, as colonial subjects, West Indians were issued the passports of the "mother country"). Consequently, Caribbean immigrants were subject to the strict immigration restrictions established in the 1920s (one hundred persons per year per colony). Among other things, the legislation was seen as a means of preventing the entry of West Indian communists.

36. See Domingo, "Gift of the Black Tropics," p. 16; *Journeys in Black: Louis Farrakhan*, BET broadcast, February 12, 2002; Louis Farrakhan, *The Charmer* (Bostrox 1999); and Paule Marshall, "Shaping the World of My Art," *New Letters* 40 (autumn 1973), p. 103. The emergence of a number of other black women writers in the post–civil rights era also brought questions of Caribbean-American identity to the surface. Worth noting in this regard are the fiction and nonfiction publications of June Jordan, Michele Wallace, Audre Lorde, and Shirley Chisholm.

37. Alphonso "Dizzy" Reece and Wynton Kelly were both born in Jamaica in 1931. Kelly lived in Brooklyn from the age of four. Regarding Reece, who moved to New York in 1959, Christopher Porter writes, "Reece . . . says he faced discrimination from some American black musicians because of his West Indian heritage—which may seem odd since a large number of jazzers, from Randy Weston and Sonny Rollins to Wynton Kelly and Henry Minton (Minton's Playhouse founder), have family lines that can be traced to the Caribbean. While Reece wouldn't talk in depth about the prejudice, it's something he readily acknowledges." See Christopher Porter, "Overdue Ovation for Dizzy Reece," *Jazztimes*, October 2004, p. 46. It should be noted Reece's experiences might not be comparable to those of the other individuals Porter mentions, as they were born in the United States, or immigrated early in their lives, or made their music in different eras. Regarding the role of West Indians in jazz, the work done in England by Jamaican immigrants Joe Harriott and Coleridge Goode, and Vincentian expatriate Ellsworth "Shake" Keane, particularly in the free jazz mode, is worth noting.

38. See Ashley Khan, *Kind of Blue: The Making of the Miles Davis Masterpiece* (New York: Da Capo, 2000), p. 7; Arthur Taylor, *Notes and Tones: Musician-to-Musician Interviews* (New York: Da Capo, 1993), p. 24; Paul Bradshaw, "Spiritual Healing: Randy Weston," *Straight, No Chaser* (winter 2001), pp. 34–37; Ted Panken, "Approaching Enlightenment: Sonny Rollins Executes the Impossible in a Quest for His Musical 'It,'" *Down Beat*, February 2001, p. 27; Sonny Rollins, "Don't Stop the Carnival" (*What's New*, RCA Victor 1962), "St. Thomas" (*Saxophone Colossus*, Prestige 1956), and *Now's the Time* (RCA Victor 1964). Wynton Kelly did record albums with the Canadian pianist and child of West Indian immigrants Oscar Peterson. In his autobiography, Miles Davis (with whom Kelly played on the classic *Kind of Blue*) remarks, "A lot of [Thelonious Monk's] music reminds me of the West Indian music being played today, that is his accents and rhythms and the way he approached melody." See Miles Davis with Quincy Troupe, *Miles* (New York: Simon and Schuster, 1990), p. 79. Eric Dolphy is featured on the track "Garvey's Ghost," along with the vocalist (and actor) Abbey Lincoln, from Max Roach's

album *Percussion Bitter Sweet* (Impulse 1964). Albert Ayler's "Ghosts," also released on Impulse (*Love Cry,* 1968), suggests a calypso influence. Finally, among the post-Marsalis generation of jazz musicians, the clarinet player Don Byron has signified his Caribbean connections in his work (and aesthetically, perhaps, with his dreadlocks). In this regard, see Byron's "Shake 'Em Up" (*You Are #6,* Bluenote 2001), which in the Rollins tradition is calypso-inspired (and indeed Byron's recording features his calypso-playing father Don Byron Sr. on bass). As an example of the influence of Rollins's example on contemporary jazz, see pianist Marc Cary's "Down De Road" (*Listen,* Arabesque 1997); saxophonist (and Virgin Islands native) Ron Blake's *Sonic Tonic* (Mack Avenue 2005); and St. Thomas native and bassist Reuben Rogers's *The Things I Am* (Renwick Entertainment 2006).

39. His comments in the liner notes for his 1966 release *Compulsion* (reissue, Blue Note 2007) offer another possibility: "[A]s the American Negro advances [if he does not maintain awareness of his history], he will lose sight of his own traditions . . . forgetting the distinct values of his own culture." As late as 2001, Hill would state, "My family moved here [Chicago] from [Haiti] so we could starve a little better." In a March 2006 feature, John Murph writes, "Hill says that the Haitian rumor started when he and drummer Andrew Cyrille (who's from Haiti) used to run tight. By association, people assumed that Hill was from the island. But instead of correcting people, he built a mythos around the confusion. Hill says some insiders were privy to the truth, including A. B. Spellman, who wrote the liner notes for *Black Fire* [1963; reissue Blue Note 2004]. He even says that Spellman helped fuel the myth by giving him Haitian literature." Indeed, in his liner notes for Bobby Hutcherson's *Dialogue* (1965; reissue, Blue Note 2002), Spellman writes, "Andrew Hill is a pianist-composer from Port-au-Prince, Haiti and Chicago." Bob Blumenthal, in the new liner notes for the 2002 reissue of *Dialogue,* which features Hill and four of his compositions, gets it half-right: "Spellman, like several writers of the time, was under the misperception that Hill was born in Haiti. The pianist was born in Chicago to Haitian immigrant parents." See *Los Angeles Weekly,* April 6–12, 2001, p. 150; John Murph, "Now's the Time: Andrew Hill Finds Beauty as Music Helps Him Survive Cancer," *Down Beat,* March 2006, p. 44; Bobby Hutcherson, "Les Noirs Marchant" (*Dialogue,* 1965; reissue, Blue Note 2002); Nat Hentoff (1966) and Bob Blumenthal (2007), liner notes, Andrew Hill, *Compulsion* (1966; reissue, Blue Note 2007); and Andrew Hill, "Le Serpent Qui Danse" (*Andrew!!!* Blue Note 1968).

40. The songwriting talents of Trinidadian immigrants Peggy Thomas and Joe Willoughby, and Vincentian Walter Merrick, encouraged Louis Jordan to record a number of calypsos (e.g., "Run Joe" and "Push-Ka-Pee-She-Pie"). Released in October of 1945, Ella Fitzgerald and Jordan's record "Stone Cold Dead in the Market" (*The Best of Ella Fitzgerald,* Verve 1996) became a hit the following year. The calypso was based on a Barbadian melody adapted by Trinidadian immigrant, former seaman, and artist Frederick "Wilmoth Houdini" Hendricks (1895–1973), originally titled "He Had It Coming," and released as part of a collection of three 78s by Decca (*Decca Presents a Special Collection of the World Famous Music of Trinidad,* 1939). Hendricks released another album, *Harlem Seen through Calypso*

Eyes (Decca 1940), an interesting take on black immigrant life in the United States. "Stone Cold" was subsequently covered in instrumental form by Jimmy Smith with Stanley Turrentine on their session *Prayer Meetin'* (Blue Note 1963). Rupert Westmore "Lord Invader" Grant successfully sued Morey Amsterdam, who was credited as the composer of the lyrics for "Rum and Coca-Cola," which he likely heard while participating in a United Service Organizations (U.S.O.) tour of Trinidad in 1943. The melody itself was adapted from a Martiniquan folk song by Trinidadian composer Lionel Belasco, who also sued successfully for compensation. Regarding the pre–World War II popularity of calypso and the linkages between the United States and Trinidad in this period, see Joseph Mitchell, "Houdini's Picnic," *New Yorker*, May 6, 1939, pp. 45–55; John Chilton, *Let the Good Times Roll: The Story of Louis Jordan and His Music* (Ann Arbor: University of Michigan Press, 1994); Donald Hill, "'I Am Happy Just to Be in This Sweet Land of Liberty': The New York City Calypso Craze of the 1930s and 1940s," in *Island Sounds in the Global City: Caribbean Popular Music and Identity in New York*, Ray Allen and Lois Wilcken, eds. (Urbana: University of Illinois Press, 2001), pp. 74–92; and Harvey R. Neptune, *Caliban and the Yankees: Trinidad and the United States Occupation* (Chapel Hill: University of North Carolina Press, 2007).

41. See Henry Louis Gates Jr., *Thirteen Ways of Looking at a Black Man* (New York: Random House, 1997), p. 168; Michael Eldridge, "Remains of the Day-O: A Conversation with Harry Belafonte," *Transition* Issue 92, Vol. 12, no. 2 (2002), p. 121; Hill, "I Am Happy"; "Calypso Songs Use Biting Satire to Criticize Colonial Rule," *Freedom* 1, no. 2 (1951), p. 6; and Hollis Liverpool, *Rituals of Power and Rebellion: The Carnival Tradition in Trinidad & Tobago* (Chicago: Research Associates School Times, 2001), pp. 431–43.

42. Irving Burgie, *Day-O!!! The Autobiography of Irving Burgie* (New York: Xlibris, 2007), p. 195.

43. Though later purchased and distributed by Twentieth-Century Fox, the film was an independent production by Darryl F. Zanuck, based on a bestselling novel by Alec Waugh that probed many of the same kinds of anxieties his earlier studio efforts, among them *Gentlemen's Agreement* (1947) and *Pinky* (1949), had engaged (i.e., anti-Semitism and racial passing, respectively). *Island* was shot in Barbados and Grenada. It is interesting to consider the filmic representations of the United Kingdom and the United States in terms of the correlation between perceptions of relative power and the willingness to commit to moral and egalitarian principles (e.g., *Amistad*).

44. See Donald Bogle, *Toms, Coons, Mulattoes, Mammies, and Bucks: An Interpretive History of Blacks in American Films* (New York: Continuum, 1997), p. 172. The bill in question was not passed into law. Regarding the constructions of the Caribbean, see Belinda Edmondson, *Caribbean Romances: The Politics of Regional Representation* (Charlottesville: University Press of Virginia, 1999), p. 6; and Krista A. Thompson, *An Eye for the Tropics: Tourism, Photography, and Framing the Caribbean Picturesque* (Durham, N.C.: Duke University Press, 2007).

45. Lisa D. McGill, *Constructing Black Selves: Caribbean American Narratives and the Second Generation* (New York: New York University Press, 2005), p. 26.

46. The colon can mark ratios (4:1) and time (11:25 PM) and refers as well to middle persons in the colonial hierarchy. It joins power and punctuation, and processes, to borrow from Fela Kuti, usually less than expensive shit. On this general point, see Jennifer DeVere Brody, *Punctuation: Art, Politics, and Play* (Durham, N.C.: Duke University Press, 2008).

47. Quoted in Gates, "Belafonte's Balancing Act," in *Thirteen Ways of Looking at a Black Man*, p. 159; and the documentary *Sidney Poitier: One Bright Light*.

48. See Sidney Poitier, *This Life* (New York: Knopf, 1980), pp. 86–87; and Nelson George, *Blackface: Reflections on African-Americans and the Movies* (New York: HarperCollins, 1994), pp. 17–18 (italics added). *Cry, the Beloved Country* also featured Canada Lee in a lead role. There is also a point in *No Way Out* (1950) where it sounds as if Poitier, his character under great stress, breaks into Bahamian patois; thanks to Krista Thompson, Harvey Neptune, and Michael Hanchard for sharing this observation with me.

49. Besides the Cold War factor, labor market pressures increased the call for the elimination of national quotas, and the labor movement itself, especially following the 1955 merger of the American Federation of Labor and the more liberal CIO, assumed a proimmigration posture, in marked contrast to its support for immigration restrictions in the 1920s. Regarding the changes that led to the 1965 reform, see Desmond King, *Making Americans: Immigration, Race, and the Origins of the Diverse Democracy* (Cambridge, Mass.: Harvard University Press, 2000); and Daniel J. Tichenor, *Dividing Lines: The Politics of Immigration Control in America* (Princeton, N.J.: Princeton University Press, 2002). The 1948 British Nationality Act established the right of Commonwealth members to migrate to the United Kingdom; the Commonwealth Immigrants Act of 1962 represented a significant restriction on that ability.

50. *Come Back, Charleston Blue* (Warner Brothers 1972) was the second in the series of movies, after *Cotton Comes to Harlem* (United Artists 1970), based on Chester Himes's novels featuring Grave Digger Jones (Cambridge's character) and Coffin Ed Johnson (played by Raymond St. Jacques). In *The River Niger* (1976), James Earl Jones's character refers, affectionately, to his best friend, played by Louis Gossett Jr., a West Indian doctor, as a "Jamaican tree climber" and a "monkey chasing son of a bitch." Interestingly, the lead part in *To Sir with Love* was offered to Poitier after Belafonte reportedly turned it down (for lacking depth and a sexual dimension). See David Montgomery, "Tally Man Come, Name Belafonte," *Washington Post*, April 2, 2006, p. D1. *Pressure Point*'s narrative structure implies that Nazis and black nationalists represent possibly equivalent threats to the health of the republic (the film was directed by Sidney Kramer).

51. See Poitier, *This Life*, pp. 320, 335–53; and *The Measure of a Man: A Spiritual Autobiography* (San Francisco: HarperSan Francisco, 2000); Clifford Mason, "Why Does White America Love Sidney Poitier So?" *New York Times*, September 1, 1967, sec. 2, pp. 1, 21; Colin A. Hughes, *Race and Politics in the Bahamas* (New York: St. Martin's Press, 1981), pp. 124–64, 307; and Michael Craton and Gail Saunders, *Islanders in the Stream: A History of the Bahamian People*, vol. 2 (Athens: University

of Georgia Press, 1992). Bahamian audiences were allowed to see *No Way Out* in October 1950, after the beginning of the protests (which included the resignation of the only nonwhite member of the Censorship Board, A. F. Adderley). The Bahamas became independent on July 10, 1973. With regard to the effects of tourism, Poitier writes, "People even danced to Bahamian musicians playing other people's music— Jamaican music or American artificial calypso music; tunes from the American hit parade or the American 'soul' top ten." For traces of junkanoo in American R & B, see Betty Wright's "Clean Up Woman," Gwen McCrae's "Rockin' Chair," and the early recordings of KC and the Sunshine Band.

52. Michael Veal cites the following recordings as revealing Fela's influence: the JB's "Hot Pants Road" (1971), Bootsy's "Stretchin' Out (In a Rubber Band)" released in 1976, Bootsy and the Sweet Band's "Jamaica" (1980), and George Clinton's "Nubian Nut" (1983). See Lloyd Bradley, *Bass Culture: When Reggae Was King* (London: Viking, 2000), pp. 279–80; James Brown with Bruce Tucker, *James Brown: The Godfather of Soul* (New York: Macmillan, 1986), p. 221; Michael E. Veal, *Fela: The Life and Times of an African Musical Icon* (Philadelphia: Temple University Press, 2000), p. 258; and Trevor Schoonmaker, ed., *Fela: From West Africa to West Broadway* (New York: Palgrave Macmillan, 2003). During this period, Caetano Veloso and Gilberto Gil were both in exile in London (and in this context it is interesting to consider Gil's recording of Blind Faith's "Can't Find My Way Home," *Gilberto Gil,* Philips 1971).

53. The Impressions' Curtis Mayfield coproduced a compilation of ska recordings, *The Real Jamaican Ska* (Epic Records 1964; Jimmy Cliff was one of the featured artists). The impact of southern radio stations on Caribbean peoples also explains the popularity of country and western music in Jamaica (beyond Charley Pride), an influence that was evident, for example, in the early work of Toots and the Maytals, among others. An example of the continuing popularity of this form in Jamaica is the song "Ain't Gonna Figure It Yet" on Beenie Man's collection *Many Moods of Moses* (VP Records 1997).

54. Continuing, Prince Buster contends that American R & B "penetrated deep into the fabric of [Jamaican] society and had a devastating effect on our folk music, our dialect, even our dress code." Buster, who joined the Nation of Islam in Jamaica in the early 1960s, assembled the musicians for the Folkes Brothers' "Oh Carolina" in 1959, the first popular recording featuring Rastafarian musicians (drummers led by Count Ossie). See Bradley, *Bass Culture*, pp. xv, 153.

55. See Bradley, *Bass Culture*, pp. 51, 53, 57; Grant Farred, "Wailin' Soul: Reggae's Debt to Black American Music," in *Soul: Black Power, Politics, and Pleasure*, Monique Guillory and Richard C. Green, eds. (New York: New York University Press, 1998), p. 60; and Timothy White, *Catch a Fire: The Life of Bob Marley* (New York: Holt, 1998), p. 20.

56. Cary Fraser, *Ambivalent Anti-Colonialism: The United States and the Genesis of West Indian Independence, 1940–1964* (Westport, Conn.: Greenwood Press, 1994), p. 3.

57. Manley's decision to accept Fidel Castro's offer to travel on the Cuban leader's jet to the September 1973 meeting of the Non-Aligned Movement in Algiers was

seen as a threat to the status quo and specifically United States–Jamaica relations. Guyana's Forbes Burnham also accepted the offer. Trinidad's Eric Williams, who was similarly invited, declined, as he was not intending to participate in the meeting. Regarding Cuba's significance in Jamaican discourse in this period, it is the island to Jamaica's north that figures as the site of liberation in Perry Henzell's film *The Harder They Come* (1972). See Michael Manley, "Overcoming Insularity in Jamaica," *Foreign Affairs* 49, no. 1 (October 1970), p. 106; Evelyne Huber Stephens and John D. Stephens, *Democratic Socialism in Jamaica: The Political Movement and Social Transformation in Dependent Capitalism* (London: Macmillan, 1986), p. 92; and Jervis Anderson, "Home to Jamaica," *New Yorker*, January 19, 1976, pp. 64, 73, 78.

58. Regarding Delroy Wilson's insistence that "Better Must Come" was not meant as a political endorsement, see Bradley, *Bass Culture*, p. 281. Max Romeo also has suggested, using a familiar albeit awkward logic, that the adoption of his song did not necessarily signify his interest in formal politics: "I did the song 'Let the Power Fall On I.' I have nothing to do with politics, but Michael Manley was campaigning. He thought it would make a new political slogan. He asked me to use it. I was an admirer of Manley's politics. There was no political side, I'm an artiste, I entertain everybody." *The Harder They Come* was initially blocked by Jamaican censors until Michael Manley, with whom Henzell was then on good terms, intervened. Henzell broke with the PNP after Manley announced his commitment to democratic socialism. See Howard Campbell, "Honouring a 'Reel' Jamaican Legend," *Jamaica Gleaner*, December 3, 2006; and "Selected Entries from Charles Hyatt's Diary," *Jamaica Gleaner*, January 14, 2007.

59. See Rex Nettleford, "Cultural Action in Independence," in *Jamaica in Independence: Essays on the Early Years*, Rex Nettleford, ed. (London: James Curry, 1989), p. 318; Anderson, "Home to Jamaica," p. 78; and Gilroy, *Against Race*, p. 24. The Manley-Marley collaboration also drew on the alliances Walter Rodney had forged during his short stint as a lecturer at the University of the West Indies in 1968—among the urban poor, Rastafarians, and students—and the new politics that followed the riots that took place after he was barred from returning to Jamaica from a black writers' conference in Montreal. On this point, see Walter Rodney, *The Groundings with My Brothers* (London: Bogle-L'Ouverture, 1990); Anthony J. Payne, *Politics in Jamaica*, rev. ed. (Kingston: Ian Randle, 1994), pp. 22–30; and Prince Buster, "Doctor Rodney" (seven-inch release b/w "Taxation," Fab 1968).

60. See Vivien Goldman, *The Book of Exodus: The Making and Meaning of Bob Marley and the Wailers' Album of the Century* (New York: Three Rivers Press, 2006), p. 63; and Linton Kwesi Johnson, "Bob Marley and the Reggae International," *Race Today*, June–July 1977, p. 93. "Smile Jamaica" would be used later as the music for advertisements by the Jamaican Tourist Board.

61. Anthony Spaulding was seen as one of the more ardent socialists in Manley's cabinet: "As socialists, our purpose in Jamaica is that as vanguards of the conscience of society, we must ensure that we preside over the death of capitalism, the naked ruthlessness of the rich." See Stephens and Stephens, *Democratic Socialism*

in Jamaica, p. 180. In *Catch a Fire*, Timothy White implies that the gunmen were upset with Marley for failing to pay the debts incurred by his friend, soccer player Alan "Skill" Cole. The CIA documents are included in the appendix to White, *Catch a Fire*, pp. 427–32.

62. Quoted in Stephen Davis, *Bob Marley: Conquering Lion of Reggae* (London: Plexus, 1993), p. 178, and Robin Denselow, *When the Music's Over* (London: Faber and Faber, 1990), p. 131 (italics in original).

63. Quoted in Davis, *Bob Marley*, p. 196. The raid on Fela Kuti's home by Nigerian government troops in 1977 led to the death of his mother and involved the mass rape of a number of the women living there (whom Fela symbolically married shortly afterward). Marley and the Wailers recorded their final two studio albums, *Survival* and *Uprising*, in Jamaica.

64. See Farred, "Wailin' Soul," p. 56; and Bradley, *Bass Culture*, p. 471. At the 1978 Peace Concert, Peter Tosh lit up a spliff (marijuana cigarette) in front of Manley, Seaga, and the other officials assembled at the event. That act, it is suggested, led to a savage beating from the police in retaliation afterward. At the height of the PNP's popularity with the reggae community, and the Manley regime's closeness to Cuba and, by extension, sympathy with the war in Angola, a number of songs expressing support for Jamaican involvement in the struggle were released, including Tappa Zukie's "MPLA," Pablo Moses's "We Should Be In Angola," and "Angola" and "Leftist" by Channel One's house band, the Revolutionaries.

65. See Stephens and Stephens, *Democratic Socialism in Jamaica*, pp. 134–37; Payne, *Politics in Jamaica*, pp. 52–58; and White, *Catch a Fire*, p. 304. Political violence was responsible for most of the 889 killings of people in the lead up to the elections in 1980 (and the 351 killings in 1979). Jamaica's population, in this period, was just over two million.

66. After being elected to Parliament in 1959, Seaga became the leader of the JLP in 1970, a position he continued to hold into the twenty-first century. For evidence of Seaga's anthropological expertise regarding Jamaican culture, see his 1956 liner notes to the album *Folk Music of Jamaica* (Ethnic Folkways Library no. FE4453). The Jamaica Tourist Board organized tours of the United States before Seaga's 1964 effort to encourage travel to the island. For instance, in 1955, the government-sponsored Silver Seas Calypso Band—in reality, a mento group—performed on *The Steve Allen Show*, *The Home Show*, and at Brooklyn's Abraham and Straus department store. See Denselow, *When the Music's Over*, p. 126; and Bradley, *Bass Culture*, pp. 58, 133–34.

67. The vinyl album version of *Catch a Fire*, when it was subsequently rereleased (with much less expensive artwork), was credited to Bob Marley and the Wailers (instead of just the Wailers), although both Peter Tosh and Bunny Livingstone were still fully involved members of the group when the album was recorded (and released). Perceptions that Island was trying to promote Marley as the leader of the group alienated Peter Tosh. Bunny Wailer simply refused to tour abroad to promote the Wailers' albums, largely because of the cold weather he experienced in the United Kingdom and the United States. By the time of the band's third release, *Natty*

Dread, in 1974 (after the 1973 releases *Catch a Fire* and *Burnin'*), the group was called Bob Marley and the Wailers, and Tosh and Livingstone were gone. See Nigel Williamson, "Catch a Fire," *Uncut*, March 2001, pp. 49–50; White, *Catch a Fire*, p. 251; and Goldman, *The Book of Exodus*, p. 223.

68. In fact, the first outside guitarist to work with the Wailers would have been white American Wayne Perkins, who contributed overdubs under Blackwell's direction to the album *Catch a Fire* in London. Al Anderson rejoined the band in 1978 (for the tour during which the live album *Babylon by Bus* was recorded), and the Wailers featured both Anderson and Junior Marvin from that point until their last studio album, *Uprising*. See Linton Kwesi Johnson, "Some Thoughts on Reggae," *Race Today*, December 1980, p. 58; Davis, *Bob Marley*, p. 134; and Timothy White, "Bob Marley's Jamaica," *Crawdaddy*, January 1976, p. 40.

69. Marley first left Jamaica for Wilmington the day after his wedding to Rita Anderson, and his second son, Stephen, was born there in 1972. After he became financially more secure, he bought two homes in Wilmington—one for his mother, her husband, and her three other children, and one for himself and his family—and then later one in Miami.

70. Nash also had hits in 1968 with "Hold Me Tight" and a reggae version of Sam Cooke's "Cupid," which were recorded in Jamaica. He also recorded Marley's "Nice Time," "Comma Comma," "Reggae on Broadway," "Rock It Baby (We've Got a Date)," "Mellow Mood," and "Guava Jelly."

71. Danny Sims was able to secure airplay and an album release in Canada: "Canada was different—Canada had a lot of Jamaicans, and I got good action on Bob Marley and the Wailers there. Canada was the only country that put out the album."

72. See George, *Blackface: Reflections on African-Americans and the Movies*, p. 17; and Coombs, "On Being West Indian in New York," pp. 184, 194–95.

73. See Steve Greenberg, liner notes, *The Very Best of Booker T & the MG's* (Rhino 1994), p. 4; Teddy Pendergrass and Patricia Romanowski, *Truly Blessed* (New York: Berkley Boulevard, 1999), p. 96; and Roger Steffens, "Wailers' Scrapbook," *Beat* 19, no. 3 (2000), p. 61. Danny Sims and Johnny Nash brought members of the Atlantic records studio house band down to Kingston to record tracks for Nash and Marley for the JAD label. Besides Purdie, Chuck Rainey and future Stuff members Richard Tee and Eric Gale were also involved in the sessions (as was South African trumpeter Hugh Masekela).

74. In light of Marley's experience, it is interesting to contemplate the role of violence in pushing individuals either into the popular or deeper into the vernacular. As Grant Farred notes, (personal) crises in general, often involving implicit violence exercised by the state, can be causally linked with such turns and reinvestments—Paul Robeson and W. E. B. Du Bois's passport restrictions and their subsequent identifications with Harlem and Ghana, respectively, and C. L. R. James's battles with Eric Williams in Trinidad over the American naval base located at Chaguaramas Bay that led to the publication of *Modern Politics*, *Party Politics*, and most significantly *Beyond a Boundary*. At the same time, explicit violence can play a particular function for men in triggering these reconfigurations.

Here I am thinking of Muhammad Ali's response to being drafted during the Vietnam War, Marley's exile and diasporic reawakening after the 1976 assassination attempt, Fela Kuti's lyrical turn from the indirect to the explicit after the raid on his Kalakuta compound, and in a slightly different respect, Stuart Hall's turn to race and questions of coloniality (first in evidence in *Policing the Crisis*) following the Handsworth riots that occurred while he was still at Birmingham University's Centre for Contemporary Cultural Studies. See Grant Farred, *What's My Name? Black Vernacular Intellectuals* (Minneapolis: University of Minnesota Press, 2003), pp. 20–22; and Veal, *Fela*.

75. See Barney Hoskyns, "Burnin'," *Mojo*, March 1995, p. 73; White, *Catch a Fire*, p. 378; Denselow, *When the Music's Over*, p. 173; Arnold Shaw, *Black Popular Music in America* (New York: Schirmer Books, 1986), p. 269; and Davis, *Bob Marley*, pp. 192, 219. It is important to note that Marley and reggae likely received more exposure on college radio stations and the public radio network, airwaves that were accessible to black listeners. Fredrick C. Harris brought this likelihood to my attention. On a separate point, bravado aside, Peter Tosh subsequently recorded and released disco-oriented material (under the influence of Mick Jagger and Keith Richards at Rolling Stones Records). With regard to Tosh's more commercial work, see *Bush Doctor* (Rolling Stones Records 1978), which includes his duet with Mick Jagger "(You Gotta Walk) Don't Look Back." Finally, Gil Scott-Heron's estranged father, Giles Heron, was the first black to play for Glasgow's Celtic Football Club. Before joining Celtic, he served in the Canadian Air Force, and was also a skilled hockey player.

76. Many of these calypsonians eventually left England: Roberts was there, largely based in Manchester, between 1948 and 1962; Moore between 1948 and 1961; Charles from 1951 to 1962; and Grant only briefly before returning to New York City, where he died in 1961. Trinidad and Tobago's independence in 1962 also drew many of these expatriates back to the Caribbean. Roberts's tours of Africa are said to have influenced the development of Ghanaian high-life music, and it is important to note the dialogues that the presence of West African and Caribbean musicians in London in this period made possible and their effects on developments throughout the diaspora. For evidence of this crossfertilization, see the four volumes of *London Is the Place for Me* (Honest Jons Records 2002, 2005, 2006, and 2006). Quevedo, aka Atilla the Hun, became involved in politics in Trinidad, running successfully for a seat on the Port of Spain city council, and subsequently the Legislative Council of Trinidad and Tobago, before dying in 1962.

77. In a 1976 interview, Marley noted, "Before me sign with Island I had three albums out that I didn't even know about." See Timothy White, "Bob Marley's Jamaica," *Crawdaddy*, January 1976, p. 38; and Goldman, *The Book of Exodus*, p. 128. Rita Marley's sister and brother (under the tags "Ranking Miss P" and "DJ Lepke") launched one of the pioneering pirate reggae radio stations (i.e., unlicensed and therefore illegal) in London in 1980, the Dread Broadcasting Corporation (DBC). It ceased operation in 1984.

78. Accordingly, both the novelist Caryl Phillips and the dub poet Linton Kwesi Johnson, among others, have suggested that their earliest role models were African

Americans. See Caryl Phillips, *The European Tribe* (Winchester, England: Faber and Faber, 1992), p. 1; "Interview: Linton Kwesi Johnson Talks to Burt Caesar," *Critical Quarterly* 38, no. 4 (winter 1996), p. 64; and Trevor Phillips and Mike Phillips, *Windrush: The Irresistible Rise of Multi-racial Britain* (London: HarperCollins, 1998), p. 316 (italics added).

79. See Barnor Hesse, "Diasporicity: Black Britain's Post-colonial Formations," in *Un/settled Multiculturalisms: Diasporas, Entanglements, Transruptions*, Barnor Hesse, ed. (London: Zed, 2000), p. 96; and Bradley, *Bass Culture*, pp. 385–86. For a discussion of the emergence of black British theatre against the backdrop of the impossibility of black Britishness, see Michael McMillan and SuAndi, "Rebaptizing the World in Our Own Terms: Black Theatre and Live Arts in Britain," in *Black Theatre: Ritual Performance in the African Diaspora*, Paul Carter Harrison, Victor Leo Walker II, and Gus Edwards, eds. (Philadelphia: Temple University Press, 2002), pp. 115–27. It is important to note that Jamaican cultural forms—including music, food, and language—were emerging not only as the modal black cultural forms but also as appealing and significant submodal formations within the broader British context for many intersecting youth constituencies, whether white, Asian, African, and/or Caribbean. On a separate point, as a result of touring with Marley and the Wailers, the members of the Handsworth, Birmingham-based group, Steel Pulse, became Rastafarians. See *Mojo*, November 2007, p. 154.

80. See Kevin Howes, liner notes, Noel Ellis, *Noel Ellis* (summer 1983; reissue, Light in the Attic 2006). Ellis, son of Alton Ellis, who migrated from Kingston to Toronto and then later to London, released a twelve-inch single in 1978, "Reach My Destiny," recorded and produced in Toronto, based on the rhythm track from Willie Williams's classic "Armigideon Time"—with Williams, who was also based in Toronto in this period, among the musicians on the track (released by Summer Records). "Made in Jamaica" was stamped on the label for that record. See Bradley, *Bass Culture*, p. 393; and Lloyd Bradley, liner notes, Dennis Bovell Presents 4th Street Orchestra, *Scientific, Higher Ranking Dubb/Yuh Learn!* (1977; reissue, RAMA 2006).

81. See Lloyd Bradley, liner notes, Dennis Bovell Presents 4th Street Orchestra, *Scientific, Higher Ranking Dubb/Yuh Learn;* and Bradley, *Bass Culture*, p. 389.

82. For useful overviews and reviews of the album *Exodus*, see Goldman, *The Book of Exodus*; and Linton Kwesi Johnson, "Bob Marley and the Reggae International," *Race Today*, June–July 1977, pp. 92–94.

83. "Is like you fishing and the fish kinda pick up the sweet bait and you give him a little length, like, and you just jerk him in," suggested Garrick. See Gregory Stephens, *On Racial Frontiers: The New Culture of Frederick Douglass, Ralph Ellison, and Bob Marley* (New York: Cambridge University Press, 1999), p. 181; Goldman, *The Book of Exodus*, pp. 203–4, 270; and Malika Lee Whitney and Dermott Hussey, *Bob Marley: Reggae King of the World* (San Francisco: Pomegranate, 1994), p. 161.

84. According to Carol Cooper, Marley's music sought to "accomplish a particular international goal: to resurrect the political ethic of Garveyism." Quoted in Cooper, "Tuff Gong," pp. 33, 79. Marley's own feelings about Garvey seem not to have been signifi-

cantly affected by Garvey's racialism, despite Marley's own mixed-race background (his father was, as far as he knew, white). In *On Racial Frontiers*, Gregory Stephens argues otherwise and contends that Marley's work represents a rejection of Garvey's hyperracialism while upholding his Pan-Africanism and (p. 155) that he was "a paradoxical choice as a patron saint for Marley-era Rastafarian reggae." Marley was clearly aware of the possible implications of his supposed biracialism (especially in the mid-1970s), as was Island. In one interview, he offered, "Me don't dip on the black man's side or the white man's side. Me dip on God's side, who cause me to come from black and white." See Lloyd Bradley, "Uprising!" *Mojo*, March 2005, p. 76. He seems, though, to have abandoned any particular concern with the issue of his racial makeup by the end of the decade. Indeed, Stephens's extended examination of the album *Survival* to support his thesis is striking, given that it is probably the Marley album least supportive of such an interpretation. In *Before the Legend*, Christopher John Farley presents evidence that Marley's father was in fact himself of mixed race.

85. The reference to "preaching on the streets of Harlem" is actually made after the commercially released version of the recording fades out. The reference to "rock" in the title and lyrics of the song also marks it as compatible with Blackwell's attempts to market Marley to white audiences. Garrick also contends that an interview was done with *Ebony*, including a photo shoot, that was never published: "We went to Chicago and went and tour[ed] *Ebony* magazine, the Johnson Building, and spend the whole day with them and did an interview, did a photo session, met the staff in the entire building, you hear me, and *Ebony* has never printed a word about Rasta or reggae music." See Neville Garrick's comments quoted in Whitney and Hussey, *Bob Marley*, pp. 160–61.

86. Suggested Du Bois ("Pan-Africa and New Racial Philosophy," *Crisis*, November 1933, p. 147), that if the "young, black American is going to survive and live a life, he must calmly face the fact that however much he is an American, there are interests which draw him nearer to the dark people outside of America than to his white fellow citizens." Stephen Davis (*Bob Marley*, p. 218) suggests that Marley was affected by reading the Du Bois article in 1978.

87. Quoted in Cooper, "Tuff Gong," p. 79 (italics in original). It should be noted that Marley's responses to questions in interviews sometimes were rendered in patois and sometimes in the Queen's English. This difference probably reflected two factors: the interviewer's own priorities regarding "authenticity" and "accessibility," and Marley's own habit of mocking and playing with the expectations of different interviewers.

88. On the *Billboard* general or "pop" charts, *Exodus* reached number twenty, *Kaya* number fifty, *Survival* number seventy, and *Uprising* number forty-five. *Exodus* might have done even better if not for the cancellation of the U.S. portion of the tour scheduled to promote the album (on account of an injury to Marley's toe associated with what turned out to be cancer). See *Joel Whitburn's Top R & B Singles 1942–1995* (Menomonee Falls, Wisc.: Record Research, 1996), p. 286, and George Albert and Frank Hoffmann, eds. *The Cashbox Black Contemporary Singles Charts, 1960–1984* (Metuchen, N.J.: Scarecrow Press, 1986), p. 320.

89. Consistent with its previous marketing strategies, Island had persuaded Marley to modify the album's original title, "Black Survival." See Bradley, *Bass Culture*, p. 419. The Wailers' 1974 release *Natty Dread* was also incorrectly titled because of miscommunication between Island and Marley, who had intended to call the album "Knotty Dread," which of course made more sense than the awkward and confusing title the release eventually received. Nevertheless, Marley eventually embraced the term: one of the tracks on the album *Survival* was called "Ride Natty Ride." It should also be noted that Wailers' albums were regularly "sweetened" and remixed throughout this period (though none as radically as *Catch a Fire*, Island 1973, 2001). The bass and percussion elements that were prominent on the versions of the albums and singles released by Marley's Tuff Gong label (which owned the rights to the Wailers' music in Jamaica) in the Caribbean were watered down in the versions of the tracks released in the rest of the world. This is not an unusual practice. African recording artists commonly release different versions of their albums at home and in North America and Europe. Regarding the difficulties African recording artists face trying to break through in North America and Europe, see David Hecht, "Walking Out on Uneasy Success," *New York Times*, March 19, 2000, sec. 2, pp. 31, 35.

90. See White, *Catch a Fire*, pp. 304, 378.

91. "Could You Be Loved" is published by Bob Marley Music Ltd. BV and administered by Rondor Music (Ldn) Ltd.

92. See Davis, *Bob Marley*, pp. 184, 219; and "Marley Parley," in *Reggae, Rasta, Revolution: Jamaican Music from Ska to Dub*, Chris Potash, ed. (New York: Schirmer Books, 1997), p. 62.

93. Reggae would prove popular outside of the anglo-Caribbean circuit as well: e.g., Nigeria's Majek Fashek, the Ivory Coast's Alpha Blondy, South Africa's Lucky Dube, and Brazil's Gilberto Gil. One could even step outside the realm of music and consider the effects of late twentieth century-competition in the areas of track and field, e.g., Gail Devers, Merlene Ottey, Carl Lewis, Ben Johnson, Linford Christie, Donovan Bailey, Ato Bolden, Frankie Fredericks, Maurice Greene, and Michael Johnson, and perhaps boxing, e.g., Mike Tyson, Frankie Bruno, Lennox Lewis, and Evander Holyfield, on black diasporic sensibilities. In particular, the identity of the boxer Lennox Lewis, of Jamaican parentage, has been a site of contestation, with both England and Canada claiming him.

94. Accordingly, Marley's first question to Johnson, when Johnson was working at a community center in London's Islington district, was, as Johnson remembers, "Why wasn't I a Rasta? Why wasn't I saying 'Jah!'?" Indeed, Johnson acknowledges that he "identified a lot with Rastafarian ideas, particularly the anticolonial aspects of Rasta, the rejection of the domination of white European culture, language, religion and so on." While providing Caribbean-descended youth in the United Kingdom (and elsewhere) with a mode of resistance that they might adapt to their circumstances—for example, the black British reggae bands Aswad, Matumbi, and Steel Pulse, the Canadian band Messenjah, and the American punk-reggae outfit Bad Brains—Johnson was concerned that Rastafarianism represented an inad-

equate means of substantively challenging black marginalization. With regard to what he termed "the Rasta trap," Johnson argued, "For many youngsters in Britain, particularly the unemployed and working youth, who supply most of the musicians, the discovery of Rasta is like a spiritual awakening. It opens up the creative potential and the creative possibilities of this section of our community. They seem, in the main, to have been stuck there. . . . But for this Rasta trap we could have gone much further." Johnson had also, as a young man in his early twenties, "completely renounced all religions . . . having realised the role that religion had played in the enslavement of black people." Overall, the ways alienated black youth throughout the diaspora engaged, and often later rejected, different versions and aspects of Rastafarianism constituted one of the most fascinating cultural developments of the late twentieth century (for example, the contrast between the second-generation, expatriate Rastafarianism of Steel Pulse and the dread but secular aesthetics of Soul II Soul). See "Interview: Linton Kwesi Johnson Talks to Burt Caesar," p. 68; interview with Linton Kwesi Johnson, *Los Angeles Weekly*, July 13–19, 1984, p. 42; Johnson, "Some Thoughts on Reggae," p. 59; Linton Kwesi Johnson, "Reality Poem" (*Forces of Victory,* Mango/Island 1979); Bob Marley and the Wailers, "Survival" (*Survival*, Tuff Gong/Island 1979).

95. The song's title includes the common mispelling of the name of the street in question ("Eglington" as opposed to "Eglinton"). Reggae singer Denroy Morgan also had a big R & B hit with the song "I'll Do Anything for You" at the end of the disco era (produced and cowritten by Bertram Reid of Crown Heights Affair). Crocker's methodology in this period is difficult to classify, though he was one of the more open-minded disc jockeys and programmers in black radio. (By this point Inner City Broadcasting owned stations in New York, Detroit, and Berkeley, and Crocker was the program director for all three.) *Billboard* noted, "Crocker, long known as an unorthodox programmer, has done some unusual things in recent months such as an in-depth interview with himself on a recent program." See Doug Hall, "Crocker, Like Knight on Horse, Vows to Up WBLS-FM Ratings," *Billboard*, February 3, 1979, p. 30; and "Word 'Disco' Dirty in New York Radio," *Billboard*, December 8, 1979, p. 24.

96. See the O'Jays, "A Letter to My Friends" (*When Will I See You Again*, Philadelphia International 1983); Cameo, "A Tribute to Bob Marley" (*She's Strange*, Atlanta Artists/Polygram 1984); and "Little Boys—Dangerous Toys" (*Single Life*, Atlanta Artists/Polygram 1985); and War, "Just Because" (*Outlaw*, RCA 1982). In 1998, the album *Midnight Love* was rereleased including a number of alternate versions of the songs on the original 1982 release, including two previously unavailable versions of "Third World Girl." See Steve Turner, *Trouble Man: The Life and Death of Marvin Gaye* (London: Michael Joseph, 1998), p. 206; David Ritz, *Divided Soul: The Life of Marvin Gaye* (New York: Da Capo Press, 1991), p. 51; and Paul Gilroy, *The Black Atlantic: Modernity and Double Consciousness* (London: Verso, 1993), p. 96. Stevie Wonder was supposed to tour with Marley at one point (the plans were dropped when Marley became ill), and they did play one memorable show together at the 1979 Black Music Association convention in Philadelphia. Wonder

would later record Marley's "Redemption Song" for the soundtrack of Spike Lee's film *Get on the Bus*.

97. Bell, along with Kenny Gamble and Leon Huff, one of the main architects of the sound of Philadelphia, has observed that he spells his first name "Thom" rather than "Tom" in observance of West Indian custom. The Jamaican native—he moved to Philadelphia at age four in 1947—also recalls his parents telling him "You're different. In order to succeed, you're going to have to work ten times harder than the black man and a hundred times harder than the white man." Quoted in John A. Jackson, *A House on Fire: The Rise and Fall of Philadelphia Soul* (New York: Oxford University Press, 2004), p. 12. Other bands with West Indian American membership, in this period, would include the Five Stairsteps (including future solo star Keni Burke), Black Ivory (lead singer Leroy Burgess), Mandrill, Crown Heights Affair, Starpoint ("Object of My Desire"), and later Brooklyn's Full Force. Starpoint's bassist and drummer, brothers Orlando and Greg Phillips, recorded reggae and calypso after the band's dissolution. Solomon Burke, one of the early pioneers of the soul movement, is a second-generation Caribbean American as well. Regarding Randy Muller's role in shaping the sound of 1970s Brooklyn funk, see Andrew Mason, "Disco Architect: Randy Muller," *Waxpoetics* 10 (fall 2004), pp. 108–14. On a humorous note, Guyanese immigrant and producer Dennis King's accent is the subject of Kleeer's "De Ting Continues" (*Taste the Music*, Atlantic 1982).

98. See White, *Catch a Fire*, p. 18; and Michael E. Veal, *Dub: Soundscapes and Shattered Songs in Jamaican Reggae* (Middletown, Conn.: Wesleyan University Press, 2007). Products of West Indian deejay culture would include Jamaica's King Tubby and Sir Coxsone; the Americans Kool Herc, Afrika Bambaataa, Grandmaster Flash and Pete Rock; and in the United Kingdom, Soul II Soul's Jazzie B, Norman Jay, and the drum and bass crew (Goldie, Grooverider, Roni Size, Randall, Fabio, Krust, LTJ Bukem, and 4 hero's Dego and Marc Mac).

99. Quoted in William Shaw, "A Bronx Tale," *Details*, November 1998, p. 179. The Original Jazzy Jay, his cousin Kool DJ Red Alert, and Fab 5 Freddy (Fred Brathwaite), besides Herc, Flash, and Bambaataa, were also first-generation hip-hop artists with West Indian backgrounds.

100. For many of these individuals, an awkward language of identification and categorization developed. For example, when Luther Campbell suggests "My father is a Jamaican, but Mamma was born and raised in Miami," or KRS-One states "My father is a Jamaican [and] . . . my mother is American . . . or born in America," it does not mean that both artists' mothers were not of West Indian parentage but rather reflected the dilemma of how to speak of American blacks whose roots included the Caribbean. Indeed, Campbell's mother is of Bahamian parentage. See Shaw, "A Bronx Tale," p. 179; Luther Campbell and John R. Miller, *As Nasty as They Wanna Be: The Uncensored Story of Luther Campbell and the 2 Live Crew* (Fort Lee, N.J.: Barricade Books, 1992), pp. 4, 12; *allhiphop.com*, February 8, 2006; and Michael Lipscomb, "Can the Teacher Be Taught? A Conversation with KRS-One and Michael Lipscomb," *Transition* 57 (1992), p. 175.

101. Similarly, Luther Campbell notes, "Back when I was a DJ, I was the only one spinning hip-hop and reggae in the clubs in Miami. But my mother is from Nassau, and my father being from Jamaica, definitely played a role in the way I used bass to create music, if you listen to it, Miami bass sounds a lot like music from the West Indies, but with our own Miami spin on it." Indeed, although the New York area has been predominant in terms of producing a fusion between African American and Caribbean sensibilities, Miami, Marley's last home, has also played an important role in this regard. See David Toop, *Rap Attack 2: African Rap to Global Hip Hop* (London: Pluto Press, 1991), p. 69; Bill Brewster and Frank Broughton, *Last Night a DJ Saved My Life* (New York: Grove Press, 2000), p. 211; David Bry, "Song of the South," *Vibe*, June 2002, p. 94; and *allhiphop.com*, March 8, 2006. Herc also was associated with the enduring popularity of the recordings of the Caribbean British group Cymande. Samples of their songs would be used by the Fugees ("Dove" on "The Score"), De La Soul ("Bra" on "Change In Speak"), Heavy D ("Fug" on "Cuz He's Always Around"), Master Ace ("The Message" on "Me and the Biz"), and R & B group Jazé ("Bra" again on "It's Alright," produced by Herby "Luv Bug" Azor), among others. "Bra," a 1972 recording, was a regular feature of Kool Herc's sets during that decade (along with the Incredible Bongo Band's "Apache"). British reggae group Aswad's 1988 cover of "The Message" can also be read as a salute to Cymande's pioneering role in establishing a space for black British expression.

102. See Brian Coleman, "Classic Material," *XXL*, December 2004, p. 192; Robbie Busch, "Back to the Future: New York's Kool DJ Red Alert Transports Listeners to Another Dimension," *Waxpoetics* 19 (October–November 2006), p. 124; and Bonsu Thompson, "Back For the First Time," *XXL*, December 2001, p. 69. Dancehall-influenced intonations can also be detected in the recordings of rappers DMX and Ja Rule. The list of individuals who were either immigrants from the Caribbean or the offspring of West Indian immigrants, among the second (post-1982) hip-hop generation, includes LL Cool J, Stetsasonic's Daddy-O, Doug E. Fresh, and British immigrant Slick Rick. Third-generation hip-hop Caribbean Americans would include KRS-One, Biz Markie, Salt-n-Pepa, Heavy D, Pete Rock and C. L. Smooth, Brand Nubian's Grand Puba, Charlie Brown and Busta Rhymes of Leaders of the New School, Main Source, Pos and Trugoy of De La Soul, the Jungle Brothers, Q-Tip and Phife of A Tribe Called Quest, Special Ed, Organized Konfusion's Pharoah Monche, Gang Starr's Guru, Jeru the Damaja, Das EFX, and producers Herby "Luv Bug" Azor and Salaam Remi. Remi's father is Van Gibbs, who produced, among others, the Fat Boys and Taana Gardner ("Heartbeat"). Remi would produce the Fugees ("because of their West Indian roots"), as well as dancehall artists Supercat, Ini Kamoze, Beenie Man, Patra, Shabba Ranks, Mad Cobra, and Elephant Man. See Beatdawg, "Gettin' Dusty," *Elemental* 7, no. 71 (2005), p. 87. The largely West Coast–situated fourth generation included fewer Caribbean American contributors (with the exception of the Miami-based 2 Live Crew's Luther Campbell, who might more accurately be included with the second generation in many respects, the Los Angeles–affiliated Tone-Loc, and Young MC), while the fifth wave that emerged in the mid- to late 1990s, in response to the recalibration of hip-hop

aesthetics and ethics that took place in the early part of that decade, involved West Indian Americans such as the Notorious B.I.G., Foxy Brown, Shyne, Jay-Z, M.O.P's L'il Fame, Canibus, Funkmaster Flex, and Cappadonna. Other artists who became popular in this period but espoused third-generation aesthetics would include dead prez's M1, J-Live, John Forté, Talib Kweli, Mos Def, and Pras and Wyclef Jean of the Fugees. West Coast rap references to reggae, and Caribbeanisms in general, have tended to focus on marijuana and the weed culture, which was one of the major selling points of reggae for the rock market in the 1970s (e.g., Warren G's cover of Bob Marley's "I Shot the Sheriff"). Vernon Reid, raised in the New York City area and one of the organizers of the Black Rock Coalition in the mid-1980s, would subtly signify his own (Afro-Caribbean) British roots in the spelling of the ensemble for which he played guitar, the rock group Living Colour. See Harry Allen, "Interview with Vernon Reid," in *Rip It Up: The Black Experience in Rock 'n' Roll*, Kandia Crazy Horse, ed. (New York: Palgrave Macmillan, 2004), p. 141.

103. Herby Azor, born in Haiti in 1965, emigrated to the United States in 1975 at age ten. For performances, the spelling used is "Hurby." "I was forced to hide my [Haitian] heritage," Kangol Kid of UTFO ("Roxanne, Roxanne") suggests; "If another rapper found out I was Haitian, in a battle it would have been a wrap." See Michael A. Gonzales, "The Understanding," *XXL*, April 2001, p. 124; and B. Boy Omega, "Time to Shine," *Source*, March 2007, p. 46. Q-Tip, of A Tribe Called Quest, has made little explicit reference to his Caribbean background in his work, except his use of patois on A Tribe Called Quest's "Oh My God" (*Midnight Marauders*, Jive/Zomba/BMG 1993) and perhaps the musical influence detectable on "You Can Do It" from his first solo release, *Amplified* (Arista 1999). There were artists—for example, Born Jamericans, Yankee B, and Shinehead ("Jamaican in New York")—who explicitly identified themselves as Jamaicans or as children of Jamaican immigrants in the marketing of their music (and generally did not do well in terms of sales).

104. For evidence of these exchanges, see Phife Dawg, "Beats, Rhymes and Phife" (*Ventilation: Da LP*, Groove Attack 2000); the video for Foxy Brown's "Oh Yeah" (*Broken Silence*, Def Jam 2001); Baby Cham, "More" (*Wow . . . The Story*, Madhouse/Artists Only! 2000); Earl Mitchell, "Baby Cham: A Brand New Vision," *Mic Check*, March 2001, pp. 16, 30; Rob Kenner, "Boom Shots," *Vibe*, May 2001, p. 169; John Leland, "When Rap Meets Reggae," in Potash, *Reggae, Rasta, Revolution*, p. 188; and Elena Oumano, "VP Records' Reggae Rapper Sean Paul to Make 'Stage One' Debut," *Billboard*, March 18, 2000, p. 11. One of the more amusing examples of clashing musical and cultural sensibilities within this emerging remix community came about as the result of Soul II Soul's efforts to break into the American market. Their first American release, "Keep On Moving," a fluid, bass-heavy, and clearly sound system–influenced production was remixed by Teddy Riley, who was at that time the mastermind behind the predominant choppy and synthesizer-dominated "new jack swing." Riley's attempt to tailor the original version was quite awkward—he basically removed the song's strongest elements—and another take produced by Soul II Soul's Jazzie B proved to be more palatable and popular.

105. See Lola Ogunnaike, "Clef Notes," *Vibe*, September 2000, p. 169; Rob Kenner, "Soundboy Burial," *Vibe*, December 2000, p. 153–54; and Frank Williams, "Baptism by Fire," *Source*, August 2000, p. 194. Jean also recorded an updated version of "Master Blaster" with Stevie Wonder for the soundtrack to the movie *How Stella Got Her Groove Back*. Jean also, quite correctly, criticized the movie for including the (unchallenged) suggestion that Haitians are a particularly high-risk group for the transmission of AIDS.

106. The album's title is, obviously, a reference to Carter G. Woodson, and there are musical references on the album to Stevie Wonder as well, among others. Hill also had children with one of Marley's sons. *Chant Down Babylon* (Tuff Gong/Island Def Jam Music Group 1999), a Marley tribute album, includes a cut-and-paste "duet" between Hill and Marley on "Turn Your Lights Down Low."

107. "She has no platform," Owens argued during the campaign. "We agree on just about every issue." If elected, Clarke would have joined Sheila Jackson-Lee in Congress (Democrat, Texas, Eighteenth district), the daughter of Jamaican immigrants, who was first elected in 1994. Clarke was facing term limitations on her city council seat (and, according to sources, was hoping to be replaced by her daughter) and had been found guilty of campaign finance irregularities. Owens, in the eyes of many observers, seemed to have lost his interest in politics and was preparing, it was rumored at the time, to hand his seat to his son Chris. Owens also had been perceived as failing in the area of constituency service (particularly with regard to his district's immigrant populations), and Clarke claimed to have been picking up the slack through the powers she exercised as a city councillor. The standard political considerations (i.e., careerism, reputation, and spite) determined different local politicians' choice of whom to endorse (e.g., mayoral hopeful Mark Green, Ed Koch, and Queens borough president Claire Schulman). Clarke's daughter was indeed elected to replace her mother in the 2001 city council elections and would run successfully for Owens's congressional seat in 2006 after he retired, defeating, among others, Owens's son Chris. See Jamila Daniel, "A Rift Grows in Brooklyn," *Village Voice*, March 14, 2000, p. 26; Wayne Barrett, "Brooklyn Betrayal," *Village Voice*, September 12, 2000, pp. 52–53, 55; Peter Noel, "BrooklynRATS," *Village Voice*, September 26, 2000, pp. 46–50; Jonathan P. Hicks, "Bitter Primary Contest Hits Ethnic Nerve Among Blacks," *New York Times*, Thursday, August 31, 2000, p. B6; and Yvonne Bynoe, "The Connection between Name and Identity," *politicallyblack.com*, March 14, 2000, p. 2 of printed transcript. Regarding the interaction of Caribbean immigrants and American blacks in the political and cultural arenas, see Philip Kasinitz, *Caribbean New York: Black Immigrants and the Politics of Race* (Ithaca, N.Y.: Cornell University Press, 1992); Philip W. Scher, *Carnival and the Formation of a Caribbean Transnation* (Gainesville: University Press of Florida, 2003); and Reuel R. Rogers, *Afro-Caribbean Immigrants and the Politics of Incorporation: Ethnicity, Exception, or Exit* (New York: Cambridge University Press, 2006).

108. It is in this context that victims of police violence—e.g., Eleanor Bumpurs, Michael Stewart, Yusef Hawkins, Patrick Dorismond, Nicholas Heyward Jr., Abner Louima, Malcolm Ferguson, Amadou Diallo, Ousmane Zongo, and Sean Bell—regardless

of "ethnicity," were claimed by a more-than-imagined community that collectively recognized the alliterative effect of these shootings and assaults. Thinking of the diaspora as, among other things, a set of discourses through and by which things are made, it is not surprising that the politics that would derive from this sense of being in a "world that forces lifelong insecurity," as Marley suggests, would typically be articulated in the arenas of popular culture, including but not limited to hip-hop. The Marley lyrics can be heard in the fade-out to the title track from the album *Survival*.

109. On this point, see Toni Morrison's comments about American identity and Ralph Ellison quoted in Paul Gilroy, "Living Memory: A Meeting with Toni Morrison," in *Small Acts: Thoughts on the Politics of Black Cultures* (London: Serpent's Tail, 1993), pp. 179–80; and the remarkable shifts in Caryl Phillips's identifications evident in *The European Tribe* (London: Faber and Faber, 1987); *The Atlantic Sound* (New York: Knopf, 2000); and his interview with Chinua Achebe, "Out of Africa," *Guardian*, February 22, 2003. On a separate point, it is worth remembering that the United States first exercised its veto privileges at the United Nations in defense of Rhodesia (just as it had blocked inclusion of a racial equality plank in the constitution of the League of Nations after World War I).

Chapter 7

1. See Joy James, "The Profeminist Politics of W. E. B. Du Bois," in *W. E. B. Du Bois: On Race and Culture*, Bernard W. Bell, Emily R. Grosholz, and James B. Stewart, eds. (New York: Routledge, 1996), p. 142; Hazel Carby, *Race Men* (Cambridge, Mass.: Harvard University Press, 1998), p. 10; and Tony Martin, "Women in the Garvey Movement," in *Garvey: His Work and Impact*, Rupert Lewis and Patrick Bryan, eds. (Kingston, Jamaica: Institute of Social and Economic Research and the Department of Extra-Mural Studies, University of the West Indies, 1988), p. 67; and, more generally, regarding Du Bois's and Garvey's views regarding issues of gender and sexuality, Alys Eve Weinbaum, "Reproducing Racial Globality: W. E. B. Du Bois and the Sexual Politics of Black Internationalism," *Social Text* 67, Vol. 19, no. 2 (summer 2001), 15–41; David Levering Lewis, *W. E. B. Du Bois: The Fight for Equality and the American Century, 1919–1963* (New York: Holt, 2000); Susan Gillman and Alys Eve Weinbaum, eds., *Next to the Color Line: Gender, Sexuality, and W. E. B. Du Bois* (Minneapolis: University of Minnesota Press, 2007); and Winston James, *Holding Aloft the Banner of Ethiopia: Caribbean Radicalism in Early Twentieth Century America* (London: Verso, 1999), pp. 138–53.

2. Marcus Garvey, "Editorial," *Negro World*, September 11, 1920, p. 1. For a more detailed consideration of the role played by women within the UNIA, see Barbara Bair, "True Women, Real Men: Gender, Ideology, and Social Roles in the Garvey Movement," in *Gendered Domains: Rethinking Public and Private in Women's History: Essays from the Seventh Berkshire Conference on the History of Women*, Dorothy Helley and Susan M. Reverby, eds. (Ithaca, N.Y.: Cornell University Press, 1992), pp. 154–66; and Ula Taylor, *The Veiled Garvey: The Life and Times of Amy Jacques Garvey* (Chapel Hill: University of North Carolina Press, 2002).

3. See Harvey Neptune, "Manly Rivalries and Mopsies: Gender, Nationality, and Sexuality in United States–Occupied Trinidad," *Radical History Review* 87 (fall 2003), p. 79; and The Neville Brothers, "Africa" (*Nevillization*, Kryptic 1995). The civilizationist perspective found expression in the Fortunate Fall thesis, especially popular in the nineteenth century, according to which new world blacks were seen as having been saved from barbarism and savagery by the Middle Passage. Regarding this particular history, see James H. Meriwether, prologue to *Proudly We Can Be Africans: Black Americans and Africa, 1935–1961* (Chapel Hill: University of North Carolina Press, 2002), pp. 11–26. For a compatible narrative, see Babyface's "Simple Days" (*The Day*, Epic 1996)—"Bring back those simple times of yesterday when a man was a man"—and see, regarding the reconstructions of a doubly tropic "Africa," Kamari Maxine Clarke, *Mapping Yorùbá Networks: Power and Agency in the Making of Transnational Communities* (Durham, N.C.: Duke University Press, 2004); and J. Lorand Matory, *Black Atlantic Religion: Tradition, Transnationalism and Matriarchy in the Afro-Brazilian Candomblé* (Princeton, N.J.: Princeton University Press, 2005).

4. A different perspective, I believe, became increasingly dominant in James's politics and theory over the course of the century: one that delinks gender, sexuality, position, and function. It can be argued that this shift occurred as a result of James's extended engagements with Grace Lee Boggs and Raya Dunayevskaya during his involvement with the Johnson-Forest group and the fugitivity that characterized this period, which he spent "underground," which might have encouraged/compelled his abandonment of certain conventions. See Carby, *Race Men*, p. 126; Michelle Ann Stephens, *Black Empire: The Masculine Global Imaginary of Caribbean Intellectuals in the United States, 1914–1962* (Durham, N.C.: Duke University Press, 2005), p. 239; and C. L. R. James, "Three Black Women Writers: Toni Morrison, Alice Walker, Ntozake Shange," in *The C. L. R. James Reader*, Anna Grimshaw, ed. (Oxford: Blackwell, 1992), pp. 411–17.

5. See Neptune, "Manly Rivalries and Mopsies," p. 78; and, more generally, *Caliban and the Yankees: Trinidad and the United States Occupation* (Chapel Hill: University of North Carolina Press, 2007); Brent Hayes Edwards, *The Practice of Diaspora: Literature, Translation, and the Rise of Black Internationalism* (Cambridge, Mass.: Harvard University Press, 2003); and T. Denean Sharpley-Whiting, *Negritude Women* (Minneapolis: University of Minnesota Press, 2002). Regarding the Manchester Pan-African Congress and the significance of Ghana's independence, see, among others, Meriwether, *Proudly We Can Be Africans*; W. E. B. Du Bois, "Selections from 'Africa, Pan-Africa, and Imperialism,'" in *W. E. B. Du Bois: A Reader*, David Levering Lewis, ed. (New York: Holt, 1995), pp. 655–67, 670–75; Cedric J. Robinson, "W. E. B. Du Bois and Black Sovereignty," in *Imagining Home: Class, Culture and Nationalism in the African Diaspora*, Sidney Lemelle and Robin D. G. Kelley, eds. (London: Verso, 1994), pp. 145–57; and Kevin Gaines, *American Africans in Ghana: Black Expatriates and the Civil Rights Era* (Chapel Hill: University of North Carolina Press, 2006).

6. The calypso in question is Hollis "Chalkdust" Liverpool's recording "They Ain't See Africa at All" (*Kaiso With Dignity*, Hot Vinyl 1984). The song refers to the

singer's belief that some Afro-Caribbeans tend to celebrate every aspect of their heritage (the European, the Asian) except the "African."

7. See LeRoi Jones, "American Sexual Reference: Black Male," in *Home: Social Essays* (Toronto: Penguin, 1998); Eldridge Cleaver, *Soul on Ice* (New York: McGraw-Hill, 1968); Norman Mailer, *The White Negro* (San Francisco: City Lights, 1957); Anthony Paul Farley, "The Black Body as Fetish Object," *Oregon Law Review* 76 (1997), pp. 457–535; Michael Hanchard, "Jody," *Critical Inquiry* 24 (winter 1998), pp. 473–97; Eddie Murphy's concert film *Raw* (Paramount 1987); and Klaus de Albuquerque, "In Search of Big Bamboo," *Transition* 77, no. 1, pp. 48–57. Ralph Ellison dismissed Mailer's work, rather accurately, as the "same old primitivism crap in a new package." See Ralph Ellison, *Living with Music: Ralph Ellison's Jazz Writings*, Robert G. O'Meally, ed. (New York: Modern Library, 2001), p. 250. "Jody" is the subject of Johnnie Taylor's 1971 hit "Jody's Got Your Girl and Gone" and has figured historically as a disciplinary figure of sorts in prison work songs as well as military cadence calls ("Ain't no use in going home, Jody's got your girl and gone. Ain't no use in feeling blue; Jody's got your sister too. Ain't no use in looking back; Jody's got your Cadillac"). "Jody's that fella," observed Rufus Thomas at Wattstax, "that when you leave home at six o'clock, he's in your house at six-[oh]-one." It is worth considering the fact that the name "Jody" is not gender-specific and that it can indeed float. Finally, in *A Raisin in the Sun*, Younger Jr. suggests that Murchison is wearing "faggotty white shoes."

8. See Jay-Z, "Girls, Girls, Girls" (*The Blueprint*, Roc-A-Fella/Universal 2001); and the conflict between the character played by Angela Bassett and the mother of the man she is pursuing in *How Stella Got Her Groove Back* (although issues related to age difference are also relevant here).

9. Chappelle's representation of Africa is complicated somewhat by the other stereotypes he invoked in response to stories that he sought psychiatric help while abroad. He said to Oprah Winfrey, "Who goes from America to Africa for medical attention?" See the transcripts of Chappelle's appearances on *The Oprah Winfrey Show* (February 3, 2006) and *The Actor's Studio* (2006); and Kevin Powell, "Heaven Hell Dave Chappelle: The Agonizing Return of the Funniest Man in America," *Esquire*, May 2006, pp. 92–99, 147–48. His mother, Yvonne Lee Chappelle, worked with Patrice Lumumba in the Congo and was, indeed, in the country when he was assassinated.

10. See Maureen Rowe, "The Woman in Rastafari," *Caribbean Quarterly* 26, no. 4 (1980), p. 14; and Carolyn Cooper, *Noises in the Blood: Orality, Gender and the "Vulgar" Body of Jamaican Popular Culture* (London: Macmillan, 1993), p. 131. In this category, one might also include Black Uhuru's "Shine Eye Gal"—"a shine eye gal is a trouble to a man"—(*Liberation: The Island Anthology*, Island 1993) and Barrington Levy's similarly titled and focused "Shine Eye Girl" (*Too Experienced: The Best of Barrington Levy*, VP Records 1998).

11. See Grant Farred, "Wailin' Soul: Reggae's Debt to Black American Music," in *Soul: Black Power, Politics, and Pleasure*, Monique Guillory and Richard C. Green, eds. (New York: New York University Press, 1998), p. 65; Stephen Davis, *Bob Marley: Conquering Lion of Reggae* (London: Plexus, 1993), p. 210; and Cedella Booker

with Anthony Winkler, *Bob Marley: An Intimate Portrait by His Mother* (London: Viking, 1996), p. 132. Gayle McGarrity, an acquaintance of Marley, has made reference to another dimension of the reggae star's world: "I think that Skill [Cole, Marley's football-playing friend] had some very ugly sides to him and I think his relationship with Bob was a strange one. I just want to leave it at that. There were levels of . . . homoerotic violence. . . . [At] Hope Road . . . there'd be like fourteen guys upstairs and as you'd come up they'd be like 'Is just man and man idea here. We don't want a woman for contaminate the vibe.' I remember always thinking, fourteen guys and they're all sleeping up there together? I'm not saying they were having sex, that's why I say homoerotic rather than homosexual." Quoted in Roger Steffens, "High Tide or Low Tide: Dr. Gayle McGarrity," *Beat* 20, no. 3, 2001, p. 62.

12. See Imani Tafari Ama, "Muta and Yasus Defend the Culture," *Sistren* 16, nos. 1–2 (1994), p. 8; and Leland, "When Rap Meets Reggae," p. 187. The primacy of the domestic/international dynamic is observable in the following comment from Beenie Man regarding his 2004 release *Back to Basics* (Virgin): "I was getting too international, I think. So then I went back to Jamaica and took over back dancehall, and it was back to basics. I really wanted to do a dancehall album. And with no R & B. So the people know, say, I'm not leaving. I'm not going anywhere." Interestingly, Moses equates "R & B"—i.e., African American music—with the "international" and by implication "foreign." See *Source*, August 2004, p. 164. "Nineteen eighty, that's when I knew I had to leave [Jamaica]," recollects Clement "Coxsone" Dodd, about the timing of his decision to relocate to Brooklyn. See Michael Deibert, "Sir Coxsone Turns on the Power from Kingston to Brooklyn," *Village Voice*, March 13, 2001, p. 65

13. Elena Oumano, "Women Increase Number, Scope of Roles in Reggae," *Billboard*, January 27, 1996, p. 37.

14. Cooper, *Noises in the Blood*, pp. 141, 171; and Paul Gilroy, *"There Ain't No Black in the Union Jack": The Cultural Politics of Race and Nation* (London: Hutchinson, 1987), p. 187–88. I will use *culture* with a lowercase *c* to signify what Cooper labels "Culture."

15. Quoted in Cooper, *Noises in the Blood*, p. 150. In the same way the emergence of hip-hop has brought about a certain nostalgia among older generations of R & B consumers, and the tendency to romanticize earlier eras, dancehall's predominance since the mid-1980s has encouraged a certain romanticization of earlier generations of reggae artists. Accordingly, it is forgotten that it was the same rude boys (e.g., Max Romeo, the Wailers) who made relatively explicit and "slack" recordings in the 1960s who went on to promote "consciousness" in the 1970s. In the early 1970s, John Holt, then the most popular reggae singer in Jamaica and with expatriate audiences abroad, lamented, with regard to the emergence of deejays, "Really and truly, I think that the deejay records were one of the things that lowered the standard of Jamaican music." Quoted in Gavin Petrie, ed., *Black Music* (London: Hamlyn), p. 73.

16. See Ossie Davis and Ruby Dee, *With Ossie and Ruby: In This Life Together* (New York: Morrow, 1998), p. 77; and "Radio Suicide Threat Unnerves Jamaicans," *Toronto Star*, March 31, 2000, p. A17.

17. The song was originally recorded in 1988. It became popular in 1993 partly because it used the same rhythm as Mad Cobra's "Flex," which was a success on the American R & B charts that year. (The song's producer sought to take advantage of Banton's increasing dominance of the dancehall genre by releasing an old recording.) The song continues to be popular and has achieved near anthemic status in some corners, where a session cannot be complete until at least a couple of choruses have been sung (and certain boundaries reinforced).

18. Trainer suggests, "The controversy over 'Boom Bye Bye' . . . represents a clash of Jamaican and American [sensibilities]. . . . In Jamaica . . . homosexuality is condemned from the pulpit, 'batty-man' better remain in the closet." Indeed, after a government-appointed committee (organized partly in response to pressure from Britain) recommended in 2001 that same-sex activity between consenting adults be decriminalized, Roman Catholic and Protestant clergy led the outcry and reaction. Accordingly, Trainer argues, "For Buju to offer an apology to the gay community would be tantamount to committing professional suicide. Shabba [Ranks] 'bow' [i.e., eventually offered an apology when faced with a similar uproar] and look what happened"—i.e., his credibility was undermined in Jamaica, with the consequence that his career collapsed abroad. Quoted in Trainer, "Buju Banton: Dancehall's Cultural Griot," in *Reggae, Rasta, Revolution: Jamaican Music from Ska to Dub*, Chris Potash, ed. (New York: Schirmer Books, 1997), pp. 211–12. "Trainer" is the full name under which the article was published.

19. For evidence of the conflation of anticolonial and postcolonial discourse, and religious concerns, with debates regarding homophobia, see Elena Oumano, "Jah Division," *Village Voice*, February 15, 2005; Shirley Richards, "Canada's C38: Redefining Marriage," *Jamaica Gleaner*, July 10, 2005; "A Word of Advice to Asafa," *Jamaica Gleaner*, May 16, 2006; Devon Dick, "No Homo Genes," *Jamaica Gleaner*, June 13, 2006; Teino Evans, "Reggae Writes Back: Active Stance Taken against Gay Rights Activists," *Jamaica Gleaner*, October 6, 2006; Andre Jebbinson, "As Gay Pressure Mounts, Artistes out in the Cold," *Jamaica Gleaner*, October 8, 2006; and Kavelle Anglin-Christie, "Haunted by One Song," *Jamaica Gleaner*, October 8, 2006. Some argued that the term "batty man" or "battybwoy" is only meant to refer to pedophiles. Beenie Man suggests, "[N]obody [outside Jamaica] really knows what 'batty man' means. That's what it is . . . a child molester." This equation of homosexuality and pedophilia again draws on colonial discourses—white British men traveling in search of Jamaican boys—while avoiding the fact that most pedophiles are heterosexual. See Rob Kenner, "Time Out," *Vibe*, June 2005, p. 120. It should be noted that the antisodomy laws on the books in Jamaica became the subject of debate (as they did in India as well, as a result of the actions of writers and artists in general) and that these laws were the result of colonial legislation British imposed in the late nineteenth century. Homosexuality was criminalized in the United Kingdom in 1885, with the Criminal Law Amendment Act, and only overturned with the passage of the Sexual Offences Act in July 1967. Antisodomy laws were ruled unconstitutional in the United States in *Lawrence v. Texas* (02–102) 539 U.S. 558 (2003). See, on this point, "Mr. Dalley's Unfortunate Retreat," *Jamaica*

Gleaner, July 2, 2006; Randeep Ramesh, "India's Literary Elite Call for Anti-gay Law to Be Scrapped," *Guardian*, September 18, 2006; and Tanya Stephens's antihomophobia recording "Do U Still Care" (*Rebelution*, VP 2006).

20. Quoted in Peter Akinti and Michael Fountaine, "Talk Like a Champion," *Untold*, May–June 2000, pp. 48, 51.

21. Quoted in Rob Kenner, "Collateral Damage," *Vibe*, June 2002, p. 114; and Kennedy Mensah, "Look Into My Eyes," *Untold*, June–July 2002, p. 92. Regarding "Who Am I," Davis has suggested that the punctuation is important, i.e., "How could I make love to a fella [full stop or question mark]. In a rush [comma], pass me the keys to the truck." Regarding his archnemesis, he notes, "He [Bounty Killer] used to have people wonder if me straight or if me lean. Now a fi him turn. What goes around comes around, and that him fi know." On a side note, as Carolyn Cooper has noted, the six-foot, six-inch dancehall artist Eek-A-Mouse has played a significant role in undermining the foundations of yardie (Jamaican) machismo. In 2006, Buju Banton and Beenie Man had shows canceled in Britain and the United States in response to allegations of homophobic content in their music. A number of dancehall artists signed agreements in 2007 not to promote homophobic sentiments in their creations, in response to pressure from American and particularly British interests.

22. See Rob Kenner, "Catch a Fire," *Vibe*, October 2001, p. 122; and *Reggae Collector* 2 (summer 2002), p. 20. In the lyrics to his 2000 recording (incidentally featuring Bounty Killer) "Another Level," Baby Cham commanded: "Tell the brother that mess up the economy to read Chapter Three Deutoronomy; tell them we have to secure our family, government corruption ah go down like sodomy." See Baby Cham featuring Bounty Killer, "Another Level" (*WOW . . . The Story*, Madhouse/Artists Only! 2000). Although he was never as deeply involved in the music industry as his opponent, Seaga, P. J. Patterson did represent the Skatalites, Jamaica's pioneering ska band, for a brief period in the early 1960s. In March 2002, dub poet Mutabaruka (aka Allan Hope) would release "Dem Lie," a song criticizing the government, and the political class as a whole, for the high homicide rate and the effects of the drug trade (with the Caribbean being a major transshipment point for cocaine). The song borrowed its rhythm from American rapper Afroman's comedic 2001 hit "Because I Got High" and followed in the tradition of previous recordings by the poet (e.g., "People's Court" in 1992) criticizing the government. The recording, predictably, received little exposure on Jamaican radio but sold respectably in the island (and in New York).

23. See Norman C. Stolzoff, *Wake the Town and Tell the People: Dancehall Culture in Jamaica* (Durham: Duke University Press, 2000), p. 5.

24. Quoted in *Weekly Star* (Jamaica), August 19–25, 1999, p. 9. Attendees included Arnold Bertram, minister of local government, youth and community development, music industry executive Louise Fraser-Bennett, and recording artists Bounty Killer, Buju Banton, Tony Rebel, and Mutabaruka. The laying of obscenity charges against DMX in Trinidad after a 1999 performance and the many complaints about the frequent use of expletives in the live shows of the Notorious

B.I.G. and Jay-Z in Jamaica point to perhaps another "cultural difference" between the United States and the Caribbean.

25. The ganja was returned to Jendau. See *Pride* (Canada), September 2–8, 1999, p. 20; *Weekly Star* (Jamaica), August 19–25, 1999, p. 9; and Bounty Killer (*5th Element*, Blunt/TVT 1999). British-based reggae singer Maxi Priest stated afterward with regard to the summit: "One should look at what they put down on paper. Should I be telling someone to fire two shots or fire a nine-millimetre? I shouldn't be telling anybody that. The only thing I tell anybody to do is love, love, love." Quoted in "Maxi Makes the Music of Love," *Toronto Star*, September 5, 1999, p. D5. "The clowns are getting a break presently," suggested prominent old-school reggae vocalist Beres Hammond. "We have to get it back to where it was in the late seventies when the music was beautiful, and people went out to have fun. They didn't want to shoot nobody." Quoted in John Masouri, "Life Signs," *Echoes*, March 2001, p. 32.

26. Orlando Patterson, "Race, Gender, and Liberal Fallacies," *New York Times*, October 20, 1991, reprinted in *Reconstruction* 1, no. 4 (1992), p. 65.

27. Patterson, "Race, Gender, and Liberal Fallacies," p. 76 (italics added). Class, gender, and generational differences have also been reflected in the different audiences that calypso, reggae/dancehall, and R & B/rap attract in Caribbean communities in the West Indies, the United Kingdom, the United States, and Canada. Generally, calypso draws an older audience and is more favored by women than men, and the upper classes more than lower-income constituencies. Reggae and dancehall, and black American music, are the preferred musics of the younger generations, with R & B perceived as the more upscale scene, more likely to be supported by those who are disconnected "from their Caribbean roots." Regarding the connection between gender and calypso lyrics, see Roy L. Austin, "Understanding Calypso Content: A Critique and an Alternative Explanation," *Caribbean Quarterly* 22, nos. 2–3 (June–September 1976), pp. 74–83.

28. See Patterson, "Race, Gender, and Liberal Fallacies," p. 76; Belinda J. Edmondson, "Trinidad Romance: The Invention of Jamaican Carnival," in *Caribbean Romances: The Politics of Regional Representation*, Belinda J. Edmondson, ed. (Charlottesville: University Press of Virginia, 1999), pp. 67–68.

29. Jacqueline Nassy Brown suggests and theorizes a useful outline of this geography in her discussion of the relationship between blacks in Liverpool—to be precise "Liverpool-born blacks"—and black communities elsewhere as structured through the filters of popular culture, the shipping industry, the slave trade, expanding American military power, and most important, gender and race (in a specific and unique sense, as most of the subjects of Brown's research are products of interracial unions). See Jacqueline Nassy Brown, *Dropping Anchor, Setting Sail: Geographies of Race in Black Liverpool* (Princeton, N.J.: Princeton University Press, 2005). Similarly instructive and useful are Katherine McKittrick, *Demonic Grounds: Black Women and the Cartographies of Struggle* (Minneapolis: University of Minnesota Press, 2006); and Katherine McKittrick and Clyde Woods, eds., *Black Geographies and the Politics of Place* (Boston: South End Press, 2007).

30. I could elaborate here and restate the argument I made in the previous chapter that we should think of the diasporic as taking place not only at the level of

Afro-national sensibilities but also at the regional and local levels and, accordingly, potentially between places marked within the same national borders (e.g., London and Liverpool, Los Angeles and New Orleans, Cape Town and Johannesburg). For example, as Stacy Morgan suggests, the social realism that emerges in Chicago in the 1930s can be read as a response to, and rejection of, the more adventurous—i.e., not consistently supportive of heterosexist norms—spirit of the Harlem Renaissance. See Stacy Morgan, *Rethinking Social Realism: African American Art and Literature, 1930–1953* (Athens: University of Georgia Press, 2004). Long Island is marked in similar fashion in relation to Brooklyn and Harlem, and Montego Bay in relation to Kingston.

31. The collaboration between the United Kingdom's Massive Attack and Mos Def, "I Against I" (*Blade 2* soundtrack, Virgin/EMI 2002), falls neatly into this tradition.

32. See "Interview: Linton Kwesi Johnson Talks to Burt Caesar," *Critical Quarterly* 38, no. 4 (winter 1996), p. 67.

33. On his 1980 album *Bass Culture*, Linton Kwesi Johnson has a track entitled "Inglan [England] Is a Bitch." Although the phrase is employed by a character (a fifty-five-year-old Caribbean immigrant who has lost his job) whose voice Johnson is using, the usage does contrast quite neatly with the notion of Africa as the "motherland" (Johnson, it should be made quite clear, has never promoted this type of Garveyist sentiment). On the subject of gender, Johnson has stated: "I was always a little bit ambivalent about feminism because there were some aspects of it I could identify with, but it seems to me that it was a confused ideology. . . . I just had some difficulties with it. . . . I don't particularly care much for Alice Walker's work, but Toni Morrison I think is a brilliant writer. As women, writers like Toni Morrison have broadened the black experience, and the human experience, by bringing a woman's perspective to bear on the core questions of Black Liberation, and individual liberation and freedom." See Oscar Cabarcas, "Hip Hop 101," *Source*, June 1997, p. 45; "Interview: Linton Kwesi Johnson Talks to Burt Caesar," pp. 73–74; Mel Cooke, "J'can-born Poet to Read from Penguin Collection," *Jamaica Gleaner*, May 27, 2005; Isaac Julien and Colin McCabe, *Diary of a Young Soul Rebel* (London: BFI, 1991), p. 2; and Michael E. Veal, *Fela: The Life and Times of an African Musical Icon* (Philadelphia: Temple University Press, 2000), p. 238. In Julien's film *Young Soul Rebels*, about two soul deejays, it is worth noting that one of them (Chris) slips into patois at moments when he is resisting authority (e.g., the police, condescending radio station managers). Throughout the movie, reggae and R & B are coded as marking different masculinities.

34. It is important to note that Jamaican films (using the term loosely) have tended to be rather consistent in terms of their depiction of Jamaican realities (e.g., *The Harder They Come, Dancehall Queen, Third World Cop*) and have avoided, for obvious reasons, the romanticization of island life (e.g., American films ranging from *Island in the Sun* to *How Stella Got Her Groove Back*).

35. One other iconic presence worth noting is Pam Grier, and particularly her "Foxy Brown" character (from the 1974 movie of the same title). The character's name was appropriated by a Jamaican dancehall singer (known for her cover of Tracy

Chapman's "Fast Car") and by the Caribbean American rapper Inga Marchand. (To square the circle, perhaps, at one point in *Coffy* [1973], Grier assumes a West Indian accent.)

36. It should be noted, though, that reggae artists such as Gregory Isaacs, Dennis Brown, and Freddie McGregor were able to record both love songs and "culture"/political tunes and maintain credibility in both realms, and that Tosh did record a remake of the Temptations' "Don't Look Back" with Mick Jagger of the Rolling Stones, in an attempt to curry mainstream support. See Cooper, *Noises in the Blood*, p. 151.

37. See Tupac, aka Makaveli, "Blasphemy" (*The Don Killuminati: The 7Day Theory*, Interscope 1996); Lauryn Hill, *The Miseducation of Lauryn Hill* (Ruffhouse/Columbia 1998); Method Man, "Cradle Rock" (*Tical 2000: Judgement Day*, Def Jam/Polygram 1998); Queen Latifah, "U.N.I.T.Y." (*Black Reign*, Motown 1993); and Jill Scott, "Watching Me" (*Who Is Jill Scott? Words and Sounds* 1, Hidden Beach/Epic 2000). Worth noting in this context is the R & B singer Bilal's reggae-inspired "Home" (*1st Born Second*, Interscope/Universal 2001), which is about just that, going home.

38. See 50 Cent and Kris Ex, *From Pieces to Weight: Once upon a Time in Southside Queens* (New York: MTV Books, 2005); and *Get Rich or Die Tryin'* (MTV/Paramount 2005). In both the print and film versions of his life story, Jackson does not know his father.

39. Regarding the relationship between diasporas and queer spaces, see Rinaldo Walcott, *Black Queer Diaspora: Reading from a Queer Place in Diaspora* (forthcoming); and "Outside in Black Studies: Reading from a Queer Place in the Diaspora," in *Black Queer Studies: A Critical Anthology*, E. Patrick Johnson and Mae G. Henderson, eds. (Durham, N.C.: Duke University Press, 2005), pp. 90–105. In this light, it is interesting to contrast Spike Lee's and Isaac Julien's respective takes on the year 1977, as reflected in *Summer of Sam* (40 Acres and a Mule/Touchstone 1999) and *Young Soul Rebels* (ILC 1991).

40. See Brian Coleman, "Classic Material," *XXL*, December 2003, p. 183; and Kool G Rap and DJ Polo, "The Polo Club" (*Wanted: Dead or Alive*, Cold Chillin'/Warner Brothers 1990). "We did Saturdays for a long time," recalls Philadelphia deejay, artist, and producer King Britt with regard to his sessions at the city's Silk City, "but the crowd changed over the years. We couldn't play hip hop and house on the same night anymore." Quoted in DJ Statik, "King Britt," *B.INFORMED* 5 (2004), p. 38. Interesting in this context is Blaze's *25 Years Later* (Motown 1990), a house music concept album espousing black nationalist sentiments.

41. See The Notorious B.I.G., "Friend of Mine" (*Ready to Die*, Bad Boy/Universal 1994); "Family Business: The Making of *Ready to Die*," *XXL*, April 2004, p. 130; and "25 Years of Hip Hop on Wax," *Blues and Soul*, December 14–27, 2004, p. 37. By "white" I mean "categorically other." The British music scene has been marked by a higher degree of interracial and multiracial formations and collaborations featuring Caribbean, African, Asian, and (white) European artists: e.g., Soul II Soul, Talvin Singh, Roni Size and Reprazent, MJ Cole, Incognito, Massive Attack, and Nitin Sawhney.

42. Regarding Canada's place in this field, when LL Cool J was attempting to ridicule Canibus, another rapper (in "Back Where I Belong"), he suggested that his challenger was "really from Canada" (i.e., by definition illegitimate and inauthentic). In a debate about whether hip-hop was truly "dead," generated by the release of Nas's album *Hip Hop Is Dead*, Young Jeezy, a southern rapper opposed to the suggestion dismissed Monie Love, a former rapper and radio show host, by drawing attention to her British nationality.

43. Adds Benjamin, regarding "B.O.B.": "It's influenced by UK drum & bass beats, because right now the UK is killing it with beats. I don't think jungle will ever make it in America. That's why we needed to make it harder and more American with southern-style bass." See Tricia Romano, "Junglist's Delight," *Paper*, November 2000, p. 60; and Mansel Fletcher, "Southern Comfort," *Hip Hop Connection*, January 2001, p. 34. Ahmir "?uestlove" Thompson of the Roots has spoken of the refuge London provided to him and his band in the early 1990s, at a point when West Coast rap was beginning to emerge as a hegemonic form within hip-hop and the British music scene was producing musics—drum and bass, trip hop, and acid jazz (later configured in the United States as "neo-soul")—and supporting artists—the Young Disciples, Incognito, Omar, Massive Attack, Portishead, Goldie, Roni Size and Reprazent, Wookie, and 4 hero—whose conceptions of the boundaries of black performance were more elastic than those being promoted in the American market. "Living in London," he recalls, "I learned the culture isn't as disposable as I thought it was. Just because it was thrown away in the United States, doesn't mean the rest of the world has forgotten about it." See *5 Conversations about Soul* (Image Entertainment 2003). As a testament to this understanding of the potential reach of black music, the Roots recorded "You Got Me," a track featuring Erykah Badu and Eve, with lyrics discussing a trans-Atlantic romance, that dissolves at its conclusion into a drum and bass breakdown.

44. "When I was growing up," Chuck has observed, "I listened to Sly and the Family Stone, James Brown, George Clinton, but I also listened to rock music. The music in Public Enemy is a reflection of what I listened to in the early 70s. Led Zeppelin and all the inroads made in rock. I grew up when there was a melting pot in music." See Dan Goldstein, ed., *Rappers Rappin'* (Surrey: Castle, 1995), p. 107; Tricky, "Black Steel" (*Maxinquaye*, Fourth and Broadway/Island 1995); and Public Enemy, "Black Steel in the Hour of Chaos" (*It Takes a Nation of Millions to Hold Us Back*, Def Jam/Columbia 1988).

45. Alexander G. Weheliye, *Phonographies: Grooves in Sonic Afro-Modernity* (Durham, N.C.: Duke University Press, 2005), pp. 188, 195. The guitar sound on Tricky's version recalls, to my mind, the late 1970s Manchester-based group the Buzzcocks. Tricky recorded two other cover versions of American hip-hop classics by Eric B and Rakim ("Lyrics of Fury") and Slick Rick ("Children's Story") that can be read as an effort on his part to realize new space within the genre. See Tricky, "Lyrics of Fury" (*Pre-Millenium Tension*, Island 1996); and "Children's Story" (*Nearly God*, Island 1996).

46. It is not surprising, in this matrix, that there has been a resistance to discussing the issues brought to the surface by the emergence of AIDS not only in the United

States but throughout the diaspora. The narratives associated with the disease replicate exactly those constructions of "Africa," and "Africans" that many have expended considerable energy to resist and disrupt. The sad irony is that AIDS is in many respects the ultimate linked fate issue, yet it is at the same time a concern that generates very little substantive attention and creative energy on the part of black policy-makers in the arenas of formal politics (a situation explained in large part by the complicated relationship between the black churches and homophobia). With regard to the American context, the members of the CBC have been more engaged with the issue—and those connected to gay and lesbian rights—than many of their colleagues. As Barney Frank has suggested, "*The* demographic group that has by far the best record on gay and lesbian issues is the Congressional Black Caucus. They have a better record than the gay caucus. Not [though] the *openly* gay caucus." See "Relations: Friends and Allies Across the Divide," *New York Times Magazine*, July 16, 2000, p. 50. Nevertheless, as Cathy Cohen has written, "[There is] little evidence to suggest that most black representatives engaged in any public activity beyond voting 'the right way. . . .' Rarely [have] black legislators attempt[ed] to draw attention to the disproportionate impact of AIDS on African-American and other communities of color." Continuing, she adds, "Very few black congressional members demonstrated any interest in linking the political battles around AIDS in black communities to the development of AIDS in, for instance, central Africa." See Cathy Cohen, *The Boundaries of Blackness: AIDS and the Breakdown of Black Politics* (Chicago: University of Chicago Press, 1999), pp. 311, 313.

Chapter 8

1. "The last time I looked at my children's globe," the film director Spike Lee stated, "New Orleans was part of the United States." George W. Bush, president at the time, would eventually weigh in as well: "You know there's a debate here about refugees. Let me tell you my attitude. . . . The people we're talking about are not refugees. They are Americans, and they need the help and love and compassion of our fellow citizens." Kilpatrick, Watson, and Cummings were speaking as part of a press conference held by the CBC on the morning of September, 2, 2005. The Lee quotation is from George Vescey, "Film on a City's Despair Offers Lessons in Humility," *New York Times*, October 29, 2006, sec. 8, p. 7. The Jackson quotation is from "Calling Katrina Survivors 'Refugees' Stirs Debate," *msnbc.msn.com*, posted September 7, 2005 The statement by the flood victim and the Bush quotation are from Robert E. Pierre, "'Refugee': A Word of Trouble," *Washington Post*, September 7, 2005, p. C1 (italics added). On this point, see Donnie, "Impatient People" (*Daily News*, Soulthought 2007).

2. Another recurring image in CNN's coverage was of two white Barbie-style dolls hanging from a piece of string as if they were symbols of what would happen to whites if they should venture anywhere close to these black masses. See Michel Foucault, *Society Must Be Defended: Lectures at the Collège de France, 1975–76*, Mauro Bertani and Alessandro Fontana, eds., David Macey, trans. (New York: Picador, 2003), p. 256.

3. As Michael Dawson and Lawrence Bobo have demonstrated, while most participants in the post-Katrina discourses, regardless of race, agreed (or, at least, came to agree) that the victims were not refugees but citizens, blacks and whites disagreed sharply in their interpretations of the flood itself. Blacks were apparently far more likely than white respondents to contend that those who remained in New Orleans did so because they were unable to leave (as opposed to choosing to stay), to be convinced that the federal response was delayed and lacked vigor because the stricken were disproportionately black, to think it proper that the federal government commit the expenditures necessary to restore New Orleans, to assert that the persistence of racial inequality was underscored by the catastrophe, and to "believe that racial equality will either never be achieved in the United States, or at least not in their lifetime." See "After the Storm: In the Wake of Katrina," *Du Bois Review* 2, no. 2 (2005), pp. 155–58.

4. Regarding the instabilities of human rights and citizenship discourses, see Jacques Rancière, "Who Is the Subject of the Rights of Man?" *South Atlantic Quarterly* 102–103 (spring–summer 2004), pp. 297–310.

5. A week later, on *The Ellen DeGeneres Show*, September 9, 2005, West explained, "A lot of times, people let fear get in the way of their dreams and what they need to do. And being in the situation I'm in, you have everything to lose. You can lose your endorsements [he had a contract with Pepsi], you can lose this, you can lose that. But there's a whole lot more I could have lost; how about if I like . . . what if I had drowned? What if I didn't eat for five days? People are so concerned about what they can lose." In a show nearly three months later, Dave Chappelle quipped, regarding West, "I don't know if you agree with him or not, but give it up for him. I've got a lot of respect for him. And, I'm going to miss him." Taking the joke to its logical conclusion, he added, "I'm not risking my entire career to tell white people obvious things." See Dave Itzkoff, "Dave Chappelle Is Alive and Well (and Playing Las Vegas)," *New York Times*, November 27, 2005, Arts and Leisure sec., p. 32. West's comments were deleted in the delayed West Coast broadcast of the concert. Myers and West made fun of the moment shortly afterward on the NBC show *Saturday Night Live* (October 1, 2005). While many, including other artists, subsequently endorsed his comments, Curtis "50 Cent" Jackson criticized West and made public his own identification with President Bush (partly on account of their sharing a birthday). Wynton Marsalis, a native of New Orleans, in true Ellisonian fashion, referred to the flood as a test the "national character" of the United States would survive, and expressed confidence that the residents of the flooded city were "blues people" and accordingly "resilient." See *The Tavis Smiley Show*, September 8, 2005. Other creative artists offered responses, including Mos Def ("Katrina Clap," subsequently retitled on rerelease as "Dollar Day"), Public Enemy ("Hell No We Ain't All Right"), Ed Motta and Incognito's Bluey ("Where the Levees Broke"), Gloria Anne Muldrow ("New Orleans"), Terence Blanchard (*A Tale of God's Will: A Requiem for Katrina*), Spike Lee (*When the Levees Broke: A Requiem in Four Acts*), and Kara Walker (*After the Deluge*). Finally, before the flood, West had taken stances against certain forms of materialism (i.e., the

purchase of "blood" or "conflict" diamonds, mined under extraordinarily unfair labor conditions, to put it mildly) and homophobia within the hip-hop industry. Along with Sean Price, Erick Sermon, and Keith Murray, Kanye West is one of the few artists in hip-hop not to employ a moniker.

6. See Chris Heath, "Kanye West: Graduate," *GQ*, December 2007, p. 382.

7. For evidence of this aspirational sensibility with regard to modernity, see among others, Houston A. Baker Jr., *Modernism and the Harlem Renaissance* (Chicago: University of Chicago Press, 1987); and *Turning South Again: Re-thinking Modernism/Re-reading Booker T.* (Durham, N.C.: Duke University Press, 2001); Guthrie P. Ramsey Jr., *Race Music: Black Cultures from Bebop to Hip Hop* (Berkeley: University of California Press, 2003); and Louis O. Chude-Sokei, *The Last "Darky": Bert Williams, Black-on-Black Minstrelsy, and the African Diaspora* (Durham, N.C.: Duke University Press, 2006). For a powerful challenge to contemporary understandings of race, see Barnor Hesse, *Creolizing the Political: A Genealogy of the African Diaspora* (Durham, N.C.: Duke University Press, 2009).

8. For Scott, the new question pertains to "the conceptual and institutional dimensions of our modernity." One might argue that the problem spaces, questions, and answers Scott defines and distinguishes are not that easily separated and that the concerns underlying what he calls the anticolonial, postcolonial, and "after postcolonial," unless defined extremely narrowly, cannot be cleanly disentangled, especially if we are attentive to the relationship among colonialism, coloniality, and modernity. Accordingly, Aimé Césaire, Frantz Fanon, and C. L. R. James are engaged with anticolonialism, postcoloniality, and the "new" question Scott proposes. See David Scott, *Refashioning Futures: Criticism after Postcoloniality* (Princeton, N.J.: Princeton University Press, 1999), p. 15; and *Conscripts of Modernity: The Tragedy of Colonial Enlightenment* (Durham, N.C.: Duke University Press, 2004), pp. 2–3.

9. Worth considering in this light as well is the work of Me'Shell NdegéOcello. Consider her recent disruptions of R & B conventions by means of strategic breaks in texture and engagements and injections of antiwar sentiment in her covers of Earth, Wind & Fire's "Fantasy" (*Interpretations: Celebrating the Music of Earth Wind and Fire*, Stax 2007), and Eugene McDaniel's "Compared to What?" (*Talk to Me* soundtrack, Atlantic 2007).

10. See Zora Neale Hurston, "Characteristics of Negro Expression," in *African American Literary Theory: A Reader*, Winston Napier, ed. (New York: New York University Press, 2000), pp. 31–44. Thanks to Sandra Richards, Dwight McBride, and Dana Weiner, for providing the language and references I needed to complete this last paragraph.

ACKNOWLEDGMENTS

Much thanks to those who have, usually patiently, put up with the work-induced absences, silences, and minor personality disorders, this book generated: Anusha Aruliah, Dave Austin, Cameron Bailey, Maxine Bailey, Joe Brewster, Lloyd Charlton and family, George Elliott Clarke, Perryne Constance, Warren Crichlow, Kevin George, Michael Hamilton, Rick Harris, Wayne Harris, Kingsley Henry, Dwayne Hopkinson, Judy Mapp, Randy McDowall and family, Dave Messam, Faizal Mirza, Darrell Moore, my senior amigo Ron Nash, Ron Nazon, "broMAN" Mark Anthony Neal, Jacqueline Nichol-Hamilton, Janet Nichol, Sharon Othello, Ron Peters, Chris Ramsaroop, Michelle Ray, Martin Ruck, the Saunders family, Gary St. Fleur, Michèle Stephenson, Clement Virgo, Rinaldo Walcott, Ignatius Watson, Shirleen Weekes, Ruth White, Dulcina Wind, and the Each One Teach One crew—Marwan Lucas, Sirak Abebe, Richard Babb, Richard Frederick, Randy Messiah, and Everton Rodney—for disputing every claim of musical expertise I made. Special thanks to Cameron, Joe, Michèle, and Clement—filmmakers all—for letting me observe the creative process up close and to Ron Iton and Hilary Fletcher, Claudia Iton, Gaylene Gould, Michael McMillan, and Henry Bonsu, for making London feel very much like home.

Colleagues at the University of Toronto provided much-appreciated encouragement when I started writing this book. Thanks to Joe Carens, Dickson Eyoh, Jennifer Nedelsky, Melissa Williams, Rob Vipond, and Joe Wong. Much thanks, too, to the following members, past and present, of the new Chicago School for fostering a unique intellectual community: Badia Ahad, Armstead Allen, Kara Allen, Ana Aparicio, Kevin Bell, Kathleen Bethel, Henry Binford, Martha Biondi, Michelle Boyd, Jennifer Brody, Sherwin Bryant, Tracy Burch, Corey Capers, Tiffane Cochrane, Michael Collins, Huey Copeland, Suzette Denose, Souleymane Bachir Diagne, Madhu Dubey, Marsha Figaro, Kesha Fikes, Tyrone Forman, Dilip Gaonkar, Doris Garraway, Adam Green, David Grinblatt, Jessica Harris, Melissa Harris-Lacewell, Rejji Hayes, Robin Hayes, Darlene Clark Hine, Sharon Holland, Bayo Holsey, Bonnie

Honig, Johari Jabir, Lynette Jackson, Marissa Jackson, E. Patrick Johnson, Waldo Johnson, Richard Joseph, Aaron Kamugisha, John Keene, Tim King, Amanda Lewis, Tessie Liu, Minkah Makalani, John Márquez, Kate Masur, Dwight McBride, Marjorie McDonald, Nancy McLean, Omar McRoberts, Charles Mills, Aldon Morris, Toni-Marie Montgomery, Larry Murphy, Dylan Penningroth, Barbara Ransby, Sandra Richards, Jennifer Richeson, Beth Richie, Dorothy Roberts, Kerry Ann Rockquemore, Reuel Rogers, Nitasha Sharma, Victoria DeFrancesco Soto, Hendrik Spruyt, Robert Starks, Butch Ware, Celeste Watkins-Hayes, Dana Weiner, Erin Winkler, Harvey Young, Paul Zeleza, and Linda Zerrilli.

A number of individuals read draft chapters and provided useful and timely feedback. For service beyond the boundary, thanks to Rob Brown, Robert Gooding-Williams, Michael Hanchard, Patrick Bernard Hill, John Jackson, Dean Robinson, Todd Shaw, Lester Spence, Deborah Thomas, and Alexander Weheliye. Rogers Smith, Cary Fraser, Tyrone Forman, Desmond King, Mark Anthony Neal, S. Craig Watkins, and Madhu Dubey, provided congenial spaces in which I could test some of this material in public. Andrea Simpson and Jane Junn were generous co-conspirators when it came to organizing conferences. A very special thanks to Joseph McCormick, who has supported this project—and its author—in a number of ways going back to the late 1980s. I owe similar longstanding debts to Germaine Hoston and the late Milton Cummings Jr.

Others were exposed to multiple drafts and always responded with good cheer. Among these interlocutors, my very special thanks go to Mary Pattillo for curbing (slightly) my appetite for the pretentious; Tracy Vaughn for her art, spirit, and attention to detail; Harvey Neptune for reminding me that the Caribbean is a great theoretical space and that time is indeed a construct; Joe Carens for the kind of support one only expects from family members; Barnor Hesse for providing much-appreciated community and raising the bar (higher and higher); and Krista Thompson who read more draft chapters than anyone else—including the author!—and for pushing me to take the book's title seriously.

Fred Harris and Cathy Cohen have played crucial roles in the writing of this book. Their scholarship helped inspire it, their friendship sustained the author, and their collegiality helped find the book a home with Oxford. (And Fred would want me to mention that everything I know about African American art history, I learned in his living room.) Dedi Felman signed the book at Oxford, and her enthusiasm kept me going long after I would have otherwise quit; David McBride understood the book better than I did, and his personal investment in the book's success raised my spirits at every turn. My franglais patois has been moved ever closer to understandable English by Angela Chnapko and Joellyn Ausanka; Angela, Joellyn, Brendan O'Neill, and Woody Gilmartin helped, far beyond the call of duty, bring this project to completion. Nathan Jalani Taylor kindly granted permission for his artwork to be used on the book's cover, a piece which in the last stages of writing, revising, and copy-editing, helped inspire me considerably.

Much love to my parents, Carmen and John, who provided the laboratory in which this project was first conceived; my aunts, uncles, and cousins who still let me use the family name; and my brothers Tony and Brian—my best friends—and their families including my nieces, Carmen and Angela, and my nephew Justin, who keep me plugged into the real world.

There are a number of Caribbean restaurants in Toronto, Brooklyn, London, and Chicago that kept this jerk chicken and roti addict going; the Jazz Showcase in Chicago provided many a Sunday evening of great music, very good tea, and just enough light so that I could do revisions between sets. Finally, thanks to the many guiding spirits, both sacred and profane, who made writing this book possible: 4 hero, Joan Armatrading, Arsenal FC, A Tribe Called Quest, Erykah Badu, the Beatles, Andy Bey, Black Uhuru, Charles Burnett, Terry Callier, le Club de Hockey Canadien de Montréal, Betty Carter, Tracy Chapman, the Clash, John Coltrane, Robert Cray, Cymande, Nick Drake, Shaun Escoffery, Fela Kuti, Rachelle Ferrell, Marvin Gaye, Gilberto Gil, the Guess Who, Donny Hathaway, Phyllis Hyman, Incognito, Garland Jeffreys, Linton Kwesi Johnson, Chaka Khan, Barrington Levy, Robert Nesta Marley, Curtis Mayfield, Frank McComb, Joni Mitchell, Toni Morrison, Ed Motta, Me'Shell NdegéOcello, Jair Oliveira, Omar, Greg Osby, Richard Pryor, Paul Robeson, Santana, Gil Scott Heron and Brian Jackson, Ousmane Sembène, Wayne Shorter, Zadie Smith, Soul II Soul, Wole Soyinka, Steel Pulse, Lewis Taylor, Thin Lizzy, Lilian Thuram, Gino Vannelli, War, Cassandra Wilson, Bill Withers, Stevie Wonder, Lizz Wright, and the Young Disciples.

One love.

INDEX